THROUGH THE JADE GATE

CHINA TO ROME

A Study of the Silk Routes during the

Later Han Dynasty

1st to 2nd Centuries CE

An annotated translation from the *Hou Hanshu*

'The Chronicle on the Western Regions'

Updated and Expanded

VOLUME II

APPENDICES AND BIBLIOGRAPHY

John E. Hill

2015

Volume II:
ISBN-13: 978-1503384620
ISBN-10: 1503384624

VOLUME II

APPENDICES

Appendix A: Introduction of Silk Cultivation to Khotan 1
Appendix B: The Story of Sea Silk 3
Appendix C: Wild Silks 11
Appendix D: Gan Ying's Journey to the Persian Gulf 16
Appendix E: Routes from the Tarim Basin, Gandhāra and Sindh to the West 21
Appendix F: The Kingdom of Jibin (Kapisha & Gandhāra) 36
Appendix G: The Kingdom of Puda 65
Appendix H: The Kingdom of Wuyishanli (Arachosia & Drangiana) 76
Appendix I: The Wusun People 91
Appendix J: Chigu - The Court of the Wusun Ruler 102
Appendix K: The Yuezhi people 106
Appendix L: The Yuezhi migrations 116
Appendix M: The Kingdom of Daxia 133
Appendix N: Lanshi (Baghlan) - principal city of Daxia and later the Da Yuezhi 162
Appendix O: The title *xihou* 185
Appendix P: The Early Kushans 192
Appendix Q: Names and Titles of the Kushan Kings - Kujula to Kanishka 208
Appendix R: Qingbi = Azurite/Lapis lazuli? 220
Appendix S: Jade 229
Appendix T: The linking of the Jade and Lapis lazuli Routes 234
Appendix U: The *xuandu* - the 'hanging passages' 239
Appendix V: Rhinoceroses and Rhinoceros Horn 245
Appendix W: Notes on the Saka or Se/Sai peoples 261
Appendix X: The Significance and Use of Skull Cups 270
Appendix Y: The Adventures of Zhang Qian 275
Appendix Z: Lijian (Ptolemaic and Roman Egypt) 286

ABBREVIATIONS AND BIBLIOGRAPHY

Abbreviations 288
Bibliography 291

Appendix A: Introduction of Silk Cultivation to Khotan in the 1st Century CE

This story of how silk technology arrived in Khotan is told in the 7th century account of the famous Chinese Buddhist pilgrim monk, Xuanzang, and summarised by the Hungarian -British explorer and archaeologist, Sir Aurel Stein:

> "In old times the country knew nothing of either mulberry trees or silkworms. Hearing that China possessed them, the king of Khotan sent an envoy to procure them ; but at that time the ruler of China was determined not to let others share their possession, and he had strictly prohibited seeds of the mulberry tree or silkworms' eggs being carried outside his frontiers. The king of Khotan then with due submission prayed for the hand of a Chinese princess. When this request had been acceded to, he dispatched an envoy to escort the princess from China, taking care to let the future queen know through him that, in order to assure to herself fine silk robes when in Khotan, she had better bring some mulberry seeds and silkworms with her.
>
> The princess thus advised secretly procured mulberry seeds and silkworms' eggs, and by concealing them in the lining of her headdress, which the chief of the frontier guards did not dare to examine, managed to remove them safely to Khotan. On her first arrival and before her solemn entry into the royal palace, she stopped at the site where subsequently the Lu-shê convent was built, and there she left the silkworms and the mulberry seeds. From the latter grew up the first mulberry trees, with the leaves of which the silkworms were fed when their time had come. Then the queen issued an edict engraved on stone, prohibiting the working up of the cocoons until the moths of the silkworms had escaped. Then she founded this Saṅghārāma on the spot where the first silkworms were bred; and there are about here many old mulberry tree trunks which they say are the remains of the trees first planted. From old time till now this kingdom has possessed silkworms which nobody is allowed to kill, with a view to take away the silk stealthily. Those who do so are not allowed to rear the worms for a succession of years.
>
> That the legend here related about the origin of one of Khotan's most important industries enjoyed widespread popularity is proved by the painted panel (D. iv. 5) discovered by me in one of the Dandān-Uliq shrines, which presents us, as my detailed analysis will show, with a spirited picture of the Chinese princess in the act of offering protection to a basketfull of unpierced cocoons. An attendant pointing to the princess's headdress recalls her beneficent smuggling by which Khotan was supposed to have obtained its first silkworms, while another attendant engaged at a loom or silk-weaving implement symbolizes the industry which the princess's initiative had founded. A divine figure seated in the background may represent the genius presiding over the silkworms." Stein (1907), Vol. I, pp. 229-230. For more information consult: Boulnois (2004), pp. 179-190; Stein (1921), Vol. III, pp. 1278-1279; Watters (1904-1905), pp. 287, 302.

The story is retold in the *Li yul luṅ-btsan-pa* or '*Prophecy of the Li Country*' – a Khotanese Buddhist 'history,' completed about the middle of the 8th century, and survives in Tibetan, was probably translated by Khotanese Buddhist monks who had fled to Tibet to escape persecution at the hands of an anti-Buddhist king in Khotan.

Aside from the usual pious Buddhist flourishes, its chronological list of kings has proved to be surprisingly accurate when checked against dated accounts in the Chinese histories. The list of Khotanese queens, however, is less detailed and not in chronological order. See: note 4.1, and Hill (1988), pp. 179-190.

The saga is set during the reign of King Vijaya Jaya, who is said to have married the princess who brought the silkworm eggs and mulberry seeds to Khotan. It provides several clues to dating the story.

The *Li yul luṅ-btsan-pa* states that King Vijaya Dharma was the youngest of the three sons of King Vijaya Jaya. He is probably identical to the *daren* ('Noble' or 'High Personage') named Dumo in the *Hou Hanshu*. See: note 20.15. He was killed in 60 CE.

> "**Dumo** 都末 of Yutian [Khotan] (d.60). A man of noble family, in 60 Dumo led his kinsmen to assassinate Junde, the oppressive governor who had been appointed by the hegemon King Xian of Suoju [Yarkand].
> Soon afterwards Dumo and his associates were themselves killed by the chieftain Xiumoba and the Chinese Han Rong. -*HHS* 88/78:2925." de Crespigny (2007a), p. 192. See also: ibid, pp. 277-278; 300, 780, 885, 899.

The name 都末 = Dumo has been reconstructed as: K. 45e[1] + K. 277a: *tomwât; EMC: *tomat or *tuomat). Schuessler (2009), 1-38e', p. 53, gives tɑ for the Late Han and gives as examples the transcriptional forms of Middle Han: 都賴 tɑ-lɑs Talas; 都密 tɑ-mɨt (*tâmrit) Tarmita, Termes. For 末 he gives a Late Han rendering of mɑt (21-37a, p. 238).

都末 = Dumo (*Tɑ-mɑt) therefore seems to have been an attempt to transcribe the Khotanese version of *Dharma* (Pāli: Dhamma), making it probable that Duma and Vijaya Dharma were one and the same person.

Furthermore, the record says King Vijaya Jaya was followed by his son, King Vijaya Dharma, followed by his son, King Vijaya Siṃha and who, in turn, was followed by King Vijaya Kīrti.

King Vijaya Siṃha is said to have conquered the king of Ga-hjag/Kashgar, and King Vijaya Kīrti to have assisted Kanishka/Kanika in his conquest of So-ked/Saketa with the king of Gu-zan/Kucha.

Kanishka's conquest of the central Ganges Valley is confirmed by the inscription bearing his name from year 2 at Kosam/Kauśāmbī), and the two inscriptions of year 3 from Sarnath, to the east of Saketa.

The Rabatak Inscription makes it clear that this campaign took place early in Kanishka's era, which Harry Falk (2001) and (2004) has identified as beginning in 127 CE. See: Appendices P and X.

This evidence points to the reign of King Vijaya Dharma as occurring roughly 60 or 70 years earlier, or around 60 CE – exactly the period indicated for the 'noble' named 'Dumo' in the *Hou Hanshu*.

F. W. Thomas in the notes to his translation of "The Annals of the Li Country [Khotan]" adds support to my dating for the arrival of silk technology in Khotan in the early first century CE:: "The introduction of silk-culture into Khotan probably took place early, perhaps about the beginning of the Christian era." Thomas (1935), page 110, n. 9. Also see: Emmerick (1967), pp. 33-47, and Thomas (1935), pp. 110-119.

Although it is impossible to date these events exactly, the evidence is sufficient to declare that silk technology probably arrived in Khotan sometime during the first half of the 1st century CE. Khotan is still famous today for its exquisite silks.

Appendix B: The Story of Sea Silk

For over 2,000 years there were stories of a mysterious, fine, and rare cloth, usually referred to as "sea silk" or "sea wool," made in the Roman Empire. By the mid-20th century, it was commonly dismissed as a legend:

> "Various sources also mention particularly beautiful cloths, veritable symbols of these deeply monarchic societies with strict hierarchies, fabrics made exclusively for kings, which could not be exported on pain of harsh punishment, such as a caliph's robe woven at Tennis in Syria, certain Byzantine silks reserved for use in the palace and Chinese silks which were not allowed to be sold to merchants. In particular the cloth made of marine silk, from the hair of the *abû qalamûn*, as soft as silk and golden coloured, mentioned by Al-Muqaddasi in the 10th century as a product of North Africa. The sovereign forbade its export, but, says the author, it was exported in secret. Unfortunately this cloth is known to us only through literature, and no museum has been fortunate enough to preserve any. It is not even represented in painting. Like the dragon and the unicorn, we can but dream of it." Boulnois (2004), p. 287.

Other writers have gone even further than Boulnois, denying there ever was such a fabric as sea-silk. They believed that the so-called 'water-sheep' of the Chinese texts were fictional, and that reports of marine 'fine wool' or 'down' in the *Hou Hanshu* and the *Weilüe* were either simple fables, or the cloth referred to was, in fact, a wild silk, as claimed in the *Hou Hanshu*. See, for example: Pelliot (1963), pp. 509-510; Raschke (1976), p. 854, n. 849.

In Chinese literature there are two early references to *shuiyang* 水羊 – literally 'water-sheep' and the cloth made from them. The first reference is in the 'Chronicle on the Western Regions' of the *Hou Hanshu* (see Section 12). It says:

> "They [of Da Qin = the Roman Empire] also have fine cloth [細布 *xibu*] which some say [或言] is made from the down [毳 *cui*] of 'water sheep,' but which is, in fact, made from the cocoons of wild silkworms."

The *Hou Hanshu* states that the claim the cloth was made from "water-sheep" was false and, instead, it actually referred to wild silks. This critical comment may have been added to the original report by the compiler, Fan Ye, in the 5th century, possibly based on the hints in the 3rd century *Weilüe*.

Nevertheless, this account is interesting as it shows that the authors of both the *Hou Hanshu* and the *Weilüe* had a healthy scepticism about the story of the "water sheep," and presented a seemingly more logical alternative.

Both the *Hou Hanshu* and the *Weilüe* describe the 細布 *xibu* 'fine cloth' as 毳 *cui*, implying that the cloth was exceptionally fine and soft. It is defined as:

> "**1. a. Down** from birds; fine hair. **b.** (*Anat. - Embryol.*) Lanugo [fine hair of a newborn infant]. **2.** Knitting of animal hair. **3.b** :: *n. 11532* 脆 **ts'ui**4 **Fragile;** delicate; frail. . . ." Translated from *GR* Vol. VI, p. 175, No. 11518. See also: Kroll (2015), p. 69; *OCD*. Part II, p. 130.

> "The down on birds; the fine fur next [to] the skin; furry, downy; soft, velvety; crisp; delicate; fragile, easily broken." Williams (1909), p. 839;

These terms would not have been used to describe the wild silks produced in China which were considered "very coarse." See the quote from Gray in Appendix C.

> "They [the subjects of Justinian] were still more intimately acquainted with a shell-fish of the Mediterranean, surnamed the silk-worm of the sea ; the fine wool or hair by which the mother-of-pearl affixes itself to the rock is now manufactured for

curiosity rather than use ; and a robe obtained from the same singular materials was the gift of the Roman emperor to the satraps of Armenia.[67]

[67] Procopius de Ædif. 1. iii. c. I. These *pinnes de mer* are found near Smyrna, Sicily, Corsica, and Minorca; and a pair of gloves of their silk was presented to Pope Benedict XIV. [This cloth is the *byssus* woven from the threads of the *pinna squamosa*.]."

Gibbon (undated), p. 33.

A thousand years later, in the *Zhufan zhi* by Zhao Rugua, published *circa* 1125 CE, we find reference to sea-silk in Chinese sources under a different transcription:

"The products of the country ("Rum" – identified as Asia Minor) are: 鮫綃 (?byssus), gold-spangled *yüé-no* cloth (金宇越諾布), brocades with alternating stripes of gold and silk, bezoar stones, *wu-ming-i*, rose-water, gardenia flowers, liquid storax, borax, and a superior quality of engraved opaque glassware." Hirth and Rockhill (1911), p. 141.

Hirth and Rockhill indicate some doubt as to the identification of 鮫綃 *jiaoxiao* as sea-silk by placing a question mark before the identification as "byssus" above, but, it is not possible to maintain serious doubts any longer. Here is how "*le Grand Ricci*" dictionary defines the term, its constituent characters and related terms:

"鮫綃 – (*Myth.*) silk material made by the nymphs of the southern seas (see *jiaoren* 鮫人).
鮫 – *jiao* "鮫 CHIAO[1] **1.** (*Ichtyol.*) Shark; elasmobranchii (a branch of fish including sharks and rays); dog-fish. **2.** ;: *n. 1304* 蛟 **chiao**[1] (*Myth.*) Marine dragon resembling a big serpent with four feet.
鮫人 – [*jiaoren*] (*Myth.*) Nymph of the southern seas, who spins under water (and whose tears are pearls)" *GR* Vol. I, p. 715.
綃 – *xiao* – "**1. raw silk;** naturally coloured silk. **2.** Very light silk cloth; gauze." *GR* Vol. II, p. 1066. Translated and adapted from the French original. (JEH)

"The reference to byssus is important. Although this product — the threads of the pima squamosa, is found throughout the Mediterranean, it is more abundant near Smyrna than elsewhere. It was much prized for making fabrics by the Emperors of Byzantium, even after the introduction of the silkworm into Europe. Conf. also infra, p. 153, lines 23—25." Hirth and Rockhill (1911), p. 142, note.

The *Weilüe* also reports on what must surely be the same fabric:

"They have a fine cloth that is said to be made from the down of 'water-sheep'. It is called Haixi ('Egyptian') cloth. This country produces the six domestic animals, which [are said to] all come from the water.

It is said that they [the people of Da Qin] not only use [ordinary] sheep's wool but also bark from trees, or make silk from wild cocoons." Translated by the author.

Yu Huan, who composed the *Weilüe*, carefully qualified the reports in the *Hou Hanshu* that the Romans had "the six domestic animals" which all lived in the sea, and hints that the sea-silk may have come from wild cocoons rather than from the 'down' of 'water-sheep.'

A parallel passage in chapter 330 of Ma Duanlin's magisterial encyclopaedia, the *Wenxian Tongkao*, published in 1317 CE, refers to this cloth simply as *xibu* 細布 or "fine cloth" which is called *haizhongbu* 海中布, or "cloth from the sea." Hirth (1875), p. 80.

Emil Bretschneider, in his *Arabs and Arabian Colonies* (1871), p. 24, was the first to propose that the 'down of the water-sheep' referred to in the Chinese accounts was " . . . perhaps, the *Byssus*, a cloth-stuff woven up to the present time by the Mediterranean coast, especially in Southern Italy, from the thread-like excrescences of several sea-shells, especially *Pinna squamosa*." Hirth (1875), p. 262.

"'Fine cloth, also called down of the water-sheep', which according to the *Hou-han-shu* was made from the cocoons of wild silk worms, seems a most exotic material. It was probably byssus, a cloth made from the silk-like hairs by which certain shell-fish, such as the *Pinna squamosa*, attach themselves to rocks. These shell-fish are found in many parts of the Mediterranean, and the material made up from their 'hair' was highly prized in the ancient world. It is not produced commercially any longer, although Gibbon records that in the early eighteenth century Pope Benedict XIV was presented with a pair of gloves made from this material." Thorley (1971), p. 77.

"[The Romans] were still more intimately acquainted with a shell-fish of the Mediterranean, surnamed the silk-worm of the sea; the fine wool or hair by which the mother-of-pearl affixes itself to the rock, is now manufactured for curiosity rather than use; and a robe obtained from the same singular materials, was a gift of the Roman emperor to the satraps of Armenia.†

† Procopius de Edif. Lib. 3, c. 1. These *pinnes de mer* are found near Smyrna, Sicily, Corsica, and Minorca; and a pair of gloves of their silk was presented to pope Benedict XIV."

Gibbon (1867), Chap. XL, p. 313 and note †.

Early in the 17th century, reports from Russia arrived in England about a cloth attributed to fabulous creatures, half animal and half plant, supposedly coming from Scythia. Sir Richard Lee, the British ambassador to Russia (July 1600 to April 1601), was given a 'gowne or long cloake, made after the fashion of that cuntrie with the skins of those Tartar lambes.'

"Francis Bacon also noted, in his comments on zoophytes ["a creature on the borderline between an animal and a plant"], in the *Sylva sylvarum* (1627) that:

There is a Fabulous Narration, that in the Northern Countries, there should be an Herbe that groweth in the likenesse of a Lambe, and feedeth upon the Grasse, in such sort, as it will bare the Grass round about. But I suppose, that the Figure maketh the Fable; For so we see, there be Bee-Flowers, &c. And as for the Grasse, it seemeth the Plant, having a great Stalke and Top, doth prey upon the Grasse, a good way about by drawing the Iuyce ['juice"] of the Earth from it." Appleby (1997), p. 24.

But, by the early 18th century, it became known in England that this remarkable cloth was made from the byssus of the *Pinna marina*, and several specimens of both the byssus and the shells were already in the collections of the Royal Society.

"The *Journal Book* records that on 14 May 1719 he [John Busby] presented the Society with:

a Stocking resembling Soft Silk made of the beard of the Shell fish Pinna together with some fragments of the Shell and an Account of it was read. In which by his Own Order at Tarentum in the Kingdom of Naples from the Beards which he Saw taken from Several Shells of a Ffish which much frequents that Branch of the Sea leading to the Bay of Tarentum called Mare De Pesco. The Ffish is Called by Some of the Inhabitants the Scooda and by others the Parachella.

A comparison of the shell with a *Pinna* shell fetched from the Repository proved them to be identical.

Although it has not yet been verified, several writers claim that Pope Benedict XIV was presented with [a pair of] *Pinna* byssus stockings in a sliver snuffbox during 1754. On 18 March, 1804, [Admiral Lord] Nelson, on board the *Victory*, while blockading the French off Toulon, sent Emma Hamilton: a comb, which looks handsome, and a pair of curious gloves; they are made only in Sardinia of the beards of mussels, I have ordered a muff; they tell me they are very scarce, and for that reason I wish you to have them." Appleby (1997), p. 31.

" 'The *pinna* belongs, like the common edible muscle [sic = mussel], to the order of the *Vermes testacea.* The animal is a limax, its shell is bivalve, fragile, and furnished with a beard; the valves hinge without a tooth. The pinna does not fasten itself to rocks in the same situation as the muscle, but sticks its sharp end into the mud or sand, while the rest of the shell remains at liberty to open in the water." Browne (1832), pp. 280-281.

The Treasury of Natural History or A Popular Dictionary of Zoology, by Samuel Maunder (1878), p. 526, contains the following entry on the Pinna genus:

PINNA. A genus of Molluscs, called also *wing-shell*, which in many respects approaches the Mussels. It has two equal wedge-shaped valves, united by a ligament along one of their sides ; and obtains a very considerable size, sometimes being nearly three feet long. The animal fixes itself, by its *byssus* which is remarkably long and silky, to submarine rocks and other bodies ; where it lives in a vertical position, the point of the shell being undermost, and the base or edge above. Sometimes large bodies of them are found even attached to a sandy bottom at the depth of a few fathoms. They are common in some parts of the Mediterranean ; and are not merely sought as food by the inhabitants on the coasts, but they gather the byssus, of which a stuff may be formed which is remarkable for its warmth and suppleness. The filaments are extremely fine and strong, and the colour, which is a reddish-brown, never fades. The finest byssus of the ancients was fabricated from these filaments ; and in Sicily they are still sometimes manufactured into gloves and other articles of dress, though, it must be confessed, more as an object of curiosity than use." Maunder (1878), p. 526.

"Among other marine productions for which the Alghero coast is famous is the pinna flabellum, or pinna marina as it is also called. The following passage in "Swinburne's Travels in the Two Sicilies," (section 32,) [Henry Swinburne, 4 Vols., first published 1783-85] gives an account of it as found and used by the Tarentines on the coast near Capo St. Vita, and the description is applicable, in many respects, to the Sarde use of it. "This bivalve shell (the pinna marina) of the muscle tribe, frequently exceeds two feet in length. It fastens itself to the stones by its hinge, and throws out a large tuft of silky threads, which float and play about to allure small fish. Amid these filaments is generally found, besides other insects, a small shrimp, called by the ancients cancer pinnotheres, by the modern Tarentes, caurella. This little crustaceous animal was imagined to be generated with the pinna, and appointed by nature to act as a watchman in apprising it of the approach of prey or enemies; and that, upon the least alarm, this guard slipt down into the shell, which was instantly closed; but more accurate observers have discovered that the poor shrimp is no more than a prey itself, and by no means a sentinel for the muscle, which, in its turn, frequently falls a victim to the wiles of the polypus octopedia. In very calm weather this rapacious pirate may be seen stealing towards the yawning shells with a pebble in its claws, which he darts so dextrously into the aperture, that the pinna cannot shut itself up close enough to pinch off the feelers of its antagonist, or save its flesh from his ravenous tooth. The pinna is torn off the rocks with hooks, and broken for the sake of its bunch of silk, called lanapinna, which is sold in its rude state for about fifteen carlini a pound to women that wash it well with soap and fresh water. When it is perfectly cleaned of all its impurities, they dry it in the shade, straighten it with a large comb, cut off the useless root, and card the remainder, by which means they reduce a pound of coarse filaments to about three ounces of fine thread. This they knit into stockings, gloves, caps, and waistcoats; but they commonly mix a little silk as a strengthener. This web is of a beautiful yellow brown, resembling the burnished gold on the back of some flies and beetles. I was told that lanapinna receives its gloss from being steeped in lemon juice, and being afterwards pressed down with a tailor's goose."

The Sardes call the fish nachera, and the lanapinna, known to naturalists as the byssus, is termed the barba; this, when cleaned and prepared, sells for 8*s* the lb.; and it takes four ounces to make a pair of gloves, which are sold at eleven reals (4*s* 2¾*d.*) the pair.

Many of the pinna were nearly three feet long, of a most brilliant mother-of-pearl surface in the interior; and the pearls obtained from them are more curious than valuable.

Plutarch, in his "Solertiâ Animalum," speaks of the pinnothera attaching itself to the pinna, and acting as a kind of jackal or provider, for it bites the pinna by way of informing it that there is a little fish inside his shell which he then closes, and they eat their prey together." Tyndale (1849), pp. 77-79.

" 'It is said that the pinna fastens itself so strongly to the rocks, that the men who are employed in fishing it are obliged to use considerable force to break the tuft of threads by which it is secured fifteen, twenty, and sometimes thirty feet below the surface of the sea.

'The fishermen at Toulon use an instrument called a cramp for this curious pursuit. This is a kind of iron fork, whose prongs are each about eight feet in length and six inches apart, and placed at right angles to the handle, the length of which is regulated by the depth of water. The pinnæ are seized, separated from the rock, and raised to the surface by means of this instrument.

'The threads of the pinna have from very ancient time been employed in the manufacture of certain fabrics. This material was well known to the ancients, as some suppose, under the name of byssus, and was wrought in very early times into gloves and other articles of dress and ornament. It appears that robes were sometimes made of this produce, since we learn from Procopius that a robe composed of byssus of the pinna was presented to the satraps of Armenia by the Roman emperor.

'A writer of the year 1782 evidently refers to the pinnæ marinæ, when he says, "The ancients had a manufacture of silk, and which, about forty years ago, was revived at Tarento and Regio in the kingdom of Naples. It consists of a strong brown silk, belonging to some sort of shell, of which they make caps, gloves, stockings, waistcoats, &c., warmer than the woollen stuffs, and brighter than common silk. I have seen such kind of silk in shells myself; I think it was of the pectin kind, but cannot be sure."

'Several beautiful manufactures are wrought with these threads at Palermo. They are in many places the chief objects of the fishery, and the silk is found to be excellent. The produce of a considerable number of pinnæ is required to make only one pair of stockings. The delicacy of this singular thread is such that a pair of stockings made of it can be easily contained in a snuff box of ordinary size. Some stockings of this material were presented, in the year 1754, to pope Benedict XIV; and, notwithstanding their extreme fineness, were found to protect the legs alike from cold and heat. Stockings and gloves of this production, however thin, are too warm for common wear, but are esteemed useful in gouty and rheumatic cases. This great warmth of the byssus, like the similar quality in silk, results probably from both being imperfect conductors of heat as well as of electricity.

'It is not probable that this material will ever be obtained in much abundance, or that it will cease to be a rarity, except in the places of its production. It is never seen in England save in the cabinets of the curious." Browne (1832), pp. 285-286. Also see the entries on Byssus in the *Oxford English Dictionary* (2011).

After extensive enquiries about this rare, beautiful and elusive cloth, and with the kind help of Valérie Lefebvre-Aladawi, President of the SYTCOS - the Syrian Textile and Costume Squad in France, I contacted Dr. Felicitas Maeder who had recently started a "Project Sea-silk" at the Natural History Museum in Basle, Switzerland. She sent me her fascinating article, "The Project Sea-silk – Rediscovering an Ancient Textile Material," see: Maeder (2002), pp. 8-11. She also included a copy of "Oriental Translations: Pinna Wool, Aquatic Sheep and Mermaid Fleece," in McKinley (1988), pp. 67-75.

Felicitas Maeder's article includes a beautiful full-page colour reproduction of a 14th century knitted cap of sea-silk and points out, on page 10 that:

"Proof of the reality of the use of sea-silk for textile production at least in late antiquity is a fragment of a woven textile of the 4th century. It was found in 1912 in a woman's grave in Aquinicum (Budapest), at that time a Roman town at the north-east frontier of the empire. It was described in 1917 by F. Hollendonner and 1935 by L. Nagy. J. P. Wild mentions this fragment in his study of textile manufacture in the Northern Roman provinces (1970) and adds that it supports the assumption that the 'marine wool' of Diocletian's Price Edict meant sea-silk."

This evidence of the existence of sea-silk textiles in the Roman Empire as early as the 4th century, and the fact that the 'marine wool' mentioned in Diocletian's Price Edict of 301 CE probably refers to sea-silk, led me to re-examine the references in both the Chinese and Western accounts.

"The most famous product produced by the Pinnidae is the byssus fiber, which is an extremely fine and soft but strong fiber produced by a gland in the foot of the animal for the purpose of anchoring the shell. The byssus fiber of some of the larger species in this family is sufficiently long so that it can be spun and then woven or knitted to make small garments. It has a beautiful golden bronze sheen and was often combined with silk when used in making larger garments. Most authorities believe that the use of the byssus as a fiber in making garments probably originated in India near Colchi. This is based on the fact that the earlier Greek and Roman writers referred to *Pinna* but did not mention the use of the byssus before the time of Tertullian (150-222 A.D.) Tarento was the center of the industry in Italy, and Procopius, who wrote on the Persian wars about 550 A.D., stated that the five hereditary satraps (governors) of Armenia who received their insignia from the Roman Emperor were given chlamys (or cloaks) made from *lana pinna* (*Pinna* "wool," or byssus). Apparently only the ruling classes were allowed to wear these chlamys. Even today a small remnant of the former industry remains in Italy and a few articles such as gloves, hats, shawls and stockings are made mainly for the tourist trade. According to Simmonds (1879) in "The Commercial Products of the Sea," the byssus formed an important article of commerce among the Sicilians, for which purpose considerable numbers of *Pinna* were annually fished in the Mediterranean from a depth of 20 to 30 feet. He also said, "a considerable manufactory is established at Palermo; the fabrics made are extremely elegant and vie in appearance with the finest silk. The best products of this material are, however, said to be made in the Orphan Hospital of St. Philomel at Lucca." Though the modern gloves and shawls are knitted, the chlamys, gloves and stockings of the ancients were woven, for knitting was not known until about 1500 according to Yates (1843). Articles made from *Pinna* byssus are extremely strong and durable except that they are readily attacked by moths so that great care must be taken in their preservation. There are, as a consequence, very few examples of the early garments in existence. On Plate 153 are shown the cleaned byssus of *Atrina rigida* Solander ; the shell of *Pinna nobilis* Linné, the species from which the byssus was obtained for the Italian industry ; and a glove made from byssus fibre at Tarento, Italy [presently displayed at the Smithsonian in Washington, D.C.]." Turner and Rosewater (1958), pp. 292, 294.

The word *byssus* not only refers to the excretions of seashells, as sometimes assumed, but was originally used to describe fine threads of linen, and later, of cotton and silk. It is derived from Latin *byssus* via Gk. *byssos* = flax, linen. It is of Semitic origin related to Hebrew *būts* – fine linen. This word is possibly related to the material "'Böz,' an exotic cloth in the Chinese Imperial Court." See the discussion in Ecsady (1975), pp. 145-153.

"A triangular form, ventral flattening, and secure attachment to firm substrates by byssal threads (byssus; proteinaceous threads secreted by a gland on the foot) have allowed certain bivalves to colonize hard surfaces on wave-swept shores. The byssus is a larval feature that is retained by adults of some bivalve groups, such as the true mussels (family Mytilidae) of marine and estuarine shores and the family Dreissenidae of fresh and estuarine waters." *EB*. Retrieved 19 September, 2011 from: http://www.britannica.com/EBchecked/topic/67293/bivalve.

"The Pinnidae have considerable economic importance in many parts of the world. They produce pearls of moderate value. In the Mediterranean area, material made from the holdfast or byssus of *Pinna nobilis* Linné has been utilized in the manufacture of clothing for many centuries: gloves, shawls, stockings and cloaks. Apparel made from this material has an attractive golden hue and these items were greatly valued by the ancients.

Today, pinnidae are eaten in Japan, Polynesia, in several other Indo-Pacific island groups, and on the west coast of Mexico. In Polynesia, the valves of *Atrina vexillum* are carved to form decorative articles, and entire valves of larger specimens are sometimes used as plates." Rosewater (1961), pp. 175-176.

Sea-silk continued to be a much sought-after luxury product throughout the Middle Ages, as these references from the 10th century make clear:

"Beyond the examples already cited, one could note the Spanish vizier Mansūr's bestowal on the Christian and Muslim princes who had helped him in a victorious campaign in A.H. 387/A.D. 997 of "two thousand two hundred and eighty-five pieces of various kinds of *tirāzī* silk, twenty-one pieces of sea-wool, two *'anbarī'* robes [i.e., perfumed with ambergris], eleven pieces of *siqlātūn* [silk in a variety of colors dependent on its place of origin] . . . seven brocade carpets . . . and two marten furs." For the complete catalogue, see al-Maqqart, *Analectes* (as above, note 40), 1:271." Quoted from: "Gifts and Gift Exchanges as Aspects of the Byzantine, Arab, and Related Economies" by Anthony Cutler in *Dumbarton Oaks Papers No. 55* Ed. Alice-Mary Talbot (2001), p. 265, n. 102. Downloaded from: http://www.doaks.org/DOP55/DP55ch13.pdf on 8 April, 2003.

"The "delicate cloth which some say is the wool of sea sheep, but is really made from the cocoons of wild silkworms" may refer to the filaments which cover certain Mediterranean mussels, mentioned in other texts and which form a sort of "marine silk". The Arab author, Al-Muqaddasi, writing at the end of the 10th century, describes a mussel which was gathered in the Mediterranean and which he calls *abû qalamûn*: "a creature which scratches itself on the rocks on the seashore. It leaves some of its fur there, which has the softness of silk and the colour of gold. The people do not leave a thread of it behind, because it is very rare. It is gathered, and cloths are woven from it; and in the course of a day it assumes various colours. The ruler has forbidden the export of it, though, of course, some is exported secretly. One garment of it may fetch ten thousand *dînârs.*[26]

26. *In: AL-MUQADDASI.* The Best Divisions for knowledge of the Regions, *translated by Basil A. Collins. Centre for Muslim Contribution to Civilization, Garnet Publishing, Reading, 1994, p. 215.*"

Boulnois (2004), pp. 117-118, 437, note 26.

Felicitas Maeder, through her "Project sea-silk", mounted a spectacular sea silk exhibition at the Natural History Museum in Basle, Switzerland from 19 March to 27 June, 2004, which featured a variety of pieces ranging from a knitted 14th century cap to a woven tapestry cloak embroidered with sea silk made for Mussolini in 1929.

A magnificently illustrated exhibition catalogue in both Italian and German was published in 2004, with detailed notes on all aspects of the history, production and uses of sea silk, entitled: ***Bisso marino**: Fili d'oro dal fondo del mare* – ***Muschelseide**: Goldene Fäden vom Meeresgrund*. Edited by Felicitas Maeder, Ambros Hänggi, and Dominik Wunderlin. Naturhistoriches Museum and Museum der Kulturen, Basel, Switzerland.

A second exhibition, called "Sea-silk - golden threads of the sea" was held from 18 October 2008 - 1 March 2009 in the Villa Ciani, Lugano, Switzerland.

In July 2008, I visited the Division of Mollusks at the Smithsonian National Museum of Natural History in Washington, D.C. I was thrilled to be taken by the Curator, Mr. Paul Greenhall, behind the public displays to see the 17th century sea silk glove from Sorrento, Italy which they have in their reference collection. The glove is in perfect condition, incredibly light and soft and the golden sheen is still brilliant – it looks as if it was knitted only recently. They also had several *Pinna nobilis* shells and raw byssus threads which I was kindly allowed to handle and photograph.

In 2012, Dr. Felicitas Maeder developed a website called "Project Sea-silk," now accessible in four languages: German, French, Italian and English. It is well-illustrated and freely available online at: http://www.muschelseide.ch/en.html.

From the accounts in both the *Hou Hanshu* and the *Weilüe* I believe it is now beyond question that sea silk was offered to the Chinese by Roman traders in the 2nd and 3rd centuries CE.

Sea silk was a beautiful, rare, valuable, light, non-perishable, and easily transported item, making it an ideal product to trade for Chinese silks.

In spite of the fantastic stories of its origin, the passage in the *Weilüe* quoted above which states that Da Qin had "a fine cloth that is said to be made from the down of 'water-sheep'," clearly shows that it was known in China by the 3rd century, at least, and that it was not a type of wild silk, but truly 'silk from the sea.'

Appendix C: Wild Silks

"Wild silks" have been woven in China from early times, although the scale of production has always been far smaller than for cultivated silkworms. The term used here in the *Hou Hanshu*, *yecan* 野蠶 - literally 'wild cocoons,' is defined as: *tussah* [from Hindi टसर – *tasar*]; 'wild silkworm'. *ABC*, p 1130.

> "[Hindi *tasar*] **1 :** an Oriental silkworm that is the larva of a moth (*Antheraea paphia*, syn. *A. mylitta*) and that produces a brownish silk; *also* **:** a sometimes cultivated Chinese silkworm (*A. pernyi*) producing a similar silk **2 a :** the uneven tan filament produced by the wild silkworms of China and India that is coarser, stronger, and shorter than cultivated silk **b :** any of various fabrics (as pongee and shantung) made of this silk and used in its natural tan color or dyed." *WTNID* under: **tussah.**

Commercially reared silkworms are normally killed before the pupae emerge - either by pricking them with a needle, or dipping the cocoons into boiling water - thus allowing the whole cocoon to be unravelled as one continuous thread, approximately a kilometre long. The result is a strong, very fine, warm, and beautiful cloth.

Some wild silks are difficult to dye, but many have naturally attractive colours, such as the highly-valued rich golden sheen of the silk of the muga silkworm from Assam. Wild silks are favoured by Buddhists as they don't require the killing of the pupae.

> "That which is properly known as silk is the unbroken thread unwound from the cocoon of the silkworm, *Bombyx mori*, which feeds mainly on the leaves of the white mulberry tree (*Morus alba*). This caterpillar turns into a chrysalis, but is not permitted to transform itself into a moth, so that the cocoon is not perforated. Thus a continuous unwound thread is what distinguishes cultivated silk from the various forms of wild silk, made from the cocoons of other caterpillars, in which the moth leaves the cocoon by piercing a hole through it, thus breaking the thread which the caterpillar has wound around itself. In this instance, the silky substance has to be woven just as one would cotton, and the thread obtained is less fine and inferior in quality than thread from an intact cocoon. Wild silks, produced by various insects, exist in many parts of the world from Assam to Madagascar; the Mediterranean countries also produced their share of them, around the same time that Seric cloth appeared there. This has led to a certain confusion in the use of the various terms for these fabrics, as we shall see." Boulnois (2004), p. 47.

> "In places like Ch'ing-chou and Yin-shui [both in Shantung province] there is a wild silkworm [3] that makes the cocoon [without human care], its natural habitat being old trees. Garments made of this silk are rainproof and dustproof. The moth flies away immediately upon emerging from the cocoon, and its eggs are not preserved on paper sheets. Wild silkworms are found but rarely in other localities.
>
> 3. Wild silk is produced by caterpillars other than the mulberry silkworm, or *Bombyx mori*. The term "wild" implies that these silkworms are not capable of being domesticated and artificially cultivated like the mulberry worms." Sung (1637), p. 37 and p. 71, n. 3.

> "The tussah silkworm, *Antheraea pernyi*, a native of China, feeds exclusively on one type of oak tree, *Quercus serrata*, and only out of doors on trees of shrub height. Although it can produce both a spring and an autumn crop, only the autumn crop is usually used for silk production. Tussah cocoons contain more gum and calcium compounds than mulberry worm cocoons, and must be boiled in sodium carbonate solution for one and a half hours, followed by the normal boiling procedure before reeling." *NEB*, Vol. 7, p. 288c.

"The use and production of wild silk was known to geographically widely diverse areas of the ancient world. In this case the larvae are not cultivated or fed. They spin the cocoon and then chew their way out of it. The cocoons are then collected and unwound. The domesticated silkworm is killed, either by scalding the cocoon or by the insertion of a needle, to insure that the thread remains undamaged from the efforts of the larvae to escape. Wild silk is coarser and somewhat less expensive and is the product of a considerable variety of larvae of the sub-order *bombycina*. It is to this class that the famous Coan silk of the ancient world belonged. Such wild silk was produced in China and possibly also in India, Central Asia and Mesopotamia. How much, if any, was exported to the West is unknown." Raschke (1976), p. 623. (Also see the discussion of Coan silk, ibid. p. 722, nn. 380, 381).

"The more than 500 species of wild silkworms fend for themselves, feasting on oak and other leaves. When they become moths, they are bigger and more gorgeous than the commercial *Bombyx*. More robust than their domesticated cousins, wild silkworms produce a tougher, rougher silk, not as easily bleached and dyed as the mulberry silk.

China is the chief supplier of an off-white wild silk known as tussah. India has a monopoly on the muga caterpillar, which thrives in the humidity of the Assam Valley and produces a shimmering golden silk. The eri silkworm, raised on the castor plant in India, produces silk that is extremely durable, but that cannot be easily reeled off the cocoon and must be spun like cotton or wool." Hyde (1984), p. 14. Also consult: Good (1995), pp. 959-968; Adams (2002); Gopal (1961), pp. 61-69.

"Not only has early evidence for silk been assumed to be Chinese, but the techniques of degumming and reeling are also considered exclusively Chinese silk industry 'secrets'. The process of de-gumming, is where the sericin gum is removed from the silk, by submerging the cocoons into a weak alkaline solution. Reeling silk is a process by which the long silk strands (gummed ot not) are collected onto a bobbin rather than needing to be twisted as short segments into a spun thread. These two important silkworking processes have been thought to be part of a 'package' of Chinese technology known only to China until well into the early centuries AD, although the evidence presented here indicates that wild *Antheraea* silks were also known and used in the Indus as early as the mid-third millennium BCE, and that reeling was practiced. The implication of evidence for silk reeling is that the silkmoth was stifled, leaving the cocoon intact in order to be unraveled. When wild silk cocoons are collected on the ground, usually after the silkmoth has eaten its way out, the remaining silk fibers must be spun rather than reeled, as they are short.

This new discovery of silk in the Indus Valley pushes back the earliest date of silk outside of China by a millennium. Specific contributions of the present paper include discussion of new silk finds from Harappa and Chanudaro along with SEM imaging of modern wild specimens of *Antheraea assamensis* and *A. mylitta* silk." Good et al. (2009), p. 2.

"Before concluding this chapter, I ought to add that in China Proper, more particularly, I believe, in the neighbourhood of Cheefoo, in the province of Shan-tung, and also in Mongolia, and Mantchuria, there are silkworms which produce what is termed by Chinese silk merchants "mountain silk." These worms are very large, and are found upon oak trees. The silken stuffs made of mountain silk are very coarse." Gray (1878), p. 230.

Shanchou 山紬 (literally, 'mountain silk') is a general term for cloth made from wild silks. See: *GR* Vol. V, p. 104. Wild silks used for stringing beads have been found and identified from two Indus sites, Harappa and Chanhu-daro, dating to *circa* 2450-2000 BCE, "roughly contemporaneous with the earliest Chinese evidence for silks."

> "At least two separate types of silk were utilized in the Indus in the mid-third millennium BC. Based on SEM image analysis there are two thread forms in the samples from Harappa, which appear to be from two different species of silkmoth (*Antheraea* sp.) [*A. mylitta* and *A. assamensis*]. The silk from Chanhu-daro may be from yet another South Asian moth species *Philosamia* spp. (Eri silk). Moreover, this silk appears to have been reeled." Good, et al. (2009), p. 8.

There are significant indications in the literature that wild silks were in use in Persia and Greece by the late 5th century BCE, apparently referred to as "Amorgina" or "Amorgian garments" – see: Richter (1929), pp. 27-33.

Pliny the Elder, (1st century CE) provides a strange mix of real knowledge and fanciful ideas:

> "Another species of insect is the silk-moth which is a native of Assyria. It is larger than the insects already mentioned [i.e. bees, wasps and hornets]. Silk-moths make their nests of mud, which looks like salt, attached to stone; they are so hard they can scarcely be pierced by javelins. In the nests they make wax combs on a larger scale than bees and produce a bigger larva.
>
> Silk-moths have an additional stage in their generation. A very big larva first changes into a caterpillar with two antennae, this becomes what is termed a chrysalis, from which comes a larva which in six months turns into a silkworm. The silkworms weave webs like spiders and these are used for *haute couture* dresses for women, the material being called silk. The technique of unravelling the cocoons and weaving the thread was first invented on Cos by a woman named Pamphile, the daughter of Plateas. She has the inalienable distinction of having devised a way of making women's clothing 'see-through.'
>
> Silk-moths, so they say, are produced on Cos, where a vapour from the ground breathes life into the flowers – from the cypress, terebinth, ash and oak – that have been beaten down by the rain. First, small butterflies without down are produced; these cannot endure the cold so they grow shaggy hair and equip themselves with thick coats to combat winter, scraping together down from the leaves with their rough feet. They compact this into fleeces, card it with their claws and draw it out into the woof, thinned out as if by a comb, and then they wrap this round their body.
>
> Then they are taken away, put in earthenware containers and reared on bran in a warm atmosphere. Underneath their coats a peculiar kind of feather grows, and when they are covered by these they are taken out for special treatment. The tufts of wool are plucked out and softened by moisture and subsequently thinned out into threads by means of a rush spindle. Even men have not been ashamed to adopt silk clothing in summer because of its lightness. Our habits have become so bizarre since the time we used to wear leather cuirasses that even a toga is considered an undue weight. However, we have left Assyrian silk dresses to the women – so far!" Pliny *NH* (77 CE) (a), pp. 157-158. (XI, 75-78).

> "Ta Ts'in State [Da Qin – the Roman Empire] weaves carpets out of the silk of wild cocoons, mixed with the many coloured wools of all sorts of animals, and representing birds, beasts, men, scenery, and all manner of strange things. This is evidently tapestry, known to the Eastern nations long before it was improved by the Greeks, and described by Rawlinson (Syria) and Beeton in precisely the same words as K'ang-hi. The word 罽 has the same meaning as 氍毹 [*qulu* or *qushu*],* and,

probably, as is the case with many Chinese proper names, combines the name sound of the foreign State with the leading feature of that State's productions. In Syria and Persia the carpet is still the chief feature in households, and the skill of the Mongols in weaving camel's hair carpets probably dates from the introductions from Syria." From the *Peiwenyunfu* composed during the reign of the Qing Emperor Kangxi (1662-1723). In: Parker (1885), Vol. 14 No. 1, p. 42. ***NOTE:** the original text has alternate forms of 氍毹 in which the radical no. 82 element comes first in each character – otherwise they are identical. (JEH)

"*Wild Silks*,—The ravages of pebrine and other diseases had the effect of attracting prominent attention to numerous other insects, allies of the mulberry silkworm, which spin serviceable cocoons. It had been previously pointed out by Captain Hutton, who devoted great attention to the silk question as it affects the East Indies, that at least six species of *Bombyx*, differing from *B. mori*, but also mulberry-feeding, are more or less domesticated in India. These include *B. textor*, the boropooloo of Bengal, a large species having one generation yearly and producing a soft flossy cocoon; the Chinese monthly worm, *B. sinensis*, having several generations, and making a small cocoon; and the Madrasi worm of Bengal (*B. croesi*), the Dassee or Desi worm of Bengal (*B. fortunatus*) and *B. arracanensis*, the Burmese worm—all of which yield several generations in the year and form reelable cocoons. Besides these there are many other mulberry-feeding *Bombycidae* in the East, principally belonging to the genera *Theophila* and *Ocinara*, the cocoons of which have not attracted cultivators. The moths yielding wild silks which have obtained most attention belong to the extensive and handsome family *Saturnidae*. The most important of the species at the present time is the Chinese tussur or tasar worm, *Antheraea pernyi* . . . , an oak-feeding species, native of Mongolia, from which is derived the greater part of the so-called tussur silk now imported into Europe. Closely allied to this is the Indian tussar moth . . . *Antheraea mylitta*, found throughout the whole of India feeding on the bher tree, *Zizyphus jujuba*, and on many other plants. It yields a large compact cocoon . . . of a silvery grey colour, which Sir Thomas Wardle of Leek, who devoted a great amount of attention to the wild-silk question succeeded in reeling. Next in promising quantities is the muga or moonga worm of Assam, *Antheraea assama*, a species to some extent domesticated in its native country. The yama-mai worm of Japan, *Antheraea* (*Samia*) *yama-mai*, an oak-feeder, is a race of considerable importance in Japan, where it is said to be jealously guarded against foreigners. Its eggs were first sent to Europe by Duchêne du Bellecourt, French consul-general in Japan in 1861; but early in March following they hatched out, when no leaves on which the larvae would feed were to be found. In April a single worm got oak-buds, on which it throve, and ultimately spun a cocoon whence a female moth issued, from which Guérin Méneville named and described the species. A further supply of eggs was secretly obtained by a Dutch physician Pompe van Meedervoort in 1863, and, as it was now known that the worm was an oak-feeder, and would thrive on the leaves of European oaks, great results were anticipated from the cultivation of the yama-mai. These expectations, however, for various reasons, have been disappointed. The moths hatch out at a period when oak leaves are not ready for their feeding, and the silk is by no means of a quality to compare with that of the common mulberry worm. The mezankoorie moth of the Assamese, *Antheraea mezankooria*, yields a valuable cocoon, as does also the Atlas moth, *Attacus atlas*, which has an omnivorous larva found throughout India, Ceylon, Burmah, China and Java. The Cynthia moth, *Attacus cynthia*, is domesticated as a source of silk in certain provinces of China, where it feeds on the *Ailanthus glandulosa*. The eria or arrinidi moth of Bengal and Assam, *Attacus ricini*, which feeds on the castor-oil plant, yields seven generations yearly, forming loose flossy orange-red and sometimes white cocoons. The ailanthus silkworm of Europe is a hybrid between *A. cynthia* and *A. ricini*, first obtained by Guérin Méneville, and now spread through many silk-growing regions. These are only a few of the moths from which silks of various usefulness can be produced; but none of these presents qualities, saving perhaps cheapness alone, which can put them in competition with common silk." *EB* (1911), Vol. 25, pp. 100-101.

Appendix D: Gan Ying's Journey to the Persian Gulf

A diplomatic envoy, Gan Ying, was sent on a mission in 97 CE to reach Da Qin (the Roman Empire), by the well-known Chinese general, Ban Chao, who was then stationed in the "Western Regions," or modern Xinjiang.

Gan Ying did not actually reach Da Qin territory, but, according to the *Hou Hanshu*, he did reach the shores of the "Great Sea," that is, the Persian Gulf, which was, quite logically, considered to be part of the 'Great Sea' = the modern 'Arabian Sea'.

He was allegedly discouraged from going further because the Parthians did not want direct communications to develop between China and the Roman Empire, and thus lose control of the trade and its profits.

In spite of being discouraged, Gan Ying a great deal of accurate information about Da Qin, probably from sailors in the Persian Gulf ports. However, his account certainly also contained some rather fanciful details - which may have been the result of deliberate misinformation or yarns spun by sailors in Persian Gulf ports.

His itinerary has been a subject of considerable speculation and debate. See notes 9.1 and 10.9. He presumably started his journey from somewhere in the Tarim Basin where Ban Chao was based. He may have set out from Kashgar travelling through Bactra/Balkh, or the 'hanging passages' in Hunza, to Jibin near Jallalabad, and then crossing into Parthian-controlled territory on his way to Kandahar and points further west.

It has often been assumed, following Friedrich Hirth's pioneering work *China and the Roman Orient* in 1885, that Gan Ying travelled through Sibin (identified as Ctesiphon), Alüan/Aman (identified as Hamadan/Ecbatana), to the Persian Gulf, and then back via Mulu or Merv.

The many discrepancies in this reconstructed itinerary have been explained by assuming that the Chinese had only vague notions of the region, or had copied information from imperfect foreign sources. The geographical directions and distances were considered deficient and a number of rather dubious phonetic reconstructions of the place names have been devised to justify them.

However, I believe Gan Ying did not go via Hamadan/Ecbatana and Ctesiphon at all, but took a quite different route.

Faxian clearly states (in the early 5th century) that neither Zhang Qian nor Gan Ying reached the *xuandu* (the 'hanging passages') of the Indus gorges, so we can discount this route. See: Appendix U; Rémusat (1836), pp. 36-37; Legge (1886), p. 27; Petech (1950), pp. 15-16.

Gan Ying could have travelled through the *xuandu* in Hunza, or by one of the other routes through Badakhshan and/or Gilgit to Gandhara. From there, he would have followed the Indus into Sind, which was still held by the Indo-Parthian successors of Gondophares. After that, Gan Ying would have headed west to Kandahar, probably across the Bolan Pass [1,649 m. or 5,410 ft.], which is open all year and links Sindh with Quetta, and the main route to Kandahar.

> "In the vast chain of mountains which extend from Baluchistan along the natural North-West Frontier of the sub-continent, there have been seven main corridors through which invasions and commerce have historically flowed between Central Asia and the Indus plains. Local tribesmen have between them known and utilised scores of ways through the chain, but only this small handful of routes has ever been viable to travellers from farther afield. Of the seven principal corridors through the mountains, the Bolan Pass is the most southerly and the longest; sixty-seven miles [108 km] from start to finish, which is almost thrice the length of the Khyber Pass away to the north. No one knows when man first discovered this way of reaching ancient India from the plateau of Afghanistan, but it may well

have been the first passage used; it certainly pre-dated the Khyber by several hundred years." Moorhouse (1984), p. 83. See also: Anonymous (1842), "The Bolan Pass."

It is logical that Gan Ying would refer to the Sind region and Arachosia and Drangiana, as "Anxi," or Parthia, as these territories were still controlled by Indo-Parthian princes, who were related to, and apparently allied with, the rulers of "Parthia proper," which included most of Mesopotamia and modern Iran. See the quote in note 14.3 from Puri (1994), p. 199.

My interpretation of the text in the *Hou Hanshu* is that Gan Ying travelled from the Tarim Basin to Gandhara and then turned south, crossing the Kushan-Parthian frontier near modern Uch.

Located at the final confluence of the five main rivers of the Punjab, Uch was at the junction of the Indus and the Chenab. The other major tributaries, the Jhelum, Ravi, Sutlej and Beas, join the Indus further upstream.

Uch is said to have been founded by Alexander the Great, but it may well be older. Today it is about 60 miles or 100 km. south of the present junction of the rivers, which over time, has gradually shifted north. It traditionally formed the frontier between the Punjab and Sind. See: Cunningham (1871), p. 220.

"Down to the time of Timur and Akbar, the junction of the Chenab and Indus took place opposite Uchh, sixty miles above the present confluence at Mithankot. It was unchanged when Rennell wrote his "Geography of India," in 1788, and still later in 1796, when visited by Wilford's surveyor, Mirza Mughal Beg. But early in the present century the Indus gradually changed its course, and leaving the old channel twenty miles above Uchh, flowed to the south-west, rejoining the former channel at Mithankot." Ross (1883), p. 65.

"At Mithankot, 500 miles [805 km.] from the sea, the Indus receives the accumulated waters of the five Punjab rivers, viz., the Jhelum, Chenab, Ravi, Beas, and Sutlej. Above the confluence its single breadth is 600 yards, its velocity five miles an hour, depth twelve to fifteen feet, and discharge of water 92,000 cubic feet per second. The five united streams are called the Punjnad, which, above the point of junction with the Indus, is 1,076 yards [984 m.] wide, and about 15 feet [4.6 m.] deep, flowing two miles per hour, with an estimated discharge of 69,000 feet per second. Below the junction the river has a breadth of from 2,000 yards [1,829 m.] to several miles, according to the season of the year. The tidal influence is experienced up to Tatta, seventy miles from the sea." Ross (1883), p. 32.

"After crossing the Sutlej the Punjab is entered. The Land of the Five Rivers has been the scene of the principal events in the history of India from the earliest period up to the time of its annexation to British territory. All invaders of India, excepting the English, have crossed the streams of the Punjab—the Jhelum, the Chenab, the Ravi, the Beas, and the Sutlej. These rivers eventually run into the Indus—the Nile of India—which forms a sixth stream of the Punjab, though it is not reckoned among them which give their collective name to the country. The Indus, for many long centuries before British occupation, was the boundary separating India from Afghanistan; to cross the Indus at Attock was to pass out of India. The Jhelum and the Ravi run into the Chenab; the former about 100 miles [161 km], the latter about 30 miles [48 km] north of Multan; the Beas joins the Sutlej at the southern boundary of the Kapurthala State; the Sutlej joins the Chenab at Jallapur, about 50 miles [80 km] below Multan; and the Chenab flows into the Indus at Mithankot, about 100 miles [161 km] below Multan; the Indus then flows on through Sindh, carrying the waters of these five magnificent rivers to the sea. Ross (1883), p. 67.

> "Mithankot is thirty miles [48 km.] west of Khanpur, on the right bank of the Indus, in the British district of Dera Ghazi Khan, and opposite the point where the five rivers of the Punjab unite with the waters of the river Indus, and flow thence to the sea as one grand stream. The site of Mithankot has frequently been changed, owing to the encroachments of the Indus. The town has now been removed five miles from the river, and has lost all its commercial importance in consequence. In the vicinity of the town there is a handsome shrine sacred to Akil Muhammad. A species of sambhar [*Rusa unicolor unicolor* – a large species of deer] is found in the dense jungles adjoining the Indus." Ross (1883), p. 64.

> "In describing the geography of Multân it is necessary to bear in mind the great changes that have taken place in the courses of all the large rivers that flow through the province. In the time of Timur and Akbar the junction of the Chenâb and Indus took place opposite *Uchh*, 60 miles above the present confluence at Mithankot. It ·was unchanged when Rennell wrote his 'Geography of India,' in A.D. 1788, and still later, in 1706, when visited by Wilford's surveyor, Mirza Mogal Beg. But early in the present century the Indus gradually changed its course, and leaving the old channel at 20 miles above *Uchh,* continued its course to the south-south-west, until it rejoined the old channel at Mithankot.
>
> The present junction of the Râvi and Chenâb takes place near *Diwâna Sanand,* more than 30 miles above Multân; but in the time of Alexander the confluence of the Hydraotes and Akesines was at a short distance below the capital of the Malli, which I have identified with Multan. The old channel still exists, and is duly entered in the large maps of the Multan division." Cunningham (1871), pp. 220-221.

It appears that Gan Ying continued his journey west (then northwest) from the Indus Valley to Herat; then west and southwest to Susa, and then south, across the Karkheh/Karkhen River. From there, he would have continued *southwest* (as stated in the text) to the port city of Charax Spasinou and the coast of the Persian Gulf. He may have travelled further, as far south as Fars, the seat of Manchihr I.

Parthia, at the time of Gan Ying's visit, was in great turmoil. It seems likely that the southern provinces, including Fars, were, to all intents and purposes, independent about this time, at least until the invasion of Trajan in 116 CE.

It seems likely that this instability explains the fact that "Manqu" (<*man-khut) 滿屈 – probably Manchihr (or Manuchihr) I of Persis – is said to be a king of Anxi in the text. Wang (2007a), p. 101. It is of more than passing interest that Manqu sent envoys and presents to China in 87 and 101 CE, both before and after Gan Ying's visit in 97 CE.

Although the information provided is meagre, Gan Ying probably returned along much the same route as far as Herat, and then turned north to the Merv Oasis (Mulu – described here as 'Eastern Anxi' – see: note 10.4), then under Parthian control, which explains its inclusion in this account. From Merv, he would have headed eastwards back to the Tarim Basin. There are three possible routes: he could have travelled either through Daxia and through Wakhan via Tashkurgan to Kashgar, or through the lands north of the Middle Oxus and along the Alai Valley to Kashgar or, possibly, via Sogdiana and Ferghana to Kashgar.

Two of the distances given in the *Hou Hanshu* agree remarkably well with the measurements given by modern maps for the places I have identified along his route:-

- The distance from Uch in the Indus Valley via Quetta, Kandahar and Farah to Herat is almost identical to that given in the *Hou Hanshu* of 3,400 *li* (1,414 km) between the eastern frontier of 'Anxi' (at Uch) and Alüan/Aman (= present day Herat – see: note 10.10).

• From Herat through Nishapur, the Caspian Gates and Qom to the site of ancient Susa is 1,500 km on my maps; the *Hou Hanshu* gives 3,600 *li* (1,497 km.) between Alüan/Aman/Herat and Sibin. See: Section 12 of the translation.

• The site of Spasinou Charax seems firmly located now. John Hansman (1984), pp. 161-166, makes a very strong case for locating it at Karkh Maisān/Naisān about 48.5 km northwest of modern Basra. I have measured from Susa southwest to this site, which is only about 175 kilometres as the crow flies. However, this is nowhere near the 960 *li* (399 km) given in the *Hou Hanshu* from Sibin to Yuluo. I can find no likely city in a 400 km arc from Spasinou Charax, so I assume that if I am correct in my locations, there is probably an error in the text.

However, we are told by Pliny in *NH* (77 CE) (b) VI. xxxi, 134, that the shoreline of the Persian Gulf had extended some 120 Roman miles (178 km.) from Charax. If Gan Ying was recording the distance from Susa to the shore of the Persian Gulf in the kingdom of Characene, rather than just to the town of Charax Spasinou, we get a total of about 353 km, which is far closer to the 399 km of the *Hou Hanshu*. See the quote from Pliny in note 10.12.

Pliny adds that the shoreline had extended some 70 Roman miles further out to sea (104 km. - roughly 2 km a year), between the time of Juba II (died *circa* 24 CE) and Pliny (who was writing in 77 CE).

If the shoreline continues moving south at about this rate from the time of Pliny's information (sometime prior to 77 CE, when he wrote his book) and 97 CE, when Gan Ying visited the region, the journey from Susa to the sea would have been more than 40 km. further than that given by Pliny's informants. This makes the measurements given in the *Hou Hanshu* very accurate indeed. See also: note 10.9.

> "Gan Ying seems to record a precise political situation. The Arsacids seem to have militarily occupied the entire area, transforming Mesene into a Parthian Satrapy and nominating an Army official as responsible for the points of major economic interest: the cities and river harbours.
>
> From the dates reported by Ban Zhao's envoy it is possible to conclude that the gap of monetary emissions of the independent kingdom Characene that took place in those years was due to a military or even political occupation of the client potentate. Characene harbours had in that period become Arsacid harbours and the authority that regulated and controlled the commercial traffic and transactions depended directly on the Great King or on his military representative in the area. Given the goals of Gan Ying's mission it would predictably have been unfruitful, in search of collaboration, to turn to the members of the ruling Arsacid class in Ctesiphon, the fulcrum of the State of Anxi. As the Chinese seemed to know well, the Arsacid leadership would never have facilitated contact between the two greatest economic powers of the known world, one the producer, the other the main purchaser, of most of the goods that travelled across Arsacid territory.
>
> For the Great King it was vital, not only that the two states not be able to entertain reciprocal diplomatic relationships, but it was extremely important to avoid, as much as possible, that the merchants coming from the two Empires should meet. If that had happened the tangible risk would have remained, in the light of the impressive resources and inexhaustible means which the two states would have had, that an agreement and a direct collaboration between the Romans and Chinese would have excluded the Parthian merchants from the long-distance trade between East and West, depriving them of their role as mediators and of the high earnings related to the difference between the sale and purchase costs, and the Arsacid crown of the substantial revenue derived from the taxation of the transported goods.

> It is easy to comprehend how it would have seemed more reasonable, to Ban Zhao and his entourage, in order to gain collaboration in the attempt to reach the Roman territory, turning to merchants and ruling classes of a Kingdom, that of Characene, who during the previous years had demonstrated a considerable openness towards foreign economic initiatives, as well as a conspicuous independence from Arsacid directives. Unfortunately for Gan Ying and his explorative mission, upon their arrival in Mesene, the region had been occupied by the Great King's troops who had put an end to the Characene trade apogee and to a phase of wide political autonomy.
>
> In the occupied lower-Mesopotamia it is likely that the officials and merchants with whom the Chinese mission was in contact were governmental agents or men properly trained to provide information and answers in line with Arsacid interest. The Great King Pacorus II ()?, perhaps the most attentive of all the monarchs to the economic revival of his kingdom, anxious to re-establish fruitful contacts with the Celestial Empire could not risk the degeneration of the relationships between the two Empires – by preventing the diplomats from crossing his territory – but he nonetheless possessed the means for causing, discreetly, their mission to fail." Gregoratti (2012), pp. 113-114.

The southern route I have outlined for Gan Ying's journey fits the information given in the *Hou Hanshu* very closely, and is the only route proposed to date that does so.

Appendix E: Routes from the Tarim Basin, Gandhara and Sindh to the West

The routes from the Tarim Basin, Gandhara and Sindh to the West, which cross through the forbidding ranges and deserts of Afghanistan, have been pivotal in the history of the Indian sub-continent. They have provided access for travellers, pilgrims, traders and invaders, cultures, religions and the arts.

• The location and significance of Ptolemy's 'Stone Tower'

Claudius Ptolemy (*circa* 90-168 CE) the great Greco-Egyptian polymath, lived in Alexandria, Egypt. His major work, the *Geographia*, probably completed *circa* 150 CE, gave an outline of the main trade route from the Euphrates to China based on the accounts of the merchant Marinus of Tyre which, in turn, were collected from his employees' reports who had travelled with his caravans all the way to and from China.

From Ptolemy's account, it is clear that the 'Stone Tower' was located at a key point on the main caravan route between Balkh and the Tarim Basin. It marked the spot where caravans from both the Roman Empire and China would meet, barter, and exchange cargoes before turning back to their original points of departure.

There have been many attempts to locate the site of Ptolemy's Stone Tower (*λίθινος πύργος* - *Lithinos pyrgos*) but it appears that only one location – in the Alai Valley, meets with the geographical indications given in Ptolemy and is supported by the accounts of the "kingdoms" in this region given in the *Hanshu.*

Aurel Stein makes a strong case for locating Ptolemy's 'Stone Tower' in the Upper Alai Valley on the most direct and favourable route from ancient Baktria to the Tarim Basin:

> "From Termez, where traffic coming from Balkh and its modern successor as a trade-centre, Mazār-i-Sharīf, usually crosses the Oxus, an easy route up the Surkhan river brings the traveller to the wide and fertile plain in the centre of the Hisār tract. In this we may safely recognize 'the plain country' which the ravine mentioned by Marinus' authority adjoins. In the comparatively narrow main valley of Kara-tegīn, stretching for some 155 miles [250 km] from Āb-i-garm where the regular road from the Hisār side enters it, up to Daraut-kurghān where the Alai is reached, there is more than one defile by the river. But it is practicable for laden transport, even camels, throughout and owing to its plentiful agricultural produce offers a convenient line of communication. Then below Daraut-kurghān, now the highest village on the Kizil-su, the valley opens out into the great Pāmīr-like valley of the Alai. It is in the vicinity of Daraut-kurghān, where cultivation is carried on at an elevation of about 8000 feet [2,438 m.] and where I found a Russian post in the place of a former fort, that we may place the 'Stone Tower' where, according to Marinus, the traveller arrives after having ascended the ravine.
>
> It is there that those following the route now towards Kāshgar would have to take their food supplies for their onward journey. But I noted in 1915 patches of recent or old cultivation for fully 27 miles [44 km] above Daraut-kurghān up to an elevation of about 9000 feet [2,743 m.]. The Alai valley in general physical character resembles a Pāmīr, being an open trough with a width at its floor nowhere less than six miles But owing to its lower elevation, from about 8000 feet at Daraut-kurghān to not more than 11,200 feet [3,414 m.] at the Taun-murun saddle as its eastern end, and owing to a somewhat moister climate, the steppe vegetation is here far more ample than on the Pāmīrs. In consequence the Alai forms, or, until the Soviet régime, formed, favourite summer grazing-ground for very numerous camps of Kirghiz nomads.
>
> With its open ground and excellent grazing, the great Alai valley seems as if intended by nature to serve as a very convenient channel for traffic from east to west

such as the traders bringing silk from the Tārīm basin needed. Another important advantage was that, what with the cultivation at one time carried on above Daraut-kurghān in the west and still at present to be found at Irkesh-tam to the east of the Taun-murun saddle, the distance on the Alai route over which shelter was not to be found scarcely exceeded 70 miles or three easy marches on such ground.

This route remains open for eight or nine months in the year for laden animals, including camels. Even in the months of December to February when snow is deep, it would be practicable in the same may as is the trade route from Irkesh-tam across the Terek pass (12,700 feet [3,871 m.] above sea-level), provided there were enough traffic to tread a track through the snow. But such traffic between Kāshgar and the Oxus region as was once served by this ancient 'silk route' no longer exists. The trade of the Tārīm basin from Kāshgar now proceeds towards Farghāna, reaching the Russian railway at Andijān across the Terek pass, while what trade in sheep and cattle there comes up Kara-tegīn from the hill tracts towards the Oxus is diverted at Daraut-kurghān towards Marghilān and the railway. However during the months of May and early June when the melting snow closes the Terek pass, the eastern end of the Alai sees some of the Kāshgar trade to Farghāna making its way across the Taun-murun to the easier Taldik pass over the Alai.

At Irkesh-tam, the present Russian frontier and Customs station, we may safely locate 'the station at Mount Imaus whence traders start on their journey to Sera', as suggested long ago by Baron Richthofen. It is here that the Alai route is joined by another, much frequented in modern times and probably in antiquity also, which leads from fertile Farghāna across the Terek pass to Kāshgar. This location of the 'traders' station' at Irkesh-tam is strongly supported by Ptolemy's statements elsewhere which place it due east of the Stone Tower and at the north-eastern limits of the territory of the 'nomadic Sakai', the Iranian predecessors of the present Kirghiz." Stein (1932b), pp. 22-23. For more details, see: Stein (1928), Vol. II, pp. 847-850.

The only two plausible alternative sites are:

- Tashkurgan (literally "Stone Tower" or "Stone Castle") in Xinjiang, to the south of Kashgar on the main route from northern India and Badakshan to the Tarim Basin through the Wakhan corridor in modern Afghanistan.
- On a mountain near Osh in Ferghana, to the north of the Terek Pass which leads into the Alai Valley and then either east to Kashgar via Sary Tash and Irkeshtam in the Alai Valley, or west and then south to Bactria. See: Rapin (1998), pp. 218-219. **NOTE:** See the brief dismissal of this position in note 67 of the quote from Bernard (2005), pp. 953-957, below.

At first glance, the town of Tashkurgan would seem to be a likely choice for Ptolemy's "Stone Tower," as it was on the main route from northern India and eastern Afghanistan to the Tarim Basin, plus its name literally means "Stone Tower." As a result, some scholars still favour Tashkurgan as the most likely site. This position is argued convincingly and in detail in the 2014 paper, "Travelling along the Silk Road: A new interpretation of Ptolemy's coordinates" by Tupikova, Schemmel and Geus, although they admit that Stein's proposed locations are possible:

"Concerning the Northern Route, an important fact has to be underlined here. We have shown that the traditional identifications of the Ptolemaic positions along the Northern Silk Road are supported by a system of distances and directions measured to these locations relative to the *Stone Tower* identified as Tashkurgan. Nevertheless, due to the intricate geometry of the Ptolemaic mapping, our result does not exclude the possibility that the *Stone Tower* can also be identified with Daroot-Korgon." Tupikova, Schemmel and Geus (2014), p. 52.

The name "Tashkurgan" is relatively common in these regions as many settlements contained a stone castle or tower, and could be referred to as "Tashkurgan." For example, the important Afghan town of Kholm/Khulm, about 84 km east of Balkh, is also known as Tashkurgan, and there are others in Kyrgyzstan and Tajikistan.

However, the journey from Bactra to Tashkurgan necessitates a particularly long and difficult journey through the gorges of Badakhshan and the Wakhan Corridor, over the formidable Wakhjir Pass (4,927 m/16,165 ft), and then north to Tashkurgan and Kashgar, or northeast to Yarkand.

Moreover, this route, "is closed for at least five months a year and only opens irregularly for the remainder.... In the opinion of a source near the Afghan-Chinese border this route is impossible for half the year and challenging for the other half" (Townsend 2005, pp. 36, 38). There is a branch of this route that cuts across the southeastern corner of Tajikistan from the Wakhan Corridor to Tashkurgan, but this shortcut is considered even more difficult.

The distances via the three possible routes from Balkh to Kashgar on modern maps are approximately:

1. Balkh to Termez – 122 km; Termez via the Surkhab-Wakhsh Valley and the Alai Valley to Kashgar = 799 km. Total = 921 km.

2. Balkh to Termez = 122 km; Termez to Khujand = 540 km; Khujand to Osh = 342 km; Osh to Sary Tash = 184 km; Sary Tash to Kashgar = 321 km. Total = 1509 km.

3. Balkh to Konduz = 180 km; Konduz via the Wakhan Corridor to Tashkurgan = 690 km; Tashkurgan to Kashgar = 292 km. Total = 1162 km.

These distances show that the most direct route from Balkh to Kashgar was the first – the one favoured by Aurel Stein, P. Bernard and others - through the Surkhab-Wakhsh and Alai valleys. In addition, there were fewer passes to cross and more abundant water and fodder available than on the other two routes.

Interestingly, Ptolemy specifically notes that the "Stone Tower" was located in the territory of the Sacae or Sakas.

This corresponds with the account in *Hanshu* 96A which lists two tiny 'kingdoms' west of Kashgar - Xiuxun 休循 in the upper Alai region, and Juandu 捐毒, or modern Irkeshtam, which was east of Xiuxun, and about 200 km west of Kashgar).

Like Ptolemy's 'Stone Tower,' these 'kingdoms' are the only places in the region which the *Hanshu* says were inhabited by Sakas - except the previous inhabitants of the Wusun Kingdom. Also, see: *CICA*, pp. 138-139, and notes 2.16, 21.17; Appendix W.

Here are translations of the key Western and Chinese texts:

• **The 'Stone Tower' and the 'Territory of the Sacae' in Ptolemy's *Geographica.*** From the English translation by Italo Ronca:

"1

"The territory of the Sakai is bounded in the west by Sogdiana along the already mentioned side (see above, ch. 12); in the north by Scythia, along the <approximately> parallel line between the bend of the Iaxartes [Syr Darya] and the border point lying at 130° / 49°; in the east it is also bounded by Scythia along the lines, one of which starts at the position last mentioned and runs across the adjoining Askatankas range to the trading post near the Imaon range belonging to the merchants who trade with Sera — this post lies at 140° / 43° —; the other (line) runs across the northern branch of the Imaon to the border point situated at 145° / 35°; in the south (it is bounded) by the Imaon mountains themselves, along the line joining the previously mentioned border points.

2

In the territory of the Sakai there rises the already mentioned mountain ranges of the Komedai – the ascent to this mountain region of Sogdiana lies at 125° / 43°, the position of its terminal point near the ravine of the Komedai is at 130° / 39°; the so-called Stone tower lies at 135° / 143° [sic – read 43°, not 143° – see p. 38].

3

The Sakai dwelling along the Iaxartes are called Karatai and Komaroi; those (living) in the entire mountain region, Komadai; those along the Askatankas Massagetai, those in between, Grinaioi and Toornai; below these, along the Imaon, there are the Byltai. [The land of the Sakai belongs to nomads: they have no towns, but dwell in forests and caves]." From: Ptolemy (1971), pp. 107-108.

The *Hanshu* 96A, 10B (*CICA*, p. 105) states that (the people of) Xiuxun and Juandu "are all of the Sai race." Therefore, it seems, the Da Yuezhi controlled the fertile basin to the north of the middle Oxus, while remnants of the Sai still controlled the main route from the Oxus up the Alai Valley and into the Tarim Basin. The control of this key trade route by the "Sakai" (= Chinese "Sai" – as quoted from Francke (1907), p. 677, in Appendix W is confirmed in the quote from Ptolemy 6.13.2 (see where above) and Ammianus Marcellinus 23.6.60:

> "Bordering on these [the Sogdians] are the Sacae [Sai], a fierce nation dwelling in a gloomy-looking district, only fit for cattle, and on that account destitute of cities. They are at the foot of Mount Ascanimia and Mount Comedus, along the bottom of which, and by a town called the Stone Tower, is the long road much frequented by merchants which leads to China." Ammianus Marcellinus 23. 6. 60. Downloaded from: http://www.tertullian.org/fathers/ammianus_23_book23.htm 18 February, 2012, See also note 13.7, and at the end of Appendix W.

- **Notes on the kingdoms of Xiuxun/Hsiu-hsün and Juandu/Chüan-tu in *Hanshu* 96A:**

"The state of Hsiu-hsün[355]

The seat of the king's government is the Niao-fei valley[356] it is west of the Ts'ung-ling, and is distant by 10210 *li* from Ch'ang-an. There are 358 households, 1030 individuals with 480 perons [sic – read 'persons'] able to bear arms. To the east it is a distance of 3121 *li* to the seat of the protector general, and 260 *li* to Yen-tun valley, [in the state of] Chüan-tu; to the north-west it is a distance of 920 *li* to the state of Ta-Yüan; and 1610 *li* to the west, to the Ta Yüeh-chih. The popular way of life and clothing are the same as in Wu-sun, and in company with their stock animals they go after water and pasture. Originally they were of the Sai race.

355. ". . . . Hsü Sung points out that this country is also mentioned in the *Shui-ching chu* 2.3b f., where it is said that the "West River" coming from the country of Chüan-tu (see below, note 358) flows westward through Hsiu-hsün and then "descends to the South into the country of Nan-tou", ... Chavannes (1905), p. 555, note 4, locates this state in the Irkeštam area on the road between Kashgar and Osh. This is where Matsuda (1956), p. 152ff., locates Chüan-tu, placing Hsiu-hsün 'in the Alai" (p. 156f.).

It is in this area that western authors locate the Stone Tower, Πύργος λιθικός mentioned by Ptolemy's basic informant, Maes Titianos; see Stein (1933), p. 47 and pp. 292-295, followed by Herrmann (1938), p. 103ff., and by Innes Miller (1969), pp. 126-132. Both Herrmann and Innes Miller give a survey of the earlier literature on this subject. Stein believed the Stone Tower to have been situated in the Alai valley, near the village of Chat, from where the route led to Irkeštam on the Sino-Russian border. The Chinese expression *shih ch'eng* 石城, "stone walled-city" or "stone fortress" occurs occasionally, but it is not applied to the Stone Tower; cf. note 638." *CICA*, pp. 138-139.

Xiuxiu 休脩 [W-G: *Hsiu-hsiu*] is obviously the same place as Xiuxun 休循 in the *Hanshu* and Xiuxiu 休修 in the *Hou Hanji* Bk. 15 (see *CICA*, p. 138, n. 355). It has been identified as being in the Alai Valley, in the region of the modern settlement of Daraut-kurghān or of Chat to the west of Kashgar, and the site of Ptolemy's 'Stone Tower' (*Lithinos Pyrgos*). See: Stein (1932b), pp. 22-23. Also: *CICA*, pp. 138-139 and n. 355; Shiratori (1957), p. 27, Bernard (2005), p. 955; Stein (1928), Vol. II, pp. 847-850; Stein (1932b), pp. 22-23.

"The state of Chüan-tu[358]

The seat of the king's government is at Yen-tun valley and it is distant by 9860 *li* (4,100 km) from Ch'ang-an. There are 380 households, 1100 individuals and 500 persons able to bear arms. To the east it is distant 2861 *li* (1,190 km) to the seat of the protector general [at Wulei 烏壘 = Yangisar (W-G: Yang-hsia), 350 *li* (166 km) east of Kucha (*CICA*, p. 164] ... [text defective] to Shu-lo [Kashgar]. To the south it adjoins the Ts'ung-ling; there are no human inhabitants. By ascending the Ts'ung-ling on the west, one is at Hsiu-hsün. To the north-west it is a distance of 1030 *li* (428 km) to Ta Yüan, and to the north [the state] adjoins Wu-sun. Clothing is of the same type as that of Wu-sun. [The people] go after water and pasture, keeping close to the Ts'ung-ling. Originally they were of the Sai race.

358. . . . . Wang Hsien-ch'ien tries to provide modern identifications; Chavannes (1905), p. 555, note 3, locates this state West of Kashgar, on the northern slopes of the Pamirs, in the Karategin area. Matsuda 91956), p. 152 ff., places it near Irkeshtam." *CICA*, p. 139. [Also in: Shiratori (1957), *M.T.B.* 18, p. 27; Bernard (2005), pp. 953-957 and nn. 63-68 (see below).

Modern scholars add weight to the information provided in the early texts:

"Of the numerous points to cross the *Oxus*, today's Amu Darya, available to those leaving Baktra, Maes' men had to choose one of them which gave them the most rapid access for the ascent of the Surkhan Darya valley through which probably went the easiest approach to Chinese Turkestan : preferably Termez-*Taramita*, where the Greeks had founded an important establishment which reached its apogee under the Kushans, or down-steam the passage at Kampyr-tepe, where the Greeks had also created a port on the Oxus, the closest to Baktra, but of less importance than Termez, or a little upstream, that of Patakesar[63]. Once the Oxus was crossed one was in the province of Sogdiana which the summary description of Maes' itinerary does not name. In four days, through the Surkhan Darya Valley, one reached Denau (anciently *Chaganyan*[64]) and Regar, then one turned towards the east in the direction of Qaratagh (*Hamvaran*); then, always continuing eastward through the Kafirnigan Valley via Hisar (*Aban Kasavan*), Dushanbe (*shuman*), Kafirnigan. Via Fayzabad (*Weshegird*) one then reached the upper valley of the Surkhab-Wakhsh which one ascends towards the northeast : there one enters the "mountainous country of the *Comedes*" (Section 8), that Marin and Ptolemy speak of[65], which they link with the "country of the Sakas" (Ptolemy VI.13). The "ascension" (ἀνάβασις) (Section 9) first crosses the part of the valley which was called *Rasht* during the Middle Ages, *Karategin* in Turkic (today the region around Garm), and which then marked the eastern frontier of Khorasan, where the Barmekid Fadl abu Yaya (end of the 8th cent.) who stood against the incursions of the Turks, had (p. 955) constructed some fortified "Gates", which did not always resits attacks[66] : the enterprise at least testifies to the importance that the authorities who governed the Oxus Valley gave to this opening towards China.

A little before Daraut Kurgan, after the constrictions of Karategin, the Surkhab Valley opens into the Alai to the north and the Transalai to the south in a thalweg

["The line in the bottom of a valley in which the slopes of the two sides meet, and which forms a natural watercourse" From the online *OED*] 9 to 15 km wide and 125 km long. This is close to Daraut Kurgan which is the generally agreed site of the *Stone Tower* (*Lithinos Pyrgos*) (Section 10) (alt. 3,121 m), doubtless, as the name indicates, a fortification built of irregular stone[67], which marked an important halt on the route which led up a gentle slope towards Irkeshtam, at the foot of the Taun Murun Pass (alt. 3,420 m), where one crosses the line of division of the watersheds between the river system of the Oxus Basin and the Tarim depression towards which the Kashgar River descends. Irkeshtam, according to some, was the *Hormeterion*, of which Ptolemy made "the departure base of the merchants who traded with the Seres"[68], while others prefer to situate it further east, on the eastern rim [p. 956] of the Tarim Basin, at Kashgar or Yarkand[69] : the *Hormeterion* is not mentioned in the passage relating to the itinerary of Maes but appears in Ptolemy in the description of the "Scythia beyond Imaos", that is, the region straddling the saddle of the Alai and the eastern part of Chinese Turkestan (Ptolemy, VI.13,1 ; 14,1 ; 15,3). It is, however, leaving from the "Stone Tower," and not the *hormeterion*, that Maes' agents have measured the length of the journey that remained to be made before their final destination, the capital of the Seres, as if this fortification marked a political frontier between two worlds, that from which the Greco-Syrian merchants came and from Iran and West Central Asia they crossed, were, in their eyes, an extension [of their world] that retained affinities with their own, and, beyond, an unknown world, with Seres and Chinese confused, which (because it was) little known, made them uneasy because of their strangeness and the various difficulties of entering into contact with them. The suggestion I make here would be in the sense of a recent hypothesis which situates in the upper valley of the Wakhsh one of the five principalities into which the Yuezhi nomads had divided the Greek possessions on the right bank of the Oxus which they had conquered just as the Chinese sources report[70]. The one named *Hsiu-mi* [pinyin: *Xiumi*] had *Ho-mo* [pinyin: *Hemo*] for its capital, which could be an adaptation in the Chinese of the local toponym-ethnonym that the Greeks had transcribed by *Comedes* and (p. 957) the Arabo-Persian authors by *Kumedh*. In the *Han-shu* [pinyin: *Hanshu*], which lists the five *hsi-hou* [pinyin: *xihou*] in order of increasing distance from the Governor General of the Tarim Basin, *Hsiu-mi* [pinyin: *Xiumi*] is cited at the head of the list[72], which effectively corresponds to its geographic situation on the assumed route of a migration, leaving from the Tarim, the most direct and easy way to the valley of the Oxus, which was that of the Wakash-Surkhab. If the "*Stone Tower*" marked the north-eastern frontier of the Yuezhi-Kushan possessions, the depression of the Alai which followed it has played the part of a buffer zone between the masters of the valley of the Oxus and those of Chinese Turkestan.

63. On these sites see H.-P. Francfort, *Études de géographie historique sur la plaine d'Aï Khanoum*, Paris, 1978, pp. 56-61, pl 5. There were other crossing points which allowed one to reach the other valleys (Kafirnigan, Wakhsh itself, Qizil su) to rejoin the upper valley of the Wakhsh, but the importance of the town and the interest it presented to merchants gives priority to Termez.

64. I give the modern names and between parentheses the high Middle Age equivalents such as are found in the *Hudūd al-'Ālam* (*op. cit.* [n. 57]), pp. 114-115, 353-354, 361-363 (with commentaries).

65. Also Ammianus Marcellinus XXIII.6.60 [probably published before 391 CE] ; the country of the Sakas is dominated by the Ascantacas, Imaus and Comedus Mountains : *praeter quorum radices et vicum quem Lithinon Purgon appellant, iter longissimum patet mercatoribus pervium ad Seras subinde commeantibus.* [See the translation from Yonge (1862), p. 340 in Appendix M]. . . . Among the Arab geographers see in particular, Ibn Rusta quoted by J. Marquart 1901, *op. cit.* (n. 41), p. 233 : the country of *Komedh* is mentioned on the Wakhsh downstream of Rasht. . . .

66. A. Sprenger 1864, *op. cit.* (n. 45), pp. 43-44 ; *Hudūd al-'Ālam*, p. 361. There are 13 to 14 days' marches between Termez and Garm.

67. 5 km from Daraut Kurgan, at the confluence of the Surkab and the Kok Su, at the village of Chat, in a cultivated zone less windy than Daraut itself and planted with trees, A. Stein 1928, *op. cit.* (n. 65), p. 850, noted the presence of an undulation demarking a wall base forming an irregular oval of 300 x 250 m ; previously J. Markwart, *Wehrot und Arang. Untersuchungen zur mthischen und geschichtlichen Landeskunde von Ostiran.* Leyde, 1938, p. 63 ; presently E. Rttveladze, *Velikij šjolkovyi put'. Encyclopedičeskij spravočnik, Drevnost' I rannee srednevkov'e,* 1999, p. 219. It seems difficult to me to identify the Stone Tower with the mountain which dominates Osh, as Cl. Rapin proposes, in *Alexander's Legacy in the East. Studies in Honor of Paul Bernard.*, Bull. Asia Institute 12, 1998, p. 218. Such localisation implies a detour to the north through the Ferghana Valley, illogical and extends the route ascending the Wakhsh Valley unnecessarily. The author concedes that "the ascent of the Wakhsh-Komedes which had its hour of glory in the 1st century CE [*the exact period of Maes*] was an alternative detour through the Gates of Iron and Samarkand at the time of periods of tension with Kangju power" (p. 218). No one thinks of denying the existence of an access route from China through Ferghana and the Terek Pass, but this was not the one taken by Maes' merchants. I find no explanation of the "plains" (or "plateaux") which, according to Marin-Ptolemy, follow (or precede [?]) the "gorge" and which are named before the Stone Tower situated at a distance of 50 schones (that is 277 km) : .... (I.12,7-8) ; I do not see any one has given any. The geographical coordinates of Ptolemy confirm that the ascent of the Comedes (125° 43'), the Gorge-Pharynx (130° 39') and the Lithinos Pyrgos (135° 43') follow in this order to the west. The word τά πεδια ['the fields'] attached to the mention of the Gorge could therefore only correspond to the large depression of the Alai, the only part of the region which could merit this qualification.

68. At Irkeshtam the route remounts the Alai and rejoins that which, by the well-frequented Terek pass (3,870 m), connects Fergana to Kashgar and the rest of Chinese Turkestan.

Bernard (2005), pp. 953-957 and nn. 63-68. See also: Piankov (2014), pp. 204-219.

"Traders' Station on Mt. Imaos

There is a second point mentioned in Ptolemy's account of the trade route to the Seres as extracted from Marinus which concerns us here. It is 'the station (*ὁρμητήιον*) at Mount Imaos, whence traders start on their journey to Sēra'. It is mentioned in Book VI. xiii, I, where the eastern limits of the territory of the nomadic Sakai, including also the mountain district of the Kōmēdoi and the Stone tower, are described. From the previously quoted statement of Marinus it is certain this station for the traders to the Sēres lay due east of the Stone Tower. This and the distinct statement that the *ὁρμητήιον* must, as rightly pointed out by Baron Richthofen, be looked for close to where the route coming from Kara-tegīn, the valley of the Kōmēdoi, crossed the watershed towards the Tārīm basin. This consideration has already led me to express my concurrence in the belief that the vicinity of Irkesh-tam, the present Russian frontier and customs station, about 16 miles [25.75 km] by road from the watershed at Taun-murun, would have been a likely position for the ancient traders' station. Such a location, as justly observed by Baron Richthofen, finds support in the fact that the route from the Alai valley is joined at Irkesh-tam by another, much frequented in modern times and probably in antiquity also, which leads from Farghāna over the Terek pass to Kāshgar. If at the period to which the information recorded by Maēs refers (probably the last quarter of the first century A. D.) direct Chinese control over the 'western regions' did not extend beyond the watershed between the Tārīm basin and the Oxus, the vicinity of Irkesh-tam would have offered a very suitable position for one of those frontier control stations, such as Chinese administration has always been accustomed to maintain on the borders of the Empire proper; for the elevation, about 8,500 feet [2,591 m.], permits of some cultivation, and facilities for irrigation are assured." Stein (1928), Vol. II, p. 850. **NOTE:** Tupikova, Schemmel and Geus (2014), p. 33, n. 40 admit that Stein "makes a strong case for identifying *hormeterion* as modern Irkeshtam, about 200 km west of Kashgar."

Taken together, I believe these indications make it almost certain that the 'Stone Tower' was located in the 'kingdom' of Xiuxun in the Alai Valley, somewhere west of Sary Tash and the turnoff to the north of the branch route to Ferghana in the region of Daraut Kurgan.

Further east of Sary Tash, and about 200 km west of Kashgar, is the modern customs station of Irkeshtam, which was almost certainly the site of ancient Juandu as there are no other places in the regions so well located to control the route, and which provide sufficient arable land, fodder and water to support a small year-round population. Irkeshtam was most probably also the site of Ptolemy's *ὁρμητήιον* [*hormeterion*].

- **Other routes from the Tarim Basin, Gandhara and Sindh to the West**

"Modern roads and other infrastructure has perhaps made the Tarim Basin far more accessible than before but studying satellite photos shows that the routes and access points are still severely restricted by the natural conditions and especially by the surrounding mountains. Approaching from the east the Hexi (Gansu) corridor provides a natural entrance to the Basin from the area around the upper Yellow River Valley. This "corridor" runs between the Kunlun Mountains to the south and Gobi desert to the north, and is an area of mostly barren flats with forests and greener areas along the slopes of the mountain. The other "easy" access to the Tarim Basin is on the western edge where caravans can cross over the Pamir and Karakoram ranges both westwards and southwards. Frank Harold in his article *Over the High Passes* states that besides the multitude of smaller routes used by locals there are essentially six routes going west and south, three to the Indian subcontinent, two to ancient Bactria i.e. today's Afghanistan and one to Sogdiana, as well as one going northwards. They usually follow the rivers and passes through the mountains which, as noted earlier, are comparatively smaller in the west.

There are three main routes to cross from India; the southernmost of these routes, the one leading directly to the Indian plains, is the famous Karakoram route which for a caravan would take roughly sixty days to cross. It lies directly south of Yarkand and after crossing the great Himalayas themselves the caravan would descend to Leh on the Indus in Ladakh. Further west in today's Pakistan lies the less arduous but more dangerous Gilgit route. From Gilgit the route makes it way north past Tashkurgan to end near Kashgar, passing through the land of Hunza renowned for its caravan robbers. Harold quoting Skrine states about the gorges of the lower Karakorum that they are "as difficult a tract of country as can be found anywhere in the world". The third route from India runs up along the Kabul River by way of Chitral and crosses the Hindukush at the Baroghil Pass which gives access to the area of Wakhan, the upper headwaters of the river Oxus (Amu Darya). Following the Oxus and then crossing the Pamir this route then reaches Tashkurgan and from there runs on to Kashgar.

Running westwards are the two main routes into Bactria and to Samarkand in ancient Sogdiana; the southernmost one being the Faizabad route going from Faizabad by way of the previously mentioned Wakhan gorges to reach Kashgar. A far more inviting route however is the one that runs up the Kyzyl Ssu valley in today's Tadzhikistan and crosses the grassy and low Irkeshtam pass before going onwards to Kashgar across the Pamir Highland. Both British col. [sic] Henry Yule and Stein argued that this would have been an important route for traffic in ancient times, based on the ease of crossing and the rich pastures in the valley which would have been ideal for caravans.

The northern Tian Shan range can also be crossed, mainly in its eastern and western ends. In the east one can cross north of Turfan through the mountains and into the massive Dzungarian depression which affords access to the vast Eurasian steppe. In the west are the two last crossings, one going northwest and one due north. From Samarkand travellers can travel along Syr Darya up the Ferghana valley before crossing the Terek pass southwards. The route then turns east and crosses the previously mentioned Irkeshatam pass to end in Kashgar. The final route in the western Tian Shan crosses either the Bedel pass near Aksu or the Muzart pass further northeast between Aksu and Kucha, both passes entering into the steppes near lake Issyk Kul. The Tian Shan are rugged and high, making both crossings challenging prospects even for well-equipped and supplied travellers while the Muzart pass is open only in summer." Høisæter (2013), pp. 24-25.

The main ancient trade route from Afghanistan into the Gandharan plains was the route Saifar Rahman Dar refers to as the 'Karappah Pass Route':

"*Karappah Pass Route*

The Karappah Pass Route ran along the northern bank of the Kabul River over a short distance. It is generally accepted that during the period under discussion, the Afghan highlands were connected with Gandhāra through this northern, rather than southern, route by means of two alternate passages, namely the Kapiśa (Begram)—Puṣkalāvatī-Taxila . . . passage or the Kapiśa-Bajaur (Khar)-Swat-Taxila passage . . . .

The Karappah Pass Route bypasses the more difficult Khyber Pass Route on its south. From Begram, it first follows King's Highway and shares all the ascents and descents until Dhaka/Lalpura. On this sector, travelers desirous of going to Alishang and Alingar would cross the river at the ferry of Mandawar, while those intending to proceed towards Nur Gal, Kunar, and Pashat would use a ferry at Jalalabad. Those destined to journey to Purusapura and Puṣkalāvatī and beyond into the plains of the Panjab had two options: after reaching Dhaka/Lalpura, they could go directly to Peshawar by the Ali Masjid-Jamrod-Tahkal route, or they could take a relatively easier or less cumbersome route starting from Lalpura on the bank of River Kabul opposite Dhaka. By means of this second route, they would proceed towards Gandab, Karappa Ghashaey, Shab Qadar and, after crossing the little river Jindai at Bala Hissar, they would reach Puṣkalāvatī (modern Shaikhan Dheri at Charsada), the capital of Gandhāra in the second century B.C. From here, Puruṣapura was only eighteen miles [29 km.] to the south. Travelers for long distances would go straight to Taxila via Shahbazgarhi—the site of Aśoka's Rock Edicts—and thence to Ohind on the Indus. By both these routes, the distance between Begram and Puruṣapura remained almost the same, i.e., about 110 *kuroh*. A *kuroh* is slightly less than two English miles [3.2 km.].

There is no doubt that the Kapiśa (Kapiśi)-Puṣkalāvatī-Ohind-Taxila road was more popular in ancient times than the Kapiśa-Puruṣapura-Taxila route. This is demonstrated by the fact that a number of archaeological sites pertaining to the period under consideration exist much more frequently along the former route than along the latter one. Whereas between Peshawar and Ohind, there exist a few minor archaeological sites from the first two or three centuries of our era, the road from Shaikhan-dheri (Puṣkalāvatī) to Ohind is littered with a great number of sites from this period. When Aśoka decided to install edicts in this area, he selected the city of Shahbazgarhi on this route for the purpose. Beside the site of rock edicts from the third century B.C., there are some well-known sites, such as Mekhasanda, Chanaka-dheri, Surkh Dheri, Aziz Dheri, Tor Dheri, Ranigat, Rata Pind, Salatura, (the birthplace of the third-century B.C. grammarian, Pāṇini) and Ohind. At Ohind, boats were needed to cross the River Indus to Hazro, then on the opposite bank. The district of Hazro is again full of archaeological sites that are now being ruthlessly damaged by treasure hunters. Along the present Grand Trunk Road, there are only two archaeological sites of which I know—one at Haji Shah Morr, and the other at Bihari Colony, Hasanabdal.

The Bajaur-Buner-Taxila route remained popular during the Indo-Greek and also the Parthian periods. The most significant finds of this period from this area are a number of so-called Buner Stair-Risers now divided among The British Museum, the Victoria and Albert Museum, The Cleveland Museum of Art, Royal Ontario Museum (ROM), and Peshawar Museum. Particularly, three of these panels in The Cleveland Museum and ROM present Dionysian themes in a very refined manner. These possibly belonged to some stage performers of the Parthian period (i.e., the first century A.D.) who traveled along this historic route to Taxila. Marshall, who has illustrated the maximum number of these panels, dates them between 25 and 60 A.D. A few similar stair risers recently have been excavated *in situ* fixed in the steps of the staircase of the main *stūpa* at Gangue Dher on the ancient road between Puṣkalāvatī-Shahbazgarhi-Ohind. But these risers belong to a late phase of history of Gandhāra, i.e., *circa* 5th–6th century A.D." Dar (2007), pp. 39-41.

The description of the routes south of the Karappah Pass Route from Gandhara and Sindh to Afghanistan by Major-General Sir George K. Scott-Moncrieff written to an unnamed British parliamentarian, "in the autumn of one of the early years of the present [20th] century," is illuminating.

Scott-Moncrieff outlines five other major routes that led into various parts of Afghanistan. I have quoted him at some length, as it may be difficult for readers to locate the original article:

> "So after a pause I replied that it was very far from being the case that there was only one route into Central Asia. In the North-West Frontier Province alone there were five such trade-routes leading to Afghanistan, not to mention other and important roads farther south, by Quetta to Kandahar, and in the north towards Chitral, and north-east through Kashmir, into Central Asia.
>
> This roused his curiosity at once. Alert for all useful information, he asked for more details.
>
> Laying my right hand, palm downwards, and fingers out-spread on the table, I replied –
>
> "My fingers represent the five routes from this province, not to scale, of course, not in length proportionate to their importance, but still with sufficient accuracy for the purposes of a diagram. These fingers show the valleys, and the blank wedge-shaped parts indicate the mountainous country lying between the valleys, country which is only partially surveyed, and is inhabited by fierce tribes, constantly at war with each other, and owing allegiance neither to the Amir of Afghanistan nor the British. To-day you saw the blockhouses guarding here and there the road through the Pass. These are placed on the trade-routes for the protection of the trader ; otherwise highway robbery would be universal and trade almost impossible. The four knuckles of my hand represent the four towns in this province from which the routes proceed – Peshawar, Kohat, Bannu, and Dera Ismail Khan [note: 'dera' means 'camp'], – though here again the proportionate distances are imperfectly represented, for the distance between the first two is less than half the intervals between the others respectively. There is a good road, recently made, from Peshawar to Kohat, and a still better road, finished about ten years ago, from Kohat to Bannu and Dera Ismail, but this is the only lateral road ; all the others project, like my fingers, into the valleys, with no lateral connections, and terminate at Afghan territory.
>
> "You saw to-day (in the Khyber, represented by my little finger) some of the traders, or *powindahs*, as they are called, who bring goods from Samarkand and Bokhara, by Kabul, to the Peshawar market. If you had driven on about a dozen miles farther you would have reached the Afghan border, but you would still have about

fifty miles farther to go before you reached the first town of importance, Jalalabad, and beyond that you would still have about 100 miles of wild mountainous country before you reached Kabul.

"There is a good road the whole way, which was made by us in the winter of 1879-80, and presumably has been maintained ever since. Part of the road which you drove over to-day was made by the British in 1838-40, and we found it forty years later in quite useful condition. It takes a good deal to destroy a road. Some of those over passes within fifty miles of us here were made by Alexander the Great, and with a little addition can still be used for pack animals, if not for the carts. Of course a road is a most potent factor in the civilisation and settlement of a country, for by it merchandise comes and goes, and, as Alexander and Cæsar found, it is necessary for the passage of troops to maintain law and order. I think, for the defence of a frontier such as this, money is more profitably spent on roads than on forts. You saw some of the latter to-day, and I quite admit that they are necessary for the protection of the Pass. But, personally, I think we go in for too elaborate a system of work in them, and I think a cheaper and rougher form would be equally effective and less costly. Whereas all money spent on roads is useful both for commerce and military movements."

"What about the four other routes?"

"My third finger represents the Kurram Valley route from Kohat, penetrating far nearer to Kabul than any of the others. The scenery is beautiful in parts, and the climate more bearable than in the others, but the route crosses in Afghan territory a high pass about 10,000 feet above sea-level, which is blocked with snow for several months every year. But for this the road would be used for commercial purposes more than it actually is. Our present jurisdiction extends to the foot of the Peiwar Pass, where Lord Roberts defeated the Afghans in 1878, and it was by this route that he entered Kabul the following year. I have been over that route once, and the impression it left was one of beauty and fertility, but full of practical difficulties for road construction.

"The middle finger corresponds to the Tochi Valley, leading from Bannu to the Afghan city of Ghazni, a route which presents no great physical difficulties. We had a lot of trouble with the tribes there a few years ago, and we have done a good deal of work in making a good road fit for wheeled traffic, like that you were on to-day, as far as our farthest outpost, sixty miles or so beyond Bannu. We have built also many defensive posts, so I hope we shall not have much trouble there in the immediate future. Hordes of nomad traders come that way every cold weather. They leave their families at Bannu, and go off to sell their wares all over Kurram, returning again when the weather gets warm.

"The forefinger corresponds to the Gomal Pass, which debouches at a place about fifty miles north-east of Dera Ismail Khan. Here, too, vast numbers of the *powindah* people come, leaving their wives at Dera Ismail for the cold weather, and going off as far east, I am told, as Calcutta. The road through the Pass has begun, but a great deal remains to be done. The gorges of the Gomal River are for the most part sheer precipices, and the river is subject to sudden and violent floods. Besides this, the tribesmen are about the most savage of any on the border, and that is saying a good deal. One of my survey parties was ambushed the other day, and, escort and all, cut to pieces, very few escaping. Still, we must make that road, difficult though it may be, for not only can we join up with some of the routes from Quetta to Kandahar by it, but the alternative to ten miles of difficult gorges along the river is a waterless and shadeless climb of nineteen miles over a rugged mountain pass. The *kafilas* do come that way now, but some of them avoid it by a route farther south (represented by my thumb, the fifth route I have spoken of), which also is terminated at Dera Ismail.

"This is, to my mind, a very important route, for at its west end it joins one of the roads in the Beluchistan agency at Fort Sandeman, and troops could come by this way from Quetta to Dera Ismail and the northern frontier without going round the long circuitous route by Sind. The road has barely been begun. It passes through a wild and rugged tract of country at the back of a mountain called the Takht-i-Suleiman (throne of Solomon), and part of it necessarily traverses for about two miles a narrow rift or gorge, where the rocks rise in almost vertical precipice in height about 800 feet [244 m.], and a stream brawls over the debris at the bottom. Over the sharp rocks in the bed of this stream the laden camels stumble, cutting their legs, and sometimes tumbling down, poor brutes ! but at least they have not the long waterless climb that at present they have to face in the Gomal. After passing through the rift they have seven or eight miles of very rough mountain paths ; then easier going for another twenty miles, until the road emerges from the plains near a little village about forty miles from Dera Ismail Khan. The intervening country is a bare waterless desert, but easy enough for travelling. We are beginning road work, and have collected tools and plant, explosives, &c., at the entrance to the mountain part ; but the young civil assistant engineer is evidently not happy about it. . . .

"So you see that the position is that in the Khyber, where you were to-day, we have a useful driving road, with many twists and corners, it is true, but quite fit for wheeled traffic throughout. The same applies to Kohat and the Kurram Valley for about 120 miles, only there we have one or two important bridges yet to be built. To a somewhat less extent this applies also to the Tochi. But in the Gomal and on the Fort Sandeman road we are only beginning to substitute a properly graded road, suitable for camels, for the old native tracks. Of course there are many subsidiary roads for military purposes only in various directions, but these do not affect the main commercial routes." Scott-Moncrieff (1924), pp. 746-749.

"There are no fewer than 19 passes over the Hindu Kush proper, but most of them are of only local significance, because of steepness and height and the fact that they are blocked by snow during much of the year. Only three can be considered as major routes historically—the Khawak, Salang, and Shibar Passes.

The focal point of the three routes is the town of Charikar (5200 feet) [1585 m], some forty miles [64 km.] due north of Kabul where the Ghorband and Panjshir Rivers debouch on the plain of Kohistan. This is a natural site for an emporium, and archeological remains in the neighborhood justify the belief that it was near this site that Alexander the Great built his town of Alexandria-under-Caucasus.

The Khawak route ascends the Panjshir Valley in a general northeasterly direction for some 75 miles [121 km.] to the Khawak Pass (11,640 feet) [3548 m.], whence it runs due west for 30 miles [48 km.] to Sangburan (5250 feet) [1600 m.]; here it turns due north, and after 10 miles it crosses the Murgh Pass (7400 feet) [2256 m.] and descends into the region of Narin. Another pass, the Tawa Shah (4700 feet) [1433 m.], leads into the valley of Jabardagh and Shorab and so to Khanabad (1270 feet) [387 m.], some 70 miles [113 km.] from the Murgh Pass, where the route joins that from China. The distance from Kabul to Khanabad by this route is about 225 miles and is counted as 17 days' travel.

It is evident that this road, which crosses one high and two low passes, is often blocked in winter. Nevertheless, it is fairly direct, and the gradient is easy; there is ample water and forage; and the valleys are relatively open, so that there is little danger of ambush. Of all the routes to the north and to China, this has been perhaps the most popular; and tradition asserts that it was by this way that Alexander the Great penetrated Central Asia.

The Salang route via Bajgah runs due north and then north-northwest from Charikar for about 25 miles [40 km.] to the pass of the same name (12,000 feet) [3658 m.] and then falls away sharply for 25 miles [40 km.] to Khinjan (3720 feet). From Khinjan it runs straight west for 15 miles to Doshi (also called Keilaki; 2800 feet) [853 m.], where it turns north in the valley of the Surkh, or Ghori, River and proceeds about 85 miles [137 km,] to Khanabad (1270 feet) [387 m.]—a stretch that is hard going because of the sand and marshes. The Salang route has the advantage in distance, for it is only some 190 miles [306 km.] from Kabul to Khanabad, or 14 days' travel. However, because of the steepness of the approaches to the pass and the unfavorable terrain, this route has never been favored by caravans. It has been used chiefly by couriers or private travelers to whom time was a prime consideration. Occasionally it has been used by armies for the same reason.

The Shibar route runs almost due west from Charikar up the thickly settled valley of the Ghorband for about 70 miles [113 km.] to the Shibar Pass (9800 feet) [2987 m.], the lowest pass over the Hindu Kush. From this point the road descends into the narrow, precipitous gorge of the Shikari River, which for 38 miles [61 km.] offers little in the way of camping sites, forage, or protection. From it, however, easy connections can be made with the western routes passing through Bamian (see below) as well as with the route to Khanabad. In spite of the lowness of the pass, the distance involved and the difficulties of the terrain have made this route a *pis aller*, to be used only when all other ways are blocked by snow.

We cannot, however, dismiss the question of the Hindu Kush by a consideration of the passes over the range proper. We must also look at the routes that skirt it, in particular the route that leads from Kabul to Mazar-i-Sharif by way of Bamian, which for want of a better name will be called the Unai-Dandan Shikan route.

The Unai-Dandan Shikan route leads straight west from Kabul, through Arghandeh and Jalrez to the Unai Pass (11,000 feet) [3353 m.], 50 miles [80 km,] distant. There it swings to the northwest, and after about 25 miles it traverses the Hajigak Pass (11,000 feet) [3353 m.] and descends via the Panjfilan Pass (10,000 feet) [3048 m.] to Bamian (8342 feet) [2543 m.], another 25 miles [40 km.] away. From Bamian the road follows a general northerly direction, going over a series of passes: Ak Robat (10,255 feet) [3126 m.], Katar Sum (10,200 feet) [3109 m.], Dandan Shikan (8830 feet [2691 m.], a very steep pass—hence its name of "tooth breaker"), Kara (9320 feet) [2841 m.], and Chambarak (7500 feet) [2286 m.]. After about 140 miles [225 km.] in the mountains the road descends to Haibak (3657 feet) [1115 m.] and from that point runs through low hills to Tashkurghan (1500 feet) [457 m.], about 45 miles [72 km.] distant, where it joins the great east-west road from China. From Tashkurghan it is 35 miles [56 km.] almost due west to Mazar-i-Sharif (1240 feet) [378 m.], which now replaces the ancient city of Balkh as the metropolis of the north. This route covers about 320 miles [515 km.] and is counted as 21 days' travel.

Despite the fact that this is the longest route and traverses eight passes, four of which lie at more than 10,000 feet [3048 m.], it has been very popular. This is in part due to the excellent forage, easy gradients, and comparatively open valleys. Moreover, during the last century and a half (the period of our best records) this route has been freer than any other from the disorders caused by feudal and civil wars." Howland (1940), pp. 273, 276-277.

There is further information on these routes given by H. C. Verma:

• **The Khyber Pass** west to Jalalabad and then west to Kabul, northwest via Bamian to Mazar-i-Sahrif (near ancient Bactra/Balkh), or north towards Badakhshan:

> "Ab'l Fazal mentioned the Khaibar route as one of the five routes that led to the province of Kabul. It was so difficult to negotiate before the time of Akbar that even horses and camels found it difficult to tread, but Akbar by the able superintendence of Qāsim got it improved to the extent that now wheeled carriages could pass over it with ease, and the Turānīs and Hindus generally use it. . . ." Verma (1978), p. 72.

It is easy to see from this account why the easier Karappah Pass Route (which led directly to Charsadda/Pushkalavātī) was preferred over the Khyber Pass Route in ancient times.

• **The Kurram Valley** from Kohat through the Peiwar/Paiwar Pass to Kabul:

> "*The Kurram Route* : the Kurram Pass, being the direct road from Bannū to Ghazni (and Bannū to Kabul), has been for centuries looked upon as one of the most important routes across the Sulamain mountains. This was an alternative to Khaibar route which was separated from it by the range of Safed Koh. It went via the Kurram valley at the head of which is the historic Paiwar Pass. The Khaibar and the Kurram routes might be regarded as a "twin system, with Kabul as the common objective." But there is no practicable pass across the Safed Koh, so that no force moving along either line could depend on direct support from the other side of the mountains. It will be convenient here to regard the Kurram as an alternative to the Kabul route, and to consider the two together as forming a distinct group." Verma (1978), pp. 101-102.
> **NOTE:** I have included a detailed description of the Kurram Valley by C. R. Markham (1879), pp. 47-48 in Appendix G (JEH).
>
> "**KURRAM,** a river and district on the Kohat border of the North-West Frontier province of India. The Kurram river drains the southern flanks of the Safed Koh, enters the plains a few miles above Bannu, and joins the Indus near Isa-Khel after a course of more than 200 miles. The district has an area of 1278 sq. m.; pop. (1901), 54,257. It lies between the Miranzai Valley and the Afghan border, and is inhabited by the Turis, a tribe of Turki origin who are supposed to have subjugated the Bangash Pathans five hundred years ago. It is highly irrigated, well peopled, and crowded with small fortified villages, orchards and groves, to which a fine background is afforded by the dark pine forests and alpine snows of the Safed Koh. The beauty and climate of the valley attracted some of the Mogul emperors of Delhi, and the remains exist of a garden planted by Shah Jahan. Formerly the Kurram valley was under the government of Kabul, and every five or six years a military expedition was sent to collect the revenue, the soldiers living meanwhile at free quarters on the people. . . ." *EB* (1911), vol. 15, p. 953.

• **The Tochi Valley** from Bannu to Ghazni:

> "*The Tochi Valley Route* : South of the Kurram was the open rump of the Tochi valley, and the route traversing this valley through the Tochi Pass was yet another link between the kingdom of Kabul and the Indian frontier. This was formerly known as the Farmūl route. Bābur once decided to use this route on his return journey to Kabul from Bannū in AD 1505. The route went through the Plain[33] and Farmūl[34] via Birk whence it took a north-westerly direction to Ghazni. The Tochi route does not figure frequently in history, but it has been used in the past for sudden raids from Ghazni in spite of the difficulties which "Nature has strewn about its head".
>
> 33. Also known as Dasht or Bāzār situated to the southwest of the Bannū lands.
> 34. Farmūl is the modern Urganj or Aurgun." Verma (1978), pp. 104-105, and nn. 33, 34.

"**TOCHI VALLEY,** or DAWAR, one of the chief routes into Afghanistan in the North-West Frontier Province of India. It leads from the Bannu through tribal country, and is inhabited by the Dawari (q.v.). The valley is divided into two parts, known as Upper and Lower Dawar, by a narrow pass called the Taghrai Tangi, some three m. long. Between Dawar and British territory is the low range of uninhabited hills, which skirt the Bannu district. It was by this route that Mahmud of Ghazni effected several of his raids into India and the remains of a road flanking the valley and of defensive positions are still to be traced. . . ." *EB* (1911), Vol. 26, p. 1043.

- **The Gomal Route** From Dera Ismail Khan via the Gomal Pass to Ghazni, or south to Quetta:

"*The Gomal or Ghwāliri Route* : This route ran to the north of the Tochi Pass [**NOTE:** Scott- Moncrieff above seems to indicate it was to the south (JEH)] and like the latter, it also led to Ghaznī. The route followed the course of the Gomal stream, crossing and recrossing it at every mile. To quote Bābur ". . . persons well-acquainted with the roads, represented that going by the Gūmāl road, this torrent (The Gomal) must be crossed several times, that there was always uncertainty on the Gūmāl road". The route met the famous Gomal-Ghaznī road via Farmūl.[37] From Dera Ismail Khan on the river Sindh to the Gomal Pass the route went north ascending the beautiful oasis which broke the monotony of the desolate and deadly plain that was to start from the Gomal Pass to the Ghaznī highlands. The Gomal had, too, like both the preceding routes (the Kurram and the Tochi routes) the disadvantage of debouching into an arid desert, intersected by ravines, ramifying into numerous fan-like branches, which would oblige the invaders to advance in long unwieldy columns. In length, and from the point of view of the physical difficulties to be overcome, it may be classed with the Bolan. Commenting on the Tochi and the Gomal routes Holdich writes that they were the two highways to Ghazni, but "there is no comparison between the two as regards their facilities or the amount of traffic they carry. All the carrying of trade of Ghazni province is condensed into the narrow ways of Gomul. Trade in the Tochi hardly extends farther than the village at its head".

37. At Farmūl the route united with the Tochi route, and from Farmūl, the route to Ghazni was the one and the same." Verma (1978), pp. 105-106, and n. 37.

"It lies in Lat. 32° N and Long. 70° E, and about 100 miles [161 km.] to the south-east of Surgurgai near Āb-i-Istādah in Afghanistan. The Gomal Pass which connects Ghazni with Dera Ismail Khan, is also known as the Ghwālīrī Pass. . . .

The Gomal Pass is, in several respects, the most interesting in the whole range, for it has been the great trade route between India and Central Asia during several centuries." Verma (1978), pp. 273-274.

- **From Dera Ismail to Quetta to Takht-i-Sulaimān and Waziristan:**

"The country of Waziristan is situated between the southern extreme of the Kurram basin and the peak of Takht-i-Sulaimān. The eastern Sulaimān Range is more distinctly developed here as a lofty chain of mountains with several parallel ridges. Appearing like a wall from Sindh, this range is pierced at numerous points by stream[s] . . . .

Takht-i-Sulaimān, situated opposite the town of Dera Ismail Khan on the Sindh, is the highest peak of this Range. Its summit is described as a narrow plateau about five miles [8 km] long, stretching from north to south, with culminating points at either extremity, the northern peak being 11,300' [3,444 m] and the southern 11,110' [3,386 m] above the level of the sea." Verma (1978), p. 272. Also: Markham (1879), pp. 38-62.

Appendix F: The Kingdom of Jibin (Kapisha & Gandhara)

There has been heated debate about the location of Jibin 罽賓 (W-G: *Chi-pin*) during the Han era for well over a century.

> 罽 *jì* – 'kind of hair cloth,' 'woollens,' 'rug of rough material, of hair or fur.' This character is not listed in Karlgren, and reconstructed pronunciations are not given in *GR*; but Petech (see below) gives *k̭iad/kiäi. Pulleyblank gives the EMC as kiaj^h.
>
> 賓 *bīn* – 'guest,' 'to greet a guest or a host,' 'to lay out,' to honour.' Both *GR* and Karlgren 389a give: *p̭iĕn / p̭iĕn; EMC is pjin.

> "In the time of the Emperor Ching-te (B.C. 32-7) [read: Cheng Di], Ke-pin [Jibin] again sent an envoy with offerings and an acknowledgement of guilt. The supreme board wished to send an envoy with a reply to escort the Ke-pin envoy home; but Too Kin [a Chinese official] addressed the Generalissimo Wang Fung to the following effect:— ... "From Pe-Shan [Pishan] southward there are four or five kingdoms not attached to China. With only a hundred men to keep a look-out, and to beat the five night watches for self-protection, they will be at times exposed to attacks by robbers, carrying off their asses and cattle bearing provisions: and will thus be rendered dependent on these countries for food, for which they must make some requital. The countries may be small and poor, and unable to furnish food; or the inhabitants may be cruel and crafty and refuse to give, even intercepting them at the boundary. The Chinese Commission will in such circumstances be left to starve among the hills and valleys begging food to sustain life, with no means of obtaining it. In some ten or twenty days men and animals will die in the desert, and be never more heard of. Again, on passing the Great Headache Mountain, the Little Headache Mountain, the Red Land, and the Fever Slope men's bodies become feverish, they lose colour, and are attacked with headache and vomiting. The asses and cattle being all in like condition. Moreover there are three pools with rocky banks along which the pathway is only 16 or 17 inches wide for a length of some 30 *le* [*li* = 12.5 km], over an abyss of frightful depth where the travellers whether on horse or afoot are all attached, and lead each other by ropes. After more than 2,000 *le* [*li* = 832 km] the Hindu Cush is reached; more than half the cattle having perished by falling down the chasms, their bodies lying scattered about and dashed to pieces. Men lose their grasp, and they are unable to save each other. In fact, viewing the dangers of these precipitous gorges, the difficulties are beyond description." Wylie (1881) pt. 1, pp. 36-38. See also Appendix U.

The Chinese sources differ, but the most common identifications of "Jibin" assert that Jibin referred to a state centred in Kapisha (north of Kabul), or to "(the Vale of) Kashmir," in and around Srinagar in the modern Indian state of Jammu-Kashmir. At times Jibin's territory extended to regions to the north, particularly the routes through the Chitral Valley to Gilgit and Hunza. Both theories allow for the fact that borders changed as rulers changed and Jibin's political fortunes varied:

> "Coming back to the Records [of Xuanzang] we find a Chinese editorial note added to the word Kashmir telling us that Ki(-Ka)-p'in (罽賓) was an old and incorrect name for the country. But in many Chinese treatises Ka-pin is a geographical term of vague and varying extension, and not the designation of a particular country. It is applied in different works to Kapis, Nagar, Gandhāra, Udyāna, and Kashmir. The region first called Kapin was once occupied by the Sakas (塞), a great nomad people who spread themselves over vast regions to the north-west from what is now the district of Kashgar. Afterwards applied less vaguely Kapin was the name of a country south of the Ts'ung-Ling and subject to the Great Yue-ti (*Getæ*), and it is said to have been a

synonym for the *Tsao* (漕) [sic – should read *Ts'ao* or *Cao* in pinyin] of the Sui period." Watters (1904-1905), pp. 259-260.

> "The east of Afghanistan, Swāt, Dīr, and Gandhāra then formed a cultural, religious and, at many periods, a political unity. It was the heart of what R. Salomon proposed to call "*Greater Gandhāra*", an expression I have not used because of the potential risks of confusion, which D. Jongeward does not use anymore, but which corresponds to a reality he did not consider." Translated from Fussman (2013), p. 130.

Although it is undeniable that Jibin referred to Kashmir in a few later Buddhist records, it is now certain that, during both Han Dynasties at least, Jibin was centered in Kapisha and, at times, controlled western Gandhara including Taxila, Swat, and the routes leading through Chitral to Wakhan and as far as the *xuandu* or 'hanging passages' of northern Hunza.

During the Former Han Dynasty, Jibin was of special interest to China because it sat astride the main trade routes into northern India as well as those to the southwest, through Kandahar, and on to the Persian Gulf. This confirms its key role in our understanding the history of the period, particularly the rise of the Kushan Empire, and the opening of the south-western Silk Routes.

By the time of the *Hou Hanshu*, Jibin had been swallowed up by the Kushans and, no longer independent, and therefore of not much interest to the Chinese, who referred to it simply as a region, no longer as a 'country' or 'kingdom.'

The identification of Jibin with Kophen was first made by Jean-Pierre Abel-Rémusat, who also proved that Kophen referred to the Kabul River. See: Abel-Rémusat (1836), p. 23, n. 2; Prinsep (1844), p. 81, and Cunningham (1871), pp. 29, 31-32.

The reconstructed pronunciations, *k̭iad/kiäi – p̭iĕn/p̭iĕn (or in Pulleyblank's own EMC: kiaj^{h}–pjin), seem to provide closer transcriptions of the Greek *Kophēs*, *Kophēn* than Pulleyblank's reconstruction of it as *Kaspir, or Kashmir. Pulleyblank (1963), pp. 218-219.

> "Again, there was no other considerable country south of the Hindoo Kush besides Ki-pin known to the Chinese of 2,000 years ago ; and it is plain that the situation they assign throughout the course of ages to this land in relation to India, Gandhâra, Udyâna, Balti, &c., corresponds perfectly to the traditional site of the Greek and Roman Cophes and Cophene of Alexander's generals, whose personal observation was after all the main evidence utilised by Arrian, Pliny, &c. If we remember that 'Cabul' is even now pronounced 'Cawbl,' with the accent on *Caw*, and that the Chinese syllables used have (by the living tests indicated above) the value *Kaw-bu*—with the accent invariably on the first syllable—we need have no hesitation in accepting the Kao-fu[35] conquered from Ki-pin by the Indo-Scythians as Cabul (the Cabura of Ptolemy) conquered from the Sakya princes of Cophene by Kanishka.
>
> [35]A syllable *fu* (having the same ' power ') is used by the Chinese *(ante*, p. 629, n. 11) to express the Hindoo word Djambu, not to mention the common word *Fu-t'u* or *Budh*."
>
> Parker (1905), p. 636. **NOTE:** Parker also gives a detailed account of Jibin after the Kushan period, see: Parker (1905), pp. 629-634.

> "A great deal of error has crept into our interpretation of the geography and history of the Kabul valley through a rather general failure to appreciate the sense in which the Hellenistic writers used the name Kophen. It does not represent the length of the Kabul River of our day but rather the united stream of the Kabul and the Kunar rivers below Jelalabad.[5] The district of Kabul, the Kabulistan of the early Arab geographers, from above Jelelabad to the Ghorband valley was attached to, but not an integral part of, the Paropamisadae. In all periods it appears as a passageway rather than as a center of power.

[5] Arrian, *Anab.*, IV, 22, 5-7. Coming from Bactria on his way to India Alexander arrived at Alexandreia, near Charikar. While there he appointed Turiaspes satrap of "the country of the Paropamisadae and of the rest as far as to the river Kophen." From Alexandreia he proceeded to Nikaia, which is generally identified as Kabul City. From Nikaia he "advanced toward the Kophen", at the same time sending heralds to the Indian princes of the Indus ordering them to come to meet him. "Here he divided the army"; this can apply only to his point of contact with the princes on the Kophen, which must have been some distance below Kabul. It is clear that the name Kophen cannot be applied to any stream much above the junction of the Kunar (the Choes of Arrian and the Koa of Ptolemy) with the Kabul, and so this junction seems to provide the basis for a new name. There are repeated instances in this same area of the application of a new name to the union of two steams."

McDowell (1939), p. 784. See also Smith (1908), p. 46.

"**KABUL RIVER,** a river of Afghanistan, 300 m. [300 miles - 483 km] in length. The Kabul (ancient Kophes), which is the most important (although not the largest) river in Afghanistan, rises at the foot of the Unai pass leading over the Sanglakh range, an offshoot of the Hindu Kush towards Bamian and Afghan Turkestan. Its basin forms the province of Kabul, which includes all northern Afghanistan between the Hindu Kush and the Safed Koh ranges. From its source to the city of Kabul the course of the river is only 45 m. [72 km], and this part of it is often exhausted in summer for purposes of irrigation. Half a mile east of Kabul it is joined by the Logar, a much larger river, which rises beyond Ghazni among the slopes of the Gul Koh (14,200 ft.)[4,238 metres], and drains the rich and picturesque valleys of Logar and Wardak. Below the confluence the Kabul becomes a rapid stream with a great volume of water and gradually absorbs the whole drainage of the Hindu Kush. About 40 m. [64 km] below Kabul the Panjshir river joins it; 15 m. [24 km] farther the Tagao; 20 m. [32 km] from the Tagao junction the united streams of Alingar and Alishang (rivers of Kafiristan) ; and 20 m. [32 km] below that, at Balabagh, the Surkhab from the Safed Koh. Two or three miles below Jalalabad it is joined by the Kunar, the river of Chitral. Thenceforward it passes by deep gorges through the Mohmand hills, curving northward until it emerges into the Peshawar plain at Michni. Soon afterwards it receives the Swat river from the north and the Bara river from the south, and after a further course of 40 m. [63 km] falls into the Indus at Attock. From Jalalabad downwards the river is navigable by boats or rafts of inflated skins, and is considerably used for purposes of commerce." *EB* (1911), Vol. 15, p. 625.

The 'Paropamisadae,' or the land "above the eagle" (possibly from Avestan, meaning "higher than an eagle can fly"), was previously of one of the Achaemenid Persian satrapies known as Sattagydia. It included the mountainous central portion of Afghanistan including the Kabul, Bamiyan and Panjshir valleys. See Mac Dowell and Taddei (1978b), p. 187. Toynbee (1961), pp. 112-113; 130.

"From the climate, the geographical features, and the produce, the central area in Han times must have been in Gandhāra, including Taxila. Kaspeiria and Paropamisadae were possibly subject to Jibin, but cannot be regarded here as part of the metropolitan territory of Jibin. . . .

Since the metropolitan territory of Jibin lay in the middle and lower reaches of the River Kabul, "Ji-bin [*kiat-pien*]" was very likely a transcription of "Kophen", an ancient name for the River Kabul." Yu (1998), p. 149.

Cunningham describes the region of Kapisha, which he refers to as 'Kapaisene, or Opiân,' in considerable detail, identifying places named in both Xuanzang and Western Classical sources. See: Cunningham (1871), pp. 16-27.

Cunningham identifies the main route from the region of Lanshi, the capital of Daxia (which I identify as Baghlan, see: Appendix N), as crossing the Kushan Pass, and continuing down the Kushan Valley to the ancient town of Kushân near modern Begram. Cunningham (1871): 2006 reprint, pp. 21, 23-24. Surely, the use of the name 'Kushan' for the main pass south of Baghlan, and for the valley leading from the pass south to the town of Kushân in Kapisha is more than just coincidence?

It seems almost certain that, during both Han dynasties, Jibin was based in Kapisha and Gandhara, with the summer 'capital' at Kapishi (the capital of Kapisha according to Xuanzang), and the winter 'capital' at Peshawar. It controlled Swat, the Kunar/Chitral Valley and the route to the much-feared *xuandu* or 'hanging passages' in Hunza.

The borders and rulers of Jibin and neighbouring regions were fluid, as the 'Chronicle on the Western Regions', Section 14 states:

> "They [Gaofu/Kabul] have not always been ruled by the same masters. Whenever one of the three kingdoms of Tianzhu, Jibin, or Anxi [Parthia] became powerful, they took control of it; when weakened, they lost it."

As already noted, some scholars maintain that Jibin referred to the Kashmir Valley, and possibly included western Gandhara, as well as northern areas such as Gilgit and Hunza. This identification is based in part on linguistic grounds, but mainly on the fact that a few later Buddhist texts did indeed use 'Jibin' to refer to the Kashmir Valley. See: Pulleyblank (1963), pp. 218-219, (1999), p. 75, and the discussion in Bailey (1985), pp. 44-46.

> "Chipin must be identified with the modern state of Kashmir, southeast of the Yuezhi yabghu of Xuimi [sic – read Xiumi](in the Wakhan?) and Zhuangmi (around Chitral?), and southwest of the Gilgit River state of Nandou. The length of nine days' journey north to Nandou seems wrong, given that the distance was only 330 li, or *c.* 140 km. Far to the west was Herat in southern present-day Afghanistan." Benjamin (2007), p. 110.

Benjamin fails to give any evidence for his statement that "Chipin must be identified with the modern state of Kashmir," or his identification of Nandou as a "Gilgit River state." Moreover, the placing of Chipin (Jibin) to its southwest is impossible, as the Gilgit River is almost directly north of Srinagar, and not to the northeast. Hulsewé discusses this hypothetical identification of Jibin in *China in Central Asia*:

> "Petech (1950), pp. 63-79, has devoted an exhaustive study to the subject; he admits that Chi-pin indicates, especially in later times, Kashmir, but concludes (p. 79): "the name Chi-pin... in the dynastic histories from the 1st century B.C. to the end of the 5th century A.D. ... indicates the Indian territories of the great political power of the North-West, whatever it was at the time of writing (Saka, Kushan, Hephthalites)". However, Pulleyblank (1963), p. 218, sharply criticises Petech's solution; he believes Petech's "alleged" geographical and historical grounds to be invalid and finds further support for the traditional identification with Kashmir in linguistics, namely: "if ... we have to suppose a final sibilant for the first character in the Han period", reconstructing for Middle Chinese (i.e. Karlgren's Ancient Chinese) k̂iei/-pyin, derived from kā̠(t)s-pin (< pēn) = *Kaspir." *CICA*, p. 104, n. 203.

Daffinà examines this note by Hulsewé in a review article:

> "The Authors [Hulsewé and Loewe] have accepted Pulleyblank's identification of Chi-pin with Kāśmīr, relying confidently on his reconstruction of the consonantal system of 'Old Chinese' and overlooking the plain fact that throughout the period to which the *Han shu* account of Chi-pin refers, and even beyond, Kāśmīr was a historical nonentity. Pulleyblank's attempt at reconstructing 'Old Chinese' has certainly been a meritorious effort, but one open to serious criticism (see for instance

B. Karlgren, 'Loan Characters in Pre-Han Texts', *BMFEA*, 35. 1963. pp. 18-20). Besides, Pulleyblank's **Kaspir* as supposed original of Chi-pin is not even a complete novelty, having been preceded by Laufer's **Ki-spir* (see B. Laufer, *The Language of the Yüeh-chi*, Chicago, 1917, p. 12 n. 1). The Authors will agree that geographical and historical facts cannot be deduced, as a general rule, from nasal initials and sonant stops. In dealing with the foreign names to be met with in Chinese historical texts, one should always keep in mind, as a healthy warning, Maenchen-Helfen's 'History in Linguistics', *JSAOS*, 68, 1948, pp. 120-124. To my humble opinion Petech (1950) p. 64 is conclusive in showing that in *Han shu* Chi-pin is not so much a geographical notion as rather a political one, denoting the Śaka realm in India and comprising "Gandhāra, Kāpiśi, parts of Western Panjāb, but probably excluding Kashmir" *pace* Pulleyblank. See also Narain (1957) p. 136. Our text says that communications with Chi-pin "started from [the time of] Emperor Wu" (A, 25a, 2-3 = p. 107). The statement is perhaps not to be taken literally, as the *Han shu* shows a tendency to refer to the times of emperor Wu (141-87 B.C.) as the starting of the communications with all of the Western Regions. Anyhow Chi-pin was unknown to Chang Ch'ien, and also to Ssŭ-ma Ch'ien who probably finished his work shortly before 90 B.C. (p. 8). Hence it appears that the Chinese could hardly have come to know of Chi-pin prior to that date. This means that Chi-pin, as a name, probably came to North-West India with the Śakas and was therefore something new, denoting a political formation not previously existing but emerging in the first or second decade of the 1st century B.C. The large dogs 大狗 mentioned among the products of Chi-pin (24b, 1 = pp. 106-107) point indirectly to Pañjāb as they probably are the ferocious dogs, known in antiquity, bred in the region of Kekaya, between Bias and Satlāj (see V.S. Agrawala, *India as Known to Pāṇini*, Varanasi, 1963[2], p. 75; and also here below, p. 334). *Shan-hu* 珊瑚 'coral', *hu-po* 虎魄 'amber', and *pi-liu-li* 璧流離 'beryl' (24b, 5-6 = p. 107) which certainly were not indigenous to Chi-pin but imported into it, prove that the area had been for a long time under the sway of Greek civilization; as it was actually the case of Kāpiśa, Gandhāra and Pañjāb, but not of Kāśmīr. The Chinese *hu-po* shows that amber was known locally by the Greek name of ἅρπαξ. *Pi-liu-li* points to some Middle-Indic form like Pāli *veḷuriya-* or Prākrit *verulia-*, later sanskritized as *vaïḍūryami* (see M. Mayrhofer, *Etymologisches Wöterbuch des Altindischen*, III, Heidelberg, 1976, pp. 267-268). As no Middle-Indic text containing either Pāli *veḷuriya-* or Prākrit *verulia-* can be safely said to be older than the *Han shu* account of Chi-pin, Chinese *pi-liu-li* is virtually the first evidence of the word. This makes it highly probable that the Indian term had a north-western origin and derived from Greek βήρυλλος, βήρύλλος, and not *vice versa* as it is generally believed (but see J. Halévy, 'Mélanges étymologiques', *Mémoires de la Société de Linguistique*, 11, 1900, p. 82). Kāśmīr probably never went under Greek rule and even if it did, it was so only in its southern portion and for a very short time (Tarn, 1951, pp. 155, 238; but cf. Narain, 1957, p. 80)." Daffinà (1982) , pp. 316-318.

"As pointed out several years ago (Daffinà, 1967, pp. 47-48 n.), in the Chinese *Aśokarājāvadāna*, translated by An Fa-ch'in between 281 and 306 A.D., Chi-pin corresponds undoubtedly to Kāpiśa-Lampāka, modern Kāfiristān (see *Taishō Issaikyō*, vol. 50, p. 102, b. 14; and Ét. Lamotte, *Le Traité de la Grande Vertu de Sagesse*, I, Louvain, 1944, pp. 548n., 550.). **Up to the time of An Fa-ch'in there is not a single instance where Chi-pin can be safely said to mean Kāśmīr.**" Daffinà (1982), pp. 317-318. Also: Sen (2003), pp. 3-4; Lévi (1896), pp. 161-162. **NOTE:** bold highlight added by author. (JEH)

"Kāśmīra and Uddiyāna [Swat] were recorded as Jibin in some ancient Chinese documentations. As to the territory of Jibin, however, there has been a considerable disputation in the academic circles. In the Han Dynasties 206B.C.~220A.D.), Jibin laid [sic] to the west of Sindu river and also to the south of Hindukush Mountains, covering an area of the plains of the river valleys of the middle and lower reaches of Kabul River and its tributaries, Kapisa, Gandhāra, Takṣaśilā, Uddiyāna and some other kingdoms were included." Li (2005), p. 1.

The lower part of the Kabul River, from the region of modern Jalalabad to the point where it flows into the Indus River at Attock, was known as *Kubhā* in the Ṛgveda Saṃhitā, and *Kophēs* or *Kophēn* in Greek – see Witzel (2003), p. 46.

"Strabo and Ptolemy agree with Huen Tsang [Xuanzang] that Gandhara consisted of the lower Kabul valley, between the Choastes (Kunar) and the Indus, that is to say, the Jalalabad valley and the Peshawar plain, including the hill tracts lying in between, as far as Bajaur, through which early trade routes ran to India." Codrington (1944), p. 38.

"Half a mile above Attock the Indus receives the Kabul river. Its channel up to this point runs through about 872 miles of wild mountainous country, inhabited by fierce fanatical tribes, little known and less explored by Europeans. Attock is the first important point on the Indus within British territories. From thence to the sea is 972 miles, thus giving the total length of the river from its source as 1,844 miles. Up to Attock it falls on an average about twenty feet per mile, and thence to the sea only one foot per mile. Attock is about 2,000 feet above sealevel. The river is navigable for flat-bottomed steamers to Kalabagh, 100 miles below Attock." Ross (1883), p. 32.

It was vital for whoever controlled the region of Jalalabad and/or Peshawar in the Kabul River Valley to also control the fortifications at Kapisha (the Kapisha-Kanish of the Achaemenids) in the Begram Valley to the northwest of Kabul. See: Vogelsgang (2002), pp. 99, 104, 107, 121. Its strategic position made it critical to regulate trade, and prevent invasions from northern and western Afghanistan.

It was also essential for controlling trade and possible invasion routes to the northeast, to extend their power (as the Kushans did) up the Kunar/Chitral Valley and then east to the easily defended gorges of Yasin, Gilgit and Hunza.

"Begram is situated at the confluence of the Ghurband and Panjshir Rivers of eastern Afghanistan, 80 kilometers north of Kabul and approximately 250 kilometers northwest of the legendary Khyber pass. Looking at a topographic map of the region, the location of the site at Begram is particularly striking. To the south, the Kohdaman Plains stretch all the way to Kabul. To the southeast, the Panjshir River and Valley flow down toward the Jalalabad Plains from which it is a relatively easy journey to the Khyber Pass, today connecting Afghanistan with Peshawar in Pakistan. To the north, a number of passes and river valleys lead to the plains of ancient Bactria, along sites such as Surkh Kotal and Bactra, the capital of ancient Bactria. These passes of the western Hindu Kush mountains were renowned lines of communication between Bactria and India, which carried along their paths not only people and materials but also the cultures attendant thereon. These passes also connected the area of Begram with stations along the Silk Roads from China to the Mediterranean." Mehendale (1996), pp. 48-49.

"The plain of Begrâm is bounded by the Panjshir and the Koh-dâman rivers on the north and south; by the Mahighir canal on the west; and on the east by the lands of Julgha, in the fork of the two rivers. Its length, from Bayân, on the Mahighir canal, to Julgha, is about 8 miles [12.9 km]; and its breadth, from Kilah Buland to Yuz Bashi, is 4 miles [6.4 km]. Over the whole of this space vast numbers of relics have been discovered, consisting of small images, coins, seals, beads, rings, arrowheads, fragments of pottery, and other remains, which proves that this plain was once the site of a great city.

Al-Bīrūnī further says . . . , "In the mountains bordering on the kingdom of Kāyabish (Kāpiśa), i.e. Kābul, rises a river which is called the *Ghorvand* on account of its many branches. It is joined by several affluents : 1. The river of the pass of Ghūzak; 2. The river of the gorge of Panchīr (Panjshir falling into the Ghorvand), below the town of Parvān (about 8 miles to the north of Chārikar) ; 3-4. The river Sharvat and the river Sāva, which latter flows through the town of Lambagā (Lampāka), i.e. Lamghan ; they join the Ghorvand at the fortress of Drūta ; 5-6. The rivers Nūr and Kīrāt.—Swelled by these affluents, the Ghorvand (Kābul) is a great river opposite the town of Purshāvar (modern Peshāwar) being there called *the ford*, from a ford near the village of Mahanāra on the eastern bank of the river, and it falls into the river Sindh (Indus) near the castle of Bītūr, below the capital of al-Kandahār (Gandhāra), i.e. Vaihand (Und near Attock)." Sircar (1971), pp. 51-52, n. 3. **NOTE:** 'Und' here refers to Hund or Ohind, now just a small village, where there was an important ancient ford of the Indus, about 15 km upstream from Attock. This was where Alexander's army crossed the great river. The Attock ford is about 80 km east of Peshawar and just 3 marches from Taxila. (JEH)

- **An alternative theory for the origin of the name 'Jibin'**

"There is no mention of the considerable state which the Chinese call Ki-pin until the beginning of the first century before Christ. The Chinese had then for a generation or so already discovered the West: they were not only able to assert themselves up to the same mountain limits that bound the empire now, but they also had some knowledge of Parthia—that is, Persia—of the whole Oxus and Jaxartes region, and of a large state which completely barred their way to the Indus valley and India. This state, in imitation of the native sound, they called *Ki-pin* or 'Shawl-guests.' In naming new states the Chinese either gave them, and still give them, a well-known Chinese name with a differentiating word added—as, for instance, we say New South Wales;—or they imitated as closely as convenient the foreign sound by using one or more Chinese characters, either as pure phonetics or as also descriptive of some striking local peculiarity. Thus Ki-pin was noted for its *ki* or 'shawls,' 'rugs,' &c.; and to *pin*, or 'to guest,' meant 'to come to court with presents or homage.' " Parker (1905), p. 625.

- **Jibin to *circa* 125 CE**

Jibin receives extensive comment in the *Hanshu*, but is only briefly mentioned on three occasions in the later 'Chronicle on the Western Regions' of the *Hou Hanshu*. By the time of the *Hou Hanshu* account (c. 125 CE), Jibin had been conquered by Kujula Kadphises, and absorbed into the Kushan empire.

After the Da Yuezhi were defeated and humiliated by the Xiongnu under Chanyu Jizhu in 166 BCE, and their king's skull was made into a drinking cup, they first fled to the region of the Ili valley and Issyk Kol (Chinese: 熱海 – *Rehai* or "Hot Lake" – because it never freezes), according to the *Hanshu*, displaced many, but not all, of the Sakas previously settled there. See: Appendix X and note 13.3.

Hanshu 96B informs us that:

"When the Ta Yüeh-chih turned west, defeated and expelled the king of the Sai, the latter moved south and crossed over the Suspended Crossing [*xuandu*]; and the Ta Yüeh-chih took up residence in his lands. Later, when the *K'un-mo* of Wu-sun attacked and defeated the Ta Yüeh-chih migrated to the west and subjugated the Ta Hsia; and the K'un-mo of Wu-sun took up residence here." *Hanshu* 96B from *CICA*, pp. 144-145.

This passage from *Hanshu* chap 96A implies that the Saiwang moved out of Daxia/Bactria - not from the Ili Valley region – but from Baktria *after* the Yuezhi invaded that country:

> "When, formerly, the Hsiung-nu conquered the Ta Yüeh-chih, the latter moved west and established themselves as master of Ta Hsia [pinyin: Daxia, i.e. Baktria]; it was in these circumstances that the king of the Sai moved south and established himself as master of Chi-pin. The Sai [Saka] tribes split and separated and repeatedly formed several states. To the north-west of Shu-lo [Kashgar], states such as Hsiu-hsün [pinyin: Xiuxun] and Chüan-tu [pinyin: Juandu] are all of the former Sai race." *Hanshu* 96A from *CICA*, pp. 104-105.

This scenario ostensibly places the conquest of Jibin by the Saiwang three decades later – around 130 BCE. However, Hulsewé's phrase: "it was in these circumstances," is based on only one word in the Chinese text: 而 *er* – which could be better translated as: 'and'; 'and then'; 'and yet'; or 'but'.

Replacing the phrase, 'it was in these circumstances' with the more correct 'and then,' resolves the apparent contradiction, and makes it obvious there is really no reason to doubt the statement in *Hanshu* 96B that the Saiwang moved south over the *xuandu* - the 'hanging passages,' - presumably the ones in Hunza - and into Jibin after being expelled from the Ili/Issyk Kol region by the Da Yuezhi; *not later*, after the Da Yuezhi conquered Daxia/Baktria, as Narain makes explicit:

> "When the Yüeh-chih reached the Upper Ili they displaced the Sai (Śaka) people; some of the Sai princes (Sai-wang) moved south and ultimately reached Chi-pin. The Yüeh-chih, on the other hand, were soon attacked by the Wu-sun, and hence they moved west beyond Ta-yüan to occupy Ta-hsia. It is important to note that the Chinese evidence is consistent and explicit in saying that the Sai moved to the south and the Yüeh-chih to the west; the two peoples did not travel in the same direction." Narain (1957), p. 134.

Some scholars have proposed that the 'Saiwang' could represent the 'Royal Sakas' = the *Sakaraukai* of Western sources and the *Śaka-muruṇḍa-* of the Indian sources. See: Lebedynsky (2006), pp. 63, 174; Harmatta (1994b), p. 409. However, this seems unlikely.

It is true that Chinese *wang* sometimes carries the sense of 'royal,' but if the Chinese had wished to use the term to represent a meaning similar to 'Royal Sakas,' they could have ordered the words to read 王塞 - *Wangsai*, or used a more appropriate term to represent 'Royal Sai.'

> "The combination Sai Wang 'King of the Sakas' has been taken by some scholars as a transcription of the ethnic name Sacaraucae, a people referred to in Western sources in connexion with the end of the Greek kingdom in Bactria. This completely arbitrary [sic] identification has no linguistic basis whatever and attempts to draw together the historical accounts of the King of the Sakas, who, according to the *Han shu*, went to Kashmir [more probably, Kapisha-Gandhara], and the Sacaraucae in Sogdiana and Bactria have only added to the general confusion in which the obscure history of these events is immersed." Pulleyblank, (1970), p. 159 n. 12.

Communication between Jibin and China began during the reign of Emperor Wu (141-87 BCE) but the king of Jibin, Wutoulao (presumably a descendant of the *Saiwang*), believing he was too far from China for the Han to reach him, "frequently menaced or killed Han envoys." When Wutoulao died, his [unnamed] son took his place.

During the reign of Emperor Xiao Yuan (49-33 BCE) the Chinese sent an envoy to Jibin, who, feeling threatened, plotted with Yinmofu, "son of the Rongqu 容屈 king" (probably the son of a subordinate ruler), and killed the king. Yinmofu was then installed on the throne. He later rebelled and put seventy members of a Chinese mission to death – at which point the two countries severed relations.

Sometime prior to 22 BCE, during the reign of Emperor Cheng (33-7 BCE), Jibin apologised. This event is recorded in an address by Du Qin to Wang Feng, the supreme general, who died in 22 BCE – *CICA*, p. 108 and n. 237.

Although official envoys from China were ended, trade continued to prosper, and the *Hanshu* reports: "In fact Chi-pin [Jibin] was seeking to profit from the imperial gifts and from trade, and its envoys came [to Han] once every several years." From: *Hanshu* 96A in *CICA*, pp. 108-112; Sen (2003), pp. 3-4.

The *Hou Hanshu* states that, after Kujula Kadphises conquered the other four *xihou* and formed the Guishuang (= Kushan) kingdom:

> "He [then] invaded Anxi (Parthia) [i.e. "Indo-Parthia"] and took the Gaofu (Kabul) region. He also defeated the whole of the kingdoms of Puda (Paktiya), and Jibin (Kapisha-Gandhāra)."

Mark Passehl suggests that the rulers of Puda and Jibin overthrown by Kujula were probably Aspavarna of the Apracarajas, and Abdagasha, the Gondopharean ruler of Taxila (personal communication, 25 April, 2013).

- **Jibin during the Later Han dynasty**

> "Southwest of Pishan [modern Pishan/Guma in the southern Tarim Basin], you pass through Wucha [Upper Hunza and the Tāghdumbāsh Pamir], cross over *xuandu* [the 'hanging passages' in Hunza], cross Jibin and, at the end of more than 60 days march, you arrive at the kingdom of Wuyishanli [Arachosia and Drangiana]. [Wuyishanli] extends for several thousand *li*." See *Hou Hanshu*, Section 8.

The *Hanshu* describes Jibin as adjoining the Da Yuezhi in the northwest and Wuyishanli/ Arachosia to the southwest. If it bordered the Da Yuezhi at that time, it must have extended to the mountain range just north of Kapisha, which forms a natural boundary with Badakhshan. The physical description in the *Hanshu* suggests its heartland was in western Gandhāra:

> "The land of Chi-pin is flat and the climate is temperate. There is lucerne [= alfalfa - *Medicago sativa*], with a variety of vegetation and rare trees. . . . [The inhabitants] grow the five field crops, grapes and various sorts of fruit, and they manure their orchards and arable land. The land is low and damp, producing rice, and fresh vegetables are eaten in winter. . . . They use gold and silver to make coins, with [the image of] a mounted rider on the obverse and a human face on the reverse. The [state] produces humped cattle, water-buffalo, elephant, large dogs, monkeys, peacocks. . . ." *Hanshu* 96A in *CICA*, pp. 105-106.

Hulsewé's translation is misleading, stating that a mounted rider is on the "obverse" of their coins, and a human face on the "reverse." Numismatists describe coins as having the ruler's image on the "obverse" or front side, and any other designs on the "reverse." However, such technical numismatic terms just did not exist in Han period Chinese.

The Chinese text (以金銀為錢，文為騎馬，幕為人面) in fact, does not indicate that the "human face" is on the reverse at all. There is no word in the text to indicate which side of the coin the "mounted rider" is on, while the translation of the word 幕 mu[4] as "reverse" in connection with the "human face" is unwarranted.

The sentence should read: "They use gold and silver to make coins inscribed with a mounted rider and, on the other side, a man's face."

An AR (silver) tetradrachm of Kujula Kadphises/Heraios found at Bamiyan (which is south of the Hindu Kush), shows a mounted king on one side and a king's portrait on the other. Downloaded from: http://www.grifterrec.com/coins/kushan/kushan.html on 28 March, 2012. See also the AE (bronze) tetradrachms and drachms of 'Soter Megas'/Vima Takhtu accessed from: http://www.grifterrec.com/coins/kushan/kushan2.html on 28 March 2012.

The references to coins with the portrait of the king on one side and a horseman on the other could refer to some coin issues of Indo-Greek Kings, but not the Saka kings, such as Azes I or Vonones, whose coins did not feature portraits on the obverse.

> "There are no gold coins I know of with head/horseman, only silver. Here are examples, I'm not sure this is exhaustive. Philoxenus and Nicias are probably late second century BC. Hippostratus, Menander II and Hermaeus first century BC. In my view the horseman is Alexander the Great.
>
> The only coinage of gold and silver featuring head and horseman are the Eucratides coins which feature two horsemen (the Dioscuri), c. 170-140 BC.
>
> If Jibin is the Kabul/Begram area, then Hermaeus is the most likely candidate, if Taxila is meant, then Hippostratus is the most likely." Joe Cribb (personal communication, 27 April, 2013).

The reference to gold coins with such designs has remained a puzzle, but recently, a single gold coin of Abdagases II was found near Kandahar that featured a mounted horseman on one side spearing an unidentified quadruped – although this does not fit the description in the *HHS* as it has no human face on the other side. See: Bivar (2007), pp. 33-34 and n. 20 quoted in Appendix H.

The gold coin of Eucratides I Megas (who reigned *circa* 170–145 BCE in Bactria and for some time in north-west India) meets the description in the *Hou Hanshu*. It shows a portrait of the king on one side, and, as Cribb mentions above, *two* mounted horsemen on the other. The Chinese characters do not indicate number; therefore, the text can be read as referring to either one or more horsemen. The main question is the early date of Eucratides, but there is no reason why such a coin might not have been kept for a century or so, and then become known to the Chinese.

Details of the reigns of these kings and the territories they controlled are poorly known, so it is impossible to say which coins, if any, were circulating in Arachosia when the information was collected for the *Hanshu*.

The *Shiji* states that: "The coins of the country are made of silver and bear the face of the king. When the king dies, the currency is immediately changed and new coins are issued with the face of his successor." See: Wang (2007a), p. 90. The later *Hanshu* records an interesting change:

> "The description of the Parthian coinage is also different from that in the *Shiji* account, by describing the king's portrait on the obverse and the queen's head on the reverse [read: "on the other side" – see the discussion above]. The majority of Parthian coins are either of the Greek or Scythian tradition, with royal portraits and divine images. But there is indeed a type of Parthian coinage to match this account, the drachm with a bust of Phraataces and Queen Musa, issued between 2 BCE and 4 CE. The account also accurately noted that the coins issued in the Scythian tradition: while the coins had the royal portrait on the front, there was a horse-rider on the obverse ["on the other side"]." Wang (2007a), pp. 94-95.

Some early coins of Kujula Kadphises and Soter Megas feature a mounted horseman on one side and the king's portrait on the other. Although Kushan control is not thought to have extended as far as Arachosia, their coins may have been in use there.

However, an early silver tetradrachm of Kujula Kadphises/'Heraios' found at Bamiyan (which may have been considered part of Arachosia at the time) shows a mounted king on one side and a king's portrait on the other. See the illustration of the coin described as "Senior ISCH B1.2T; Mitchiner ACW 2836, Mitchiner ECCA 97". Accessed on 28 March, 2012 from http://www.grifterrec.com/coins/kushan/kushan.html.

Perhaps Heraios' territory extended to the southern side of the Hindu Kush, or maybe this was an isolated find. See also: the AE (bronze) tetradrachms and drachms of 'Soter Megas'/Vima Takhtu at: http://www.grifterrec.com/coins/kushan/kushan2.html, accessed on 28 March, 2012

"This hub of the Kushan empire came to be known as Gandhara. It extended for about 250 miles [402 km] on all sides of Purashapura [Peshawar]: north over the Malakand pass into Uddiyana in the Swat valley, south across the Indus river as far as the Jhelum and westwards up the Kabul river valley, past the fertile valley of He-lo (now Jalalabad) and deep into Afghanistan as far as Kapisha, the summer capital of the Kushans (now the Russian air base at Begram)." Allen (1999), p. 190.

"What used to be the village of Begram lies thirty-five miles [56 km] north of Kabul, above the confluence of the Ghorband and Panjsher rivers. It now forms part of the largest air base in Afghanistan, built by the Russians in the early 1980s in their fruitless attempt to bring the Afghans into the twentieth century. It is said that the sandy soil hereabouts used to give up more than 10,000 copper coins every year. This was once Kapisha, the summer capital of the Kushans — probably the least known and the most undervalued of all the many dynasties of kings who ruled in Asia.

The village itself stood on a long mound encircled by high walls. Only a fraction was ever excavated: digging in the bazaar area of the old city in 1937 and 1939, French archaeologists unearthed two hoards in adjoining rooms at the foot of a tower in the outer wall. Both rooms had been hastily walled up as though in an attempt to hide the treasures of what was obviously an extremely wealthy - if not royal - household. The Begram Treasure added up to some 2400 objects, including exquisitely carved ivories from central India, painted glassware from Alexandria, Han dynasty lacquer ware and Roman bronzes." Allen (1999), pp. 182-183.

"Most glassware uncovered at Begram has Roman parallels and is thought to have been transported along the Silk Road to Begram. The mosaic or "Millefiori" bowl and a large number of glass goblets with decorative patterns consisting of honeycomb designs find their parallels in Roman Egypt and Europe. Analysis of Begram's fascinating painted glass beakers has revealed that the base glass is of a soda-lime-silica variety, a type analogous to ancient glassware found in Egypt and the Near East. Supporting the theory of Egyptian provenance are ancient sources that mention Egypt in general and Alexandria in particular, along with Syria, as centers of glass manufacturing.

If Roman Egypt or Syria was the place of origin of much of the Begram glassware, the exact route by which the commodities traveled to Begram might be indicated by the distribution pattern of the ribbed bowls uncovered at Begram. Examples of such ribbed bowls are known throughout the Roman world, and a number of them have been discovered at the site of Ed-Dur in the Arabian Gulf Emirate of Umm al-Qaiwain, on the island of Bahrain, and in the coastal site of Arikemedu in Tamil Nadu, southern India. Dated firmly in the first century, their coastal distribution seems to suggest that some, if not all, of the Begram glassware first traveled by sea to the ancient port cities of the Indian Ocean and then was distributed overland to the north. The Periplus of the Erythraean Sea, a first century trading manual, mentions that Barbaricum near modern Karachi, Pakistan, and Barygaza in Gujarat, western India, were the two main ancient ports where Roman products were offloaded in return for goods produced in India and silk yarn and cloth from China." Mehendale (2008a) p. 140.

For recent accounts of the importance of Begram and magnificent illustrations of the treasures discovered there, see: Mehendale (1996), pp. 47-64; Mehendale (2001) [2004], pp. 485-514., Mehendale (2008a and b) and Cambon (2008).

> "Qiujiuque [Kujula Kadphises] invaded Anxi with the result that he took the country of Gaofu, which shows he took Paropamisadae from the Gondophares family. He then destroyed Jibin, of course, in order to put an end to the rule of the family in Gandhāra and Taxila. As mentioned above, the last year of Gondophares was at latest A.D. 45 and it is generally believed that the family of Gondophares had also at least one [later] ruler, Pocores, and their reign in the valley of the Kabul River ended in A.D. 60-65. After that, Jibin was subject to Guishuang." Yu (1998), p. 160. **NOTE:** The dates given here, according to new evidence, were probably about 11 years later – see: Appendix P.

Assuming the Takht-i Bahi inscription was in the Azes era, Gandhāra must have remained under the rule of the Indo-Parthian king Gondophares until *circa* 56 CE. See: Falk and Bennett (2009), pp. 197 and 207, and the discussion in the Introduction and Appendix P.

The Pantjar Stone Inscription, from Pantjar on the Indus, on the border between Peshawar and Hazara districts in Pakistan, is dated in year 122 of the Ajasa (Azes) era (i.e. *circa* 75 CE) and contains the title "Maharaya Gushana." From this we can deduce that less than 19 years (and probably considerably less) passed from the time of Gondophares to the conquest of the Indo-Parthian rulers of Gandhara by Kujula Kadphises. See: Simonetta (1958), p. 171.

The itinerary given in Section 8 of the 'Chapter on the Western Regions' in the *Hou Hanshu* makes it clear that travellers heading south entered Jibin, or Jibin-controlled territory, immediately after crossing the mountains from Wucha [the Tāghdumbāsh Pamir and Upper Wakhan – see: note 8.2]. Then, continuing southwest, they apparently remained within Jibin's territory all the way to Wuyishanli or Arachosia. The *Weishu*, or *History of the Northern Wei*, adds further information on the location of Jibin:

> "The History of the Northern Wei [covering the period 386-534 CE] mentions an embassy from Jibin in the 1st Zhengping year of Taiwu Di (451-452 CE). The notice on the Peoples of the West inserted in this history reproduces that of the Han, but adds a few precise details. The capital of Jibin is SW of Bolu [= Bolor or Gilgit-Baltistan], 14,200 *li* from the capital of the Beiwei (Northern Wei); the country is surrounded by four chains of mountains. It is 800 *li* [333 km] in length from west to east, 300 [125 km] from north to south." Translated and adapted from Lévi and Chavannes (1895), p. 374. **NOTE:** The distance from Kapis/Begram in the east to Taxila is about 350 km. confirming the account of the *Weishu*. (JEH)

The distance given in the text of about 300 *li* or 125 km. from the north to the south of Gandhara is, roughly, the distance from the mountains of Swat in the north to the district of Kohāt in the south. The distance of 800 *li* [333 km] given from west to east in the text is close to the actual distance from Taxila to Jalalabad in Afghanistan plus about 60 km extra – not quite far enough to reach Kapisha, but not far short. As the figure given has been rounded, one can assume the distance was meant to approximate the distance from Taxila to Kapisha as representing the east-west length for Jibin at this period.

Xuanzang, who first visited Taxila in 634 or 635 CE made it clear that in earlier times all of Gandhāra as far as Taxila had been controlled by Kapisha, and only later by Kashmir:

"The chiefs were in a state of open feud, the royal family being extinguished; the country had formerly been subject to Kapis but now it was a dependency of Kashmir." Watters (1904-1905), I, p. 240. Refer also to the translations by Beal (1884), pp. 136-137, and Li (1996), pp. 93-94.

When Xuanzang returned in 644 CE, the King of Kapisha was established at the town of Hund – north of Attock, above the junction of the Indus and the Kabul rivers. Hund was ancient Udabhandapur or Uḍakhāṇḍa city – see: Li (1995), pp. 85, 60, 156. Li (1996), pp. 80, 82, and 93, refers to it as Uḍakhand city).

Evidently, the new king of Kapisha had regained control of all of Gandhāra west of the Indus, and as far as the borders of Badakhshan. He personally escorted Xuanzang past Kapisha and provided him with "a great officer accompanied by a hundred men, as an escort whilst he crossed the Snowy Mountains [over the Kawak Pass], and to convey fuel, provisions, and other requisites for the journey, which the king provided." See: Beal (1911), pp. 192-194; Li (1995), pp. 156-158.

There is more information on the history of Hund and its role as the eastern capital of Gandhāra-Kapisha, in the booklet, *Hund: The Forgotten City of Gandhara* by Sehrai (1979), and its useful foldout map of archaeological sites in Gandhara at the end.

The Chinese pilgrim, Wu Kong, after travelling through Swat to the Indus River, entered Gandhāra in 753 CE. His account helps to locate Jibin both in Kapisha and in Gandhāra. The conditions that he reports were probably typical of the political situation of Jibin for many centuries:

"On the 21st day of the second month of the 12th Guisi year (753) [= 15 March, 753], he [Wu Kong] arrived at the kingdom of Qiantuoluo 乾陀罗– the Sanskrit pronunciation is correctly Gandhâra [Jiantuoluo] (健馱邏); this is the eastern capital of Jibin (罽賓).

The king lives in winter in this place; in summer, he lives in *Jibin*; he seeks out the warmth or coolness to promote his health." From the itinerary of Wu Kong (750-790). Translated and adapted from Lévi and Chavannes (1895), p. 349.

Jibin during the Han dynasty:

• Did Jibin include northwestern Kashmir and Swat/Udiyana?

"The Chinese sources tell us that the key to Chi-pin was the Hanging Pass. We would expect therefore that Chi-pin was not far from the Hanging Pass, probably to the south or south-east. The identification of Chi-pin is not yet finally settled, because in the different periods of Chinese history the term denoted different regions, though all these regions were contiguous to each other. According to Shiratori, Chi-pin denoted Gandhāra in the Han period, Kashmir in the time of the Six Dynasties, and Kāpiśa in the T'ang period.[1] But the earliest mention of Chi-pin is in the *Ch'ien Han Shu* and we are concerned with the region it denoted in the period of the early Huns. Franke concluded that, while Chi-pin specially denotes Kashmir, the Śaka dominion included the north-western portion of modern Kashmir and the area we have called the Swat valley; roughly this region would be that called Udyāna,[2] which was sometimes included in the geographical term Gandhāra. In the *Ch'ien Han Shu* Chi-pin is described as a fruit-growing country, famous for embroidery and other handicrafts.[3] It seems that, though Chi-pin later denoted the Kashmir valley and gradually became a geographical expression for the Kuṣāna empire in India, in our period it was roughly the Swat valley and the adjoining areas. The findspots of the coins and inscriptions of the earliest Śaka kings in India also suggest the same identification. The old view that Chi-pin was Kabul[4] does not seem probable, because the Chinese also knew the latter by the name Kao-fu.[5]

[1] Shiratori, op. cit., pp. 377-462.
[2] Franke, op. cit., pp. 58-59.
[3] Wylie, p. 35.
[4] Also supported and discussed in detail by Tarn, in Appendix 9, pp. 469-73. He found in Chi-pin the old name Ko-phen for Kabul. Cf. also Lohuizen, op. cit., p. 372.
[5] *Hou-han Shu*, Bk. 88. Cf. *infra*, pp. 159-60." Narain (1957), pp. 135-136, and nn. 1-5.

- **Was the capital of Jibin Xunxian 循鮮 in Gandhāra or 脩鮮 Xiuxian in Kashmir?**

Some scholars have proposed that the name 循鮮 Xunxian (W-G: Hsün-hsien), given as the capital of Jibin in the *Hanshu*, might represent the old capital of Gandhāra, Pushkalavātī or Pushkaravātī (= modern Charsadda). Others have maintained that it might represent the capital of Kashmir, Śrīnagara, (modern Srinagar) – given in the Tang histories as Xiuxian (W-G: Hsiu-hsien) 脩鮮

> "Hsün-hsien 循鮮 *sic*; however, as indicated by Hsü Sung [1781-1848] and Wang Hsien-ch'ien [1842-1918], an early quotation and references show that this should be read Hsiu-hsien 脩鮮, GSR 1077e and 209a: si̯og/si̯ə̯u-si̯an/si̯än; the confusion between *hsün* and *hsiu* is not uncommon." From *Hanshu* 96A in *CICA*, p. 104, n. 204.

> "For the name of the head town of Chi-pin the Authors [Hulsewé, and Loewe, in *CICA*, p. 104, n. 204] accept the reading *Hsün-hsien* 循鮮 of the text. But in note 204, following Hsü Sung and Wang Hsien-ch'ien who quote the *T'ang-shu* and the *T'ai-p'ing yü-lan*, they seem to prefer, without any apparent reason, the reading *Hsiu-hsien* 脩鮮 which is the name the capital of Chi-pin has in the *T'ang shu*. This preference is all the more surprising as in the T'ang official history Chi-pin is Kāpiśa (see Éd. Chavannes, *Documents sur les Tou-kiue occidentaux*, Sanktpeterburg, 1903, pp. 130-132), an identification which the Authors, in accepting Pulleyblank's equation of Chi-pin with Kāśmīr, have implicitly rejected. From their point of view, therefore, Hsün-hsien and *Hsiu-hsien* ought not to be interchangeable, as the capital of Chi-pin/Kāśmīr could hardly be the same place or have the same name as the capital of Chi-pin/ Kāpiśa." Daffinà (1982), p. 318.

Whichever form was the most accurate, it seems certain that 循鮮 Xunxian and Xiuxian 脩鮮 were both meant to be transcriptions of the same name. Additionally, it seems they could have been intended as translations.

Pushkaravātī represents in Sanskrit 'abounding in Lotuses,' (see Monier-Williams, p. 639). However, the more common spelling of the name, Pushkalavātī, actually translates as something like: 'abounding in richness, strength, magnificence or excellence.' (*CICA*, p. 104, n. 203).

The character 循 *xun* can be translated as – '**good**,' well' – see: *GR*, Vol. III, page 84, No. 4770, **11.** The alternative form, 脩 *xiu* can be read in Chinese as: *xiu* – 'beautiful; good; excellent'; to cultivate (an art or a virtue) – see: *GR*, Vol. II, page 1221, No. 4579, **4b.**

The second character in each case is 鮮 *xian* – 'beautiful; clear; brilliant; good; excellent; savoury; delicious' – see: *GR*, Vol. II, page 4479, No. 1141, **5** to **7.**

Thus, Xunxian or Xiuxian have the same meaning, each providing an excellent translation of Pushkalavātī, making it almost certain that Pushkalavātī/Pushkaravātī/ modern Charsadda was the ancient winter capital of Jibin.

Pushkalavātī is no longer mentioned as the winter administrative centre or the seat of the king of Jibin after the time of its conquest by Kujula Kadphises. In fact, we know that by Kanishka's time, if not before, the local centre of power had been relocated to nearby Peshawar. See, for example: Smith (1908), p. 243.

• What were the routes from the Tarim Basin to Jibin and beyond?

Examining maps of northern Pakistan and the adjoining parts of Afghanistan and Chinese territory, one can see the long range of very high mountains, stretching roughly east to west, dividing northern Pakistan from the Tāghdumbāsh Pamir and the Wakhan corridor.

The route from China to Wuyishanli/Arachosia-Drangiana, as described in both the *Hanshu* and the *Hou Hanshu*, reaches Jibin after crossing through the fearsome *xuandu* (or 'hanging passages') in Hunza.

Parallel routes run to the north and south of this range and are linked at a few intervals via passes. The northern route through the Tāghdumbāsh Pamir and the Wakhan corridor leads to Badakhshan in northern Afghanistan. The southern route runs from Hunza and Gilgit to Mastuj.

> "**CHITRAL,** a native state in the North-West Frontier Province of India. The state of Chitral (see also HINDU KUSH) is somewhat larger than Wales, and supports a population of about 35,000 rough, hardy hillmen. Previous estimates put the number far higher, but as the Mehtar assesses his fighting strength at 8000 only, this number is probably not far wrong. Both the state and its capital are called Chitral, the latter being situated about 47 m. [76 km] from the main watershed of the range of the Hindu Kush, which divides the waters flowing down to India from those which take their way into the Oxus. Chitral is an important state because of its situation at the extremity of the country over which the government of India exerts its influence, and for some years before 1895 it had been the object of the policy of the government of India to control the external affairs of Chitral in a direction friendly to British interests, to secure an effective guardianship over its northern passes, and to keep watch over what goes on beyond these passes. This policy resulted in a British agency being established at Gilgit (Kashmir territory), with a subordinate agency in Chitral, the latter being usually stationed at Mastuj (65 m. [105 km] nearer to Gilgit than the Chitral capital), and occasional visits being paid to the capital. Chitral can be reached either by the long circuitous route from Gilgit, involving 200 m. [322 km] of hill roads and the passage of the Shandur pass (12,250 ft.) [3,734 metres], or (more directly) from the Peshawar frontier at Malakand by 100 m. [161 km] of route through the independent territories of Swat and Bajour, involving the passage of the Lowarai (10,450 ft.) [3,185 metres]. It is held by a small force as a British outpost.
>
> The district of Chitral is called Kashgar (or Kashkar) by the people of the country; and as it was under Chinese domination in the middle of the 18th century, and was regarded as a Buddhist centre of some importance by the Chinese pilgrims in the early centuries of our era, it is possible that it then existed as an outlying district of the Kashgar province of Chinese Turkestan, where Buddhism once flourished in cities that have been long since buried beneath the sand-waves of the Takla Makan." *EB* (1911), Vol. 6, pp. 251-252.

Mastuj, on the Yarkhun River (a tributary of the Chitral/Kunar River), is the main centre in the upper reaches of the Chitral/Kunar valley, from where, when the political situation allowed, there was relatively easy, year-round access to the region of Jalalabad at the junction of the Kunar and the Kabul River. This was the easiest and most direct route to Kandahar and the Persian Gulf from the north.

The route leading to Jibin from the Tarim Basin, though not suitable for laden animals, was open for most of the year and was the quickest and most direct route for a person on foot heading to the north Indian plains, or to Kabul and/or Kandahar. Travellers went over either the Kilik or the Mintaka Pass, through Hunza and Gilgit and then via Mastuj and Chitral and down the Kunar Valley to the region of modern Jalalabad in Afghanistan.

> "Most of the European explorers, sportsmen, missionaries and others who have visited Central Asia from India have travelled by this route [*via* Leh and over the Karakoram Pass], and we might have followed in their steps. But I was more fortunate than they, for I was travelling to Kashgar on duty, and a shorter and less arduous, yet even more interesting, route was open to me. This was the last of the three mentioned above, that *via* Gilgit, the Mintaka Pass and the Chinese Pamirs. For several reasons this route is not practicable for trade or regular traffic. For one thing, the gorge of the Hunza River between Baltit and Misgar (six marches) is in many places quite impossible for loaded ponies, and all baggage has to be carried in fifty-pound loads from village to village on the backs of the few porters available." Skrine (1926), p. 5.

From Gilgit it was considered a relatively easy journey east across the low Shandur Pass (3,725 m. /12,221 ft.), which is about 20 kilometres from Mastuj in the upper Chitral/Kunar valley. From Mastuj there was all-season access via Chitral to the region of Jalalabad on the middle section of the Kabul River, in modern Afghanistan, which, in turn, controlled the easiest and most direct routes to Kabul and Kandahar or east to Peshawar.

The great distance between the Kashmir Valley and the Upper Kabul River Valley would alone seem to eliminate the possibility of Kashmir being the centre of Jibin, though it might have controlled Jibin at times.

Nor could Kashmir possibly be described as a "flat" country that produced elephants – the winter is far too severe for elephants. The western part of Gandhara, often considered part of Jibin, is indeed fairly flat, is considerably warmer than the Kashmir Valley, and contains plenty of water, thus providing good conditions for maintaining herds of war elephants.

Temperatures in Srinagar, the capital of Kashmir, usually stay below freezing all night in January and there are often heavy falls of snow.

On the other hand, it never snows in Taxila, the ancient capital of Gandhara. Islamabad, only 32 km from Taxila, is described as having a "typical version of a humid subtropical climate." See: http://en.wikipedia.org/wiki/Climate_of_Islamabad .

> "The classical writers are unanimous in their accounts of the size and wealth of Taxila. Arrian describes it as "a large and wealthy city, and the most populous between the Indus and Hydaspes [modern Jhelum]." Strabo also declares it to be a large city, and adds, that the neighbouring country was "crowded with, inhabitants, and very fertile." Pliny calls it "a famous city, situated on a low but level plain, in a district called *Amanda*. These accounts agree exactly with the position and size of the ancient city near Shah-dheri [within the modern city of Peshawar], the ruins of which are spread over several square miles." Cunningham (1871), pp. 105-106.

During the period covered by the *Hou Hanshu*, all regions east and north of the Kashmir Valley (including the strategic and commercially important routes into northern Afghanistan, to reach the Wakhan Corridor, and the Tarim Basin), were considered part of the territory of Jibin.

The territory containing the routes that led through Chitral, Gilgit, Hunza, and adjoining regions, was usually under some degree of control by the kings of Kashmir or Jibin, except when they became part of a larger empire, such as the Kushans or later, the British. See: Section 8.

From Chitral, the easiest route for those travelling to the south and west led down the Gilgit/Kunar River valley to Jalalabad and then on to Kabul, and southwest through Kandahar, or northwest to the region of Kapisha near modern Begram. This route was free of snow all year. Today, the border between Afghanistan and Pakistan cuts through the Kunar Valley preventing free travel along this otherwise superior route.

A more difficult route led south from Chitral and across the Lowari Pass (3,200 m/10,499 ft.), 365 km. (227 miles) to Peshawar. Another route led west, connecting Chitral via the Dorah Pass (over 4,300 m/14,000 ft.), into Badakhshan in northern Afghanistan.

Before the partition of the subcontinent in 1947, 'Kashmir' referred to the princely state of Jammu-Kashmir. As well as the so-called 'Vale of Kashmir' it included Gilgit and the territory along the Indus River past Chilas, and around the great bend of the Indus River, down to the plains of the Punjab (in modern Pakistan). To the north, it included the Gilgit and Wakhan valleys; to the west, it stretched past Gupis to the relatively easy Shandur Pass (3,725 m. or 12,221 ft.), which is about 20 kilometres from Mastuj, and links Chitral with Gilgit.

> "Summing up these quasi-historical indications, we are justified in concluding that Gilgit and the adjacent Hindukush tracts were under the suzerainty of the dynasty which held sway at the time over the north-western borderlands of India along the Kābul river and lower down on the Indus. Popular belief, as Al-Bērūnī's statement shows, claimed for them distant descent from the great Kushan rulers. Direct access from the Peshawar valley up the Indus must at all times have been extremely difficult, as I had the occasion to convince myself on my exploration of 1942, owing to the character of the river-gorges in the Indus Kohistan. But connection from Gilgit could be maintained with the Kābul river valley, always a main seat of that dynasty, either up the Kūnar river and thence via Chitrāl or else with territory immediately to the east of the Indus via Chilās and the Kāgān valley, and also by the longer and more difficult route via Astōr and Kashmir." Stein (1944), p. 9.

> "Both from Chitrāl proper and from upper Kāshkār or Mastūj the Indus Valley can be readily reached by a number of routes leading across the headwaters of the Swāt and Panjkōra rivers, and the remarkable extension which in recent years the Khān of Dir's power has taken in the direction of the Swāt Kōhistān and the Indus Valley presents a curious parallel. Chilās and the other Dard communities along the Indus, if left to themselves, could without great difficulty have been overawed by the Chinese garrison placed in Gilgit and Yasīn; but when controlled and supported by a neighbouring hillstate of such resources as Chitrāl, they were bound to become a serious menace to the Kashmīr-Gilgit route, which they flanked, and upon which the maintenance of that garrison depended." Stein (1907), p. 17.

> "While the bulk of the trade between Peshawar and Kabul took place along the overland routes, the Kabul river was an important conduit for the local trade from Kunar, Bajaur, Kafiristan and Chitral. During the warm season traffic on the river was brisk. Bajaur and Kunar exported wax, hides, ghi, rice, walnuts, and honey; Bajaur also sent large quantities of iron ore to Peshawar; finally, gold dust, hawks, falcons and slaves from Kafiristan and Chitral floated down the river [on rafts made of wood and inflated hides]." Noelle (1997), p. 183.

Travellers heading from the Tarim Basin area for Badakhshan could travel west through the Wakhan corridor. Caravans heading for northern India had to avoid the precarious 'hanging passages' in northern Hunza (which laden animals could not cross) by proceeding further west along the Wakhan corridor to Sarhad ('Frontier') and then cross over the Baroghil Pass (3,798 m/12,460 ft.), which led to Mastuj.

The Baroghil is a relatively easy pass during the summer, though it is closed for about three months during winter. It was the only pass in the region that laden pack animals could cross. From Mastuj they could travel to either Jalalabad or Peshawar via Chitral. At times, the Baroghil Pass was even practicable for carts, and certainly was for armies:

> "All details recorded of it [i.e. the passage of Ko Hsien-chih's troops in 747 CE] agree accurately with the route which lies over the Barōghil saddle (12,460 feet above the sea [3,798 metres]) to the sources of the Mastūj river, and then, crossing south-eastwards the far higher Darkōt Pass (15,200 feet [4,633 metres]), descends along the Yasīn river to its main junction with the main river of Gilgit. Three days are by no means too large an allowance of time for a military force accompanied by baggage animals to effect the march from the Oxus to the summit of the Darkōt Pass, considering that the ascent to the latter lies partly over the moraines and ice of a great glacier. The Darkōt Pass corresponds exactly in position to the 'Mount T'an-chü' of the Annals and possibly preserves the modern form of the name which the Chinese transcription, with its usual phonetic imperfection, has endeavoured to reproduce. The steep southern face of the pass, where the track descends close on 6,000 feet [1,829 metres] between the summit and the hamlet of Darkōt, over a distance of five or six miles [8 to 9.7 km], manifestly represents 'the precipices for over forty li in a straight line' which dismayed the Chinese soldiers on looking down from the heights of Mount T'an-chü.
>
> From the foot of the pass at Darkōt a march of about twenty-five miles [40 km] brings us to the village of Yasīn, the political centre of the valley. . . ." Stein (1907), Vol. I, pp. 9-10.
>
> "Chitral, unlike Gilgit, is not blocked [to the south] for eight months in the year by Nature. If there were no such things as states, frontiers, and feuds, Chitral could be reached with ease from Peshawar any day in the year. It could be reached via Jallalabad. For, at Jallalabad, the Kabul River is joined by the Kunar River; and Chitral is simply another name for the upper Kunar valley. Unseal the sealed frontier that cuts this valley in two like a travel-proof bulk-head, and that grim annual toll of deaths on the Lowari Pass could be remitted." Toynbee (1961), p. 143.
>
> "Accordingly from here I retraced my steps, and Lennard and myself marched down the Oxus valley to Sarhad, the frontier outpost of Afghan arms in Wakhan. From there we recrossed the Hindu Kush by the low depression known as the Baroghil Pass, beyond which we separated-Lennard to return over the Darkot Pass, with its formidable snow and glaciers, to Yasin and Gilgit;. . . I to follow the gorge of the Yarkhun river (which in its later course is variously known as the Mastuj, Chitral, Kashkar and Kunar river) to Mastuj." Curzon (1896), p. 17.
>
> "That remarkable offshoot, the Shandur range, which, starting from the head of the Yarkhun, or Chitral, or Kunar river (for it is all the same river), shuts off the narrow valley of Chitral from the headwaters of the Gilgit and the Swat and Panjkora-across which lies the dreaded Darkot pass to the north and the Shandur pass between Chitral and Gilgit–continues as a strictly conscientious water–divide, admitting of no breaks, down the eastern side of the Kunar valley. Here it lowers its crest and allows the existence of several passes, which were once somewhat easy links on the high-road from Kabul to India; then rising again slightly where the Kabul river forces its passage by a devious course between conglomerate cliffs (the first break in its continuity since its commencement), it finally culminates in the great level range of Sufed Koh, the dominating feature both of the Kabul and the Kuram valleys." Holdick (1901), p. 463.

> "As we stood on the terrace together [at Drosh, south of Chitral], the Colonel [of the Chitral Scouts] pointed to a ridge high above the valley, four or five miles away. Turning to me, he said, "There's your Durand Line." I hadn't realised that they ever went up there on exercise or patrol. "Of course, we do it regularly. There are forty-two passes between Chitral and Afghanistan, and it's our job to keep an eye on every one. Especially now." Moorhouse (1984), p. 257.

> "From Sarhad ['Frontier'] starts the well-known route which leads southwards over the Barōghil pass to the headwaters of the Mastūj river, to this day representing the easiest line of access from the Upper Oxus to Chitrāl as well as to Gilgit." Stein (1907), Vol. I, p. 8.

There are other routes a traveller could take from Gilgit. One led to Srinagar in the Kashmir Valley. From Srinagar, one could cross over the relatively easy Baramula Pass - 1,570 metres (5,150 ft) to Taxila, the capital of Gandhara. This route is usually open, "except in January, February, and part of March, when it is liable to be blocked by snow over the Muree hill and between Rampur and Baramula." Younghusband (1909), p. 57.

From Taxila it was easy travelling west to Peshawar and Jalalabad, or east through the Yamuna and Ganges Valleys.

However, this route from Gilgit via Kashmir to Peshawar and Jalalabad would have been unnecessarily long and circuitous for someone heading from Gilgit to Wuyishanli /Arachosia.

Another route led south from Gilgit to the Indus and then down the river valley via another set of difficult and dangerous *rafiqs* (*xuandu* or 'hanging passages') to Taxila, and then west, as in the previous route.

> "After leaving behind Misgar, the northernmost hamlet of Hunza, the natural difficulties of the route decrease. The valley widens as we approach the watershed which separates the headwaters of the Hunza river from those of the Oxus on the one side and the Tāghdumbāsh Pāmīr on the other. Lord Curzon, in his exhaustive Memoir on the Pāmīrs, has duly emphasized the important geographical fact that the water-parting in this part of the Hindukush lies considerably to the north of the axial range and is also far lower. This helps to account for the relative ease with which the Kilik and Mintaka passes, giving final access to the Tāghdumbāsh Pāmīr, can be crossed, even with laden animals, during the greater part of the year." Stein (1907) Vol. I, p. 21.

A more hazardous route from Chitral over the Lowari Pass to the region of Peshawar is reluctantly used nowadays as an alternative to the Kunar River route that is blocked by the Pakistan-Afghan frontier. There was also a vital route from Chitral north to Zebak in Badakhshan:

> "After five marches [from Faizabad, the capital of Badakhshan] they reached the small village of Zebak, from whence there is a road to Chitrál. This route is said to be dangerous on account of the inroads of the Siyaposh Kafirs; but still a considerable traffic is carried on by this route between Badakshan and Chitrál." Montgomerie (1871), p. 155.

There are further detailed studies on the location of Jibin, such as the essays in Lévi and Chavannes (1895), pp. 371-384; Petech (1950), pp. 63-80; Tarn (1984), pp. 469-473; and Yu (1998), Chapter 8, "The State of Jibin," pp. 147-166. Also worth checking are: Stein (1900) Vol. II, Chap. II, especially, pp. 351-362; Molè (1970), p. 97, n. 105; Rapson, ed., (1922), p. 501; Keay (1977), pp. 130, 146, 222, 224; Toynbee (1961), pp. 1, 48, 51-52 130, 125-126; and Pugachenkova, et al. (1994), p. 356.

• What and where was the vassal Kingdom of Nandou 難兜 ?

The *Hanshu* contains an account of the former "kingdom" of Nandou 難兜 (literally: 'difficult detour,' 'small pocket,' or 'pouch'), which was subject to Jibin. It is not mentioned in the *Hou Hanshu* or later works, presumably because it had been absorbed into the Kushan Empire by then.

Nandou, which, in the early literature, is only briefly mentioned in the *Hanshu*, has proved to be difficult to identify, partly because there appear to be errors in the *Hanshu's* account and the fact that there are no other references for comparison.

Here is the translation of the passage from *Hanshu* 96A according to Hulsewé:

> "The state of Nan-tou
>
> The seat of the king's government is at ... [text defective], and it is distant by 10150 *li* from Ch'ang-an. There are 5000 households, 31000 individuals with 8000 persons able to bear arms. To the north-east it is a distance of 2850 *li* to the seat of the protector general. To the west [*] it is a distance of 340 *li* to Wu-lei, and, to the south-west, 330 *li* to Chi-pin. It adjoins [the land of the] Ch'iang tribes who are termed Ch'o in the south, Hsiu-hsün in the north and the Ta Yüeh-chih in the West. [The inhabitants] grow the five field crops, grapes and various fruits. There is silver, copper and iron, and [the inhabitants] make weapons in the same way as the various other states. It is subject to Chi-pin." From: *Hanshu* 96A in *CICA*, p. 103. **NOTE:** Both Chinese texts I have accessed say that Wu-lei was 340 *li* to the *south* of Nan-tou, not to the *west*. If the identification of Wulei as the Great and Little Pamir Valleys is correct (see: note 20.3), both versions are wrong and should read "to the north-east." (JEH)

The missing seat of the king's government in this text is said to be at the "walled town of Nandou" (難兜城) in the massive Song dynasty encyclopaedia, the *Taiping Yulan*.

Placing the Erh Ch'iang (pinyin: Er) or Ch'o (pinyin: Jo) Qiang = 'Unconquered Qiang,' see: note 1.10) to the south of Nan-t'ou (pinyin: Nandou) seems out of place, though not impossible. The only other references we have to the Jo Qiang locate them in the mountains to the south of the Tarim Basin and on the northern Tibetan plains or Changthang, stretching from Dunhuang in a long line west to the mountains south of Khotan. No other text places them anywhere near the position indicated here.

I have identified Hsiu-hsün (pinyin: Xiuxun) with some confidence (in note 2.16), as being well to the north, in the Alai Valley, just west of Kashgar. Unless I have made a gross error, or one or other of these 'kingdoms' was really very extensive, there is no way Xiuxun could adjoin Nandou to the south. These complications are likely due to the lack of detailed geographic knowledge of the area at the time by the Chinese.

The only other references to Nandou are almost identical descriptions in later works and brief comments elsewhere in the same chapter (96A) of the *Hanshu* stating:

- "Wu-ch'a adjoins Nan-tou in the west" – see: *CICA*, p. 98. This is possible if I am correct in identifying Wu-ch'a as Upper Hunza and the Taghdumbash Pamir – see: note 8.2.
- that it is said to adjoin the Da Yuezhi in the west.
- that, from Chi-pin [Jibin] one can reach Nan-tou [Nandou] after a nine days' journey (see *CICA*, p. 104). It is difficult to equate this with the earlier claim that it is only 330 *li* (137 km) south-west to Chi-pin.

> "Wang Hsien-ch'ien supposes that the figure "nine" [days] is wrong, because the distance between the two states is said to be a mere 330 *li* or ca. 140 km [actually only 137.2 km]." *CICA*, p. 104, note 207.

While this certainly seems a long time for a journey (行 = 'walk') of 137 km (at just 15.2 km per day average), it must be remembered that roads, passes and tracks in Bajaur are very mountainous and often cut by avalanches, snow, ice, heavy storms and fog during winter, and by flooding rains in the spring. The length of the journey may well have been based on the time taken by one traveller when conditions were not ideal, rather than an average trip between the two centres.

Alternatively, it could be that it was only 330 *li* (137 km) from the frontier of Nandou to (the capital of Jibin), but 9 days' journey (say 230 km) between the two capitals.

In spite of the fact that the information on Nandou in the *Hanshu* apparently contains some errors, it probably refers to the important ancient trade-route which went north-east from the region of modern Jalalabad at the junction of the Kabul and Kunar/Chitral rivers, and via Gilgit to Mastuj, and then either through the Baroghil Pass into the Wakhan Corridor, or west to Yasin, Gilgit and Hunza.

Nandou is usually thought to refer to the to the lower Gilgit River – see: *CICA*, p. 103, n. 95, and Benjamin (2007), pp. 109-110.

I believe that the Bajaur Valley in the presently semi-independent "tribal areas" of western Pakistan is the most likely position for Nandou. This is based on a number of arguments including the fact that the *Hanshu* clearly states it adjoins the Da Yuezhi in the west, and Badakhshan (then controlled by the Da Yuezhi), was directly over the mountains, to the west of Bajaur. Neither the Swat Valley nor the lower Gilgit River directly adjoined Da Yuezhi territory to its west.

Moreover, Bajaur was the usual route from Afghanistan to India before the use of the Khyber Pass became more popular. This was the route Alexander took to invade Swat. As Verma (1978), p. 72, points out (see quote above) even horses and camels found the Khyber Pass difficult to negotiate until Akbar improved the road.

After the conquests of Kujula Kadphises, Kushan rule extended throughout Bajaur and the fertile Swat Valley bordering it to the east.

It is very difficult to obtain detailed information on the passes and routes across Bajaur. For several centuries, and still today, it has remained under the control of fiercely independent tribes. Even the British did not manage to conquer or survey the area. However, the following quotes supply some details:

> "This road [from Chakdarra – just north of the Malakand Pass] to Dir and Chitral first crosses the watershed between the Swat River and its north-eastern tributary the Panjkora ["Panjkora means 'Five Districts'. Each of the five is a valley ploughed by a river whose waters are rushing to join the main stream." Ibid, p. 140]. Then it runs up the Panjkora valley. Finally it serves to the left and runs up a tributary of the Panjkora that bears the same name–Lowarai–as the pass and as the mountain below whose left shoulder the pass runs. The watershed itself is not impressive. It is just a low divide between the heads of two side valleys. But, when the northward-running valley narrows into a gorge and the road swings away and up over the shoulder of a mountain, the northward view from the top is a grand one. At one's feet, far below, lies the Panjkora valley, with the river running down it south-westwards. To the left rise the jagged mountains of Bajaur. This wild country is included in the Malakand Agency, and its people come out, when they wish, through Chakdarra to see the World. But no British official was ever allowed to enter Bajaur, and no Pakistani official, either, has gained admittance there yet. Across the Panjkora valley, towards the north, the mountains lie within the state of Dir, up to a range that marks the frontier between Dir and Afghanistan. Like the mountains in the foreground, this range is snow-less in June; but, above its crest, two snow-covered mountain-masses

just emerge. The mass on the left is the snow-crown of Nuristan. The mass on the right is Loawari Mountain." Toynbee (1961), p. 139.

"The next day, at a mile and a half north of Alladand, they reached the Swat River, a very large stream, which they crossed on rafts: continuing their march the same day, they ascended the opposite mountains, and, by an easy pass, crossed over the Lurrum Mountains into the Talash district, and, descending to the Punjkora River, crossed it on the 17th. This river appeared to be even larger than the Swat River. From the Punjkora River they marched on through Jundul, the largest district of Bajaur, reaching, on the 18th August, Miankilai, the chief town of Jundul, and the capital, in fact, of the province. Bajaur is divided into three districts, viz., Jundul (Miankilai), Nawagai, and Shahr, each of which is ruled by a separate Khan ; the two latter, however, being, in a measure, subordinate to the present Khan of Jundul, Faiz Talab Khan, styled Haji-Saheb-Zada in consequence of his having made the pilgrimage to Mecca, and who has, owing to this and his general uprightness as a ruler, become much respected, . . ." Montgomerie (1872), p. 182.

"The Malakand Pass gives access to the valley of the Swat, a long and wide trough running east and west, among the mountains. Six miles further to the east, at Chakdara, the valley bifurcates. One branch runs northward towards Uch, and, turning again to the west, ultimately leads to the Panjkora River and beyond to the great valley of Nawagai. For some distance along this branch lies the road to Chitral, and along it the Malakand Field Force will presently advance against the Mohmands. The other branch prolongs the valley to the eastward. A few miles beyond Chakdara a long spur, jutting from the southern mountains, blocks the valley. Round its base the river has cut a channel. The road passes along a narrow stone causeway between the river and the spur. Here is the Landakai position, or as the tribesmen have for centuries called it, the "Gate of Swat." Beyond this gate is Upper Swat, the ancient, beautiful and mysterious "Udyana." This chapter will describe the forcing of the gate and the expedition to the head of the valley.

Another mile or so brought us to the Watelai River, a stream about thirty yards broad, which flows into the Jandul, and thence into the Panjkora. Crossing this and climbing the opposite bank, the troops debouched on to the wide level plateau of Khar, perhaps ten miles across and sixteen in length [16 by 26 km]. Standing on the high ground, the great dimensions of the valley were displayed. Looking westward it was possible to see the hills behind the Panjkora, the sites of the former camps, and the entrance of the subsidiary valley of the Jandul. In front, at the further end, an opening in the mountain range showed the pass of Nawagai. Towering on the left was the great mass of the Koh-i-mohr, or "Mountain of Peacocks"--a splendid peak, some 8000 feet [2438 m.] high, the top of which is visible from both Peshawar and Malakand. Its name is possibly a corruption. Arrian calls it Mount Meros. At its base the city of Nysa stood in former times, and among many others fell before the arms of Alexander. Its inhabitants, in begging for peace, boasted that they conducted their government "with constitutional order," and that "ivy, which did not grow in the rest of India, grew among them." City, ivy, and constitutional order have alike disappeared. The mountain alone remains. A little to the northward the Ramlat Pass was distinguishable. On the right the smooth plain appeared to flow into the hill country, and a wide bay in the mountains, roughly circular in shape and nearly twelve miles across, opened out of the valley. The prominent spurs which ran from the hills formed many dark ravines and deep hollows, as it were gulfs and inlets of the sea. The entrance was perhaps a mile broad. I remember that, when I first looked into the valley, the black clouds of a passing storm hung gloomily over all, and filled it with a hazy half-light that contrasted with the brilliant sunshine outside. It was the Watelai, or as we got to call it later--the Mamund Valley.

Early next morning the 3rd Brigade and three squadrons of the 11th Bengal Lancers moved on to Nawagai and crossed the pass without opposition. The general and Headquarters staff accompanied them, and we found ourselves in a wide and extensive valley, on the far side of which the Bedmanai Pass could be plainly seen." Churchill (1898), Chapter X.

"I do not agree with Mr. Pincett that Alexander went as far north as Chitral (*J. R. A. S.*, 1894, p. 681) ; but at present it is not possible to determine the point at which he turned eastwards, and crossed the mountains into Bajaur. It is, however, certain that he used one of the regular passes, which remain unchanged, and by which alone Bajaur territory can be entered. Raverty describes, from native information, two routes from Kābul to Bajaur ; and it may well be that Alexander followed the 'left-hand,' or eastern one, which goes through a village named Kūz Danāhi, where two roads diverge, of which one leads to Chitrāl, and the other by the Shahr, or capital of Bājaur. (*Notes*, 112-118)." Smith (1908), p. 47, n. 2.

Google maps show that from Nawagai (34° 41' N; 71° 22' E), the modern 'capital' of Bajaur, it is about 140 km by road southwest to Jalalabad in Afghanistan, which was certainly in Jibin, if not the 'capital.' It is also 140 km north of Peshawar.

"**BAJOUR,** or BAJAUR, a small district peopled by Pathan races of Afghan origin, in the North-West Frontier Province of India. It is about 45 m. [72 km] long by 20. [32 km] broad, and lies at a high level to the east of the Kunar valley, from which it is separated by a continuous line of rugged frontier hills, forming a barrier easily passable at one or two points. Across this barrier the old road from Kabul to India ran before the Khyber Pass was adopted as the main route. Bajour is inhabited almost exclusively by Tarkani (Tarkalanri) Pathans, sub-divided into Mamunds, Isazai, and Ismailzai, numbering together with a few Mohmands, Utmauzais, &c., about 100,000. To the south of Bajour is the wild mountain district of the Mohmands, a Pathan race. To the east, beyond the Panjkora river, are the hills of Swat, dominated by another Pathan race. To the north is an intervening watershed between Bajour and the small state of Dir; and it is over this watershed and through the valley of Dir that the new road from Malakand and the Punjab runs to Chitral. An interesting feature in Bajour topography is a mountain spur from the Kunar range, which curving eastwards culminates in the well-known peak of Koh-i-Mor, which is visible from the Peshawar valley. It was here, at the foot of the mountain, that Alexander found the ancient city of Nysa and the Nysaean colony, traditionally said to have been founded by Dionysus. The Koh-i-Mor has been identified as the Meros of Arrian's history—the three-peaked mountain from which the god issued. It is also interesting to find that a section of the Kafir community of Kamdesh still claim the same Greek origin as did the Nysaeans; still chant hymns to the god who sprang from Gir Nysa (the mountain of Nysa); whilst they maintain that they originally migrated from the Swat country to their present habitat in the lower Bashgol. Long after Buddhism had spread to Chitral, Gilgit, Dir and Swat; whilst Ningrahar was still full of monasteries and temples, and the Peshawar valley was recognized as the seat of Buddhist learning, the Kafirs or Nysaeans held their own in Bajour and in the lower Kunar valley, where Buddhism apparently never prevailed." *Encyclopaedia Britannica* (1911), Volume 3, p. 226.

"BAJOUR, on the north-east of Afghanistan, is a territory containing a town of the same name. Though at no great distance from the Punjab and the plain of Peshawur, scarcely any thing is known concerning it beyond what was gleaned by the sagacity and industry of Elphinstone from native information. It is a plain, or rather a spacious valley, on the south side of the Hindoo Koosh, from which a lofty ridge runs southwards, dividing Bajour on the west from Kafiristan. On the north-east it opens to Panjkora, by a tract of no great elevation called Berawul. On the east it is bounded by the hills held by the Otmaunkhail; on the south it communicates with the Suwat and the Eusufzai country, by the valley, through which the Lundye river flows. It lies between lat. 34° 45'—35° 10', long. 71° 5'— 71° 35', and is about twenty-five miles and fifteen broad. The mountains which inclose it are nearly inaccessible from their steepness, and the forests, principally of oak and cedar, which cover them, are so thick as to exclude the rays of the sun. These afford covert for numerous wild beasts. The plain Bajour resemble that of Peshawur, and is very productive, especially in wheat. It is held by the Afghan tribe of Turcolaunee, who, unlike their neighbours, the Esufzai, are ruled by a chief having considerable power, and bearing the title of *Bauz*. The number is probably about 70,000 or 80,000; but as there are other inhabitants, descendants of Kafirs, Hindoos, Moguls, and others, the total number may be about 120,000. The chief is said to have an income of about a lac [100,000] of rupees annually, and has usually, on emergencies, furnished a body of troops to the Afghan government. In the battle of Jelalabad, in April, 1842, he was among the discomfited parties. Bajour contains an inexhaustible supply of iron-ore of the finest quality. It is found in the form of a black sand, washed down by the torrents from the deposits in the mountains, and from this source the greater part of Northern Afghanistan and the neighbouring states are supplied. The two chief towns, Bajour and Nawagye, have each about 5,000 inhabitants. Bajour is supposed to be the Bazira mentioned by the historians of Alexander. Lat. 35° 2', long. 71° 23'." Thornton (1844), pp. 65-66.

It is significant to find a reference to the presence of good quality iron ore in Bajaur, which confirms the mention in *Hanshu* 96A in Nandou (quoted above from *CICA*, p. 103). Interestingly, iron is referred to as a product in only five other kingdoms among the many the notices contained in *Hanshu* 61, 96A, and 96B.

"Though we cannot follow the details of Alexander's operations by the river Khōēs, it is certain that they took him for a considerable distance up the large and populous valley of the Kūnar river. Then he crossed the mountains to the east and had more than one hard fight in the territory which the Greek records and geographical considerations combined clearly show to have been the present Bajaur. The river Guraios, which the Macedonians had to cross before Alexander could lead them into the country of the Assakēnoi, has long ago been proved to be identical with the Panjkōra, the Gaurī of Sanskrit texts. Coming from the mountains of Dīr, it flows past Bajaur on the east and then joins the Swāt river, where it passes through difficult gorges towards the Peshawar plain.

With the passage of the Guraios or Panjkōra, we are told, began the invasion of the country of the powerful nation of the Assakēnoi, and reference to the map shows that this could be no other than Swāt, as has also been long since recognized. . . .

Only for the initial stages of Alexander's march was definite guidance available, and that was supplied by plain geographical facts. It is certain that in ancient times, as at present, the direct route led from the Panjkōra through Talāsh and across the easy saddle of Katgala into the wide open valley which thence stretches down to the Swāt river and its strategically important crossing now guarded by the fort of

Chakdara. Geographical considerations would further show us that the several fortified towns which Alexander successively besieged and captured were probably situated in the main Swāt valley; for this at all times must, as now, have been the most fertile and populous portion of the territory." Stein (1929), pp. 41-43.

"The origin of the word Bajaur is uncertain and nothing is exactly known as to when and how this name was given to this area. However, according to one version it was derived from the Persian word Baj (tribute) and awardan (to bring). Legend is that the area of Bajaur once belonged to a tribe called Arab up to the time of the Pathan conquest and was ruled by the Chief of Arab tribe, therefore, it denotes the area which paid tribute to the Chief, or which paid tribute to the Hindu dynasty of the day. According to the version of the common man of the area the word Bajaur denotes an area which has been ruled by powerful tribal chiefs with force Bajaur in the annals of history. However, the empirical facts and historical data support the first version about the origin of the word Bajaur. It's administrative headquarters is at Khar town, at a distance of about 140 kilometers north of Peshawar connected through a metalled road via Mohmand Agency and Malakand Agency. The land mass of the agency lies between 34° 30' and 34° 58' north latitudes and 71' 11° and 71' 48° east longitudes. The green valleys of Bajaur Agency are situated in the north – west of NWFP. The agency is surrounded by Dir district on the north – east, Afghanistan on the north – east, Mohmand Agency on the south – west and Malakand Agency on the south – east. The total area of the agency is 1,290 square kilometers [498 sq. miles]. . . .

The terrain of the agency is mountainous and hilly. In the northern part mountain ranges are 3,000 meter [9,843 ft] high. Towards the south the height gradually decreases and on the southern border, peaks are slightly over 2,500 meters [8.202 ft] high, in the central part, the height further decreases. In the north – western half, the land slopes down to the south –east direction while the central parts slopes to the north – east through the Jandol Khwar and Panjkora river. The Panjkora River flows in southern direction till it joins the Swat River, which flows along the eastern boundary of Bajaur Agency. . . . Alexander the great reportedly camped at Sikandaro, in Bajaur Agency and this place is known after his name." "Historical and Administrative Profile of the Bajaur Agency" by The Bajaurian's Society, December 12, 2010. Accessed from: http://www.facebook.com/note.php?note _id=173044499385796 on 28 Feb. 2012. Note: this link was broken when I last looked on 30 October, 2014.

There are at least two passes from Bajaur into Afghanistan. One of them is marked as Nawe Khotal, (altitude approximately 6,000 ft. or 1,829 metres) in Haye & Crone (1933), map on p. 352. This pass on the Pakistan side of the border (altitude 2,302 metres/7,552 ft.) is now known as the "Nawa" in Google Maps. Its position is at 34° 45' 30.42 N, 71° 13' 48.07 E, and is 15.5 km NW of Nawagai, as the crow flies. The Nawa Pass is the first major border crossing between Pakistan and Afghanistan north of the Khyber Pass.

Another pass further north (9.30 km NE of the Nawa Pass) leads via the Kunar-Bajaur Link Road in Pakistan, through Petaw towards Asadābād, on the western bank of the Kunar River in Afghanistan. It is about 18 km. in a straight line NNW of Nawagai, altitude about 2,100 metres (6,890 ft.) above sea level.

"NAAGHI, in Afghanistan, a village situate about twenty miles south-west of the town of Bajour. Some supposed it to be the Aornus of the historians of Alexander, the capture of which was one of the most arduous exploits of that conqueror." Lat. 34° 49', long. 71° 15'. Thornton (1854), pp. 69-70.

> "NARANG, in Northern Afghanistan, a village situate on the right bank of the river Kooner, twenty-six miles north-west of the town of Bajour." Lat. 35° 20', long. 68° 2'. Thornton (1854), p. 73.

Nandou is said (*CICA* p. 103) to border on the land of the Er Qiang (or 'Unconquered Qiang') to the south, which is almost certainly an error as the Er Qiang were only known as living on or very near the Tibetan plateau (see: note 1.10 for information on the Er Qiang). Perhaps the original report was that Nandou was south of the Er Qiang. This error is, however, not sufficient to throw the general picture of Nandou's position into doubt.

According to Hulsewé's translation Wulei 無雷 (The Great and Little Pamir Valleys) were 340 *li* (141 km) to the *west* of Nandou. *CICA*, p. 103. However, this appears to be a mistaken translation. The Chinese text I have available (downloaded from: http://zh.wikisource.org/wiki/%E6%BC%A2%E6%9B%B8/%E5%8D%B7096%E4%B8%8A) on the 21st February, 2012, reads: 南至無雷三百四十里 - "[From Nandou] it is 340 *li south* to Wulei." However, neither version makes sense. Wulei, if it does refer to the Pamir Valleys would be northeast of either Bajaur or Swat.

There is also confusion regarding Wulei's position as it related to Puli (Tashkurgan) in *CICA* – see the discussion in note 20.3.

Ancient Bajaur was a busy place in the first few centuries BCE. The main route went through here from Afghanistan to the Indian plains via Swat before, for unknown reasons, it changed around the turn of the Common Era to travel through the Khyber Pass and on to Charsadda and Peshawar, and then east into northern India.

> "*Gandhāra - Swat - Bajaur*: The ancient region of Gandhāra comprises a plain around the confluence of the Kabul and Indus Rivers, with two major urban sites at Taxila and Charsadda, and mountain valleys to the north and north-west (Swat, Bajaur) with important Buddhist remains. Gandhāra historically had close connections to regions to the north-west. It had been part of the Achaemenid Empire, and was on the route of Alexander's campaigns (for an interesting early twentieth-century attempt to trace this route on the ground, see Stein 1929). On Gandhāra's cultural heritage, illicit excavations and the antiquities trade see Ali and Coningham 2002. The Buddhist archaeology and Graeco-Buddhist art of Gandhāra lie largely outside the scope of this survey (but see Allchin 1997 for a collection of useful studies). As in Bactria, many sites which were probably settled under the Indo-Greeks have thus far only yielded material of later periods, or it has been difficult to discern much about earlier occupation under the later strata. Callieri 1995 reviews and provides a useful critical discussion on archaeological material of the period of the Indo-Greek kingdoms in northwestern India, from the time of the Graeco-Bactrian invasions in around 180 BC to the last Indo-Greek kingdoms in the Panjab in the late first century BC or very early first century AD. For earlier archaeological activities in the region, see e.g. Barger 1941 and Faccenna 1964, the latter including accounts of several sites with some material from the last three centuries BC.
>
> The most substantial archaeological evidence for the Indo-Greek presence in the region comes from Bīr-kot-ghwaṇḍai (Barikot) in the Swat Valley, with its fortification wall of the second century BC (Callieri 1990a; Callieri 1992; Callieri, et al. 1992; Callieri 1993; summarised in Callieri 1995, 302-304). Significantly, the site also yielded a small number of Indo-Greek coins, as well as terracottas and ceramics with similarities to those of the Graeco-Bactrian kingdom. On imported items and the coins from Bīr-kot-ghwaṇḍai, see Taddei, et al. 2004.

In Gandhāran art of later periods the legacy of the Indo-Greeks is plain to see. Of particular note are two schist reliefs depicting the Trojan Horse (Allan 1946; Khan 1990)." Mairs (2011), p. 36.

"A small number of items with Prākit inscriptions in the Kharoṣṭhī script from northwestern India contain transcribed Greek personal names or titles (summarised in Callieri 1995, 302, and Karttunen 1994, 330). These are for the most part later in date than the actual Indo-Greek occupation of the region, and attest the continuing use of Greek administrative or other official titles. A Buddhist reliquary from Shinkot in Bajaur bears the name of the Indo-Greek king Menander and is apparently palaeographically contemporary to his rule, in the mid-second century BC (Konow 1947; Majumdar 1937; on Menander see also Bopearachchi 1990b and Fussman 1993a). A later inscription added to same casket, in the first century BC, names an individual with a Saka name holding the Greek title *anagkaios*: with little contemporary evidence for official titles in the region, it is difficult to determine precisely what this title implies. It recurs in the inscription of King Seṇavarma of Oḍi, from Swat, of the first half of the first century AD (Salomon 1986). In both these cases the bearer of the title has a non-Greek name. Another Buddhist reliquary, from Swat, dated to the first half of the first century BC, contains the name Theodoros and the administrative title of meridarch (Konow 1929, 1-4), a title which again recurs in the Seṇavarma inscription (Salomon 1986). Another Kharoṣṭhī inscription containing a Greek name comes from a stone seal from Bajaur of the first half of the first century AD: it names one Theodamas (Konow 1929, 6). *Strategos*, too, appears as an official title on two objects, a silver saucer from Taxila and a reliquary: both post-date the Indo-Greeks and refer to officials who do not bear Greek names (Marshall 1951, 613, 777ff; Fussman 1980, 4, 25, 28ff). On a Greek (*yona*) era, datable to 186/185 BC [now thought more likely to refer to 175/174 BCE – see Falk & Bennett (2009)], in a Kharoṣṭhī inscription on another reliquary of uncertain provenance, see Salomon 2005, with further discussion by Jakobsson 2009 and Rapin." Mairs (2011), pp. 42-43.

There have been two major coin hoards discovered in Bajaur:

"In the north he [Menander] occupied Hazara and the Swat valley. Two hundred drachms of his in mint condition have been found in Swat, and 721 further specimens, showing little signs of circulation, in the first Bajaur hoard; the second Bajaur hoard contained 92 coins of Menander out of 120 examined by Houghton. And now, with the discovery of the Bajaur casket inscription of the reign of Menander, it is quite certain that the Swat valley was included within his kingdom and was under the governorship of Viyakamitra, who, as the name shows, must have been a prince of Indian origin. The inscription consists of two groups of small epigraphs of different periods ; the first mention of the name of *Mahārāja Minadra* and can be dated in the middle of the second century B.C., while the second refers to the reconsecration of the casket in the time of a certain Vijayamitra who has been identified with the Vijayamitra named on certain Indo-Scythic coins, and is dated some time in the first century B.C. Unfortunately the portion of the lid of the casket which may have contained a date is broken. Nevertheless, this small and fragmentary inscription is of great value." Narain (1957), pp. 79-80.

"Menander was born in the Caucasus; but the Greek biographer Plutarch calls him a king of Bactria, and Strabo, the Greek geographer and historian, includes him among the Bactrian Greeks "who conquered more tribes than Alexander [the Great]." It is possible that he ruled over Bactria, and it has been suggested that he aided the Seleucid ruler Demetrius II Nicator against the Parthians. His kingdom in the Indian subcontinent consisted of an area extending from the Kabul River valley in the west to the Ravi River in the east, and from the Swat River valley (in modern Pakistan) in the north to Arachosia (the Kandahar region) in Afghanistan in the south. Ancient Indian writers indicate that he probably led expeditions into Rajputana and as far east along the Ganges (Ganga) River valley as Pataliputra (now Patna), in the present-day Indian state of Bihar.

Menander was probably the Indo-Greek king who was converted to Buddhism by the holy man Nagasena after a prolonged and intelligent discussion, which has been recorded in the *Milinda-panha.* The style may have been influenced by Plato's dialogues. The wheel engraved on some of Menander's coins is probably connected with Buddhism, and Plutarch's statement that when Menander died his earthly remains were divided equally between the cities of his kingdom and that monuments, possibly stupas (Buddhist commemorative monuments), were to be erected to enshrine them indicates that he had probably become a Buddhist.

The only inscription referring to Menander has been found in **Bajaur**, the tribal territory between the Swat and Kunar rivers; but large numbers of Menander's coins have been unearthed, mostly of silver and copper, attesting to both the duration of his reign and the flourishing commerce of his realm. According to Buddhist tradition he handed over his kingdom to his son and retired from the world, but Plutarch relates that he died in camp while on a military campaign." *Encyclopædia Britannica Online.* Downloaded 15 February, 2012 from: http://www.library.eb.com.au/eb/article-9051960.

"The two Bajaur hoards and the Yagistan find, all in the Swat region, consisted predominantly of the coins of Menander in almost mint condition, and the only inscription which mentions Menander has been found in the same area; the Swat relic vase of the Meridarch Theodorus and the Bajaur seal of Theodamus are further indications pointing to the same conclusions." Narain (1957), p. 173.

"It is significant that not a single coin of Antimachus II [who preceded Menander] was found in Taxila excavations. On the other hand, the Bajaur hoards contain a good number of his coins, and the Mir Zakah Treasure has 133." Narain (1957), p. 96.

There have also been two inscribed reliquary caskets discovered in Bajaur, the most recent one containing a key date:

"The **Bajaur casket** is an ancient Buddhist reliquary from the area of Bajaur, in Gandhara. It is dated to around 5-6 CE [read "around 15-16 CE" – see: Falk and Bennett (2009), p. 212]. It proves the involvement of the Indo-Scythian kings of the Apraca, in particular King Indravarman, in Buddhism. The casket is made of schist. The inscription which is written in Kharoshthi, translates into English as:

"In the sixty third year of the late great king Aya (Azes), on the sixteenth day of the month of Kartia (Kartika), at this auspicious (?) time, Prince Indravarma (Indravarman), son of the king of Apraca, establishes these bodily relics of Lord Sakyamuni; .... He produces brahma-merit together with his mother, Rukhunaka, daughter of Aji.... And these bodily relics having been brought in procession from the Muraka cave stupa, were established in a secure (?), safe, deep (?), depository... —Text of the Bajaur casket, Metropolitan_Museum_of_Art." Downloaded from: http://www.metmuseum.org/Collections/search-the-collections/60005057 28 Feb., 2012.

"The re-interpretation of this inscription enables us to more fully reconstruct the previously obscure dynasty of kings who ruled Apraca or Avaca (modern Bajaur in north-western Pakistan) in the 1st centuries B.C. and A.D. Moreover, the date of the inscription *saṃvatsarae treṣṭhimae 20 20 20 3 maharayasa ayasa atidasa* ('in the year 63 of the late King Azes [I]') provides the long-awaited explicit evidence that the Indo-Scythian king Azes was the founder of the "Vikrama" era of 58-7 B.C. [according to Falk and Bennett (2009), p. 212, this should read *circa* 48-7 BCE]. . .

> "*Avaca* refers to the name of the kingdom of the rulers (the Apraca- or Avaca-rājas) in the inscription, not to its findspot. The latter is not mentioned and is presumably unknown; the inscribed casket is located only "in the collection of Professor Samuel Eilenberg"... . The casket may be assumed, however, to have come from the same region as the related Bajaur (Shinkot) relic casket." Salomon (1982), p. 59, and n. 1.

Bhagamoya's reliquary inscription is dated in the Azes year 77 = *circa* 29/30 CE. Salomon (1996), p. 450, n. 7; Falk and Bennett (2009), pp. 197-215. This means that Indo-Scythian kings were ruling the region to at least 30 CE.

However, there is some evidence, "that by the second decade [read "3rd decade" according to the new dating] of the first century CE, the Apraca kingdom was in a state of fragmentation, with various portions of its territories falling into the hands of local satraps, at least one of whom, Bhagamoya, seems to have laid claim to the Apraca throne itself." Salomon (1996), p. 449.

The Indo-Scythians were overthrown by Kujula Kadphises soon after the middle of the 1st century CE; the territory then lost its independence and was incorporated into the Kushan Empire. Jibin was no longer mentioned as a separate 'kingdom', either in the *Hou Hanshu* or later Chinese accounts.

Appendix G: The Kingdom of Puda.

Many attempts have been made to identify Puda 濮達, but no consensus has yet been reached. See: *CICA*, p. 112, n. 253.

Nevertheless, archaeological information has become available in recent years which strongly supports early suggestions made by Otto Francke (1904), p. 93, n. 1; and Marquart (1905), pp. 175 ff., that Puda referred to the country of the Paktues mentioned by Herodotus.

Background

The *Hanshu* only briefly and incidentally mentions Putao (W-G: P'u-t'ao) in its note on the kingdom of Wuyishanli (W-G: Wu-i-shan-li) centred in Kandahar:

> "It [Wu-i-shan-li] adjoins Chi-pin in the east, P'u-t'ao in the north, and Li-kan and T'iao-chih in the west ; after travelling for some one hundred days one then reaches T'iao-chih." From: *Hanshu* 96A in *CICA*, pp. 112-113.

The *Hou Hanshu* provides some additional geographical information regarding Puda's position. It says it could be reached by travelling southwest from Pishan (modern Pishan or Guma) in the Tarim Basin, through Wucha (Upper Hunza and the Tāghdumbāsh Pamir), and then crossing over the *xuandu* or 'hanging passages' in Hunza. See: Appendix U.

One then travelled across Jibin before arriving at the kingdom of Wuyishanli. Here are some 19th century estimates of the times taken for sections along this route:

> "The pace of the caravans generally varied between 8 and 25 miles [13 to 40 km] per day. Thus the distance of 191 miles [307 km] between Kabul and Peshawar was covered in two weeks.... The distance of 308 miles [496 km] between Kabul and Qandahar was considered a journey of 15 days." Noelle (1997), p. 284.

Taking 60 days for the journey between Pishan in the Tarim Basin to Kandahar by foot, as described in the text, is plausible. At, say, 25 km per day average, this gives a total of 1,500 km, which roughly approximates the true distance.

The *Hou Hanshu* also records that Qiujiuque [Kujula Kadphises] "invaded Anxi [Indo-Parthia] and took the Gaofu [Kabul] region. He also defeated the whole of the kingdoms of Puda 濮達 and Jibin." This suggests that Puda was in the general region of Kabul and Jibin (Kapisha-Gandhara) – see: Appendix F.

• The name 'Puda'

Petech (1950), p. 69, reconstructs the early pronunciation of Puda as *b'uok-d'ât*. Other reconstructions include **p'uk* or **b'uk* - **d'ât* or **t'ât* (*CICA*, p. 112 n. 253, from Karlgren Nos. 1211j and 1145o).

Pulleyblank (1963), p. 101, says that the Putao 鏷挑 M. **phuk-deu** < ***pok-δat** of the *Hanshu* (to the north of Wuyishanli or Arachosia) "must be the same" as Puda 濮達, for which he gives M. **puk-dat** < ***pok-δat.**

There is little doubt that Puda and Putao refer to the same place especially when the geographic indications are added to the phonetic similarities. Pulleyblank, however, attempts to identify them both with Puśkalāvatī; though unsuccessfully in my opinion:

> "Both names must represent a Prakrit form of Puśkalāvatī, Greek Πευκελεαώτις, the present Charsada. The use of M. **d-** (**< δ-**) for foreign *-l-* will be discussed and further illustrated below. Here we are concerned rather with the vocalism. We have evidently two alternative attempts to render the Indian ***-lavat***(in Prakrit ***-laot-***?). The first represents the diphthong but leaves the final ***-t*** unrecorded. The second represents the final ***-t*** at the expense of the diphthong." Pulleyblank (1963), p. 101. See also: *CICA*, p. 112, n. 253.

In his *Lexicon of Reconstructed Pronunciation in Early Middle Chinese, Late Middle Chinese and Early Mandarin* (1991), Pulleyblank gives pəwk/tʰat, or pəwk/dat as reconstructed pronunciations for Puda 濮達 in "Early Middle Chinese." Pulleyblank (1991), pp. 243, 299, and 69.

The various pronunciations reconstructed from the Chinese would seem more likely to be representations of the Paktyike of Herodotus and the Pakthas people of the *Rigveda*, than of Puśkalāvatī, as Pulleyblank suggested.

"For 撲挑 the Authors [Hulsewé and Loewe of *CICA*, see p. 112] adopt the reading P'u-t'ao, without excluding (n. 253) that P'u-tiao and P'u-t'iao are also possible. Of course in cases such as these the choice of a reading becomes a matter of personal taste. I notice, however, that in GSR 1145o the reading t'iao comes first. As for the location of the place on the map, the Authors are inclined to rely, once again, on ever hypothetical phonetic reconstructions rather than on more solid geographical and historical arguments. Nobody has ever denied, as far as I know, that the P'u-t'iao of Han shu is one and the same with the P'u-ta 濮達 which according to *Hou han shu* the Kuṣāṇa Kujūla Kadphises conquered after gaining possession of Kao-fu and before seizing Chi-pin (*HHSCC* Mem. 78, 14b, 10f. = p. 122 n. 292). This rules out as simply absurd the identification of P'u-t'iao/P'u-ta with Bactria as was proposed by Wylie and since then maintained by a number of scholars (see P. Daffinà, 'The Return of the Dead', *East and West*, 22, 1972, p. 91). When Kujūla Kadphises started his conquering march, Bactria had been for a long time in the hands of the Kuṣāṇas (see Daffinà, 1967, p. 80). If Kujūla's conquests follow a logical route, as Pulleyblank (1968) p. 248 n. 1 among others believes, P'u-t'iao/P'u-ta must be sought for somewhere between Kao-fu (*i.e.* Kābul, p. 122 n. 296) and Chi-pin. Therefore its location on the map depends not so much on the reconstruction of the 'Old Chinese' forms of its name, as rather on the precise identification of Chi-pin. Pulleyblank's equation of P'u-t'iao/P'u-ta with Puṣkalāvatī (which the Authors appear to accept) does not stand by itself but is consequent on his preconceived equation of Chi-pin with Kāśmīr. As original of his 'Old Chinese' *phok-δeauĥ and *pok-δa̱t, Pulleyblank postulated an unspecified "Prakrit form of Puṣkalāvatī". It escaped him that this form does exist and is known to have been *Pakhalavati* (see Tarn, 1951, pp. 237-238 n.; and now also M. Mitchiner, *Indo-Greek and Indo-Scythian coinage*, I, London, 1975, p. 85, type 162). It may then be questioned whether 'Old Chinese' 'phok-δeauĥ [should read *phok-δeauĥ] and *pok-δa̱t can really be renderings for *Pakhalavati.* Actually they seem to correspond better to Vedic *Pakthāḥ*, Greek Πάχτυες. The Πάχτυες have been located in either the Gardez Province or in the Kābul Valley (see A. D. H. Bivar, 'Indo-Bactrian Problems', *Numismatic Chronicle*, seventh series, 5, 1965, p. 95 n. 2; H. Treidler, in Pauly-Wissowa-Kroll, *Realencyclopädie der klassischen Alterumswissenschaft*, Supplementband 10, 1965, cols. 475-476). Both position [*sic*] are fairly consistent with a Chi-pin corresponding, geographically, to Kāpiśa, Gandhāra and West Pañjāb." Daffinà (1982), pp. 319-320.

Chris Dorn'eich (Dorn'eich (2008), pp. V - VI.) makes a strong case to identify Puda with Bactra (rather than with Bactria or Puṣkalāvatī) but, I believe, his position is equally weakened by Daffinà's article.

It seems to me that if Daffinà's argument is accepted, there can be only one plausible identification of Puda - that it refers to Paktiya, not Bactria or Bactra (= Zariaspa/Balkh), or Puṣkalāvatī.

- **Puda = the Paktyike or Paktyia?**

The theory that Puda = the Paktyike (*Πακτυϊκὴ γῆ*) mentioned by Herodotus, was first proposed by Otto Francke in his "Beiträge aus chinesischen Quellen zur Kenntnis der Türkvölker und Skythen Zentralasiens," in *Abhandlungen der Berliner Akademie der Wissenschaften* (1904), p. 93, n. 1; and J. Marquart in his *Untersuchungen zur Geschichte von Eran*, zweites Heft (Leipzig, Dieterich, 1905), pp. 175-176.

> "On the other hand, the Parsuytai, one of the five tribes of the Paropanisadae mentioned by Ptolemy, probably get their name from *Pashto, Pushta,* a mountain; the name of the language, Pashto, itself seems to be derived from the same root. It is interesting that in India the Afghans adopted the identical *nom de guerre,* Rohilla, men of the mountains. On the other hand, Hekataeus [of Miletus, flourished *circa* 560-418 BCE] wrote of Kaspapyrus as being in the country of the Paktyike and the name recurs elsewhere. In spite of its seeming likeness to the *Pakhto-Pakhtun* of the hard Peshawari dialect, the etymology remains obscure, though it is accepted by such authorities as Grierson and Trump. Pashto, the national language of modern Afghanistan, exists as an ancient scion of the Iranian group; there is no doubt of its antiquity, for it is not of the direct descent. Huen Tsang, once again, supplies a clue, when he reports that the people of Tsao-kiu-tch'a spoke a unique language. It may well have been Pashto. He says that the country had two capitals, cities of considerable size, well equipped and defended. The walled city of Ho-si-na is probably Ghazni itself, while Ho-sa-lo, the second capital, is certainly Mukkur, for Huen Tsang mentions its distinctive water-supply, a spring divided into many channels, by which Bellew camped in 1857." Codrington (1944), pp. 39-40.

Herodotus, III, 93, mentions the territory of Paktyike, as part of the 13th satrapy or division of peoples subject to the Achaemenid Persian emperor Darius, "along with Armenia, and the countries reaching thence to the Euxine [Black Sea]." He also states:

> "Besides these, there are Indians of another tribe, who border on the city of Caspatyrus, and the country of Pactyica; these people dwell northward of all the rest of the Indians, and follow nearly the same mode of life as the Bactrians. They are more warlike than any of the other tribes, and from them the men are sent forth who go to procure the gold. . . ." Herodotus, Bk. III.102 – Translation from Rawlinson (1910), p. 270.

> "The Caspians [in Xerxes' army] were clad in cloaks of skin, and carried the cane bow of their country and the scimitar. So equipped they went to the war, and they had for their commander Ariomardus the brother of Artyphius.
>
> The Sarangians had dyed garments which showed brightly, and buskins which reached to the knee: they bore Median bows, and lances. Their leader was Pherendates, the son of Megabazus.
>
> The Pactyans wore cloaks of skin, and carried the bow of their country and the dagger. Their commander was Artyntes, the son of Ithamatres.
>
> The Utians, the Mycians, and the Paricanians were all equipped like the Pactyans. They had for leaders, Arsamenes, the son of Darius, who commanded the Utians and Mycians; and Siromitres, the son of Oeobazus, who commanded the Paricanians." Herodotus, Bk. VII, 67-68, – Translation from Rawlinson (1910), p. 539.

About 515 BCE, Darius I of Persia commissioned Scylax of Caryanda (521-485 BCE) to travel overland to India from where he and his companions sailed down the Indus, finally reaching the Red Sea in thirty months:

"Of the greater part of Asia Darius was the discoverer. Wishing to know where the Indus (which is the only river save one that produces crocodiles) emptied itself into the sea, he sent a number of men, on whose truthfulness he could rely, and among them Scylax of Caryanda, to sail down the river. They started from the city of Caspatyrus, in the region called Pactyica, and sailed down the stream in an easterly direction to the sea. Here they turned westward, and, after a voyage of thirty months, reached the place [Arsinoë near modern Suez] from which the Egyptian king, of whom I spoke above, sent the Phoenicians to sail round Libya. After this voyage was completed, Darius conquered the Indians, and made use of the sea in those parts." Herodotus, Bk. IV, 44.

"The first Greek record of navigation in the Erythraean Sea is likewise found in Herodotus (4, 4):

> "A great part of Asia was explored under the direction of Darius. He being desirous to know in what part the Indus, which is the second river that produces crocodiles, discharges itself into the sea, sent in ships both others on whom he could rely to make a true report, and also Scylax of Caryanda. They accordingly, setting out from the city of Caspapyrus and the country of Pactyice[1] sailed down the river toward the east and sunrise to the sea; then sailing on the sea westward they arrived in the thirtieth month (*τριηκοστῷ μηνί*) at that place where the king of Egypt despatched the Phoenicians, whom I before mentioned, to sail around Libya. After these persons had sailed round, Darius subdued the Indians, and frequented this sea. Thus the other parts of Asia, except toward the rising sun, are found to exhibit things similar to Libya".
>
> The truth of this story in Herodotus has been seriously questioned in voluminous arguments which are now so much waste paper, as we have written records of Hindu trade with Babylon, which they called Baveru, more than a century before that time, and we have the discovery of teak logs in buildings at the ancient Ur reconstructed by Nabonidus. These logs came from western India, from the Cambay region; and in the Periplus of the first century, we have a written record of the same trade still existing. . . .
>
> 1 Caspapyrus, Sanscrit Kasyapapura. This was the Indus valley in the neighborhood of the confluence of the Kabul river, more or less the Peshawar district. Hecataeus mentions this place as a city of the Gandharians. Pactyice, or the Pactyan land, was the upper course of the Kabul valley; or more generally the territory in which Pukhtu was spoken-southeastern Afghanistan, See Lassen, 1, 142-2, 631. Vincent Smith, *Early History*, 2nd edition p. 35; Schoff, *Periplus of the Erythraean Sea* pp. 42, 189."

Schoff (1913), pp. 351-352 and n. 1.

"The city of Kaspatyros in the Paktyan land (*Πακτυικὴ γῆ*), from which Skylax began his voyage, is called Kapapyros, a city of the Gandharians, by Hekataios. The site cannot be identified, and it is impossible to say which form of the name is correct. Gandhāra was the modern Peshāwar District and some adjacent territory. Kaspatyros or Kaspapyros, has nothing to do with Kashmīr, as many writers have supposed (Stein, *Rājataraṅgiṇī*, trans. ii, 353)." Smith (1908), p. 35, n.

"Herodotus' remark that they sailed towards the east most probably did not come from Scylax himself, since the Indus flows mainly towards the south-west. But in Herodotus' time the size of Asia was not known, and he must therefore have concluded that such a distant river as the Indus would naturally have run towards the east, towards the outermost edge of the world, which was envisaged as a disc at that time." Landström (1966), p. 29. **NOTE:** Herodotus was probably referring to the fact that Scylax would have first sailed east along either the Kabul or Kurram river before joining the Indus, only after which they would have headed southwards. (JEH)

There is an interesting account of another people who were influenced by the Pactyans:

> "The wandering tribe known by the name of the Sagartians – a people Persian in language, and in dress half Persian, half Pactyan, who furnished to the army as many as eight thousand horse. It is not the wont of this people to carry arms, either of bronze or steel, except only a dirk; but they use lassoes made of thongs plaited together, and trust to these whenever they go to war." Herodotus, Bk. VII, 85 (ii).

The Pactyans are briefly mentioned in the *Rigveda*, where they are called Pakthas or Paktues:

> "Of the ten tribes [with notices in the *Rigveda* VII, 18, 7] five are of little note, the Alinas, perhaps from the north-east of Kāfiristān, the Pakthas, whose name recalls the Afghān Pakthūn, the Bhalanases, possibly connected with the Bolān Pass, the Çivas from near the Indus, and the Vishāṇins." Rapson, ed., (1922), p. 73.

> "The confederacy against the Sudas consisted of 10 peoples. Five of them were to the west of the Indus and their names were the Alinas, the Pakthas, the Bhalanases, the Shivas and Vishanins." Mahajan (1978), p. 97.

The references to Puda in the *Hanshu* and *Hou Hanshu* agree with the general location indicated in Herodotus (*c.* 430-424 BCE) for Paktyike, and the Rigveda for the Pakthas. It therefore seems probable that Puda was located in the rich valleys to the south and southeast of Kabul, where the modern towns of Ghazni, Gardez and Bannu are situated.

Chavannes, in a review of J. Marquart's *Untersuchugen zur Geschichte von Eran* in *T'oung Pao* 6 (1905), pp. 512-515, criticises Marquart's view that Puda referred to the Paktues mentioned by Herodotus (VII, 67), and proposed instead that it represented Bactra or Balkh. Consult, *CICA* p. 112 n. 253, and Chavannes (1907), p. 191 n. 3. However, this view has never received widespread acceptance:

> "Dr. Franke (*Beiträge* [1903], p. 99 n.) considers as doubtful the current identification of Po-ta (P'u-ta, Cantonese Pok-tiu) with Bactria, and suggests as the true equivalent the 'Paktyan land' (*Πακτυικὴ γῆ*), which he places to the north of Arachosia." Smith (1908), p. 259, n.

The region to the south of the Kabul Valley is still known for its fertility and seems to have been both wealthy and well populated throughout the Kushan period:

> "South of the Safid-Koh, where the Sulimani ranges begin, there is a drainage system extending over a large area, the steams of which converge to the Kurram, a river flowing in a south-east direction across the Bannu district to the Indus. The Kurram rises at the junction of the western Sulimani Range with the Safid-Koh ; being formed by the Keriah, the Hariab (Huryab of Elphinstone), and streams from the Mangal country, which unite below a place called Ali-khel (7500 feet [2,286 m] above the sea). Thence the combined waters enter the valley, and flow eastwards past the Kurram fort to the village of Thal in Miranzai, which is 42 miles [68 km] from Bannu. The river then turns south-east, receiving the Shamil and Tochi rivers from Khost and Dawar. The river-basin within the hills, between the eastern and western Sulimani ranges, is of considerable extent, including the main valleys of Kurram, Khost, and Dawar, besides some subsidiary valleys, such as Furmul, at the back of Khost, which is watered by the Tochi, in its upper course. On the north it is bounded by the snowy

heights of the Safid-Koh, and on the west by the western Sulimani Range, which forms the water-parting between the Indus and the Afghan drainages.

The Kurram district is about 60 miles [97 km] long by some 3 to 10 [5 to 16 km.] wide. The valley is very beautiful, with the Safid-Koh looking down in great majesty on the smiling green fields and pleasant orchards. The climate is agreeable, and the clear and rapid river renders the supply of water abundant, and irrigates the rice-fields on either side. The water rushes in a winding and rocky bed down the centre of a deep fillet of rich cultivation sprinkled with villages, each with its clump of magnificent plane-trees, while the distance is everywhere closed by the ever-varying aspect of the noble mountains which tower over the valley in its whole length. The road enters the valley at Thal, 66 miles [106 km] from Kohat and 50 [81 km] from the Kurram fort, and proceeds along the banks of the river. There is an alternative route, leaving the main road about 36 miles [58 km] further on, and passing over the Darwaza Pass, where there is a square enclosure with round towers at the angles and in the centre of each face, and an inner square forming a citadel. At a distance of 25 miles [40 km] from the Kurram fort, up the valley, is the village of Paiwar, at the foot of a narrow gorge. Here it is necessary to cross a steep spur which forms one root of the Sikaram Peak, the loftiest of the Safid-Koh Range. Over this spur there are two roads, one by the Paiwar Pass, and the other, higher up, called the Ispingwai Pass. By the Paiwar, the road leads over several deep ravines with oak jungle, and then up a zigzag ascent, with the hills on either hand covered with pine forests. The descent on the other side is gradual. The fine timber grown on these mountains is floated down the river to Bannu. The actual ascent was estimated at 1000 feet [305 m], and the crest of the Paiwar Pass is about 8000 feet [2,438 m] above the sea. From the Paiwar there is a descent to Ali-khel, and then an ascent to a camping-ground called Hazaradarakht ("Thousand trees"), which is covered in snow in winter ; but in summer the short sweet grass, with stunted growth of *artemesia*, orchises, and lilies, affords good pasture. From this place a pass leads over the Safid-Koh into the Kabul basin, which is frequented by traders of the Jaji tribe. Masson visited a place called Murkhi Khel in the plain of Jalalabad, which is at the foot of another road leading over the Safid-Koh into the Kurram Valley. Here he saw many Jajis who had come over the pass. From Hazaradarakht the Shutar-Gardan Pass ("Camel's neck") is reached, which crosses the Safid-Koh. The *Shutar-Gardan* is 11,200 feet [3,414 m.] above the sea. The descent into the Logar Valley is long and steep, with sharp zigzags. The pass is overhung with huge masses of naked limestone rock cropping out in every direction, and the mountains have a rugged aspect. The country between the Paiwar and Shutar-Gardan passes, comprising the Upper Kurram Valley, is called Huryab by Elphinstone, and is the Iryâb of Timur's historians." Markham (1879), pp. 47-48.

"*The Kurram Valley Route*

There is an old route south of Khyber Pass. The Spin Gar (*Safed Koh*) separates the two from each other. Both the Khyber and the Kurram routes emanate from a single point, and both aim to reach the same destination—the fertile plains of the Panjab—though they use different intermediary stations—Puruṣapura on the one hand, and Bannu on the other. The latter emanates from the Kabul Valley and runs towards the Kurram Valley at the head of the historic Peiwar Pass (*Paiwar Kotal*) under the shadow of Sikaram (Sitaram?), which sits 15,620 feet [4,561 m.] above sea level, on the Durand Line. Because of the rigid line of the range, there is no lateral communication between the two routes.

The most important archaeological landmark of the Kabul-Bannu route is the huge mound of Akra that has been yielding remarkable finds for many years. Among other things, this site has yielded a marble toilet tray depicting the Hellenistic theme of Artemis and Actaeon from the first century A.D., a 68 mm high cameo in dark blue chalcedony or onyx depicting in white the head of Heracles in profile that is dateable to the first century A.D. (The British Museum Reg. No. G&R 1893.5-2, 1 and The Walters Museum 1026, Catalogue no. 3558), a finely carved dark hard stone intaglio depicting a standing lion looking left (The British Museum Reg. No. OA. 1956. 4-2, 4), and, most remarkable, the semi-precious stone carvings from Akra in the form of a carved garnet of prodigious size—c. 60 mm [2.36 inches]—in the form of a *hamsa* or goose with outspread wings (the Victoria and Albert Museum, Reg. No. IM 34.1935) dateable to the first century A.D. More recently, excavations currently being conducted at Akra by a team from The British Museum also have yielded many hundreds, if not thousands, of seals and intaglios probably for the most part dateable to the last centuries B.C. and to the early centuries A.D. The toilet tray, the cameo and intaglios, and a number of copies of terracotta Roman lamps from this site on the Peiwar Pass route suggest either direct contact through trade with the classical Hellenistic world or, as in the case of the copied Roman lamps, perhaps "a local rendering of a highly desirable scarce trade item, in this case, a luxury object probably of very high value." These finds are a good illustration that Akra was linked to the rest of Indo-Greek or Parthian world of the period. Two Hindu stone sculptures also were found in the area, namely from Wanda Shahabkhel four kilometers [2.49 miles] northeast of Bannu, both of which date between the second and third centuries A.D. One represents Varāha and the other depicts Ekamukhaliṅga." Dar (2007), pp. 48, 50-51. Also, see: Appendix E.

"Gardez itself is a small town with a big rectangular mound and a castle, which the army still uses. The mound is about seventy yards by a hundred and fifty [64 by 137 metres], and the quantity, variety and condition of Bactrian Greek coins which are found in it and are for sale in the bazaar is unparalleled in Afghanistan; there are also Kushan and Ephthalite Hunnish coins. No road runs from Gardez into Pakistan, but a frontier officer I met in a teahouse told me it was an easy three hour ride on horseback, and the frontier valleys go straight down to the Indus. The province called Paktya, which lies between Gardez and Pakistan, is difficult for foreigners to visit. It is the home territory of the frontier Pathans; a lot of smuggling goes on, particularly of wood from the coniferous forests . . ." Lévi (1972), p. 122.

"[Sir Herbert] Edwardes's first impression [in 1847] of the Kurram valley was ecstatic. Like the Kabul valley it is well watered by snow-melt and rain, fertile with wheat and maize and oranges, shady with poplars and eucalyptus and chenars, and bright with irises and wild roses. 'In spring,' wrote Edwardes, 'it is a vegetable emerald; and in winter its many-coloured harvests look as if Ceres had stumbled against the Great Salt Range, and spilt half her cornucopia in this favoured vale . . . Altogether, nature has so smiled on Bunnoo, that the stranger thinks it is a paradise.'

As the centre of this rich district, Bannu is still a busy town, its streets crowded with men and cattle, and donkeys loaded with stacks of wheat or wood, its bazaars bustling with traders." Fairley (1975), p. 194.

"Kabul, on the other hand, was connected with India by the commercial routes passing through Jalalabad and Ghazni in the latter case via Kurram, Khost, or the Gomal Pass. To the north, Kabul was linked with Balkh, Qarshi and Bukhara by the Bamiyan route." Noelle (1997), p. 281.

"Some thirty miles [48 km.] below Kalabagh the last right-bank tributary of any importance, the Kurram, joins the Indus. It rises in the great mountains of the Afghan border which, from the eastern side of the Indus, looked to Burnes 'very imposing, the absence of ruggedness in their outlines giving the appearance of a vast fortress formed by nature, with the Indus as its ditch'. From these fortress walls, through defiles that lead down from Afghanistan, hordes of savages and warriors have been loosed upon India over the centuries; even more than ever came over the more northerly passes through the Hindu Kush: always 'wild, strange and new'." Fairley (1975), p. 173.

"Another Kushan text, in various versions, was discovered in 1967 near the Dasht-i Nawar plain, about 50 km west of Ghazni and south of the Hindu Kush watershed. The group of inscriptions, five in total, was placed at a height of more than 4,000 metres. Unfortunately the reading of the texts is still problematic and it is not even known whether all five inscriptions, in different scripts and languages, contain the same message. One version is written in the same Greek script and Bactrian language as were used at Surkh Kotal and at Rabatak. Next to it is an apparently identical text in Middle Indian and with Kharoshthi script. The same text is also written in a hitherto unknown language (perhaps Saka), apparently in Kharoshthi script. The two other inscriptions are in Greek and Kharoshthi script respectively, but impossible to read. The Bactrian and Middle Indian texts refer to Vima, but whether this is Vima Kadphises or his predecessor, Vima Tak[to], is still unclear. The location of these inscriptions is of great interest. Nowadays this part of Afghanistan is only thinly populated, but in Kushan times the situation may have been very different. Archaeological exploration in this part of Afghanistan may one day elucidate this problem. One of the most fascinating sites that await controlled archaeological excavations is that of Wardak, some 30 km northwest of Ghazni. Surveys have shown that the site reflects a large fortified urban settlement with a regular street plan. Outside the ramparts there are the remains of other structures, including a number of stupas and what appears to be a monastic complex. From one of the stupas an inscribed relic casket was obtained that is now in the British Museum." Vogelsang (2002), p. 150.

"Akra is the most prominent site in the Bannu region and has been known to European visitors and scholars for more than 150 years.... The discovery of coins and numerous fine art objects in the 19th century in particular suggested to these scholars that the site was most important during the Historic period (ca. 250 B.C. to A.D. 1000). These discoveries coupled with the site's size led Stein to argue that Akra was the ancient capital of Bannu, and he drew attention to the records of the Chinese Buddhist pilgrims Faxian and Xuanzang who visited the Bannu region in the fifth and seventh centuries A.D., respectively. Stein also made the prescient observation that the ample irrigation and remarkable fertility in the north-west of the Bannu Basin bore a resemblance to the typical oases of eastern and western Turkestan in Central Asia..... In 1996 this initial theodolite survey was extended beyond the main mounded area to the north, along the course of the nullah. It showed that an additional 48 ha of mounds and material scatters are still preserved on the right bank of the nullah, indicating that the total preserved area of Akra might be around 80 ha.... At present it appears that the site was inhabited as early as ca. 2000 B.C. and up to as late as ca. A.D. 1200, including two distinct phases of Iron Age occupation.... Nevertheless, there is evidence that suggests that Akra continued to be occupied extensively in the final centuries B.C. and the first centuries A.D. The most telling evidence for the exact chronology of the settlement at this time is available from the many coins that have been found on the surface and those that have been excavated since 1996. While their definitive publication is not yet complete, it is sufficient to state that the collections of coins from the site currently held in the British Museum, Ashmolean Museum, and Peshawar Museum include those of the Indo-Greek kings Apollodotus, Hermaeus, Demetrius, Strato, Atimachus [sic – read Antimachus], Menander, the Parthian king Gondophases, the Skythian kings Maues and Azes, the Kushan king Kidara Kushan, as well as those of Hepthalite rulers, Hindu Shahi rulers, and a lone silver coin of Mahmud of Ghazni, dating to the 11th century A.D." Magee et al. (2005), pp. 719-720, 731.

"**BANNU,** a town and district of British India, in the Derajat division of the North-West Frontier Province. The town (also called Edwardesabad and Dhulipnagar) lies in the north-west corner of the district, in the valley of the Kurram river. Pop. (1901) 14,300. It forms the base for all punitive expeditions to the Tochi Valley and Waziri frontier.

The district of Bannu, which only consists of the Bannu and Marwat tahsils since the constitution of the North-West Frontier Province in 1001, contains an area of 1680 sq. m. [4,351 sq. km] lying north of the Indus. The cis-Indus portions of Bannu and Dera Ismail Khan now comprises the new Punjab district of Mianwali. In addition to the Indus the other streams flowing through the district are the Kurram (which falls into the Indus) and its tributary the Gambila. The valley of Bannu proper, stretching to the foot of the frontier hills, forms an irregular oval, measuring 60 m. [97 km] from north to south and about 40 m. [64 km] from east to west. In 1901 the population was 231,485, of whom the great majority were Mahommedans. The principal tribes inhabiting the district are: (i) Waziri Pathans, recent immigrants from the hills, for the most part peaceable and good cultivators; (2) Marwats, a Pathan race, inhabiting the lower and more sandy portions of the Bannu valley; (3) Bannuchis, a mongrel Afghan tribe of bad physique and mean vices. The inhabitants of this district have always been very independent and stubbornly resisted the Afghan and Sikh predecessors of the British. After the annexation of the Punjab the valley was administered by Herbert Edwardes so thoroughly that it became a source of strength instead of weakness during the Mutiny. The inhabitants of the valley itself are now peaceful, but it is always subject to incursion from the Waziri tribes in the Tochi valley and the neighbouring hills. Salt is quarried on government account at Kalabagh and alum is largely obtained in the same neighbourhood. The chief export is wheat. A military road leads from Bannu town towards Dera Ismail Khan. The Indus, which is nowhere bridged within the district, is navigable for native boats throughout its course of 76 m. [122 km]. The chief frontier tribes on the border are the Waziris, Battannis and Dawaris. All these are described under their separate names." *EB* Vol. 3, p. 355.

In 2002 an ancient city was discovered at Kotale Kharwar (33°57'N; 69°03'E), about 105 km (60 miles) south of Kabul, and northeast of Ghazni. It contains numerous remains of buildings and Buddhist relics. Unfortunately, because of the war it has not been fully excavated, and is being heavily looted for saleable artefacts. Four police out of nine sent to protect it in 2003 were murdered. "Plunder goes on across Afghanistan as looters grow ever bolder: Trade in antiquities worth up to £18 bn as thieves excavate sites." James Astill. Downloaded: www.guardian.co.uk/world/2003/dec/13/highereducation.artsandhumanities on 19 March 2009.

EXCAVATIONS AT MES AYNAK UNEARTHING TREASURES BUT SITS UPON A COPPER MINE THAT CHINA AIMS TO EXPLOIT

Archaeology Briefs. Sunday, November 20, 2011.

The gold still glistened after a more than 1,000 years underground; the gemstones glinted at their first touch of sunlight, undimmed by a millennium in the dirt. "It's a necklace," said a Polish archaeologist breathless with excitement. "They've found a gold necklace!"

As the fine grey sand of Afghanistan's sun-bleached mountains was gently sieved away, there was treasure in the pan: tiny golden orbs adorned with even smaller gold beads, tulip-shaped pendants no bigger than a fingernail, red gemstones and swirling gold bowls, like acorn lids. Next to them were two spoons and a brooch made of copper, green from corrosion, and two copper hairpins embellished with gold.

Excavations at Mes Aynak have already unearthed three Buddhist monasteries and an ancient copper mine replete with statues, coins, reliefs and murals – which is more than enough to secure its place as one of the most significant archaeological digs in a generation.

Yet last week's discovery was the first time since archaeologists started work in 2009 that anyone has found jewelery in the mountains, 35km south of Kabul, and with at least three more monasteries still to be explored, Afghan officials hope the discoveries will elevate Mes Aynak into the archaeological pantheon, alongside Tillya Tepe, home of the Bactrian hoard. The archaeological remains in Logar province date from the 1st to the 7th centuries; first settled by the Khushan dynasty and eventually abandoned by the Hephtalites [sic], with the advent of Islam to Afghanistan.

"The gold, the wall paintings, the statues all suggest that the inhabitants of the site were quite wealthy," said Hans Curvers, leading archeologist on site. "Not a surprise when you live in the place were the Khushan empire mines, its main financial resources." But the treasure is both a blessing and a burden for the Afghan government, which is desperate to start exploiting its minerals as a source of income.

The archaeological sites sit directly on top of a world class copper deposit which a Chinese state mining company paid $3 billion (£1.9bn) to acquire, in 2008. It was Afghanistan's largest foreign investment, and allegedly came with a $30m bribe to the then minister of mines. The Afghan government hopes to earn up to $350m a year in royalties – equivalent to 20 per cent of Kabul's tax revenue – once the mine is operational, but recently agreed a 12-month delay, to give the archaeologists more time.

"The artifacts are right on top of the copper," said Nasir Ahmad Durrani, deputy minister of mines. "Unless we remove them we can't get to the mine." The government has also spent $6.5m clearing Soviet-era landmines from the site. "The landmines and artifacts amounted to a force majeure," Mr Durrani added. "The original timelines didn't take into account the realities on the ground ... but we believe that by 2014 we will be able to start commercial production."

Western officials are less sure. The Chinese have improved the road to the mine and built a camp to house their workers but they are yet to start work on the railway or the power station, stipulated in their contract, which they will need to purify the copper and then export it. Omar Sultan, the deputy minister of culture, said he was confident the archaeologists would excavate the areas in immediate danger before the Chinese "start blowing it up".

"We are not going to let anybody destroy our culture and I haven't seen any intention to go and do that from the Chinese or anybody else," he said. He hopes to relocate the monasteries, block by block, in a purpose-built museum nearby.

"This was a crossroads of civilizations," he said. "We have a cultural heritage that doesn't just belong to Afghanistan. It belongs to all of humanity." Posted by Nancy B. Downloaded on 13 December, 2011 from: http://archaeologybriefs.blogspot.com/2011/11/excavations-at-mes-aynak-unearthing.html

As detailed above, two massive hoards of coins and other treasures were discovered near the village of Mir Zakah (Myrazykali), in 1947 and 1992. The find spot is about 60 km due east of Kotale Kharwar, in modern Paktia Province, and 32 km northeast of Gardez on the ancient route from Ghazni to Gandhara, approaching the Peiwar Pass leading into Pakistan. See: Bopearachchi & Raman (1995), pp. 11-13; Holt (2005), pp. 140-141, 143-145; Vogelsang (2002), pp. 128, 140.

The second find alone contained items made of gold and other precious materials and an estimated 300,000-400,000 coins including thousands of Greco-Bactrian, Indo-Greek, Indo-Scythian and Kushan coins, the latest being those of Vasudeva (early 3rd century).

The fertile Upper Kurram Valley controlled the two main southerly routes from Kabul - to Kandahar in the southwest, and to Sind in the southeast, and supplied fresh produce for Kabul. It also contains the ancient city at Mes Aynak described in the news item above. It would have been a logical region for Kujula to turn his attention towards after his conquest of Kabul. He could have then surrounded the rich Gandharan plains to both the east and south of the Kurram Valley before moving to subjugate them.

> "The [Bannu] basin is a small, topographically defined region in the east of the Sulaiman Range, and is separated from the Gomal Plain in the south and the Indus River and plain to the east by a series of substantial ranges. This is a climatically marginal area, between western winter and eastern summer precipitation zones, and does not receive regular rainfall from either. It is, however, fed by a number of ephemeral streams that flow out of the various ranges, and by two perennial rivers, the Kurram and the Tochi, which flow from the Sulaiman Range and have created passes through the mountains between the eastern low- and western highlands. The ancient and modern settlements are concentrated in the northwestern part of the basin, in the area between the two perennial rivers." Magee et al. (2005), p. 718.

The evidence strongly suggests that this region in what is now eastern Afghanistan must have been of significant importance from the time of the early Greco-Bactrians and throughout the period of the Great Kushans. The extensive coin finds tell us that it was part of Kushan territory from the time of Kujula, and the inscriptions mentioning Vima Takhtu or Vima Kadphises provide further evidence of Kushan rule.

It is likely that Puda/Paktyike included the regions of the Khost Basin, the modern provinces of Paktia and Lowgar in Afghanistan plus the present district of Kurram, and the Bannu Basin in Pakistan. It certainly extended over a large area - from the fertile valleys south of Kabul to the point where the Kurram (the Krumu of the Rigveda) and Tochi rivers join the Indus in modern Pakistan.

Appendix H: The Kingdom of Wuyishanli (Arachosia & Drangiana)

Wuyishanli 烏弋山離 is also called **Wuyi** 烏弋 = the combined provinces of Arachosia and Drangiana (also known as Sakastāna), with Kandahar as its administrative centre.

The city of Kandahar is located on the Tarnak River, a tributary of the Helmand, and has been a major trade centre for many centuries. The old city, which was sacked by Nadir Shah in 1738, was located about 6 km west of the present city, was the capital of the Arachosian region since Achaemenid times.

Wuyishanli is mentioned as 'Wuyi' in *Hanshu* 96B – see: *CICA*, p. 197, as well as in the *Weilüe*. See: Chavannes (1905), pp. 555, 558.

Schuessler (2009), p. 51, n. 1-28 gives ?ɑ-jik-ṣan-liɑi (Alexandria) as the "Middle Han" reconstruction for 烏弋山離.

Note that the transcription (烏) 遲散 (Wu) Chisan [(*Wu*) *Ch'ih-san*] in the *Weilüe*, represents the city of Alexandria in Egypt. See: Hill (2004), and Hirth (1875), pp. 68-69.

According to Schuessler, (烏) 遲散 should be represented in "Middle Han" as (?ɑ), and "Late Han" -ḍi-sɑn^{B}. See: Schuessler (2009), p. 51, n. 1-28; 279, n. 26-16; 261, 24-44.

"On the name of Alexandria in Indian literature, cf. in the first place S. Lévi's paper of 1934, reprinted in *Mémorial Sylvain Lévi* (Paris, 1937, 413-423). Lévi concurs with the opinion I first upheld in 1914 (*JA*, 1914, II, 413-417) that the Alasanda of the *Questions of King Menander* was the Egyptian Alexandria. Moreover, *ālisaṃdaga*, the name of a bean, and *ālakandaka*, a name of the coral, must be nouns derived from Alexandria.

In Chinese Buddhist texts, the Chinese version of the *Questions of King Menander* gives a form 阿荔散 A-li-san (* ·Â-ljie̯-sân), nearer to the Greek original for the vowel of the second syllable than Pâli Alasanda. Lévi (*loc. cit.* 418) also thought he had found the name of Alexandria in the Chinese version of Nāgārjuna's commentary on the *Prajñāpāramitā*; but he elicited it through a correction which I hold as very doubtful.

Apart from Buddhist texts, I proposed in *TP*, 1915, 690-691, to identify with Alexandria of Egypt the name 黎軒 Li-hsüan (* Liei-χi̯ɐn), Li-kan 犁軒 (* Liei-kân), etc., known in China from the end of the 2nd cent. B. C. Although others entertain different views, I still think that the equivalence is substantially correct. It remains doubtful whether, in the first half of the 3rd cent. A. D., the name of Alexandria underlies the transcriptions 遲散 Ch'ih-san (* D''i-sân) and 烏 遲 散 Wu-ch'ih-san (*·Uo-d''i-sân) of the *Wei lio*; cf. HIRTH, *China and the Roman Orient*, 181-182 (but the equivalence has gained in probability now that we know for certain that 烏弋山離 Wu-i-shan-li [*·Uo-i̯ək-ṣăn-ljie̯, still more anciently ·O-di̯ək-săn-ljia], certainly renders the name of another Alexandria; cf. *ZDMG*, 1937, 252; *TP*, 1938, 148). Chao Ju-kua, writing in 1225, has a whole paragraph on 遏根陀 O-ken-t'o (*·Ât-kən-d'â), and describes its Pharos with the wonderful mirror (*HR*, 146-147; cf. LE STRANGE, *Nuzhat-al-Qulūb*, transl., 239-241); this last transcription is made the Arabic form Iskandariya." Pelliot (1959), p. 29.

"A better phonetic correspondence to Alexandria in a western context [than Lijian] is provided by Chísăn 遲散 or Wūchísăn 烏遲散 EMC ?ɔ dr̯i san' (or san^{h}) [Schuessler (2009), pp. 211, 18-1; 126, 7-23; and 261, 24-44: "Late Han": ?ɑ < ?ɑi-le^{C},-lie^{C}-sɑn^{B}], said in the *Wèilüè* to be the first place one reaches in Dà Qín and identified by Hirth as Alexandria. The first syllable *wū* 烏 (truncated in the first case) is the regular equivalent in Han times for a foreign initial *a*-, replaced by *ā* 阿 EMC ?a, in the new-style transcriptions that appear in the early Buddhist texts. The few *xiéshēng* connections of *chí* 遲, which appears to have *xi* 犀 EMC sɛj as phonetic, do not give

> the kind of clear-cut evidence for *l- as the source of the Middle Chinese retroflexed stop, dr̯, that we find in the cases of EMC d < *l cited above; but neither do they support a connection with Old Chinese dental stops. It is relevant that, as Hirth noted, Middle Chinese dr̯- was sometimes used in transcriptions of Sanskrit to represent the voiced retroflex stop *ḍ*, a sound that is rather close to [l].” Pulleyblank (1999), p. 76.

> “A good example of a Han transcription that shows both Old Chinese *r > Middle Chinese *l and Modern Chinese *l*-, corresponding to foreign -*r*-, and Old Chinese *l > Middle Chinese *j- corresponding to foreign -*l*- is the name Wūyìshānlí EMC ˀɔ jik ʂəɨn liə̯̂, long accepted as equivalent to the name Alexandria (not the great metropolis in Egypt but one of the other cities by this name founded by Alexander in present Afghanistan). Greek -*r*- is correctly represented by Middle and Modern Chinese *l*-, while Greek *l*- is represented by the initial consonant of the second syllable. The graph *yì* 弋 (a Type B syllable) is phonetic in *dài* 代 EMC dəjʰ (a Type A syllable) showing the typical pattern of Han dynasty *l-.” Pulleyblank (1999), pp. 73-74. Also, Pulleyblank (1963), p. 116.

The name Arachosia derives from **Saravastī* > Avest. *Haraxᵛaⁱtī* > O. P. *Harauvatish* or *Harahvatish*. See Chavannes (1905): 555, n. 6; Pelliot (1914), pp. 413-417; Pelliot (1959), p. 29; Pulleyblank (1963), pp. 116, 128; and *CICA*, p. 112, n. 250; Witzel (2003), p. 57.

Many authorities believe that its capital was at Kandahar, and named ‘Alexandria’ or ‘Alexandropolis,’ after Alexander; however there is still some doubt:

> “The city’s name—its origin, still controversial, and its history, complicated by its variations—is a related problem. From the Muslim period on, it has borne the name Kandahār (in Pashto; Pers. Qandahār), which appears for the first time in the works of the Arabic historian Aḥmad b. Yaḥyā Balāḏori (d. 892, q.v.; ed. de Goeje, p. 434). Writing about the Arab raid in the region at the time of the Omayyad caliph Moʿāwiya (r. 661-80), he reports on the capture of a city located at the Indian border by the name of al-Qandahār. . . .
>
> Archeology [sic] also is needed to clarify the time before the 7th century, for which the study of names can only lead to conjecture. The origin of the name Kandahar remains debatable and subject to speculation. One should attach no importance to popular etymologies that derive the name from *Eskandar* (that is, Alexander the Great, q.v.), based on the tradition of the Macedonian conqueror as founder of the city (discussion in *Gazetteer of Afghanistan* V, p. 262; cf. below). Several plausible, if unproven, interpretations have been offered by scholars. One might theorize that the origin of the name Kandahar is to be sought in that of the kingdom of Gandhāra (q.v.; Old Persian *Gandāra*, Elamite *Kan-da-ra*: see refs., Hallock, p. 708), which occupied the lower basin of the Kabul river. H. W. Bellew (1880, pp. 22-23; cautiously, Caroe, pp. 169-70) conjectured that the name was applied to the entire region of present-day Kandahar by refugees fleeing the Hephthalite (q.v.) invasion in the 5th century CE. Another suggestion—of even earlier use of the name—is that “Kandahar” might derive from a hypothetical Greek town name **Gondophareia*, after the name of the Indo-Parthian sovereign Gondophares (r. 20-50 CE, q.v.), of whom coins have been found in the area (Marquart and de Groot, p. 269; Herzfeld, p. 63; Fischer, p. 210). The modern name has also been sought in the first part of *Condigramma* (the second member, *grama*, means ‘village’ in Sanskrit [see Mayrhofer, II, p. 353]), which is a town in Ariana (see ARIA) mentioned by Pliny (*Natural History* 6.25), and in the name of a district in Arachosia (q.v.) called *Gandutava*. The latter was the site of a battle between the Achaemenid satrap and rebels against Darius I, as described in the king’s Bisotun inscription (DB 3.66; Agravala, p. 19; cf. Fischer, p. 205; see also ibid., p. 209).

> In any case, there existed an important city on the western border of India from the 3rd century BCE on, as witnessed by a Greco-Aramaic inscription of the Indian emperor Aśoka (r. ca. 265–238 BCE, q.v.) found on a rock one kilometer east of the northern part of Qaytul (Schlumberger et al., 1958). Even if the city on this site did not yet necessarily bear the name Kandahar, we cannot avoid the question of whether to identify it with the city of Alexandria in Arachosia . . . , which the Macedonian conqueror was said to have founded when he passed through the region. The question is complicated (Tscherikower, pp. 102-3; Fischer, pp. 194-99). In fact, the tradition regarding this "foundation" (or, more often, re-foundation) is recent. It was not mentioned in the older Alexander literature; the 3rd-century BCE geographer Eratosthenes recorded in Alexander's itinerary "the city of Arachosians" (Strabo, 11.8.9), that is, the people on whom Alexander imposed a satrap on his way to Bactria (Arrian, 3.28). The names *Alexandropolis metropolis Arakhosias,* and *Ellenis* only appear in late texts: Isidore of Charax in the 1st century CE (q.v.; ed. and tr. Schoff, p. 37), repeated by Stephen of Byzantium (fl. 6th century) and others. Attempts have been made to identify the Arachosian Alexandropolis with Kandahar (Schoff, p. 34), but the claim was by no means proved. At least the existence of the Aśoka inscription and the late classical tradition of an Alexander foundation indicate the impact of the introduction of Hellenism (q.v.) in this region at the time of the great conqueror. Further archeological work may help define the exact locations of the oldest urban centers in the Helmand region." Xavier de Planhol in: "KANDAHAR i. Historical Geography to 1979." *Encyclopædia Iranica.* Last updated: November 10, 2010. Downloaded 8th December, 2011, from: http://www.iranicaonline.org/articles/kandahar-historical-geography-to-1979. For further discussion on the origin of the name, see: Yu (1998), p. 168.

For thousands of years the rich lands along the Helmund River between Seistan and Kandahar have provided a practical route for caravans between Persia and India.

There were two main routes from Kandahar to the west. The shortest went directly west from ancient Arachosia to Drangiana (modern Sistan) and then via Bam to Stakhr (near Persepolis), and then to ports on the Persian Gulf.

The second route, more favourable to caravans, headed northwest via Farah to Herat, then joined the major route which led south of the Caspian Sea to ancient city of Rayy (south of modern Tehran) or, alternatively, southwest to Susa and the major port of Charax Spasinu at the head of the Persian Gulf.

> "Drangiana, the steppe country of the lower Helmand river and Hamun lake — modern Seistan (i.e. Sakastene) which derives its name from the Saka tribes who were settled there after their invasion in the second century B.C.
> Arachosia, the east of Drangiana — the valley of the upper Helmand, modern Farah and Kandahar and the centre of Achaemenid ruling over the tribes as far as the Indus in the east and the sea to the south" Mac Dowell and Taddei (1978a), p. 187, nn.

> "*Alexandria of Arachosia* (Stephanos Byzantinos 12, "Alexandria;" Isidore of Charax 19, "Alexandropolis;" Strabo 11.8; Pliny 6.61; Ammianus Marcellinus 33.6, "City of the Arachosians"). Capital of Arachosia, located either at Ḡaznī or, more probably, at old Qandahār, where the ancient ramparts were being excavated and two bilingual inscriptions of Aśoka have been discovered." P. Leriche, "Alexandria." *Encyclopædia Iranica.* (Updated, August 1, 2011). Downloaded on 8 January, 2012, from: http://www.iranicaonline.org/articles/alexandria-general-designation-of-cities-whose-foundation-is-credited-to-alexander-the-great-356-23-b.

"The ruins, therefore, in a way, corroborate the evidence of inscriptions. The importance of the site is such that we clearly understand that Aśoka had seen fit to engrave a (complete?) series of edicts on rock: this is without a doubt the location of the Ἀραχωδίας μητρόλις mentioned by Isidore of Charax (3). Unfortunately, the date of the ancient wall cannot be certain. It is tempting to see in A the Greek town, made larger by the AA extension of the Kushan period, but this would be purely hypothetical. Only excavations would allow a response to this problem, among others. . . .

3) It is difficult to know what the ancient name of the town was : Alexandria (of Arachosia) or Alexandropolis. See lastly, U. Scerrato, *A bilingual graeco-aramaic edict by Aśoka*, pp. 19-22. The question will only be resolved by the appearance of new documents."

Fussman (1996), p. 41. **NOTE:** The Chinese transcription 'Wuyishanli' strongly favours Alexandria rather than Alexandropolis. It would have been simple for the Chinese to indicate a **poli(s)* at the end of the name. (JEH)

"The name *Wu-i-shan-li* 烏弋山離 is at length discussed by the Authors [Hulsewé and Loewe - in CICA, p. 112 and n. 250] who agree it is "evidently a transliteration of Alexandria", although they seem unable to decide between Alexandria in Aria (Herāt) and Alexandria in Arachosia (Qandahār). Details often impede [a] general view and one cannot see wood for trees. Wu-i-shan-li was not merely a town but a state and what the non-sinological reader or perhaps any reader would expect of a note on Wu-i-shan-li, is an answer to the simple question: What in the end was, politically, Wu-i-shan-li? Far from giving the answer, the Authors do not even put the question. Yet it should not have been difficult for them to explain that Wu-i-shan-li whose boundaries were Chi-pin to the north-east (23b, 1-2 = p. 104), P'u-t'iao to the north (27b, 3 = p. 112), and An-hsi/Arsacid Persia to the west (29b, 8-9 = p. 116), could correspond to nothing else but the Indo-Parthian state as it roughly was in the first quarter of the 1st century A.D., and that the Alexandria rendered by the four Chinese syllables was, therefore, most probably Qandahār (see Daffinà, 1967, pp. 93-96). But of course all this implies that identification of Chi-pin with the Śaka realm of North-West India which the Authors are reluctant to admit. However, setting apart its geographic position and few others [*sic*] particulars, Wu-i-shan-li almost looks like a duplicate of Chi-pin. Except for antelopes, lions and rhinoceros (29a, 5 = p. 114), its products are explicitly said to be identical with those of Chi-pin (28b, 12-29a, 5 = ibid.). The passage on its coinage (29a, 9-10 = p. 115) is practically the same as that on the coinage of Chi-pin (24a, 11 = p. 106). Besides the text says, further on, that the popular way of life of Arsacid Persia is identical with that of Wu-i-shan-li and Chi-pin (30a, 1-2 = p. 116). All this seems to denote the existence of close similarities among Wu-i-shan-li, Chi-pin, and An-hsi, such as cannot be accounted for as due to confusion derived from "loose talk or unauthenticated traveller's tales" (p. 27 and n. 66). Two at least of the three countries, viz. An-hsi and Chi-pin are known to have been officially visited by Han envoys. The similarities can therefore be explained only as due to a common Iranian stock to which Parthians, Indo-Parthians and Śakas belonged, as well as to that Hellenistic cultural heritage which they alike shared." Daffinà (1982), p. 319.

The earlier Persian name for Kandahar was Kapisakaiš, but it was renamed Alexandria or Alexandropolis after Alexander's visit in the spring of 329 BCE. According to most authorities, both Wuyi(shanli) and the modern name, Kandahar ultimately derive from Alexandria.

Isidore of Charax, writing about the turn of the 1st century CE, described Arachosia and its metropolis:

"Beyond [Sacastana, or modern Seistan] is Arachosia, 36 shoeni [approx. 266 km – as 1 shoeni traditionally = 40 stade; or about 236 km according to the estimation of the stade used by Apollodorus of Artemis and Pliny by Hansman (1981), p. 3]. And, the Parthians call this White India; there are the city of Biyt and the city of Pharsana and the city of Chorochoad and the city of Demetrias; then Alexandropolis, the metropolis of Arachosia; it is Greek, and by it flows the river Arachotus. As far as this place the land is under the rule of the Parthians." Schoff (1914), p. 9.

"Alexander moved on swiftly [from the west] to Kandahar, where he founded another town, Alexandria in Arachosia (the part of Baluchistan which lies behind the Quetta Hills). Again, this has been a strategic site throughout Afghan history, and Kandahar has been occupied from then till now. In the old citadel, a temple to the deified Alexander has been discovered, along with an inscription in Greek and Aramaic by the Indian emperor Ashoka who lived a few decades after Alexander. (This is a place where the Indian and West Asian culture zones have always overlapped.) In the bazaar in the old town, the hakims (traditional doctors) claim descent from the doctors who went with Alexander – descendants of the physicians Philip and Critobulos. They still practise the Yunnani (Greek) herbal medicine which can be found right across Pakistan and North India." Wood (1997), p. 136.

"The exact extent of Arachosia is not clear. With the Arḡandāb valley as its center, it seems not to have reached the Hindu Kush, but it apparently extended east as far as the Indus river (Strabo 11.10.1), particularly in view of the reference to its ivory. According to Ptolemy 6.20.1 (cf. Strabo 15.2.9), Arachosia bordered on Drangiana in the west, on the Paropamisadae (i.e., the satrapy of Gandāra) in the north, on a part of India in the east, and on Gedrosia (or, according to Pliny, Natural History 6.92, on the Dexendrusi) in the south. . . . The metropolis of Arachosia, which bore the same name as the land and its main river (Strabo 11.8.9, eis Arachōtoùs tȇn pólin; Pliny, op. cit., 6.61 *Arachosiorum oppidum*; Stephanus Byzantius, p. 110, 13 M.), has to be sought at the site of modern Kandahar (see P. Bernard in *Studia Iranica* 3, 1974, pp. 171-85), all the more so since the importance of the Greek colony Alexandria or Alexandropolis (called "metropolis of Arachosia" by Isidorus Characenus 19) [or 'Isidore of Charax,' a geographer of the 1st century BCE/1st century CE], newly founded on the ancient site in post-Achaemenid times, has been corroborated by the discovery of both a Greek and a Greco-Aramaic edict of the Indian king Aśoka (q.v.). . . . Later on, the land was under the control of the Seleucid Antiochus III, Demetrius of Bactria (seemingly the founder of Demetrias), and the Parthian king Mithridates I; in the time of his successors Phraates II (ca. 138-128 B.C.) and Artabanus II (ca. 128-123 B.C.), nomad Saka tribes invaded from the north, i.e., from Central Asia, and occupied Arachosia and especially the neighboring Drangiana, whose name thereafter was Sakastāna (later Sīstān). At what time (and in what form) Parthian rule over Arachosia was reestablished can not be said with any authenticity. In Isidorus Characenus (sec. 19) there is at least evidence for Arachosia, if only a little part of the original province of this name, being under the rule of the Parthians, who called it Indikȇ Leukȇ́ "White India." (R. Schmitt, 1986) From the *Encyclopædia Iranica*. Updated: August 10, 2011. Accessed from: http://www.iranicaonline.org/articles/arachosia. On 24 September, 2011.

"Other groups of nomads moved south and west, through the Herat corridor onto the Iranian Plateau. They subsequently came into contact with the young empire of the

Parthians, in present-day Iran. For years to follow the newcomers and the Parthians waged a merciless war. Within a decade, between 130 and 120 BC, the immigrants killed two Parthian kings (Phraates II and Artabanus II) and almost managed to completely defeat their opponents. If the newcomers had succeeded, they would have appeared in West and Northwest Iran and perhaps even further west, just like their ancestors so many years before and just like the Turkic tribes a thousand years later. However, history never repeats itself exactly, and the Parthians were eventually saved by the military genius of Mithradates II (*r.* 123-88 BC), who rallied the Parthian forces and warded off the enormous threat that had suddenly appeared along the northeastern and eastern frontiers." Vogelsang (2002), p. 138.

"The Greek and Macedonian army passed by Kandahar, a site built up by Alexander and still bearing his name (derived from Iskandariya, *Alexandria* in Arabic)." Holt (2005), p. 31.

"Still on the etymological side of the problem: how far back in the city's history can one take its name? The allegation that Kandahar (Pushtu) or Qandahār (Arabic and Farsi) comes somehow from Alexander the Great (via Iskandarabad for example) has been long rejected. That somehow one can make Kandahar out of Γανδίφθορα (Helms 1982) may be possible, but rather far-fetched at present. The stem *Kand* or *Kund,* as in many Central Asian city names (Samar*kand*, Tash*kent*, etc.) variously meaning fortress or simply place, can in the first place add little more than typifying a durable and common practice. Its source in Avestan literature *(kang > kaŋha)* 'fortress' in Iranian epics, or Old Iranian *kan* (to dig) > *kand*(a), Avestan *kanta,* Sogdian *kanth* or Choresmian *kāth* from *kātha,* meaning perhaps 'fortress' merely underlines this while adding little of real applicable historical value (Vogelsang 1981 and pers. comm.).

Returning to early Islamic sources, Mas'ūdi's (died AD 956) note on Kandahar in the Indian Kingdom of Gandhara is perhaps still the best origin for our city's long-lived Islamic name. He says 'it was from this Kandahar that the name was carried to the settlement of the Gandharians on the banks of the Arghastan' which afterwards became famous as the modern Kandahar. This Indian Kandahar, according to al-Baladhurī (futūh al-buldān: 445) was taken by Hishām ibn 'Amr at-Taghlibi, the governor of Sind under the Abbasid al-Mansūr. Hisham threw down the 'Budd' and built a mosque in its place, repeating perhaps an act that caused the Gandharians to flee westwards when the capital of Gandhara was captured by the Hephtalites, according to the Chinese pilgrim Sung-yun who visited the region about AD 520. Thus the begging bowl of Buddha in the Wais shrine of Kandahar could be regarded as a relic of those times and the existence of a Buddhist Stupa and Vihara at the summit above Old Kandahar take on even more meaning for this period." Helms (1983), pp. 343-344.

"About 4 m. [6.5 km] west of the present city, stretched along the slopes of a rocky ridge, and extending into the plains at its foot, are the ruins of the old city of Kandahar sacked and plundered by Nadir Shah in 1738. From the top of the ridge a small citadel overlooks the half-buried ruins. On the north-east face of the hill forty steps cut out of solid limestone, lead upward to a small, dome-roofed recess, which contains some interesting Persian inscriptions cut in relief on the rock, recording particulars of the history of Kandahar, and defining the vast extent of the kingdom of the emperor Baber. Popular belief ascribes the foundation of the old city to Alexander the Great.

Although Kandahar has long ceased to be the seat of government, it is nevertheless by far the most important trade centre in Afghanistan, and the revenues of the Kandahar province assist largely in supporting the chief power at Kabul. There are no manufactures or industries of any importance peculiar to Kandahar, but the long lines of bazaars display goods from England, Russia, Hindustan, Persia and Turkestan, embracing a trade area as large probably as that of any city in Asia. . . .

Immediately to the south and west of Kandahar is a stretch of well-irrigated and highly cultivated country, but the valley of the Arghandab is the most fertile in the district, and, from the luxuriant abundance of its orchards and vineyards, offers the most striking scenes of landscape beauty. The pomegranate fields form a striking feature in the valley the—pomegranates of Kandahar, with its "sirdar" melons and grapes, being unequalled in quality by any in the East. The vines are grown on artificial banks, probably for want of the necessary wood to trellis them—the grapes being largely exported in a semi-dried state. Fruit, indeed, besides being largely exported, forms the chief staple of the food supply of the inhabitants throughout Afghanistan. The art of irrigation is so well understood that the water supply is at times exhausted, no river water being allowed to run to waste. The plains about Kandahar are chiefly watered by canals drawn from the Arghandab near Baba-wali, and conducted through the same gap in the hills which admits the Herat road. The amount of irrigation and the number of water channels form a considerable impediment to the movements of troops, not only immediately about Kandahar, but in all districts where the main rivers and streams are bordered by green bands of cultivation. Irrigation by "karez" is also largely resorted to." *EB* (1911), Vol. 15, p. 649.

By the Kushan period, Wuyishanli (which remained independent) included Arachosia and Drangiana (O.P. *Zranka* = 'waterland') or modern Sistan - directly west of Arachosia and east of the Parthian province of Fars. This is made clear in the *Hou Hanshu*, where travellers were said to have travelled directly from Wuyishanli to Tiaozhi [Characene and Susiana], which bordered on the Persian Gulf. See: Section 8 and Yu (1998), pp. 168-169.

The accounts of Wuyishanli in both the *Hanshu* and the *Hou Hanshu* mention only the one state, Wuyishanli, between Jibin to the northeast and Tiaozhi and Lijian to the west. This extensive territory appears to have been a legacy from the time it was a Persian satrapy:

"What made Arachosia into a 'worthy' *dahyu*? The answer may be simple: it was the seat of an important Persian satrap.... In this context, reference should be made again to Vivāna, Darius' loyal satrap in Arachosia.... His jurisdiction, as may be inferred from the Akkadian version of the Bisutun text, could easily have extended to the *dahyu* of Sattagydia.* The same deduction can be made about Drangiana: in the Bisutun passage under discussion there is no mention of Drangiana, although the army of Vahyazdāta, on the way from Persis to Arachosia, must have passed through Seistān. Thus it seems likely that Vivāna, the *Harauvatiyā xšaçapāvā*, administered as large an area as was controlled two centuries later by the Persian satrap Barsaentes.... F.W. König (1972: 57) has suggested that Vivāna was one of the few 'Reichshüter' of the Empire, the Warden of the South-Eastern Marches. It shows that the jurisdiction of a satrap was not necessarily restricted to a *dahyu*; indeed, it may have comprised a much larger area including several *dahyāva*. There is also reason to suggest that sometimes the name of the residence of the satrap (in this case Arachosia) was applied to all the lands controlled by that satrap." Vogelsang (1985), pp. 88-89.

It appears that the Kushans never conquered Arachosia. Instead, it was governed by a series of more or less autonomous "Indo-Parthian" rulers until the arrival of the Sasanians about 240 CE. See: Simonetta (1978), p. 186. This conclusion has been further supported by two finds of Indo-Parthian gold coins. The second is of most interest to us here:

"Only three years after the appearance of this slightly enigmatic coin, the same editors reported the appearance of yet a second, entirely distinct, gold coin [apparently found near Kandahar] in the name of Abdagases II.[20] This specimen, perfectly struck and preserved displays on the obverse the figure of a mounted horseman spearing with a lance the fallen figure of a quadruped, which may be a wolf, or more probably a deer. He wears the rounded and jewelled tiara seen on the previous specimen, with diadem ties trailing behind. A miniature figure approaches from the front, the male Iranian version of the Classical Nike, extending a ring of sovereignty. Once again, the inscription is in elegant Parthian: 'bdgšy MLKYN MLK' BRY S'nbry MLK' *Abdagaš Šāhān Šāh puhr Sānabar Šāh* "Abdagases King of Kings, son of Sānabares, King." The reverse represents a human figure leading a bridled horse to the left; whether, as the editors suggest, for a sacrifice, or as a rendering of the deity Druvaspa as on coins of Kanishka, is uncertain. The inscription mentions "Abdagases, King of Kings, the Great" but the remainder, which might explain the image, is largely off the flan. To compare the headgear and splendid costume of such an Indo-Parthian prince we can look at the reproduction by E. Herzfeld of a mural painting discovered by him at the site of Kuh-i Khwaja across the Iranian frontier.

This is again a spectacular and original coin, which together with his assumption of the elevated title King of Kings, suggests that this late Indo-Parthian achieved a quite unexpected level of affluence and prosperity. Despite the rather inconclusive discussion by the editors of this coin of the date of Abdagases II, one could, perhaps, taking him as contemporary with Soter Megas, place him around 70 CE. At this relatively late date the Indo-Parthians must have lost most of their possessions in the Punjab to the Kushans, but it appears that they retained undisturbed the regions of Kandahar and Sistan, and even enjoyed there considerable opulence.

[20] Grenet, F. and Bopearachchi, O. (1999), "Une nouvelle monnaie en or d'Abdagases II", *St Ir* 28, 1 :73-82."

Bivar (2007), pp. 33-34 and n. 20 (and details from the book's bibliography).

Arachosia and Drangiana had been closely associated since they formed adjacent provinces of the Achaemenid Empire. In the time of Aśoka (reigned *circa* 273-232 BCE) and the Seleucid king, Antiochus II (*r.* 261-246 BCE): "it is clear that the two kingdoms were then contiguous with a frontier west of Kandahar. . . ," Sherwin-White and Kuhrt, p. 80. Michael Witzel provides further confirmation of the combination of these two satrapies:

"The extent of Arachosia has shifted over time (cf. also GNOLI 1980: 36), see the distinction in the O.P. inscriptions and Greek sources which distinguish between Arachosia and Drangiana. . . . Strabo [writing *circa* 23 CE] 11.560, on the contrary, has both Drangiana and Arachosia within one satrapy; the Avestan *Drangiana/Sistan and Arachosia indeed share the same x^v dialect, as is clear from the very name, *Harax^{v}aitī*, and not the usual Avestan *-huu....*" Witzel (2000), p. 26, n. 59.

"Arachosia, which appears in the cuneiform inscriptions of Darius, is a curious subject altogether. The original name is Harakhwati (equivalent to the Sanscrit Saraswati), from whence came the Greek Arachotos and the Arab Rakhaj (which seems to have been applied to Kandahar), and the modern representative of which title is the Arghand-ab River.

The town of Kandahar was certainly the Greek Alexandria or Alexandropolis, and was quite distinct from the capital of Arachosia." Rawlinson (1842), p. 113.

"Arachosia (Old Persian *harahuvati*, corresponding to Sanskrit *sarasvati* 'rich in rivers') was the well-named land of present southern Afghanistan, the valley of the

Upper Helmand (Avestan *Ha'tumant* 'rich in dams') and the tributaries where the Thamani (Herodotus III.93, 117) lived . . , the people of Arachosia must have been settled agriculturalists from an early time in this fertile land comparable to Bactria in the north. Similar to Bactria in the north, Arachosia was the centre of Achaemenid rule over neighbouring tribes to the south and east and Darius was fortunate to have a loyal satrap who, after a number of battles with the rebels sent against him from the west, was able to consolidate the rule of the new king.

The lower course of the Helmand river and the Hamun lake was occupied by the Zrangi (Old Persian *Z(a)ra(n)ka*, with local *z-* for Old Persian *d-*), which name has been explained as 'sea land' by many scholars, unsuccessfully, I believe. The name survived into Islamic times as Zarang, the capital of the country. The Hamun lake area played an important role in Zoroastrian tradition and as the homeland of the hero Rustam. By geography and history it has been connected with Arachosia and the upper Helmand rather than with Fars province or the west. The invasion of Saka tribes in the second and first centuries before our era undoubtedly changed the population for their name was applied to the land which has held to this day, Seistan. In pre-Achaemenid times as today it is a land where the steppe and sown are intermingled and nomads are on all sides of the lake which is large in winter while almost vanishing in the late summer." Frye (1963), pp. 71-72.

Pavel Lurje (personal communication, 18 May 2002) said the form *Ha'tumant* in the above quotation is incorrect: "Avestic Haetumant-, (Greek Etymandres), *not* Ha'tumant. The Kandahar inscription of Ashoka seems to be not in Aramaic language, but some local Iranian or Indian language in Aramaic script . . . ."

"The main features of all the larger rivers of the Sistan basin may be illustrated by a single example. The Helmund of the Afghans, the Etymander of the ancients, is the only large river between the Tigris and the Indus. Rising among great mountain peaks which tower to heights of over 15,000 feet [4,572 m.], the Helmund flows through the land of the Hazara Mongols (Holdich, *a*, p. 42), "a wild mountainous country of which no European has seen much more than the outside edge. It is a high, bleak, and intensely inhospitable country, where the snow lies for most months of the year, where little or no fuel is to be found, and cultivation is confined to the narrow banks of the Helmund and its tributaries." Farther downstream, near the edge of the mountains, Zamindawar, northwest of Kandahar "is a beautiful country, filled with a swarming population of well-to-do cultivators" (p. 43). From Zamindawar the river flows southward, and not far below Girishk enters the desert, through which it flows for 300 miles [483 km.] to Sistan, first southward, then westward, and lastly northward. On the left lie the deserts of Registan and northern Baluchistan, which McMahon (*a*, pp. 13, 14, 16; *b*, p. 290) and Holdich (*a*, p. 104-105) describe as consisting of flat plains of fine alluvium and dark gravel over which the fierce north winds drive fields of sand-dunes. On the southern edges of the desert the dunes often attain a height of 200 feet [61 m.], and enormous drifts of sand bury the volcanic mountains of northern Baluchistan to depths of one or two thousand feet [305 or 610 m.], or even more (McMahon, *b*, p. 290). North of the Helmund River the Dasht-i-Margo, or Desert of Margo, which was crossed by Ferrier (*a*, p. 400), appears to be of much the same character, although the sand-hills are not so high apparently, and the area of fine silt exceeds that of gravel.

The river itself flows in a distinct valley of erosion, which Colonel McMahon described to me as being broadly open, with three or four persistent terraces of gravel, like those which will be described later as occurring along other streams nearer to the Hamm-i-Sistan. Between these receding terraces lies what Holdich (*a*, p.

106) calls "the curious green ribbon of Helmund cultivation which divides the great untraversed wastes of the Dasht-i-Margo from the somewhat less formidable sand deserts to the south." "Here in a narrow green space of a mile [1.6 km.] or so in width we found the great river shut in with a green abundance, infinitely refreshing and delightful." Jungles of tamarisks border the river, and here and there nomad Baluchis feed their flocks, or even cultivate fields of grain. Far more impressive than the modern villages, however, are the innumerable evidences of a far greater population which finally disappeared not many hundred years ago. Every writer on the region dwells on the "cities of the dead, spreading out like giant cemeteries for miles on either side of the river, gaunt relics of palaces and mosques and houses, upright and bleached, scattered over acres of debris, masses of broken pottery, mounds of ancient mud ruins. . . . The extent of these Kaiani ruins (dating their final destruction from a century and a half ago) would be incomprehensible were it not for the extent of the indications of that canal system which was developed from the Helmund to assist in supporting the crowd of humanity which must have dwelt in the Helmund Valley" (Holdich, *a*, p. 107)." Huntington (1905), Vol. 1, pp. 276-277.

"Modern Seistan is a flat, unwholesome country, distributed geographically on either side of the Helmund between Persia and Afghanistan. It owes its place in history and its reputation for enormous productiveness to the fact that it is the great central basin of Afghanistan, where the Helmand and other Afghan rivers run to a finish in vast swamps, or lagoons. Surrounded by deserts, Seistan is never waterless, and there was, in days which can hardly be called ancient, a really fine system of irrigation, which fertilized a fairly large tract of now unproductive land on the Persian side of the river. The amount of land thus brought under cultivation was considerable, but not considerable enough to justify the historic reputation which Seistan has always enjoyed as the "Granary of Asia." This traditional wealth was no doubt exaggerated from the fact that the fertility of Seistan (like that of the Herat valley, which is after all but an insignificant item in Afghan territory) was in direct contrast to the vast expanse of profitless desert with which it is surrounded—a green oasis in the midst of an Asiatic wilderness." Holdich (1910), pp. 201-202.

SEISTAN, or SISTAN (SEJISTAN), the ancient *Sacastane* ("land of the Sacae") and the *Nimruz* or "Meridies" of the *Vendidad*, a district of Persia and Afghanistan, situated generally between 30° 0' and 31° 35' N., and between 61° 0' and (including Rudbar) 62° 40' E. Its extreme length is about 100 and its breadth varies from 70 to over 100 m., but the exact limits are vague, and the modern signification of the name practically comprehends the peninsula formed by the lower Helmund and its embouchure on the one side and the Hamun (lake) on the other. Its area is 7006 sq. m. [18,145 sq. km.]; 2847 sq. m. [7374 sq. km.] are Persian territory, while 4159 sq. m. [10,772 sq. km.] belong to Afghanistan. When British arbitration was brought to bear upon the disputed claims of Persia over this country in 1872, it was found necessary to suppose two territories one compact and concentrated, which was called "Seistan Proper," the other detached and irregular, called "Outer Seistan."

1. Seistan Proper is bounded on the north by the Naizar, or reed-bed which fringes the Hamun; west by the Hamun itself, of which the hill called Kuh-i-Khwajah marks the central point; south by a line shutting in Sikuha and all villages and lands watered by the main Seistan canal; and east by the old bed of the Helmund, from 1 m. [1.6 km.] above the dam at Kohak to the mouth. Kal'ab-i-nau and Rindan are among the more northerly inhabited villages. The Kuh-i-Khwajah is a sufficient indication of the western side. Burj-i-'Alam Khan should be included within the southern

boundary as well as Sikuha. Khwajah Ahmad and Jahanabad, villages on the left bank, or west of the true bed of the Helmund, denote the eastern line. The whole area is estimated at 947 sq. m. [2453 sq, km.]. The fixed population may be roughly stated at 35,000 some 20,000 Seistanis and 15,000 settlers the greater part of whom are Parsiwans, or rather, perhaps, a Persian-speaking people. To the above numbers may be added 10,000 Baluch nomads.

Taking the aggregate at 45,000, we find nearly 48 persons to the square mile [18.5 people per sq. km.]. These figures are eight times in excess of the proportional result found for the whole of Persia. It should be explained that the designation Seistan Proper is not arbitrarily given. The territory comprehended in it is spoken of as Seistan by the dwellers on the Right bank of the Helmund, in contradistinction to their own lands. At the same time it could only be but a fractional part as indeed the whole country under consideration could only be of the Seistan of Persian history.

Seistan Proper is an extensive tract of sand and clay alluvium, generally flat, but irregular in detail. It has heaps, but no hills; bushes, but no trees, unless indeed three or four tamarisks of aspiring height deserve the name; many old ruins and vestiges of civilization, but few monuments or relics of antiquity. It is well watered by rivers and canals, and its soil is of proved fertility. Wheat or barley is perhaps the staple cultivation; but pease, beans, oil-seeds and cotton are also grown. Among fruits, grapes and mulberries are rare, but melons and water-melons, especially the latter, are abundant. Grazing and fodder are not wanting, and besides the reeds peculiar to Seistan there are two grasses which merit notice that called *bannu*, with which the bed of the Hamun abounds on the south and the taller and less salt *kirta* on the higher ground.

2. Outer Seistan, the country on the right bank of the Helmund, and east of its embouchure in the Hamun, extends more than 100 m. [160 km.] in length, or from a point between the Charboli and Khuspas rivers north to Rudbar south. In breadth the district of Chakhansur, measuring from the old bed of the Helmund, inclusive of Nad Ali, to Kadah, may be estimated at some 30 m. It produces wheat and barley, melons, and perhaps a few vegetables and oil seeds. Beyond the Chakhansur limits, southward or up to the Helmund, there is probably no cultivation save that obtained on the river bank, and ordinarily illustrated by patches of wheat and barley with melon beds. On the opposite side of the river, in addition to the cultivated portions of the bank, there is a large tract extending from south of Kuhak, or the Seistan dam (band), to the gravelly soil below the mountain ranges which separate Seistan from Baluchistan and Narmashir. The distance from north to south of this plain may be computed at 40 m. [miles] [64 km.], and from east to west at 80 or 90 m. [129 or 145 km.]. Lands north of the Naizar not belonging to the Afghan district of Lash Juwain may also be included in Outer Seistan; but it is unnecessary to make any distinction of the kind for the tract marked Hamun on the west, where it merges into the Persian frontier. The inhabitants are Seistanis or Parsiwans, Baluch nomads and Afghans. Between the Kuhak band and Rudbar they are mainly Baluch. Most of the less nomad tribesmen are Sanjurani and Toki, the sardars jealously claiming the former appellation.

The most remarkable geographical feature of Seistan generally, in the modern acceptation of the term, is the Hamun, which stretches far and wide on the north, west and south, but is for a great part of the year dry or a mere swamp. It is a curious feature in the physical conformation of northern and western Afghanistan that none of the rivers flow to the sea, but that the Helmund and all the other rivers of western Afghanistan empty themselves into these lagoons, which spread over thousands of square miles. A noteworthy feature of the Seistan lagoon is that in times of excessive flood it overspreads a vast area of country, both to the north and south, shutting off the capital of Seistan (Nusretabad) from surrounding districts, and spreading through a channel southwards, known as Shelag, to another great depression, called the Gaud-i-Zirreh. This great salt swamp is about 1000 ft. [305 metres] lower in elevation and is situated so close to the Helmund as to leave but a few miles of broken ridge between. By that ridge all communication with Seistan must pass in time of flood. Seistan becomes a promontory connected with the desert south of the Helmund by that isthmus alone. In the early spring the existence of a lake could only be certified by pools or hollows of water formed at the mouths of the principal feeders, such as the Khash Rud on the north-east, the Farah Rud on the north-west, and the Helmund, where its old bed terminates at no great distance from the Khash Rud. Bellew describes the aspect of that portion of Seistan limited to the actual basin of the Helmund as indicating the former existence of a lake which covered with its waters a considerable area. On the north this tract has been raised to a higher level than the remainder by the deposit at the mouths of rivers of the solid matter brought down. It is still, however, from 200 to 500 ft. [61 to 152 metres] below the level of the desert cliffs that bound it, and at some former period formed the shores of the lake ; and it is from 50 or 60 to 200 ft. [15 or 18 to 61 metres] or or above the level of the beds of the rivers now flowing into the existing Hamun. The water-supply of Seistan is about as uncertain as that of Sind, though the general inclination to one bank, the left, is more marked in the Helmund than in the Indus. Therefore the boundary lines given must be received with slight reservation. It is easy to see that a good year of inundation extends the borders of the so-called lake to within the Naizar; and there are well-defined beds of dry canals intersecting the country, which prove the existence formerly of an extensive water-system no longer prevailing. The main canal of Seistan, confounded by some writers with the parent river, bears the waters of the Helmund westward into the heart of the country. They are diverted by means of a large band or dam, known indifferently as the "Amir's," the "Seistan" or the "Kuhak" band, It is constructed of horizontally laid tamarisk branches, earth and perpendicular stakes, and protected from damage by a fort on the left and a tower on the right bank of the river. Although this diversion of the stream may be an artificial development of a natural channel, and undoubtedly dates from a period long prior to recent Persian occupation, it appears that the later arrangements have been more maturely and better organized than those carried on by the predecessors of the amir of Kaian. The towns of Deshtak, Chelling, Burj-i-'Alam Khan, Bahramabad, Kimmak and others of less note are actually on the banks of this main canal. Moreover, it is the indirect means of supplying water to almost every town and village in Seistan Proper, feeding as it does a network of minor canals, by which a system of profuse irrigation is put in force. The yearly rainfall is only 2 to 3 in. [5.1 to 7.6 cm.]. The Seistan depression receives the drainage of a tract of country over 125,000 sq. m. [323,748 sq. km.] in area. Provisions in Seistan are as a rule sufficient, though sheep and oxen are somewhat poor. Bread is cheap and good, being procurable to natives at less than a halfpenny the pound. Vegetables are scarce, and rice is chiefly obtained from Herat. The inundated lands abound with water-fowl. Partridges and sand-grouse are occasionally seen. River fish are plentiful enough, but confined to one species, the barbel.

The population is about 205,000, but the country, even with the lazy methods of the present day, furnishes a very large amount of grain and food-supplies in excess of local requirements, and it could, of course, be made to furnish very much more. Under improved government Seistan could with but little trouble be made into a second Egypt.

The inhabitants of Seistan are mainly composed of Kaianis, descendants of the ancient rulers of the land; Sarbandis and Shahrakis, tribes supposed to have consisted originally of immigrants from western Persia; and Baluchis of the Nharui and Sanjurani (Toki) clans. Bellew separates the "Seistanis"; but it is a question whether this term is not in a large measure applied to fixed inhabitants of the country, whatever their descent and nationality. The dense reed-beds (Naizar) skirting the Hamun, often several miles in width and composed of reeds 10 ft. [3 metres] or more in height, look impenetrable, but narrow winding lanes exist in them, known only to the Sayads (Arab, for "hunter"), a strange aboriginal race of Seistan, who live by netting fish and water-fowl. These people live all the year round at the water's edge, in huts made of reeds, and change their abodes as the waters advance or recede. They have a language of their own, and are an unsociable people, suspicious of strangers, ever ready to decamp if they think a tax-collector is near.

History.— The ancient Drangiana (Zaraya, Daranka, "lake land") received the name of "land of the Sacae" after this country was permanently occupied by the "Scythians" or Sacae, who overran Iran in 128 B.C. It was included in the Sassanian empire, and then in the empire of the caliphs. About A.D. 860, when it had undergone many changes of government under lieutenants of the Bagdad caliphs, or bold adventurers acting on their own account, Yakub b. Laith al-Saffar made it the seat of his power. In 901 it fell under the power of the Samanids, and a century later into that of the Ghaznevids. An invasion of Jagatais and the irruption of Timur are salient points in the history of Seistan prior to the Sefavid conquest (1508). Up to 1722 Seistan remained more or less a Persian dependency. . . ." *EB* (1911), vol. 24, pp. 592-593.

"But as collective ruins covering an area of 500 square miles [1295 sq. km.] have been noted by Mr. Tate, the surveyor of the late Seistan mission, who camped in their midst to the north of Kala-i-Fath, the exact site of Pulaki may yet require careful research before it is identified. Seistan is the land of half- buried ruins. No such extent of ruins exists anywhere else in the world. It seems probable, therefore, that, like the sites of many another ancient city of Seistan, Pulaki has been either partially or absolutely absorbed in the boundless sea of desert sand, which envelops and hides away each trace of the past as its waves move forward in irresistible sequence before the howling blasts of the north-west." Holdich (1910), p. 336.

"The ruins of Eastern Persia and the neighbouring countries are incredibly abundant. The mighty cities of the dead crowding the shores of the lake of Sistan in the centre, and the abundant vestiges of a former population much denser than the present in Kirman to the west, Baluchistan to the south, and the Helmund Valley to the east, have already been mentioned. Examples might be multiplied indefinitely, for the tale of every traveller is full of them. North of Sistan the same is true. Half-way from Herat to Kandahar the plain of Dasht-i-Bakwa, where, according to an Afghan prophecy, a great battle will some day take place between the English and the Russians, is now inhabited only by nomads, although this has by no means always been the case. Yate [Yate, C. E. *Kurasan and Sistan*, London, 1900, pp. 442] (p. 12) "found the plain covered with the marks of old karezes, or underground water-channels, and it had evidently been thickly populated by a cultivating class at some time, while water was said to be obtained all over it. When I passed it was all a waste." Ferrier, in the same region, describes the ruins of city after city. To a certain extent these might be returned to prosperity under good government, but there are certain places which no amount of government, good or bad, could affect." Huntington (1905), Vol. 1, pp. 305-306.

"The seat of the king's government [of Wuyishanli] is at . . . [the text is defective here] and it is distant by 12,200 *li* [5,073 km] from Ch'ang-an. It is not subject to the protector general . . . [There are many] households, individuals and persons able to bear arms, and it is a large state. To the north-east it is a distance of 60 days' journey to the seat of the protector general. It adjoins Chi-pin in the east, P'u-t'ao in the north, and Li-kan and T'iao-chih in the west ; after travelling for some one hundred days one then reaches T'iao-chih. The state is situated in the Western Sea; . . . [a passage on Tiaozhi (T'iao-chih) is inserted here in the Chinese text – in the middle of the section on Wuyi].

The land of Wu-i [-shan-li] is very hot ; it is covered in vegetation and flat. For matters such as grass, trees, stock-animals, the five field crops, fruit, vegetables, food and drink, buildings, market-stalls, coinage, weapons, gold and pearls, [conditions] are identical with those of Chi-pin, but there are antelope, lion and rhinoceros.

The way of life is such that a serious view is taken of arbitrary murder. The obverse of the coins shows only a human head with a rider on horseback on the reverse. Their staves are embellished with gold and silver.

[The state] is cut off and remote and Han envoys reach it only rarely. Proceeding by the Southern Route from the Yü-men and the Yang barriers, and travelling south through Shan-shan one reaches Wu-i-shan-li, which is the extreme point of the Southern Route; and turning north and then proceeding eastward one arrives at An-hsi." *Hanshu* 96A from: *CICA*, pp. 112-113.

The use of *Wuyi* (W-G: Wu-i), the shortened form of the name *Wuyishanli*, in this passage is analogous to the 3rd century *Weilüe's* use of *Bei Wuyi* 北烏伊, or 'Northern Wuyi', to refer to Alexandria Eschate, or modern Khujand. See: Chavannes (1905), p. 558.

The Chinese name *Bei Wuyi* is a shortened form of *Bei Wuyishanli* or 'Northern Alexandria,' just as *Wuyi* was sometimes used for *Wuyishanli*. See also: note 19.1.

That pearls are mentioned suggests an active pearl trade, perhaps from the Persian Gulf, Indian waters, or both. Pearls are also mentioned in the account on Jibin.

The reference in the *Hanshu* to the "serious view taken of arbitrary murder" may reflect the influence of Buddhism or to the local effect of Ashoka's inscription. The early arrival of Buddhist ideals in the region is confirmed by a bilingual inscription (in both Greek and Aramaic) by Aśoka (died *circa* 238 BCE) which advocates a vegetarian diet and the avoidance of, or restraint in, the hunting and killing of animals.

The *Hanshu's* report of lions and rhinoceroses in Wuyishanli is quite possibly accurate:

"Even within the historic period the geographical range of the lion covered the whole of Africa, the south of Asia, including Syria, Arabia, Asia Minor, Persia and the greater part of northern and central India." *EB* (1911), Vol. 16, p. 737.

Rhinoceros, though now extinct in the region, were still being hunted in the Afridi hills northeast of Kandahar in the sixteenth century:

"c. 1555. – "We came to the city of Purshawar, and having thus fortunately passed the *Kotal* we reached the town of Joshāya. On the Kotal we saw rhinoceroses, the size of a small elephant." – *Sidi 'Ali*, in *J. As.* Ser. 1. tom. ix. 201." Yule and Burnell (1886), p. 700.

"1519. – "After sending on the army towards the river (the Indus), I myself set off for Sawâti, which they likewise call Karnak-Khaneh (*kark-khâna*, 'the rhinoceros-haunt'), to hunt the rhinoceros. We started many rhinoceroses, but as the country abounds in brushwood, we could not get at them. A she rhinoceros, that had whelps, came out, and fled along the plain; many arrows were shot at her, but. . . she gained cover. We set fire to the brushwood, but the rhinoceros was not to be found. We got sight of another, that, having been scorched in the fire, was lamed and unable to run. We killed it, and everyone cut off a bit as a trophy of the chase." – Baber, 253." Quoted from *Baber* in: Yule and Burnell (1886), p. 762. Also see Chandra (1977), p. 9.

The "antelope" mentioned in the *Hanshu* is discussed by Hulsewé and Loewe on page 114, n. 262. They point out that *tiaoba/taoba* 挑拔 was said to be another name for the *fuba* 符

拔. A specimen was sent as a present to Emperor Zhang in 87 CE by the king of Parthia. It was probably a Persian or Goitered Gazelle – *Gazella subgutterosa*. See note 10.5.

Arachosia was one of the few places where elephants were bred and raised successfully in captivity. The hot and steamy conditions and abundant fodder along the river made the transport and trade of elephants from India to Persia possible.

> "Suitable sites for elephant-parks are rare in both Syria and Afghanistan. And the Seleucids' war-elephants, like the Ghaznavids', were sinews of war in the literal sense. In discussing Ashoka's inscription at Qandahar, I have recalled that the first Seleucus ceded all his provinces west of Qandahar and south of the Hindu Kush to Chandragupta Maurya in exchange for 500 of the Indian emperor's elephants; and the price in terms of ceded territory turned out not to be excessive from Seleucus's point of view. Those 500 elephants were trumps. They won him his victory over his rival Antigonus 'One-Eye'. In fact, they won him his empire. No wonder that he and his successors took trouble to provide their elephants with congenial accommodation." Toynbee (1961), p. 72.

> "Not only ivory, but also elephants were probably transported to the west via Arachosia. Indeed South-East Afghānistān offers the easiest route for the passage of these bulky animals to the west. Alexander's general Craterus, on the return journey from the Indus Valley to Persis, took with him all the elephants of the Macedonian army (Arrianus, *Anab. Alex.* VI. 17.3). And reference has already been made to the fifteen elephants belonging to the 'Indians on this side of the Indus' who were probably allied to Barsaentes, the Achaemenid satrap in Arachosia and Drangiana. In later years, Antiochus III, while campaigning in the East, received a number of elephants from the Indian king Sophagasenus. These animals were transported to the west via Arachosia (Polybius XI. 39.11-16). The same route may have been followed also by Seleucus I when he returned to the west after signing the treaty with Candragupta Maurya (see chapter 1). This treaty included the gift of five hundred elephants to the Macedonian monarch. Finally, reference should be made to an event during the Early Islamic Period when the local ruler of *ar-Ruxxaj* (Arachosia) offered a number of elephants to a contestant of Ya'qub b. Laith, the founder of the Ṣaffārid dynasty (C.E. Bosworth 1968: 119)." Vogelsang (1985), pp. 81-82.

Arachosia was famous throughout Afghanistan for its pomegranates, melons and grapes.

There is an abandoned gold mine about 3 km north of the present city of Kandahar which may have had some importance in antiquity. Finally, gold is mentioned as a product of Wuyishanli in *Hanshu* 96 A: 24a, 29a. See: *CICA*, p. 114; Dubs (1955), p. 512, n. 3.

Wusun 烏孫 [literally, *wu* = 'crow,' 'raven;' or 'black' + *sun* = 'grandson,' or 'Grandson(s) of the raven(s)']. For details on their territory during the time of the Later Han, see: note 1.64 and Appendix K.

The Wusun are generally thought to have been partly of Caucasoid background. Yan Shigu (581–645 CE) added the following comment to the opening passage in *Hanshu* 96 B, 1A on the Wusun:

> 〔一〕 師古曰：「烏孫於西域諸戎其形最異。今之胡人青眼、赤須，狀類彌猴者，本其種也。」
>
> Downloaded on 3 January 2012, from: http://www.guoxue123.com/shibu/0101/01hsyz/111.htm. Also, see: Mallory and Mair (2000), p. 93; Yu (1998), pp. 141-142.

My translation follows:

> "**1.** [Yan] Shigu says: The Wusun of the Western Regions are the most unusual looking of the Rong (peoples). The present Hu ('barbarians') have blue (or green) eyes and red beards, and look like apes, are also of the same stock (as the Wusun)."

Mallory and Mair remark that when the Chinese first encountered the Russians, they thought they were descendants of the Wusun because of their similar looks. They add:

> "Skulls presumed to derive from the Wusun and excavated and studied by Soviet archaeologists and anthropologists have ranged in their descriptions from primarily Caucasoid with some Mongoloid admixture (like Uzbeks or Tadjiks) all the way to pure European on the basis of six skulls dating to the first centuries BC/AD at Semirech'e. In any event, the Wusun are one of the historically named peoples of a European physical type who occupied East Central Asia." Mallory and Mair (2000), pp. 93-94.

The *Hanshu* claims that the Wusun "originally" lived next to the Yuezhi in the Hexi/Gansu Corridor. *Zizhi tongjian, juan* 18, reports that in 115 BCE:

> "The King of *Wusun* having resolved not to return to their former homeland, the *Han* government decided to take over the land that belonged to them and set up a new prefecture – *Jiuquan* [*circa* 104 BCE], immigrants were relocated to settle in the area. Later the prefecture was split into two, one of them retained the former name, and the other was named *Wuwei*. Upon the founding of the two prefectures, they had cutting off [sic – should read 'cut off'] communications between the *Xiongnu* and the *Qiang* tribes that settled south of the *Qilian* Mountain." Yap (2009), p. 201.

The Wusun are described in *Hanshu* 96B, along with the Da Yuezhi and the Sai, as being a *zhong* 種 — meaning a 'race' or 'tribe,' indicating that the Chinese saw them as distinct peoples. *CICA*, p. 145. See also the quote from Francke (1907), p. 677. See: Appendix W.

The history of the Wusun is exceedingly difficult to determine as the Chinese histories are contradictory and inconsistent. These inconsistencies were probably best summed up by Edwin Pulleyblank:

> "This account of the Wu-sun which Chang Ch'ien allegedly learned at second hand from the Hsiung-nu can be summarized as follows: (1) in the time of the present ruler's father, the Wu-sun were a small people on the western borders of the Hsiung-nu ; (2) they were conquered by the Hsiung-nu and their ruler was killed ; (3) the present ruler, named K'un-mo, was a new-born infant at the time; he was abandoned in the wilderness but miraculously saved by wild animals, a crow and a she-wolf; (4)

K'un-mo was brought up at the court of the ruler of the Hsiung-nu ; (5) when a grown man, K'un-mo was put in command of his own people and given a fief to the west of the Hsiung-nu (in their original grazing grounds?); (6) K'un-mo was a successful general and caused a revival of his people ; when the *shanyu* died, he moved away from the Hsiung-nu and successfully established his independence, though he was still regarded by the Hsiung-nu as a vassal.

The miracle in item (2) is clearly a part of a tribal origin myth of a familiar type. The abandoned infant, suckled by a she-wolf, immediately reminds one of Romulus and Remus. The part played by the crow seems to be an embellishment based on the meaning of the Chinese characters used for the name of the Wu-sun, i.e. 'crow grandson'. Since these characters are undoubtedly a transcription of a non-Chinese word, one can only suppose that this punning interpretation was added by Chang Ch'ien himself or some other Chinese.

The mythological elements, which must be of much earlier origin, have evidently got confused with the history of the actual ruler. What we are told of the latter agrees quite well with the other information we have. According to the chapter on the Hsiung-nu in the *Shih-chi* (copied in the *Han shu),* the Hsiung-nu subjugated the Wu-sun along with Lou-lan and the Hu-chieh, a nomadic people in the Altai region, and 26 neighbouring countries (evidently the states of the Tarim Basin) after inflicting a crushing defeat on the Yuezhi in 176 B.C. That the Wu-sun prince should have been brought up at the court of the Hsiung-nu ruler and later put over his own people as a dependent ruler would be quite in keeping with what we know of the practice of nomadic rulers. The *shanyu* after whose death K'un-mo established his *de facto* independence can only have been Lao-shang (c. 174-160 B.C.). Lao-shang's successor, Chien-ch'en (160-126) was still living when Chang Ch'ien was a prisoner among the Hsiung-nu. When Chang Ch'ien visited K'un-mo sometime after 119 B.C., the latter was already an old man. He was still living in the period 110-105 when a Chinese princess was sent to be his bride but the date of his death is unknown. This is all quite consistent." Pulleyblank (1970), pp. 155-156.

"It should not be overlooked that Wu-sun is not merely a transcription of a foreign name. It is at the same time an attempt to etymologize it. According to the well-known tradition of the Turks the ten girls, one of whom became the ancestor of their ruling clan, were the children of a prince and a she-wolf. The prince, the only one left after all his people had been slain, was saved by a she-wolf; he took her for his wife. In a north-asiatic variant of the swan-maiden tale (J. Batchelor, *Uwepekere Stories* 101 [Sapporo 1924]); B. Pilsudski, *Materials for the study of the Ainu language and folk-lore* 25-8 [Cracow 1912]) it is a bird-woman who becomes the wife of the hero who has survived a catastrophe, usually the slaying of all his relatives. In the Wu-sun tradition these two tales are merged. After his father was killed and his country annihilated the hero lived alone in a desert. A raven brought him meat and a she-wolf suckled him, cf. De Groot, *Urkunden zur Geschichte Asiens* 2.23-4. Wu-sun means 'the grand-sons of the raven.' How the foreign name really sounded is unknown." Maenchen-Helfen (1945), p. 74, n. 32.

The legendary account of their origins and the name 'Wusun' is also found in the *Shiji*:

"During this time [i.e. *circa* 119 BCE] the emperor occasionally questioned Zhang Qian about Daxia and the other states of the west. Zhang Qian, who had been deprived of his marquisate, replied, "When I was living among the Xiongnu I heard about the king of the Wusun people, who is named Kunmo. Kunmo's father was the ruler of a small state on the western border of the Xiongnu territory. The Xiongnu attacked and killed his father, and Kunmo, then only a baby, was cast out in the wilderness to die. But the birds came and flew over the place where he was, bearing meat in their beaks, and the wolves suckled him, so that he was able to survive. When the *Shanyu* heard of this, he was filled with wonder and, believing that Kunmo was a god, he took him and reared him. When Kunmo had grown to manhood, the *Shanyu* put him in command of a band of troops and he several times won merit in battle. The *Shanyu* then made him the leader of the people whom his father had ruled in former times and ordered him to guard the western forts. Kunmo gathered together his people, looked after them and led them in attacks on the small settlements in the neighbourhood. Soon he had 20,000 or 30,000 skilled archers who were trained in aggressive warfare. When the *Shanyu* died [i.e. Jizhu – the "Old Chanyu" died *circa* 158 BCE – Watson (1993), p. 147], Kunmo led his people far away, declared himself an independent ruler, and refused any longer to journey to the meetings of the Xiongnu court. The Xiongnu sent surprise parties of troops to attack him, but they were unable to win a victory. In the end the Xiongnu decided that he must be a god and left him alone, still claiming he was a subject of theirs but no longer making any large-scale attacks on him.

"Now the *Shanyu* is suffering from the recent blow delivered by our armies, and the region formerly occupied by the Hunye king and his people is deserted. The barbarians are well known to be greedy for Han wealth and goods. If we could make use of this opportunity to send rich gifts and bribes to the Wusun people, and persuade them to move farther east and occupy the region which formerly belonged to the Hunye king [who surrendered to Han with 30,000 or 40,000 men in the fall of 121 BCE – see ibid, pp. 67, 153, 173], then the Han could conclude an alliance of brotherhood with them and, under the circumstances, they would surely do as we say. If we could get them to obey us, it would be like cutting off the right arm of the Xiongnu! Then, once we had established an alliance with the Wusun, Daxia [now controlled by the Da Yuezhi] and the other countries to the west could all be persuaded to come to court and acknowledge themselves our foreign vassals." *Shiji* chap. 123, from Watson (1993), pp. 237-238. See also: Beckwith (2009), pp. 6-7, and Jila (2006), pp. 161-177.

Compare the similar passage in *Hanshu* 61, which contains a number of interesting, but sometimes questionable, additions:

"The Son of Heaven asked [Chang] Ch'ien about the states such as Ta Hsia. Since he had already lost his noble rank, [Chang] Ch'ien took the opportunity to report as follows:

"When I was living among the Hsiung-nu I heard of Wu-sun; the king was entitled *K'un-mo*, and the *K'un-mo's* father was named Nan-tou-mi; originally [Wu-sun] had lived with the Ta Yüeh-chih between the Ch'i-lien [mountains] and Tun-huang; and they had been a small state. The Ta Yüeh-chih attacked and killed Nan-tou-mi, seizing his lands, and his people fled to the Hsiung-nu. An infant *K'un-mo* had recently been born, and the Pu-chiu *Hsi-hou*, who was his guardian, took him in his arms and ran away. He laid him in the grass and searched for food for him; and on coming back he saw a wolf suckling the child, furthermore there were ravens holding meat in their beaks and hovering at [the child's] side. Believing this to be supernatural, he then carried [the child] back to the Hsiung-nu, and the *Shan-yü* loved and reared him. When he had come of age, [the *Shan-yü*] delivered to the *K'un-mo* his father's people; he had him lead troops, and on several occasions he did so meritoriously.

"At the time the Yüeh-chih had already been defeated by the Hsiung-nu; making for the west they attacked the king of the Sai. The king of the Sai moved a considerable distance to the South and the Yüeh-chih then occupied his lands. Once the *K'un-mo* had grown to adulthood, he asked permission of the *Shan-yü* to avenge his father's wrongs. Going west he attacked and defeated the Ta Yüeh-chih, who again fled west, moving into the lands of the Ta Hsia. The *K'un-mo* despoiled the population of Ta Hsia, and then remained there in occupation.* His forces gradually grew stronger, and at the death of the *Shan-yü* he was no longer willing to attend at the court of the Hsiung-nu and serve them. The Hsiung-nu sent forces to attack him, but they had no success; and with an even greater respect for his supernatural powers they kept their distance.

"At the present the *Shan-yü* has recently suffered at the hands of the Han and the *K'un-mo's* lands[809] are empty. Barbarians love their old homelands and also greedy for Han goods. If we could only make use of the present opportunity to send generous presents to Wu-sun, and induce [its people] to move east and live in their old lands;[810] and if Han would send a princess to be the consort of [the king][811] and establish brotherly relations, the situation would be such that they would agree, and[812] this would result in cutting off the right arm of the Hsiung-nu [Gansu]. Once a link has been forged with Wu-sun, the states such as Ta-Hsia to its west could all be induced to come to court and become outer subjects[813] of Han."

From: *Hanshu* Chap. 61, in *CICA*, pp. 214-218.

***NOTE:** I wrote to Professor Hulsewé years ago about the mistake here regarding the Wusun "despoiling" the population of Ta Hsia (Daxia). This has been repeated by scholars claiming that the Wusun actually invaded Daxia. Professor Hulsewé replied suggesting this new rendering:

> "The K'un-mo despoiled the [Ta Yüeh-chih] horde and remained in occupation [of the Ta Yüeh-chih's original area]." Hulsewé – personal communication, 10 Aug. 1981.

This corrected one error – that of the Wusun (rather than the Da Yuezhi) invading and occupying Daxia. However, there is another error in the first sentence. The Wusun did not attack and "despoil" the Da Yuezhi in their "original homeland" (which was in and around the Gansu Corridor and Dunhuang), but only after they had displaced some Sakas and settled in the region of the Ili River and Issyk Kol. I translated this key passage again, correcting the two errors:

> "Now that the Kunmo was strong, he asked the Chanyu permission to seek revenge for his father. Thereupon, he stormed the Da Yuezhi to the west. The Da Yuezhi again fled west, on foot to the territory of Daxia. The Kunmo invaded this multitude [i.e. the Da Yuezhi in the Ili Valley and around Issyk Kul], and then settled there. His troops gradually grew stronger; then the Chanyu died, and he no longer agreed to attend the court and serve the Chanyu."

Hanshu 96B gives a shorter version of these events:

> "Later, when the *K'un-mo* of Wu-sun attacked and defeated the Ta Yüeh-chih, the Ta Yüeh-chih migrated to the west and subjugated the Ta Hsia; and the K'un-mo of Wu-sun took up his residence here. It is said : "For this reason, among the people of Wu-sun there are [elements of] the Sai race and the Ta Yüeh-chih race." From: *Hanshu* 96B in *CICA*, p. 145.

During the Later Han, the Wusun occupied Dzungaria, the region of (Lake) Issyk Kul and expanded further west at times through Semirechye to the region of Talas.

Some Yuezhi and Se/Sai reportedly stayed behind after the Wusun conquest. This implies that after they invaded the region some decades earlier some Sai had remained in the area.

Furthermore, the Xiao Yuezhi remained, seeking refuge among the Qiang in the mountains to the south and west of the Gansu Corridor after the original flight of the Da Yuezhi.

It is tempting to speculate in such cases that, perhaps, those who stayed behind were smaller tribes within the larger confederations of the Yuezhi or Sai, possibly differing in linguistic, ethnic or cultural backgrounds from the central tribal group.

Several scholars relate the Asiani with the Wusun due to the apparent similarity of the names. This makes it difficult to say how the Asiani became the rulers of the Tacharoi/Tocharoi in what is now Afghanistan when the Chinese texts indicate the Wusun remained well to the north and northwest of the regions finally settled by the Da Yuezhi.

> "The Asiani have been equated with the Wu-sun. It is true that 烏孫 wu-sun< .uo-suan< .o-swən (possibly år-swan, ➔ P. Boodberg, *HJAS* 1. 304, note 73, 1936) could be a transcription of Asiani. But besides the phonetic similarity there is little which would favor the equation and much that is against it, cf. Haloun, Zur Üe-tṣi-Frage 252-4." Maenchen-Helfen (1945), p. 74, n. 32.

Pulleyblank points out there are a number of serious inconsistencies between the accounts of the *Shiji* and the *Hanshu*:

> "The variations [in the *Hanshu*] from the *Shih-chi* may be summed up as follows: (1) K'un-mo's father's name is given as Nan-tou-mi; (2) the original home of the Wu-sun is specified as having been 'with the Great Yüeh-chih between Ch'i-lien and Tun-huang'; (3) Nan-tou-mi is said to have been killed, not by the Hsiung-nu, but by the Yüeh-chih; (4) this, not conquest by the Hsiung-nu, is given as the reason for the submission of the Wu-sun to the Hsiung-nu; (5) circumstantial details are added to the story of how the infant was miraculously saved; (6) the young K'un-mo, with the *shan-yü*'s permission, led his people west to take vengeance on the Yüeh-chih, who had meanwhile migrated westwards into the territory of the King of the Sakas—the Wu-sun defeated the Yüeh-chih, impelling them on further westwards against Ta-hsia; (7) just then the *shan-yü* died and thereafter K'un-mo no longer acknowledged allegiance to the Hsiung-nu (whereas in the *Shih-chi* the departure of the Wu-sun to the west only occurred *after* the *shan-yü's* death)." Pulleyblank (1970), p. 157.
>
> "The whole story of the Wu-sun vendetta against the Yüeh-chih is, I suspect, an imaginative reconstruction without any genuine historical basis, introduced partly for dramatic effect—vendetta as a motive for war was as familiar to the Chinese from the tales of the Spring and Autumn period as it was to the Greeks—partly to account for the ethnic distribution in the Wu-sun territory in the first century B.C. when it came under direct Chinese observation. We are told that there were both Saka and Yüeh-chih elements in the Wu-sun population, as well as Sakas in neighbouring small states in the Pamir. Moreover, when the Chinese made contact with Kashmir (Chi-pin) [see: Appendix F] over the Hanging Pass, they learned that the ruler there too was a Saka who had come from the north. They were told, or assumed, that the King of the Sakas had been driven out of his original home in the Pamir by the Yüeh-chih. Whether or not this particular detail had an historical foundation would be impossible to say but, at any rate, it is clear that no reliance can be placed on the way in which everything is tied together in the *Hanshu*." Pulleyblank (1970), p. 159.

The Wusun are said to have originally lived beside the Yuezhi, and were probably under their control until the Yuezhi were defeated (*circa* 176 BCE) by the Xiongnu king. See the quote from Enoki, et al. (1994), pp. 174-175; also Appendix L.

Some scholars argue that the claim the Wusun originally lived near the Yuezhi between Dunhuang and the Qilian Range was unlikely as the area was too small to support such a large population, and that it was, therefore, probably a later fabrication.

Others have speculated that, because of this apparent lack of space, the name 'Qilian,' during the Early Han referred to a longer range, and probably included the Barkol Range and the Tianshan/Tängri Tagh ('Heavenly Mountains') of today. See: Barber (1999), p. 122. Consult also Watson (1993), pp. 152, 171-172, 237; Harmatta (1994c), p. 488.

This claim seems invalid: see Appendix K – The 'Homeland' of the Yuezhi.

The Juyan Valley juts out into the Gobi desert for hundreds of kilometres and, during the Han era, was a very fertile region, but it has since largely dried up. See: note 12.23 and Appendix K. Benjamin adds:

> "The difficulty scholars have had in allowing for the possibility of an original Gansu location for the Wusun stems from research by Haloun, published in 1937. Haloun collected all the references to the original homeland of the Yuezhi, and argued that they must have occupied the whole of the Gansu corridor, as well as additional areas further to the east and northeast, leaving no room for the Wusun anywhere in the Gansu. However, whilst being very particular in collecting textual references to the Yuezhi, he simply ignored or waved aside similar specific references to the Gansu as also being the home of the Wusun. Thus, with apparently no room for the Wusun in the Gansu (even though this conclusion was based on the use of selective evidence), and with a general (although unjustified) assumption amongst modern scholars that the Xiongnu must have dominated the *whole* of Mongolia, the Wusun were automatically relegated to northern Xinjiang or the Altai, despite there being no evidence to justify this. As a result, Haloun (and later Pulleyblank) both incorrectly located the Wusun in the Altai. But a careful reading of evidence for the pre-expansion (i.e. pre-209 BCE) homeland of the Xiongnu shows that their western territory lay mainly in the Ordos region, extending beyond the Huanghe into the southeastern Gansu. This left an area in the northeastern Gansu where the early Wusun could very well have been lodged 'as a small state on the western border of Xiongnu territory', and thus there is no need to doubt the evidence of the Chinese sources." Benjamin (2007), pp. 51-52.

> "[The Xiongnu] . . . conquered the Loulan, Wusun, and Hujie [呼揭] tribes, as well as the twenty-six states nearby, so that all of them have become a part of the Xiongnu." *Shiji* Chap. 123, in Watson (1993), p. 140.

The *Hanshu* suggests that soon after the defeat and displacement of the Yuezhi [*circa* 166 BCE], the Wusun settled in Dzungaria and the Semirechiye/Zhetysu ('Seven Rivers') region, particularly the Ili River Valley and the region around the great lake of Issyk Kul.

> "[*Hanshu* 96B, according to *CICA*, p. 144, says Wusun] . . . adjoins the Hsiung-nu in the east, K'ang-chü in the north-west, Ta Yüan in the west and the various states of the walled towns in the south". Besides, from other passages of the sa/me chapter we learn that Wu-sun lay north of Chüan-tu which was either Qarategin or Irkeštam (A. 40b, 4 = p. 139), north of Ch'iu-tz'ŭ/Kučā (B, 14b, 2 = p. 164), and north of Yen-ch'i/Qarašahr (B, 24a, 10 = p. 178). Chapter 61 (5b, 7 = p. 218) locates Wu-sun east of Ta Hsia/Bactria. There is no doubt that all these indications refer to the territory briefly described in B, 1b, 6 = p. 144, and said to have been originally the land of the Sai/Saka (2a, 11 = ibid.). As K'ang-chü corresponds to the basins of the Ču, the Talas and the middle Syr-darya, and as

Ta Yüan is the Ferghāna Valley while the various states of the walled towns are the oases of the Tarim basin, the original land of the Sai/Saka – south-east of K'ang-chü, east of Ta Yüan and north of the states of the walled towns – must necessarily be sought for somewhere north of the T'ien-shan. That leads to its location around Issyk-Kul and along the upper courses of Ili, Naryn and Ču, as rightly pointed out by Haloun (1937) p. 246. So this is the territory the Wu-sun occupied after having expelled the Ta Yüeh-chih out of it (2a, 11–2b, 5 = pp. 144-145)." Daffinà (1982), p. 326.

"The Wu-sun were bounded by the Hsiung-nu to the east, by the settled peoples of East Turkestan to the south, by Ta-yüan (Ferghana) to the south-west and by K'ang-chü to the west. Their federation included locally conquered Saka tribesmen, as well as some Yüeh-chih. The question of the ethnic origin of the Wu-sun themselves remains debatable, and contradictory hypotheses have been advanced. The one thing that is clear is that the majority of the population consisted of linguistically Iranian Saka tribes." Zadneprovskiy (1994), p. 459. For details on the ancestry of the Wusun see the quote from Yu (2000), pp. 1-2, in note 1.64.

Per Petrovich Semenov, the remarkable Russian botanist who travelled through the Tianshan regions in 1856-1857, made some interesting comments about the Wusun:

"The Atban and Dulat tribes of the Great [Kirgiz] Horde still retained a common name of *usun* in the middle of the nineteenth century. Their sultans considered their clan to have originated from more ancient rulers than the Chinghiskhanids, the forefathers of many sultan families of the Middle Horde; it is quite possible that the sultans of the tribes which preserved the name *usuns* originated from the ancient *usun* rulers (*kun-mi*), with whom the Chinese dynasty had become connected as far back as the second century BC." Semenov (1998), p. 137.

"The Usuns remained the undisputed rulers of the Issyk-kul' basin for five centuries, and it would seem they must have left behind some monuments, of which one should refer the local stone images, the Bronze Age weapons found here, and generally the most ancient objects among those cast ashore by the waves of Issyk-kul'. . . .

Undoubtedly, what contributed most of all to the fall of the Usun state was the fact that the Huns, gradually forced out by Chinese policies from the vicinity of the province of Gan-su and from Tangut, also moved away to the west and found for themselves a second fatherland in Dzhungaria, having subordinated all the nomads who lived between the Tian'-Shan' and the Altai, and who belonged mainly to the Eastern Turkic tribes (Tu-kiue). Chinese chroniclers vigilantly observed the movements of their enemies, gathering detailed information about them, but at the beginning of our era they had already lost sight of them, contenting themselves with a final statement that they had left for Si-khai, that is 'the western sea', by which the Chinese historians meant the Aral-Caspian basin. It appears that the Chinese Huns, according to the testimony of their chroniclers, could not have gone to the west by any other route from Dzhungaria but that through the present-day Kirgiz steppes and across the river Ural into the Trans-Volga region, where for the first time the European Huns became known in the basin of the river Itil (Volga), which apparently gave its name to the famous Attila. Only the European Huns came into Europe from their second fatherland, not solely in their tribal composition, but as an agglomeration, composed of various tribes of nomads who lived between the Tian'-Shan' and Altai, and who recognized the political domination of the Huns. By no means all these tribes followed the Huns, and many remained on the beautiful pastures of

Dzhungaria; instead of them, during their further movement the Asiatic Huns carried away peoples whom they came upon on their way, mainly Finnish tribes.

Chinese chroniclers mention the Usuns as far back as before the beginning of the fourth century AD. Forced out of their Tian'-Shan' nomadic encampments at that time by the wave created by the great movement of the Huns, they fled partly to the south-west towards the upper Jaxartes and Trans-Oxiana, and partly to the north-west into the Kirgiz steppe, where they submitted to Turkic tribes (Tu-kiue), who had moved there, became mixed with them in unions, which in comparatively modern times received the name of Kirgiz-Kazakhs, and since then have now disappeared from the theatre of history. It is obvious that one should look for the remains of the Usuns among the tribes of the Karakirgiz and Kirgiz of the Great Horde, among whom on the one hand I met from time to time blue-eyed and red-haired people, and on the other hand, there survived the word 'Usun', by which the Kirgiz of the Great Horde designate two of their clans, but the Sarybagish – one of *their* clans. It is clear that no monuments, besides those stone images and some bronze weapons, could have survived from the nomads who lived here before the beginning of our era, but on the other hand the nature of the Tans-Ili region and the Tian'-Shan' foothills has here and there preserved its typical features, which were so well noted by the Chinese two thousand years ago." Semenov (1998), pp. 170-172.

"According to the *Hanshu* [96B], the Wusun numbered 120,000 households with 630,000 people and 188,800 under arms, which, if these figures are to be believed, would render them over twice as numerous as the entire settled population of the oasis states. . . .

As to their origins, the *Hanshu* emphasizes that they had only recently taken up their positions in the west and that their present territory had been previously occupied by the Sai. This name, in its earlier pronunciation (**sək* or **səg*), is commonly equated with the Iranian word *Saka*, the name applied in Iranian sources to the peoples rendered as Scythians in Western sources (the earliest reference to Scythians is in Near Eastern sources where an Assyrian document of Esarhaddon (680-669 BC) renders their name *iš-ku za-ai*, taken to derive from **škūz-*, hence our Greek *skythos*). The Sai were reputedly pushed out of their territory first by the Yuezhi (*c.* 177 BC) and then the Wusun, who at the time of the Han incorporated elements of both the Sai and the Yuezhi 'races'. It has been suggested that the Wusun may also be identified in Western sources as their name, pronounced the **o-sən* or **uo-suən*, is not far removed from that of a people known as the Asiani who the writer Pompeius Trogus (1st century BC) informs us were a Scythian tribe. There is another school of thought that has regarded the Wusun as the Issedones of Herodotus (see ill. 37 for another)[where it is proposed that "the name here may actually be cognate with that of the Ossetes, an Iranian people of the Eurasian steppes, who have survived only in the Caucasus"]." Mallory and Mair (2000), pp. 91-92. See Beckwith (2009), p. 405, n. 53.

". . . the name Wu-sun is regularly reconstructed for the period as *A-swin, which is a perfect transcription of Asvin [Aśvin], the name of the twin equestrian warrior-gods in the Vedas. I am inclined to think that is what both 'Wu-sun' and 'Asiani' represent, but of course I will probably never find anything that would confirm this beyond doubt, so other interpretations are possible, though I personally think they are much less likely." Christopher Beckwith (personal communication, 12 April, 2008). Also, Beckwith (2009), p. 376.

"As you know I currently think that Wu-sun and Asiani are the Chinese and Roman names for an authentic Iranian tribal name of *Asiyan, and that it was perhaps the

> oldest and most prestigious (royal?) tribe of the Sakas. But that's just a theory and I'm certainly interested in all other plausible suggestions.
>
> I think that Asianoi was the correct term in Greek too, faithfully reproduced in Latin by Pompeius Trogus (it is impossible for the Roman writers to have had a tradition independent of the Greek writers in this matter) but that most Greek writers tended to prefer Asioi (even after the initial use of Abioi was rejected as an obvious Homerism to appeal to Alexander), because of its closer similarity to the influential name of the Abioi in Greek culture, but chiefly because it removed the exact correspondence with the term Asianoi for ALL inhabitants of Asia which currently troubles modern researchers, and must have irritated the ancient Greeks too.
>
> I also think the earlier "Issedones" represents authentic *Asiyan too, and that the -y- was pronounced in a sufficiently "hard" way as to be misunderstood by Herodotus' source, the poet Aristeas, as more like a delta. Aristeas was one man (perhaps with a small retinue) whose ability to misconstrue (and/or mis-recall, when he later came to write) novel names spoken by novel peoples he encountered was rather greater than after Alexander's conquests brought large numbers of Greeks into permanent contact with these Saka peoples for hundreds of years unbroken." Mark Passehl (personal communication, 13 April, 2013).

Alternatively, Pulleyblank (1963), p. 136, says that the Wusun: "M. **·ou-suən** < ***·ậh-smən**, a nomadic people north of the T'ien-shan during the Later Han period, are probably to be identified with the Ἀσμίραιοι [Asmiraioi] of Ptolemy." Pulleyblank, ibid. p. 227, and he adds: "There is good reason to think that the Wu-sun spoke a Tocharian type of language."

However, there is evidence mounting that they actually spoke a Saka language though, as far as I know, these recent developments are still to be published.

Whatever their language and ethnic origins, the Wusun were a nomadic or semi-nomadic people who, after the Da Yuezhi moved to Daxia, raised horses and grazed their flocks on the rich steppe-lands in the basins of the Ili, Naryn and Chu rivers in Semirechye to the north of the Tianshan ranges, and the fertile pasturelands around Issyk Kul.

The Wusun king had his residence near the southeastern end of Issyk Kul, surrounded by mountains, and easily defended. The Ili River valley was doubtless the basis of their wealth, providing extensive rich pasturelands and control of major trade routes:

> "Kulja [Yining], it may be seen, has an air of its own; but that air is rightly come by, for it is the capital of the Nine Cities of Ili. This is a frontier, and the most vulnerable and hazardous frontier for a journey of many hundred miles. All the contrasting peoples that congregate there are aware that the possibility of upheaval and terror underlies the prosperity and ease of life, and for that reason take on a spirit of recklessness and devil-may-care. The town populations especially are unruly and dissipated.
>
> The valleys of the Ili River and its tributaries are the richest ground in Central Asia. As we talk of "white man's country" in Kenya or some other territory that lies outside of our natural heritage, so the Chinese talk of the Ili, as a fat, desirable land, but one in which, in that phrase which has no parent language, "the natives must be kept in order." Not only is there an abundant supply of water in the streams, but there is also an ample rainfall, so that almost no true desert is to be found between the streams or between the towns. Bread is cheaper here than anywhere else in a province of cheap food. In the mountains, iron is easily accessible, besides gold and other metals, while coal is even more readily obtained, and there is a great supply of timber. All the materials of necessary clothing, and even more solid comforts, are also produced in this sub-province, so that imports of Chinese origin are restricted to tea, silks, and articles of luxury requiring skilled manufacture. The tendency to be at

the same time claimed by a ruling Chinese population and divorced from economic dependence on China explains much of its bloody and revolutionary history; but indeed, its modern history is only a pendant to a long and savage past of invasion and war.

The Ili valley opens on to what must have been one of the most important of the intermediate regions on the cardinal route of migration between Mongolia and Southern Russia, the route used in the epoch-making migrations of the nomads. The forest shelters for winter and inviting pastures for summer seem to have tempted every tribe in temporary occupation to abandon the long trek and make a bid for permanent possession. Yet it was a trap, for the very fact that it was intermediary between the two great steppe regions, that of Southern Russia and that of Mongolia, laid it open to every horde in passage; and whatever tribe had occupied it, instead of having the freedom of movement of the open steppe, and the ability of evasion (so necessary in the warfare of mounted nomads), was bottled up by the T'ien Shan at its back. Thus the Tur Qara, the Yueh-chih,[1] the Huns, and the proto-Turkish tribes were halted for longer or shorter periods on the lower Ili, and from the early Middle Ages we have an increasingly coherent record of the successive rise to power, decline, and migration into new regions, of the Uighurs, Qara-Khitai, Mongols, and Qazaqs, and their different sub-tribes.

[1] If indeed these two are not alternative or successive names of the same people, who may have been connected with the "Scythians" of earlier time, and who were probably a blond Indo-Germanic race. Von Lecoq (*Auf Hellas Spuren*), bringing to bear the knowledge gained from manuscripts and even portraits recovered in Turfan, suggests the possibility of new identifications of the very highest importance in respect of the shadowy but fascinating study of the earliest tidal folk-movements."

Lattimore (1930), pp. 221-222 and note 1.

"In its upper reaches, as it comes down from the glaciers of the Tyan'-Shan', the Chu follows a southerly course at first, but twelve kilometres from Lake Issyk-Kul' it makes a right-angled bend and goes on to flow from east to west. This sudden change of course is caused by a stony ridge stretching over the whole twelve kilometres, which prevents the waters of the Issyk-Kul' from spilling into the Chu where it flows, twenty metres below the level of the lake. Only during the rainy season, when the level of the waters in the lake is high, does it overflow into the Chu along a bed running over the ridge.

It is the opinion of an engineer, supported by survey data of the Chu, that attempts were made at some time to deepen this bed and regulate the flow of water. He also thought that in the distant past the Chu must have flowed through the valley of the Issyk-Kul', gathering on its way the waters which now form the lake and which are rapidly evaporating, and was thus able to reach the sea. There were signs, he said, that after the volcanic upheaval which threw up the barrier between the river and the lake the inhabitants had made superhuman efforts to avert the catastrophe which threatened their valley by trying to pierce the twelve kilometre-long ridge. Apparently the task was insuperable with the technical means then available and the inhabitants were driven out of the land and settled elsewhere. The engineer claimed to have studied the ancient Hindu Vedas, and said that their description of this part of the country unmistakably pointed to the Jany-Dar'ya and the Chu. The theory that the plain covered by Lake Issyk-Kul' was once inhabited is further strengthened by the many domestic articles washed ashore in stormy weather, such as fragments of quaint-looking barrels, copper vessels of all sorts, etc., now exhibited in the museum at Przheval'sk or to be seen in the posting inns strung along the shore of the lake."
Pahlen (1964) – From: *Mission to Turkestan: Being the Memoirs of Count K.K. Pahlen, 1908-*

1909. Downloaded, from: http://www.iras.ucalgary.ca/~volk/sylvia/Pahlen.htm#thirteen on 11 December, 2005.

The Wusun first became of real importance to the Chinese after they fled to the west and took possession of Dzungaria, Issyk Kul, and Semirechye during the Early Han Dynasty. They controlled the main northern branches of the Silk Routes, providing a buffer for the Chinese against the raids of the Xiongnu, and became significant exporters of fine horses.

The Chinese began a complex course of diplomacy and bribery to win their favour and prevent them from becoming allies of the Xiongnu. A princess was sent to marry their leader, the 'Kunmi' (or Kunmo), *circa* 110 BCE, but she had to take second place to a princess sent earlier by the Xiongnu. *CICA*, p. 148, n. 400.

The capital of the main branch of the Wusun, referred to as the 'seat of the Greater Kunmi' in the *Hanshu*, was Chigu 赤谷 – literally 'Red Valley'. This town has so far remained unidentified but I believe it is now possible to locate it with a high degree of precision and confidence. See: Appendix J.

In 5 BCE, Bihuanzhi (or Beiyuanzhi) 卑爰疐 the younger brother of Mozhenjiang, the 'Lesser Kunmi' of the Wusun, (recently killed by the 'Greater Kunmi'), led a group of over 80,000 persons to the north and attached himself to the Kangju. From here, he harassed both the 'Greater Kunmi' and the new 'Lesser Kunmi.' The Chinese Protector General killed him in a surprise attack sometime between 1 and 3 CE. See: *CICA*, pp. 161-162, and n. 496.

There are only occasional references to the Wusun in the *Hou Hanshu*. However, there is the remark in Section 1 of the 'Chapter on the Western Regions' that, following the re-establishment of Chinese control in the Tarim Basin in 127 CE, "the Wusun and the countries of the Congling, put an end to their disruptions to communications to the west."

Chavannes incorrectly translated this passage so it reads that the Wusun, and the countries of the Congling, "broke (all relations with China)." Chavannes (1907), p. 167.

> "Little is known of the Wu-sun during the early centuries of the Christian era. Under pressure from the Ju-jan, a new group of nomadic tribes from Central Asia, the Wu-sun were obliged to abandon Semirechye and seek refuge in the T'ien Shan mountains. The last reference to the Wu-sun in the historical sources is in A.D. 436, when a Chinese diplomatic mission was dispatched to their country and the Wu-sun reciprocated. It is probable that by the middle of the fifth century A.D., the Wu-sun, with other neighbouring peoples, had succumbed to the Hephthalites."
> Zadneprovskiy (1994) p. 461.

Paul Pelliot and L. Hambis (*Histoire des compagnes de Gengizkhan*, vol. I. Leiden, 1951, p. 72) have suggested that the modern Sary-Uysuns among the Kirghiz, the Uzbek Ushuns and Uyshuns, and the Uysuns of the Kazakh Senior Juz, are descended from the Wusun.

> "Separate Wusun princedoms, remains of the ancient Huno-Wusun of northern and northwestern China, existed for a long time in Khangai and Beitin - Bishbalyk." Zuev (1960), p. 18.

Some of these tribes were living in territories previously inhabited by the Wusun until recent times. See: http://en.wikipedia.org/wiki/Uysyn#Uysyns_of_Middle_Ages

Appendix J: Chigu - The Court of the Wusun Ruler

According to the *Hanshu*, the 'seat of the Greater Kunmi', later 'the Greater Kunmo' (= 'Leader' or 'Shah') was named Chigu 赤谷 (literally 'Red Valley').

The titles Kunmo 昆莫 or Kunmi 昆彌 appear to be interchangeable. While they seem to be attempts to transcribe an indigenous Wusun title, it is of interest to note that the first character, *kun* 昆, means 'elder brother' in Chinese.

During the Yuanfeng period (110-105 BCE) the Kunmo of the Wusun was given a Chinese princess in marriage. *Hanshu* 96B in *CICA*, p. 148, records that "she had buildings constructed for her residence," but her poetry indicates that she had to live in a yurt for some time beforehand.

> "According to the Chinese chronicles, which were always detailed, there were 120,000 families of Usuns, who established themselves in this their second fatherland [the Issyk'-kul' basin], while their army comprised 188,000 horsemen. Their country, according to the descriptions in the Chinese chronicles, abounded in excellent pastures and herds, which made up their principal wealth, but it was cold and very rainy, and its mountains were covered with fir-trees and deciduous forests. The Usuns were primarily engaged in horse-breeding: the wealthy ones had more than four, and even five, thousand horses. Although the Usuns were under the supreme domination of the Huns, all the same they had their own quite powerful sovereigns, who bore the title of *kiun'-mi*. The Chinese readily sought an alliance with these Usun rulers in order to instigate wars, in case of need, in the rear of their powerful enemies. That is why in 107 BC the Chinese Court gave their princess in marriage to the Usun king with the title of *kiun'-di*. The first Chinese palace was built for this queen in the main nomad camp of the Usun king. This royal residence the Chinese called Chi-gu-chin, that is 'the town of the red valley'. This 'red valley', according to the idea which I formed on the spot, could only have been the valley of the Dzhargalan, but in any case Chi-gu-chin was not on the shore of Issyk'-kul', but at some distance from it, as is confirmed by ancient Chinese maps, and that was brought about by the need of the Usun rulers to be surrounded by rich pastures and not by water.
>
> A plaintive song of the Usun queen, written by her even before the building of the palace at the end of the second century BC, has been preserved by the Chinese chroniclers. Here is a translation of it:
>
> My relatives gave me in marriage
> And forced me to live in a far country
> My poor *iurta* [yurt] serves me as a palace
> Its walls upholstered with thick felt.
> Raw meat is my food,
> And sour milk is my drink.
> My senses long for my fatherland,
> And my heart is deeply wounded.
> Oh, if I could be a little bird of passage,
> How quickly I would fly there.
>
> But already during the reign of the queen's grandson, by the name of Ud-zy-ty, the kingdom became divided into bigger and smaller portions, and the temporary capital of Chi-gu-chin was abandoned for ever." Semenov (1998), pp. 170-171.

While Semenov's account is of interest, I disagree with him locating Chigu beyond the northeast end of Issyk Kul in the Dzhargalan Valley, which is much further from Wensu/Uch Turfan than the 610 *li* (254 km) indicated in *Hanshu* 96B. See *CICA*, p. 163.

If he is correct in his statement that Chigu was "abandoned forever" in the 1st century BCE, it would explain why it is not mentioned in either the *Hou Hanshu* or the *Weilüe*. Certainly, Wusun power was split between contesting chiefs and had begun to wane by the time of the Later Han.

Chigu is not mentioned again until the *Tangshu* (presented to the Emperor in 945 CE), where it is identified with a town called Chishan 赤山 or 'Red Mountain.'

The itinerary in the *Tangshu*, chap. XLIII, b, p. 14a, leads from the town of Dashi (*Ta-shih*) in the district of Wensu (modern Wushi) across the Bedel Pass to: "Tun-to cheng, which is none other than the town of Ch'ih-shan (lit. "Red Mountain"), capital of the Wusun."

Tun-to ch'eng ['the town of Dunduo'] is recorded to be some 160 *li* south of Issyk Kul, over a mountain range, and past a 'Lake of Snow.'

Although many of the distances in this account from the *Tangshu* are clearly incomplete or incorrect, it does indicate that the site of the capital of the Wusun should be sought some 160 *li* south of Issyk Kol. However, as there is no agreed estimated length for the *li* during the Tang era, and estimates vary widely, it is impossible to decide exactly how far south of Issyk Kol Chishan was located. All one can really do is to suggest that, as the Tang *li* was likely somewhere between a third and a half of a kilometre – Chishan/Chigu was probably somewhere between about 53 and 80 km. south of the lake.

This makes it likely that Chishan should be sought in the region of modern Kara-Say (approx. 77° 52' E, 41° 33' N), in the fertile Naryn Valley to the south of Issyk Kul. See: Chavannes (1900), pp. 9-10. Kara-Say is 100 km south of Barskoon/Barskon on the southern bank of Issyk Kol. From Barskoon, the ancient road to China headed through Kara-Say and over the Bedel Pass (4,284 m 14,055 ft) via Wushi to Aksu.

Because the Han *li* is known to have been 415.8 m. long, the Chigu 赤谷 or 'Red Valley' of the Han period can be located with some certainty. There is a very dramatic red-coloured mountain and valley not far south of the present town of Karaköl at the eastern tip of Issyk Kul:

> "About 25 km west of Karakol, at the mouth of the Jeti-Öghüz canyon is an extraordinary formation of red sandstone cliffs that has become a kind of tourism trademark for Lake Issyk Kul.
>
> A village of the same name is just off the main around-the-lake road. Beyond it the earth erupts in red patches, and soon there appears a great splintered hill called Razbitoye Serdtse or Broken Heart. (Legend says two suitors spilled their blood in a fight for a beautiful woman; both died, and this rock is her broken heart.)
>
> Beyond this on the west side of the road is the massive wall of Jeti-Öghüz. The name means Seven Bulls, and of course there is a story here too – of seven calves growing big and strong in the valley's rich pastures. Erosion has meant that the bulls have multiplied. They are best viewed from a ridge to the east above the road. From that same ridge you can look east into Ushchelie Drakanov, the Valley of Dragons.
>
> Below the wall of the Seven Bulls is one of Issyk Kul's surviving spas, the ageing Jeti-Öghüz Sanatorium, built in 1932 with a complex of several plain hotels, a hot pool, a restaurant and some woodland walks. . . .
>
> From here you can walk up the park-like lower canyon of the Jeti-Öghüz river to popular summer picnic spots. Some five km up, the valley opens out almost flat at Dolina Svetov, the Valley of flowers. . . . There are also said to be pre-Islamic petroglyphs up here, similar to those at Cholpon-Ata." King, et al. (1996), p. 392.

I am confident that Jeti-Öghüz is the 'Red Valley' and 'Red Mountain' of the early Chinese accounts. This is confirmed by the distances given in the *Hanshu* between Chigu and the town of Wensu or Uch Turfan (see: note 21.18), to the south of the mountains.

Hanshu 96B (*CICA*: 162) states the distance from Wensu to Chigu is 610 *li* (254 km). Wensu was in the valley of the Dashigan He (also known as the Taushkan Darya), and identified with the region of modern Wushi (Uch Turfan/Uqturpan), 85 km west of Aksu.

My measurements make it close to 254 km from Wensu to the Jeti-Öghüz Sanatorium. The route goes over the relatively low (4,284 m or 14,055 ft.) Bedel Pass, and via the main route across the Zauka or Dzhunkukucha Pass (3,833 m or 12,576 ft.) to Kyzyl Suu near the lake and from there a few kilometres east and then south up the Jeti-Öghüz Valley, past the famous red rock formations, to the old sanatorium and hot springs. I have checked these routes on Russian Military Topographic maps 1:100,000, 1970 and 1973, and the U.S. Defence Mapping Agency Aerospace Center map ONC6, Sheet F6, 1:1,000,000, revised Feb. 1981).

These measurements on modern maps corresponding to those in the Chinese texts add to the evidence that Chigu was located in the Jeti-Öghüz Valley.

> ". . . . Zauka Pass lies at 3,388 metres [11,116 ft.] in the Terskei Alatau, overlooking Issyk-kul'. The river Zauka, originating in perpetual snows near its summit, is some 64 km long and drains to the upper Naryn from an alpine lake, ice-covered for ten months of the year. The pass was already known in the seventh century by the Buddhist missionary Huan-tsang and was used by several nomadic hordes during the era of great folk migrations." Colin Thomas in Semenov (1998), p. 160, n.1.

> "On 11 June [1857] we left our camp and, having crossed the Dzherty-oguz, began climbing the saddle-like foothills which separated the main ridge of the Tian'-Shan' from its frontal chain, which the Karakirgiz called Orgochor. Having climbed up the sloping plain, we were now going further to the west-south-west at the same level, and after about twelve *versts* [12.84 km] we reached the river Bol'shaia Kyzyl-su. To the right of us opened up a magnificent view of the blue lake and of its beautiful quadrangular bay, protected by spits; the rivers Bol'shaia and Malaia Kyzyl-su discharged into it. To the left there was a marvellous view of the main Tian'-Shan' chain with its continuous row of snowy peaks. Along the way we came upon several graves and tumuli.
>
> After a further five *versts* [5.35 km] we crossed the Malaia Kyzyl-su, and still further on we now came out at the river Zauka, on which there was the famous mountain pass over the main crest of the Tian'-Shan', leading into Kashgaria and Fergana. . . .
>
> The terrain across which we came to the river Zauka was called Kyzyl-dzhar. It derived its name of 'Krasnyi Iar' (Red Cliff) from a huge outcrop of rather loose sandstone, filled with boulders and beautifully stratified with a clear alignment from east to west and a dip of 15° to the south. This interesting rock formation was Issyk-kul' conglomerate, of very ancient origin, found by me in this way for the first time at a distance of more than twenty *versts* [21.4 km] away from the lake and at a considerable height above its level.
>
> In historical terms the terrain was of no less interest. The historical role of this locality began as early as the seventh century AD. At that time (in the year 630) there penetrated hither the first traveller before me, an eye-witness who supplied geographical information about the Tian'-Shan' and Issyk-kul'. This was Huan-tsang, a Chinese Buddhist pilgrim, who passed through here on his way from one of the towns of Semigrad'e, situated to the north of the Tian'-Shan', namely Ak-su, the capital of the Turkic *kagan* (khan). The pilgrim's route went through the Tian'-Shan', probably over the Zauka Pass, came down to the southern (Terskei) shore of Issyk-kul', along which it went further across the river Barskuan, came out from the

western extremity of the lake to the river Chu, and passing through the Baum gorge, reached the upper reaches of the river Talas and the country of a 'Thousand springs' (Min-bulak). In this land there was at that time the headquarters of the Turkic Tugieu *kagan*, bearing the name of Suiab. . . .

At that time the interesting area of Kyzyl-dzhar, where I was on 12 June, was occupied by the tribe of Dzhikil', an offshoot of the Kharluk tribe, who established their seat here, which received the name of Dzhar (Iar). Since the end of the eighth century the locality of Iar (Kyzyl-dzhar) rivalled in its population and culture other similar areas on the northern slope of the Tian'-Shan', namely Suiab in the country of 'a thousand springs' and Barskaun near the discharge of the river of that name into Issyk-kul'. In all these areas, even at the time of my travels in 1857, ancient ruins were visible, the remains of ancient irrigation canals and orchard plantations, which were very ancient and had become completely wild, in the form of whole groves of apple-trees and apricot-trees." Semenov (1998), pp. 153-155.

"He [Abdullah Sultán, Governor of Turkistán, in 1545] assembled his forces in Káshgar. . . . On reaching Káfir Yári [they were joined by] Aiman Khwája Sultán, who had come by way of Sárigh-at-Akhuri. In the night it was decided that the Khán should proceed by way of Báris Káun, and Aiman Khwája Sultán by way of Janku.[1]

On the next day, Aiman Khwája Sultán marched off in the direction of Báris Káun. As they were descending from the pass of Báris Káun, Khwája Ali sent two men of the Kirghiz, whom he had captured, with news that [Muhammad Kirghiz] and his followers were lying on the shores of Issigh Kul, at the mouth of the Báris Káun [stream], ignorant [of the approach of the enemy]. Now Issigh Kul is a month's march from Káshgar. . . .

1. Evidently the passes of *Barskun* and *Zauka* (as shown on our maps) which lead across the range bounding the Issigh-Kul valley on the south. *Káfir-Yári* must have been near the southern end of these passes, and *Sárigh-At* some distance to the south-east. See Kostenko's *Turkistan*, vol. ii., pp. 66-7.)"

From the *Tarikh-i-Rashidi* [composed in 1541-42 CE]; Elias (1895), p. 350 and n. 1. **NOTE:** The Báris Káun or Barskun was probably the Bedel Pass (4,284 m or 14,055 ft.) (JEH).

"Having completed the additional survey of the Kyzyl-dzhar locality, we quickly set off to catch up with our detachment, which was slowly going down along the road towards Issyk-kul'. We went straight by the ancient ruins across the steppe foothills of the Tian'-Shan', and having caught up with our detachment, by five o'clock in the afternoon we came out to that beautiful lake's bay, into which both Kyzyl-su rivers discharged." Semenov (1998), p. 163.

Zuev (1960), p. 21, claims that Chigu's "other names were "Kün (Hun) city": Kün-kat, and "City of Bag."

To sum up, it now seems almost certain that Chigu was situated close to the original site of the Kunmo's encampment in the Red Valley near the southeastern end of Issyk Kul – not far from modern Karakol City.

Appendix K: The Yuezhi people

Understanding the rise of the Kushan Empire is essential to comprehending Central Asian history as a whole, including the development of both the overland and maritime Silk Routes linking countries from Japan to the Atlantic and the east coast of Africa. These routes were crucial to the early spread of Buddhism and Christianity, and the exchange of technologies, art and philosophies, and much more.

The study of the Da Yuezhi and the following Kushan Empire was hampered by a lack of firm evidence for the dating and the line of succession of their various kings and the relationships between them. Consensus was elusive. Each time scholars appeared to be on the brink of solving one or other of these puzzles some counter-evidence or argument appeared, throwing everything back into doubt.

The discovery of the renowned 'Rabatak inscription' found in 1993 at Rabatak, near Surkh Kotal in Afghanistan has led to a breakthrough in our knowledge of the Kushan Empire. It relates to the rule of the great Kushan Emperor, Kanishka I. Inscribed on rock in the Bactrian (or 'Aryan') language written in Greek script, it gives details of Kanishka's family from the time of his grandfather, Kujula Kadphises, to Kanishka, and refers to the establishment of Kanishka's era.

This era was used on many inscriptions from Kanishka's lifetime and those of his successors - well into the 3rd century CE. The later dates often have "dropped-hundreds" (first proposed by Lohuizen-De Leeuw (1949), pp. 271-272; 307), so that a date of, say, 27 – can be read as 27, 127, or 227, as the case may be, depending on the context.

The "dropping of hundreds" is a common process and one we still use today. For example, a person might say: "I was born in '82" – meaning 1982 - and this meaning would be clear for a long period of time – at least until sometime after 2082.

> ". . . that this continued era is nothing but the old Kuṣāṇa era, in continuous use at Mathura in the fourth and early fifth centuries, always returning to 1 after the lapse of one century, while the newly introduced Gupta dates continue to grow without such a feature." Falk (2012), p. 134.

The newly deciphered inscriptions provide clarification of relationships, while new dates have been proposed for the inception of both the Azes and Kanishka eras – as discussed in the Introduction.

The new information about the Da Yuezhi and their successors, the Kushans, now established with reasonable certainty, allows a far more informative and accurate reconstruction of events than was possible just a few years ago.

The 'Homeland' of the Yuezhi

Both the *Shiji* 123 and *Hanshu* 96A claim that the Yuezhi first lived between Dunhuang and the Qilian Shan or 'Heavenly Mountains.' See Dubs (1993), p. 234 and *CICA*, p. 120.

Many scholars have found this a stumbling block as, at first glance, there does not appear to have been enough room for such a large group as the Yuezhi to flourish, much less share this area with the Wusun tribe, as claimed. See: note 1.64 and Appendix I.

However, these descriptions only mention the northwestern side of the territory. There are a number of Chinese texts which indicate that the Yuezhi originally lived in a much larger area than that indicated in these brief notices in *Shiji* 123 and *Hanshu* 96A.

One can be found in the *Hou Hanshu* itself, in its chapter on the Qiang people, the Qiang juan, 84.48, which reads:

> 湟中月氏胡，其先大月氏之別也，舊在張掖、酒泉地。Downloaded from: http://ctext.org/hou-han-shu/xi-qiang-zhuan 2 February, 2014. This translates as:

"The Huangzhong[1] Yuezhi Hu (= "barbarians" or "Westerners") were a part of the former Great Yuezhi, (and) used to be from the region of Zhangye and Jiuquan [commanderies]."

NOTE: the modern town of Huangzhong is located at: 36° 25'N; 101° 34'E., or about 80 km east of Lake Koko Nor (Qinghai Hu), and about 10 km southwest of modern Xining. The Huangzhong Yuezhi were among the Yuezhi who fled to the mountains, remaining there when the Da Yuezhi fled far to the west. They, and perhaps other related mountain peoples were later referred to as the Xiao (or 'Lesser') Yuezhi. Zhangye and Jiuquan were commanderies centered in the Gansu corridors [see: Appendix I] – but with significant fertile territories extending beyond the corridor itself, in particular, the rich and well-watered Edsin Gol which thrust some 300 km northwest into Mongolia was capable of supporting a large population.

The *Tangshu* adds that the Yuezhi originally lived in the town of Zhaowu 昭武 to the north of the Qilian Mountains. The historical geography of Li Chaoluo (1769-1841), places the town of Zhaowu to the north-west of Ganzhou 甘州 (an early name for modern Zhangye City), in the province of Gansu. Chavannes (1900), p. 133, and n. 1.

"It was the Yuezhi who previously lived in the town of Zhaowu, to the north of the Qilian Mountains. Having been beaten by the Turks [sic - read Xiongnu], they gradually moved south dwelling in the Tsungling Mountains, and, entering them, took possession of this territory." *Tangshu*, 221, b, p. 1. Translated and adapted from Chavannes (1900), pp. 133-134.

Zhaowu 昭武 is also the name of a commandery founded in 117 BCE, in the modern county of Zhangye 張掖, in the centre of Gansu province. See: *GR*, Vol. I, p. 234.

This strategic position suggests that the Yuezhi originally controlled traffic through the Gansu corridor, the main route from China to the west. As Zhangye was at the main entrance to the Juyan corridor that leads towards the heart of Mongolia, the Yuezhi very likely controlled and occupied that territory as well.

Alternatively, perhaps, this was the "original homeland" of the Wusun who were described as being a 'small nation' at this period, living just west of the Xiongnu.

The *Kuodi zhi,* or "Complete Geographical Treatise," which was, according to Wilkinson, p. 739, by Li Tai et al, an "Early Tang geographical work that was recovered in the Qing from scattered sources such as annotations to the *Shiji*. . . ." provides us with further details of the extent of the Yuezhi's 'homelands'. It says:

括地支云
凉甘肅延沙州等地本大月氏。 This translates as:

"The *Kuodi zhi*, says: "Liang, and Gansu, as far as Shazhou [Dunhuang], etc., (was) the original territory (of the) Da Yuezhi."

The economist Guan Zhong (*circa* 720-645 BCE) referred to the Niuzhi 牛氏 (thought to be an early form of the name Yuezhi 月氏) supplying jade to China in 645 BCE. See: Lebedynsky (2006), p. 59. Further, all the jade items found in a Shang Dynasty tomb (early 12th century BCE) came from Khotan. Liu (2001), p. 265; see the quote in Appendix S.

If the identification of the name Niuzhi with the Yuezhi is accepted, it establishes that they used, and presumably controlled, the routes through the Gansu Corridor, and via Dunhuang to Khotan as early as the 7th century BCE (and perhaps earlier). They were still in the area almost five hundred years later when the Xiongnu forced them out *circa* 176 BCE. Therefore, it seems reasonable to accept this region as their "homeland."

The Gansu corridor provided the main conduit for communications between China and countries to the northwest and west. It offered opportunities for limited areas of intensive agriculture, and extensive grazing lands. However, even with the addition of the important oasis of Dunhuang (which is said to have had a population of 76,000 in the 2nd century CE – see: Bonavia (2004), p. 162), it would probably still have been insufficient to provide enough food and animal fodder for such a large a group. This explains why many scholars have sought to expand the home territory of the Yuezhi far to the north.

One theory suggests that, during the early Han Dynasty, the Qilianshan referred to a more extensive range that included the Barkol ranges as well as parts of the Tianshan to the north of the Tarim and Turfan basins. However, this claim lacks support in the literature and has always seemed unnecessary and unconvincing to me.

There are three large territories mentioned in the Chinese sources in addition to those mentioned in the brief notices in *Shiji* 123 and *Hanshu* 96A that may have formed part of the "original" territory of the Yuezhi. Together with Gansu and Dunhuang, they could have supported the large population indicated in the historical texts. These three territories are:

1. Liang. A large, but poorly defined ancient territory, most of which was included in the prefecture of Liangzhou during the Western (Former) Han, just prior to 100 BCE.

> "**Liang** (Liang) 凉(州). **liang² chou¹** (Liangzhou) **1.** (*Historical geography*) *Prefecture* instituted under the Western Han controlling a part of Gansu and Ningxia, Qinghai and part of modern Inner Mongolia. . . ." *GR* vol. IV, p. 13, no. 6972.

There are some interesting notes on Liang in Rafe de Crespigny's *Northern Frontiers* (1984):

> "The Liang province of Later Han was divided in two by the Yellow River, flowing eastwards from the Tibetan massif and then north towards the desert land of the Ordos. In this region, unlike other territories, the Yellow River was of only minor importance as a communications route: its valley and its waters provide some opportunity for travel upstream or down, but river transport is generally practicable only during the high water of summer, and there were, in any case, few places of interest or value along the stream. On the contrary, in fact, in the time of Qin and at the beginning of Former Han the Yellow River served as the frontier line of the empire, and during later centuries it was a barrier to be overcome between China and central Asia.
>
> According to *Shi Ji*, the Great Wall of the empire of Qin began at Lintao, in the valley of the Tao river south of present-day Lanzhou, then ran north to the region of Lanzhou, and then northeast below the Ordos. It was not until the time of Emperor Wu, shortly before 100 BC, that the Han established a military and political presence northwest across the Yellow River and founded the commanderies of Hexi "West of the River". Jiuquan, Zhangye and Dunhuang were probably established in 104 and subsequent years, Wuwei and Jincheng in the half-century following." de Crespigny (1984), p. 7.

The name, Zhangye ("to extend the arm") was an abbreviation of: "To extend the arm of the country, through to the Western Regions." See the quote in Psarras (2003), note 1.25.

> "At this time the Han forces in the east had conquered the barbarian states of Huimo and Chaoxian and made provinces out of them, while in the west the Han had created the province of Jiuquan [in 104 BCE, or shortly after] in order to drive a wedge between the Xiongnu and the Qiang barbarians and cut off communications between them. It had also established relations with the Yuezhi people and Daxia (Bactria) farther west and had sent an imperial princess to marry the ruler of the Wusun people, all in an effort to create a split between the Xiongnu and the states to the

west which had up to this time aided and supported them. In addition, the Han continued to expand its agricultural lands in the north until the frontier had been pushed out so far as Xuanlei [胘雷]. In spite of all these moves, however, the Xiongnu did not dare to voice any objections. This year Zhao Xin [趙信], the marquis of Xi, who had been acting as adviser to the *Shanyu*, died [*circa* 111 BCE]." *Shiji* 110 in Dubs (1993), p. 156.

NOTE: The Huimo, also known as the Yemaek, were living in Manchuria and the Korean Peninsula and are said to be one of the tribes that later made up the Koreans. The Chaoxian were an ethnic group living on the Korean Peninsula. So far, I have been unable to locate Xuanlei. (JEH)

As seen above, the Yuezhi were a large, powerful confederation living in the region for several centuries at least. They controlled the Hexi/Gansu Corridor, which is the main route from the west to the northern Chinese plains in the basin of the Huang He/Yellow River. The Yuezhi made great profits from trading of jade and horses into the Chinese empire. The text adds: "Formerly they were very powerful and despised the Xiongnu." Dubs (1993), p. 234. The Xiongnu bordered them to the east:

"The [Xiongnu] kings and leaders of the right [west] live in the west, the area from Shang Province west to the territories of the Yuezhi and Qiang tribes." *Shiji* 110, from Watson (1993), p. 136.

An estimate of the population size of the Da Yuezhi may be inferred from the claim of *Shiji* 123 that, after they had been defeated and fled to the west, they still had 100,000 to 200,000 "archer warriors." This indicates a total of up to 800,000 people, and perhaps more.

The original population of the Yuezhi must have been significantly larger, as the figures in the *Shiji* refer to the period after they had suffered at least two major defeats and some tribes who had fled into the mountains for safety among the Qiang had been left behind:

"Those [of the Yuezhi defeated by the Xiongnu] who could not make the great trek westwards remained behind among the Qiang barbarians, generally considered to be Proto-Tibetans, in the 'Southern Mountains' (another ambiguous location but probably corresponding to today's Qilian and Altun ranges, southwest of Dunhuang) where they constituted the Lesser Yuezhi." Mallory and Mair (2000), pp. 58-59.

2. Juyan. As mentioned above, Juyan was a well-watered and fertile corridor that stretched some 300 km from Zhangye in Gansu, northeast towards the heart of Mongolia. It ended in a large region of lakes and grasslands at the south-west edge of the Gobi Desert. it has become far more arid in recent times.

"**JUYAN** 居延. **1.** County. WESTERN HAN: seat: southeast of Ejin Qi, west Inner Mongolia (Tan v. 2:33-34, ②6). **2.** [Zheluzhang 遮虏障]. Border pass in the Juyanze area. WESTERN HAN: 102 BC–. **~ HAI** -海 [Juyanze -澤; Xihai 西海]. Lake, in north Ejin Qi, west Inner Mongolia (Tan v. 2:33-34, ①6)(DSFY 63.2976, 2979). Xiong (2008), p. 274.

"It is within the district of Kanchow [Zhangye] that the great Black River dashes out through a gorge in the Richthofen Range [the Qilian Mountains] and spreads itself across the plain. Having watered Kanchow, it rushes on to create the oasis of Kaotai, then turns direct north into Mongolia, changing its name to that of Edsin Gol. The enchanted forests on its banks owe their beauty to its flow. Then, suddenly, it ceases to function and finds a grave in the twin salt-lakes of Gashun Nor and Sogo Nor." Cable (1934), p. 17.

The Hexi/Gansu corridor stretches northwest all the way from the upper basin of the Huang He/Yellow River to the region of Dunhuang. Two rivers flow northeast from the Gansu corridor past the ancient major oasis and city of Zhangye (Kanchow) – see the end of note 1.27. They then travel through the Juyan Valley some 300 kilometres towards Mongolia ending in a vast inland delta and region of lakes covering about 10,000 sq. km (3,900 sq. miles).

These lakes were quite substantial until modern times. Goshun Nur or the 'Western Lake' reportedly still covered an area of 267 km^2 (103 sq. mi.) as recently as 1958 but had dried up completely in 1961, but has been reported to have increased slightly to cover 38 km^2 (15 sq. mi.) by August 2012. See the 'Lake area as of August 2012 according to the Ejin Weather Station.' Downloaded from: http://www.weather.com.cn/neimenggu/sy/tqyw/08/1695728.shtml (in Chinese) on 7 August 2013. Also, see: note 12.23.

This note from *circa* 61 BCE illustrates there were a number of other, smaller fertile valleys accessible to whoever controlled the Gansu Corridor:

> "Furthermore, both Wuwei district and Rile in Zhangye have open valleys with water and grass on their northern borders. We fear that the Xiongnu and the Qiang are in collusion, and that they plan a great invasion of Zhangye and Jiuquan in the hope of cutting off the Western Regions." *Hanshu* 69, from: Dreyer (2008), p. 684.

In ancient times, the region was clearly capable of supporting quite a large population:

> "**Hei River** [黑河, lit. "black river"; *Hei He*] river rising in central Gansu province, China, and flowing into the western Alxa Plateau (Ala Shan Desert) in western Inner Mongolia Autonomous Region. The river is formed by a series of small glacier-fed rivers flowing north from the Nan and Qilian mountain ranges in Gansu, between Zhangye and Jiuquan. It then flows northward across the desert into a depression filled with salt marshes and swamps that vary greatly in size from one season to another. Between Dingxin and Ximiao it is called the Ruo River. At Ximiao in Inner Mongolia the river bifurcates into two streams, the Xi (Morin) and Dong (Narin) rivers, which empty, respectively, into Lakes Gaxun (Gashun) and Sub (Sogo).
>
> The Hei valley is virtually the only part of the Alxa Plateau that has any permanent agriculture or permanent population. It was colonized on a small scale as long ago as the 1st century BC; its permanent settlement is comparatively recent. Even with irrigation, however, which is imperative in the arid climate of the area, the intense salinity of the soil is a major problem for agriculture.
>
> The lower course of the Hei River from about 102 BC formed a forward defense line for the armies of the Han dynasty (206 BC–AD 220), defending the region against the nomadic Xiongnu. In 1930–31 a Sino-Swedish expedition in the area discovered great numbers of documents written on wooden strips and dating from the period before the Dong (Eastern) Han (AD 25–220). Most of them date from 73 to 48 BC and are the earliest surviving Chinese official documents." From: *Encyclopaedia Britannica Online*. Downloaded on 16 November, 2011.

Juyan was sometimes referred to as 沙陰地 *Shayindi*: 'The 'Land Hidden in the Sands.' See: Dreyer (2008), p. 677 and 678, n. 38.

Two thousand years ago, the rivers were considerably larger and emptied into substantial lakes at the northeast end of the valley. This provided a long fertile strip of land, watered by two roughly parallel rivers, ending in a large, well-watered delta and lake system. It also held an important strategic position controlling the easiest and shortest communication routes from the heartland of Xiongnu territory across the Gobi Desert, to China and the 'Western Regions.'

> "The cost of maintaining the Han hold in these parts had involved further work and continual expense to the east, where it had become necessary to extend the earthworks and watchtowers far beyond the limits of the defences built in the time of the First Ch'in emperor. The new line of communications led westward as far as Tun-huang. At the same time a supplementary branch was built in a northerly direction, at right angles to the main line, to take advantage of the water supplies of the Edsen gol at Chü-yen, and set up agricultural garrisons there. These were intended to supply the conscript troops stationed on the main east-to-west line. Fragments of the written records made by these forces testify to their professional standard and give some idea of the extent of the supplies needed for the maintenance of the garrison."
> Yü (1986), p. 412.

The Juyan valley with its rivers and lakes, as well as the Dunhuang oasis, and the Gansu corridor were probably all controlled by the Yuezhi until their final defeat by the Xiongnu in 166 BCE – see: Dorn'eich (2013). The western forces of the Xiongnu under the Hunye (W-G: Hun-ya) king quickly occupied much of the territory abandoned by the Yuezhi, including Juyan, and remained there until late in the 2nd century BCE.

The Chinese then sought to consolidate their control of the region by building fortifications. To bolster Han forces in the Gansu Corridor they stationed military units near the entrance to the Juyan Valley made up of some of the Xiao Yuezhi left behind after the bulk of the confederation moved to the west .

The Emperor sent Zhang Qian on a mission to the Wusun *circa* 118 BCE to encourage the Wusun to move back into the Gansu region, which was unsuccessful. However, relations between Han and Wusun improved after some Wusun envoys were taken to the capital and impressed with China's might. "For the first time the states of the north came into communication with Han," and the northern Silk Route was open for trade. Finally, the Han strengthened the relationship by sending a princess in the Yuanfeng period (110-105 BCE) to marry the Wusun Kunmo, "with a very rich store of gifts." See: Watson (1993), pp. 238-240 and *Hanshu* 61 and 96B – in *CICA*, pp. 145 ff., and 218 ff.

> "According to *Shiji*, the Great Wall of the empire of Qin began at Lintao, in the valley of the Tao River south of present-day Lanzhou, then ran north to the region of Lanzhou, and then northeast below the Ordos. It was not until the time of Emperor Wu, shortly before 100 BC, that the Han established a military and political presence northwest across the Yellow River and founded the commanderies of Hexi "West of the River". Jiuquan, Zhangye and Dunhuang were probably established in 104 and subsequent years, Wuwei and Jincheng in the half-century following.
>
> Under Later Han, the commanderies of Wuwei, Zhangye, Jiuquan and Dunhuang stretched in that order from southeast to northwest along the present-day Gansu corridor. On the southwest, they were backed by the Qilian Shan and the mountainous region of present-day Qinghai. To the north and east they faced the Helan Shan, the Tengger and other deserts on the edges of the Gobi. The cities and settlements were based on oases, supplied by the snowmelt streams which flow from the high ground to the south and then disappear into marshes in the desert. As in the Tarim basin of central Asia, irrigation agriculture was maintained around these cities, and the settled farming economy was sufficient to provide a frontier defence for the trade and communications of the Silk Road which led through the Western Regions to India and Rome.
>
> This region of the Gansu corridor was not necessarily and naturally the base for an agricultural economy. It had formerly been taken over from chieftains of Xiongnu states, whose people had no doubt found adequate grazing grounds and pastures

among the marshes and along the rivers of this territory. Though the military presence of Han was reinforced by agricultural colonies and settlements, the water supply of the rivers today is still changeable, and ruins in the desert testify to the loss of oases and the need for new settlement elsewhere. The maintenance of Chinese colonisation during the Han period was by no means impossible, but it required constant effort and care.

In one part of this region, now known by the Mongol name of Edsin Gol, the Ruo Shui flows past the present city of Jiuquan for more than three hundred kilometres into the desert. Nowadays, the Edsin Gol provides little more than brackish water and salt pans, but in the time of Han these marshes were fertile, and abundant with wild life. The whole river system then provided a salient of arable land stretching into the heart of the desert.

This territory [established as in 102 BCE – see: Psarras (2003), p. 236], called Juyan by the Han Chinese, was maintained and garrisoned by the empire from the time of Emperor Wu until the last century of Later Han. Militarily, the outpost of the Great Wall was important for two reasons: as a supply point for the garrisons in the northwest and, perhaps more significant, as a means to deny this prosperous region to the northern nomads. Left undefended, Juyan would have provided an ideal route for attack against the Chinese commanderies of the corridor itself.

During Former Han, therefore, the Zhelu Zhang (Fortress to Block the Enemy), had been constructed by the marshes of the Edsin Gol, and it was from this base, for example, that the general Li Ling went forth on his disastrous attack against the Xiongnu in 99 BC.

South of the Juyan salient, the main line of defences followed the Great Wall, which ran in this region from the passes of Yumen Guan and Yang Guan in Dunhuang commandery of the far west along the northern edge of the Gansu corridor past Jiuquan, Zhangye and Wuwei." de Crespigny (1984), pp. 7-9.

"Quite soon, however, his [Sang Hongyang's] proposal bore fruit, with the establishment of the garrison lines in the north-west (*ca.* 100 BCE) where conscripts were assigned to the production of food and the necessary work of irrigation (at Juyan 居延, in modern Gansu)." Loewe (2006), p. 153.

"Juyan Site spreads across Jinta County of Gansu Province and the Erjina Banner of the Inner Mongolia Autonomous Region.

Juyan is the site of the beacon towers and walls of the frontier fortress under Ju Yan and Jian Shui of the Zhangye prefecture during the Han Dynasty (206BC-220AD). The frontier fortress stretches from the northeast to the southwest, with a total length of about 250 kilometers. Built in 102BC, it was abandoned in the late Eastern Han (25-220). The frontier fortress acted as a strategic pathway to the West and a barrier along the Gansu Corridor. It also played an important role in severing the connection between the Huns and the Qiangs [sic], and held a special position in the Han strategy towards the Huns.

During excavations in 1930, over 10,000 bamboo and wooden slips were unearthed from the Han Dynasty. Between 1972 and 1976, another 20,000 slips were unearthed at the Pochengzi Jiaqu Palace Site, the fourth beacon-fire tower ruins of the Jiaqu and Jianshui Jinguan Site. These three sites all have their own special features, providing important clues to forming a comprehensive understanding of the architectural style of beacon-fire towers of the Han Dynasty.

The Pochengzi Jiaqu Palace Site comprises constructions of the Zhang and Wu, both located in the northwest. Covering an area of 23.3 square meters, the small castle contains houses, kitchen ranges and sties. Unearthed cultural relics include bows, arrows, bronze arrowheads and armor, together with iron farm implements, tools and various daily articles.

The fourth beacon tower of Jiaqu is very large; it has a remnant 3.4 meters high. The cone-shaped tower is made of tampered earth on an eight-meter-long base on each side. In the southwest corner of the beacon tower is a kitchen range with a chimney where smoke was released into the sky in emergencies.

The Jianshui Jinguan Site is built on a mountain pass and contains a large number of cultural relics, such as knives, swords and arrowheads; fragments of clothing made of silk, gunny [a coarse jute or hemp fabric], hide and leather; and torches used for igniting the beacon fire. These findings reflect the military activities of the period.

Han slips found at the site provide a wide range of records that can be applied to many fields, including politics, military affairs, the economy, culture, science and technology, law, philosophy, religion and different ethnic groups. They not only recorded military activities in the Juyan area, but also kept official documents from the mid-Western Han to early Eastern Han periods, providing important materials for the study of Han history and culture." Downloaded on 17 November, 2011 from: http://www.chinaculture.org/gb/en_travel/2003-09/24/content_33524.htm

"The ancient settlement of Juyan is today known as Ejina Banner (Ejin Qi), in Inner Mongolia, and lies 90 km northeast of Jinta county, Gansu province, northwest China. It occupies a very strategic location between two vital areas: Mongolian grasslands to the north and the Hexi corridor in Gansu. The grasslands range east-west and were home to the powerful Xiongnu tribal confederacy. The Chinese thought of these nomadic or semi-settled nomadic peoples as uncivilized barbarians who raided Chinese settlements for food and other goods.[3] The Hexi Corridor was China's main conduit from the Han dynasty capital at Chang'an (modern day Xi'an), and subsequently at Luoyang. To Central Asia, India, Afghanistan, Iran and further west to Europe.

By 177 BCE the Xiongnu had overcome most of the oasis kingdoms in eastern Central Asia, and were able to draw on the resources of the region. These resources were significant, and the region became known as "the right arm of the Xiongnu". In 138 BCE China sent its first envoy Zhang Qian to seek military alliance with the enemies of the Xiongnu and cut off "its right arm". As a result of this and other early missions, the Han government at great expense set out to develop, maintain and guard the route through the Hexi corridor. Fortifications were built, and farms and settlements were established to house and feed both the great numbers of troops that were stationed there and the people who passed through on official and unofficial business. The Han defeated the greater Xiongnu confederacy in 102 BCE. They took over the homeland of the Juyan tribe of the Xiongnu, and installed a Chinese county level administration at Juyan. Juyan was one of nine counties in Zhangye prefecture and comprised two townships and 82 villages. It was temporarily renamed Jucheng during the Wang Mang period (9-23 CE), and was gradually abandoned from 31 CE.[4]

The Juyan sites were built on the fertile land alongside the Ruoshui River and near the Juyan Lake. The river originates in the Qilianshan Mountains, and flows north through the prefecture-seat of Zhangye, where it splits east-west and then flows in a northwesterly [sic – north-easterly] direction through the desert to the

Juyan Lake. It is understandable that the Han fought the Xiongnu for this strategic location and set up farming garrisons on the fertile land.[5]

3 This stereotyping has been questioned, for example by di Cosmo, "Ancient Inner Asian Nomads."

4 He, "Han jian – xiangli zhi".

5 Gansu Juyan yuanjiudui, "Juyan Handai Yizhi"."

Wang (2008), p. 61.

"On two different occasions, in 1927 and 1934, I have spent several weeks in the lower Etsin-gol, and I have never been able to find this region anything but wonderful and delightful, an earthly paradise after the long journey through the eastern Gobi ; one is fascinated at the sight of the ancient poplars, enjoys the shade of the foliage in summer, and in the winter listens in delight to the rustling of the wind in their leafless tops. The sand dunes stretch their curved banks like giant dolphins, now quite naked and shifting before the wind, now covered with vegetation and held fast by tamarisks, whose handsome violet sprays blossom in spring, and whose impenetrable thickets afford a refuge to the shy, graceful pheasants. And amid this curious, genuinely Central Asiatic scenery the river cleaves its course sword-like through the Gobi, the world's greatest desert.

When, after resting awhile, one quits this region and its inexhaustible store of water, pasture and fuel, and fares westward through the fearful desolation of the Black Gobi, one feels as if one were on board a ship leaving a luxuriant South Pacific isle, and steering out to sea again over the endless water spaces." Hedin (1938), pp. 70-71.

"We reached the left bank of the Etsin-gol at Manin-tsaghan and took a short rest. The river here runs in one single channel, 150 yards [137 m] wide and then covered with a 20-inch [51 cm] layer of ice, on which was a sanded track for camels. On our bank poplars grew in small copses, on the other side were firm vegetation-clad dunes. This was a place where a bridge should be made.

We went on west-south-west over hard *gobi* of fine gravel, where not a blade of grass grew. Three of the motor-lorries were far ahead. The mirage made them hover a little above the horizon, so that they looked like aeroplanes which had just taken off. To the right an old ruined fort appeared with the remains of yellow-brown walls of sun-dried brick. Its name is Mu-durbeljin, or "the bad square", and it is one of a cluster of fortifications which at this point form a *limes* 2,000 years old.

White-tailed antelopes dashed past us. To the west and south-west wide shining surfaces extended, resembling lakes or snow-fields ; but they too were a trick of the mirage. Here the great caravan road to Hami ran through sheer *gobi*, which afforded the most splendid surface. We passed a dry river bed called the Narin-köll. . . .

Soon the eastern arm of the river Möruin-gol came in sight, a river which branches off from the Etsin-gol at various points, then combines and later separates again into two arms. We had soon reached the first arm, which Kung examined. The arm of the delta was 173 yards [158 m] wide, but the ice-covered stream only 127 yards [116 m]. The greatest depth was only 4 feet [122 cm], of which 2 feet 7 inches [79 cm] were solid ice. We could see that this ice had been formed by new water flowing down over the older ice, layer above layer.

The second, or western arm is rather more than 2 miles [3.2 km] away, and is rather larger than the eastern. Its bed was 203 yards [186 m], its ice-crust 175 yards [160 m] wide. The maximum depth was 4 feet 3 inches [130 cm]." Hedin (1938), pp. 84-85.

3. **Zhenfan** (镇番; W-G: Chen-fan) - now known as the Minqin Oasis - associated with Shiyang River (石羊河), (previously called the Gu River (谷水). Like the Juyan corridor to the north, it extended out from the Gansu corridor, northeast towards Mongolia. It was, and is, part of Wuwei commandery, anciently known as Liangzhou - a name retained today for the central urban district.

> "The commandery of Wuwei also extended a salient to the north, less marked than Juyan, but also presenting a forward defence and a frontier pass to the steppe and desert. The area of Chinese control was based upon the river system of the Shiyang He in the region of modern Minqin." de Crespigny (1984), p. 10.

While it was a fertile region during the Han Dynasty, overpopulation and over exploitation of water resources have seriously affected it recently:

> "The "lake district" of Minqin, comprises five villages and towns: Xiqu, Zhongyu, Donghu, Shoucheng, and Hongshaliang. They are right in the frontline, facing the advance of the Tengger and Badain Jaran deserts. In Zhongqu village where Qingtu Lake could once be found, there are huge clouds of dust in place of an abundance of water and lush pasture." From: "Will the Desert claim Minqin?" Zhang Tingting (2004). Downloaded from: http://www.china.org.cn/english/2004/Sep/105977.htm on 3 June 2014.

Appendix L: The Yuezhi migrations

Among the most significant and far-reaching events in Central and South Asian history was the collapse of the Greco-Bactrian state centred in the north of modern Afghanistan, and the arrival of the Yuezhi and other nomadic groups into the Bactrian region during the 2nd century BCE. These rapid changes affected the whole of the known world at the time, changing cultures over much of Eurasia and Africa forever.

The Chinese records provide a relatively clear and accurate summary of events from the period shortly after the Yuezhi arrived on the banks of the Oxus. They are based on the report to the Chinese Emperor by a Chinese envoy, Gan Ying, who spent "more than a year" in the region in 129-128 BCE, and a number of years 'on the road' and in captivity among the Xiongnu where he married a Xiongnu wife.

Unfortunately, Gan Ying gives no account of the events in Bactria leading up to the arrival of the Da Yuezhi, or details on their apparently rather easy subjugation of the local people, whom he described as being "unwarlike" settled agriculturalists and urban dwellers, with no overall leader. See: Appendix D.

The Chinese histories sketch an outline of historical developments regarding the Da Yuezhi and Daxia. These include: the movement of the Da Yuezhi across the Oxus; the division of the country into five *xihou* or 'duchies;' the forced unification of the five *xihou* into one empire by the leader of the Guishuang *xihou* early in the first century CE; and expansion into the region of Kabul and across northern India in the 1st and 2nd centuries CE.

The records on the Da Yuezhi and Daxia in the *Shiji*, *Hanshu* and *Hou Hanshu*, are complimented by the records of Roman and Greek historians. It is interesting that this is the first time that same historical events are discussed in both Eastern and Western sources. However, the details often remain murky and are sometimes contradictory.

The historical accounts have been augmented by recent archaeological finds that include inscriptions, vast quantities of coins, and remains of ancient cities. These finds have been supplemented by recent decoding of eras, greatly aiding the dating of inscriptions and providing the framework for assembling a coherent history of the period.

The first historical "western" record of the collapse of Greco-Bactria and the arrival of the Da Yuezhi and other nomadic groups is from Apollodoros of Artemita (*circa* 130-87 BCE). He wrote *Parthika*, a history of the Parthian Empire. This long lost work in at least four volumes, was probably completed it in the early 1st century BCE, and was a major source for both Strabo and Ptolemy.

> "Both records [those of Strabo and Ptolemy] went through a common intermediary, who on several indications was Poseidonios of Apamea [*circa* 135-51 BCE]. The intermediary subjected Apollodoros' evidence to a significant remaking, for example in replacing the name of the river *Tanais* with *Jaxartes*." Piankov (2010), p. 99.

Other invaluable work is found in Gnaeus Pompēius Trōgus, a Roman historian of the 1st century BCE who wrote the *Historiae Philippicae* in forty-four books. The central theme was the Macedonian empire founded by Alexander's father, Phillip. Unfortunately, the original has not survived.

Marcus Junianus Justinus, (or, simply, 'Justin'), a late 2nd or 3rd century Roman historian, wrote an 'epitome' or very condensed version of Trogus' history. Some *prologi* (summaries or chapter headings) by an unknown author have also survived, though they are so brief that the entries are often open to various interpretations.

The last event recorded by Justin that can be confidently dated relates to the recovery of the Roman standards captured by the Parthians in 20 BCE, although Trogus' original history may have covered events into the first decade of the 1st century CE.

Of course, Justin could have made some changes, interpretations, and additions to Trogus, but for simplicity, I refer to Justin's abbreviated versions of Trogus' work simply as 'Trogus' throughout.

> "The second tradition is reproduced in Pompeius Trogus (Prol. 41) who states that "Baktria and Sogdiana were captured by Scythian tribes of Saraucae and Asiae". Trogus is perhaps closer to the original forms; he says nothing about crossing the river, nor does he mention the Tochari among the nomads who invaded Baktria and Sogdiana.[12] But, he knows the Tochari, and the context in which they are mentioned testifies in favour of greater proximity of the Trogus' account to Apollodoros, and the latter one to the Chinese evidence." From Piankov (2010), p. 3.

• Theories regarding the identity and background of the Yuezhi

1. Some authorities consider that the *Daxia* of the Chinese accounts refers to the inhabitants of the Bactrian region prior to the arrival of the Da Yuezhi, and that the name *Daxia* is a Chinese transcription (*Ta-cha, *Ta-char) equivalent to the Classical *Tochari.*

Many believe that the name Tochari was gradually transmitted to the Da Yuezhi after they had settled in the region for some time, and later formed the 'Kushan' Empire.

Most of these scholars, accept that the Da Yuezhi together with, or possibly identical to, the Asii/Asiani, formed one of only two bands of "Scythian tribes" said in Trogus' *Prologue 41* to have occupied Bactra and Sogdiana; the other tribe was the Sacaraucae. In Trogus' *Prologue 42*, the Sacaraucae (variant spellings: Sacarauli or Sakaraukai), are said to have been destroyed - in which case, the Asii/Asiani must be the Da Yuezhi.

This means the Daxia of the Chinese accounts refers to the people conquered by the Da Yuezhi. Further support for this position is found in *Prologue 41* which says that the Asiani became the rulers of the Tochari, neatly fitting the *Hanshu*'s account of Daxia.

The Chinese histories, on the other hand, make a point of stating that the Chinese retained the old name of Da Yuezhi rather than using Guishang/Kushans).

Almost all the Greeks and Macedonians who stayed in Bactria would have been ex-soldiers, and many would have found local partners or wives. By the time the Yuezhi arrived some two centuries later, a large proportion of the local population, referred to as the Daxia (estimated by Zhang Qian in 129-128 BCE to be about a million – see: Appendix M) could probably still trace their family line back to a Greek or Macedonian ancestor.

A problem with this theory is that the usual translation of Prologue 41 says that the events recorded took place during the reign of Diodotos, the founder the independent state of Bactria around the middle of the third century BCE. If this is correct, it means the Asii/Asiani invaded the country more than a century before the Yuezhi and almost certainly would be a different people.

However, the text of the Prologue by its nature is much abbreviated, and there are differences between the many Latin editions.

2. Some contemporary scholars maintain that the 'Tochari' of the western sources must refer to the Yuezhi. This position depends heavily on linguistic analyses. These scholars tend to arrive at similar conclusions, i.e. the Da Yuezhi and the Tochari were the same people. They also postulate relationships between these groups and toponyms that appear to be etymologically related.

> "The name Tokharian (or Tocharian) current in English and other European languages has been much discussed. Among philologists specializing in early Central Eurasia and China a consensus on the main issues was reached long ago, despite some unresolved problems. However, due to the nature of the sources—mainly Chinese historical and geographical texts, in which the names must be interpreted via

> Chinese historical phonology, an extremely arcane field—research on the topic remains a highly contentious subject that is largely opaque to scholars unfamiliar with Chinese philology and phonology. As a result, there is more confusion about the name or names of the Tokharians than about any other name in premodern Central Eurasian history.
>
> The identity of the Tokharoi and Yüeh-chih *people* is quite certain, and has been clear for at least half a century, though this has not become widely known outside the tiny number of philologists who work on early Central Eurasian and early Chinese history and linguistics. It is known that the Tokharoi and the Tokharians were the same people because the Tokharoi-Tokhwar-Yüeh-chih-Tukhâr- of Bactria and the Tukhâr-Toχar-/Toɣar-Yüeh-chih of the Tarim Basin are identified as one and the same people in every source that mentions them." Beckwith (2009), p. 380.

Inconclusive debates continue as to whether the Yuezhi were mostly descended from 'Caucasian' ('Europoid') or from 'Mongoloid' ('Mongolic') stock, and what language or languages they "originally" spoke.

Until other evidence becomes available, I think we should accept that the Yuezhi were probably a confederation of tribes from a range of ethnic, cultural, and linguistic backgrounds. There is not enough evidence yet to say what the background of the "core" or ruling group was, although it seems likely that they were of a mix of both 'Caucasian' and 'Mongoloid' stock, like the Xiongnu. See, for example: Kim et al (2010), pp. 429-440.

We know that, after the Da Yuezhi moved to Daxia, they began using an Eastern Iranian language known as "Bactrian," or "Aryan" in their inscriptions, which probably became an 'official' language. Bactrian, being an Iranic language, could well have been spoken by the people who had lived in the region from when it was under Persian rule in Achaemenid times, before being gradually adopted by the newcomers.

'Bactrian' is closely related to other satem Indo-European languages in the region, particularly Persian, Sakan, and some north Indian languages, so it would have been a useful *lingua franca* for communication between the various peoples under Da Yuezhi control, and their immediate neighbours and trading partners.

Yet, this still gives us no indication as to what "original" language of the Da Yuezhi was. Many scholars believe it was one of the so-called "Tokharian" languages – which were *centum* Indo-European languages and, therefore, affiliated with most western and southern European languages - which had survived in the Tarim Basin into the first millennium CE. Others remain equally convinced they spoke a Sakan, or eastern-Iranian language (belonging to the *satem* branch of the great Indo-European family), and some think it was '(Proto-)Turkic'.

• Background to the arrival of the Yuezhi

Most scholars agree that the Greco-Bactrian state was close to collapse shortly before the arrival of nomadic groups in the 130s BCE. Justin records that Eucratides I Megas was murdered by his own son while returning from India to Bactria, and his body desecrated.

When the Saka or 'Scythic' peoples arrived in Bactria, closely followed by the Yuezhi, they found a feeble Greco-Bactrian state, weakened by disastrous foreign campaigns and incessant internal squabbling, and perhaps civil war.

The inhabitants may have surrendered, been annexed, or made a treaty with the invaders, but managed to retain some limited autonomy over certain local regions and cities. This is indicated in Zhang Qian's account where he emphasises the differences between the Daxia people, which he describes as dwelling in towns and cities, with local chiefs who were agriculturalists and "unwarlike," compared to the "nomadic" Da Yuezhi, still camped on the north bank of the Oxus.

• Chinese accounts of the migrations

The only early references to Yuezhi interactions with Se/Sai people and the Wusun are in the *Hanshu*; there are none in the *Shiji*, or the *Hou Hanshu*,

The accounts of the interaction between the people mentioned in the *Shiji* and the *Hanshu* are difficult to interpret and the details vary widely. The accounts are based on discussions held between Zhang Qian and Emperor Wudi sometime after he was forced to relinquish his marquisate between 123 CE and 119 CE, and long after the first report he made to the Emperor soon after he returned to China in 126 BCE. See: Watson (1993), p. 237-238. See: the discussions in Appendix I.

• *Shiji* 123 states:

> "Formerly they [the Yuezhi] were very powerful and despised the Xiongnu, but later, when Maodun became leader of the Xiongnu nation, he attacked and defeated the Yuezhi. Some time afterwards his son [Jizhu], the Old *Shanyu* ['*Laoshang*,' died 158 BCE], killed the king of the Yuezhi and made his skull into a drinking cup. The Yuezhi originally lived between the Qilian or Heavenly Mountains and Dunhuang, but after they were defeated by the Xiongnu they moved far away to the west, beyond Dayuan, where they attacked and conquered the people of Daxia and set up the court of their king on the northern bank of the Gui [Oxus] River. A small number of their people who were unable to make the journey west sought refuge among the Qiang barbarians in the Southern Mountains, where they are known as the Lesser Yuezhi [Xiao Yuezhi]." Watson (1993), pp. 234; 147.

• The parallel passage from *Hanshu* 96A:

> "Ta Yüeh-chih [Da Yuezhi] was originally a land of nomads. The people moved around in company with their stock-animals and followed the same way of life as the Hsiung-nu. There were more than 100000 trained bowmen, and for this reason they relied on their strength and thought lightly of the Hsiung-nu [Xiongnu]. Originally [the people] dwelt between Tun-huang and Ch'i-lien [Dunhuang and Qilian]. Then the time came when the *Shanyu* Mao Tun [Maodun or Modun] attacked and defeated the Ta Yüeh-chih, and the *Shan-yü* Lao-shang killed [the king] of the Yüeh-chih, making his skull into a drinking vessel. The Yüeh-chih thereupon went far away, passing Ta-Yüan [Dayuan] and proceeding west to attack and subdue Ta Hsia [Daxia]. The principal city was established north of the Kuei [Gui] River to form the king's court. The remaining small group [of the Yuezhi] who were unable to leave sought protection among the Ch'iang [Qiang] tribes of the Southern Mountains and were termed Hsiao Yüeh-chih [Xiao Yuezhi]." From: *Hanshu* 96A in *CICA*, pp. 120-121.

> "The same text with a few minor variations of wording appears in the account of the Great Yüeh-chih [Da Yuezhi] in chapter 96A on the 'Western Regions' in the *Han shu*. It will be noted that there is no reference to either the Wu-sun or the Sakas. The Wu-sun are mentioned separately in Chang Ch'ien's [Zhang Qian's] report as a powerful nomadic people located some 2,000 *li* [832 km] north-east of Ta-yüan [Dayuan = Ferghana]. It is stated that they had formerly been subject to the Hsiung-nu [Xiongnu] but no allusion is made to any relations, hostile or otherwise, with the Yüeh-chih. Sakas (Sai 塞, Middle Chinese *Sək*) are not mentioned anywhere in the *Shih-chih* [*Shiji*]." Pulleyblank (1970), p. 154.

- **The parallel passage from *Hou Hanshu* on the Yuezhi move to Daxia**

  The *Hou Hanshu* gives this very brief account: "Formerly, the Yuezhi were defeated by the Xiongnu. They then moved to Daxia and divided up this kingdom between five *xihou* . . . ."

There is no mention of the Wusun or Sakas here. In fact, the *only* people mentioned as playing a part in the Da Yuezhi move to Daxia are the Xiongnu. This is undoubtedly because the account is so brief, and the fact that the *Hou Hanshu* focuses on a later period than the *Hanshu*, long after these events had taken place.

- **The struggle between the Yuezhi and the Xiongnu**

Due to the inconsistencies between the various texts and references, there has been uncertainty about the dates and details of the struggles between the Yuezhi and Xiongnu confederacies. Now at last, some can be resolved.

The *Shiji* and the *Hou Hanshu* both mention that the Da Yuezhi, after their final defeat at the hands of the Xiongnu, *circa* 169/168 BCE, fled to the west, eventually conquering Daxia, a state roughly corresponding with the territory of the previous Baktria/Bactria/Bactriana, centred in the plains on both banks of the middle Syr Darya.

We know from the texts that this conquest took place shortly before the Chinese envoy, Zhang Qian, found the king of the Da Yuezhi with his court on the northern shore of the Oxus River/Syr Darya in the summer of 129 BCE.

The only accounts of the Da Yuezhi between these two dates, and references to their involvement with the Wusun and Sai or Sai Wang, are to found in the *Hanshu*.

There seems to be no reason to doubt the story in the *Hanshu* that the Da Yuezhi first fled from the Gansu corridor to the region of the Ili River and Issyk Kul, displacing some Sai/Se (Saka) peoples, and settled there for two or three decades. It is not clear whether they left that region and moved on to Daxia because they were defeated by the Wusun or the Xiongnu, or by both, as the extant records give contradictory accounts. Perhaps they simply decided to move further away to avoid conflict.

- **The flight of the Da Yuezhi to the West**

  "Finally Qin overthrew the other six states, and the First Emperor of the Qin [Qin Shi Huang who reigned as King of Qin 247 – 220 BCE, and as Emperor of China from 220 – 210 BCE] dispatched Meng Tian to lead a force of 100,000 men north to attack the barbarians. He seized control of all the lands south of the Yellow River and established border defences along the river, constructing forty-four walled district cities overlooking the river and manning them with convict labourers transported to the border for garrison duty. He also built the Direct Road from Jiuyuan to Yunyang. Thus he utilized the natural mountain barriers to establish the border defences, scooping out the valleys and constructing ramparts and building installations at other points where they were needed. The whole line of defences stretched over 10,000 *li* [4,158 km] from Lintao to Liaodong and even extended across the Yellow River and through Yangshan and Beijia.

  At this time the Eastern Barbarians were very powerful and the Yuezhi were likewise flourishing. The *Shanyu* or chieftain of the Xiongnu was named Touman. Touman, unable to hold out against the Qin forces, had withdrawn to the far north, where he lived with his subjects for over ten years. After Meng Tian died [210 BCE] and the feudal lords revolted against the Qin, plunging China into a period of strife and turmoil [which lasted until after the first Han Emperor, Gaozu, began his rule over China in 202 BCE], the convicts which the Qin had sent to the northern border to garrison the area all returned to their homes. The Xiongnu, the pressure against them relaxed, once again began to infiltrate south of the bend of the Yellow River until they had established themselves along the old border of China." *Shiji* 110. From: Watson (1993), pp. 133-134.

Touman, the Chanyu of the Xiongnu, according to *Shiji* 110, sent his eldest son Modu 冒頓 (209-174 BCE) as a hostage to the Yuezhi. Modu's name is "usually mistranscribed" as Mao-tun (or Maodun). See: Golden (2006), p. 140, quoted in Appendix M.

"Touman's oldest son, the heir apparent to his position, was named Maodun, but the *Shanyu* also had a younger son by another consort whom he had taken later and was very fond of. He decided that he wanted to get ride [sic – read 'rid'] of Maodun and set up his younger son as heir instead, and he therefore sent Maodun as hostage to the Yuezhi nation. Then, after Maodun had arrived among the Yuezhi, Touman made a sudden attack upon them. The Yuezhi were about to kill Maodun in retaliation, but he managed to steal one of their best horses and escape, eventually making his way back home. His father, struck by his bravery, put him in command of a force of 10,000 cavalry." From: *Shiji*, 110, in Watson (1993), p. 134.

Within a few years, Modu conquered the powerful Donghu or "Eastern Barbarians," and the Xiongnu quickly became the major military power to the north of China:

"The Eastern barbarians had up until this time despised Maodun and made no preparations for their defence: when Maodun and his soldiers arrived, they inflicted a crushing defeat, killing the ruler of the Eastern Barbarians, taking prisoner his subjects, and seizing their domestic animals. Then he returned and rode west, attacking and routing the Yuezhi, and annexed the lands of the ruler of Laofan and the ruler of Boyang south of the Yellow River. Thus he recovered possession of all the lands which the Qin general Meng Tian had taken away from the Xiongnu: the border between his territory and that of the Han empire now followed the old line of defences south of the Yellow River, and from there he marched into the Chaona and Fushi districts and then invaded Yan and Dai.

At this time the Han forces were stalemated in battle with the armies of Xiang Yu, and China was exhausted by warfare. Thus Maodun was able to strengthen his position, massing a force of over 300,000 skilled crossbowmen.... When Maodun came to power, however, the Xiongnu reached their peak of strength and size, subjugating all of the other barbarian tribes of the north and turning south to confront China as a rival nation." *Shiji* 110. From: Watson (1993), pp. 135-136.

"Following this successful campaign [when Modu completely destroyed the Donghu] *Maodun* led his men and started to push west against *Yuezhi*, which succumbed before the advancing *Xiongnu*. . . . Turning to the south *Maodun* and his cavalry conquered the *Loufan* and *Baiyang* tribes. Later he laid waste to the *Yan* and *Dai* prefectures of *Han* and he finally recovered the land that was lost to *Meng Tian*. . ., now the Kingdom of *Xiongnu* shared its border with the *Han* Kingdom from the *Henan* Pass to *Chaona* and *Fushi* counties." From the *Zizhi tongjian* in: Yap (2009), pp. 68-69.

• The first defeat of the Yuezhi by the Xiongnu between 206 and 203 BCE

For almost the whole of the 3rd century BCE the Yuezhi were the pre-eminent power to the north-west of China – see: *Shiji* 123, in Watson (1993), p. 234 (quoted at the end of this Appendix).

In early December 207 BCE, Ziying, the King of Qin, surrendered to the rebel Han leader Liu Bang. Liu Bang was forced to hand the city over to Xiang Yu whose forces were superior. Xiang Yu killed Ziying and, in the spring of 206 BCE, set fire to the town of

Xianyang 咸陽 - a former capital, about two kilometres north of the later Han capital of Chang'an (literally: 'Forever Safe'). See: Cotterell (2008), p. 37. Sadly, the Imperial library in Xianyang with its priceless collection of unique historical works was destroyed in the fire.

The *Shiji* states that Modu conquered the Donghu (the major tribe to the northeast of China) and later the Yuezhi to the west, while the forces of Liu Bang and Xiang Yu were struggling for control of China.

Therefore, we can place the first defeat of the Yuezhi by the Xiongnu sometime between 206 and 203 BCE, as Xiang Yu committed suicide in December 203 or January 202 BCE, after his army was defeated by the Han forces. See: *Hanshu* – the Imperial Annals 1B: 2a. From Dubs (1938), p. 97; and see: the *Shiji* in Dubs (1961), p. 106.

Although Benjamin places the first attack against the Yuezhi "*c.* 207 BCE," rather than 206 or later, he sums up the situation well:

> "This first attack against the Yuezhi was inconclusive, and certainly no rout. It would be another forty-five years before the Xiongnu were able to inflict a final 'knock-out' blow, which is further evidence of both the previous and continuing strength of the Yuezhi dynasty. They were apparently able to withstand a serious and potentially fatal attack from a powerful enemy (Maodun with some 300,000 troops at his disposal) without having to give up any of their lands . . . . None the less, the fact that a people whom the Yuezhi had previously treated with contempt (and who only eight years previously had sent their heir apparent to them as hostage) had attacked and defeated them in what was clearly a major raid must have come as a considerable shock...." Benjamin (2007), pp. 64-65.

• The second defeat of the Yuezhi by the Xiongnu in 176 BCE

In the 6th month of 176 BCE (i.e. between 24 July and 22 August) a messenger arrived in the Xinwang region with a letter from the Chanyu (Modu) for the Chinese Emperor boasting that he had sent one of his subordinates, the "Wise King of the Right [or West]" on a successful campaign which the *Shiji* describes as follows:

> "Through the aid of Heaven, the excellence of his fighting men, and the strength of his horses, he has succeeded in wiping out the Yuezhi, slaughtering or forcing to submission every member of the tribe. In addition he has conquered the Loulan, Wusun, and Hujie tribes, as well as the twenty-six states nearby,* so that all of them have become part of the Xiongnu nation. All the people who live by drawing the bow are now united into one family and the entire region of the north is at peace.' *Shiji* 110; from: Watson (1993), pp. 140-141.
>
> ***NOTE:** This paragraph appears to have been only roughly translated by Watson. The Chinese text reads:
>
> "以天之福，吏卒良，馬彊力，以夷滅月氏，盡斬殺降下之。定樓蘭、烏孫、呼揭及其旁二十六國，皆以為匈奴。諸引弓之民，并為一家。北州已定 . . . ." I translate this as:
>
> "With the blessings of Heaven, good officials, excellent soldiers, and superior powerful horses, he wiped out the Yuezhi, killing many by beheading and murdering them. He pacified Loulan, the Wusun and Hujie, and asserted [that he had also pacified] twenty-six nearby states. All (or 'many' or 'several of') the peoples who live by drawing the bow are now one family. The northern region is now settled. . . ."
>
> Joseph Yap kindly pointed out (personal communication 16 March 2014) that the Hujie were a nomadic tribe living to the north of the Xiongnu and often mentioned along with the Dingling 丁零 who lived to the south and east of Lake Baikal in modern Siberia.

This attack was apparently not quite as devastating to the Yuezhi as the *Shiji* suggests, for the Yuezhi remained in Gansu for another decade. See: Dorn'eich (2010), who establishes that the Yuezhi fled to the west in 166 BCE, 10 years after the Xiongnu attack reported to the Chinese in 176 BCE.

• Was it the Xiongnu or the Yuezhi who attacked the Wusun?

The *Shiji* and *Hanshu* have conflicting accounts of a Xiongnu attack on the Wusun *circa* 173 BCE. One of the most significant differences is that the *Shiji* says that the Xiongnu killed the father of the Wusun Kunmo, Nandoumi, while *Hanshu* 61 (*CICA* p. 214) blames it on the Yuezhi. These accounts are both attributed to Zhang Qian's (W-G: Chang ch'ien's) report to the Emperor. See the quote from *Shiji* 123 in Watson (1993), pp. 237-238 in Appendix I.

The parallel passage in *Hanshu* 61 clearly states that it was the Da Yuezhi rather than the Xiongnu who killed the Kunmo's father. See the quote from *Hanshu* Chap. 61, in *CICA*, pp. 214-218 in Appendix I.

Some scholars have suggested that the *Shiji's* account was primary and the *Hanshu* account stating that the Da Yuezhi killed the Wusun king's father, Nandoumi (Nan-tou-mi), was altered for political or other reasons. See, for example: Pulleyblank (1970), pp. 154-160 and Pulleyblank (1981), pp. 278-286; also, Honey (1999), especially pp. 67-82, and Lu (1995), pp. pp. 51-68.

Others, such as Hulsewé and Loewe, believe the *Hanshu* account of the Wusun is primary, and sections of the *Shiji* that had been lost were recreated from the accounts in the *Hanshu*. See: *CICA*, pp. 11-39.

It is critical to the understanding of this whole period of history to decide whether the accounts in the *Shiji* or those of the *Hanshu* should take precedence.

Carefully rereading the arguments, particularly those between Professors Hulsewé and Pulleyblank, while comparing the Chinese texts of contested passages, I find myself convinced by the plausible and detailed arguments of Professors Pulleyblank and Lu, who find that the accounts in the *Shiji* were primary:

> "In an appendix to the article 'Chinese and Indo-Europeans' it was shown that, contrary to the view put forward but never demonstrated by the eighteenth-century scholar Ts'ui Shih, and adopted by the eminent sinologists Paul Pelliot and G. Haloun, chapter 123 of the *Shih-chi* on 'Ta-yüan' could not have been reconstituted from parallel passages in the *Han shu* but must have been the source for the latter—as one would naturally assume if doubts had never been raised. In summing up the evidence I noted that the most important discrepancies between *Shih-chi*, 123, and the Han shu concerned the Wu-sun and Sakas and I argued that one must assume that the Han shu had grafted separate, additional, material on to the account in the *Shih-chi*. I did not, however, go into the matter in detail. This is the burden of the present article. . . .
>
> The information that *k'un-mo* was really a royal title and not a name is introduced in the *Han shu* article on the Wu-sun just after the point where it finally leaves the *Shih-chi* account behind. The fact that up to this point the *Han shu* (in spite of the fact that its editor had different information) had used *k'un-mo* as a proper name shows as clearly as anything could that it was copying the *Shih-chi* text. The insertion of the name Nan-tou-mi at the beginning is, however, tell-tale evidence that Pan Piao[8] did not simply copy the text he had in front of him but tampered with it in order to insert information that could not conveniently be brought in any other way.
>
> An example of a change introduced arbitrarily in order to make the story tidier is the statement in the *Han shu* that the Wu-sun had originally lived along with the Yüeh-chih between Tun-huang and the Ch'i-lien mountains, i.e. in western Kansu. This has the effect of turning Chang Ch'ien's proposal to move the Wu-sun eastwards

into an invitation to return to their original homeland, an implication which is not found in the *Shih-chi.* Haloun noticed this discrepancy between the two sources and suggested that it might have arisen from a textual corruption, namely a misreading of K'un-ya as K'un-mo (K'un-ya being a variant of Hun-ya).[9] This conjecture (which implies the priority of the *Shih-chi* text) might account for the origination of the *Han shu* interpretation but would not absolve its editor from the charge of having embellished the story by references to the Wu-sun's 'former territory' *(ku ti)* both in the cited passage and later in the account of Chang Ch'ien's actual attempt to persuade the Wu-sun ruler. This can only be a case of improving the story for dramatic effect.

If we have caught the *Han shu* out in one instance of this kind, it will make us wary of accepting other departures from the *Shih-chi* account as based on solid evidence rather than imaginative reconstruction. There are in any case difficulties of chronology in the *Han shu* account. The *Han shu's* statement that the Wu-sun's submission to the Hsiung-nu came, not as the result of conquest but because they were fleeing from the Yüeh-chih is hard to reconcile with the statement in the Hsiung-nu chapter of the *Shih-chi* (repeated in the *Han shu)* that the Hsiung-nu conquered the Wu-sun after they had already severely defeated the Yüeh-chih in 176 B.C.[10]

The story of the enmity between the Wu-sun and the Yüeh-chih, of which there is not a trace in the *Shih-chi,* has the effect of turning the westward migration of the former into a vendetta against the latter. The *Shih-chi* simply states that the Yüeh-chih, after setting out on their migration around 174 B.C., eventually reached the banks of the Oxus, where Chang Ch'ien found them in 128 B.C. Since we know from Western sources that their arrival in Sogdiana cannot have been very long before that date, it is clear that they must have spent longer or shorter periods at places in between, but of this the *Shih-chi* knows nothing. Into this lacuna the *Han shu* inserts *(a)* the Yüeh-chih attack on the Sakas, *(b)* K'un-mo's vengeance on the Yüeh-chih, which impelled the latter still further westwards. Both these events are placed before the death of the *shan-yu* who brought K'un-mo up, that is, before 160 B.C. (see p. 156 above), which is much too early for the conquest of Bactria, a fact that has troubled commentators in the past.

The whole story of the Wu-sun vendetta against the Yüeh-chih is, I suspect, an imaginative reconstruction without any genuine historical basis, introduced partly for dramatic effect-vendetta as a motive for war was as familiar to the Chinese from the tales of the Spring and Autumn period as it was to the Greeks - partly to account for the ethnic distribution in the Wu-sun territory in the first century B.C. when it came under direct Chinese observation. We are told that there were both Saka and Yüeh-chih elements in the Wu-sun population, as well as Sakas in neighbouring small states in the Pamir. Moreover, when the Chinese made contacts with Kashmir (Chi-pin) over the Hanging Pass,[11] they learned that the ruler there too was a Saka who had come from the north. They were told, or assumed, that the King of the Sakas[12] had been driven out of his original home in the Pamir by the Yüeh-chih. Whether or not this particular detail had an historical foundation would be impossible to say but, at any rate, it is clear that no reliance can be placed on the way in which everything is tied together in the *Han shu.*

To sum up : a detailed comparison between the accounts of the Wu-sun in the *Shih-chi* and *Han shu* confirms the conclusion enunciated in my previous article. The discrepancies can be readily accounted for on the assumption that the *Shih-chi* text is primary and the *Han shu* based on it, with the addition of some genuine new information and some arbitrary embellishments. The opposite hypothesis, that the

Han shu text was primary and that a forger deliberately excised just those details does not make sense—apart from the fact that it is totally lacking in supporting evidence.

[8] For evidence that Pan Piao, Pan Ku's father, who died in A.D. 54, was responsible for *Han shu,* 96, 'The Western Regions', see G. Haloun, *ZDMG,* XCI, 1937, p. 250, n. 1. See also E. G. Pulleyblank, 'Chinese evidence for the date of Kaniṣka', in A. L. Basham (ed.), *Papers on the date of Kaniṣka,* Leiden., 1968. This is the revised version of an article prepared for a conference held in 1960. There it is shown that three items can be identified as having been added by Pan Ku to the chapter as completed by his father.

[9] G. Haloun, art. cit., 295.

[10] See p. 156, n. 5, above.

[11] *Han shu pu-chu,* 96A, p. 5463 ff."

Pulleyblank, (1970), pp. 154 and 158-160 plus nn. 8-11.

- **Did the Yuezhi flee to Daxia after being defeated by the Wusun, or by the Xiongnu?**
  - *Hanshu* 96A (*CICA,* pp. 104-105) says the Da Yuezhi were defeated by the Xiongnu before they moved west to Daxia. This text seems to be abbreviated and may be defective – missing out on the story that the Da Yuezhi, after fleeing from the Xiongnu, displaced the Saka living in the Ili/Issyk Kol region and lived there for some decades before they were chased out and fled to Daxia.
  - *Hanshu* 96B (*CICA,* p. 145) says the Da Yuezhi were defeated by the Wusun before they moved west to Daxia.
  - *Hanshu* 61 (*CICA* pp. 216-217) again says the Da Yuezhi were defeated by the Wusun before they moved west to Daxia.
  - *Hou Hanshu* simply says: "Formerly, the Yuezhi were defeated by the Xiongnu. They then moved to Daxia [Bactria] and divided up this kingdom between five *xihou* [princes]."

Hanshu 96B (*CICA* pp. 144-145) states that the Da Yuezhi, after being defeated by the Xiongnu, headed west and attacked the king of the Sai who then moved far to the south while they occupied his lands [in the Ili region]. Some years later, the Wusun Kunmo attacked and defeated the Da Yuezhi forcing them to flee again to the west finally ending up in Daxia. This must have occurred sometime *before* Modu Chanyu died, *circa* 158 BCE. The Wusun remained in occupation of the lands vacated by the Da Yuezhi.

It is difficult to understand why the author of *Hanshu* 61 blamed the Yuezhi for killing the first Kunmo; or to explain the confusion about the dates relating to Modu Chanyu.

Perhaps the *Hanshu* concocted a "politically correct" version of the story designed to curry favour with the Wusun? It is certainly true that this account, which postdates that of the *Shiji,* refers to the discussions between Zhang Qiang and the Emperor *circa* 119 BCE, when they were trying to find some way to get the Wusun to move back to the Gansu region to provide a buffer against Xiongnu advances. It may have been designed to blame the Yuezhi for killing the Kunmo's father, Nandoumi, thus providing an excuse for the Wusuns' attack on the Da Yuezhi (who had previously been considered allies by the Chinese). It might have allowed the Emperor to avoid chastising the Wusun for this hostile action while he was trying to encourage them to move back closer to China.

It is of interest to note that, of the early Chinese accounts, only *Hanshu* 61 makes any mention of the Yuezhi killing the father of the Wusun Modu Chanyu, or of later defeating the Sai. Neither the *Shiji,* the *Hou Hanshu,* or *Hanshu* 96A and 96B make any reference to these events.

Shiji 123, reports that Zhang Qian, *circa* 119 BCE, told the Emperor that early on, when the Wusun were still a small state, the Kunmo was killed by the Xiongnu and his son, later known as Modu/Maodun, was raised by the Xiongnu. Watson (1993), pp. 237-238.

Zhang Qian suggested to the Emperor that the Chanyu might be persuaded to get the Wusun to settle (or resettle) in the Hexi/Gansu corridor now that it had been emptied of both the Yuezhi and the Xiongnu.

> "The emperor approved of this suggestion and, appointing Zhang Qian as a general of palace attendants, put him in charge of a party of 300 men, each of whom was provided with two horses. In addition the party took along tens of thousands of cattle and sheep and carried gold and silver worth 100,000,000 cash. Many of the men in the party were given imperial credentials making them assistant envoys so that could be sent to neighbouring states along the way." Watson (1993), p. 238.

Ultimately, however, the Wusun could not be persuaded to move back to the region of the Gansu corridor.

• The third defeat of the Yuezhi by the Xiongnu

In 174 BCE, or shortly after, "Maodun died and his son Jizhu was set up with the title of [Laoshang] Old *Shanyu*." *Shiji* 110, from: Watson (1993), p. 142. The title or nickname of 'Laoshang' would suggest that Jizhu was somewhere between 50 and 70 years of age – the traditional age range ascribed to the word *lao* 老. See: *GR* Vol. III, p. 1116, No. 6722. The word *shang* 上 means 'Emperor', 'sovereign', or 'king'. *GR*, Vol. V, p. 123, No. 9554, **6.**

The *Shiji*, the *Hanshu*, and the *Zizhi tongjian*, *juan* 18, all agree that the Yuezhi were again defeated during the reign of Jizhu/Laoshang (reigned *circa* 174-158 BCE), this time definitively, and with the added humiliation of having their king's head made into a drinking cup by the Xiongnu Shanyu. See the quote from *Shiji* 123 in Watson (1993), p. 234 earlier in this appendix. Also see: Appendix X on the significance and use of skull cups.

The defeat leading to the flight of the Da Yuezhi to the west certainly occurred sometime between the death of Modu in 174 and that of Jizhu in 158.

This defeat most likely took place in 166 BCE, as the Xiongnu had become so powerful and self-confident by then that the Chanyu invaded China in this year with 140,000 horsemen and wreaked havoc to within a short distance of the capital. Then he "remained within the borders of the empire for a little over a month and then withdrew." It seems probable that his defeat of the Yuezhi occurred during this invasion. *Shiji* 110. See: Watson (1993), p. 145.

Chris Dorn'eich's 2010 paper, "The Great Yuezhi/A(r)si Exodus of 166 BCE" makes a strong case that the Xiongnu defeated the Yuezhi in the little more than a month after they advanced close to Chang'an in 166 BCE. The Da Yuezhi probably fled to the west not long after their king was killed, probably late in the same year, or early in 165 BCE after they had time to mobilise.

This theory fits with dates estimated by, among others, Julius Klaproth (1826), pp. 57 and 132-133, and Chavannes (1895): "Introduction aux Mémoires Historiques de Se-Ma Ts'ien," LXX (p. 44).

However, Benjamin makes an interesting case that the migration of the Yuezhi could have begun rather later, *circa* 162 BCE:

> "This passage follows the *Han shu* account of the defeat of the Wusun by the Yuezhi and the flight of the infant *Kunmo* [of the Wusun] to the Xiongnu *Shanyu* which,... most probably occurred in 173 BCE. The tale describes the education of the young *Kunmo* at the hands of Jizhu, and states that 'when he had come of age (the *Shanyu*) delivered to the Kunmo his father's people...'. Daffina has translated the relevant Chinese characters as 'adult age' and used examples in the handbook on ritual, the *Lishi*, to argue that adult age was 30. But Hulsewe and Loewe dispute this conclusion and note that the *Hou Han Shu* states: 'Anciently one was given arms at 15, to return

> these at sixty'. If they are correct, then the *Kunmo* (if he was aged one or less at the time of his father's death) would have reached the age of 15 by *circa* 158. However, the *Han Shu* states that by the time the *Kunmo* had come of age, the Yuezhi 'had *already* been defeated by the Xiongnu', and further implies that they had already settled in the Ili Valley by then. This confirms the defeat of the Yuezhi by the Xiongnu sometime before 158."
> Benjamin (2007), pp. 72-73.

> "A more precise *terminus post quem* can also be provided by the fact that in or immediately after 162 Jizhu signed a peace treaty with the Han and thereafter apparently remained at home for the rest of his life. It is reasonable to suggest, therefore, that the third and final defeat of the Yuezhi at the hands of the Xiongnu probably took place in 162 BCE, just before the signing of this peace treaty. With the defeat and expulsion of the Yuezhi, and the concluding of peace with the Han, Jizhu [or 'Laoshang'] was able to spend the remaining four years of his life in relative tranquillity, content in the knowledge that the Xiongnu had now gained control of the vital Gansu Corridor, and hence potentially of all the Tarim Basin beyond."
> Benjamin (2007), p. 73.

Hulsewé and Loewe certainly made an error in their assumption about when one was considered to have "come of age," which has led Benjamin astray in the quote above.

The word *zhuang* 壯, according to William's 1909 dictionary, means: 'full-grown, manly; manhood, at age of thirty.' *GR*, Vol. II, p. 183, No. 2624, **1c.**, gives: 'In the prime of life. Aged thirty years,' while Kroll 92015), p. 622 says: "**2.** In the prime of life, traditionally 30 years of age."

Babies are considered to be one year old at birth in China, so thirty years of age actually means thirty-one according to Western reckoning. *Zhuang* 壯 did not refer to 'coming of age,' but in the 'prime of life,' that is, 31 or older, if taken literally.

Using this reckoning, all that can be inferred from this passage is that the Xiongnu probably defeated the Yuezhi sometime before *circa* 142 BCE.

The letter from the Chinese Emperor to the Chanyu in 162 BCE outlines the terms of the new peace treaty between the Xiongnu and the Han:

> "According to the decree of the former emperor, the land north of the Great Wall, where men wield the bow and arrow, was to receive its commands from the *Shanyu*, while that within the wall, whose inhabitants dwell in houses and wear hats and girdles, was to be ruled by us; thus might the countless inhabitants of these lands gain their food and clothing from agriculture, weaving, or hunting; father and son live side by side; ruler and minister enjoy mutual security; and all forsake violence and rebellion. Now we have heard that certain evil and deluded men, succumbing greedily to the lure of gain, have turned their backs upon righteousness and violated the peace alliance, forgetting the fate of the countless inhabitants and disrupting the concord which existed between the rulers of our two states.
>
> This, however, is an affair of the past. In your letter, you say that "since our two countries have been joined again in peace and the two rulers are once more in concord," you desire "to rest your soldiers and turn your horses to pasture, in order that generation after generation may know prosperity and joy and we may make a new beginning in peace and harmony." We heartily approve these words. . . .
>
> Our two great nations, the Han and the Xiongnu, stand side by side. Since the Xiongnu dwell in the north, where the land is cold and the killing frosts come early,

we have decreed that our officials shall send to the *Shanyu* each year a fixed quantity of millet, leaven, gold, silk, cloth, thread, floss, and other articles.

Now the world enjoys profound peace and the people are at rest. We and the *Shanyu* must be as parents to them. . . ." *Shiji* 110, from: Watson (1993), p. 146.

After their final defeat by the Xiongnu (*circa* 166 or 162 BCE), the majority of the Yuezhi, referred to as the Da Yuezhi ('Great' Yuezhi) by the Han, went northwest, settling in the region of the fertile Ili Valley and the grazing grounds around the great Issyk Kul or 'Warm Lake' (so-called because it never freezes over). According to the *Hanshu*, as we have seen above, they displaced the local Saka tribes, most of whom fled to the south, some reaching Jibin which they conquered.

This group of Sakas, who presumably spoke an Iranic language, should be distinguished from the other Sakas who Benjamin believes the Yuezhi encountered later, on their way to Daxia, i.e. the so-called 'Amyrgian' Sakas of the Ferghana Valley, and 'Tigraxauda' (or Sacaraucae) Saka who were "probably in occupation of northern Bactria" when the Da Yuezhi arrived on the scene. Benjamin (2007), pp. 97-100.

A smaller group of Yuezhi tribes, later known as the 'Xiao' or 'Lesser' Yuezhi, fled into the mountains to the west of the Gansu corridor, where they settled among the local Qiang tribes near modern Xining. See: *Hanshu* 96A in *CICA*, p. 121 and Appendix J.

• The Da Yuezhi migrate from the Ili region to northern Bactria

According to *Hanshu* 61, the Wusun reportedly attacked the Da Yuezhi about 133 or 132 BCE.

They fled via Ferghana and Sogdiana into Daxia/Bactria, arriving there *circa* 131/130 BCE. Pulleyblank argues convincingly that "the vendetta against the Yüeh-chih" by the Wusun must have been a fiction. See: the quotes in Appendix I from Pulleyblank (1970), pp. 157 and 159.

Taishan Yu makes an almost unassailable case that this move must have taken place sometime between 133 and 129 BCE, and probably in 130 BCE. As this is such a key date for the reconstruction of the period, I have quoted his reasons in full:

"The Da Yuezhi who migrated west to the valleys of the Rivers Ili and Chu were driven off by the Wusun and moved farther west to the valley of the Amu Darya later. On this dating, there are also two theories: a) during the reign period of Chanyu Laoshang (174-161 B.C.) and b) reign period of Chanyu Junchen 軍臣 (161-126 B.C.). I think that the latter is correct.

1. In the *Hanshu,* ch. 61, it is recorded that Da Yuezhi were driven off by· the Wusun, when the Kunmo of the Wusun was at the age of "*zhuang* 壯". Since a man was "*zhuang*" at thirty, if we suppose Kunmo to have been at the age of 30-50 when he drove the Da Yuezhi away, then, according to the date of Kunmo's birth (c. 185-175 B.C.), the date that the Da Yuezhi gave up the valleys of the Rivers Ili and Chu must have been between 155 and 125 B.C. This was exactly the reign period of Chanyu Junchen.

2. In the *Shiji,* ch. 123 it is recorded:

Zhang Qian was a native of Hanzhong 漢中. During the reign period Jianyuan = (建元, 140-135 B.C.), he was a *lang* 郎 [Gentleman-in-waiting]. At that time, the Son of Heaven made inquiries among the Xiongnu who had surrendered and they all reported that the Xiongnu had defeated the king of the Yuezhi and made a drinking-vessel out of his skull. The Yuezhi had fled and were furious with the Xiongnu, but had no ally to join them in attacking the Xiongnu. The Han, wishing to be engaged in wiping out the Hu, upon hearing of this report, desired to communicate [with the Yuezhi]; but the road passed through [the territory of] the Xiongnu, the Emperor recruited thereupon men who were able to undertake the mission. Zhang Qian, in his capacity as a *lang*, responded to the call and enlisted for the mission to the Yuezhi. Starting from Longxi [prefecture], in company with Ganfu 甘父, a Hu slave of the Tangyi 堂邑 family [Tangyi was an ancient locality situated to the north of the subprefecture of Liuhe at modern Jiangsu – *GR*, Vol. V, p. 828], he passed through [the territory of] the Xiongnu. The Xiongnu captured him and sent him to the Chanyu. The Chanyu said: "The Yuezhi are to the north of us; how can Han send envoys to them? If I wish to send envoys to Yue 越 [south of China], would Han be willing to allow us?" He detained [Zhang] Qian for more than ten years ...."

It is generally believed that Zhang Qian was sent to the Da Yuezhi in the 2nd year of the reign period Jianyuan of Emperor Wu (139 B.C.) and returned in 3rd year of the Yuanshuo 元朔 (126 B.C.), and that he consequently escaped from the Xiongnu and went to the Da Yuezhi in 129 B.C. In the same chapter it is recorded: "[Zhang Qian] escaped in the direction of the Yuezhi. Having sped westward for several tens of days he arrived in the state of Dayuan." Since the state of Dayuan was situated in the present Ferghāna Basin, the route Zhang Qian took shows that he knew the Da Yuezhi had given up the valleys of the Rivers Ili and Chu. Thus this date must have been between 139 and 129 B.C.

3. In the *Hanshu*, ch. 52, it is recorded that in the 2nd year of the reign period Yuanguang 元光 (133 B.C.), Wang Hui 王恢 reported to Emperor Wu:

> Now, given the prosperity of Zhongguo 中國 ['Middle Kingdom' = China], the dispatch of one per cent of its vast resources to attack the Xiongnu, could no more be resisted than a bolt from a powerful crossbow fired at an ulcer which is about to break. If [Your Majesty] acts thus, the Northern Fa 北發 and the Yuezhi can be brought into subjection.

According to the same chapter, "Wang Hui was a native of Yan 燕 He served frequently as a frontier official, and consequently was familiar with the situation of the Hu (the Xiongnu)," He would not make assertions without good grounds. This shows that the Da Yuezhi still lived in the valleys of the Rivers Ili and Chu. Therefore, the date when the Da Yuezhi gave up the area can be narrowed to between 133 and 129 B.C.

4. According to Western historical records, in *circa* 129 B.C., Phraates II (139/8-128 B.C.), the Arsacid king, made an expedition to the Syrian kingdom under the Seleucids. However, he had to tum round to fight against the Sakas, and was killed in action in the next year, because the Sakas broke through his north-eastern frontier and mounted a large-scale invasion. The Sakas who invaded the Arsacids may have been the Asii, the Tochari and other tribes who had lived in Sogdiana and Bactria. By suffering assaults from the Da Yuezhi who migrated west, a group of the Sakas was forced to rush within the boundaries of the Arsacids. Therefore, the date that the Da Yuezhi gave up the valleys of the Rivers Ili and Chu can further be specified to 130 B.C.

5. In the *Hanshu*, ch. 96A, it is recorded:

[The Da Yuezhi] originally lived between Dunhuang and Qilian. Then the time came when the Chanyu Modu attacked and defeated the Yuezhi, and the Chanyu Laoshang killed [the king] of the Yuezhi, making his skull into a drinking vessel. The Yuezhi thereupon went far away, passing Da-yuan and proceeding west to attack and subjugate Daxia. The principal city was established north of the River Gui 媯.

At first glance, it seems that the Da Yuezhi gave up the valleys of the Rivers Ili and Chu during the reign period of Chanyu Laoshang. However, it seems the corresponding records of the *Hanshu*, which were based on the account of the *Shiji*, ch. 123, missed the original meanings to some extent. The original text of the *Shiji*, ch. 123, is as follows:

> When Modu ascended the throne, he attacked and defeated the Yuezhi. By to [sic] the reign period of Chanyu Laoshang, [the Xiongnu] killed the king of the Yuezhi, and made a drinking vessel out of his skull. The Yuezhi originally lived between Dunhuang and Qilian. Having been defeated by the Xiongnu, they went far away. Passing [Da]yuan and proceeding west, they attacked and subjugated Daxia ....

According to this, Sima Qian, the editor of the *Shiji*, only generally attributed the western migration of the Yuezhi to the attack of the Xiongnu, and never mentioned that this migration of the Yuezhi took place during the reign period of Laoshang. There is no reason to consider that, in the mind of Sima Qian, the Yuezhi migrated west because of their king's being killed by Laoshang.

By an oversight, Ban Gu, the editor of the *Hanshu*, moved the statement, "the Yuezhi originally lived between Dunhuang and Qilian", ahead of this passage, and deleted the statement, "having been defeated by the Xiongnu", in order to give consideration to the ensuing statement of the same chapter, part B, "later, when the Kunmo of the Wusun attacked and defeated the Da Yuezhi, the Da Yuezhi migrated to the west and subjugated Daxia", with the result of making one misinterpret that the Yuezhi's migration to the valleys of the River Gui was because of their king's being killed by Laoshang. This view contradicts the account of the *Hanshu*, ch. 96.

In fact, the immediate cause of the Da Yuezhi give up the valleys of the Rivers Ili and Chu was undoubtedly their being attacked and defeated by the Kunmo of the Wusun, but the root cause was suffering heavy casualties from Laoshang beforehand. In addition, since Kunmo's attack on the Da Yuezhi was instigated by the Xiongnu, the statement of the *Shiji*, ch. 123, "having been defeated by the Xiongnu, they went far away", is sweeping, but explains an essential aspect of the event." Yu (1998), pp. 54-55.

"Following their later defeat and eviction at the hands of the Wusun in 133/2, another sub-group of the Greater (or Da) Yuezhi apparently also chose not to continue the migration westwards with the bulk of the confederation. The *Han Shu* notes that groups of both Saka and Yuezhi remained in the Ili Basin to be assimilated with the Wusun . . . . The Sakas must have been remnants of the original occupants of the Ili who had been absorbed into the Yuezhi federation in 162, and members of both the Saka and Yuezhi confederacies then similarly decided to remain in the region following the Wusun invasion. This decision reflects a familiar pattern in pastoral nomadic politics, where both the Yuezhi king and later the Wusun *Kunmo* were able to persuade elements of the resident peoples of the region to split from the ruling dynasty and support the Yuezhi and Wusun occupations of the Ili, in return for the right to remain settled in the region.

This suggests that, as has often been the case in Inner Asian history, the ethnic makeup of many of both the Yuezhi and Wusun, and indeed of all the great tribal nomadic states, was mixed and diverse. Thus terms like 'Yuezhi', 'Wusun' and 'Mongol' more accurately refer to dynasties ruling over confederations of pastoral nomads, including tribes of different ethnicities and different languages. As such the yabghu division refers to groups that accepted Yuezhi suzerainty (and therefore in a sense were Yuezhi), but were not necessarily ethnically Yuezhi. . . . The entity that migrated to Bactria was little more than a ruling dynasty, along with the tribes that remained with them. This tradition of referring to a confederation of ethnically diverse people by the name of the ruling dynasty was well established in Central Asia, and would be continued in Bactria nearly two centuries later, when a new controlling dynasty that grew out of the Yuezhi confederation (and which may have had little or nothing in common ethnically with the 'original' Yuezhi dynasty) would assume power over that grouping, and give its name to the subsequent empire of the Kueizhuang [sic - should read Guishuang (Pinyin) or Kuei-shuang (W-G)], or Kushans." Benjamin (2007), p. 126.

"Mao-tun [the king of the Hsiung-nu or Xiongnu] was inspired by the unification of China by the Emperor Ch'in Shih-huang-ti in 221 B.C.; the first blow of the Hsiung-nu against the Yüeh-chih was given about this time. It resulted in the withdrawal of the Yüeh-chih to the western part of Gansu Province. The Hsiung-nu were originally a pastoral people in the steppes north of the Yin-shan mountain range. Szŭ-ma Ch'ien states that the Yüeh-chih were the only people who pressed the Hsiung-nu from the west. This may mean that the Yüeh-chih were seeking to control the greater part of the Mongolian plain. . . .

About 204-200 B.C. Mao-tun conquered Mongolia and subjugated several peoples. In 176 B.C. he defeated the Yüeh-chih in the western part of Gansu Province. In his letter to the Han, Mao-tun said that the Hsiung-nu had destroyed the Yüeh-chih; and Lou-lan, Wu-sun, Hu-chieh and twenty-six other countries in the neighbourhood were subjugated to the Hsiung-nu [see: *Shiji* Chap. 123, in Watson (1993), p. 140]. It is an exaggeration to say that they destroyed the Yüeh-chih, but it is clear that the Yüeh-chih were driven from the west of Gansu and probably moved from the north of the T'ien Shan mountains. What is important is that all these countries were subjugated as a result of the defeat of the Yüeh-chih, that is, they had been under the control of the Yüeh-chih up to that time.

Lou-lan, later called Shan-shan, is a country near Lop Nor in the eastern part of the Tarim basin. The Wu-sun were a pastoral people in the region of the River Ili and Lake Issîk-köl, north of the T'ien Shan mountains. The twenty-six other countries seem to have been small states in the Tarim basin, probably including Casia mentioned above. As regards Hu-chieh, no definite identification has been made. . . .

The dominion of the Yüeh-chih also extended as far south as the upper waters of the Yellow River. Szŭ-ma Ch'ien states that a small part of the Yüeh-chih, who could not follow the migration of the main horde towards the west, settled themselves in Nan-shan, the southern mountains, which separate the upper waters of the Yellow River people from the Mongolian plain.

The date of migration of the Yüeh-chih to Ta-hsia [Daxia] is not clearly known. The Hsiung-nu gave a third blow to the Yüeh-chih during the reign of Lao-shang *shan-yü* (*c.* 174-161 B.C.) [see the discussion of Chris Dorn'eich's 2010 paper, "The Great Yuezhi/A(r)si Exodus of 166 BCE" above] when Lao-shang had a drinking bowl made from the skull of the king of the Yüeh-chih]. But it is generally believed that the conquest of Ta-hsia was made sometime between 139 and 128 B.C., that is, between the departure of Chang Ch'ien and his arrival at the court of the Yüeh-chih." Enoki, et al. (1994), pp. 174-175.

"The main horde, going westward [after their final defeat by the Xiongnu in 166 BCE], fell on the Wu-sun, killed their king, and must have attempted to occupy their grazing lands and been driven out again, presumably by the Hiung-nu. Still going westward, somewhere before 160 they attacked a people called Sai-wang[4] about Lake Issyk Kul and the plain northward of the Alexandrovski range and attempted to occupy their lands; the Sai-wang, or some part of them, fled southward (pp. 277 *sq*).

But in or just before the year 160[5] the Yueh-chi were again attacked by the son of the dead Wu-sun king with the help of the Hiung-nu and were driven out of the Sai-wang county, of which the Wu-sun took possession; the main body of the Yueh-chi again went westward, though some remained and were ultimately absorbed by the Wu-sun, as were also some Sai-wang elements who had not joined in the flight southward. After 160 the Yueh-chi vanish from view for a generation—a fact which has not been noticed—till we meet them again shortly before 128 . . . .

[4] I follow Konow in keeping the Chinese name Sai-wang (Franke's view), literally 'King of the Sai', so as to beg no questions as to who they were. De Groot, p. 25, would prefer to render the name Sak-ke or Sik-ke (*i.e.* Sacas), but admits that Franke may be right; Franke in a note maintains his view. All I want myself is a word which will distinguish this Saca people from others.

[5] This date, established by Franke p. 55, is now a fixed point."

Tarn (1984), p. 276 and nn. 4-5, p. 277.

For further information on the origins and migrations of the Da Yuezhi, see: Mallory and Mair (2000), especially pp. 58-59, 94-99, 280-284, 333-334; and Benjamin (2003).

• Did the Da Yuezhi migrate further west after their defeat by the Wusun?

After the flight of the Yuezhi, the Xiongnu made many raids into China and posed a constant threat to the empire. The Emperor therefore sent Zhang Qian to see if he could obtain the help of the Da Yuezhi to defeat the Xiongnu.

When Zhang Qian set out in the spring of 139 BCE, both the Chinese and Xiongnu obviously believed the Da Yuezhi were still settled in the region of the Ili Valley and Issyk Kul. The statement made by the Xiongnu Chanyu to Zhang Qian, after he was captured, confirms this. He said: "The Yuezhi people live north of me." *Shiji* 123 in Watson (1993), p. 231.

Shiji 123 mentions that the Great Yuezhi, after their final defeat by the Xiongnu, moved "beyond Dayuan," attacked and conquered the people of Daxia and set up their court on the northern bank of the Oxus River." See the quote from Watson (1993), p. 234 in Appendix M. There is no detail on their movements en route to Daxia or any reference to a further defeat by the Wusun.

In talking about the Wusun, *Shiji* 123 says: "They were originally subjects of the Xiongnu, but later, becoming more powerful, they refused any longer to attend the gatherings of the Xiongnu court, though still acknowledging themselves as part of the Xiongnu nation." *Shiji* 123, in: Watson (1993), p. 234.

This brief account is expanded later on in the same chapter. When Shanyu Jizhu (nicknamed 'Laoshang') died *circa* 161 BCE, the Wusun Kunmo "declared himself an independent ruler, and refused to journey to the meetings of the Xiongnu court. The Xiongnu sent surprise parties of troops to attack him, but they were unable to defeat him. In the end the Xiongnu decided that he must be a god and left him alone, still claiming that he was a subject of theirs but no longer making any large-scale attacks on him." *Shiji* 123, in: Watson (1993), p. 238.

Hanshu 61 (*CICA*, p. 217, and n. 808) provides further details, although the order of events appears jumbled. For example, it implies that the Kunmo moved away to the west *before* and not *after* the death of Jizhu Chanyu, as in *Shiji* 123, which seems improbable.

The migration of the Da Yuezhi to the banks of the Oxus could not have taken longer than 10 years. The lands of Dayuan and Kangju that they are said to have traversed, would not have been able to support an extra 400,000 people (see *CICA*, p. 119) for so long. As mentioned above, the Chanyu still believed that the Da Yuezhi lived to the north of his territory *circa* 119 BCE. Also, see: Pulleyblank, (1970), pp. 158-160 and the accompanying notes quoted in Appendix I.

Appendix M: The Kingdom of Daxia

There are several theories regarding the history and derivation of the name Daxia 大夏 (W-G: Ta-hsia) = *Takha.

> "Thus it will be seen that the history of Bactria falls naturally into four divisions. Passing over the mass of legend which surrounds the earliest period, centred chiefly round the figure of Zarathustra Spitama, we find ourselves on more solid ground when we come to deal with Bactria as a satrapy of the Persian Empire. After the overthrow of Persia by Alexander we enter upon the second phase in the history of the country—its subjugation and settlement by the Macedonians. The third period begins with the revolt of Diodotus in 250 B.C, when Bactria assumes the role of an independent Greek kingdom, extending its sway not only over Sogdiana to the north, but over a great portion of the modern Afghanistan and the Panjab. The closing chapter of the history of the Bactrian Greeks commences with their evacuation of the country north of the Hindu-Kush, when they made Sâgala their capital, and ends with their final supersession by the Kushan monarchs." Rawlinson (1912), pp. xiii-xiv.

Bactria remained independent under the Greco-Bactrians, for over a hundred years until, according to some scholars, Saka tribes invaded it. This invasion by the Sakas, if it did occur, was closely followed by that of the Da Yuezhi, who conquered the region *circa* 130 BCE.

The earliest Chinese account of Daxia is in *Shiji*, Chapter 123, based on reports of the Chinese envoy Zhang Qian who visited the region soon after the Da Yuezhi conquered it from summer, 129 to autumn 128 BCE,. See: Appendix L

> "Daxia is situated over 2,000 *li* [838 km] southwest of Dayuan [Ferghana], south of the Gui [Oxus] River. Its people cultivate the land and have cities and houses. Their customs are like those of Dayuan. It has no great ruler but only a number of petty chiefs ruling the various cities. The people are poor in the use of arms and afraid of battle, but they are clever at commerce. After the Great Yuezhi moved west and attacked and conquered Daxia, the entire country came under their sway. The population of the country is large, numbering some 1,000,000 or more persons. The capital is called the city of Lanshi (Bactra)* and has a market where all sorts of goods are bought and sold.
>
> Southeast of Daxia is the kingdom of Shendu (India). "When I was in Daxia," Zhang Qian reported, "I saw bamboo canes from Qiong [a district in Sichuan] and cloth made in the province of Shu [Sichuan]. When I asked the people how they had gotten such articles, they replied, 'Our merchants go to buy them in the markets of Shendu.' Shendu, they told me, lies several thousand *li* southeast of Daxia." *Shiji* 123, 13-14, from Watson (1993), pp. 235-236. See also notes 13.3 and 13.4, and the similar passage in *Hanshu* 96A – *CICA*, pp. 120-121.
>
> *I don't agree with this identification of Lanshi as Balkh, I believe the evidence is strong that it was, in fact, Baghlan. See: Appendix N. (JEH)

The translation of this passage by Watson: "After the Great Yuezhi moved west and attacked and conquered Daxia, the entire country came under their sway," is so compressed that some of the information in the Chinese text is lost.

Rendered literally it reads: "After the Great Yuezhi moved west, they attacked and conquered Daxia (including) everything (even) government officials and livestock." (及大月氏西徙，攻敗之，皆臣畜大夏)

This historically important passage states that the Da Yuezhi controlled the *whole* of Daxia south of the Oxus at the time of Zhang Qian's visit. There is no hint that Parthians or Sakas controlled any of this territory when the Da Yuezhi arrived, as some have suggested.

"There is no numismatic evidence of any Ṣaka activity in western and southern Afghanistan. The only evidence of the Ṣaka invasion is from literary sources and all the nomadic peoples had been either destroyed or had submitted to the Parthians by about 80 B.C.

The establishment of the Ṣaka rule was solely the feat of those tribes who came to India through Wakhan and the first trace of their activity is the coinage of Maues [epigraphically MAYOY *Mauou*, r. 85–60 BCE]. The Ṣakas invading India need not have been numerous. It is worth recalling that the Longobards who entered Italy in 568 A.D. and in a few years conquered most of the peninsula numbered less than 300,000 including women and children. That there were no Ṣakas in Bactria proper is shown by many facts and particularly by the statement that the Parthian king Artabanus I was killed in 124 B.C. when fighting the Tochari, who may have been a Yueh-chih tribe, but who were certainly not Ṣakas." Simonetta & Widemann (1978), p. 167.

"Von Gutschmid says it is "remarkable that Chang [Zhang Qian] notices no difference between the Greeks and their Iranian subjects." The explanation is simple : there were no pure Greeks left. Some remains of the old Aryan (Iranian, not Greek) population may still be traced in the language of the non-Tartar people dwelling round Balkh (Rawlinson, *Herodotus*, App., Book VII., Essay 1, p. 207 ; M. Müller, *Languages of the Seat of War*, p. 33)." Rawlinson (1912), p. 94, n. 1.

In the late 2nd century BCE, territory of Daxia that was conquered extended from the southern slopes of the Zeravshan Range, which separates the Ferghana Valley from that of the Middle Oxus River, across the Oxus to the Hindu Kush in the south (with the possible exception of Bactra/Balkh, and the irrigated lands along the adjoining Zariaspa River).

To the east, Daxia incorporated what is now Badakhshan, with the Pamir Massif forming the boundary. To the southeast, it extended to the Panjshir Valley. The western border with Parthia was defined by the desert lands between Bactria and Margiana, and the province of Ariana (Greek: ἡ 'Αρειανή/Arianē), with its capital at Herat.

Strabo tells us that: "When the Greeks got possession of the country, they divided it into satrapies; that of Aspionus and Turiva the Parthians took from Eucratidas." Strabo translated by Falconer (1857). Otherwise, the names of these satrapies are unknown. Presumably, they were territories close to Margiana, possibly in the Oxus River valley to the west of Termez.

"By dividing this new realm into satrapies, the Diodotids followed the established path of Hellenistic state building. The number and names of these satrapies remain unknown, except for the two nearest Parthia to the west, Aspionus and Turiva (Tapuria?).[51] It seems possible that Bactria proper, south of the Oxus and west of Ai Khanoum, was subdivided into satrapies on the basis of habitation zones (e.g. Darya Sripul, with perhaps an administrative center at Emshi-Tepe). Sogdiana, too, might have been organized in this way. The major tributaries to the Middle Oxus formed natural valley enclaves that Alexander's army had invaded in separate missions and subsequently colonized. In two of these valleys archaeologists have identified what appear to be regional administrative centers of the third century B.C.: Dalverzin Tepe in the heart of the Surkhan Darya Valley and Kobadian alongside the Kafirnigan River. They resemble Ai Khanoum but on a smaller scale, with walls, a citadel, temples, palace, aristocratic quarters, and so forth. Here might be the satrapies and their local capitals in the time of Diodotus I and II.

51. Number: Seleucus I is said to have tripled the number of satrapies in his realm (Appian *Syr.* 62). For recent discussion, see Sherwin-White and Kuhrt, *Samarkand to Sardis*, pp. 44-45. Names: the usual emendation of Strabo gives Tapuria, an area somewhere between Hyrcania and Aria, in a

mountainous region once part of Media: Strabo 11.8.8; 11.9.1; 11.11.8; 11.13.3. this, however, is very far to the west of Bactria. In another case, Polybius 10.49. 1 has been emended to read Tapuria (instead of Ta Gourana) for the locale of Euthydemus's battle to forestall the punitive invasion of Antiochus the Great. The exact geography escapes us."

Holt (1999), pp. 55-56 and note 51.

There were at least two other places called Daxia 大夏 in early Chinese texts. Another 'Daxia' known to the Chinese was a town in northern Shaanxi Province (34° 40' 13 N, 107° 28' 24 E). In addition, from 407-431 CE, the Xiongnu set up a Daxia kingdom in Shaanxi Province. It is important not to confuse these places with the Daxia captured by the Yuezhi.

Further, nowadays a river known as the Daxia He 大夏河 (or Sang Qu) is located southwest of Lanzhou in Gansu Province, where the influential Labrang or Xiahe Monastery is situated, but we do not know what it was called in Han times.

Chavannes argues that the name Daxia 大夏 was used by Lu Buwei (who died in 235 BCE) to describe a state west of the Kunlun Mountains, almost certainly referring to a part of ancient Bactria:

"If the Kunlun were not mentioned in the texts, one would hesitate to recognise Bactria in *Daxia*. In fact, the name *Daxia* was applied to a part of *Shaanxi*; cf. tome II, p. 148, n. 6. In that note I have said that, in the time of Qin Huangdi [259–210 BCE], the Chinese did not know of the Bactrian *Daxia*. The texts which I now quote regarding Linglun and the sonorous flutes seems to me to prove that, from the period of Lu Buwei [291?-235 BCE] and Qin Shi Huangdi, the Chinese had knowledge of the country of *Daxia* situated near the *Kunlun*, that is to say, the country which later became the Greco-Bactrian kingdom and which, from this period, was imbued with Greek influences.

I should add that, in all the texts in which the Daxia in *Shaanxi* figures, the country is cited as the *northern* limit of the empire; on the contrary, in the texts which refer to *Linglun*, *Daxia* is given as a *western* country, and to go to the west of *Daxia*, is to enter the Far West." Translated and adapted from Chavannes' *Les Mémoires Historiques de Se-ma Ts'ien* (1899-1905), Vol. III, Appendix II, p. 328, n. a32.(120). Also, see: pp. 216-217 and n. a32. (121).

A. Franke disagrees with Chavannes' argument that the Chinese knew of a Bactrian Daxia before the time of Zhang Qian's return to China. See: Franke (1920), pp. 125, 129, 132. While I tend to agree with Chavannes, it must be admitted that the evidence is sparse.

The placename Daxia 大夏 was clearly not an attempt by the Chinese to transcribe the Greek name 'Baktria'. A more plausible suggestion is that Daxia was an attempt to transcribe *Takhar or *Tokhar into Chinese, a form which is very similar to the names of the Takhari and Tokhari people or peoples and various similar ethnic and place names in the region of the Tarim Basin recorded by western classical authors. This would also mean it was related to the later place-name of 'Tokharistan.'

"In fact, the collapse of Greek rule in Bactria was the first historical phenomenon ever recorded by both European and Asian sources. Greek, Latin, and Chinese texts mention the occupation of Bactria by nomadic peoples, who wrested the region away from the last of the Greek rulers, including the golden king Eucratides and his family. In a sense, globalism was born in Bactria, for at that same moment, the earth shrank even further when a Greek rival of Eucratides named Menander worked his solitary way into Indian literature by allegedly converting to Buddhism. Menander's massive outlay of silver coins proclaimed his name and titles in both Greek and native Indian scripts, and they carried the image of Athena Alcidemus ("Defender of the

People")—the patron deity of Macedonian Pella, Alexander the Great's birthplace. Where else in the world could anyone find such a tangle of cultural traditions, including a Greek Buddhist raja relating to his native subjects in their own language while displaying the warlike insignia of a conqueror's hometown three thousand miles (5,555 km) away?" Holt (2012), p. 2.

• The Invasions of Daxia?

The *Shiji* and *Hanshu* mention two tribes involved in the conquest of Daxia and Jibin; the Da Yuezhi are said to have conquered Daxia; and the Saiwang or "King of the Sai" who "established himself as master of" Jibin.

In the accounts that have survived from Western classical authors it is, more complex. Strabo (Στράβων; 64/63 BCE–24 CE), wrote in Greek and completed his *Geography* in 23 CE, at about the same time as Trogus was working on his '*Historiae Philippicae*'.

Unfortunately, Trogus' main work did not survive apart from the brief prologues (forewords) for each section. These were written by Justin, around the mid-2nd to the mid-3rd century CE and are, unfortunately, so brief they are often rather cryptic. They are similar in form to the chapter headings found in some 19th century books.

> "Some things about Trogus' history are reasonably clear and uncontroversial. His work fell into the genre of universal history. Somewhat earlier, Diodorus of Sicily had produced 40 books in an attempt to encompass the history of the known world from mythical times to 59 B.C. Trogus' contemporary Nicholas of Damascus produced a massive 144 books, stretching from Ninus of Assyria to 4 B.C. The difference in Trogus' work was that it was in Latin and that it concentrated on Near Eastern and Greek affairs, relying essentially on Greek sources. He also picked up on the theme of succeeding empires: Assyria, Medes, Persia, Macedonian kingdoms, Rome (but nothing substantial), Carthage, and the Parthians in Books 41 and 42. It follows that the work concentrates on the deeds and behaviour of kings and tyrants." Yardley (1994), p. 7.

• Epitome on Book 41

> "At about the same time that Mithridates ['the Great' – ruled *circa* 171-138 BCE] was beginning his rule in Parthia, Eucratides was beginning his in Bactria [ruled *circa* 170–155 or 145 BCE], both of them great men. But the fortunes of the Parthians prevailed, carrying them to the zenith of their power under this king. The Bactrians, for their part were buffeted in various conflicts and lost not just their empire but their liberty as well. Worn down by wars with the Sogdians, Arachosians, Drancae, Arei and Indians, they finally fell, virtually in a state of exhaustion, under the power of the Parthians, a weaker people than themselves. Eucratides nevertheless conducted many wars with great valour. Weakened by these, he found himself facing a siege by Demetrius [of the Bactrian dynasty of Euthydemus I which was overthrown by Eucratides], king of the Indians, but by making repeated sorties he was able to defeat 60,000 of the enemy with 300 men. Delivered from the siege after four months, he then brought India under his sway. During the return journey from India, he was murdered by his son, whom he had made partner in his royal power. The son did not conceal his parricide and, as though he had killed an enemy rather than his father, drove his chariot through his blood, ordering the corpse to be cast aside." Epitome Book 41, VI, 1-5 translated in Yardley (1994), p. 257.

- **Epitome on Book 42**

"On the death of Mithridates, king of Parthia [c. 138 BCE], his son Phrahates [ruled *circa* 138-128 BCE] was made king. Phrahates had determined to open hostilities with Syria to avenge Antiochus' attack on the kingdom of Parthia, but he was recalled to the defence of his own territory by unrest among the Scythians. These had been induced by an offer of pay to come to the aid of the Parthians against Antiochus, king of Syria; but, since they arrived on the scene only when the battle was over and were cheated of their pay on the pretext that they had arrived too late with their support, they regretted having made such a long journey for nothing and demanded either compensation for their inconvenience or another enemy to fight. Receiving a disdainful response, the Scythians took offense and proceeded to lay waste Parthian territory. Phrahates accordingly marched out to meet them . . . . Phrahates himself led an army of Greeks which he had captured in the war against Antiochus and had treated them in an offensive and brutal manner, forgetting that captivity had not diminished their hostility towards him and that, indeed, the humiliating mistreatment they had suffered at his hands had further exacerbated it. Thus it happened that, when they saw the Parthian line give ground, the Greeks went over to the enemy and took long-desired revenge for their captivity with a bloody massacre of the Parthian army along with King Phrahates himself.

Phrahates was replaced by his uncle Artabanus [ruled *circa* 128-124 BCE]. The Scythians, satisfied with their victory, merely ravaged Parthia and went back home. Artabanus then made war on the Tocharii, but received a wound to the arm from which he immediately died. He was succeeded by his son Mithridates [II; ruled 123 to 88 BCE], whose achievements earned him the sobriquet "the Great"—burning with ambition to rival the valour of his forebears, he actually surpassed them in renown by his greatness of spirit. He conducted many wars against his neighbours with great courage and added many peoples to the Parthian empire." Epitome Book 42, I, 1-5; II, 1-4, translated in Yardley (1994), pp. 258-259.

- **Trogus' Prologue 41:**

"**41.** Parthian and Bactrian history. The establishment of the empire in Parthia by King Arsaces, followed by his successors Artabanus and Tigranes, surnamed the Divine, by whom Media and Mesopotamia were brought into subjection. There is a digression on the geography of Arabia. Next comes Bactrian history; with a description of the founding of the empire by King Diodotus and then, during his reign, the occupation of Bactra and Sogdiana by the Scythian tribes, the Saraucae and the Asiani. There is also some Indian history, namely the achievements of the Indian kings of the Apollodotus and Menander." Translated in Yardley (1994), pp. 284-285. See also the translation in Pearse (2003). Downloaded on 25 March, 2012 from: http://www.tertullian.org/fathers/justinus_08_prologi.htm

This brief passage has led to disputes among scholars regarding the time of Bactria's occupation and whether the "Saraucae" and "Asiani" were the only tribes involved in the downfall of the Greco-Bactrian state.

According to Yardley, the passage states that these events took place during the reign of Diodotus, the Seleucid satrap of Bactria. He rebelled against Seleucid rule soon after Antiochus II died, probably about 246 BCE, and gained independence for Bactria. He is thought to have died about 239 BCE.

Other scholars believe that Bactria gained independence earlier, *circa* 250 BCE, and there are further arguments as to whether this happened under Diodotus I, or his son Diodotus II.

> "In this book we shall take steps in order to explain for the first time the origins of Bactria as an independent Hellenistic state. The focus must be on Diodotus I and II, the father and son who dared to break free of the Seleucid empire beginning around 250 B.C. Through the examination of ancient texts, archaeological sites, and, most important, the Bactrian coins, the Diodotids emerge from the shadows of Hellenistic history as true heirs of Alexander. An ambitious and opportunistic gambler who made good on his chances for greatness, the elder Diodotus became less a loyal satrap of the Seleucid ruler and more an autocratic dynast. He revised the Bactrian coinage and eventually, in about 246 B.C., elevated his son to a powerful position as co-ruler within the province. This Diodotus II established a second major mint in Bactria and, like his father, graced the coinage with his own portrait. Still, these men hedged their bets in their high-stakes game by keeping the name of the Seleucid king, Antiochus II, on the coin of the realm.
>
> In about 240 B.C. the fortunes of father and son took a turn for the better when their military forces drove from Bactria a renegade named Arsaces, later the founder of the Parthian empire. The victory was celebrated on the coinage and allowed Diodotus I to take the cult title Soter for saving the Greeks of Bactria from a barbarian invader. All of the elements of an independent Hellenistic monarchy were then in place, but the death of the father passed that honor to his son in about 235 B.C. Diodotus II finally put his own name on the coinage and declared Bactria the newest Hellenistic kingdom; the evolution from a Seleucid satrapy to a sovereign state was at last complete." Holt (1999), p. 19.

If we agree with Yardley, it would seem these events took place about a century before the Da Yuezhi arrived on the scene. This provide evidence that the Asiani or Asii (who are mentioned in later reports as one of the tribes who were involved in the downfall of Greco-Bactria in the 140s BCE) could not be the Yuezhi, as the latter were only very recent arrivals in the region.

In spite of this, there are some who believe that the Asiani/Asii were in fact the Da Yuezhi. This proposal is based on differences between early editions of Trogus, as discussed below.

- **Trogus' Prologue 42:**

> "**42.** Parthian history. . . . There is also a section on Scythian history, then one on the Asian [literally, 'Asiani'] kings of the Tochari, and on the demise of the Saraucae."
>
> > "In the forty-second volume are contained Parthian affairs. How the prefect of Parthia created by Phrates, Himerus, made war on the Meseni and of his brutal treatment of the people of Babylon and Seleucia: how Phrates was succeeded on the throne by King Mithridates surnamed The Great, who made war on the Armenians. Then the origins and geography of Armenia are recalled. How, after a succession of several different kings in Parthia, Orodes came to the throne, who destroyed Crassus and occupied Syria through his son Pacorus. He [Orodes] was succeeded by Phrates, who went to war both with Antony and with Tiridates. Scythian affairs are added to this. The Asian kings of the Tochari, and the demise of the Saraucae." Pearse (2003). Downloaded on the 25 March, 2012, from: http://www.tertullian.org/ fathers/justinus_08_prologi.htm
> >
> > "Trogus says that he adds the relevant Scythian history here: how the Asiani became the kings of the Tochari and how the Saraucae were destroyed — two chapters of one story. The Latin text is simple and clear." Dorn'eich (personal communication 26 July 2007).

I suggest that Trogus' text claiming the Asiani became the kings of the Tochari could mean that Kujula Kadphises was of Asiani descent. If so, by conquering and melding the five *xihous* into one empire, it would be correct to say that the Asiani became kings of the Tochari.

Kujula may have descended from a family that settled in the area following the invasion by the Sacaraucae and Asiani in the time of Diodotus (around the middle of the 3rd century BCE). However, I must stress that this is pure speculation, and I have no evidence to back it up – though it is a possible explanation for this otherwise puzzling text.

Questioned if the text might simply mean that "Asians" became the rulers of the Tochari, Mark Passehl commented that this interpretation:

> ". . . is technically possible, but meaningless since all the rulers of the Tochari were at all times Asians (in Greco-Roman eyes).
>
> I understand *reges tocharorum asiani* to mean that in the period covered by Book 42 (120s-20s BCE) the Tochari lost their native dynasty and came to be ruled by a foreign dynasty whose ethnicity was Asianic as I would say (to distinguish from the general term Asian).
>
> "Demise" is a bit soft for *interitus* which can mean "ruin" in any sense, but more usually destruction or annihilation. [See, for example, the translation in Lebedynsky (2006), p. 62] . . . .
>
> There are significant manuscript variations almost every time the Tocharian name appears in Greek or Latin texts, and Trogus *Prol.* 42 is no different, exhibiting the (genitive) forms "thoclarorum" and "toclarorum" (as well as "thodaroroum", where the "c" and "l" have been conjoined). . . .
>
> The Vatican palimpsest (*Vat. Gr.* 2306) of Strabo's text now confirms the reading "sakaraukai" at xi.2.8 – see Ciancaglini (2001), pp. 14-15." Mark Passehl (personal communication, 15 May, 2007).

> "The silence that fell later over this ethnic name ['Tochari'] probably derives from their elimination from the view of the west. Soon after [the intervention against Artabanus I in 124/123 BCE], in fact about 120 BCE, other nomads, "western" this time, occupied their place in the west : the Sacaraucae. . . .
>
> As Justin relates, the Sacaraucae disappear as an ethno-politico-military entity at a date that can be fixed about the end of the 1st century BCE [although in the 2nd century, Ptolemy VI, 14, 14 mentions 'Sagaraukai' living near the coast of the Caspian Sea, between the Jaxartes and the Oxus. Ptolemy (b), p. 110 – see quote above].
>
> Before this event, they seem to have already imposed a part of their culture on the whole of the region, as witnessed by their necropolises of the Bukhara oasis and Koktepe (a necropolis of the first phase) on the Zerafshan, as far as the Babashov and towards the headwaters of the Oxus, as far as the valley of Bishkent, where they mixed with the Yuezhi. Their disappearance occurred at the period of great social-political changes. During all of the 1st century BCE they suffered pressure from the Parthians to the west and south and the Kangju empire to the north (which ended by encompassing the territories of the Zerafshan and Kashka-darya : see the *Han shu*). A decisive frontier took shape along the Hissar chain when the Yuezhi consolidated their sedentary foundation, while beyond the Kangju protected their nomadic structure." Translated by the author from Rapin (2001), pp. 84-85; 87.

Strabo mentions four tribes: the Asioi, the Pasianoi, the Tacharoi (or Tokharoi) and the Sakaraukai, but they can be reduced to three tribes if the text is slightly "corrected."

> "But the simple historical facts (from a major Hellenistic historian [Strabo] who specialized in the epoch from 145 B.C. to Augustus) are that a very short list of

nomadic peoples seized control of Bactria from the Greeks: Sacaraucae, Tochari, Asii and Pasiani, while the fourth name here is sometimes understood as the result of a transcription error (pi supplanting eta) so that "Pasiani" disguises Strabo's true meaning "Asii or [as they are also known] Asiani". I agree with this view.

In any case the Yuezhi must correspond to one of these three (or four) people, and if there's no correspondence with any of them (which there isn't) then it follows that Yuezhi is an old Chinese label which didn't attempt to transcribe the real nomen ethnicum but had another meaning of significance to the Chinese. There are countless similar examples, perhaps most notably the fairly rude/abusive label Xiongnu for the greatest eastern steppe power of the epoch." Mark Passehl, personal communication, 5 September, 2011.

Trogus connects three tribes with Bactria: the Asiani, Saraucae and the Tochari, generally thought to be the same as the Asioi, Tacharoi and Sakaraukai of Strabo, perhaps leaving one (otherwise unattested) tribe, the 'Pasianoi' of Strabo, unaccounted for.

Trogus does not claim that the three tribes invaded Bactria, as is often assumed. In his Prologue 41, he mentions two tribes, the Asioi and Sakaraukai and the version of the text we have specifies that, *during* the reign of Bactria's first independent king, Diodotus, these tribes conquered Sogdiana and the city of Bactra – *not* the whole country of Bactria.

The third tribe, the Tochari, are said to be ruled by the Asiani. Hence, the theory that the Tochari were the people already living in the region (referred to in the Chinese accounts as the Daxia). Therefore, it was asserted that the Asiani/Asioi *must* refer to the Da Yuezhi.

The *Shiji* is specific that Daxia was *south* of the Gui/Oxus river and that: "After the Great Yuezhi moved west and attacked and conquered Daxia, the *entire* country came under their sway." (My italics) There is no mention in the Chinese records of Sakas or Parthians in Daxia.

- **The Invasions of Bactria according to Strabo XI, 11.**

"SOME parts of Bactria lie along Aria to the north, but the greater part stretches beyond (Aria) to the east. It is an extensive country, and produces everything except [olive or other seed] oil.

The Greeks who occasioned its revolt became so powerful by means of the fertility and advantages of the country, that they became masters of Ariana and India, according to Apollodorus of Artamita. Their chiefs, particularly Menander, (if he really crossed the Hypanis to the east and reached Isamus,) conquered more nations than Alexander. These conquests were achieved partly by Menander, partly by Demetrius, son of Euthydemus, king of the Bactrians. They got possession not only of Pattalene, but of the kingdoms of Saraostus, and Sigerdis, which constitute the remainder of the coast. Apollodorus in short says that Bactriana is the ornament of all Ariana. They extended their empire even as far as the Seres [perhaps as far as Juandu (Irkeshtam) just east of Kashgar – see quote from Tarn in note 2.14] and Phryni.

Their cities were Bactra, which they call also Zariaspa, (a river of the same name flows through it, and empties itself into the Oxus,) and Darapsa, and many others. Among these was Eucratidia, which had its name from Eucratidas, the king [reigned 170-145 BCE]. When the Greeks got possession of the country, they divided it into satrapies; that of Aspionus and Turiva the Parthians took from Eucratidas. They possessed Sogdiana also, situated above Bactriana to the east, between the river Oxus (which bounds Bactriana and Sogdiana) and the Iaxartes; the latter river separates the Sogdii and the nomades." Strabo XI.11 in Falconer (1857). **NOTE:** The name 'Phryni' above is given (in Latin) as Phuni in Pliny VI, 55. Aspionus and Turiva are otherwise unknown. (JEH)

There is no record of the Chinese using the name Daxia for the region in northern Afghanistan *before* Zhang Qian's arrival in the summer of 129 BCE.

- **Bactria according to Ammianus Marcellinus**

"Next to them [i.e. the Margiani] are the Bactrians, a nation formerly very warlike and powerful, and always hostile to the Persians, till they drew all the nations around under their dominion, and united them under their own name; and in old time [sic] the Bactrian kings were formidable even to Arsaces.

The greater part of their country, like that of the Margiani, is situated far from the sea-shore, but its soil is fertile, and the cattle which feed both on the plains and on the mountains in that district are very large and powerful; of this the camels which Mithridates brought from thence, and which were first seen by the Romans at the siege of Cyzicus, are a proof.

Many tribes are subject to the Bactrians, the most considerable of which are the Tochari: their country is like Italy in the number of its rivers, some of which are the Artemis and the Zariaspes, which were formerly joined, and the Ochus and Orchomanes, which also unite and afterwards fall into the Oxus, and increase that large river with their streams.

There are also cities in that country, many of them on the border of different rivers, the best of which are Chatra, Charte, Alicodra, Astacea, Menapila, and Bactra itself, which has given its name both to the region and to the people.

At the foot of the mountains [to the north] lie a people called the Sogdians, in whose country are two rivers navigable for large vessels, the Araxates [= Jaxartes, see Smith 1856, p. 188] and the Dymas [likely the Polytimetus/Zerafshan river – see Holt (1993), p. 22], which, flowing among the hills and through the valleys into the open plain, form the extensive Oxian marsh. In this district the most celebrated towns are Alexandria, Cyreschata, and Drepsa the metropolis." Ammianus Marcellinus 23. 6. 55-59. Yonge (1862), pp. 339-340.

If the Tochari were indeed the Da Yuezhi, it seems absurd that Ammianus Marcellinus would say that the "Bactrians" were rulers of many tribes "the most considerable of which are the Tochari." All the Chinese sources agree that the Da Yuezhi conquered Daxia, not the other way around.

Furthermore, it seems there were approximately double the number of Daxian people in the region as Da Yuezhi. In *Shiji* 123 the Da Yuezhi are said to have "100,000 to 200,000 archer warriors" - implying a total population of roughly half a million people - while the Daxia who lived to the south of the Oxus (where Ptolemy places the "numerous" Tochari and the inhabitants of Bactra/Balkh), are said to have had "some 1,000,000 or more persons." See: Watson (1993), pp. 234-235.

Hanshu 96A confirms the estimated population of the Da Yuezhi in the *Shiji*, saying they have: "100000 households, 400000 individuals with 100000 persons able to bear arms." *CICA*, pp. 119-120.

It seems hard to believe that, if the Asiani had become the rulers of the Da Yuezhi, and the Sacaraucae were driven from the region, there would be no mention of it in the Chinese annals. The envoy Zhang Qian reported that the king of the Da Yuezhi had established his court on the north bank of the Gui (Oxus) River after he conquered and subjugated the whole of Daxia. Such significant events would surely have been included in Zhang Qian's report to the Chinese court – as he spent over a year in the region and was acquainted with the situation. Zhang was very observant, had access to top-level sources, and even travelled south of the Oxus, across Daxia to Lanshi, its administrative centre.

Later Chinese records show contacts continued with the Da Yuezhi well into the 2nd century CE. If another tribe such as the Asiani had conquered them, as some propose, the Chinese accounts would surely have included this fact.

The main reason I cannot accept the commonly proposed hypothesis that the Tochari and the Da Yuezhi were the same people, is that Trogus' Prologue 41 says the Asiani/Asioi "became the rulers of the Tochari" and there are no references in either the Chinese or Western sources to indicate that the Da Yuezhi had been conquered at all at this time.

As discussed earlier, the king of Parthia, Phraates II, attacked and killed the Seleucid king, Antiochus VII, in Media in 129. In 130 BCE, some Sakas and Tocharoi advanced into eastern Parthia and King Phraates turned on them. However, after the Greek prisoners from the army of Antiochus (who had been pressed into service) deserted, Phraates was defeated and killed in 128 BCE.

As Zhang Qian does not mention the Parthian king, it seems Phraates' death probably occurred shortly after he left the region, possibly later in the same year.

It seems probable that the 'Sakas' and 'Tochari' moved into eastern Parthia after the arrival of the Da Yuezhi, possibly displaced by the Yuezhi. It seems it was not, as some have maintained, the Da Yuezhi, along with some Saka groups, who invaded Parthia. The Sakas apparently "occupied Arachosia and especially the neighboring Drangiana, whose name thereafter was Sakastāna (later Sīstān)." *Encyclopaedia Iranica.* Accessed at: http://www.iranicaonline.org/articles/arachosia on 18 February 2012.

• Strabo XI 8.2

The Greek text of this passage is now generally accepted as:

> μάλιστα δὲ γνώριμοι γεγόνασι τῶν νομάδων οἱ τοὺς Ἕλληνας ἀφελόμενοι τὴν Βακτριανήν, Ἄσιοι καὶ Πασιανοὶ καὶ Τόχαροι καὶ Σακάραυλοι, ὁρμηθέντες ἀπὸ τῆς περαίας τοῦ Ἰαξάρτου τῆς κατὰ Σάκας καὶ Σογδιανούς, ἣν κατεῖχον Σάκαι.
>
> "But the best known of the nomads are those who took Bactria away from the Greeks; [the] Asioi and Pasianoi and Tocharoi and Sakaraukai, who originally came from the country on the other side of the Jaxartes River that adjoins that of the Sakas and the Sogdians and was occupied by the Sakai." Translation by author.

In the 18th century, J. F. Vaillant (*Arsacidarum imperium*, II, Paris 1725, p. 61) proposed that the phrase usually given in Strabo 10.8.2 as ΑΣΙΟΙ ΚΑΙ ΠΑΣΙΑΝΟΙ . . . (= [The] Asioi and Pasianoi . . .), should be amended to ΑΣΙΟΙ ΚΑΙ Η ΑΣΙΑΝΟ (= [The] Asioi or Asianoi . . .). meaning that 'Asioi' and 'Asiani' were just two forms of the same name. See note 4 in the quote from Piankov (2010) below.

This Vatican palimpsest of *circa* late 5th century CE is by far the earliest surviving Strabo manuscript and, as the later manuscripts retain the Π of ΠACIANOI, they could have all been derived from an earlier faulty manuscript.

Vaillant had correctly noticed that Trogus (*Prologues* XLI) mentions the "Scythian" people of the Asiani, who must surely be identified with the Asioi of Strabo. This is definitely the reading of the earliest surviving copy of Strabo's *Geography*, the so-called "Vatican palimpsest" (*Vat. Gr.* 2306):

> "The history of this manuscript has only been understood since the studies consecrated to W. Aly. Copied in Byzantium about the end of the 5th century . . . .
>
> All the later manuscripts with Π and all the direct quotations of medieval times derive from a single prototype of the "Geography" carrying the title of Γεωγραφικά." Translated from: Aujac and Lasserre (1969), pp. LIII and LVII.

The Vatican palimpsest was completely written in italicised Greek capital letters arranged in three rows with no spaces between the words or punctuation, as normal in early times.

Fortunately, the section we are concerned with, Strabo 11.8.2, is well preserved, and clearly visible to the naked eye, so there is next to no chance of misreading of this passage.

Aly specifically remarks that the Greek letters Η and Π were commonly mistaken for each other. See: Aly (1956), pp. X and 242. See also: Aly (1957): *Einleitung* (Introduction, pp. 15-23), pp. 19-20. If this "correction" of the original text is applied, there are only three tribes to consider. Translations of the Greek text:

Literal translation:

"But the best known of the nomads are those who took away Baktrianē from the Greeks; the Asioi and the Pasianoi, and the Tocharoi and the Sakaraukai, who originally came from the other side of the Iaxartou [Yaxartes/Syr Darya River] that adjoins that [territory] of the Sakai and the Sogdoanou [=Sogdians], and was occupied by the Saki."

'Corrected' translation:

"But the best known of the nomads are those who took away Baktrianē from the Greeks; the Asioi, also [known as] the Asianoi, and the Tocharoi and the Sakaraukai, who originally came from the other side of the Iaxartou [Yaxartes/ Syr Darya River] that adjoins that [territory] of the Sakai and the Sogdoanou [= the Sogdians], and was occupied by the Saki." Translations by author.

- **Could the 'Paisani' have been a mistake for 'Gasiani'?**

"It has been suggested that Pasiani (Πασιανι) is a textual corruption for Gasiani (Γασιανι).[14] In my opinion, this is a reasonable suggestion, and "Guishuang 貴霜" [giuət-shiang] or Kuṣāṇa (Kushan) and Gasiani can be understood as different transcriptions of the same name."

[14] Marquart 1901, p. 206."

Yu (2011), p. 7.

Yu suggests a "correction" first proposed by Marquart that the Greek letter 'Π' was a mistake for 'Γ' (instead of for 'Η', as above, and, if this is accepted, the reading of Strabo 10.8.2, should be amended to ΑΣΙΟΙ ΚΑΙ ΓΑΣΙΑΝΟΙ . . . = [The] Asioi and Gasianoi . . , rather than [The] Asioi and Pasianoi, or the previous proposal: [The] Asioi *or* Asianoi.

Yu further suggests that the so-called "Gasiani" explains the name of the leader known in the Chinese histories as the *Xihou* 翖侯 of Guishuang 貴霜.

If correct, this would be very interesting, as the Chinese sources tell us that Kujula Kadphises, a later *xihou* of the Guishuang (which appears somewhat similar to 'Gasiani'), was the founder of the important 'Kushan' Empire in the early 1st century CE.

However, I can find nothing that supports the existence of a tribe known as the "Gasianoi," nor anyone else who accepts its existence, so, unless more evidence is forthcoming, I think this hypothesis should be discarded or put on hold.

- **Strabo XI 11.1, 2.**

"As for Bactria, a part of it lies alongside Aria towards the north, though most of it lies above Aria and to the east of it. And much of it produces everything except oil. The Greeks who caused Bactria to revolt grew so powerful on account of the fertility of the country that they became masters, not only of Ariana, but also of India, as Apollodorus of Artemita says: and more tribes were subdued by them than by Alexander—by Menander [flourished *circa* 160 to 130 BCE?] in particular (at least if he actually crossed the Hypanis towards the east and advanced as far as the Imaüs), for some were subdued by him personally and others by Demetrius, the son of

Euthydemus the king of the Bactrians; and they took possession, not only of Patalena, but also, on the rest of the coast, of what is called the kingdom of Saraostus and Sigerdis. In short, Apollodorus says that Bactriana is the ornament of Ariana as a whole; and, more than that, they extended their empire even as far as the Seres and the Phryni." (Strabo 11.11.1)

"Their cities were Bactra (also called Zariaspa, through which flows a river bearing the same name and emptying into the Oxus), and Darapsa, and several others. Among these was Eucratidia, which was named after its ruler. The Greeks took possession of it and divided it into satrapies, of which the satrapy Turiva and that of Aspionus were taken away from Eucratides [I, reigned *circa* 170–145 BCE) by the Parthians. And they also held Sogdiana, situated above Bactriana towards the east between the Oxus River, which forms the boundary between the Bactrians and the Sogdians, and the Iaxartes River. And the Iaxartes forms also the boundary between the Sogdians and the nomads." (Strabo 11.11.2). These quotes from Strabo's *Geography* (completed in 23 CE), are taken from the translation by Jones (1924).

• Ptolemy's Account

In the 2nd century, Ptolemy mentioned two tribes, widely separated geographically, but with similar names.

1. The 'Tocharoi,' who he says (VI.11.6) were "a numerous people" (the only people he specifies as 'numerous' in Bactriana) who lived 'below,' or to the south of, the 'Zariaspi' (from the Balkh oasis), and who are usually equated with the 'Tacharoi' of Strabo.

Variants of the name 'Tocharoi' in the Ptolemy's texts include: Τόχαροι, Τοχάροι; while Latin versions are: Thocari, Thacori. Ptolemy (1971), VI.12.6, pp. 27-28, 105.

These people are surely the Τόχαροι or 'Tocharoi' mentioned in Strabo XI 8.2 – see the translation above.

2. The similarly-named 'Tachoroi,' Ptolemy mentions as living with other tribes along the northern section of the Iaxartes River/Syr Darya, with the Iatioi to their west and Sakai to their east. Ptolemy (1971), VI.12.4, pp. 105, 107.

The Tachoroi were living far from the Tocharoi, and it is not known if they were related in spite of the comparable names.

• Xuanzang's Account

Four centuries after Ptolemy, the territory south of Bactra/Balkh to Bamiyan was described in the 'Biography of Xuanzang' as 覩貨邏 *Duhuoluo* - very probably a transcription of *Tukhāra.

The biography describes a number of place within this region *circa* 630 CE, including Bactra/Balkh and Tukhāra (覩貨邏 – Duhuoluo). Xuanzang travelled south from Bactra through Tukhāra "more than 600 *li*" (roughly 280 km on modern maps) and through the "Great Snow Mountains," before entering the territory of Bamiyan – see Li (1995), pp. 47-49.

Xuanzang says lands to the north of the upper Oxus, as well as Balkh to the south, were within the region of Duhuoluo/Tokharestan. See note 13.10.

• The Saka invasions

"In 141 [BCE] the curtain falls on Greek Bactria, to rise again in 128 [BCE] upon new peoples and new names; somewhere between these two dates lies the end of the Greek kingdom. The latter date[2] is the year in which the Chinese Chang-k'ien, general

> and diplomat, was in Bactria, and it is his Report to his emperor which supplies such knowledge as we have of the country immediately after the conquest.
>
> [2] I follow the Chavannes-Hirth dating for Chang-k'ien; but the year he spent with the Yueh-chi has also been given as 127-6 and 126. Nothing turns on this for my purpose."
>
> Tarn (1984), p. 274 and n. 2.

Apparently, Bactria was briefly ravaged or conquered by 塞 Se/Sai tribes displaced by the Yuezhi from the Ili-Issyk Kul region shortly before the conquest of Daxia by the Yuezhi.

It is clear that these Se/Sai people (the Saiwang of the *Hanshu*), said to have been displaced by the Yuezhi, were not the Sacaraucae – originally from beyond the Jaxartes River who Strabo, xi. 8.2 refers to as the 'Sacarauli'.

Hanshu, chap. 96B, explicitly states that the 'Saiwang' or 'king of the Sai' crossed the *xuandu* — 'hanging passages' or 'suspended crossings' — on his way to conquer Jibin, to the southeast of Daxia. See the quote from Pulleyblank, (1970), p. 159 n. 12 quoted in Appendix F.
NOTE: The *xuandu* ('rafiqs,' 'hanging passages' or 'suspended crossings') mentioned here could have been either those in Hunza, or the ones in the Indus Valley near Nanga Parbat (JEH)

The only Sai/Saka tribes mentioned as being close to Daxia in *Hanshu* 96A were the two small 'kingdoms' of Juandu and Xiuxun. They each controlled one of the two main routes to the west from Kashgar; the first going to Dayuan (Ferghana), the other down the Alai Valley to Bactria/Daxia. It is said both peoples originally "were of the Sai race." *CICA*, p. 139.

> "The Sakas, though less enthusiastically Philhellene than their Parthian successors in India, took over almost without change the political structure established by Menander. In many cases they retained Greek officials, particularly among the mint-masters and engravers. The upper stratum of society had shifted—the rulers and the warrior caste were of a different race than before—but the general shape of society remained much the same for several generations after the end of Greek rule." Woodcock (1966), p. 129.

• Daxia after the Yuezhi conquest

Shiji 123 says that the people of Daxia possibly numbered more than a million ("可百餘萬") and they "cultivate the land and have cities and houses. Their customs are like those of the Dayuan [who are described earlier as: "settled on the land, plowing the fields and growing rice and wheat. They also make wine out of grapes . . . . the people live in houses in fortified cities, there being some seventy or more cities of various sizes in the regions."]. "It has no great ruler but only a number of petty chiefs ruling the various cities. The people are poor in the use of arms and afraid of battle, but they are clever at commerce." Watson (1993), pp. 233, 235.

This makes it certain that the Daxians could not have been part of the recent invading nomadic tribes – there could not have been time for them to adapt to such a settled life. The Daxians were clearly people who had been living there well before the invasions of the 2nd century BCE.

The description of the Daxians as being "unwarlike" has been remarked upon by various writers as being incompatible with the earlier reputation of the Greco-Bactrians - warriors famed for their often-successful struggles with the Parthians and Indians.

Prior to the arrival of the Da Yuezhi, the Greco-Bactrian armies were largely destroyed by their recent punishing campaigns in India, and constant internecine struggles.

Eucratides I Megas, was murdered while returning from his extensive Indian campaigns, possibly *circa* 145 BCE (though Joe Cribb queries this date – see his quote below), reportedly by one of his sons who had his body desecrated, which may well have been followed by insurrections or civil war. It was certainly a period of great disruptions.

The weary survivors would likely have been eager to sue for peace, possibly first with the Sacaraucae, and later with the Da Yuezhi confederation. It seems the newcomers were content to allow the larger city-states retain a significant degree of independence until sometime in the first century CE.

The Daxian people probably spoke 'Bactrian,' an eastern-Iranian language closely related to modern Pashto, which is referred to as 'Āryan' in the inscriptions and documents:

> "The language of the [Surkh Kotal] inscription occupies an intermediary position between Pashto and Yidgha-Munji on the one hand, Sogdian, Khwarezmian, and Parthian on the other: it is thus in its natural and rightful place in Bactria; this is also the opinion expressed by M. Maricq (pp. 395 sqq.). It would then be best to call it *Bactrian.*" Henning (1960), p. 47.

Although the Yuezhi had temporarily established a court north of the Oxus, and had conquered or annexed Daxia by the time Zhang Qian arrived, they had not taken full possession of the territory south of the Oxus. The 'chief town' (*du*) of Daxia is said to be Lanshi, and the previous capital of the Greco-Bactrians, Bactra (modern Balkh) is not even mentioned. Bactra appears to have retained some degree of independence for a while. See: Appendix N.

> "It should be emphasized that Bactria never resembled Parthia in being a unified state. Bactria is above all a historico-geographical term, rather than a political one. During these nearly five hundred years various states were formed in this area – the Greco-Bactrian state, the empire of the Kushans (which continued to exist for a while after the fall of the Parthian state), and the various principates of the Great Yüeh-chih." Rtveladze (1995), p. 181.

The Parthians are reported to have seized two satrapies of the Greco-Bactrian state in the mid-2nd century BCE during the reign of Mithradates:

> "Precisely what part of Bactria was occupied by the Parthians during the time of Mithradates I [*circa* 171-138 BCE] is not known for certain. According to Strabo, as was mentioned above, the Parthians took the satrapies of Aspionus and Turiva [western districts of Bactria – during the reign of Eucratides, i.e. sometime before 140 BCE]. So far, however, the location of these satrapies has not been identified. Cunningham and Narain placed them in Margiana; in Tarn's opinion Turiva corresponds to the region of Tapuria, but M.E. and V.M. Masson consider this unlikely. In my view the satrapy of Turiva may be connected with the city of Fariab, which lay in north-western Tokharistan in the area of the river Shirintagao, near the border with Margiana. In the Middle Ages there was a region close to Guzganan called Fariab; it corresponds to the modern province Fariab in north-western Afghanistan, which has two main towns, Maimane (ancient Yakhutia) and Andkhui (ancient Ankhud). In the same region the use of the toponym Tariab has been constant. Now the connection between the names Turiva-Tariab-Fariab is clear; they each in fact consist of two words, of which the second originates from the word *ab* (water, river), which forms part of many Bactrian names, although it has been transformed by Greek transmission into Turiva.
>
> On the basis of this hypothesis we may place the province of Aspionus near to Turiva-Fariab. The root of the name Aspionus is clearly the word *asp* (horse), which was used to form many toponyms in Central Asia. In Bactria in particular, it was one of the main components of the name of the town Bactra-Zariaspa (golden horse), which is mentioned by Strabo and Pliny. In view of the linguistic similarities, it is a reasonable hypothesis that the satrapy of Aspionus was connected with the region of Bactra-Zariaspa. If this is true, during the reign of Mithradates I the Parthians

wrested from the Graeco-Bactrian kingdom of Eucratides the western territories of Bactria, including Bactra." Rtveladze (1995), pp. 184-185.

Mark Passehl commented on the above quote from Rtveladze (personal communication 7 July, 2003):

> "Both [Parthia and Baktria] were former Persian satrapies which became the "home territories" of successful conquests states/dynasties (Parthian Empire of the Arsakids, Baktrian empire of the Thousand Cities of the Diodotids, Euthdemids, etc.).
>
> . . . the Arsakid seizure of Baktra [i.e. the *city* of Balkh] seems quite wrong. The Arsakids probably took the two satrapies right near the end of Eukratides' reign when he was campaigning in India (ca. 146 BC), but the archaeology (Rapin's article) seems to say that even when the great nomad invasions came in the 140s-130s BC Baktra held out longest as a Greek-dynasty outpost. So either at their weakest they retook it from the Parthians (unlikely!) or never lost it when they lost the two westernmost provinces."

Retveladze's hypothesis that the satrapy of Aspionus may have been associated with Zariaspa/Balkh because of the linguistic similarities appears weak, particularly because Strabo mentions Zariaspa by name in the same paragraph as Aspionus. See the quote above from Strabo XI, 11.

> "We have seen that, after the death of Menander [c. 342-291 BCE], the Indo-Greek 'kingdoms' were controlled by several families, with inevitable wars and alliances between them. Naturally, therefore, the fall of one Indo-Greek 'kingdom' did not mean the fall of the other, and they were not destroyed simultaneously. Moreover, as we shall point out below, their fall was not the result of attack by a single power.
>
> We quote at length the passages from the literary sources which are of primary importance. Describing the situation east of the Caspian Sea, Strabo says:[1]
>
> Now the greater part of the Scythians, beginning at the Caspian Sea, are called Däae, but those who are situated more to the East than these are named Massagetae and Sacae, whereas all the rest are given the general name of Scythians, though each people is given a separate name of its own. They are all for the most part nomads. But the best-known of the nomads are those who took away Bactriana from the Greeks, I mean the Asii, Pasiani, Tochari, and Sacarauli [read Sacaraucae], who originally came from the country on the other side of the Jaxartes river that adjoins that of the Sacae and the Sogdiani and was occupied by the Sacae.[2] And as for the Däae, some of them are called Aparni, some Xanthii, and some Pissuri. Now of these the Aparni are situated closest to Hyrcania and the part of the sea that borders on it, but the remainder extend even as far as the country that stretches parallel to Aria [Herat].
>
> [1] Strabo, xi. 8. 2.
>
> [2] . . . . This is one of the most discussed passages in Strabo, and some scholars (the latest, Sten Konow in *Festkrift til Prof. Olaf Broch*, pp. 80-81, 'The White Huns and Tokharian'), who insist on putting a *καὶ* after *Σακάραυλοι*, which is found in the manuscripts, but which has been rightly cancelled both in the Teubner and Loeb editions of Strabo, needlessly confuse the import of this passage and try to bring in the Sacae. But without any prejudice to the historical discussions in question we believe that *καὶ* can be cancelled on principles of simple textual criticism, for it is quite easy for a writer who was writing *καὶ* after *Ἄσιοι*, *Πασιανοί*, and *Τόχαροι* to add one more after *Σακάραυλοι* by mistake.
>
> Tarn also does not accept (p. 332) the view of Sten Konow, which includes the Śakas and argues for five nomad peoples instead of four (cf. *Symbolae Osloenses* xxiv (1945) 148)."
>
> Narain (1957), p. 128 and nn. 1-2.

• The Greco-Bactrians after the arrival of the Da Yuezhi

It has been argued that Ai-Khanum was abandoned about the time of the death of Eucratides I, in 146 BCE. See, for example: Bernard (1994b), p. 103; Benjamin (2007), p. 179. Recent evidence contradicts this assumption, suggesting it was abandoned later:

> "MacDowall has argued that while the copper coinage found in the excavations of Ai Khanoum certainly stopped with Eucratides I (see P. Bernard, *MDAFA XXVIII* [1985] *Fouilles d'Ai Khanoum iv Les monnaies hors tresors*, pp. 51-75). Bopearachchi's claim that the silver coinage at Ai Khanoum also stops is wrong. One of the two silver hoards found at Ai Khanoum contains a silver tetradrachm of the later king Eucratides II; and in addition later silver tetradrachms are known for Heliocles, Plato, Eucratides II and Demetrius II, who were presumably rulers of more restricted parts of Bactria; in MacDowall, October 2002, private correspondence." Benjamin (2007), p. 180, n. 81.

> "The 145 BC date for the destruction of Ai-Khanum is a highly questionable construct. The arguments are: the latest coins at Ai-Khanum are issues of Eucratides I, a dated inscription found at Ai-Khanum gives a 'year 24' date. Year 24 of Eucratides I = 145 BC, therefore that is the year of the city's destruction. This cannot stand for the following reasons:
>
> 1 The latest coin from an Ai-Khanum hoard is a coin of Eucratides II (misidentified in the report by Holy 1981, pl. XII, no. 129)
>
> 2 the coins found in the excavation are all low denominations, coppers and silver obols. Eucratides I is the last issuer of coppers and obols in Bactria, his three (or four) successors do not issue these denominations, only higher value silver coins. So the found coins cannot form a terminus ad quem for the city's destruction.
>
> 3 there is no evidence to link the year 24 with Eucratides I (it might well be a year in his reign, but there is no evidence).
>
> 4 we don't know when Eucratides I began his reign, just that he was thought to be a contemporary of Mithradates."
>
> Joe Cribb, private communication, 25 August, 2011.

> "As a result, the numismatic data reveal that coinage in Aï Khanoum just prior to the Greek abandonment extended beyond the reign of Eukratides I to include the emissions of Eukratides II and Lysias [c. 120-110 BCE], and that the city's treasury was increasingly dominated by the influx of smaller denominations of a non-Attic standard minted south of the Hindu Kush, visa vie Indo-Greek drachmas and Indian punch-marked coins. Consequently, there is nothing in this evidence that precludes us from changing our earlier analysis that the Greeks of Aï Khanoum left earlier than the mid-first century B.C.E.[81]" Lerner (2011), p. 125.

> **"Abstract**
>
> The paper proposes a new interpretation of the activities that occurred in the palace treasury of the Hellenistic city of Aï Khanoum on the eve of the site's abandonment by its Greek inhabitants. A reexamination of a series of inscriptions and coins from the site reveals that the names of individuals believed to have been the treasury's directors are in actuality the names of depositors, the treasury stored three different currencies, and coins found in association with the site indicate that the city was inhabited for a longer period of time than is the standard reckoning." Lerner (2011), p. 147.

After the arrival of the Da Yuezhi, it seems that several Greco-Bactrians ruled and even issued coins in various parts of the country for a few decades. In spite of the statement in the *Shiji* that the Yuezhi had conquered and subjugated Daxia, it appears some Greco-

Bactrians retained a significant degree of autonomy. The country of Daxia was divided by the Da Yuezhi into five *xihous* ('princedoms'); one or more of the Greco-Bactrian kings may have been among these five *xihou*.

The evidence of coin finds from a series of later Greco-Bactrian kings suggests that they continued to rule in restricted territories – possibly in and around the great walled cities of Bactra/Balkh and/or Qunduz.

It is not hard to find the reasons for the continued independence of the larger Greco-Bactrian cities after the invasions of the Sakas and the Da Yuezhi.

They were large, heavily fortified cities, presumably well equipped to withstand a long siege. The invading peoples, being largely nomadic, were unlikely to have had the experience or siege equipment to breach the massive city walls. Moreover, the Yuezhi possibly wanted a period of peace to recuperate after their long and ill-fated migration and their recent conquest of the Daxia, and would, therefore, have been willing to make some sort of truce rather continue fighting.

Presumably, the larger cities would have held large stores of treasure, enabling them to pay tribute or bribes over an extended period. Finally, it may have been in the interest of the invaders to keep the cities functioning as flourishing trade centres which they could tax and would also act as buffers against further invasions.

> "In contrast to the old notion that the Yueh-Chi tribes exterminated the Greeks, suddenly and savagely replacing Hellenism with barbarism, it now seems that the transition of power was ameliorated by at least a generation of intense social and cultural contact. By the time the last Greek king was gone from Bactria, the kingdom was already under the powerful influence of the tribes settled in neighbouring Sogdiana. By the same token, traces of Hellenism can be seen in Central Asia for centuries beyond the fall of Greek Bactria. As the nomadic invaders settled the area and created the great Kushan empire, their culture betrayed much Greek inspiration. Viktor Sarianidi's extraordinary excavations of a necropolis at Tillya-Tepe (the Golden Mound) provide ample evidence of this phenomenon. Among these finds of the first century A.D. were the famous Bactrian Aphrodite, a dress clasp showing Dionysus and Ariadne, a pendant of Artemis/Anahita, and a cameo of a Greek king of Bactria (Eucratides)." Holt (1999), p. 136.

> "The issues of the last four Bactrian kings, Demetrius II, Eucratides II, Plato and Heliocles I, are more difficult to place [than the Indo-Greek issues from south of the Hindu Kush] as they issued no copper coins. Excavators are therefore unable to document their sequence or geographic range. A single Eucratides II silver coin was recorded from the hoard said to have come from Ai-Khanum (Holt). The hoard from Qunduz, south-west of Ai-Khanum and south-east of Takti-Sangin, contained a large number of silver coins of each of these four kings. Although the find spot of the hoard is known, it cannot be used to identify where these four rulers lived. However it does give a strong indication of their position after Eucratides I, as all the earlier kings except Pantaleon are represented in the hoard, but in much smaller numbers than the last four kings. The hoard shows that the coins of the last four kings were still plentiful at the time of the deposit of the hoard and that Heliocles I was the last of these.
>
> The dating of Heliocles I is therefore dependant on the fact that he is later than Eucratides I, who is identified in the Classical texts as a usurper who was a close contemporary of the Parthian king Mithradates I (171-138 BC). Eucratides can also be dated in this way on the basis of Mithradates and another contemporary imitating his coins. . . . Eucratides I's reign is, as Justin said, contemporary with Mithradates I, and from the coins found at Merv comes evidence that he may have out-lived his

Parthian contemporary. It seems sensible to place his death before 138 BC. The abandonment of copper coinage under Eucratides II and Demetrius II also suggests a major disruption of urban life taking place about the time of the death of Eucratides I, which probably relates to the nomad invasion indicated by the sack of Ai-Khanum. The Eucratides II coin reported by Holt (1981, no. 129) from an Ai-Khanum hoard suggests that the destruction of the city took place after his accession.

The dating of Heliocles I in relation to the death of Eucratides I suggests that his reign began after Eucratides II and Plato. The length of these reigns can only be guessed at. There is some basis for a guess in the ratio of the number of coins issued during them and those issued under Eucratides I. . . . It seems sensible, however, to take account of the likelihood that [Heliocles I], as the last ruler represented in the hoard, his coins would have had a higher representation. These figures are unlikely to be precisely correct, but are indicative of the likelihood of Heliocles' reign lasting into the first century BC, even as late as about the 80s BC.

Alongside the main series of Bactrian coins, the Qunduz hoard contains issues of several Indo-Greek kings. Antialcidas, Lysias, Theophilus, Philoxenus, Hermaeus, Archebius and Amyntas. The dates of these kings are no more certain than those of the late Bactrian kings. Several attempts have been made to date them and these dates are being continually revised (Senior 2004). The current opinion seems to be that the latest of these is likely to be Amyntas and that his reign is in the first half of the first century BC. The deposit of the Qunduz hoard is therefore likely to be about 70 BC. I am therefore inclined, on the basis of the above analysis, to give dates for Heliocles I later than those suggested by Tarn, Narain, Mitchiner and Bopearachchi. An earlier date can only be suggested if it is argued that the reigns of Eucratides I, Eucratides II, Plate and Heliocles I overlap.

The dating of Heliocles I to an earlier date is largely based on the statement in the Chinese sources (Pulleyblank and Zürcher) that by 128/7 BC the Dayuezhi nomads (forerunners of the Kushans) were overlords of Bactria [Daxia] ruling from a region to its north. The Chinese sources can however be interpreted from a different perspective. The control of Bactria by the Dayuezhi appears to be a loose control as the Chinese continued to send (or attempt to send) ambassadors to Bactria [Daxia] without reference to the Dayuezhi until at least 111 BC (*Han Shu*, chapter 61, parts 5–6, Hulsewé and Loewe 1979, pp. 218-222), and the first Chinese reference to the Dayuezhi in actual occupation of Bactria does not appear until about AD 75 (Pulleyblank 1968). The last successful mission to Bactria took place in about 115–113 BC, a separate mission to the Dayuezhi was sent at the same time. Embassies were sent later than 111 BC and before 90 BC, but their dates are not mentioned by the Han Chronicle.

The case for the end of the Greek kingdom of Bactria by 130 BC, and therefore Heliocles I's reign ending about the same time, is accordingly not upheld by either the numismatic evidence or the Chinese testimony. The absence of copper coinage during the last four Bactrian reigns does however suggest that the arrival of nomads including the Dayuezhi in the region had a drastic effect on monetary circulation, which was perhaps linked with the loss of the major urban centres of the kingdom. The excavations at Ai-Khanum certainly show that this city was sacked in the reign of Eucratides II, two reigns before Heliocles I [c. 125-90 BC]." Cribb (2005), pp. 212-213.

As Cribb states, Daxia continued sending ambassadors to China independently of the Da Yuezhi until at least 111 BCE. The Da Yuezhi and the Daxia are still referred to as separate peoples in the Chinese records.

"Ssu-ma-ch'ien [Sima Qian] is quite explicit that, although the Ta-Yüeh-chih had 'subjugated' the Ta-hsia [Daxia], for all practical purposes the latter were independent. The royal court of the Ta-Yüeh-chih was north of the Oxus river ; the Ta-hsia had their own capital and separate embassies could be sent them by foreign powers. It is clear that the Ta-hsia were not so thoroughly subjugated that the Ta-Yüeh-chih could establish their court south of the Oxus. It thus seems that the Ta-Yüeh-chih occupied only those parts of the Bactrian kingdom which lay north of the Oxus, but they had defeated the Ta-hsia without actually occupying their lands, and contented themselves for a time with the receipt of tribute.[1]

But the situation is quite different in the *Ch'ien-Han shu* and the *Hou-Han shu*. The former clearly says that the king of the Ta-Yüeh-chih resides at Ch'ien-shi Chêng (= Lan-shi Chêng), and the latter also notes that 'the country of the Ta-Yüeh-chih is situated at Lan-shi Chêng . . .'. We are further informed that the Ta-Yüeh-chih divided the Ta-hsia into five *hsi-hou* (*xihou*). This is definitely a picture of complete political subjugation and occupation of Ta-hsia. Moreover, we are told that both Ta-Yüeh-chih and Ta-hsia accept the order of the Chinese embassy sent by the Han Court. Ta-hsia is not separately described ; its identity is merged in that of the Ta-Yüeh-chih. And the prominence which is given to the Ta-hsia in the *Shih-chi* is not found in the *Ch'ien Han Shu*. It therefore seems evident that Bactria proper south of the Oxus river must have come under the complete political subjugation of the Yüeh-chih either after the *Shih-chi* was written or at a time near its completion, when news had not reached Ssu-ma-ch'ien, but definitely long before the composition of the *Ch'ien Han Shu*. *Shih-chi* was completed in 99 B.C.,[2] and therefore, in round numbers, we may say that the occupation took place about 100 B.C.

[1] Professor Enoki in a long communication has compared the different Chinese words used in the Chinese annals to denote degrees of 'subjugation', and he confirms our view.
[2] Hirth, p. 91."

Narain (1957), p. 140 and nn. 1-2.

The first indication we have of a degree of subjugation of the Daxia to the Da Yuezhi are the references to the "*xihou* of Shuangmi of the Dayuezhi" in 43 BCE and the "*xihou* of Xiumi of the Da Yuezhi" in 37 BCE preserved on wooden tablets near Dunhuang. See the quote from Grenet (2006), pp. 339-340, in Appendix O.

"All of the Bactrian Greek royal families appear to have died out by the time the last fragments of the Kabul valley fell into nomad hands, while war and civil strife had reduced the Greek military caste to a mere shadow of the armies whose mounted columns poured into Arachosia under the first Demetrius and under Menander across the Ganges plains. On the other hand, there is no evidence of any general or even local massacre of the ordinary Greek population after the nomad victories. In fact, the continued use of their language on local coins for more than two hundred years after the death of Hermaeus shows that they remained numerous and formed a powerful urban community which the new rulers could not ignore. The head of the Greek king dead for almost a century was still a better guarantee of credit than that of a live Kushana.

For at least a century and a half, in fact, Greek remained not only the commercial but also the patrician *lingua franca* of the Kabul valley and of Gandhara at least as far as Taxila. Merchants and kings learnt it as a matter of course, as is shown by the experiences of Apollonius of Tyana when he journeyed to Taxila in 44 AD." Woodcock (1966), p. 130.

Woodcock's theory that Kujula overstruck Hermaeus' coins because his head on a coin "was still a better guarantee of credit than that of a live Kushana," is pure speculation. Kujula may have seized large stocks of Hermaeus coins and found it faster and cheaper to overstrike than to melt them down and remint. In addition, they clearly carried the message that 'Kujula the Kushan' had replaced the Greco-Bactrian line of the great Hermaeus.

> "But whether the reign of Heliocles continued into the first century [BCE] or not, with the murder of Eucratides by his son Greek power clearly suffered a substantial and irreversible decline in Bactria. The Saka hordes that had so troubled Seleucid, Parthian and Bactrian kings alike . . . apparently seized their chance and raided across the Amu Darya from their base in northern Bactria, burning, looting, and then occupying parts of Bactria proper as far south as the Hindu Kush. Greek kingdoms south of the Hindu Kush (and any remnants remaining to the north) may have been forced to pay tribute to the Sakas, although the latter were clearly prepared to allow commercial exchanges and mercantile activity to continue within the region, as the evidence of Zhang Qian will show below. This remained the situation for a decade and a half until 130 when the Yuezhi confederation arrived in northern Bactria from Kangju/Sogdia, and defeated and evicted the Saka occupiers. Supporting evidence for this reconstructed course of events is found in textual references to the activity and role of these restive Sakan groups in the region during the second half of the second century." Benjamin (2007), p. 181.

• The Geography of Daxia under the Da Yuezhi and Kushans

It seems that Daxia in Kushan times included most of northern Afghanistan between Badakhshan in the east and the small town Antkhudh (= Andkoy or Andkhvoy), about 60 km northwest of Sheberghan, close to the desert surrounding Margiana, which was then under Parthian control. See: note 13.9.

It stretched south of the Oxus River to the Hindu Kush and included the fertile plains and valleys in the regions conquered by the Da Yuezhi to the north of the Oxus, in what is now southern Tajikistan and Uzbekistan. These northern territories contained the key regions of Termez and Khalchayan (west of the modern city of Dushanbe), north to the Zeravshan Range, which formed the southern border of Dayuan/Ferghana, to the northeast as far as the Alai Valley, and northwest as far as the "Iron Gates," past Derbent along the road to Samarkand. See the quote from Leriche (1993), p. 82 in note 13.10.

> "A substantial increase of the area under cultivation in Bactria took place in the Kushan period. New lands were irrigated, e.g., at Bīškent and along the lower course of the Vakš, while the valleys of the Balk, Kondūz, and Sorkān Daryā rivers were important producers. Urbanization showed similar progress. Some forty urban sites, including fifteen of more than 15 ha [37 acres], have now been located; all have dimensions fit for medium-sized or large towns.
>
> Besides the main cities of Bactra (Zariaspa, Lan Shi), Kondūz, and Termed (Qara Tepe), the following towns deserve mention: in southern Bactria, Delbarjīn, Begrām (famous for the find of a treasure-store containing objects from Alexandria in Egypt and from India), and the sanctuary Sork Kotal (with a great temple at the top of a flight of steps, dedicated to an apparently eclectic collection of gods headed by a deity personifying the victory of the temple's founder Kanishka; Schlumberger, le Berre, and Fussman); north of the Oxus, Delvarzīn, Aĭrtam, Zar Tepe, Qal'a-ye Kāfernegān, and Kalčajān. All these sites attest the remarkable development of urban life which characterized Kushan Bactria.

It was in the Kushan period, however, that the name Bactria fell out of use. We do not know what name the region then bore. The geographer Ptolemy, writing in the second half of the second century A.D., states that it was then inhabited mainly by Tochari. In Middle Persian and Armenian, the name Balk̲ denotes only the capital city. By the end of the Kushan period, Bactria had come to be known as Ṭok̲h̲ārestān. After the conquest of the region by the Sasanians, Ṭok̲h̲ārestān formed the core of their province of Kūšānšahr. In the Chinese sources Tu Kho Lo, undoubtedly a transcription of the new name, replaces the older Ta Hsia." Leriche (undated), p. 343.

"Archaeological evidence reveals intensive exploitation of new agricultural land and the expansion of agricultural oases at the beginning of the Christian era in the river valleys and ancient agricultural oasis areas of Central Asia, especially in the southern regions, even though the best and most suitable croplands were by that time already under cultivation. It has also been established that, with the opening up of new regions and the extension of crop-farming to the northern provinces of Central Asia on the lower reaches of the Zerafshan, on the middle reaches of the Syr Darya and in the Tashkent oasis, large numbers of nomadic livestock-breeders switched to a settled way of life and new centres of urban civilization were formed. As a result of the extensive development of irrigation networks, practically all the main provinces of Central Asia were brought under cultivation during this period and the establishment of the major crop-growing oases was completed. The extent to which northern Bactria was populated and brought under cultivation at this time can be judged from the 117 archaeological monuments of the Kushan period recorded in recent years in the territory of the Surkhan Darya province. A major channel, the Zang canal, leading from the Surkhan river, was constructed. In the zone irrigated by it a new oasis, the Angor, was established around the town of Zar-tepe. The founding of Dalverzin-tepe [about 60 km northeast of Termez] as a major urban centre also dates back to this period. The Surkhan Darya and Sherabad Darya valleys, with their flourishing agricultural oases, fortified towns and extensive grazing lands, were able to provide a strong base for unifying the domains of the Yüeh-chih on the right [northern] bank of the Amu Darya. When they were unified by the ruler of the Kuei-shuang [Kujula Kadphises], who subjugated the four other Yüeh-chih principalities, the nucleus of the Kushan Empire was formed." Mukhamedjanov (1996), pp. 265-266.

"Perhaps in the spring of 131 BCE then, the Yuezhi most probably moved from Ferghana into the 'state' of Kangju, probably the Zeravshan Valley in the heart of Sogdia. Some four or five years later [actually 2 years later, in early 129] they were followed through the region by Han envoy Zhang Qian, who was led there by guides and interpreters provided for him by the king of Dayuan. It is references to Kangju in the *Han Shu* and *Shi Ji* (and by Ptolemy in his *Geograhica*), as well as the discoveries of Soviet and Russian archaeologists, that has provided evidence identifying Kangju with Sogdia, and thus of the role of Sogdia in both the migration of the Yuezhi and the mission of Zhang Qian. The intention of this paper is to consider the origins of the relationship that developed between the Kangju and Yuezhi dynasties, a relationship that subsequently evolved to provide vital political and military stability in the region throughout the Kushan Era." Benjamin (2003).

According to *Hanshu* 61, the Wusun defeated the Yuezhi around 139 to 129 BCE and forced them out of the Ili Valley and Issyk Kul region, after which they fled further west into the Oxus River basin and conquered "Daxia." This scenario has become generally accepted. See: *CICA*: p. 217, note 13.3, and Benjamin (2003).

However, it is important to recognise that neither the *Shiji* nor the *Hou Hanshu* mention any defeat of the Da Yuezhi by the Wusun, only by the Xiongnu. The *Shiji* says:

> "The Yuezhi originally lived between the Qilian or Heavenly Mountains and Dunhuang, but after they were defeated by the Xiongnu they moved far away to the west, beyond Dayuan, where they attacked and conquered the people of Daxia and set up the court of their king on the northern bank of the Gui [Oxus] River. . . ." Watson (1993), p. 234.

As discussed in Appendix I, the story in *Hanshu* 96B of the defeat of the Yuezhi by the Wusun may have been politically motivated.

> "The coexistence of Hellenistic traditions might have continued after the Yuezhi-Kushan entered into Daxia. One Tang Dynasty scholar, who also annotated Sima Qian's *History*, quoted from a now-lost text [the *Yiwuzhi* or *Strange Things from the Southern Region* by the 3rd century scholar, Wan Zhen of the Wu kingdom] as saying:
>
> > "The Great Yuezhi is located about seven thousand *li* north of India. Their land is at a high altitude; the climate is dry; the region is remote. The king of the state calls himself "son of heaven." There are so many riding horses in that country that the number often reaches several hundred thousand. City layouts and palaces are quite similar to those of Daqin (the Roman empire). The skin of the people there is reddish white. People are skilful at horse archery. Local products, rarities, treasures, clothing, and upholstery are very good, and even India cannot compare with it."[36]
>
> It is difficult to verify the sources of this record about the Kushan, since the quoted book is perhaps lost.[37] The descriptions, however, accord very well with the horse-riding Kushans who ruled a formerly Hellenistic country. The climate and location sound like Bactria; the kings of the Kushans did indeed call themselves *devaputra*, meaning "son of heaven" or "son of god." They owned numerous good horses and cultivated nomadic skills and cultures. Yet they ruled a country that included a population of the descendants of Greeks and other immigrants from the Mediterranean, so that the architecture of the country combined Græco-Roman style with local materials and flavor. At least it looked similar to the Roman style in Chinese eyes, and the people looked fairer than Indians and some other Central Asian populations.
>
> 36. Sima Qian, *Shiji*, 123/3162.
> 37. The book entitled *Nanzhouzhi*, literally "the history of the southern states," authored by Wan Zhen [3rd century CE – see Leslie and Gardiner (1996), p. 333], was available to Zhang Shoujie, the Tang scholar who annotated the *History* by Sima Qian, as it was listed in the bibliographies of the *Tang History* with the title of *Nanzhou Yiwuzhi*, meaning "history of exotic things in the south states." However, it did not appear in the bibliographies of later official histories."
>
> Liu (2001), pp. 278-279.

Greek and Roman authors of the 1st and 2nd centuries CE were still referring to "Bactrians" and "Bactriana," although the whole region was now clearly under Kushan control:

> "Inland behind Barygaza there are numerous peoples: the Aratrioi, Arachusioi, Gandharaioi, and the peoples of Proklais, in whose area Bukephalos Alekandreia is located. And beyond these is a very warlike people, the Bactrians [Βακτριανῶν], under a king. . . ." *Periplus of the Erythraean Sea*, 47.6. (composed mid 1st century CE). From: Casson (1989), pp. 80-81.

Ptolemy, writing in his *Geography* 6.11, from material gathered in the early 2nd century CE, describes Baktriana [*Βακτριανή*, var. *Βακτριανῆ*] with the city of Baktra [*Βάκτρα* var. *Βάτρα*] specifically named as the 'royal residence'. Ronca (1971): pp. 24, 30, 105-106.

• Possible derivations of the name 大夏 Daxia

The reconstructed pronunciations for the characters of Daxia are:

大 *da* – K. 317a: *d'âd/ d'âi or t'âd/t'âi; EMC: da', dajʰ

夏 *xia* – K. 36a: *g'å/γa; EMC: ɣaɨ'/ɣɛ:

The various forms of the name given in Chinese clearly point to an original sound approximating the sound of: *Tu* (or *Du*) *ka* (or *ga*) *ra*, which is very close to *Tocharoi*, the name Ptolemy gave to the people living south of Bactra/Balkh in the 1st to 2nd centuries, and also, the place-name Tukhāra, later known as Tokharistan.

The most commonly accepted, and probably best attested theory at present, is that Daxia represented *Takha(ra), Tokhari or Tokharia. For a detailed account of this theory see, for example: Piankov (2010), pp. 97-100 and nn.

Due to its importance to the understanding of the period, I include here the other main viewpoints to date.

"These reconstructions [of the early pronunciations would seem likely to point to a derivation from *Tokha(ra) – that is, from the Tochari or Tokharians – as pointed out by several early scholars, notably J. de Groot in the Preface to his 1917 book, *Die Hunnen der vorchristlichen Zeit*, where he transcribes the two Chinese characters as "Ta-ha (Tochara)." Chris Dorn'eich (personal communication, 26 January, 2006).

"Markwart (1901), p. 206, suggests that the Tochari must have been identical with the Daxia. The Hellenic Kingdom of Bactria was destroyed by the Daxia, and the latter was destroyed by the Yuezhi. I think his theory is correct. . . ." Yu (1998), pp. 38-39, n. 18.

"Further to the west the Chinese name for Ferghana, "Dawan," and that for Bactria, "Daxia," were also variations of Tuhara.[15] Bactria, a name given by the Greeks to northern Afghanistan and Uzbekistan, was known as the "land of the Tuharans" as late as the seventh century C.E., according to the Chinese pilgrim Xuanzang.[16]

15. Yu Taishan. *A Study of Saka History*, p. 72.

16. Ji Xianlin, *Da Tang Xiyuji Jiaozhu* (An Edited Edition of the Travelogue of the Western Region by Xuanzang of the Great Tang Dynasty) Beijing: Zhonghua Shuju, 1985, p. 100."

Liu (2001), p. 268.

"The detailed discussions of the land of Tokhāristān [also written Tōγaristān, Toχāristān] have now made it clear that for the period of the fourth to eighth centuries A.D. only one region (apart from the reminiscence of the eastern *toγara* near Kanchou surviving, as we have seen above, in Greek, Khotan Saka, Tibetan and probably Chinese) was recognized to have the name *toγara*. This was the country between Sogdiana (Sughd) at the Iron Gates (*dar ī āhanīn*) and Bāmiyan (see Marquart, *Ērānšahr*, 199 ff., Pelliot, *Tokh.* 33 ff.). The capital was Balkh (*Bag-la* in Tibetan) [could this be a reference to Baghlan instead?] and the city of Tarmita was comprised in it. It was therefore the old Bactria. The evidence is furnished by Arabic, Armenian, Tibetan and Chinese sources. It is not now disputed. . . ." Bailey (1937), p. 887.

"The notion of Ṭukhāristān varies with different authors, Marquart, *o.c.*, 229. Barthold in *EI* quotes Ṭabarī, ii, 1180, where Shūmān and Akharūn belonging to Khuttal and lying north of the Oxus are reckoned to Ṭukhāristān, but usually only the region east of Balkh and south of the Oxus is understood by Ṭukhāristān." Minorsky (1937), p. 337.

"Finally, I have to mention the name of the country, 'Tukharistan'. This name is not attested in Bactrian until about 500 A.D., in the Hephthalite period, but it obviously derives from the name of the Tokharoi, Skt. Tukhāra, whom the famous Buddhist translator Kumārajīva identified with the Chinese Yuezhi." Sims-Williams (2002), p. 231.

Considering that a few centuries intervene between the Chinese Daxia (*Tadgha/Tadza) and the later forms of *toχu̯ā(r), taχu̯ā(r), toχār, tuχār and Sanskrit Tukhāra/Tuṣāra, the possibility that Daxia was an early attempt by the Chinese to render the name of Tokhāristān, or its root, must be seriously considered.

Indeed, the *Tangshu*, 121b, clearly states that Tokhāristān (吐火羅 *Tuhuoluo* and variants) was the ancient territory of (the kingdom of) Daxia. See: Chavannes (1900), p. 155; Marquart, *Ērānšahr*, pp. 204-210; Chavannes (1907), pp. 187-188, n. 2; Konow (1929), liv-lvii.

- **Did the name 大夏 Daxia derive from the name of the 'Tochars,' or 'mountain men'?**

"A second way of writing *γara* occurs in Chinese. An ancient people of the Xuang-xo (Yellow River) region, the later Ordos from the Mongol *ordo*, where Scythian, that is, Sarmatian, bronzes have been found by archaeologists,[298] was called in Chinese 夏 K 135 *hia* < *γa*, *G* 136 a *g'å*, Jap. *ka.*[299]

Foreigners reported an added sound expressed in Khotan-Saka by the syllable *-ra* and in Tibetan by a laryngeal sound *'a* (the last *akṣara* in the Tibetan syllabary). This region of which the cities *Ling* (*ḍi ttu*), *U* (*buhä: thuṃ*) and *Ṣuo-fang* (*śahvāṃ*)[300] are named in Khotan-Saka, was called in Khotan-Saka *hara-kṣīra* and referred to in the same document as *ha* without *-ra*. This *hara* will be for Chinese either *γar* or *xar.*[301] Tibetan for Chinese 夏 *hia* has *kha'a* 'summer' in a tenth-century glossary.[302]

[298] K. Jettmar, *Die frühen Steppenvölker* (1964), 159-69; E. D. Phillips, *The Royal hordes* (1965).

[299] The people *Hia* are wrongly treated as mythical by G. Haloun and that is accepted by A. F. P. Hulsewé, *China in Central Asia* (1979), 145 [note 387].

[300] *Ṣuo-fang*, K 926, 25 *ṣuo-fang* < *såk-pi̯wang*, *G* 769 a, 740 a *såk-pi̯wang* appears to be a North Iranian Saka name **saka-pruvāna-* 'the city of the fort of the Saka people' (*DKS* 256).

[301] *BSOAS* 30 (1967), 100.

[302] *BSOAS* 12 (1948), 760, note 128; *BSOAS* 30 (1967), 100; *AION* 1 (1959), 125-6."

Bailey (1985), pp. 116-117.

"In the mountainous Oxus region the east Iranian word for mountain was *γari-* (contrasting with the west Iranian in Old Pers. *kaufa-*, Zor. Pahl. *kōf-*, N. Pers. *kōh*), that is, Avestan *gairi-*, Khotan-Saka *ggari-*, gen. plural *ggariṇu*, adjective *garaja-*, Sogd. *γr-* **γar-*, adjective *γrčyk* **γarčīk*, modern Pamir languages Yidγa *γar*, Waxi *γār*, beside Sanglēčī *gar*. N Persian used the word of the mountains of the Oxus region as *γalčīk*, *γalčah* and the *γarčistān* of the Harē-rōδ.

The **tu-γara*, *ta-hia*, of the Oxus mountains could be called just 'mountain folk'. Below, however, for the eastern *gara-* name a different etymon is proposed, which could serve here if 'mountain folk' should prove too *simpliste*." Bailey (1985), p. 130. See also Vogelsang (2002), pp. 136-137 and note 3 quoted in note 1.1.

"There is such a reason and it must be sought in the historical and ethno-linguistic reality of the ancient Iranian world. The evidence lies in a passage of Strabo's *Geography*, XV, 2, 8, where he takes Eratosthenes as his source. After having described the boundaries of Ariana, Strabo writes that the name Ἀριαή could also be extended to part of the Persians and the Medes and also northwards to the Bactrians and the Sogdians,... ["and the name of Ariana is further extended to a part of Persia and of Media, as also to the Bactrians and Sogdians on the north; for these speak approximately the same language, with but slight variations." Strabo XV,2,8 translated by H. L. Jones. Downloaded on March 29th, 2012, from: http://penelope.uchicago.edu/Thayer/E/Roman/Texts/Strabo/15B*.html

"This passage explains how part of the Persians and the Medes, the Bactrians and the Sogdians, could think of themselves as 'Aryan'. Like other peoples living in Ἀριαή, they were also entitled to the name of Ἀριανοι. It also explains, as a consequence, how they could call their language 'Aryan'. Bactrian, therefore, could be called 'Aryan' just as Old Persian could, even without its speakers having a specific linguistic awareness of the profound unity of the Middle Iranian dialects.

Thus the use of 'Aryan' as a language-name referring to Bactrian and Old Persian in the inscriptions of Rabatak and Bisitun could be explained by the above-mentioned passage from Strabo's *Geography*. If, for the earlier term of comparison - namely Persian - we were to go beyond the Achaemenian period in order to draw a comparison that is contemporaneous with the Kushans, we should have to admit that we do not know what the Persians of the early Sassanian period called their language, but we do know for certain that they called themselves *ēr* or *ērān*. It was only towards the end of the Sassanian period that we have clear signs of the increasing usage of defining as *pārsī(g)* and *darī* the variants of Middle Persian that were to become the language of the whole domain of the empire, from Fars to Khorassan, according to a tendency that became more and more common with the expansion of the Muslim conquest, to which *fārsī* was to owe its fortune." Gnoli (2002), pp. 86-87.

"For the numerous vocabulary items attested exclusively in Eastern (as distinct from Western) Iranian a few examples must suffice: .. [including] **gari-* "mountain" (OInd. *girí-*, Av. *gairi-*), often also "rock" or "pass" in the modern languages: Khot. *ggara-*, Sogd. *γr-*, Yagh. *γar*, Shughni *žīr*, Yazgh.*γar*, Wakhi *γar*, Munji *γār*, Pashto *γar*, Orm. *grī*, Par. *gir*." From: "Eastern Iranian Languages" in *Encyclopaedia Iranica*. Nicholas Sims-Williams. Originally published: December 15, 1996; Last Updated: Dec. 2, 2011. Downloaded from: http://www.iranicaonline.org/articles/eastern-iranian-languages, on 6 February, 2012.

"About Tochars . . . . It is very simple, and you see it all over on the map, "tag" is mountain in Turkic, with millennium-old dialectal variations: tau, tav, tai, dag, ... I do not remember them all, but here are examples: Tuarus mountains in Anatolia before Turks, in Iran before Persians and Turks, in Syria before Turks, in Crimea before Turks; Altyn-tag (golden mountain), Ala-tau (motley mountain), Dagestan (mountainous country), Saratov (Turkic name Sary-tau, "yellow mountain")... a distinct branch of Ossetians is called Tuars/Tugars = "mountaineer" "Ar" is man in Turkic, with millennium-old dialectal variations: er, ir... Here are examples: Bulg-ar, Sav-ir, Suv-ar, Tag-ar, Tau-ar, Khaz-ar, Toch-ar....hundreds of them, with "mountaineer" and "water man" most popular (hence the Tagars and Suars, with many (variations). Incidentally, the same "ar" word is also in the Germanic languages, with the same semantics, to produce verb-derived appellations for people: teach/teach-er, drive/drive-er, eat/eat-er.... And if the Earthlings were composed with the same "ar" component, the English Earth-er would be a dialectal variation of Turkic Yer-ar. The French Coucher, English Coacher, Turkic Kocher are not only synonyms, they are dialectal variations of the same word: Koch - coach (like in stage coach, or coach van, French couch) plus "er/ar" for the man on the coach.

As you know, the oldest spelling of Tochars was Tachars (today we tend to use English for spelling, so it would be Tokhars and Takhars)."

Norm Kisamov. Personal communication, 26 March, 2008.

"These [terms] could well be exoethnonyms, exemplified by modern "mountain people" in the Caucasus, which speak hundreds of languages, but are generically called "mountaineers", with its variations in the dominating language, which were at times Persian, Turkic and Turkish, and lately Russian. Neither of these appellations makes Caucasus Kabardinians or Caucasus Nakhs Persians, Turkic or Turkish, or lately Russians." Norm Kisamov, personal communication 27 March, 2008.

"Linguists insist that the unity of the Turkic peoples is most apparent in language. Some scholars go so far as to say that no factor unites all Turks but language. Although the often-mentioned genetic connections between Turkic languages and a larger Altaic family including Mongolian and Tungusic are controversial, the resemblance among the Turkic languages is unmistakable. They have differentiated to a point where not all Turkic languages are mutually intelligible; yet they still resemble each other more closely than do Indo-European languages. Resemblances across time, between the earliest written Turkic and the modern languages, are conspicuous." Findley (2005), pp. 16-17.

The early movement of Turkic-speaking peoples is not well understood. Reconstructions are necessarily speculative, and often contentious. Proto Turkic-speaking tribes could possibly have been in the region of Sogdiana and Bactria in the 2nd century BCE when the Yuezhi arrived. Perhaps there were some proto-Turkic or Turkic-speaking tribes within the Yuezhi confederation.

"The earliest notices on Turkic peoples date back to the time of the Hsiung-nu ruler Mo-tu — the name is usually mistranscribed as Mao-tun — (209-174 B.C.E.), who launched an attack into the northern regions, most probably southern Siberia, and conquered here the tribes of Hun-yu, Ch'ü-she, Ting-ling, Ke-k'un and Hsin-li (Sima Qian 1993, 2: 138). Of these the Ting-ling, the later T'ieh-lê, the Ke-k'un (also Chien-k'un = Qïrghïz) and the Hsin-li (also Hsüeh = Sir?) are Turkic people or in the case of the Qïrghïz, a possibly Paleo-Siberian people under Turkic leadership who were in the process of Turkicization (Golden 1992, 176-179, 404-406; Janhunen 1996, 186; Karaev and Zhusupov 1996; Butanaev and Khudiakov 2000). Also noted in other Han era sources are the Hu-chieh or Wu-chieh (EMC *xɔ-giat*, *ʔɔ-giat* = *Hagaŕ = Oghur ?Oghuz; see Pulleyblank, 1983, 454-456). These are the principal groupings of Turkic speakers at that time. None of these peoples bore the name Türk at this stage of their history." Golden (2006), p. 140.

"By the second century C.E., one of their successor peoples, the Xianbi (Hsien-pi), had eclipsed them. The Xianbi were also the people who, around 265 C.E., adopted not the title chanyu but the title that later became the most prestigious for a Turkic ruler, kaghan. Another Xiongnu successor state was the kaghanate of the Rouran or Ruanruan (Jou-Jan or Juan-Juan), possibly the same people as the Avars of European sources. One of the Touran's subject tribes was the first to bear the name *Türk* as a tribal name." Findley (2005), p. 35.

"About 552 the empire of the Jouan-jouan was taken over by their vassals the Turks, whose center was in the Altai Mountains. Soon the Turks extended their own sway over neighbouring tribes in Mongolia and the western steppes, and established a large empire." Frye (1998), p. 179.

- **Does Da Xia 大夏 mean 'Great Xia'?**

"Haloun (1926), pp. 136, 201-202, has made it clear that the term Ta Hsia originally referred to a mythical or fabulous people, vaguely located in the North (but eventually shifted to the West and even to the South). He states that it was Chang Ch'ien personally who identified the Bactrians with the Ta Hsia, the westernmost people he knew, but that he did not use the words *ta* and *hsia* to reproduce their actual name. Haloun rightly stresses this last point, viz. that the pronunciation of this old-established, mythological term need not have been anything like an approximation of the name of the actual country. Henri Maspero completely endorses Haloun's views in his review of the latter's work in *JA* 1927, pp. 144-152." *CICA*: 145, n. 387.
"There remains Da Xia, which must have originally been the "Great Xia", although it could have subsidiarily become a very approximate form of the actual name of the Tokharians." From Pelliot (1936), p. 262, n. 1; see also: Pelliot (1934), p. 40.

- **Does 大夏 Daxia refer to the Dahae?**

Rapson represents the Ta-hia or Dahae as the "native inhabitants of Bactria". Rapson, ed., (1922), pp. 510-511.

"Däae is transcribed Ta-i in the *Shih-chi* (cf. Shiratori, *Sei'i Kishi Kankyu*, i. 532, ii, p. 78." Narain (1957), p. 131, n. 1.

Dayi 大益 is said to be among "the smaller states west of Dayuan". See: *Shiji* 123, in Watson (1961), p. 243. It very likely referred to the Däae, but the reconstructed pronunciations of the final character (K. 849a *i̯ĕk / i̯äk; EMC: ?jiajk) seems unlikely to have been meant as an alternative of the final character of Daxia: 夏 *xia* – K. 36a: *g'å/γa; EMC: ɣaɨ'/ɣɛ:

- **Did 大夏 Daxia refer to the Greeks?**

"(ii)Ta-hsia = Greeks: Ellis, H. Minns, *Scythians and Greeks* [Biblo-Moser, 1913], p. 129; E. Hertzfeld, *Sakastan*, [*Archäologische Mitteilungen aus Iran*. Band iv. Berlin], 1932, p. 28." Adapted and expanded from: Narain (1957), p. 131, n. 1.

I have found no other references that Daxia referred to Greeks, or any information that supports this suggestion.

- **Did 大夏 Daxia refer to the Greco-Bactrians?**

My interpretation is that the people the Chinese referred to as the Daxia were local "Bactrians" (probably speaking an East Iranian language) who had lived in the region since the time of the Achaemenid Empire. They had inter-married with the Greeks left behind by Alexander, and probably with Indians and were known to Western writers as the Takharoi or Tokharoi. However, this is simply conjecture on my part, and is not accepted by many scholars.

There was a very ancient and highly urbanised, sophisticated population in Bactria, which previously had been one of the satrapies of the Persian Empire. After Alexander, they were ruled for almost 200 years by a series of Greek-speaking kings, their culture became deeply steeped in Hellenic tradition leading to a vibrant and creative hybrid Greco-Bactrian culture. It is difficult to overstate this influence.

Alexander left behind some 23,000 Greek colonists, all men. Many would have settled and had families, although:

"Tarn's reconstruction reads all too much like a steamy chapter from the Julio-Claudian period of imperial Rome. His history of the Diodotid family hinges upon the wives and widows of the dynasty, Agrippinas of another era who steered Bactria behind the scenes. According to Tarn, "these Macedonian girls were often anything but nonentities, and the pawns sometimes queened with surprising results."[10] Unfortunately, he was playing this elaborate chess game with imaginary pieces. In Bactria, these "Macedonian girls" are indeed "nonentities" whose politics and personalities Tarn invented; they are nowhere mentioned in any ancient text. Tarn's mistake was his assumption that the later Euthydemid coins were pedigree issues giving a bloodline (partly real, partly fictitious) that entitled him to fabricate all of these female members of the Diodotid family and give them various loyalties. That erroneous assumption about the coins, now exposed like the forgeries that misled Newell, leaves us back in the dark about the elusive Diodotid dynasty.

[10] *GBI*, p. 74."

Holt (1999), pp. 70-71 and n. 10.

"When the tumultuous spring [of 327 BCE] had passed, the king ordered ten thousand infantry and thirty-five hundred cavalry to garrison Bactria while the rest of the army marched away with him to India [never to return to Bactria]. These numbers are staggering and belie any suggestion that the region had been fully pacified. Such an enormous army of occupation had no equivalent in any other province of Alexander's empire. In fact, over 43 percent of all infantry and over 95 percent of all cavalry posted to foreign garrisons were stationed in what is now Afghanistan, even though the king's realm at that moment stretched across more than nine other modern nations, including Egypt, Turkey, Syria, Iraq and Iran. Without question, the hot spot of Alexander's world was Bactria.

Even this substantial military presence does not tell the whole story, since as many as ten thousand additional Greeks and Macedonians resided as permanent settlers among the Bactrians and their neighbours. These old and disabled veterans dwelt in cities and colonies scattered throughout the area, left back to live out their days among the populations they had fought, in places that they loathed." Holt (2005), pp. 96-97.

"Greeks and Indians mixed through the groundwork of Alexander the Great; later, some of these Greeks even found themselves under foreign domination : the settlers in the Indus Valley, but also probably those of Alexandria of Arachosia [Kandahar], which were included in the territories ceded by Seleucus I to Chandragupta Maurya in 303 BCE. Besides this domination, it should also be understood that the created cities were of mixed population, and the Indian territories over which the Macedonian kings reigned were, for the most part, composed of an Indian population of Brahmanic religion, with a well-defined caste system which sidelined the foreigners, the *mlecchas* in Sanskrit. The survival of Greek cultural traits would thus be problematic, especially under Mauryan rule, and in particular, taking into account that the learning of the language is more from the mother, while the majority of Greek settlers in these cities were former [male] soldiers.

The interpretation according to Strabo of the word *épigamia*, ἐpigamía[connection by marriage], leads to this matter : *some of these riverine provinces of the Indus, which were previously dependent on Persia, and then Alexander after he went to Ariana, had peopled settlements, nowadays under India, Seleucos Nicator having ceded them to Sandrocottos to guarantee a marital agreement and in exchange for five hundred elephants.*

Strabo does not detail the nature of the *epigamia*. Understood as a marital alliance between the families of Seleucus and Chandragupta, it poses no problems ; however no trace of a member of one or the other family in the Court of either of these two kings is attested. Some specialists are tempted to see the suggestion of a convention in the broadest sense, including the possibility for the Greeks who, following this treaty, became subjects of the Mauryan King, and able to marry with local subjects, against the dogmas of caste. The situation was not unique. If this hypothesis is correct, one can probably see behind the demand of Seleucus a willingness of the Greek colonists to mingle with the local population. A perfect example may therefore be found here of the desire for Greek integration.

Another factor reinforces this assumption of the importance of the Greek communities in these Northwest Indian cities: this is the "Kandahar bilingual", a copy of the edits of Ashoka discovered in ancient Alexandria of Arachosia [Kandahar], written in Greek and Aramaic. The presence of the Greek, and of less interest for this study, of the Aramaic, firstly allows it to be considered highly probable that the local language had no writing of its own, but that they [the Greeks] also were an important presence in the population of this city, since the Buddhist proselytism of Ashoka was intended for them. The Greek would have addressed the former founders of this city, the oldest having been present for three decades, which the quality of the language corroborates, while the Aramaic portion was perhaps intended for the Kambojas, the Iranian population, for which the language and the script used is a record of the two centuries of Persian occupation in the region.

The presence of Greeks is therefore confirmed in the Mauryan Empire, but what is important is that it is understood as integrated in this empire, and Greeks are more than simple foreigners. In these edicts of Asoka, mention is made that only the Greeks do not have two groups of Brahmins and ascetics, essential components of the caste system in force in the Indian peninsula. They are also mentioned in a slightly later manuscript alongside Kambojas and "other frontier peoples" as having only two castes, masters and slaves, and it is added that it was possible to pass from one to the other "caste". The fact that the notion of caste was used is important, since it indicates that this author, and probably the great majority of Indians did not understand that other systems could exist, even among *mlecchas*. The Greeks are once again mentioned alongside Kambojas, it seems the peoples of the Northwest of the peninsula are the eyes of some of the inhabitants of the Indian peninsula, set apart, among which the Greeks were only one component. In fact, the Yavanas do not seem to appear to the Indians as a people apart, and different from those around them, so one should avoid seeing in the coexistence between Greeks and Indians a "clash of cultures," rather peoples similar in many ways like the Kambojas already in contact with the Indians for hundreds of years."

Simonin (2011), Vol. II, Appendice A : Grecs et Mauryas, pp. 203-205. Translated and adapted by the author.

Shiji 123 tells us that Daxia was south of the Oxus. However, in later Chinese accounts, "Daxia" seems to include the entire arable region of the Middle Oxus basin - including the lands to the north of the river.

Both the Greco-Bactrian realm and the territories later controlled by the Yuezhi fluctuated in extent, but I think it justified to accept that 'Daxia' essentially corresponded to the region the ancient Greeks called 'Baktria.'

Appendix N: Lanshi (Baghlan) – principal city of Daxia and later the Da Yuezhi

A condensed version of Zhang Qian's report on his extensive journeys and adventures in the 'Western Regions' is preserved in the *Shiji* (see: Appendix Y). His visited to the court of the Da Yuezhi on the northern bank of the Oxus River and briefly mentions his trip across the river to the city of Lanshi in 119 BCE. He refers to Lanshi as the 都 *du* of Daxia.

The text reads: "Its' [Daxia's] *du* is Lanshi City (其都曰藍市城)." The term *du* 都 can be translated as a 'capital', 'chief city', 'headquarters', 'big city', 'metropolis', or a 'major centre'. See: *GR* Vol. VI, No. 11668; *CED*, p. 291. Also, see: note 13.2.

Although the word *du* is often translated as "capital," there are examples of more than one *du* existing in a single state – so the translation of the term as "the capital" is only sometimes true. According to Homer Dubs, in "ancient times" it referred to "a large walled city." Dubs (1938), p. 28, n. 2.

The confusion is likely due to its use to refer to the seat of a feudal noble and there could, of course, be more than one fief within a kingdom or state. This is clarified in the definition of the term in Kroll:

> "**1.** Principal city in the fief of a feudal noble, where he establishes his primary residence and ancestral temple.
>
> **a.** metropolis, metropolitan, often the capital city of a realm; to establish a city as the capital; pertaining to the capital; e.g. ~官 *dūguān*, provincial offices staffed and controlled by central government." Kroll (2015), p. 92.

At the time of Zhang Qian's visit, Lanshi was not the "capital" of the Da Yuezhi. Although the Da Yuezhi were the rulers of Daxia, their royal court (王庭 – *wangting* – see *GR* Vol. VI, p. 521) was on the northern bank of the Gui/Oxus/Amu Darya. The *Shiji* adds: "It [Daxia] has no great ruler but only a number of petty chiefs ruling the various cities." Watson (1993), p. 235.

By the time of *Hanshu* 96A, Lanshi is no longer described as the 都 *du* of Daxia. The Da Yuezhi had moved their 'seat of government' or 'capital' (治 *zhi*; W-G: *chih*) to Jianshi (= Lanshi) 監氏: "大月氏國，治監氏城."

> "**治 zhì MC driH** . . . .
> **3.** seat of government." Kroll (2015), pp. 608-609.

> "**[a] CHIH**[4] . . . .
> **3a. To administer;** to direct; to govern. **b.** (*Adm. hist.*) To administer; Administrative residence. **C.** (*Admin. imper.*) **Capital.** . . ." Translated from: *GR* Vol. I, p. 941, No. 1763.

The reconstructions for 藍 *lan* include: K. 609k *glâm / lâm; EMC: lam; Late Middle Chinese: lan; while Schuessler (2009), 36-5, p. 347, gives: **LHan (Late Han)** as lɑm, **OCM (Minimal Old Chinese)** as râm, and **OCB** (Baxter's reconstruction of **Old Chinese**, as *g-ram.

The character 監 in the 監氏- *Jianshi* (or *Kanshi*) of *Hanshu* 96A is, doubtless, no more than a scribal error for 藍氏 Lanshi – see: *CICA* p. 119, n. 278; *GR* Vol. I, No. 1554). The ancient pronunciations of the character 監, *jian* or *kan* has been reconstructed as: K. 609a *glam; EMC: kaɨm/kɛːm, or kaɨm^{h}/kɛːm^{h}. Schuessler (2009), 36-5, p. 347 gives: **LHan** kam and **OCM** krâm.

In the *Hou Hanshu*, the name of the town is given as 藍氏, which has the same first character as the *Shiji*'s version: 藍市 - *Lanshi*. It says the Da Yuezhi 'dwell in' or 'occupy' (居 *ju*) Lanshi: "大月氏國居藍氏城".

The *Weishu* 102 (which covers the years 386 to 550 CE) says: 大月氏國，都盧監氏城 – "The kingdom of the Da Yuezhi has as its 都 'du' *Lu Jianshi cheng* ['Black Jianshi City']."

> "LAUFER also brought into the argument the name of the city of 藍市 Lan-shih, which he translated by « Blue Market », « a designation which apparently refers to the blue color of lapis lazuli ». But Lan-shih is only one among many forms given by the different texts for the old capital of the Great Yüeh-chih; there is no reason to try to explain the name by its trade in lapis-lazuli." Pelliot (1959), p. 59.

> "**藍 lán MC lam**
> **1.** indigo (*Polyganum tinctorium*), the leaves of which are a source of blue dye; the dye-color produced from the plant was usu. ref. to as *qing* 青." Kroll (2015), p. 252.

• Geographic and strategic considerations

The great east-west range of the Hindu Kush neatly divides Afghanistan into two distinct geographic regions. The southern half of Afghanistan including the Begram-Kabul valleys was blocked off by mountains from the important northern centres such as Bactra/Balkh, Ai Khanoum, Begram, and Khulm, and the main trade routes joining China with the West. Communications were only possible via a few high passes.

> "Though we know little of trade routes at the end of the third century AD, early and mediaeval Muslim itineraries as well as eighteenth and nineteenth century European explorers, all indicate that the two major caravan routes went either east or west of the present Pul-i Khumri to Doshi road. The present road was built to provide access to the Salang Tunnel and was constructed in the middle of the last century. The main route from Khulm to Bamiyan passed west of Pul-i Khumri, through Aibak (present day Samangan), Khurram and the Dandan Shikan pass, whilst to the east the ancient route to Kabul was via Baghlan, Nahrin, up the Andarab valley to the Panjshir, and then down into Charikar and the Koh Daman (le Strange 1905, 427; Ferrier 1857)." Grenet et al. (2007), pp. 246-247.

> "The plains, the useful and beautiful valleys of Badakshan, lie in the embrace of a kind of mountain horse-shoe, which shuts them off from the Oxus on the north-east and east and winds round to the Hindu Kush on the south. The weak point of the semicircular barrier occurs at the junction with the Hindu Kush, where the pass between Zebak and Ishkashm is only 8700 feet high. From the slopes of the Hindu Kush mountain torrents drain down through the valleys of Zebak (called the Wardoj by Wood), the Minjan (or Kokcha) and the Anjuman into the great central river of Kokcha. Of these valleys, so far as we know, only the Wardoj is really practicable as a northerly route to the Oxus. Shutting off the head of the Kokcha system, a lateral range called Khoja Mahomed by Wood (a name which ought to be preserved), in which are many magnificent peaks, sends down its contributions north-west to the Kunduz." Holdich (1910), p. 436.

To the east, there are several passes into Badakhshan and Wakhan, but the Khawak Pass (3,848 m. or 12,625 ft.) is the first practicable pass for caravans providing access to Tokharistan and Bactra/Balkh, and it was much used in ancient times. This route entailed a long detour to the northeast up the Panjshir Valley before crossing the Hindu Kush and then travelling back westward through the region of Andarab before reaching the plain of Baghlan where it joined routes heading to Kunduz and to Khulm.

"The travellers using the ancient Bamiyan route to Balkh had to follow a circuitous route traversing four major passes ranging in altitude from 9,000 to 12,000 feet [2,743 to 3,658 metres]. While these passes were subject to snow fall during winter, they were still more accessible than the more direct routes leading across the eastern part of the Hindu Kush. The Kawak Pass linking Panjsher and Andarab, for example, was closed entirely by snow from December to June and was only frequented by local traders." Noelle (1997), p. 283.

Other caravan routes led west from Kabul to Bamiyan and then northeast over relatively easy passes across the 'Great Snowy Mountains' or Hindu Kush, to the plains of Baghlan.

"The central section of the range, known as Kābul Kūhestān (Kohistan), was famous in antiquity as the location of the *triodon*, three great transmontane routes. The first of these was either the Khawāk Pass in the Panjshēr River valley, over which Alexander the Great passed northward, or the adjacent Thalle Pass, used by Timur; the second was the Kushān Pass (slightly to the west of the present-day Sālang road tunnel), which Alexander crossed southward; and the third was the Kipchak Pass, used by Genghis Khan in the early 13th century and by Babur in 1504." *EB* (2011): Accessed from: http://www.britannica.com/EBchecked/topic/266291/Hindu-Kush on 20 September 2011.

"Pliny further describes Alexandria [Opiân near Begram] as being situated *sub ipso Caucaso*,[3] "at the very foot of Caucasus," which agrees exactly with the position of Opiân, at the northern end of the plain of *Koh-dâman*, or "hill-foot." The same position is noted by Curtius, who places Alexandria *in radicibus montis*,[1] at the very base of the mountain. The place was chosen by Alexander on account of its favourable site at the *τρίοδον*,[2] or parting of the "three roads" leading to Bactria. These roads, which still remain unchanged, all separate at Opiân, near Begrâm.

1. The north-east road, by the Panjshir Valley, and over the Khâwak Pass to Anderâb.
2. The west road, by the Kushân valley, and over the Hindu Kush [or Kushan] Pass to Gori.
3. The south-west road, up the Ghorband valley, and over the Hâjiyak Pass to Bamian.

The first of these roads was followed by Alexander on his march into Bactriana from the territory of the Paropamisadæ. It was also taken by Timur on his invasion of India ; and it was crossed by Lieutenant Wood on his return from the sources of the Oxus. The second road must have been followed by Alexander on his return from Bactriana, as Strabo[3] specially mentions that he took "over the same mountains another and shorter road" than that by which he had advanced. It is certain that his return could not have been by the Bamian route, as that is the longest route of all ; besides which, it *turns* the Hindu Kush, and does not cross it, as Alexander is stated to have done. This route was attempted by Dr. Lord and Lieutenant Wood late in the year, but they were driven back by the snow. The third road is the easiest and most frequented. It was taken by Janghez Khan after his capture of Bamian; it was followed by Moorcroft and Burnes on their adventurous journeys to Balkh and Bokhara; it was traversed by Lord and Wood after their failure at the Kushan pass; and it was surveyed by Sturt in A.D. 1840, after it had been successfully crossed by a troop of horse artillery.

[3] Hist. Nat., vi. a. 21.

[1] Vit. Alex., vii 3. [2] Strabo, xv. 2, 8. [3] Geogr., xv 1, 26."

Cunningham (1871), pp. 20-21 and notes. Also see the map on page 15.

The quickest and most direct routes from Kabul to the northwest across the Hindu Kush, therefore, went over the Kushan Pass (about 4,370 m. or 14,340 ft.), until a tunnel was built by the Russians in the 1960s under the less frequently used Salang Pass (3,878 m. or 12,723 ft.), slightly to the east.

> "It is a matter of interest to observe that, historically, between Afghan Turkistan and the Kabul plain the fashionable pass over the Hindu Kush until quite recently was the Parwan [Salang], and this, no doubt, was due to the fact that its altitude (12,300 feet) is less by quite 2000 feet than that of the Kaoshan which closely adjoins it, although the Kaoshan [Kushan] is in some other important respects the easier pass of the two. The Khawak, at the head of the Panjshir, is lower still (11,650 feet), but it offers a more circuitous route ; whilst the Chahardar, the pass selected by the Amir Abdurrahmon for the construction of a high-road into Afghan Turkistan from the Kabul plain, is as high as the Kaoshan. All these routes converge on the important strategical position of Charikar, adjoining the junction of the Ghorband and Panjshir rivers ; and they all lead from that ancient strategical centre of Baktria, the Andarab basin." Holdich (1910), p. 357.

> "From the Khawak to the head of the Ghorband (a river of the Hindu Kush which, rising to the north-west of Kabul, flows north-east to meet the Panjshir near Charikar, whence they run united into the plains of Kohistan) the Hindu Kush is intersected by passes at intervals, all of which were surveyed, and several utilized, during the return of the Russo-Afghan boundary commission from the Oxus to Kabul in 1886. Those utilized were the Kaoshan (the "Hindu Kush" pass par excellence), 14,340 ft [4371 m]; the Chahardar (13,900 ft)[4237 m], which is a link in one of the amir of Afghanistan's high roads to Turkestan; and the Shibar (9800 ft)[2987 m], which is merely a diversion into the upper Ghorband of that group of passes between Bamian and the Kabul plains which are represented by the Irak, Hajigak, Unai, &c." *EB* (1911), Vol. 13, p. 513.

The most direct route to Badakshan left Charikar near ancient Kapisha, and travelled up the Kushan valley, past the settlement of Kushan and then over the Kushan Pass (also known as: the Kaoshan or Hindukush Pass) to Baghlan, Balkh and beyond. It was about 200 km shorter than the old caravan route through Bamiyan, thus saving about 8 days travel.

The town of Kushan, just north of Ghowr Band River, was identified by Cunningham as the probable site of ancient Kapisha. See: Cunningham (1871), p. 24.

The Kushan Pass was not too difficult, and, although it was snowed in much of winter, it was the fastest way to cross the Hindukush from Kapisha to Baghlan, Surkh Kotal, and Balkh. It is said to have been the most used pass east of Bamiyan across the Hindukush until the Soviets opened the nearby Salang tunnel in the 1960s. See: Thornton (1844), p. 408.

> "The road from Balkh to Taxila is not the only over-land route connecting India with the outside world, but it is the most important one. It has a long history: the Aryans marched along it to conquer India; after them came the Persians and held the country around it for some two hundred years; then followed the Macedonians and Greeks, the Kushanas, the Sasanians, the Hephthalites, the Turks, and the Arabs. All of them came from the northeast; and though the road was difficult and dangerous, they all took it for the same reason: at its end lay the promised land, the fertile plains of Northwestern India. What went in the opposite direction was of a very different kind; the teaching of the Buddha set out on this same route to win its glorious victories in Central Asia and China. Thus the road from Balkh to Taxila was truly a road to destiny, and therefore an enormously interesting object of study." Bachhofer (1949), pp. 100-101.

As both the Kushan/Hindu Kush and Salang passes were high and often snow-covered, they tended to be avoided by caravans, in spite of the fact they were much shorter routes than those to the east or the west. Nevertheless, they were of immense importance for rapid communications between the two regions, even providing a practical route for large armies.

It is almost certain from Strabo's account (*Geog.* xv, 1, 26) that Alexander brought his army across the Kushan Pass on his return from Bactria in 327 BCE. See: Cunningham (1871), pp. 24-25; Rapson, ed. (1922), p. 313 and note 7.

> "Broadly speaking, the whole route system to the north of Kabul can be studied under three broad categories, viz., the north-east road, the northern road, and the north-west road. . . .
>
> *The northern road* ; This road proceeded by the Kushān valley, and over the Kushān Pass to Ghori [about 30 km southwest of Baghlan on the direct route to Khulm and Bactra]. Alexander traversed this road on his return journey from Bactria. Cunningham observes, "Strabo specially mentions that he took 'over the same mountains another and shorter road' than that by which he had advanced. It is certain that his return could not have been by the Bāmiān route, as that is the longest route, of all ; besides which, it *turns* the Hindukush, and does not cross it, as Alexander is stated to have done.[157]
>
> 157. *The Ancient Geography of India*, p. 21. This route was attempted by Dr. Lord and Wood, late in the nineteenth century, but they were driven back by the snow."
>
> Verma (1978), pp. 86-87.

> "Alexander the Great entered India early in 327 B.C. Crossing the lofty Khawak and Kaoshan [Kushan] passes of the Hindu Kush, he advanced by Alexandria, a city previously founded in the Koh-i-Daman, and Nicaea, another city to the west of Jalalabad, on the road from Kabul to India." *EB* (1911), Vol. 14. P. 397.

> "The Kushān Pass, used by Alexander is over 11,000' [according to modern maps, approx. 4,370 m or 14,340 ft]. This pass leads under a great peak known as Hindukush. It starts from a point in the valley above Tūtūn darra and descends upon Khinjān [on the northern side of the range]. Henry Yule considers it the Yangī-yūl (New road) of Bābur.[27]
>
> [27] *Bābur-Nāma*, p. 205."
>
> Verma (1978), p. 265 and n. 27.

Although it does seem probable that Alexander took the shortest route, as with so many historical problems, not everyone agrees, and it is quite possible that Alexander crossed over another pass on his way south. As it was spring when he headed north, he may have taken the route through Bamiyan, which was longer, but easier, and open all year.

> "This opinion as to the locality of Alexandria ad Caucasum [Begram] receives some support from Professor Wilson ; but on the other hand, it may be urged, that as Beghram is situate nearly opposite the mouth of the Koushan Pass, or Pass of Hindoo Koosh, which is only practicable in summer ; and as Arrian relates that Alexander crossed the Caucasus in spring, he must have taken the route by Bamian, which is open all the year round ; and as, according to the same authority, his march brought him to Alexandria ad Caucasum, we must assign Bamian as its locality." Thornton (1844), p. 81.

"The communication with central Asia and Russia by the north-western frontier is far more difficult than that with Hindostan. It is principally by the passes of Hindoo Koosh or by the Bamian route. Of the passes of Hindoo Koosh, the most frequented is that of Koushan, over the north-eastern shoulder of the principal summit, and at the most elevated part of the road estimated to be 15,000 feet high. It is described by Lord as "narrow, rocky, and uneven, with a fall of 200 feet a mile, so that it was impossible that it should have ever contained any other waters than those of a headlong rapid torrent." As this is the most frequented pass through Hindoo Koosh, it is probably the best ; but it is scarcely practicable for beasts of burthen at its upper part, where the transport of goods is effected on men's shoulders, and it is totally closed by snow in winter." Thornton (1844), p. 24.

"The Ghorbund Pass proceeds from Charikar, in the Kohistan, up this valley and debauches into the Pass of Hageguk. About ten miles from its entrance, the Koushan Pass diverges to the north and crosses the Hindoo Koosh into Kunduz." Thornton (1844), p. 193.

"KOUSHAN, in Afghanistan, the most frequented of those passes over Hindoo Koosh which lie to the east of Bamian. It forms a communication with Turkestan, and is called emphatically the Pass of Hindoo Koosh, according to Leech, because the most frequented, in consequence of the protection afforded to travellers by the governments of Kabool and Kunduz; the former of which held the southern, the latter the northern portion of the pass. It is, however, more probable that it was so called from its highest part lying over the eastern declivity of the vast peak called properly Hindoo Koosh. There are three entrances to the pass from the Kohistan of Kabool. Of these the principal lies along the bed of the Ghorbund river, and in consequence is impassable when the river is swollen. The road, which is very steep, proceeds up a deep and narrow valley, cross-cutting alternating veins of mica-slate, clay-slate, gneiss, and granite, which last extends through the highest part of the pass for six miles. The elevation of the summit of the pass is estimated by Leech and Lord at fifteen thousand feet, but does not appear to have been ascertained by actual measurement. The general direction is from north to south : the inclination of the northern slope is much steeper than that of the southern, in consequence of the adjacent part of Turkestan having a far lower elevation than the Kohistan of Kabool ; still, even on the southern side, the upper part of the pass is steep, difficult, and dangerous. Lord states that "it is for wheeled carriages perfectly impassable." Leech, on the contrary, states that the Meer Timur (meaning Timur Leng, or Tamerlane) brought guns by it ; but it is well known that cannon were not used by that prince ; and though Prinsep assumes that Alexander marched from Afghanistan to Turkestan by this pass, the account given by Arrian is too general to warrant such a conclusion. The Koushan Pass appears to be that called by Baber the Pass of Kipchak. The summit is in lat. 35^0 37', long. 68^0 55'." Thornton (1844), pp. 408-409.

"The [Muhammadan] Siah-posh ['black clothed'] Kafirs have never been conquered, and they would form, in their inaccessible valleys, an admirable outpost of our Indian Empire, so that the establishment of friendly intercourse with them is much to be desired. Here would be a market for British goods, as well as a defensive post against Britain's enemies. On their western frontier is the Khawak Pass, 13,200ft. high, leading over the Hindu Kush to Badakshan, one of the lowest and most accesible of the Hindu Kush passes. It was probably used by Alexander the Great on his march from Bactria ; and it was certainly the route taken by the Chinese Pilgrim, Hiouen Thsang, in A.D. 644, who wrote one of the earliest accounts of India. Timour also used it in 1398, and Lieutenant Wood, I.N., traversed it on his way to discover the source of the Oxus. But it is very improbable that a modern Russian army would ever attempt an invasion of India by any of the Hindu Kush passes, which are closed by snow for six months in the year. If it did, there is no likelihood that it would ever return.

The Kushan Pass, a long defile with a gradual and easy ascent to a summit 15,000ft. above the sea, in the western part of the Hindu Kush, is also closed by snow from November to June ; and still further west is the Char-darya Pass, used by caravans, and practicable for artillery. This was the pass, then called Kipchak, by which the future Emperor Baber first crossed the Hindu Kush in 1504, and after passing which he first beheld the star *Canopus*. "Till then," says that most charming of memoir writers, "I had never seen the star *Soheil*" (*Canopus*), "but on reaching the top of the pass Soheil appeared below, bright, to the south." Markham (1894), p. 12.

"The Ghorband Valley is a defile running for a long distance parallel with the crest of the Hindu Kush.

The Kúshán Pass is the first of the series leading from it, and this route passes under the great peak which is visible from the city of Kabul on one side, and from Kunduz on the other. It is known as the Hindu Kush, often called by Persian writers the Hindu Koh, and it gives its name to the range. Hence the Kushan route passing under it is not unfrequently referred to as the Hindu Kush Pass.

It is a long defile, with a gradual and easy ascent, except for about a mile and a quarter, and the summit is 15,000 feet above the sea. It is closed by the snow from the 1st of November to the 15th of June. The Gwálián Pass is said to be easier than the Kushan, but the Gwázyár is a mere footpath. Next to the westward is the Char-darya Pass, which is used by caravans, and is said to be practicable for artillery. Colonel Yule holds this to be the "Kipchak" Pass, by which the Emperor Baber first crossed the Hindu Kush in 1504, and after passing which he first beheld Canopus. "Till then," he says, "I had never seen the star Soheil (Canopus), but on reaching the top of the hill Soheil appeared below, bright to the south." Westward of Char-darya come the passes of Ghalalaj, Farinjal, and Shibr. On the Farinjal Pass there is a very extensive but long-abandoned lead mine, which was examined in detail by Dr. Lord in 1837. Here the mountains are quite barren, and streaked with snow. The Shibr Pass is at the western extremity of the Ghorband Valley, and descends upon the River Surkhab, which flows from Bamian. It is, therefore, the last of the Hindu Kush passes to the westward. Colonel Yule mentions that by the Shibr Pass the Chinese pilgrim Hiouen Thsang [Xuanzang] travelled on his way to India in 630 A.D., and it was crossed by Timur on his return from Delhi. It was also the pass most commonly used by Baber, who calls it Shibrtu, and says that it is the only pass never closed in winter." Markham (1879), pp. 115-116.

". . . resolutely taking the southward road from Kundûz, we began to follow the Kundûz river up-stream. Above 'Aliabad the river drew us into a gorge, and I resigned myself to remaining imprisoned in this gorge till it deposited us at the northern foot of some pass over the Hindu Kush. But the landscape of the Iranian plateau is always springing surprises on the Western traveller. After a bit the gorge culminated in a darband, just not too narrow for road and river to squeeze through without being throttled, and then the country abruptly opened out into the broad flat plain of Baghlan. At the same moment a gang of giant snow-mountains raised their heads above the hills round the plain, and ranged themselves in a semi-circle: to right of us, to left of us, in front of us. . . .

In the middle of the plain of Baghlan stands the residency of the Governor of Kataghan Province. It is a round house, perched on the crown of a round tepe, which must once have been either a stupa or a castle or each of these in turn. We called on the Governor, drank tea with him, and drove on, till road and river once again ran the gauntlet of another darband, and once again just managed to squeeze their way through into a still larger plain that unexpectedly opened out ahead. The plain was, in fact, a double one, shaped like an hour-glass; and, coursing along the second plain's eastern side towards Pul-i-Khumri we soon saw the giant stairway of Surkh Kotal rising up from its western edge." Toynbee (1961), pp. 106-107.

"Quickly [on the way south from Surkh Kotal] the valley narrowed, as we mounted it, into a gorge. Then it opened out again, with characteristic Iranian unexpectedness. Then it narrowed once more, swept us through a bazaar chock-a-block with bivouacking buses and lorries, carried us over a bridge, and would have run us full tilt into a rock-wall, if our wary drivers had not taken a right-angle turn just in time. The crowded parking place was Doshi; the wall was the wall of the Hindu Kush, below the northern ascent to the twelve-thousand-feet-high Salang Pass, and the river that we had just crossed was not our familiar companion the Kundûz River; it was the Andarab. The two rivers meet head-on, the Andarab descending westwards from the Khawak Pass, and the Kundûz River eastwards from the Shibar Pass. Colliding just south of Doshi and turning north, they form the greater river whose course we had been following, upward and southward, since leaving Kundûz town.

As we sped over our bridge, I caught sight of a more imposing bridge over the Andarab River higher up. This is the bridge that is to carry the road from Kundûz straight on southwards towards the tunnel which Russian engineers have undertaken to bore through the Hindu Kush underneath the Salang Pass. When this tunnel is an accomplished fact, there will be a straight run, along a tarmac road, all the way to Kabul from Afghanistan's Oxus-port at Qyzyl Qala. . . . the present north-and-south road, which we were following, has to run up to the head of the Kundûz River, surmount the Shibar Pass, and then run down from the head of the Ghorband River. In fact, it has to run around three sides of a square in order to cross the Hindu Kush from Doshi to Charikar in the plain of Koh-i-Daman. The new road will run along the fourth side of the square, and then Charikar and Doshi will be within an hour or so's distance of each other. Already to-day they are as close to each other as the eagle flies—that is, if the Paropanisus does not justify its Avestan name by over-topping the ceiling of even an eagle's flight.

To-day we were bound, not for Kabul, but for Bamian; but, pending the piercing of the Salang tunnel, the same road leads to both Bamian and Kabul up to the point, not far short of the Shibar Pass, where the Bamian River drops steeply down to join the Kundûz River. This is known as the Surkhab ('Redwater') [or, preferably, 'Red River'] locally in this upper part of its course." Toynbee (1961), pp. 112-113; 130.

"At present, the main pass across the Hindu Kush is the Salang Pass and Tunnel. It directly connects the north of the country with the south and the country's capital, Kabul. The modern road crosses the mountains at a height of 3,363 metres [11,033 ft.]. Built under Soviet supervision between 1956 and 1964 it replaced a lengthy and circuitous route west of Kabul via the Shibar Pass, close to the Bamiyan Valley.[15] Another, but at present much less frequented route between north and south leads east of the Salang, through the Panjshir valley.[16]

15 Traditionally there were two main routes from Kabul to Bamiyan. The first goes north from Kabul and turns to the west along the Ghorband river and crosses the Shibar Pass

(2,987 m). The other route leads west from Kabul and crosses two passes, namely the Unay Pass (3,354 m) and the Hajigak (3,567 m) or Iraq Pass (3,963 m). From the Bamiyan valley, the ancient road proceeds north via the Aq Ribat Pass (3,117 m) and the Dandan Shikan Pass (2,744 m). A modern track, built with the help of German engineers and opened in 1933, leads north from just west of the Shibar Pass, along the Bamiyan river, to Doab-i Mekhzarin and hence down into the plains of North Afghanistan.

16 This route crosses the mountains via the Khawak Pass. Traditionally (but without any evidence) this is the route thought to have been followed by Alexander the Great in the spring of 329 BC when he led his army from the Kabul valley across the mountains to the north (compare Wood 1997:142-4)."

Vogelsang (2002), p. 9, and nn. 15-16.

"At the right-hand end (we are facing north-north-west) [at the base of the Minar-i-Chakri on the road between Kabul and Jalalabad] towers the highest mass of all: the snow-crown of Nuristan, whose east and west shoulders had given me glimpses of themselves from the plain of Peshawar and from the western foot of the Khyber Pass, before I had gained my first view of the whole crown from the Lataband. The left-hand end of the line is the eastern rampart of Afghanistan's central highlands. It hides the Hazarajat, and, beyond that, Ghor, jealously guarding the minaret of Jam. In the centre, glistening pure white against a pure blue sky, we can see the nick that is the Salang Pass. It is the highest but shortest passage between two worlds, the basins of the Indus and the Oxus. To the eye gazing out from the base of the Minar-i-Chakri, it looks as if the great white wall were not only unbroken but straight. But this is a magnificent optical illusion. The true configuration is in the shape, not of a straight line, but of a **T**-square; and the two lines that form the right-angle are broken by other and deeper gaps than the nick made by the Salang. I myself, a few days back, had profited by one of these now invisible breaks in the snow-line. I had passed out of the Oxus basin into the Indus basin over the Shibar Pass without meeting even a fleck of snow on the rolling saddle between the snow-peaks. Gazing hard, I can now make out, from where I stand, a brown ridge running down to the Koh-i-Daman plain on this side of the white horizon. It is the southern rim of the Ghorband valley, down which we had dropped from the Shibar Pass to Charikar. And then, between the Salang nick and the crown of Nuristan, the white wall sags and lets down its guard. This must be the watershed between the Panjshir and the Andarab, and my eye, travelling eastward along it, could have espied the Khawak Pass if this had not been screened by the west shoulder of the Nuristan crown." Toynbee (1961), pp. 123-124.

• Locating Lanshi as being near Baghlan and Surkh Kotal

Lanshi, described as the *du* 都 of Daxia in the *Shiji*, was definitely subject to the Da Yuezhi when Zhang Qian visited it. See: Appendix N. He reported that he found Chinese goods from the western province of Shu (Sichuan) there that had been imported via India. Watson (1993), pp. 235-236.

There are plausible strong linguistic and other arguments suggesting that Lanshi was in or near modern Baghlan, which is situated in "the valley of the southern Surkh-âb or Kunduz river, about 34 miles [55 km] south from Kunduz." Beal (1884), Book I, p. 43, n. 147. The major Kushan temple-complex of Surkh Kotal is in the valley nearby.

More pointers to a linguistic connection between the name Lanshi and modern Baghlan, can be found in the following quotes:

"The road to Kunduz branches off from the road to Mazar-i-Sharif just north of Pul-i-Khumri (5 km; 3mi.), passing through a heavily-cultivated area around **Baghlan**, capital of Baghlan Province. Medieval geographers called this area Baylan, but even more interestingly, the Surkh Kotal inscription (Chapter 22) includes the word Bagolange which closely resembles an Old Iranian word for temple altar or sanctuary. Baghlan, meaning province of the sanctuary, takes its name, therefore, from Kanishka's temple which flourished in the 2nd century A.D.

Baghlan (pop: 29,000; alt. 500 m; 1641 ft.) is actually divided into two sections. . . . .

Driving through extensive fields of sugar beet and cotton, one reaches the Administrative Centre of Baghlan at marker 262 . . . . The Governor's Office stands on top of a mound called **Cham Qala**, an ancient Buddhist monastery during the Kushan period ca. 2nd-3rd centuries A.D. While digging the foundations for the office building, several fine sculpted limestone friezes depicting scenes from the life of the Buddha were found which are now on display in the National Museum, Kabul.

Leaving Baghlan, the fertile fields gradually give way to plains dotted with mounds still guarding the remains of other ancient towns and villages. As the road approaches the low mountains softened by loess deposits which separate Kunduz from these plains, it meets a river and together they wind through low passes. In the spring these hills offer superb pasturage and large herds of horses may often be seen grazing beside the river. Horses from this area have been prized for centuries: Alexander of Macedon replenished his cavalry while he was here in the 4th century B.C.; the Kushans sent horses from here as gifts to the emperors of China in the early centuries A.D., a tradition which continued into the 15th century when horses were included among the valuable gifts presented to the Ming Emperor of China by envoys from the Afghan area." Dupree (1977), Chapter 27.

"The name [Baḡlān] originally derives from the Bactrian *bagolango* "image-temple" (< OIr. **baga-dānaka-*), a term used in the inscription of Nokonzoko (SK4) from the archeological site of Surkh (Sorḵ) Kotal in Afghanistan. In this text, the temple-complex excavated by the Delegation Archéologique Française en Afghanistan from 1951-63, is named as *Kaněško oanindo bagolango*, probably to be understood as "Kanishka-Victory-Temple." Though since the word *oanindo* represents both the name of an astral deity of victory, depicted winged and thus named on the Kushan gold coinage, and as an adjective "victorious," some scholars have taken it as an epithet referring to Kanishka.

The temple excavated at this site appeared to be a fire-temple of dynastic character, dedicated for the rulers of the Kushan dynasty. It was founded perhaps early in the reign of Kanishka (according to the unfinished inscription SK2 in the year 289 of an unstated era which is most probably a Greco-Bactrian era of about 155 B.C., thus fixing the date of construction to about A.D. 124), and restored in the year 31 of a different era, probably of Kanishka I's own enthronement, perhaps thus equivalent to A.D. 125 + 31 = 156 or shortly after.* The complex contained a *cella*, an attached subsidiary fire-temple piled with fine ashes, statues of at least two Kushan emperors, one of which seems identical with a coin-portrait of Huvishka, and a stone orthostat in poorly preserved state which appears to show an enthroned ruler in the presence of a trophy (for another theory see Fussman, p. 123).

The temple site is some 15 km northwest of Pol-e Ḵomrī in northern Afghanistan on the road to Balḵ, and about the same distance from the modern administrative center of Baḡlān, a straggling settlement on the opposite (east) bank of the Qondūz River beside the road from Pol-e Ḵomrī to Qondūz. The meaning and original location of the name were evidently forgotten during the Middle Ages, so that it attached vaguely to the district as a whole, and ultimately to its modern center. The region was no doubt closely connected with the Kushan dynasty, and it bore in the Islamic period the name Ṭoḵārestān which derives from that of the Tocharoi, the ancient horde of which they became the rulers." A. D. H. Bivar. Downloaded from: http://www.iranicaonline.org/articles/index/B/page:1/limit:1000. 21 September, 2011.

***NOTE:** These dates should be revised in light of the new work done on eras by Harry Falk and Chris Bennett. The "unfinished inscription SK2 in the year 289 of an unstated era" should be assigned to the Yonas era - now thought to begin in 175/4 BCE - giving a date of about 115 CE.

Bivar's date of 124/5 CE, according to his presumed era inception in 155 BCE, should read 134/5 CE. The restoration work is said to have taken place in year 31 - presumably in Kanishka's era, which is now thought to have started in 127/8 CE, indicating a date of 158/9 CE, and therefore, probably during the reign of Huvishka. See Falk (2001), pp. pp. 121-136; Falk and Bennett (2009), p. 212. (JEH)

"The great district of Ṭukhâristân lay to the eastward of Balkh, stretching along the south side of the Oxus as far as the frontiers of Badakhshân, and bounded on the south by the mountain ranges north of Bâmiyân and Panj-hîr. It was divided into Upper Ṭukhâristân, east of Balkh and along the Oxus, and Lower Ṭukhâristân which lay further to the south-east, on the frontiers of Badakhshân. . . .

Beyond, south-east of Siminjân, was Baghlân, Upper and Lower, and in the latter district, according to Muḳaddasî, was the capital [of Ṭukhâristân] with a Friday Mosque in the 4th (10th) century. Baghlân or Baḳlân, as the name of the district is spelt by 'Alî of Yazd, apparently lay along the road to Adarâbah, otherwise Andarâb, which is described by Muḳaddasî as having fine markets, being situated among valleys clothed with verdant forests. These valleys, which were on the northern slopes of the Panj-hîr range, had many silver mines in their recesses, according to Ibn Ḥawḳal, who speaks of two rivers, the Nahr Andarâb, and the Nahr Kâsân, as flowing through this district." Le Strange (1905), pp. 426-427.

"From the description given by M. Schlumberger it is clear that the sanctuary [of Surkh Kotal] lies within the district know to medieval geographers under the name of *Baγlān*, see e.g. Le Strange, *Eastern Caliphate*, p. 427, or Professor Minorsky's definition 'on the middle course of the Doshī river (formed by the Surkhāb (= Barfak) and Andarāb)'. The name survives to the present day. Captain John Wood, coming from Bāmiyān, left the valley of the river of Haibak a little below Ruy and, after travelling eastwards to the Qunduz river, came 'through the swampy district of Baghlan and Aliabad'. It still belongs to an eastern tributary of the Qunduz river and to a village near the junction of the two watercourses. According to Muqaddasi, 303, *Baγlān* was divided into two parts, 'upper' and 'lower'; the sanctuary should be counted to 'Upper Baγlān', where there was a 'large village, to which a well-wooded valley belonged'.

Among the fragmentary inscriptions found by M. Schlumberger and ably discussed, in all their aspects, by M. Raoul Curiel, the most considerable piece consists of three lines, of which the first two are incomplete at both sides. M. Curiel gives the following reading:—

]ΒΙΔΟΙΣΗΝΟΒΙΔΟΙΑϸΙΟ[
]ΚΙΡΔΟΜΙΒΑΓΟΛΑΓΓΟΜ[
ΔΙΑΠΑΛΑΜΗΔΟΥ

Apart from the last line, which is in Greek, the language of the inscription is not clear: M. Curiel assumes, with some measure of likelihood, that it is the Middle-Iranian dialect once spoken in Bactria. Here I wish to draw attention merely to the principal word in the second line, ΑΓΟΛΑΓΓΟ, which I regard as an older form of the name of *Baγlān* and very probably the ancient name of the sanctuary. It would be a strange coincidence if ΒΑΓΟΛΑΓΓΟ, in an inscription found within the territory of *Baγlān*, were to be unrelated to the name of the district.

ΒΑΓΟΛΑΓΓΟ, i.e. *Baγolāngo*, after the loss of the ending and compound-vowel, became *Baγlāng*, *Baγlāŋ*, finally *Baγlān*. Previously one could compare *Baγlān* with Armenian *Bagaran*, from Middle-Iranian **bagaδān*; the inscriptional spelling now shows that the Sogdian form, *βγδ'nyy*), was closest: both represent Old Iranian **baga-dānaka-* 'temple, altar, sanctuary'. Since the place-name *Baγolāngo* must be ascribed to the local Iranian dialect (whatever may have been the language of the inscription) [now referred to as 'Bactrian'], we are safe in attributing to that dialect the change of *-d-* to *-l-*, at least in intervocalic position, and the reduction of the final *-ānaka-* to *-āng-* (*-āŋ-*) as e.g. in Persian *dāng*: δανάκη. Hüan-tsang's *Fo-ka-lang* also proves *āng*.

The transparent etymology of *Baγlān* always permitted the inference that the district was called 'the sanctuary', short for 'the province of the sanctuary', after the famous temple or sacred enclosure. M. Schlumberger's brilliant discovery of *Bagolango* (as perhaps we may now be permitted to say instead of *Surkh Kotal*) has taught us where the temple lay to which *Baγlān* owed its name." Henning (1956), pp. 366-367.

Bailey says that the capital of Tokharistan was *Bag-la* in Tibetan but assumed that this must have referred to Balkh. See the quote from Bailey (1937), p. 887, in Appendix M. However, considering all the evidence, it probably referred to Baghlan, and the close phonetic correspondence adds support to this position.

Further support for the identification of 藍氏 Lanshi as Baghlan is found in the *Tangshu* XLIII, B, pp. 6-9, where there is a long list of "the protectorates, governments and districts which were created following the destruction of the Western Tujue [突厥 = 'Turks']." Grouped under the Protectorate of Anxi (Kucha) we find the "16 Governments of the Western Regions" starting with:

"1st Government of the Yuezhi 月支 (known under the name Indoscythians), established in the town of Wuhuan 阿缓 (*K* 遏换) (War-wâliz = Kunduz) of the yabghu of *Touholo* ; this government ruled twenty-five districts which were the following: a) "the district of Lanshi 藍氏, established in the town of Bobo 鉢勃 (it is known that Lanshi was, according to the *Shiji*, chap. CXXIII (completed about 109 BCE), the capital of Daxia, and that it later became the capital of the Da Yuezhi). . . ." Translated and adapted from Chavannes (1900), p. 68, note 2.

It is to be found again later in the same list of the districts of the 'Government of the Yuezhi' (under k): "the district of Boluo 鉢羅, established in the town of *Lan* 蘭". Chavannes (1900), pp. 68-69, note 2. (The reconstructed Late Han pronunciation of 蘭 is *lɑn. Schuessler (2007), p. 343. This is supported by Pulleyblank's EMC: lan See also: *GR*, Vol. 3, p. 1093).

Chavannes claims, "the town of 蘭 Lan [in the *Tangshu*] is none other than Baghlân to the south of Kunduz on the right bank of the Kunduz River." Chavannes (1900), p. 275.

Alternative locations suggested for Lanshi (藍氏)

• Bactra/Balkh

Lanshi has frequently been identified as the city of Bactra/Zariaspa (= modern Balkh; 36° 46'N, 66° 52'E) on the grounds that Bactra was by far the largest and most important city in the region. See: Watson (1993), p. 235. However, it is impossible to linguistically link Lanshi, or any variations of that name, with any of the forms given to Bactra/Balkh in the Chinese texts.

The character *lan* 藍, usually translated as 'blue' or 'indigo,' can also be read as: 'Buddhist monastery or monasteries' (– an abbreviation of *sengqielanmo* – the transcription of the Sanskrit *sanghârâma*). *GR* Vol. III, p. 1091.

The reconstructed ancient pronunciations of *lan* 藍 (K609k *glam/*lâm, – or EMC **lam*), suggest a more likely explanation for the character – that it may have been intended to represent the foreign sound, 'râ(m)'.

The second character used in the earliest example: that of the *Shiji*, is *shi* 市 (K. 963a, *đi̯əg / *źi; EMC *dʑɨ' / *dʑi'), which can be read as: 'public place', 'commercial quarter', 'town' or 'municipality'.

The character *shi* (or *zhi*) 氏, (K. 867a *đi̯ĕg / *źie̯; EMC, *dʑiĕ / *dʑi or *tɕiă / *tɕi; *GR* Vol. V, No. 9757, *śgi̯ĕg / źie̯) which replaces *shi* 市 in the transcriptions of the *Hanshu* and *Hou Hanshu* can be read as: 'family', 'line', 'sir,' and was very frequently used as a shorthand way to represent the (Da) Yuezhi (大)月氏.

Therefore, the name can be read as 'Monastery Town' or, possibly in the later accounts as 'Yuezhi Monasteries.' It could equally, represent a name which sounded something like **Rashi(g)*. Either may be correct.

Bactra was noted as a Buddhist monastic centre and this could explain its name as as 'Monastery Town' or 'Yuezhi Monasteries'. On the other hand, the name **Rashi(g)* could have been an attempt to transcribe the name Rajagriha. In this connection, it is of great interest to note that Xuanzang wrote that 縛喝 Fohe or Fuhe – usually identified with Bactra/Balkh – was commonly referred to as, "Little Rajagriha city":

> "This country was above 800 *li* from east to west and 400 *li* north to south, reaching on the north to the Oxus. The capital, which all called "Little Rajagriha city," was above twenty *li* [8.4 km] in circuit, but though it was strong it was thinly peopled." Watters (1904-5) I, p. 108. Also see Beal (1884), p. 44.

> "Today, it [Balkh] is a vast ruin field – a huge citadel, with great towered outer walls of sun-dried brick; ruined Buddhist stupas, Zoroastrian fire temples, and Nestorian Christian churches – all religions made their homes here. A medieval Muslim poet describes the city in a lovely image, surrounded by its gardens: 'as delightful as a Mani painting'. The City sits under the north side of the Hindu Kush, where the sun rises over the fertile fields, fed by a spread of tributaries fanning out from the Balkh river. It was replaced by Mazar in the last century, and there is not much left of its civic life now, beyond a few winding mud-brick lanes amid groves and gardens in the centre. Old Balkh is virtually gone, but a few people still live here. At the ancient gates, there are little shrines to ancient holy men, still neatly maintained with offering flags, and swept floors. Right in the centre of the old city, in a circle of palm trees, are the great shrines of the Timurid Age. Still especially popular with the people of the region is the grave of Rabia Balkhi. Even today she is the female protectress of the city, just as the ancient patroness of Balkh, Anahita goddess of the Oxus, was in Alexander's day. Anahita's magnificent gilded statue had been gifted by one of Darius's predecessors, Artaxerxes II. Thousands had come to licentious rites in the precinct of the 'High girdled one clad in a mantle of gold, on her head a golden crown with rays of light and a hundred stars clad in a robe of over thirty otter skins of shining fur'. . . .
> From Balkh, it was only 80 kilometres to the river, a four-day journey for Alexander's main army, but a minor disaster was narrowly averted as they ran into the sand dunes beyond the oasis and suffered very badly from heat and thirst. The time was

early summer – very, very hot – and what the Greeks experienced, modern travellers still experience." Wood (2001), p. 150.

According to Beal's *Life of Hiuen-tsiang* (1911), p. 48, the new Shah of Bactra said: ". . . men call the capital city the *little Râjagriha* – so many are the sacred traces therein." See also the translations of this passage in Li (1995), p. 47; Watters (1904-1905), I, p. 108.

Eitel (1888), p. 127, describes the original Râjagriha as: ". . . lit. the city of royal palaces. The residence, at the foot of Gridhrakûṭa, of the Magadha princes from Bimbisara to As'oka ; meeting place of the first synod (B.C. 540) ; the modern Radghir (S.W. of Bahar) venerated by Jain pilgrims. . . ."

Later forms of the town's name include *Yingjianshi* (or *Shengjianshi*) 賸監氏 in the *Peishi*, and, apparently, *Lujianshi* 盧監氏 in the *Weishu*. See: Zürcher (1968), pp. 372-373, 388. The character *lu* 盧 added in the *Weishu* simply means 'black.'

賸 *Ying* or, preferably, *Sheng*, added in the *Peishi* to the name 監氏 of the *Hanshu* translates as 'an escort,' or 'to accompany' and, perhaps, indicates here an administrative township close to the main city of Bactra itself (rather in the manner that Ctesiphon served as an administrative centre for the Parthians directly across the river from the major city of Seleucia).

None of the arguments linking Lanshi with Bactra/Balkh appears likely for two reasons:-

First, there are a number of other transcriptions of the name of this city into Chinese – none of which bear any resemblance to Lanshi. Surely, Zhang Qian would have remarked on such a huge centre in more detail if Lanshi had indeed been Bactra/Balkh.

Secondly, Bactra/Balkh, with its famously massive walls and fortifications, was unlikely to have fallen to a nomadic army, unless through treachery. There is no literary or archaeological evidence that it was conquered at this time. Also, see: Chavannes (1907), pp. 187-189, for his reasons for not identifying Lanshi with Balkh; he preferred to locate it in Badakhshan.

It seems probable to me that Bactra/Balkh managed to hold out until they could negotiate terms with the Yuezhi therefore retaining a degree of independence, although perhaps providing tribute to the Da Yuezhi. If so, Bactra could not have been Lanshi, as Zhang Qian visited it soon after the Da Yuezhi arrived and it was already dependent on them.

• **Khulm**

Pulleyblank appears to have been the first person to identify Lanshi with the city of Khulm (Tāshkurghān):

> "Another difficulty might seem to be presented by the use of 樓 M. **lu < * ĥloĥ** in Lou-lan = Krorayina. One must however remember the peculiarity already noted about transcriptions from that region, *i.e.* the use of Chinese laryngeals to represent foreign back velars or uvulars (see p. 91 above). The native pronunciation of Krorayina may have had an uvular at the beginning which prevented it from being represented by Chinese ***kl**. The same considerations may apply to 藍市 M. **læm-j̭iə** (*Shih-chi* 123), 監氏 **kam-j̭ieˊ** (or **c̭ie**) (*Han-shu* 96 A), 藍氏 **lam- j̭ieˊ** (or **c̭ie**) (*Hou Han-shu* 118) the name of the capital first of Ta-hsia and then of the Yüeh-chih in Bactria (*cf.* Haloun 1937, p. 259). The first syllable of this transcription must represent the name later known as Khulm. Khulm is a large ancient site in the heart of Tokharestan east of Balkh, strategically situated on the crossroads between the east-west road and the north-south route between Transoxianian [*sic*] and the Hindukush. It is a natural place to have made a capital city by the Yüeh-chih. I hope to give a fuller discussion

of this identification from the historical point of view elsewhere. It will suffice here to point out the variation between * ĥl- and *kl- to represent the foreign initial which was later an Iranian X-. Whether the name is originally Tokharian or Iranian, the Chinese probably first heard about it through Tocharian, perhaps as **q*-." Pulleyblank (1962), pp. 122-123. Also, see: Pulleyblank (1962), p. 247, Pulleyblank (1966), p. 122, the discussions in *CICA*, p. 119, n. 278, and Grenet (2006), pp. 328-330.

- **Could Lanshi be a transcription of Alexandria?**

"Lan-shi [*heam-zjiə*] may be a contracted transcription of "Alexandria", another name of Bactria.[34]

34. See Specht. "Tarn (1951), p. 115 suggests that "Lanshi" may have been identical with Alexandria. On the location of Lanshi, there are also various theories; for example: Puṣkalāvatī theory, see Levy; Badhakshan theory, see Chavannes (1907); and Khulm theory; see Pulleyblank (1962), p. 122; etc. I consider all of them unconvincing." Ibid, p. 41."

Yu (1998), p. 25 and n. 34.

"Bactra, 'Mother of cities' and 'Paradise of the earth', represented by the modern Balkh, was the capital [under the Greek kings], but it has never been excavated and little enough is known about it; probably we should think of a city of the type of Susa (p. 27). It was the traditional home of Zoroastrianism, and its other name, Zariaspa, may represent that of its great fire-temple, Azar-i-Asp; as Strabo (XI, 516) says that it stood on both sides of the river Bactrus, the united stream of the Band-i-Emir and the Darrah which then reached the Oxus, it is possible that the second name Zariaspa was the name of one definite part of it. It had been refounded by Alexander as an Alexandria, a name which curiously enough was used by Chinese historians though not by Greek ones;[1] it must therefore by the time of Euthydemus have possessed full Greek city forms and, besides being an important clearing-house of trade, had become a very great fortress, while the temple of its native goddess Anaïtis probably formed a centre for the native population in the same way as did E-sagila at Babylon and Nanaia's temple at Susa. The old goddess of the Oxus had now developed into a goddess of fertility on the Babylonian model, and had acquired Babylonian elements and become equated with Ishtar; her worship had been officially promulgated throughout the Persian empire by the Achaemenid Artaxerxes II, together with her festival the Sacaea during which a mock king held rule, also derived from Babylon. In her temple in Bactra stood a famous cult-image of her wearing a golden crown with eight rays and a hundred stars and clad in skins, dear to the Persians, of thirty beavers 'of a sheen of silver and gold'; she and her crown of rays figure on coins of Demetrius, which must mean that she was the city-goddess of Greek Bactra as she subsequently was of Greek Pushkalāvatī (p. 135) and as Nanaia was of Greek Susa.

[1] Lan-chi (Alexandria) was the capital of Ta-hia *i.e.* Bactria (Hirth p. 98) and subsequently, after they had occupied Bactria, of the Yueh-chi (*Hou-han-shu* chap. 118, tr. Chavannes, *T'oung Pao* VIII, 1907, p. 187). Probably it is Stephanus' Alexandria no. 11, *κατὰ Βάκτρα*. E. Specht, *JA* 1897 pp. 159–61, first saw that Lan-chi was Alexandria. De Groot p. 96 makes it Pan-ku's Kam-si, which he then interprets and locates by the aid of very much later Chinese works, a doubtful method. Why Chavannes, *loc. cit.*, and Konow, *CII* p. liv, should put the Bactrian capital in Badakshan I cannot guess. Historically, Lan-chi cannot possibly be anything but Bactra."

Tarn (1984), pp. 114-115 and n. 1.

The derivation of Lanshi from Alexandria is unlikely, as there are at least three Chinese transcriptions for various Alexandrias, and none is similar to Lanshi.

The first, in Section 8 of the 'Chronicle on the Western Regions' of the *Hou Hanshu*, is Wuyi(shanli) 烏弋(山離) representing Arachosia and Drangiana, which was centred on Kandahar (itself most likely a corruption of Alexander's name). The second, Wuchisan 烏遲散, referring to the city of Alexandria in Egypt, is in the *Weilüe*. Also in the *Weilüe* is Bei Wuyi or 'Northern Wuyi' 北烏伊, referring to Alexandria Eschate ('Alexandria the Furthest' or modern Khujand). See: Chavannes (1905), p. 558.

Furthermore, there is no evidence that Bactra/Balkh was ever called Alexandria. The name was generally used by the Greeks for cities founded (or re-established) by Alexander. Balkh was renowned for its age, size and importance long before Alexander arrived on the scene, so was unlikely to have been renamed "Alexandria."

> "The earlier Buddhist constructions have proved more durable than the Islamic period buildings. The Top-Rustam is 50 yd (46 m) in diameter at the base and 30 yd (27 m) at the top, circular and about 50 ft (15 m) high. Four circular vaults are sunk in the interior and four passages have been pierced below from the outside, which probably lead to them. The base of the building is constructed of sun-dried bricks about 2 ft (600 mm) square and 4 or 5 in (100 to 130 mm) thick. The Takht-e Rustam is wedge-shaped in plan with uneven sides. It is apparently built of *pisé* mud (i.e. mud mixed with straw and puddled). It is possible that in these ruins we may recognize the *Nava Vihara* described by the Chinese traveller Xuanzang. There are the remains of many other topes (or stupas) in the neighborhood.
>
> The mounds of ruins on the road to Mazar-e Sharif probably represent the site of a city yet older than those on which stands the modern Balkh." Downloaded on 17 April, 2006 from: http://en.wikipedia.org/wiki/Balkh#Ancient_ruins_of_Balkh. Corrected on 26 September 2011. Refer also to Leriche (1993), p. 77.

- **Could Lanshi have been Kunduz?**

> "Excavation at Kunduz may at least show what a Bactrian town of which there is no mention in classical writers was like. Some 2 miles north of the place where these remains were found, there is a huge "castle" with walls of mud 100 feet high and over 2 miles in circumference. There is a wide and deep moat, and there are four gateways. The interior consists of a series of shallow undulations or mounds well rounded by the weather, which indicate the remains of mud buildings, aligned along two roads which intersect at the centre and which connect the four gates [this is typical Hellenistic style]. The fortifications on top of the enceinte are obviously comparatively modern; they still retain the shape of walls. But because here, too, builders had been excavating earth, we were able to examine some of the lower strata of kiln-baked brick. These lower walls were very reminiscent of Sassanian building, and some of the pottery collected from these levels proves to be similar to pre-islamic Persian types which, thanks to the labours of Mr. Pope, we can now arrange in some sort of chronological order. In appearance, this impressive ruin is very similar to the Parthian fortress of Takht-i-Suleiman, which Mr. Pope has recently surveyed on the western marches of the Sassanid Empire." Barger (1939), pp. 384-385.

Rapin (2005), locates Darapsa/Adrapsa/Drapsaka/Drepsa and the 'Drepsianoi' of Alexander's historians in the region of Surkh Kotal and Baghlan - in contrast with his earlier position that it was located near Kunduz. See: Rapin (2005), p. 145 and note 10; also: Rapin et al (2006), p. 50, "*2) Carte de l'Asie centrale, avec les identifications toponymiques récents.*" Also, see: Dorn'eich (2013), p. 53.

Other suggestions for the location of Lanshi/Jianshi that never achieved widespread acceptance include Badakhshan - Chavannes (1907) p. 187, n. 2, and Khalchayan - Benjamin (2003), pp. 191-200.

• The Significance of the names 'Kushan Pass', 'Kushan Valley' and 'Kushan Town'

It seems probable that the names 'Kushan Pass,' and the 'Kushan Valley' represent genuine souvenirs from Kushan times. The route north over the Kushan Pass led directly into the heart of the Kushan dominions and was about 45 km directly south of the spectacular fortified Kushan sanctuary of Surkh Kotal. The Kushan Valley leads directly from the Kushan Pass to Charikar via the small settlement of 'Kushan'.

> "**DRÁPSAKA.** Greek name of a Bactrian city in northern Afghanistan, the first town captured by Alexander the Great after crossing the Hindu Kush (Arrian, *Anabasis* 3.29.1). Shorter forms (< ancient Iranian *drafša-* "banner") include Dárapsa (Strabo, 11.11.2), Ádrapsa (Strabo, 15.2.10), Drépsa (Ptolemy, Geography 6.12.6, confusing its location with that of Marakanda-Samarkand, probably because the rivers flowing near them were both called Dargamánēs, designating the Qondūz river and the Dargom channel), and Drepsa (Ammianus Marcellinus, 23.6.59). The name also appears in the great foundation inscription from Surkh Kotal (Sork̲ Kotal; Ball, I, no. 1123; Harmatta, pp. 453-55) in the Bactrian form Lrafo, referring to the citadel where the "gods" (i.e., statues) were transported when the temple was temporarily abandoned during the 2nd century C.E.
>
> Since Franz von Schwarz first made the suggestion in 1893 there has been a consensus that Drápsaka should be identified with the Bāl Ḥesār at Qondūz (Ball, I, pp. 222-23 no. 931; cf. Holt, p. 28 n. 67), which is the correct distance from Alexandria (q.v.) sub Caucaso (probably Begram) to correspond to the fifteen-day march mentioned by Strabo; an archeological survey (Gardin and Lyonnet, pp. 135-36) has revealed an Achaemenid occupation there. Nevertheless, two even larger fortified sites situated farther upstream should perhaps not be excluded, as they lie closer to Surkh Kotal: They are 'Alīābād (with evidence of occupation from pre-Achaemenid times; Ball, I, p. 34 no. 29) and Qal'a-ye Ḡūrī (near Surkh Kotal but still unsurveyed; Ball, I, p. 207 no. 846)." Grenet (1995). Downloaded from *Encyclopædia Iranica Online* at: http://www.iranicaonline.org/articles/drpsaka on 22 September, 2011.

The plains surrounding Lanshi/Baghlan are the meeting place of the major passes crossing from Kabul and Kapisha to the north. Lanshi controlled access to Andarab, immediately to the east and north of the Hindu Kush, which had rich mines of copper and silver. Additionally there was an extensive ancient lead mine on the Farinjal Pass to the west of the Kushan Pass. The *Ḥudūd al-'Ālam*, a Persian geography dated 982 CE, states:

> "Here dirhams are struck from the silver extracted from the mines of Panjhīr and Jāriyāna." Minorsky (1937), p. 109.

> "Andarāb lies on the south-easternmost headwater of the Doshī river (*v.s.* 77.—79.). This important valley leads up to the Khāvak pass south of which Panjhīr is situated. On the north-east Andarāb adjoins Khost. Iṣṭ., 279, names the two rivers of Andarāb ; Andarāb and Kāsān (the latter is a right affluent of Andarāb)." Minorsky (1937), p. 341.

• Lanshi/Baghlan region as a major centre of Kushan culture and power

About 20 km southeast of modern Baghlan is the major Kushan site of Surkh Kotal with its monumental stone staircase in five flights, each with a terrace, leading up from the main road towards Bactra/Balkh and Kunduz. The hilltop is crowned with an impressive dynastic sanctuary dedicated to Kanishka and his ancestors. Construction probably started during the reign of Vima Tak[to] and was completed during that of Kanishka. Harmatta, et al. (1994), pp. 320-321.

Everybody travelling here from the south would have been made dramatically aware that they were now entering Kushan territory.

"Surkh Kotal ['Red Pass'], site of a great religious temple founded by Kanishka, Great King of the Kushans, *circa* 130 A.D. is one of Afghanistan's most important archaeological sites. Destroyed by fire during the political unrest following Kanishka's death, the temple was restored and then again burned, this time by the Hephthalites, nomadic rivals and ultimate successors to the Kushans in the Afghan area. . . .

The significance of this site increases as each year passes. First there was the discovery of a large inscription written in cursive Greek script in the Kushan language (now in the foyer of the National Museum, Kabul), which created great excitement for it was the first lengthy inscription in the Kushan language ever found. Another inscription, originally a facing for the third terrace, is being pieced together, block by block, in the Museum. . . . At Surkh Kotal the Classical elements, directly inspired we now know by Bactria itself, mix with Persian motifs, but there is no evidence of India at the temple itself. About two kilometres east of Surkh Kotal, on a direct line with the staircase, however, there was a Buddhist temple with monumental figures and decorated pilasters (now [in 1977] in the National Museum, Kabul). This was, therefore, the experimental ground where the Bactrian Classical, the Persian and the Central Asian mixed. From here it moved to mix with the spirit and forms of India thereby creating one of the more expressive art forms the world has ever known. The art and architecture of Surkh Kotal, so intimately connected with the Great King had, no doubt, a particularly persuasive influence on the development of Gandharan art.

Directly across the road from Surkh Kotal archaeologists excavated a small garrison fort on top of a hill crowned with ruins called **Kona Masjid** (Old Mosque). Occupied during the Kushano-Sasanian period after Surkh Kotal had been abandoned and before the advent of Islam, *i.e.*, from the late 3rd–7th centuries A.D., the garrison was responsible for the security of the main north-south route which passed at its foot. An unique ceramic rhyton in the form of a horned goat supporting a human head was recovered from this site (now [in 1977] in the National Museum, Kabul)." Dupree (1977), Chapter 22.

"From the plain it looks as if the giant staircase mounted a spur of the hills that bound the plain on this side. But from the summit you see that the fire-temple crowns a hill that, like the hill crowned by Persepolis, is isolated by a ravine from a higher hill behind it. On the second day I climbed to the top of the deserted fortress, Islamic in date, by which this higher hill is crowned, and then found that this hill, in its turn, is separated from the main mass of the bounding hills by another ravine through which the camel-and-donkey trail runs today. Thus, together, the fortress hill and Surkh Kotal commanded three tracks, reckoning in the present wheel-road that skirts the foot of the giant staircase. This modern road must also have been an ancient one, or the foot of the staircase would not have been sited where it is.

Surkh Kotal's position is indeed a commanding one. The three tracks are so many variants of a road that comes from the south—eventually from the far side of the Hindu Kush. North of Surkh Kotal this south-and-north road bends to the left and passes between the hills and spring which bubbles out below their foot. Beyond that point the road divides. The left-hand branch runs on north-westward up a bay of the Surkh Kotal plain and over a col into the valley of the Tashkurgan River, to break out of the gorge, side by side with the river, into the Tashkurgan oasis. Since civilization began, this has been one of the perennial roads between India and Balkh, and so it still is today. As for the right-hand branch of the great north road, it bends north-eastward round the spring, runs through the waist of the hour-glass into the plain of Baghlan, and heads for Kundûz and Badakhshan. . . .

. . . . But the religion to which Surkh Kotal was dedicated by Kanishka was not Buddhism. It was a form—not necessarily, or even probably, the Zoroastrian form—of a cult of fire, or of a divinity honoured, and perhaps symbolised, in the fire kept alive on the altar.

The fire-altar stood in the middle of a four-square temple with a passage around it for the devout laity to circumambulate. This temple-plan is strikingly different from the Greek plan, in which the worship centres, not on a fire-altar, but on the statue of a divinity hidden in a holy of holies at the far end of an oblong building. The contrast between the two plans, and between the two ideas that these embody, is all the more piquant at Surkh Kotal because the Greek order of architecture has been employed here for decorating this un-Greek place of worship. This touch of Greekness is represented by the surviving stone bases of some of the columns: the four columns in the temple itself, and the series that once supported the roof of a portico surrounding the great four-square court in the middle of which the temple stands. Each time that I entered this court, I found myself moved by its majesty.

The name 'Surkh Kotal' has been given to this shrine by its French discoverers. For, before they disinterred it, the hill on which it stands was anonymous. 'Surkh Kotal' means 'Red Pass' (the soil is red, and the hill commands the passage). The shrine was fortified. There is an inner line of fortifications enclosing the shrine itself, and an outer line surrounding the whole hill-top and including the dwelling-houses on it. These houses are modest: Surkh Kotal' was both a shrine and a fort, but it was not also a palace." Toynbee (1961), pp. 108-109.

Rabatak, where the Kushan inscription that lists Kanishka's ancestors back to Kujula Kadphises was found, is approximately 20 km to the west of modern Baghlan and 20 km past Surkh Kotal along the main route leading towards Balkh.

"Finally, we should recall that it was during this [Kushan] period that the construction of large sanctuaries began on a wide scale, of which the most famous is that at Surkh Kotal. Recently, at Rabatak, not far from Surkh Kotal, another sanctuary of the same type was discovered consisting of a number of specially arranged platforms. It was from this building—about the architecture of which we shall no doubt lose all information since it is currently being destroyed by treasure-hunters equipped with bulldozers—that the famous inscription came, which at last provided us with the genealogy of Kanishka, making it possible to date the beginning of the age of Kanishka to between 78 and 127 AD." Leriche (2007), p. 136.

"Fussman, when compiling a list of the *bagolongo* (dynastic temples) established by Kanishka at Surkh Kotal, Rabatak, Airtam and Termez (if the Chingiz Tepe platform is one), confirms the key position of Bactria in the empire: 'One cannot but be astonished at the immoderate behaviour of the sovereign and the extent of work which he ordered . . . Bactria could have been covered with a veritable network of dynastic temples' (Fussman 2001, 260)." Leriche (2007), p. 138.

The *Hanshu* says: 大月氏國治監氏城 – "The kingdom of the Da Yuezhi governs Jianshi City (監氏城)." The character *jian* 監, used here, is presumably a mistake for the similar-looking character, 藍 *lan*.

The word 治 *zhi*, as used here, is a verb which means to 'rule' or 'govern.' The commonly used compound term 王治 *wangzhi*, can be translated as "the seat of the king's government," but that is not what the text has here.

Some scholars, including Hulsewé (*CICA*, p. 119), have suggested that the 王 *wang* has been omitted by mistake, and the passage should instead read: 大月氏國 (王) 治監氏城 – "The kingdom of the Da Yuezhi. The seat of (the king's) government is in Jianshi City."

I disagree. I think the character *wang* 王 = 'king,' has been left out on purpose, making it clear that the Yuezhi had, by then, divided Daxia into five *xihou* or principalities with no overall ruler.

> "Originally Ta Hsia had no major overlord or chief, and minor chiefs were frequently established in the towns. The inhabitants are weak and afraid of fighting, with the result that when the Yüeh-chih migrated there, they made them all into their subjects. They provide supplies for the Han envoys." From: *Hanshu* 96A in *CICA*, p. 121.

Significantly, there is no mention of Kujula having to unseat an overall king of the Da Yuezhi, just the other four *xihou*, or 'princes'. Nor do do any of the texts refer to Lanshi or Jianshi as a 王治 *wangzhi* (king's seat).

• **The *Hou Hanshu* says:** 大月氏國居藍氏城 – "The kingdom of the Da Yuezhi occupies Lanshi City."

The character 居 *ju* can mean to 'reside,' 'dwell,' 'residence,' or 'occupy (militarily).' See: *GR* Vol. II, No. 2797.

> **"居 *jū* MC kjo**
> **1.** site(d), situate(d), place(d)
> **a.** seat, central place of activity or authority.
> **2.** reside(nce), dwell(ing), lodge(ment); in private life, at home . . . ."
> Kroll (2015), p. 223.

The *Hou Hanshu* describes a time when the Da Yuezhi (Kushans) had conquered lands deep into northeastern India – which, as we know from the Rabatak inscription, was conquered by Kanishka. He, according to later Buddhist texts, made his 'capital' in Peshawar. Mathura seems to have become another regional or secondary Kushan 'capital.'

Mathura is 160 km southeast of modern Delhi. As the Indo-Greeks, and later the Kushans, realised, Mathura was strategically placed to oversee access between the northwest and the heartlands of north-central India in the Ganges Valley, as well as the routes to the seaports on the Gulf of Cambay on the west coast, and the Bay of Bengal in the east:

> "Menander the Great shifted his capital to a more central place of his empire than Taxila. His new capital, named 'Sakala,' or 'Sagala also called Euthymedia,' was at the site of modern Sialkot under the shade of the Jammu hills. For this reason, the Indo-Greek rulers of the Panjab might have used a more northerly route from Taxila to Mathurā, touching on the way Alexandria Boucephalos, Alexandria Nicaia, Alexandria Ioumousa, Sakala, and Alexander's Pillars on the Beas. Apollonius of Tyana mentions all these stations except Sakala [probably because it was not located at Sialkot as previously thought and was razed by Alexander's army]. Mathurā, on the

bank of River Jamuna, was the last stop on the leg of the journey leading to northern India. Beyond this point—or, more accurately, beyond Kurukṣetra—one found the gateway to the Gangetic Basin (see fig. 2.2). From Mathura, one road formerly snaked to Ujjain (Ozene) and thence to Bharukaccha (Barygaza, Broach) on the Gulf of Cambay. The main road, however, continued eastward with a course that was parallel to the alignment of the Gaṅga and Jamuna Rivers. After stopping over Kāśi, Vārāṇasī, and Sārnāth, it used to reach Pāṭaliputra (modern Patna) and finally the coast of the Bay of Bengal at the site of Tāmralipti (modern Tamluk) near Colicut or Calcutta." Dar (2007), p. 36.

- **Lanshi/Baghlan after the Kushans**

"There is, nevertheless, a consensus among numismatists (Göbl 1967, Cribb 1990, Alram 1996) to place the first king named Kidara in Kāpiśā as early as *circa* 390. This identification rests upon the reading **kidaro* on the last series of gold coins present in the hoard in Tepe Maranjān near Kabul, buried at about this date. The reading is not incompatible with what is actually written on the corrupt legend (*kioooooo*), but there is some room for doubt (for an alternative see Grenet 2002, p. 206).

There is less uncertainty concerning the continuation of the history of the Kidarites. From 457 onwards they were challenged by a rebellion of the Hephthalites, with whom the Sasanian pretender Pērōz took refuge and from whom he obtained military help. As soon as he had established himself on the throne war broke out again with a new Kidarite ruler called Kunkhas. Eventually in 467 the Kidarites were expelled from their capital "Balaam" (= Balkh?) (Priscus, 12 and 22 = Blockley, pp. 349 and 361); the Sasanians claimed the victory, but most probably it was the result of combined operations with the Hephthalites. A residual Kidarite kingdom in the Gandhāran region (possibly in Swat: Göbl 1967, II, p. 224, issue 15) continued to send embassies to China until 477." Grenet (2005).

I think that the "Balaam" mentioned above as the capital of the Kidarites by Priscus, is more likely to have been Baghlan than Bactra/Balkh, due to the obvious linguistic similarity, and that it was a closer and more convenient centre for people who also ruled Kapisha and the region of modern Begram.

Furthermore, the Hephthalites, who claimed to be descended from the Yuezhi, had their headquarters in Baghlan-Ghori (Ghori being a bit south of the present town of Baghlan) when the Chinese monks Song Yun and Huisheng visited it in 519 CE:

"The preface of the *Xiyu Tuji*, edited by Pei Ju in 606, points out that Bamiyan lies between the Hephthalite headquarters in Baghlan-Ghori to the north of the Hindukush and Kapiśi to the south while the *Suishu* locates it 700 *li* to the north of Kapiśi [over either the Salang Pass or the Kushan Pass slightly to the west]. This information may have been given by a Bamiyan emissary, which the second Sui emperor Yangdi received in 615." Kuwayama (2005), p. 140.

"Xuanzang clearly distinguishes Tokharistan from Bamiyan. Bamiyan was an independent district which did not belong to Tokharistan. It is not easy to explain in detail the boundary between these two countries. The Arab geographers divide Tokharistan into two districts, the upper (east) and the lower (west). Yet, only Ya'qubi (290) describes that Upper Tokharistan starts with Bamiyan (Minorsky 1970: 337). In the time of Burnes or Moorcroft and Trebeck, the region north of Kahmard, located to the north of Kotal-e Dandanshikan, was under the rule of Murad Beg with his residence in Kunduz, while Bamiyan and the region to the south of it was under the political influence of Kabul. Their accounts also imply that Kotal-e Dandanshikan was a socio-cultural boundary dividing Afghanistan into two parts, north and south, not only in terms of politics (Burnes 1834: 188 f.; Moorcroft & Trebeck 1837: Part IV, Chapter II, 393 f.; Adamec 1979: 301 ff. and 476 ff.)." Kuwayama (2005), p. 153.

"Song Yun was admitted to the Hephthalite ruler at his headquarter [sic] in Tokharistan and then to the Tegin of Gandhara in AD 520. He further says that some 40 countries sent their envoys to the headquarters. The "Weishu" and Song Yun's account make no mention of Bamiyan and Kapisa among the vassal states of the Hephthalites.[822] The Hephthalites had their winter quarters around the town Huoluo in the Baghlan-Gori plain according to Kuwayama. Their summer pasture was first in Badakhshan and then in Hsi-mo-ta-lo. It is possible that the Hephthalites kept the western half of Hsi-mo-ta-lo, while the Turks took the better, eastern half of Badakhshan. The Hephthalites thus seem to have been independent, even during Turkic hegemony, until the first decade of the 8th century AD. Grenet opposes the idea of Kuwayama that Kapisa was bypassed by the Kidarites and the Hephthalites as incorrect, because this appears quite unlikely in view of the role always played by the Panjshir valley in the history of invasions of northwestern India.

Sebeos also tells about the escape of the last Sasanian shahinshah Yazdegerd III (632 - 651) from the Arabs in AD 651 and his death on the territory of modern Turkmenistan. According to the Armenian historian, "... Yazkert fled from them (Arabs) but could not escape because they pursued and overtook him near the borders of the Kushans (i.e. Merv) and destroyed all of his troops. He fled to the Hephthalites ... Tetal troops captured and killed Yazkert". In the opinion of Trever Sebeos, in this report [sic], gives the Hephthalite area and ruler with his troops an ethnic identity. She remarks that country and people were identified as Kushans, but the king and the army as Hephthalites, i.e. the upper class and part of the troops belonged to other tribes, who were all part of the Kushan kingdom. The king of the Tetals used his dynastic name (of his tribe), so the king of the Kushans was a political name also indicating the country. Thereby the ethnic kinship between Kushans and the Hephthalites could be constructed."

[822] Kuwayama 1998, 332; Kuwayama 1999, 38; Since the *qishlaq* near a town is always on the lower course of the river in Tokharistan, the Hephthalite king received Song Yun somewhere on the Surkhab or the Talaqan-Kunduz, but not in Badakhshan, a site of summer pasturing: Kuwayama 1989, 114-115; Kuwayama 2002, 127."

Kurbanov (2010), pp. 198-199.

• Samangan (Aybak)

Only 35 km west of Baghlan was the large ancient city of Samangan or Aybak/Aibak (Uzbek: 'Cave Dweller'). It was on the main route heading north towards Bactra/Balkh. On a hill about 3 kilometres from the town, is the Buddhist site known as Takht-e Rostam ('Throne of Rostam') with a stupa dated to the 4th or 5th century CE. See: Califano (2011), p. 100.

"**SAMANGAN,** capital of Samangan Province, is a most ancient city near which there is an important Buddhist site dating from the 4th–5th centuries A.D. Early Arab geographers list Siminhan among the largest cities in the Afghan area and when Genghis Khan destroyed the city, its buildings extended to the foot of the mountains. Tamerlane's chroniclers reported it to be still in ruins in the 14th century but rich soil assured its revival and it was again a prominent caravan depot in the 19th century when it was called Aibak. Today, many continue to refer to it by this name even though it officially regained its ancient name in 1964." Dupree (1977), Chapter 23.

"**ČĀRĪKĀR** (also Čahārīkār), the main town of Kōhdāman and the administrative capital of the Afghan province of Parwān, located about 63 km north of Kabul.

Throughout history there has been an important urban center at the northern end of the long Kōhdāman depression, though the site has shifted back and forth between the confluence of the Ḡōrband and Panjšēr rivers, on the central axis of the depression, and the western edge about a dozen kilometers away. Kāpiśī, the capital of the Kushan empire, was established on the former site; modern Čārīkār (elev. 1,550m) stands on the latter. The succession of cities on one or the other of these sites reflects a remarkable continuity of urban life, which can be explained by the exceptional advantages of the location at a natural crossroads, where all the northern routes across the Hindu Kush between the Šebar pass on the west and the Anjoman pass on the east converge before branching off in two southern routes, one toward Kabul and the Helmand basin via the piedmont of the Paḡmān mountains, the other toward India via the Panjšēr valley and the Nangrahār. The latter route, with its northern extension through the wide Ḡōrband valley to the Šebar pass, the "old route from Bactria to Taxila" described by A. Foucher, was a major axis for the movement of men and ideas (e.g., Buddhism) before the Ghaznavid period." Downloaded from *Encyclopædia Iranica* at: http://www.iranicaonline.org/articles/carikar on 8 August 2013.

Timeline for Lanshi and Daxia - 130 to 125 BCE

• ***Circa* 130 BCE** the Da Yuezhi subjugated Daxia and established their royal court (王庭 – *wangting*) to the north of the Oxus/Amu Darya.

• **Summer 129 to autumn 128 BCE** Zhang Qian's visit to the region, Lanshi is described in the *Shiji* as the 都 *du* ('headquarters,' or 'main centre') for the Daxia.

• ***Circa* 115-113 BCE** "The last successful mission to Bactria took place, and a separate mission to the Dayuezhi was sent at the same time. Embassies were sent later than 111 BC and before 90 BC, but their dates are not mentioned by the Han Chronicle." Cribb (2005), p. 213.

• In some documents from Dunhuang, "two of which the editors presume date respectively from **87-49** and from **84-73** BCE or later, mention ambassadors from the "king of the Dayuezhi 大月氏王"." Grenet (2006), p. 339. See: Appendix O.

• The first indication we have of the division of Daxia into the 5 *xihou* are the references in some documents from Dunhuang of visits from the "*xihou* of Shuangmi of the Dayuezhi" in 43 BCE and the "*xihou* of Xiumi of the Da Yuezhi" in 37 BCE. From this we can deduce that **the Yuezhi confederation broke up into the five *xihou* sometime after 111 BCE and before 43 BCE.**

• By the time of *Hanshu* 96A (which covers events up to **23 CE**), the Da Yuezhi had moved their 'seat of government' (治 *zhi*) to Jianshi (= Lanshi). The town is no longer described as the 都 *du* for Daxia, nor is it referred to as a 'royal court' (*wangting*) – indicating that by then the Daxia had been fully conquered and assimilated, no longer a semi-independent tributary, nor was there an overall sovereign of the Da Yuezhi any longer.

• ***Circa* 125 CE** the *Hou Hanshu* account based on General Ban Yong's report to the Emperor says that the Da Yuezhi 'dwell in' or 'occupy' (居 *ju*) Lanshi. This was well after the Kushan conquest of the other four *xihou* and their invasion of northwestern India, *circa* mid-1st century CE, so we can assume that the *zhi* or 'seat of government' of the Da Yuezhi was by then established in Peshawar and/or Mathura.

Appendix O: The title *xihou*

The title 翖侯 *xihou* denotes a semi-independent ruler or 'prince' who was part of a tribal group or confederation such as the Yuezhi, Xiongnu, or Wusun, and/or the territory he controlled. See: note 8.4.

It is uncertain if the title *xihou* was originally Chinese, or whether *xihou* came into Chinese as an attempt to transcribe *yabgu/jabgu*, or its progenitor from some other language. Bailey sees *yabgu* as being of Iranian origin:

> "This *yavuga-*, from **yāvuka-* 'troop-leader', is one of the Iranian titles of the Kušans. It was written in the Han-ṣu 歙侯 K 128, 79 *hi-xou* < *xi̯əp-γə̯u*, *G* 675 q, 113 a *xiəp-g'u* which is clearly Iranian *yāvuka-*. This title is carried far down the centuries into Persian histories. Kušan has *yavuga*, *ya'uga*, Greek ZAOOY, Kroraina *yapǵu*, Mahrnāmaγ *yaβγu*, *žaβγu*, and Arabic *ǰabγu*. In Turkish it is *yapγu*. The vowel *-a-* of the Turkish transmission is valuable as proving the Iranian *-ā-* which the Kharoṣṭrī script leaves uncertain, since the Turkish has *-ä-* for Iranian *-ă-*, as in *bäγ* from *baga-*. The base *yau-* 'to assemble troops' gave also **fra-yauna-* in Khotan-Saka *hayūna-* 'companion, friend' (*DKS* 465).
>
> Since the initial *y-* varies within Iranian, from a Chinese *źiänj̯iu* one could reach back to *yāyu-* < *yāvu-* and so have a title direct from the base *yau-* without the *-ka-* suffix. The form **yāvu-* would be the common type with the long *-ā-* in the base with the suffix *-ú-* forming agent nouns and instrumental nouns. Old Ind. *kārú-*, Greek *κâρυξ* attest its early development and Avestan *bāzu-*, Khotan-Saka *bāysū-* 'arm', shows its maintenance. Such a **yāvu-* would mean again 'troop-assembler', and 'leader'." Bailey (1985), pp. 32-33. See also the discussion under "The name 'Kujula' and the title 'yavuga' in Appendix Q.

> "Pulleyblank (1966), p. 28, suggests that this word may be connected with the Tocharian word for "land", "country", **A** *yapoy*, **B** *ype.* — Pulleyblank (1968), p. 250 ff., finds good reason to assume that the following passage [on the 5 *xihou* of the Da Yuezhi in *Hanshu* 96A] was added "after the chapter on the Western Regions ... was already complete". He rightly believes that "there is strong circumstantial evidence for thinking it is based on information received in a report from Pan Ku's brother, Pan Ch'ao, dating from around A.D. 74-75", which he provides in the following pages." From: *Hanshu* 96A in *CICA*, p. 121, note 288.

Apparently it was Friedrich Hirth, in his *Nachworte zur Inschrift des Tonjukuk*: 47-50, who first suggested that *xihou* represented, and has affinities with, the later Turkish title, *yabgu*, which generally means a secondary ruler with some degree of independence, rather like the titles 'prince' or 'duke'. This has now become accepted by most authorities. See, for example: Pulleyblank (1966), pp. 27-28; *CICA*, p. 121, n. 288.

The title *yabgu* itself does not turn up in the literature until several centuries later. If it was used earlier, we have no record of it. The Turkish title may well have developed from the Chinese term.

If the title *xihou* was originally of Chinese origin, it was probably a descriptive title indicating allied, or united 'princes.' If this was so, it remains unclear whether the title indicated an alliance with the Chinese or simply with each other.

The character 侯 *hou* is a common Chinese title usually translated as "Marquis," or "Prince." On the other hand, 翖 *xi* is a relatively rare character that is only occasionally used in transcriptions, but can have the meanings of 'in agreement,' 'to join,' 'harmonious;' 'furled,' 'rolled,' or 'to close,' and, therefore, *xihou* can be translated as "allied prince".

The earliest recorded use of *xihou* is in the *Hanshu*, in an account of the history of the Wusun, referring to the 170s BCE (*CICA*, p. 215 and n. 804). He is described as the 'Bujiu (布就) xihou,' who was the guardian of the infant Wusun Kunmo (or Shah).

Aside from several bestowals of the title by the Chinese, it seems that *xihou* was exclusively used to describe princes or nobles of various foreign peoples – particularly the Xiongnu, the Wusun, and the Da Yuezhi – all originally nomadic or semi-nomadic confederations to the north or northwest of China.

Interestingly, the five divisions of the Kangju are not described in the *Hanshu* as *xihou*, but as being headed by five 小王 *xiao wang* or "lesser kings." (*CICA*, pp. 130-131).

The background, political affiliations and territories of the five *xihou* established by the Da Yuezhi in Daxia after they "attacked and subjugated" that country, are still poorly understood, and it is not known how or why they differed from the five *xiao wang* of the Kangju.

We do not know whether they were of Yuezhi origin, or whether some or all of them were subject local leaders supported by the Da Yuezhi. The wording of the text in *Hanshu* 96A seems to indicate that this was the case and implies (though never makes explicit) that there was still an overall Da Yuezhi ruler: "All the five *Hsi-hou* are subject to the Ta Yüeh-chih." From: *Hanshu* 96A in *CICA*, p. 123.

The scholar Yan Shigu (581–645 CE) said that the *xihou* of the Wusun were high dignitaries who corresponded to generals (將軍 *jiangjun*) in Han China. This could possibly indicate a primarily military role. See: Dorn'eich (2011), p. 75.

There was already a long history of such semi-independent rulers or warlords in the region before the arrival of the Yuezhi:

> "None of these insurgent warlords, called *hyparchs* (commanders) by the Greeks, claimed to be a king. They ruled, in a rough sense, no more than isolated locales. Some controlled a valley, others a mountain fortress or string of villages. When not in revolt, they normally served as local princes or chiefs, levying fighting men and taxes for the Bactrian satrap who, in turn, answered to the King of Kings. They commanded their own contingents in war. This loose arrangement gave each hyparch a great deal of autonomy and preserved the powerful sense of localism so natural in places like Afghanistan. An easygoing loyalty to the state and its representatives could vanish in a flash once parochial interests seemed threatened. When such "commanders" (a title still popular among Afghan warlords) repudiated their oaths to a king or state, they might at times band together against a common foe or break off and fight alone at the head of their own followers and kinsmen. From Alexander's day, we know of a few of the strongest by name: Ariamazes, Austanes, Orsodates, Catanes, Dataphernes, Itanes, Oxyartes, Sisimithres, and Spitamenes." Holt (2005), p. 51.

The fact that the *xihou* sometimes acted as autonomous rulers is confirmed by the discoveries of wooden tablets from Dunhuang:

> ". . . some recent Chinese publications . . . have made public some administrative documents on strips of wood discovered by archaeologists in a postal station near Dunhuang. The ambassadors of two of the already known *yabgus* are mentioned there as having been made the recipients of an official welcome in 43 and 37 BCE, and which lead to a re-evaluation of the extent of the relations they maintained with the kingdom of the "Great Yuezhi" and with China." Translated from Grenet (2006), pp. 326-327.

> ". . . , one of the new Chinese documents from Dunhuang to which I have alluded at the beginning of this article explicitly mentions "Wanruo, the ambassador of the

xihou of Shuangmi of the Dayuezhi 將大月氏雙靡翖侯使者萬若" (document from 43 BCE) which indeed seems to indicate a belonging and not a simple subordination (which obviously leaves open the possibility that the hordes controlled by the *xihou* were not solely composed of Yuezhi). Another document (of 37 BCE) talks about "escorting / accompanying (. . .) *xihou* of Xiumi of the Da Yuezhi 大月氏休密翖侯" (the mention of the ambassador would have been in the lacuna). In the same group of documents, two of which the editors presume date respectively from 87-49 and from 84-73 BCE or later, mention ambassadors from the "king of the Dayuezhi 大月氏王". One can thus assume that there was always a royal Yuezhi power above the *yabghus* (as there had been at the moment of the migration), perhaps revolving among the dynastic branches and not attached to a specific appanage, perhaps situated outside their territories, at Jianshi (Khulm?), as the *Hanshu* suggests. It is this power which would be seized by Kujula Kadphises by eliminating the other four competing *yabgus*. Another possibility is that the royal power of the Yuezhi disappeared between *circa* 80-50 (the chronological range of the two documents mentioning an ambassador of the king) and 43 (the date of the first document mentioning an ambassador of a *yabgu*), which would give some credibility to the "a little over a hundred years" - the figure provided by the *Hou Hanshu* for the elapsed time between the division between the five yabgus and the reunification by Kujula Kadphises.[40]

[40] Does the terse sentence of Justin (prologue to Book 42) *reges Tocharorum Asiani interitusque Saraucarum* indicate the temporary abolition of the Yuezhi royalty due to the dominance of the Asiani (Alans)?"

Grenet (2006), pp. 339-340 and note 40. Translated by the author from the French.

Nicholas Sims-Williams and Etienne de la Vaissière have argued that:

"Although the title *xihou* is only borne by non-Chinese rulers [which is not technically true – see above] and is invariably regarded by Sinologists as a transcription of a foreign form, Helmut Humbach (pp. 24-28) has argued that the word is in fact Chinese in origin, the syllable *hou* being a Chinese title often translated "marquis." Elaborating on this view, Nicholas Sims-Williams (2002, p. 229) has proposed to interpret *xihou* as "allied prince." Such an interpretation is particularly suited to some of the earliest attestations of *xihou*. According to the *Shiji* (chap. 19, p. 1021, and chap. 20, p. 1027), the title was bestowed twice by the Chinese emperor, in 147 B.C.E. on a Xiongnu prince and in 129 B.C.E. on a prince of the western barbarians (Hu), both of whom had allied themselves with the Han. However, the *Han shu* provides evidence for the even earlier use of this title: amongst the Wusun in the 170s B.C.E., a period before they were in direct contact with the Chinese (chap. 61, p. 2692; Hulsewé and Loewe, p. 215), and amongst the Yuezhi of Bactria, who had left Gansu or Turfan in the 170s B.C.E. and would therefore be unlikely to use a Chinese title of more recent origin (*Han shu*, chap. 96A, p. 3891; Hulsewé and Loewe, pp. 121-23). Moreover, *xi* "joined, harmonious, etc." would not have been an obvious word to employ in the political sense "united" or "allied." The earliest Chinese interpretation of *xihou* (already in the first century C.E., see the *Han shu*, chap. 17, pp. 640, 642) was "marquis of Xi," Xi being understood as the name of a village in the Huang region (Henan). Although this association must be due to folk etymology or secondary association (cf. Hirth, p. 49), its mere existence is a clear indication that the syllable *xi* was not felt to be meaningful. Later commentators of the Tang period define *xihou* as a Wusun title for a high-ranking general. It seems most likely that this view is essentially correct and that *xihou* is a Chinese transcription of a title used by the Wusun and Yuezhi, peoples from the Gansu or Turfan regions, of whose languages hardly anything is known."

From: *Encyclopædia Iranica* article: "**JABḠUYA**, Arabo-Persian form of the Central Asian title *yabḡu*." Sims-Williams and de la Vaissière (2007).

There have been several different suggestions about the locations of the five Yuezhi *xihou* (see: Grenet (2006), pp. 330-338), but their borders may have changed and territories expanded or contracted from time to time during the century or more of their existence.

Pulleyblank (1963), p. 222 (see: note 13.8), suggested that the five *xihou* mentioned in the *Hanshu* and the *Hou Hanshu* which the Da Yuezhi established in the country of Daxia after they subjugated it, "seem to have formed an arc along the north side of Tokharestan from the valley of Wakhan in the east to Tou-mi = Tarmita, Termes . . . and Balkh in the west."

Grenet (2006), pp. 330-338, proposed that, at least in the early days of Yuezhi settlement, the *xihou* were located in an arc to the north of the Oxus, though he admits that they may have extended south of the river later.

I do not agree with Grenet's descriptions of the territories of the *xihous*. Many of the discrepancies in the number of coin finds on either side of the Oxus/Amu Darya can be explained by the extensive work of Soviet archaeologists and the strict control of looting by the Soviets in "northern Bactria." Looting of sites in northern Afghanistan, south of the Amu Darya, has been a major enterprise for decades now, meaning there have been fewer recorded hoards.

The *Shiji* is clear that the Yuezhi conquered all or most of ancient Bactria, including lands on both sides of the Oxus. There are a couple of factors I assume were essential for the Yuezhi to have been able to control the region for so long:

- The Yuezhi controlled the main passes south and west as well as to the north, northwest, and northeast. They controlled the Iron Gates on the route to the northwest, the Alai Valley route to the northeast, plus access to the Wakhan Corridor over several passes, and the various routes south to the Panjshir Valley, as well as over the Kushan Pass to Kapisha, and, further west, into Bamiyan.

- The situation on their eastern border with Anxi is less clear but, although I suspect that Bactra/Balkh, and maybe Kunduz, may have been held for some time by a Greco-Bactrian king who was more or less independent of the Yuezhi, many scholars disagree, and feel that the Parthians controlled Bactra for some time—probably until Kujula took it from them.

This may be a reference to the war between Gotarzes II and his brother, Vardanes, who had laid siege to Seleucia. In about 45 CE Gotarzes advanced, "and Vardanes, compelled to raise the siege of Seleucia, encamped on the plains of Bactria." Tacitus, *The Annals*, 11.8. Accessed on 27 April 2013 from: http://www.perseus.tufts.edu/hopper/text?doc=Perseus%3Atext%3A19993A book%3D11%3 chapter%3D8.

It seems to me that the Yuezhi governed the country with the assistance of local semi-independent warlords (*xihous*) in some type of confederation (which would explain the separate "embassies" from them well into the 1st century BCE). It is likely that these relationships were strengthened by strategic intermarriages between Yuezhi and local ruling families, much as the Greeks did earlier.

Further, I cannot agree with Grenet's positioning of Gaofu north of the Hindu Kush. Not only is there the statement in the *Hou Hanshu* that the *Hanshu* was mistaken, but Gaofu clearly refers to the region of Kabul in a number of later sources. However, it may well have been that at least some of the *xihou* controlled territories both north and south of the Oxus.

For more details on proposed derivations and uses of *xihou*, see: Thierry (2005), p. 463, n. 55; Sims-Williams (2002), especially pp. 229-230, and 235; Ciancaglini (2001), pp. 73-74; Yu (1988), pp. 26-27, 41 nn. 35 and 36, 43 n. 50; Bailey (1985), pp. 32, 130; Humbach (1966) pp. 26-27; Pulleyblank (1963), p. 95; Mukherjee (1967), pp. 7-9; Frye (1962), pp. 356-358. See also the discussions in Pulleyblank (1966), pp. 27-28, and Zuev (2002), p. 31.

While there is a lack of firm evidence, I believe that Pulleyblank's suggestion is the more plausible, as it takes into account the specific statement in *Shiji* 123, that Daxia was located to the south of the Gui (Oxus) River. See: Watson (1993), p. 235. The evidence strongly suggests that, at least by the time of the *Hanshu*, the five *xihou* stretched from Wakhan to Sheberghan (Tillya Tepe), to the west of Balkh.

• The Kushans

The name "Kushan" appears to be related to the Chinese 貴霜 'Guishuang' *xihou*, one of the five *xihou* set up in the region of ancient Bactria by the invading Da Yuezhi. Not only does it look like it is phonetically related, but also it was the *xihou* controlled by Kujula Kadphises, the first of the so-called "Kushan" kings. It is worth re-examining here the pertinent section of the *Hou Hanshu*:

> "More than a hundred years later, the prince [*xihou*] of Guishuang, named Qiujiuque [Kujula Kadphises], attacked and exterminated the four other *xihou*. He established himself as king, and his dynasty was called that of the Guishuang [Kushan] King. He invaded Anxi [Indo-Parthia], and took the Gaofu [Kabul] region. He also defeated the whole of the kingdoms of Puda [Paktiya] and Jibin [Kapisha and Gandhara]. Qiujiuque [Kujula Kadphises] was more than eighty years old [i.e. more than 81 by Western reckoning] when he died.
>
> His son, Yangaozhen [Vima Takhtu], became king in his place. (He caused) a complete collapse of Tianzhu [North-western India] and installed a general to supervise and lead it. The Yuezhi then became extremely rich. All the kingdoms call [their king] the Guishuang [Kushan] king, but the Han call them by their original name, Da Yuezhi."

We do not know how closely the early Kushans were related to the Da Yuezhi who, themselves, may not have been homogenous in terms of race, culture, or even language.

The fact that the *Hou Hanshu* says the Chinese continued to call them by their "original name, Da Yuezhi" suggests, but does not negate the strong possibility that they had mixed with other groups in the region, and/or that local tribes and peoples had allied themselves with the latest wave of invaders.

> "The Yuezhi, although nomadic, did not arrive in Bactria estranged from artistic sensibilities. Some scholars have associated them with the Scytho-Siberian culture, although the Chinese sources do not permit their exact ethnological identification. This culture is associated with a vibrant form of nomadic art, at times termed 'the animal style art'. In the course of their push westward, which came to a temporary halt in Bactria, the Yuezhi made contact with other nomadic people in Central Asia. Indeed, their own migrations across the Mongolian plains and Central Asia were due to pressure from other nomadic tribes. Understandably, a nomadic component, cited in some of the papers, filters into Pre-Kuṣāṇa art. For example, a *circa* 4th century B.C. golden armlet, from Central Asia or Siberia shows contorted felines with heads raised and depicted as if seen from above. A nearly identical armlet, though dated later, was found in the Northwest of the subcontinent. The heads of fantastic creatures on a perforated ornamental plaque likewise are seen from this perspective; the plaque is tentatively dated *circa* 2nd century B.C., possibly placed in the Bacrtian [sic: Bactrian]

region, and perhaps traced to the Yuezhi. The perspective, sometimes called the "bird's eye view" is characteristic of animal style art. It reappers [sic – reappears] in an early Kuṣāṇa relief from Mathurā wherein the Warrior Goddess is struggling with the buffalo, whose head is depicted as if seen from above.

By the first century B.C., Scythian tribes known as the Śakas, having been displaced by the wandering Yuezhi, entered the Northwest by various routes. Some settled in Gandhara, displacing the Indo-Greeks there, although some minor Indo-Greeks may still have wielded authority in parts of southern Bactria. Śakas, however, seem mainly to have controlled southern Bactria, while the Yuezhi were in northern Bactria. This changed around 100 years after the Yuezhi moved into Bactria when, under Kujula, the Kuṣāṇa made forays into the Northwest of the subcontinent and in the 1st century A.D. extended their power throughout Gandhara where more than 2,500 coins of Kujula were found at Sirkap, Taxila. As these nomadic people migrated, they came into conflict with the Parthians, whose leadership itself looked back to nomadic Iranian beginnings. The Parthians, during the first half of the 1st century A.D., took over parts of Gandhara from the Śakas and ruled as far as Taxila, which is in Pakistan today.

The Parthians were a dominant force in areas of Iran and Mesopotamia which had previously been part of the Seleucid Empire. As such, they absorbed not only Near Eastern and Greek art traditions, but as neighbors, traders and rivals of Rome after 64 B.C., the Parthians brought a wide range of artistic exposures to lands in which they had a presence. Their famous ruler, Gondophares, established rule in Gandhara from *circa* 19–45 A.D. [According to the dating proposed by Falk and Bennett (2009), this date should be read *circa* 30-56 A.D.] According to recent research by Harry Falk, Gondophares likely arose from a family once in the service of Vonones, associated in some way with the imperial Arsacid family in Iran, but which had been absorbed into the Indo-Scythian rule under Azes. This finding, based on inscriptional evidence, establishes that Gondophares came from a royal house which was in the Northwest several decades before Gondophares became king. If this finding is accepted, there would have been no invasion and destabilization, but rather a return to power of a family from the region which had connections to the previous Indo-Scythian rule. This hypothesis would eliminate the notion of an Indo-Parthian conquest and posit instead an apparent continuity, demonstrated for example by the issuance of coin types and retention of an era. For the art historian this possibility is exciting. It suggests artistic patronage may have been less disruptive than previously thought and political stability, artistic patronage and continuity greater. Influences circulating in this vast region would be more apt to reinforce each other than to operate fortuitously. Classical traditions introduced by Indo-Greeks could be seen as continuing to find some receptivity through to *circa* 50 A.D. in part, since art from Parthia was also profoundly Hellenized and receptive to Roman innovations. Further, the stylistic intensity of nomadic art rendered in animal and ethnic types need find little disruption from ruling patrons—be they Indo-Scythians, or Indo-Parthians, or, the incoming. For, from *circa* the mid-1st century A.D. onward, the whole region from Central Asia, through Gandhara to northern India becomes welded under the conquests of the Kuṣāṇas.

Northern India, particularly Mathura, was already linked to the political developments of the Panjab by the middle of the 1st century B.C. Several foreign princes preceded the Kuṣāṇas as rulers of Mathura. Chief among these is Rājūvula, who as Kṣatrapa and Mahāksatrapa, issued coins in the Panjab and Jammu area. At Mathura, Mahāksatrapa Rājūvula issued coins unlike those he issued in the Northwest. At Mathura he followed local tradition. The Hindu goddess Lakṣmī stood above a *svastika* on the obverse of his coins, and on the reverse he adopted the *Abhiṣeka* Laksmi motif. His son, Śoḍāsa, continued to use the same local types on his coins. This tendency to respect local tradition should be kept in mind when we consider the characteristics that might appear in Pre-Kuṣāṇa art. Some invaders were not inclined to disturb aspects of the indigenous culture, especially pronounced in the Gangetic region; other invaders brought artistic expressions that could be assimilated because the seeds had already been planted, especially in the northwestern region. Therefore, although our timeframe represents a period of considerable political flux, stife [sic – strife] and conquest by foreign invasions into the subcontinent, this period did not create a 'dark age' or an upheaval of artistic endeavors. Were this not so, my examples of foreign forerunners for a Gandharan Maya at the Parinirvāṇa and a Pre-Kuṣāṇa Saṃkarṣaṇ/Balarāma with attributes anticipated in a Kangra painting would be unlikely." Srinivasan (2007), pp. 8-10.

Appendix P: The Early Kushans

This appendix reviews aspects of the dating of the 'Great Kushan' kings in the light of new archaeological and historical data.

> "In the same month in which rockets struck the National Museum in Kabul [May 1993] a British aid worker named Tim Porter, working in northern Afghanistan for a landmine-clearing charity, was shown a stone tablet which had been dug up on a hill known as the 'Kaffirs' [Unbelievers'] Castle', about eighty miles north of the Salang tunnel. It was a white limestone slab about three feet wide and twenty inches high, one face covered by an inscription [now known as the 'Rabatak Inscription'] written in Greek letters over twenty-three lines. Porter sent photographs to the British Museum, where the inscription was identified as being in the Bactrian language and dating from the first half of the second century CE. The discovery opened up a new era in studies of the Kushan kings of Gandhara.
>
> We now know there were twelve Kushan kings: seven absolute rulers who spanned two centuries from about 30 CE to 242 CE and another five who ruled for approximately another century and a half as tributaries of the Sasanians." Allen (1999), p. 183.

- **The Rabatak Inscription**

  "A provisional translation (by Nicholas Sims-Williams) of the twenty-three lines of Bactrian inscribed in Greek letters on the stone recently recovered at Rabatak in northern Afghanistan shows it to be an edict set up by order of King Kanishka, described as 'the righteous, the just, the autocrat, the god worthy of worship, who has obtained the kingship from Nana and from all the gods' (lines 1–2), and as 'king of kings, the son of god' (line 14). This makes it plain that the Iranian model of divine rule and the divinity of kings lay at the heart of the Kushan political system.

  The inscription sets out the extent of King Kanishka's realm and then goes on to explain that the king has ordered a sanctuary to be built in honour of King Kanishka's forebears. Of these gods, 'the glorious Umma leads the service here' (line 9). The others are then listed as 'the lady Nana and the lady Umma, Aurmuzd, Mozdooano, Sroshard, Narasa, [and] Mihr' (lines 9–10).

  The two most important deities are goddesses: one is 'the lady Nana', daughter of the moon god and sister of the sun god, the Kushan form of Anahita, Zoroastrian goddess of fertility; the other is 'glorious Umma', probably the consort of the fourth god on the list, Mozdooano, whose name translates as 'gracious one', a placatory title for Oesho, the Bactrian lord of the demons and wind god of the Kushans. Oesho has a close tie-up with the yogic god Shiva, whom we tend to think of as an essentially Hindu god, but who shares a common Iranian ancestry with Oesho in the elemental god of wind and thunder, Oado or Rudra, 'the howler', the hurler of the thunderbolt vajira, symbol of destruction. With Aurmuzd, Sroshard, Narasa and Mihr, we are on safer ground because all are Zoroastrian deities: Aurmuzd is the supreme god of light, Ahura Mazda; and Mihr, the sun god is linked with the Iranian Mithra.

  Exactly the same non-Buddhist, polytheist picture emerges when we look at the coinage of King Kanishka. He was the first ruler in history to use the device of the halo or nimbus on his coinage to emphasize his own divine status [or descent from Helios?]. He was also the first ruler in Asia to employ a monetary system based on gold rather than silver, a clear indication of the extraordinary wealth that flowed into the Kushan state coffers during his reign. . . .

  A single gold coin in the collection [in the British Museum] carries on the reverse the inscription BODDO in Greek letters. It shows Gautama Shakyamuni standing with a nimbus behind his head and a larger aureole behind his body. In this collection of twenty-nine coins he is the only deity of indisputably Indian origin. All the others have Iranian, Bactrian or inner Asian roots.

Of the twelve Kushan kings only Kanishka I issued coins with Buddhist images – and even he produced very few. Two pairs of deities dominate Kushan coinage: the sun and moon deities Miro and Mao and the rather more complex god and goddess Oesho and Nana" Allen (1999), pp. 197-199.

I am grateful to Professor Sims-Williams for his kind permission to include the revised edition of his translation of the remarkable Rabatak inscription, as presented in his 2012 article, "Bactrian Historical Inscriptions of the Kushan Period"

His first two versions were done from photographs of the inscription. Since then, he has examined the inscription itself, now housed in the Kabul Museum, and discovered that some of the letters were still partly filled with dirt. Closely examining the original has allowed him to correct some earlier errors and improve the translation. Interestingly, for the first time, he noticed "that the letters of the inscription were originally filled in with a red pigment." Here is Nicholas Sims-Williams' latest version of the Rabatak Inscription:

"Translation and notes:

[*"Year one" of Kanishka (lines 1-7)*]: ... of the great salvation, Kanishka the Kushan, the righteous, the just, the autocrat, the god worthy of worship, who has obtained the kingship from Nana and from all the gods, who has inaugurated the year one as the gods pleased. And he issued(?) a Greek edict(?) (and) then he put it into the Aryan (language) (i.e. Bactrian). In the year one there was proclaimed to India, to the cities of the *kṣatriyas* (or *kṣatrapas*?), the capture(?) of *[...]adra(g)o* and *ōzopo* and Sāketa and Kauśāmbī and Pāṭaliputra, as far as Śrī-Campā; whatever (cities) he and the other generals(?) reached(?), (he) submitted (them) to (his) will, and he submitted all India to (his) will.

[*Foundation of a temple (lines 7-19)*]: Then King Kanishka ordered Shafar the lord of the marches to make in this place the temple which is called 'God's water,' in the Kasig plains, for these gods who have come hither into the presence of the glorious Umma, that(?) (is), the above-mentioned Nana and the above-mentioned Umma, Aurmuzd, the Gracious one, Sroshard, Narasa, (and) Mihir. [*In smaller letters above the line*: 'who in the Indian (language) is called Mahāsena and is called Viśākha.'] And he gave orders to make images of the same, (namely) of these gods who are inscribed hereupon, and he gave orders to make (images of) these kings: King Kujula Kadphises (his) great grandfather and King Vima Taktu (his) grandfather and King Vima Kadphises (his) father, and himself, King Kanishka. Then, as the king of kings, the son of the gods Kanishka had given orders to do, so Shafar the lord of the marches made this sanctuary, and Pyash the lord of the marches, and Shafar the lord of the marches, and Nukunzuk the *aštowa[lgo* carried out] the king's command. May these gods who are inscribed here [keep] the [king] of kings, Kanishka the Kushan, for ever healthy, fortunate (and) victorious!

[*Chronological summary (lines 19-22)*]: And the king, the son of the gods, was pacifying(?) all India from the year one to the year six(?). [So] the temple was founded(?) in the year one; then in the third(?) year also ... according to the king's command, many rites(?) were endowed, many attendants were endowed, many ... [were endowed. And] King [Kanishka] gave the fortress to the gods, and for these freemen [who] ... in 'God's water' ...." Sims-Williams (2012), pp. 77-78. See also the earlier draft of this translation and notes in Sims-Williams 2004 [2008], pp. 55-57.

I have deliberately included only the basic translation and have eliminated Professor Sims-Williams' notes. Those who want more information should refer to his original articles cited above which contain all his notes.

It is worth mentioning that, where the inscription claims that Kanishka "submitted all India to (his) will," that claim may be not a boastful exaggeration, as "India" did not always refer to the whole peninsula in ancient times. See: the discussion in note 15.1.

• Dating Kujula Kadphises

Kujula (丘就卻 Qiujiuque) is mentioned in the *Hou Hanshu*, but not in the *Hanshu*. This suggests that his reign as emperor likely postdates 23 CE, as the five *xihou/jabgu* are only mentioned as individual units in the *Hanshu*, which covers events up to that date.

It is generally accepted that Kujula's conquest of the other four *xihou* must have occurred soon after this as the *Hou Hanshu*, which covers the period from 25 CE onward, describes his conquest of the other *xihou* as having already taken place.

The *Hou Hanshu* also informs us that Kujula "was more than eighty years old [i.e. more than 81 years old by Western reckoning] when he died," thus implying a long reign.

This is supported by his widespread copper coinage, usually with Greek legends on the obverse and Kharoshṭhī titles on the reverse. See: note 13.11, and see: MacDowall (2002), "The Rabatak inscription and the nameless Kushan king."

On some of his coins Kujula associated himself, for unknown reasons, with the Indo-Greek king, Hermaeus, thought to have reigned more than a century previously in the 90s BCE.

> "The coinage of Hermaeus was copied widely (posthumous issues), in increasingly barbarized form by the new nomad rulers down to around 40 CE (see Yuezhi article). At that time, Kushan ruler Kujula Kadphises emphatically associated himself to Hermaeus on his coins,[1] suggesting he was either a descendant by alliance of the Greek king, or that at least he wanted to claim his legacy. In any case, the Yuezhi-Kushan preserved a close cultural interaction with the Greeks as late as the 3rd century CE.
>
> 1. Since R.C. Senior suggests that the original posthumous Hermaeus coins were not struck by the Yuezhi but by Sakas, he suggests that Kujula Kadphises' use of the obverse of Hermaeus coins with his own reverse should be seen as Kadphises adapting his coinage to a popular local type after having conquered the Paropamisade. "The Decline of the Indo-Greeks," R. C. Senior, David John MacDonald, (1998), pp. 46-47."
>
> Downloaded from the Wikipedia on 24 April, 2013: http://en.wikipedia.org/wiki/Hermaeus#cite_ref-0.

Kujula assumed many exalted, imperial titles such as 'King of Kings" on his later coins many of which found at Taxila; the types included *nandipada*, Śiva's humped bull, and the *triratna*, a symbol used by both Hindus and Buddhists, clearly celebrating his conquests in India.

• Kujula and Gondophares, the Indo-Parthian ruler of Arachosia and Gandhara, were contemporaries. Kujula overstruck bronze coins of Gondophares who, in turn, overstruck late-style imitation Hermaeus bronzes. But, as far as is known, Gondophares did not overstrike coinage bearing Kujula's name. However, the events and chronology of this period remain very uncertain.

• The dating of the reign of Gondophares depends upon the Takht-i-bahi Rock Inscription (literally 'Spring Throne' – due to the spring at the top of the hill or 'throne of origins' in UNESCO document http://whc.unesco.org/en/list/140).

• The Takht-i-bahi Rock Inscription refers to year 103 of an unspecified era = Gondophares' regnal year 26. Therefore, the year 78 of the unspecified era = Gondophares' regnal year 1.

If this was the Azes era, then Gondophares became king *circa* 31 CE (according to the latest theory), and was still reigning *circa* 56 CE (his 26th year).

"The recent discovery of an inscription explicitly dated in the year 98 of Azes, equivalent to ca. A.D. 41 (Sadakata, 1996, pp. 308-11), would seem to strengthen both the presumption that the unspecified year of 103 of the Takht-i-bāhī inscription is a year of the Azes/Vikrama ere and the correlation of this event with the legend of St. Thomas' mission in India. The inscription in question places the Azes year 98 during the reign of one *avakaśa*, nephew of *guphara (gupharasa bhrataputrasa avakaśasa rajami)*, and these persons are to be identified with Abdegases and Gondophares respectively, since King Abdagases is known from his coin legends to have been the nephew of Gondophares *(guduvharabhartaputrasa maharajasa avagadaṣasa.* Senior, 2001, p. 2.159). However, there is significant doubt about the authenticity of this inscription (Senior, 2001, p. 1.125), and therefore it must be left out of consideration here. (Among the other inscriptions published in Sadakata, 1996 together with the doubtful one of the Azes year 98, one other [no. 2] is clearly a forgery (Salomon, 1999, p. 144 n. 3), but the rest [nos. 1, 3b, and 4], including the Prahodia reliquary discussed in part 5 of this article, are indubitably genuine.)" Salomon (2005), p. 369, n. 19.

"By the middle of the first century A.D. regionally powerful Śaka Kṣatrapas and Mahākṣatrapas shifted their allegiance to the Indo-Parthian Maharaja Gondophares.[79] Based on the distribution of coins produced in different mints, Gondophares expanded the territory of his realm from Seistan and Arachosia to Gandhara, Taxila, and the area around Jammu in the western Panjab.[80] A Kharoṣṭhī inscription reportedly from Takht-i-Bāhī and dated in his twenty-sixth regnal year and in year 103 of an unspecified era fixes the time of his reign from c. 20 A.D. to at least 46 A.D. if the dates are calculated according to the Azes/Vikrama era [or *circa* 31 to 57 according to the new Falk-Bennett dating]. The territorial extent and precise chronological limits for the reign of his successors remain uncertain, but it is clear from the widespread distribution of coins, archeological excavations at Taxila, and artistic developments in Gandharan sculpture that Parthian hegemony in the middle of the first century A.D. was "a period of great prosperity and cultural achievement.

[79] Two problems complicate the interpretation of numismatic and epigraphic evidence of Gondophares' reign. The first is the "homonymy problem" (Alram 1999, 37, fn. 123) of different kings named Gondophares in Seistan and Arachosia, which is suggested by Parthian-type coins of Gondophares which appear to some numismatists to belong to the first century B.C. rather than the first century A.D. cointypes adopted by Gondophares in parts of northwestern India (Robert Senior, *From Gondophares to Kaniska*, Glastonbury, Somerset, 1997, 1–11). According to B.N. Puri, ". . . it now seems that 'Gondophares' and 'Guduphara' were 'winner of glory' titles, which became a sort of family name for many subsequent members of the family" ("The Sakas and Indo-Parthians," in *History of Civilizations of Central Asia*, vol. II: The development of sedentary and nomadic civilizations: 700 B.C. to A.D. 250, ed. János Harmatta [Paris, 1994], 200). The second problem is the identification of Gondophares/Guduphara with King Gudnafar in the apocryphal account of St. Thomas, who visited India in the early first century A.D. according to late hagiographical sources. Gérard Fussman cautions against the use of these sources as evidence resolving questions about the chronology of Gondophares' reign: "Cela ne signifie ni que Thomas—. . . supposer que lui-même ait existé—l'ait rencontré, ni qu'ils étaient des contemporains. Cela nous apprend seulement que le nom de ce soverain indo-parthe étaient encore connu en Syrie vers 250 de n.è. Les *Actes de Saint-Thomas* ne datent

pas Gondopharès et permettent encore moins d'affirmer qu'il possédait Taxila" ("L'inscription de Rabatak et l'origine de l'ère Śaka," *Journal Asiatique* 286, 1998: 624–625)."

Neelis (2006), pp. 74-75 and note 79.

The Indian historical and archaeological sources give some welcome additional information. Although he is not specified by name, Kujula Kadphises can be identified in dated inscriptions that include the same titles he used on his coins.

Although most of the dates and the indications gained from archaeological finds are still being debated, the evidence seems to be mounting for a dating of the rule of Gondophares over Taxila and central Gandhara during the 50s CE, and replaced by Kujula (moving down through Kapisha/Jibin and Peshawar to Taxila) sometime around 60 CE.

The dating of Kujula's growing influence in the region during the second quarter of the 1st century CE is supported by a reference to one of his sons, Sadaṣkaṇa, otherwise unknown, in the gold-leaf inscription of Senavarma, one of the kings of Oḍi (probably Uḍḍiyāna/modern Swat); see: Appendix Q. Although the dating is admittedly rough – it does fit in with other indications:

> "Bajaur is particularly important for the history of the stūpa cult, since only here do we get relic caskets made from schist with inscriptions in Kharoṣṭhī some of which include a date, explicitly or implicitly referring to the era of Azes, which most likely is identical with the Vikrama era, starting in 57 BC [or *circa* 47 according to new dating]. That means only in Bajaur can we date the reliquaries in absolute terms. An early date is found on a small casket from the year 63 (Salomon & Schopen 1984), and finally the Śatruleka casket of the year 77 (Falk 1998)[i.e. *circa* 16 and 30 CE]. Apart from continuous reckoning, there are also some dates counting in regnal or dynastic years, parallel to what is the exclusive habit of the neighbouring Oḍis. The earliest Apraca family date is 5 on the Bajaur casket, 25 on the Indravarman reliquary, and 32 on the Prahodi casket. All dedications were made during the reign of the second Apraca king Vijayamitra, who seems to have ruled from about 15 BC to AD 20 [or *circa* 4 BCE to 31 CE].
>
> Roughly at the same time the royal house of Oḍi founded several stūpas in the Swat Valley. Their dating is solely regnal, thus preventing any chance of an absolute chronology." Falk (2005), p. 347.
>
> "*The Oḍi-rājas and their connections with the Apraca-rājas*
>
> Although the Oḍi-rājas (Gāndhārī *oḍi-raya*) or kings of Oḍi are so far known from only three inscriptions, in contrast to the fifteen of the Apraca-rājas, we are somewhat better informed as to their territory. This is mostly due to the fact that the toponym Oḍi can be securely linked to the modern town of Odigram (i.e., Oḍigrām; also spelled Udigram, etc.) in lower Swat, whose name in turn is probably derived from or at least related to *Uḍḍīyāna*, the ancient name of the Swat Valley. The inscription of Senavarma (ins. B-3) was found on a piece of gold leaf inside a large *stūpa* model which is rumored to have come from Najigram, an important stūpa site in lower Swat not far from modern Odigram, and although as usual this report cannot be reliably confirmed, it is consistent with the hypothesis that the Oḍi-rājas ruled in lower Swat.
>
> Unlike some of the Apraca inscriptions, which are dated in years of the well-known Azes/Vikrama era of 58/7 B.C. [or, rather, *circa* 47 BCE], the inscriptions of the Oḍi-rājas are dated in what appear to be either regnal years or years of their own, otherwise unknown dynastic era. However, their chronological position can be at least approximately fixed by a reference in Senavarma's inscription. This inscription, dated in the year fourteen, refers to a contemporary prince named Sadaṣkaṇa, the

son of the Great King, the King of Kings Kujula Kadphises (*maharaja-rayatiraya-kuyula-kataphsa-putro sadaṣkaṇo devaputro*; line 8g). Although the exact date of Kujula Kadphises, the first Kuṣaṇa king of India, remains unsure, this reference does suffice to locate Senavarma sometime in the earlier part of the first century A.D., and the Oḍirājas in general to the period around the late first century B.C. and early first century A.D. This timeframe makes them close contemporaries, as well as probably neighbors, of the Apraca-rājas." Salomon (2007), pp. 276-277.

"In conclusion, the main contribution to our knowledge of the history of the kings of Apraca is that it provides a firm date for the commencement of the reign of King Vijaymitra [II], namely ca. 12 B.C. [or *circa* 1 BCE according to the new dating by Falk and Bennett]. The explicit reference to a regnal year of Vijayamitra, coupled with two additional dates in the eras of Azes and of "the Greeks," confirms the unspecified lower-number dates in other inscriptions of his reign are in fact his regnal years, and thus from the latest of these, namely the reliquary of Prahoda, we know that he ruled at least thirty-two years, that is, until at least about A.D. 20 [or, rather, 31 CE]. The new chronological information on Vijayamitra confirms that he was the reigning king at the time of the several inscriptions of his brother or nephew Indravarma and of Indravama's wife Uttarā, rather than being an earlier member of the line as had been previously proposed. His exact relationship with Indravarma and with his predecessor Viṣṇuvarma, however, remains uncertain, and the surprisingly cursory references to him in the various contemporary inscriptions may be hints of tensions and disputes within the family.

One can imagine, for example, that the lavish and no doubt highly publicized pious donations of Indravarman [I]'s mother Rukhuṇa and wife Uttarā (Salomon 2003, pp. 55-6) were designated to raise his status and hence, his prospects for inheriting the throne. If this is true, however, their efforts may have been in vain, since Vijayamitra [II] was apparently succeeded by his son Indravasu, who in turn my have been succeeded by his son Vijayamitra [III], though both his relationship and succession are unsure. Indravarma [II] also ruled as king of Apraca at some undetermined time after Vijayamitra [I]. the apparent rapid succession in the later period of the Apraca dynasty, that is, in about the third and fourth decades [or, according to the new dating, in about the 4th and 5th decades] of the first century A.D., suggests that the dynasty was fragmenting and losing its territories, presumably as a result of the burgeoning power of the Indo-Parthian kingdom of Gondophares. The fact that Aśpavarma, son of Indravarma [II?] issued an abundant coinage as commander, but apparently never became king, may also reflect the same situation in the declining days of the Apraca dynasty." Salomon (2005), pp. 382-383.

We know from the Rabatak inscription that Kujula was followed by Vima Takhtu/Yangaozhen. Presumably, Vima Kadphises and Kanishka are not mentioned in the *Hou Hanshu* because neither of them had come to power before Ban Chao returned to China in 102 CE. It was probably his notes that formed the basis of his son Ban Yong's report to the emperor on the 'Western Regions,' *circa* 125 BCE.

It seems likely that Kujula's son, Wima Takhtu, was still ruling in 102 CE, and perhaps as late as 106 CE, when the Western Regions rebelled, and relations with China were cut. See: note 1.46.

According to the 'Biography of Ban Chao' in the *Hou Hanshu*, an unnamed Yuezhi king (probably Vima Takhtu) was making an alliance of marriage with the Kangju in 84 CE. The Chinese were fighting with Kashgar at the time then supported by Kangju, sent an envoy to the king of the Da Yuezhi "carrying large gifts of silk cloth to the king of the Yuezhi to intercede with the king of Kangju. The king of Kangju then ended hostilities against the Chinese and, seizing Chung, returned with him to his country. The town of Wuji immediately submitted to (Ban Chao)." See: Chavannes (1906), p. 230.

In 88 CE a Yuezhi king (probably Vima Takhtu - we also have an inscription attributable to him dated 89 CE – see below) sent "tribute" including antelope, lions and jewels to the Chinese asking for the hand of a Han princess in marriage. Relations between the Yuezhi and the Chinese soured after the Yuezhi ambassador was arrested and returned by Ban Chao. Once again, the king is not named in the text.

In the 5th month of the 2nd Yongyuan year (i.e. between 16th June and 15th July 90 CE), Ban Chao outwitted the 70,000 strong Yuezhi/Kushan army sent against him under a Viceroy (Fuwang 副王) named Xie (謝), during the reign of Vima Takhtu). Ban Chao used a "scorched-earth policy" to deny food, water and fodder to the Kushans.

He also managed to ambush troops sent by the Kushan Viceroy to Kucha for help. He seized all the gifts they were carrying for the king of Kucha, and beheaded several hundred of them, displaying their heads to discourage the Kushans, who then withdrew. See: note 1.37 and Chavannes (1907), p. 158, n. 4, and (1906), pp. 232-233.

It is almost certain that, if there had been a new Kushan king before 102, Ban Chao would have become aware of it, and it would have been mentioned in Ban Yong's report. It seems safe to say that Vima Kadphises must have come to the throne sometime after 102 CE. Indeed, as routes were not cut until the autumn of 106 (when the Protector-General Ren Shang was besieged at Karashar), and the Chinese remained in the region until 107 CE. It is unlikely the new Yuezhi king (Vima Kadphises) was enthroned before 107.

After this upheaval, unrest continued in the region with reports that the Xiongnu were vying for power. During the Yuanchu reign period (that is, sometime between 114 and 120 CE), Yuezhi troops put the Kashgari prince Chenpan, who had been a hostage with them, and favoured by the Kushan king, on the throne of Kashgar. See: note 21.4.

• Dating the inception of Kanishka's Era

During the 20th century, many scholars accepted the beginning of the well-established and still-used Śaka era of 78 CE as being the date of inception of the Kanishka era, although there was always a significant minority of dissenters.

In 2001, another important advance increased our understanding of Kanishka's era with the publication of "The *yuga* of Sphujiddhvaja and the era of the Kuṣâṇas" in *S.R.R.A.* VII, pp. 121-136, by Harry Falk. In this article, Falk makes a strong case that Kanishka's era started in 127 CE. This date has gained wide acceptance among scholars around the world. He has since given added weight to his findings with new evidence presented in a later article: "The Kaniṣka era in Gupta records." See: Falk (2004), pp. 167-176; and also: Falk (2012), pp. 132-135.

Some earlier researchers had arrived at similar conclusions, dating the beginning of Kanishka's era to this period. Among them, Dr. van Wijk presented a strong case for 128 CE – see the discussions in Konow (1929), pp. xciii-xciv quoted in Appendix Q. Also, see: van Wijk (1927), pp. 170-171; Marshall (1947), pp. 31-32 and notes, and Bivar (2000), pp. 69-75 – especially the Addendum on p. 74. I believe it is now certain that the long-held inception date of 78 CE for the Kushan era is impossible.

The apparent discrepancy of one year between Falk's and van Wijk's determinations can be easily explained, for we do not know if the era started with an elapsed year (i.e. beginning in year 0), or a current year (i.e. beginning in year 1), and/or to the overlapping of years between the Kanishka era and our own.

"It is difficult to judge from the evidence currently available how long Vima Kadphises continued to rule after the introduction of his Roman-based gold currency. There are, however, strong reasons for placing the accession of his successor, Kanishka, the most eminent of all the Kushan kings, no later than A.D. 128, and possibly a few years earlier. Kanishka reigned for twenty-three years, and was succeeded by his son Vasishka, who had a brief reign of some four or five years. After Vasishka came Huvishka, who appears to have ruled as long as forty-six years, though some of this period may have been as regent for Vasishka's son Kanishka II, who seems to have ruled only briefly around A.D. 165, being succeeded as sole ruler by Huvishka. Huvishka was finally replaced by Vasudeva (c. 202-26), the last of the major Kushan kings, who towards the end of his reign saw his kingdom dwindle considerably. Under his successors in the third century the kingdom disintegrated, largely under pressure from the rising power of the Sassanian kings of Persia.

During this period of a century or so from Kanishka's accession to the decline of the Kushan power under Vasudeva there has so far been only one discovery which gives any real help in correlating other events in Roman and Kushan history, but this is an important discovery which goes some way to confirm the chronology of the Kushan monarchs assumed in this paper. Excavations at the Ahin Posh Tope at Jalalabad revealed a deposit of Roman and Kushan coins. These consisted of three Roman aurei, one of Domitian, one of Trajan, and one issue of Sabina, wife of Hadrian, datable to A.D. 137, all well worn; together with ten dinars of Vima Kadphises, six of Kanishka, all well used, and one coin of Huvishka in mint condition. This deposit can hardly have been made before A.D. 160 when one considers the condition of the aureus of Sabina, and more probably around A.D. 170 or even later. This fits in well with the dates for Huvishka given above; in fact there is reason to believe that he minted coins only after the death of Kanishka II (apparently in year 41 after the accession of Kanishka I). This deposit certainly does not provide precise synchronous dating, but it does undoubtedly present a difficulty for those who would put Kanishka's accession in A.D. 78, a date which has formerly carried considerable authority.

There are in addition ample signs that relations between the Roman Empire and the Kushans flourished during the second and early third centuries. Both Hadrian and Antoninus Pius [r. 138-161] received ambassadors from the 'Bactrians', who must surely have been the Kushans. We do not know the precise dates of these embassies, but on the dating accepted here it is likely that one if not both came from the great Kanishka, who was responsible for developing the Kushan kingdom to its greatest extent, including the Tarim basin in Central Asia, and whose name was long revered in India as a great benefactor of Buddhism. Huvishka, whose coins depict a range of deities, minted a coin with the image of the goddess Roma in Minerva pose, complete with the title RIOM, though we do not know what event, if any, occasioned this mark of friendship, if such it was. Kanishka II described himself as KAISAR, among other titles, on an inscription found on the Indus near Attock, more out of self-glorification than any conscious fellowship with the contemporary Roman emperor, but at least both he and his readers must have been well aware of what the title meant." Thorley (1979), pp. 185-186.

"The **Antonius** [sic - Antonine] called Fulvius or Boionius, afterward also given the cognomen Pius, ruled twenty-three years [138 to 161 CE]. . . . Indeed, even Indians, Bactrians, and Hyrcanians sent legations when the justness of so great an *imperator* became known . . . ." From: Sextus Aurelius Victor, *De Imperatoribus Romanis*. XV, 4. *In*: Banchich (2000).

"The kings of the Bactrians [i.e. the Kushans] sent envoys to him [Hadrian reigned 117-138] to beg humbly for his friendship." From the *Historia Augusta* (written during the reigns of Diocletian and Constantine) – The Life of Hadrian, 21.14. Downloaded from: http://penelope.uchicago.edu/Thayer/E/Roman/Texts/Historia_Augusta/Hadrian/2*.html. 21 April, 2007. See also: Garzetti (1976), p. 422.

"Antoninus's eastern policy continued that of his predecessors. Under him too the Roman name was respected and feared, and Antoninus personally enjoyed great prestige. The distant Bactrians and Hyrcanians, and even the Indians, sought relations with Rome, evidently carried along by the vigorous commercial currents that had existed for some time and had also been encouraged by Antoninus." Garzetti (1976), p. 465.

• **Dating Kanishka's reign**

From a series of inscriptions, we know that Kanishka reigned until at least year 23 of his era, which, if it started in 127 CE, means he ruled until at least 149 CE. He was followed by further Kushan emperors until the year 98 (224 CE), and then by less powerful Kushan kings, even into Gupta times, a scenario which can finds further support if one accepts the "dropped hundreds" theory, which has now been proved correct. Falk (2012), pp. 132-135; Falk (2004), pp. 167-176. See below and also **The "dropped hundreds" theory** in Appendix K.

As seen above, it seems that the Kanishka era is actually the Yona/Indo-Greek era with "dropped hundreds", and could have been inaugurated to commemorate his extensive conquests of the central Ganges region and beyond.

It is possible that Kanishka was already on the throne for a few years before his military campaign to middle and northeastern India and the beginning of his era. Clues that have led to this theory include:

• It seems unlikely that Kanishka would have been ready to launch such a major project as the conquest of the Ganges Valley immediately after his reign began, unless there was a standing army all ready to march when he came to the throne.

• That Kanishka's conquests in middle and northeastern India took place very early his era. Tjis is shown by three early inscriptions which mention "Mahārāja Kaniṣka." The first, is dated the 8th day of the 2nd month of winter of year 2 from ancient Kosam/Kauśāmbī, and two inscriptions dated from the 22nd day of the 3rd month of winter of year 3 respectively, from Sarnath, the famous Buddhist site where Buddha preached his first sermon, near Varanasi (Benares). See, for example, Kumar (1973), p. 245.

Such early dated inscriptions in Middle India indicate that the inception of Kanishka's era must have begun around the time of the completion of this campaign.

• The Surkh Kotal complex was apparently built by or for Kanishka and its construction was originally dated in the year 289 of an unstated era.

My interpretation is that this sanctuary was dated in the Yona or "Indo-Greek" era now thought to have had its beginning date in 175/174 BCE. If correct, it would date Surkh Kotal to 114-115 CE. See: "Notes on Eras" below in Falk and Bennet (2009), pp. 208, 212.

• The *Li yul lu-bstan-pa* or 'Prophecy of the Li Country' reports that the kings of Khotan and Gu-zan (Kucha) aided Kanishka in his conquest of Saketa and brought Buddhist relics home with them.

If this story is believed, it must have occurred at some period when the Chinese had no control over these two kingdoms. The most likely window for this to have happened would have been between the time the Chinese abandoned the Western Regions (107 CE) and before Ban Yong re-established control in 127 CE. Without going into details, there are other correspondences in the *Li yul lu-bstan-pa* that indicate these dates, particularly for the king of Khotan (King Vijaya Kīrti), are approximately correct. See: Hill (1988).

• The story of the Kashgari prince Chenpan in the *Hou Hanshu*, who was exiled to the Yuezhi during the Yuanchu period [114-120 CE], and later placed on the throne of Kashgar by the (unnamed) king of the Yuezhi, is so similar to the account of the hostage prince in Xuanzang's account that I believe they must refer to the same event. See: Section 21 for the text.

Xuanzang identifies the king as Kanishka and, while his account is from the 7th century, I can see no reason to doubt him. Further, the dates are very close, though they do indicate that Chenpan was exiled and then placed on the throne of Kashgar shortly *before* the beginning of Kanishka's era. Interestingly, the date "window" here matches the one outlined above.

• It was not uncommon in ancient India for a person to rule for some period before their actual coronation. For example, King Ashoka (on whom many stories of Kanishka's life and deeds were based) was not crowned until four years after taking power, possibly because of a protracted struggle for succession. Sircar (1975), p. 14; Loeschner (2013), p. 2. Kanishka's era may have begun after a late coronation or, perhaps, to celebrate his major conquests in the Ganges Valley.

• **The "dropped hundreds" theory** – see also the first page of Appendix K.

> "From Kaniṣka onwards his own era was used for the majority of inscriptions in his realm, with the particularity that after 100 years the counting started anew, e.g., the cipher for the hundreds were dropped. This dropping was nothing but a theoretical possibility until it was given a solid basis in 1949 by J. van Lohuizen-de-Leeuw, strengthened with different arguments by Hartel 1996: 102f. It is now almost generally accepted by art historians as well as numismatists. Numbers referring to the first or second century of the Kuṣâṇas can be found on hundreds of pieces of plastic art, many from the capital Mathura, written in Brahmi, and many from Gandhara, written in Kharoṣṭhī script." Falk (2001), p. 121.
>
> "It is hardly coincidental that Kaniṣka's year 1 is now identical with year 301 in the Yavana era, and that year I of Azes is year 201 in the Arsacid era. Both "new" eras are thus nothing but continuations of older traditions. Seen this way, year 1 of Kaniṣka need not define his first year in power; likewise, year 1 of Azes could be placed anywhere in his reign." Falk and Bennett (2009), p. 211.

The same scholars have extended this research to provide dates for several other eras. In fact, Harold Falk and his colleague, Chris Bennett, seem to have successfully pinpointed the beginning dates of the Yavana (Yona) era – 175/174 BCE, the Azes era – 47/46 BCE, as well as the Kanishka era. In addition, they managed to cross-check them neatly with each other, and with two other well-known eras still in use in India today: the Vikrama era of 58/57 BCE, and the Śaka era, which began 1 April, 78 CE.

One of their important achievements has been the confirmation that some of the eras used the principle of "dropping-hundreds." This means that, once dates in a particular era reached 100, the new ones were expressed without the initial figure indicating the hundreds – much as we do today when we write "08" for 2008. Initially, this theory had many detractors, but recently it has been proven, and has this has allowed several eras to be confidently linked:

"The "dropped-hundreds" theory ceased to be a theory after dates became explicable which used the Gupta era and a "continued era" side-by-side. It was possible to show (Falk 2004) that this continued era is nothing but the old Kuṣāṇa era, in continuous use at Mathura in the fourth and early fifth Centuries, always returning to 1 after the lapse of one Century, while the newly introduced Gupta dates continue to grow without such a feature.

Rejecting the "dropped-hundreds" system leads inevitably to the conclusion that Vasiṣka (with attested regnal years in Kuṣāṇa dates: 22 [Vaskuṣāṇa], 24 [Isapur pillar], 30 [Kamra]) must be placed between Kaniṣka I and Huviṣka, with some of his years overlapping with those of Kaniṣka and Huviṣka. Kaniṣka III becomes Kaniṣka II and comes to lie right in the middle of the reign of Huviṣka. Mukherjee (1985, 12; 2004b, 409) for one accepted this absurdity without a thought, speaking of "conjoint rule," although the numismatic evidence conclusively requires us to place Vasiṣka after Kaniṣka II, who came after Vasudeva, whose reign lasted until the end of the first Kuṣāṇa Century." Falk (2012), p. 244.

Falk has illustrated the relationships between the eras in the following diagram:

"The equations arising from the research summarised above are as follows:

yavana		248/7 B.C.E. Arsacid	Śaka		175/174 B.C.E. *yavana*
→ 175/174 B.C.E.	→	48/47 B.C.E. →	78 C.E.	→	127 C.E. →
Antimachos?		= 201 = 1 Azes			= 301 = 1 Kuṣāṇa
Eucratides?					

From: Falk (2012), p. 137.

For detailed information on the new chronology, I refer the interested reader to the following articles: Falk (2001), pp. 121-136; Falk and Bennett (2009), pp. 197-215; Falk (2010), pp. 73-89; Falk (2012), pp. 131-145.

Unfortunately, the only historical accounts on the Kushan kings in the Chinese texts are the brief mentions in the *Hou Hanshu* of the first two kings, Kujula Kadphises and Vima Takhtu.

This brevity is probably due to a combination of events, including the severing of communications with the Western Regions for sixty-five years between 9 and 73 CE, the retirement of Ban Chao in 102, and the loss of communications again from 106 to 127 CE.

Fan Ye, the compiler of the *Hou Hanshu*, discusses his main sources for the 'Chronicle on the Western Regions' in his 'Commentary' at the end of the first section saying that, where the details differ from those in the *Hanshu*, they are taken from Ban Yong's report to Emperor An (107-125 CE) towards the end of his reign. See the end of Section 1, and the discussion in note 1.69.

Prior to writing the report, Ban Yong had just made one brief and unsuccessful foray into the "Western Regions" in 107 CE, reaching only as far as Dunhuang. In other words, he did not even leave the territory of 'China Proper'. Effective communication across this region to the Da Yuezhi had totally halted the previous year. The "Western Regions" are said to have been out of touch with China for a further 10 years.

Ban Yong did not travel beyond Dunhuang until 126 CE – see: Chavannes (1906), pp. 246 and 253. Therefore, most of the information in his report to the Emperor, on which this chapter is based, was almost certainly derived from the observations and notes of his father, General Ban Chao.

Ban Chao re-established Chinese power in the region in 73 CE – Chavannes (1906), p. 218, and did not retire to the capital Luoyang until the 8th month [31 August to 29

September] of 102 CE (ibid. p. 243). Sadly, Ban Chao died the following month at the age of 71 (or 72 by "Western" reckoning).

Joe Cribb makes several important points on the dating of the Kushan kings based on the finds of Kushan coins and copies of Kushan coins in Khotan:

> "On the basis of the suggested linkage between the first two Kushan kings in the Rabatak inscription and the first two Kushans in the Chinese source, it can be proposed that Vima I Tak[to] had been occupying the Kushan throne long enough before AD 107 and perhaps even before AD 90 [*when a Kushan army unsuccessfully invaded the Tarim Basin*] to "conquer India". This is clearly an important consideration for any understanding of Kushan chronology and its implications for Kushan history.
>
> *Khotanese Connections*
>
> The above references to Ban Chao's campaigns suggest that there was a close link between Chinese Turkestan and the early Kushans. This is given a concrete dimension by the discovery of coins of the first four Kushan kings at the ancient site of Khotan, Ban Chao's military base AD 73-107 [sic – should read AD 73-102]. Hermaeus imitations attributed to Kujula Kadphises were used as blanks for overstriking by a Khotanese king. Kujula Kadphises' bull and camel coin design was copied by another Khotanese king on his coins. A bull and camel coin of Vima I Tak[to] and a few regular copper coins of Vima II Kadphises have been found at Khotan. More than twenty small copper coins of Kanishka I have been found in the vicinity of the site, some together with coins of the Khotanese kings. One Khotanese king copies the denomination system of these small Kanishka I coins. The Khotanese kings associated through their coins with Kujula Kadphises should be dated before Ban Chao's occupation of Khotan AD 73-107 [73-102 – see above], and the coins associated with Kanishka I after it (Cribb 1984-5)." Cribb (1999), p. 2.

If the Śaka Era is connected at all with the 'Great Kushans,' it could have been inaugurated to celebrate the territorial gains of their ally (and possible relative) Chastana, the satrap of Ujjain; or, possibly, gains made by Vima Takhtu or those of his brother Sadaṣkaṇa. One of these brothers was probably the unnamed "Soter Megas" – "The Great Saviour" – entitled in Chinese, *Gaozhen* (高珍). This translates as something like "Precious Benefactor" and/or may have been an attempt to transcribe Guishuang (貴霜) Kushan. See: Appendix Q. This title indicates that the issuer of this coinage was responsible for at least one major victory.

Vima Takhtu possibly earned these titles when he extended Kujula's conquests of Jibin and western Gandhara across the Punjab plains as far as Mathura, which is 158 km southeast of Delhi.

Later Buddhist documents claim that, after Kanishka's conquests in Eastern India (i.e. 127 CE or soon after), he defeated the king of (?Indo-)Parthia killing "900,000 Parthians." This bloodshed is said to have led to his remorse and conversion to Buddhism). See: Zürcher (1968), pp. 386-387.

Unfortunately, we know little more about this period of Parthian history; nor is there any other evidence for the tradition that Kanishka won a great victory over the Parthians. If so, we cannot know which "Parthians" the text refers to, although it is likely to be a reference to the Indo-Parthians in Sind, Arachosia, and surrounds, or to semi-autonomous Parthian rulers in Merv, or other eastern parts of the Parthian Empire.

• The Azes era

Since the early 1980s it became the generally accepted practice to equate the Azes era mentioned in a number of important inscriptions with the Vikrama era of 58/7 BCE, which is still in use today in India.

In 2009, Harry Falk and Chris Bennett, in a seminal paper, offered the first credible argument that the two eras were, in fact, quite separate, with the Azes era beginning in 48/47 BCE rather than the 58/57 BCE inception date of the Vikrama era, necessitating the recalibration of many later dates in the Indian region:

> "King Azes has been known since the days of Charles Masson, who collected coins in the 1830s in Gandhaṛa proper and eastern Afghanistan. These coins are inscribed in a Greek genitive AZOY, and on the reverse, again in a genitive form, as *ayasa* in Kharoṣṭhī. The respective Greek nominative *AZOS has not surfaced so far. The Kharoṣṭhī form *ayasa* was first found in combination with a date comprising year, month and day on the Taxila silver scroll.[1] As early as 1914, MARSHALL suggested that this date followed an era named after king *aya*. While MARSHALL considered the possibility, RAPSON was the first scholar who firmly equated this era with the Vikrama era, starting in 58/57 BC.[2] Other solutions for the word *ayasa* were offered as well, until in 1978 BAILEY published the Indravarman reliquary, in which the era was given not as *ayasa*, but as *maharajasa ayasa*. Instantly, the meaning of *ayasa* was beyond dispute. Three scholars (BIVAR 1981, FUSSMAN 1980, SALOMON 1982) almost immediately referred to this new evidence and it became customary to speak of the "proof that the era of Azes is the Vikrama era". In fact, all that had been proved was that *aya* was king Azes. The conjectural nature of the linkage between the *aya* era and Vikrama *saṃvat* was unaffected by the new evidence.
>
> Nonetheless, the equation of Azes' era and the Vikrama era did not appear to be blatantly wrong and was defended for practical reasons by all – except for two scholars in London, Elizabeth ERRINGTON and Joe CRIBB." Falk-Bennett (2009), p. 198.

Hans Loeschner wrote a long and detailed critique of the Falk and Bennett datings in his paper: "The Stūpa of the Kushan Emperor Kanishka the Great, with Comments on the Azes Era and Kushan Chronology." Hans Loeschner. *Sino-Platonic Papers*, Number 227, July 2012, pp. 1-24.

He recommended a return to the traditional correspondence of the Azes and Vikrama eras and the incept of the Kanishka era to 78 CE.

However, close inspection of his interpretations shows that they are based on an disproven claim by János Harmatta that an unfinished inscription from Surkh Kotal dated in the year 299 was attributable to Vima Takpiso (= Tahkto). In fact, no name is legible in the inscription and the date appears to be 279. Refer to Sims-Williams (2012), p. 76.

On this basis, I have dismissed Loeschner's suggestions and continue with the now generally accepted datings proposed by Harry Falk and Chris Bennett.

This time-line corrects the dates based on the commonly-held belief that the Kushan era was equivalent to the Śaka era of 78 CE, and that the Azes era was equivalent to the Vikrama era of 58/57 BCE.

Summary of the eras according to Falk and Bennett:

Yavana (Prakrit Yoṇa, also known as the "Indo-Greek," and "Old Śaka") Era - 175/4 BCE.

Vikrama (saṃvat) Era – 58/7 BCE.

Azes era – 47/6 CE.

Saka era – 1st April 78 CE.

Kanishka era – 127 CE.

Provisional Timeline of the main inscriptions based on these eras:

175/174 BCE — **Yona, Yavana, or Indo-Greek era and also the Arsacid era.** Falk-Bennett (2009), p. 211.

59/58 BCE? — **Maghera well (or "tank") inscription (17 km from Mathura):** Dated in 116, a year of "the reign of the Yavanas." Salomon (2005), pp. 371 ff. However, Joe Cribb (1999), p. 3, thinks that the letter forms are roughly mid-first century, and tentatively suggests it be dated in the Maues era, which places it in 36 CE.

58/57 BCE — **Vikrama era begins.**

47/46 BCE — **Azes era begins. Year 201 of the Arsacid year.**

39 BCE — **Buner Plate inscription.**

"In the year 9 of the *mahārāja* Azes the Great, in month Kārttika (on day) 2; during the reign of the Mahākṣatrapa Vasa-Abdagases, son of Mahāpāla-Suśpala, (this is) the present of Saṅghamitra for the Lord, for the sage of the Śākya clan. Written (by . . . .)." Falk (2012), p. 140. Kārttika is the fourth month of the rainy season, so the dating should be placed in late 39 BCE.

36 BCE — **Buner Reliquary inscription.**

"In the year eleven of the Mahākṣatrapa Namipāla, on the fourth day of month Kārttika, these relics of the Lord Śākyamuni were established. (This) was written (by) Balamitra." Falk (2012), p. 139. Kārttika is the fourth month of the rainy season, so the dating should be placed in late 39 BCE.

1 BCE/**1** CE — **Apraca Dated Reliquary.** 1st year of Vijayamitra's reign.

26 CE — **Apraca (Rukhuṇa) Dated Reliquary.** In July of the 27th year of Vijayamitra's reign.

"The inscription records the establishment of a stūpa jointly by Rukhuṇa, the wife of the King of Apraca, by Vijayamitra, the king of Apraca, and by the Stratega (Commander) Indravarma, who, as we know from other inscriptions, was Rukhuṇa's son. . . .

The inscription bears a triple date, referring to the eighth day of Śrāvaṇa [the 1st month of the rainy season - therefore it was in 26 CE] in the regnal year 27 of Vijayamitra, the year 73 of "the year which is called 'of Azes'," and the year 201 "of the Greeks" (*yoṇaṇa*)." Salomon (2005), p. 361.

29/30 CE — **Gondophares comes to the throne** - if the **Takht-i-bahi Inscription** is dated in the Azes era; or 18/19 CE - if it is dated in the Vikrama era.

55/56 CE — **Gondophares still on throne** - if the **Takht-i-bahi Rock Inscription** in 103 of an unspecified era was actually in the Azes era; and the 26th year of his reign. See Salomon 1982. 103 - 47 = 56 CE. 56 -26 = 30 CE. So, if the era was, in fact, the Azes era of *circa* 47 BCE, as most scholars agree, Gondophares must have ruled *circa* 30 (29-30) to at least *circa* 56 CE (55-56).

75/76 CE — **Panjtār Stone Inscription** of "Maharaya Gushana." Panjtar is situated on the Indus on the border of the Peshawar and Hazara districts of Pakistan. As it is dated in Śrāvana (July), in the year 122 it must relate to 75/76 CE.

"This is a Kharōshṭhī record from the Yūsufzai country, on the banks of the Indus : it seems to have been actually found at a place named Salīmpūr, near Panjtār ; but it has come to be known as the Panjtār inscription. The original stone being now not forthcoming, we are dependent on the two figurings of the record given by

Cunningham in JASB, vol. 23 (1854), plate at p. 705, and *Reports*, vol. 5 (1875), plate 16, No. 4." Fleet (1914), p. 372.

78 CE – **The Śaka era** began on April 1st of this year. Falk (2012), p. 132.

84 CE – **An unnamed Yuezhi king (probably Vima Takhtu)** was making an alliance of marriage with the Kangju according to 'Biography of Ban Chao' in the *Hou Hanshu.*

87 CE – **Kalawān Copper Plate Inscription.** 23rd day of Śrāvana (1st month of the rainy season) in 134. Name of ruler not given. Situated SE of the Sirsukh near Taxila. Calculations based on the Azes era for 134 give a date of 87/88 CE. However, because it is dated in Śrāvana (1st month of the rainy season), we can be sure it was from 87 CE. See Ruegg (2005), pp. 3-9.

88 CE – A Yuezhi king (who was most probably **Vima Takhtu** - as we have an inscription attributable to him dated in 88/89 CE - see below) sent "tribute" including antelope, lions and jewels to the Chinese asking for the hand of a Han princess in marriage.

88 CE – **Taxila Silver Scroll** (from the Dharmarājikā stupa in Taxila), dedicated to the health of an ailing *Maharaja Rajatiraja Devaputra Khushana* and includes the distinctive "Nandi-pāda" symbol. Dated in the month of Āshāḍha (June) in Azes' year 136, therefore it must have been in 88/89 CE. See: Appendix Q. **NOTE:** Joe Cribb (2005), p. 222 places this as a year of **Vima Takhtu.**

90 CE – The Kushan king asked for the hand of a Chinese princess in marriage and was refused. Therefore, between 16th June and 15th July, a 70,000-man Yuezhi army under a viceroy named Xie – (副王謝) Fuwang Xie was sent to the region of Khotan but was outwitted by Ban Chao and forced to return.

95/96 CE – **Vima Takhtu.**

"Another indicator of the length of Wima Takto's reign comes from an inscription from Mathura, referring to a *maharaja rajatiraja* in the year 270. As Wima Takto was the first Kushan to rule at Mathura (Sims Williams and Cribb 1996, p. 102). It seems plausible to identify him as the king whose name is missing from the year 270 inscription (due to a fracture of the stone bearing this inscription)." Cribb (2005), p. 214.

104-105 CE – **Vima Takhtu.** Dasht-i-Nāwūr inscription "dated year 279 Gorpiaios 15 under the Kushan king Vima Takhto." (clear in both Bactrian and Kharoṣṭhī versions of the trilingual).

"Apparently a royal proclamation of Vima Taktu, one of a group of inscriptions on a boulder near the peak of Mt. Qarabāy. Dated in the year 279 of an unnamed era, perhaps equivalent to 104/5 CE." Sims-Williams (2012), p. 76. See also: Falk-Bennett (2009), p. 207; and Fussman (1974).

104-105 CE? – **Surkh Kotal inscription SK2** dated 279; or 299 according to Harmatta 1992: 427, which would place it ca. 124/125 CE.

Circa **107** CE – an "Indian" envoy, presumably sent by the Kushan ruler, was received by Trajan, the Roman emperor. See, for example: Smith (1903), p. 31 and n. 2.

112/113 CE – **Vima Kadphises (?).** Khalatse Inscription of dated 287 in Indo-Greek era?

114-120 CE – **Kashgari prince Chenpan** in the *Hou Hanshu*, was exiled to the Yuezhi during the Yuanchu period [114-120 CE], and later placed on the throne of Kashgar by the (unnamed) king of the Yuezhi - following Xuanzang's account, probably, Kanishka.

124/125 CE — The Mathura inscription of an anonymous *maharaja rajatiraja* of the year 299 - presumably in the Yavana/Indo-Greek era. Cribb (2005) assumes it was Vima Kadphises rather than Kanishka before of his era began.

124-125 CE? — Surkh Kotal inscription SK2 dated 279; or 299 according to Harmatta 1992: 427, which would place it *circa* 124/125 CE - see also entry on this inscription under 104-105 CE.

125 CE. 24 September — **"Traṣaka" reliquary of 172.** See Falk and Bennett (2009).

127 CE — Kanishka era begins. Year 301 of Yona/Indo-Greek era.

129 CE — Mahārāja Kaniṣka. 2nd month of winter at Kosam (the city of Kosāmbi on the Jumna river).

130 CE — Mahārāja Kaniṣka. Two inscriptions on the 22nd day of 3rd month of winter from Sarnath.

138 CE — Sui Vihār Copper-Plate Inscription. Found in a large ruined stupa about 16 miles (25.8 km) north-west of Bahāwalpur at 71° 34' E. and 29° 18' N. Probably the southernmost known Kushan inscription near the ancient border between the Punjab and Sindh. Dated in the 28th of Daisos of the year 11 of the Kanishka era (June, 138 CE). Dedicated (in Kharoṣṭhī script) to: "mahajajasya rajatirajasya devaputrasaya Kan[i]shkasya." Adapted from Konow (1929), pp. 138-141.

148 CE — Mahārāja Kāṇiska. Mathura. 4th month of winter = *circa* February, 148

155 CE, August — Blessings invoked for **Devaputra Shāhi Huviṣka.** Mathura. 1st day of Gurpiaios.

156 CE — Mahārāja Devaputra Huksha (Huviṣka). Mathura.

187 CE — Mahārāja Devaputra Huvaṣka (Huviṣka). Mathura. 10th day of 4th month (= June).

191 CE — Vāsudeva (titles not clear). Mathura. 2nd month of rainy season (c. August).

214 CE — Mahārāja Rājātirāja Shāhi Vāsudeva. Mathura. 30th day of 2nd month of winter (c. December or January 215, CE).

225 CE — Rājan Vāsudeva. Mathura. 11th day of 4th month of rainy season (October).

229 CE — Bodiao (波調) (Vāsudeva) sent an envoy with "tribute" to Cao Rui, a Chinese emperor of the Wei dynasty according to the historical work the *Sanguozhi* (3rd year of Taihe 太和).

232 CE — Kaniṣka II. Falk (2001), p. 130; Falk (2012), p. 134.

249 CE — Vasiṣka. [Vaskuṣāṇa]. Falk (2012), p. 134.

251 CE — Vasiṣka. [Isapur pillar]. 30th day of the 4th month of summer (*circa* October). Falk (2012), p. 134.

257 CE — Vasiṣka. [Kamra]. Falk (2012), p. 134. Also at Ayrtam, 18 km east of Termez on the north bank. "King [is] Ooeṣko, the Era-year [is] 30 when the lord king presented and had the Aerdoxṣo-Farro image set up here." Harmatta (1994b), p. 432.

268 CE — Mahārāja Rājātirāja Devaputra Kisara ('Caesar') Vajeṣkaputra ('son of Vajeṣka') Kaṇiṣka. Ara near Attock. 25th day of the month of Jyaiṣṭha (May or June of the Year 41, which, without the 'dropped hundred,' would give 168 CE).

Appendix Q: Names and Titles of the Kushan kings - Kujula to Kanishka

This appendix examines some aspects of the Chinese, Brāhmī, and Kharoṣṭhī names and titles of the 'Great Kushans.'

Titles are notoriously difficult to translate accurately from one language to another, and scholars often disagree, even when an original inscription is clearly legible.

Qiujiuque 丘就卻 in the *Hou Hanshu* almost certainly refers to Kujula Kadphises, and Yangaozhen 閻高珍 to one of his sons — either Wima Takhtu, or his brother (or half-brother), Sadaṣkaṇa. See note 13.16.

• The Chinese name Qiujiuque 丘就卻 = Kujula Kadphises

Both Chavannes and Pelliot sometimes made the mistake of substituting 郤 *xi* for the very similar-looking character 卻 *que*. See: note 13.11; Chavannes (1907), p. 191, n. 2; Pelliot (1929), p. 201. However, Pelliot's main point is still valid:

> "If there is now a secure point in the interpretation of the Chinese texts relating to the Indo-Scythians, it is really due to the respective equivalence of the names of 丘就郤 [should read: 丘就卻] Qiujiuque (*K'i̯e̯u̯-dz'i̯e̯u̯-kiak) and of 閻高珍 Yangaozhen (*I̯äm-kâu-t'i̯ĕn) with those of Kuzulakadphises and Vemakadphises. The phonetic correspondence is not, however, perfect for either of the two names." Translated and adapted from Pelliot (1929), p. 201.

The initial two syllables of this name, *Qiujiu*, provide an acceptable transcription of the first two syllables of *Kuju(la)*. See: note 13.11. The final character, *que* 卻, is less easy to explain.

> "The relationship between the names of Qiu-jiu-que 丘就卻 and his son Yan-gao-zhen 閻高珍, the Kushan chieftains referred to in the Later Han chronicle, and their presumed counterparts Kujula and Vima represents a long-standing problem. In discussing the historical implications of the Rabatak inscription, Joe Cribb has again drawn attention to the apparent mismatch, but he concludes that the evidence of the Rabatak inscription, which for the first time allows us to identify the son of Kujula Kadphises as Vima Takhtu, together with the numismatic data, corroborates these equations (Sims-Williams and Cribb 1996, pp. 102-3).
>
> Qiu-jiu-que should derive from *k^huw-dzuw-k^hɨak* in Early Middle Chinese as reconstructed in Pulleyblank 1991. It has been suggested (Pelliot 1914, p. 401; Pulleyblank 1962, p. 109) that the third character *que* 卻 is a mistake for *jie* 劫, EMC *kɨap*, which would represent the first syllable of Kujula's surname Kadphises. As an alternative, one might consider the possibility that the Chinese derives from a hypocoristic form **Kujuk(a)k*: cf. Sims-Williams 1992,p. 34, on *-kk* as a hypocoristic suffix in Sogdian onomastics. A parallel for the use of **Kujukk* beside *Kujula* as the name of the same person may be found in the occurrence of *πopoκo* = *Puruk* beside *πop[..]πo*, perhaps to be restored as *πop[ασ] πo* = **Pur-asp*, in two copies of a single later Bactrian document, where both forms clearly refer to the same man." From the "Appendix: The names of Kujula Kadphises and Vima Takhtu in Chinese," in Sims-Williams (1998), pp. 89-90.

> "Since the occasion presents itself, I will remark that, for the name of Kuzulakadphises, whose name the Hindu legends give in the genitive in the form Kujulakapasa, the Chinese form has the irregular ancient final *k* of *-que* (*-kh^iak*). But I strongly doubt that the responsibility for this inconsistency was the responsibility of the actual scribes who noted the name for the first time. In all probability, 卻 *que* or

> 却 *que* (*$kh^{i}ak$*; the two forms were used interchangeably) is a simple copyist's mistake for 劫 *jie* (*$k^{i}ap$*), and the Chinese transcription thus implies an original *Kudzu[la]kap, fully conforming with the Greek and Hindu forms. The very natural confusion between 却 *que* and 劫 *jie* is in a way illustrated by an unquestionable example: in Mr. Watanabe's article on Kalmāṣapada (*J. Pāli Text Soc.*, 1909, p. 308 and 309), the name of Kalmāṣapada, transcribed in a Prakrit Kammāsa, was written one time with *que*, and another time with *jie*; it ought to be *jie* in both cases." Translated and adapted from Pelliot (1914), p. 401, n. 1.

Another alternative character that could have been intended here is: 郤 *xì* – crack, opening, cleft; rift. It is of interest that the proposed reconstruction given for the pronunciation of this character [Medieval Chinese: khaekb] is quite similar to those for 卻 *que* (*-$kh^{i}ak$*) and the interchangeable 却 *que* (*$kh^{i}ak$*):

> "N.B. this graph [卻 *que*] sometimes confused with 郤 *xì* 1. Cleft, reft; 2. Rift, discord; but they are quite distinct." Kroll (2015), p. 381; also p. 490.

> "A number of examples of clusters of velars or laryngals + l from the Han period have already been given and more could be added.... We probably have 劫 M. **k̭ap** earlier in the transcription of Kujula kadphises [sic], if we accept Pelliot's emendation of the last syllable 卻 M. **k̭ak** (1914, p. 401). Pelliot noted this as a transcription in which foreign l was not represented by the Chinese. If we restore ***klāp** we have ***khūĥ-dzūh-klāp** which can represent a *kujūl(a)kap- by metathesis." Pulleyblank (1962), p. 123.

This interpretation works. The first two syllables *Qiujiu* 丘就 provide a very accurate transcription for Kujula (or Kuzula), especially when one keeps in mind that the Chinese commonly dropped the final **la* when transcribing Indian names.

The final character 卻 *que* (interchangeable with 却) *may* have given rise to a copyist's mistake for 劫 *jie* (*$k^{i}ap$*), and represented the first syllable of Kadphises as Pelliot suggests above. Schuessler (2009), 2-2, p. 96, gives for: 卻劫: **Mand** què; **LHan** k^{h}ɨak; **OCM** khak.

However, it could equally have been an attempt to render one of his titles. *Jie* 劫 was commonly used to transcribe the sound *ka* in Indian languages – as in the abbreviation for 劫波 – *jiebo* = Pali *kappa* and Sanskrit *kalpa*. See: *GR* vol. I, p. 743; Kroll (2015), p. 208. It is even possible that 卻 *que* (read as 劫 *jie*) represented the word *kara* which appears on many of Kujula's coins:

> "The word *Kara* appears in the Kharoshṭhī inscription on the reverse of a class of copper coins (camel: bull). The legend can be read as *Maharayasa* (or Mahatasa) *Rayarayasa* (or *Rayatirayasa*) *Devaputrasa Kuyula Kara Kaphasa* (or *Kuyula Kara Kaphasa*, or *Kuyla Kara Kapasa*, or *Kayala Kara Kapasa*, or *Kujula Kara Kaphasa*, or *Kujula Kaphasa*, or *Kujula Kara*, or *Kuyula Kaphasa*). Kuyula has been identified with the Kushāṇa king Kujula. . . . The term *Kara* has been related by F. W. Thomas to the term *Kāla*, occurring in certain Kharoshṭhī documents of Chinese Turkestan. T. Burrow thinks that *Kāla* may mean «prince». At least from the context of its use it appears to have stood for a title. The term *Kara* may also be compared with the word *Ka'ra*, used in some Khotanese texts probably as a title.
>
> The expression *Kara* occurs in the term *Καραλραγγο* (*Karalrańgo*), which appears as a title in the Great Bactrian inscription of the Kushāṇa age discovered at Surkh-Kotal. W. B. Henning takes *Karalango* as meaning «lord of the marches», and consider it

«same» as «Persian Kanārang, a title of governors of provinces bordering on the lands of the former Kushan empire».

. . . . Thus the expression *Karalranga* comprises two words *Kara* and *lraṅga* (= *draṅga*). Here *Kara* cannot be taken in the sense of denoting «a prince». On the other hand, in a few Central Asian Kharoshṭhī documents, referred to above, the word *Kāla* (*Kara*) is used as a title of a «Son of a Great King» (nos. 622 and 634). This apparent contradiction may be obviated if the term *Kara* is taken to mean «lord». A prince as well as a person in-charge of a lranga (or draṇga) may be referred to as a «lord» (c.f. *draṅgādhīpa* or *draṅgeśa*, meaning «lord of draṇga».

Such an import for the term *Kara* fits well with its appearance as a title of Kujula Kadphises in the legend on coins struck by him as a king and not as a prince. King Kujula could well have been described as «lord» (of the Kushāṇa kingdom). Thus the Kushāṇa royal epithet *Kara* may perhaps be taken to mean «lord»." Mukherjee (1977), pp. 8-9.

It should be noted that the Sanskrit word *kāra* has among its meanings those of 'a husband', 'master', or 'lord' – see Monier-Williams (1899), p. 274; while *kāla* was sometimes used as a name for Śiva and for Rudra (ibid. p. 277).

"The base ***kar-*** 'to fight' gave O. Pers. ***kāra-*** . . . .

This *kara-*, *kāra-* belongs with Indo-European (Pok. 615-6) *koro-*, Lit. *kāras* 'war', *kārias* 'army', Got. *Harjis*, O.Engl. *here* 'army'. See earlier Mélanges E. Benveniste, 1974, 19-20." Bailey (1979), p. 98.

On the other hand, it is possible that it is closely related to the later Turkic epithet *kara* = "black":

"Othman is celebrated by the Oriental writers for his personal beauty, and for "his wondrous length and strength of arm." Likc Artaxerxes Longimanus, of the old dynasty of Persian kings, and like the Highland chieftain of whom Wordsworth sang, Othman could touch his knees with his hands when he stood upright. He was unsurpassed in his skill and graceful carriage as a horseman ; and the jet black colour of his hair, his beard, and eyebrows, gained him in his youth the title of "Kara," that is to say, "Black" Othman. The epithet "Kara," which we shall often find in Turkish history,* is, when applied to a person, considered to imply the highest degree of manly beauty. . . ."

**E. g.* Karadhissar, "The Black Castle;" Kara-Denis, "The Black Sea;" Kara Mustapha, "Black Mustapha;" Karadagh, "Black Mountain;" Kara-Su "Black Water."

Creasy (1854), p. 12.

Fussman (1998), p. 632, also considers the identification of Qiu-jiu-que 丘就卻 with Kujula as certain, though he admits the Chinese transcription of the name is not very accurate. Consult: Pulleyblank (1963), pp. 109, 123, 223.

Joe Cribb suggests an approximate date for Kujula's reign of 30-80 CE – see Sims-Williams and Cribb (1995/6), pp. 105-107. Fussman suggests that Kujula died *circa* 45-50, perhaps as late as 60 CE – see Fussman (1998), p. 638.

As this debate remains unresolved, the interested reader should check the articles mentioned by Sims-Williams, Cribb and Fussman for further information on the Kushans that flows from the discovery of the Rabatak inscription. Also see: note 13.16.

• The name 'Kujula' and the title 'yavuga'

Kujula appears to be a personal or family name and not a title. On later coins he took grand titles such as one might expect of an emperor: *Maharayasa Rayarayasa* and

Maharajasa Rajatirajasa ('Great King, King of Kings'), and *Devaputrasa* ('Son of Heaven'). For the title 'Son of Heaven,' see: Lévi (1934), pp. 1-21, and Chen (2002), pp. 289-325.

Kings of Shanshan from the 3rd century CE also took the title 'Devaputra' or 'Son of Heaven.' See, for example, Brough (1965), pp. 598-599; Burrow (1940), Document Nos., 115, 169, 180, and numerous others.

The Kushans, or the Chinese, or both could have influenced them. The population of Shanshan possibly also contained descendants of the Xiao ('Lesser') Yuezhi who were said to have fled into the mountains to the south after the defeat of the Yuezhi by the Xiongnu in 176 BCE. Pelliot carefully analysed the use of this title by the Kushans:

> "Very similar to Chinese *t'ien-tzŭ* and Iranian *faγfur* is Skr. *devaputra,* «son of the gods», a title to which S. LÉVI has devoted a learned monograph (*JA,* 1934, 1-21). As a title, the term has never been met with in Sanskrit literature, except in a passage of the *Suvarṇaprabhāsa;* yet it is of frequent occurrence in the epigraphy of the Kuṣaṇa, as the royal title of that dynasty. The apparent exception of the *Suvarṇaprabhāsa* may almost be said to confirm, rather than to qualify the exclusive use of the title by the Kuṣaṇa, as it seems that the work was composed under their rule, and merely extolls the title of the dynasty. Since the Kuṣaṇa had come from China, and remained in touch with the land of their origin, the conclusion seems almost necessary that they had followed the example of the Chinese «Son of Heaven». Here, there seems to be some contradiction in LÉVI's views. On the one hand, he says (p. 15) that the notion of the «divine Heaven», *dyu Dyaus pitā,* had not outlived Vedic times, so that the secondary notion of *deva,* «a god», remained the only available. On the other hand, taking into account the fact that, on their way from China to the west, and before reaching India, the Yüeh-chih or Kuṣaṇa had been in close touch with Iranian nations, LÉVI thinks that *t'ien-tzŭ* first became *bagpuhr,* and that «it is probably through the intermediary of *baγpuhr* that *t'ien-tzŭ* became *devaputra*» (p. 18-19). But, in such a case, it is not the meaning of *t'ien* which ought to be compared with that of *deva,* but the meaning of *baγ-*. Whatever the case may be, the equivalence, direct or indirect, of *t'ien-tzŭ* with *devaputra* was so well felt that *devaputra* was used later in Indian Buddhist circles as the designation of the Chinese Emperor, in the same way as *baγpūr, baγūur* and *faγfūr* in Iranian and Arabic countries (cf. CHAVANNES, *Relig. éminents,* 56, 82; TAKAKUSU, *A Record of the Buddhist Religion,* 136; LÉVI, *loc. cit.,* 17). About the year 1000 there reigned a king in Ladakh who had the title of Lhazi-bu (= *devaputra);* cf. A. H. FRANCKE, *Antiq. of Indian Tibet,* I, 41.
>
> Recently, Mrs. BAZIN-FOUCHER (*JA,* 1938, 504) has taken exception to the theory which ascribes a Chinese origin to the royal title *devaputra* of the Kuṣaṇa. Starting from the «divine character» of the Seleucid kings, and from the ancient «monarchic cult» inherited from the Achaemenids by the Arsacids and Sassanids, Mrs. BAZIN-FOUCHER concludes : «So it seems to me purposeless to look in China, as has been sometimes attempted, for the origin of Skr. *devaputra.* The Yüeh-chih did not have to bring this title with them from the borders of Kan-su : they found this royal epithet already in common use in Iran with exactly the same meaning, in Greek as Theopator or in Parthian Pahlavi as *baγpuhr.* » To me this seems to take the question by the wrong end. The Kuṣaṇa, on their way from Kan-su to Bactria, are not likely to have been influenced by the Greek term Theopatôr. On the other hand, *baγpuhr* is so little attested as a common royal epithet in Parthian Pahlavī that the only example of it known hitherto is in the sense of « Son of God», with reference to Jesus. And when Sogdian *baγpur* and the later *baγbūr, faγfūr* make their appearance [sic], it is in connection with the Emperor of China. The explanation of *devaputra* as modelled on *t'ien-tzŭ,* in the same way as and perhaps through the intermediary of *baγpūr,* makes,

in my opinion, a strong case which Mrs. BAZIN-FOUCHER's argument has not weakened. LÉVI was even tempted to go further and to establish a connection between the title of *devaputra* of the Kuṣaṇa and the epithet of «Son of God» used for Jesus in the «first Judaeo-Christian communities» (pp. 19-21); but this is a much more debatable proposition.

When I say that *t'ien-tzŭ*, «Son of Heaven», and its Iranian and Sanskrit counterparts *baγpūr* and *devaputra* are originally the designation of the Chinese Emperor, this does not mean that the use of this title always remained as narrowly restricted. The epigraphy of the Kuṣaṇa already shows that they had appropriated the designation, and so did the kings of Khotan. Among Altaic nations, the Hsiung-nu and the Turks, T'u-chüeh as well as Uighur, had done or did the same *(tängri-dä qut bulmïš*, etc.). The notion of various «Sons of Heaven» was even erected into a regular system, which is not of pure Chinese origin but which has found its clearest expression in Chinese texts. We can trace it back to the 3rd cent. A.D., but it is probably older. The earliest text speaks only of three regions of plenty : plenty of men in China, plenty of jewels in the Mediterranean Orient (Ta-Ch'in), and plenty of horses among the Yüeh-chih (Kuṣaṇa). But the theory was soon evolved that there were four «Sons of Heaven» : that of the men in China, that of the elephants in India, that of the jewels in the Mediterranean Orient, and that of horses among the Kuṣaṇa." Pelliot (1963), pp. 653-655.

On one coin (Senior ISCH type 6v), Kujula styles himself: *Maharajasa Khushanasa Yavugasa Kushana Katisa* which roughly translates as: *The Great King (and) Yabgu of the Kushans, Kushan Katis.* This seems to be an intermediate form, indicating he no longer saw himself as just a *yabgu* of the Kushans, but was beginning to take on royal trappings.

On his earlier coins, we find Kujula using forms of the lesser title *yavuga* (= later *yabgu*) such as: *yavugasa, yavuasa, yauasa* = 'satrap' or 'governor.'

The name *Kujula* and the title *yavuga* were used by earlier Saka rulers in India, probably indicating a close connection, possibly even a family connection, between the early Kushans and the Sakas:

"The Taxila copper-plate of the year 78 [probably of the Azes era, and, therefore, probably *circa* 31 CE, see Falk and Bennett (2009)] mentions Liaka Kusuluka, who is characterized as a *kshaharata* and as kshatrapa of Chukhsa, i.e. probably present Chachh, immediately west of Taxila.

The designation *kshaharāta* is well known from a different part of India. It is used about some members of another Saka dynasty, the so-called Western Kshatrapas of Kāṭhiāwār and Mālava. In a Nāsik inscription of the 19th year of Siri Puḷumāyi a *Khakharātavasa*, i.e. evidently *Kshaharātavaṁśa* is mentioned, and it is possible that *kshaharāta* was the name of a family or clan.

The term *kusuluka* is also known from other sources. Liaka Kusuluka is evidently the same person who has issued coins with the legend ·ΛΙΑΚΟ ΚΟΖΟΥΛΟ. These coins are imitations of those of Eucratides, but we are more justified to draw chronological conclusions from this fact than in the case of Maues.

The Greek spelling shows that the actual sound was *kuzūla*, and this *kuzūla* is possibly the name of a family, as suggested by Professor Lüders, in which case the Kuzūlas must have belonged to the larger group of the Kshaharātas.

We shall see later on that the same designation *κοζουλο* ['Kozoulo'] is used about the oldest of the Kushāṇas, who came to India not via the Indus country, but from the north-west. It is therefore probable that Liaka was descended from the ancient Saka rulers of Ki-pin, and that his family had not come to India from Seistān.

There is another detail which seems to point in the same direction. Liaka had a son, Patika, who seems to be spoken of in the copper-plate as a *jaüva*, and this *jaüva* is most probably the same title which is used by the early Kushāṇa ruler designated *Κοζουλο* in the forms *ζαοος*, and *yavuga*. We learn from Chinese sources that this title was used in a series of principalities extending from Wakhān and towards Kābul, i.e. in, and in the neighbourhood of, Ki-pin." Konow (1929), pp. xxxii-xxxiii.

"For *yabgu*, various origins have been proposed, *i.a.* Iranian, Chinese and Turkish. Latest research saw an early loan into Chinese (Sims-Williams and de la Vaissière 2007) or a late loan into Turkish (Lüders 1940: 789; Frye 1962: 356–358), with possible origins in Iranian (Frye), Tocharian, or Wusun-Yuezhi languages (cf. Sims-Williams and de la Vaissière 2007). Sogdian princes seem to carry it, written as *zhao'wu* in Chinese annals (Malyavkin 1989). Sanskrit forms in Hun inscriptions are *javūḫkha* and *jaūvkhaḥ*, if a title and not a personal name (Bühler 1892: 240 l. 10; Melzer 2006: 261). An independent form *yabuva* in Ceylonese Pali (Mahāvaṃsa 51,4) seems possible.[3]

The term was translated by Konow (1929: 27) as *jaüvañae* in the Taxila Silver Scroll of Patika, now in the British Museum, taking it as "the well-known title yavuga". However, his conclusion was erroneous, since the clear letters read *jaüvanae*, Skt. *jambuvane*, "in the Jambu woods".

After Kujula, the term *yabgu* disappears in Kuṣāṇa texts, only to re-surface in Hūṇa times, on Hephthalite coins and documents.

On Kujula's coins, *yabgu* usually specifies the Kuṣāṇas, as e.g. *khuṣaṇa-yavuga(sa)*, or ΧΟÞΑΝΟΥ ΖΑΟΟΥ. As long as Kujula used to refer to "Hermaios" on the Greek obverse, a ΣΥ ΕΡΜΑΙΟΥ makes Hermaios a ΖΑΟΣ too. Only on one issue does Kujula use the title *yavugasa ṣaaṇa*, "of the Yabgu of kings" (Falk 2006b: 148, fig. 5).

The title *yavuga/yaüa* was not used in Gandhara by any other group prior to the Kuṣāṇas. In 1996, R. Salomon read *yaguraṃña* on a silver beaker once belonging to the treasury of Kharahostes, allegedly corresponding to a hybrid title *yabgu-rāja*. My reading, however, is *egaraṃña* (Falk 2001: 311 n. 5; 2002: 86 n. 11), genitive of the well-attested title *ekarāja*, "monarch", known *i.a.* from the Arthaśāstra. In our context it really matters if this **yabgu-rāja* ever existed. If it did we would have to assume that a title from the Kuṣāṇas was adopted by an unrelated group of Śakas already in the early decades of our era. Since Kujula succeeded the Kharahostes family soon later,[4] a very close contact, friendly or inimical, can be assumed. Nonetheless, palaeography forbids[5] such an adoption for Kharahostes.[6]

4 The coins of a son of Kharahostes show a *tamka* looking like three spokes inside an interrupted circle. The same *tamka* is the only one Kujula ever uses for himself. The text reads *kharaosta-putrasa majuvriasa*, v.l. *mujavriasa*, i.e. Skt. *Mañjupriya or *Muñjapriya, still read and listed under "Hajatria" in Senior 2001: 125f. #145–148. For a synonymous *mijupria*, Skt. Mañjupriya, in the Gilgit valley cf. Fussman 1989: 7, § 2.3.

5 In his edition of 1996: 424a, Salomon read *mahakṣatrapaputrasa (ya)guraṃña khara(yo)(sta)sa*. A reading *yaguraṃña* seems hard to defend, since the alleged *ya* is pointed, with a long right leg and a short beam pointing right, and a short left leg, looking like a perfect initial *e*. The *ya* in *yo* is of a completely different shape, being wide and angular instead. What Salomon took as the *-u-mātrā* in *ga* of alleged *yagu*, is nothing but a footmark resembling a small hook downward to the left. This very same footmark is also present in the letters *kṣa, sa, ña, kha, ra, yo, sta, sa, i.e.* in almost all the letters of this short text, whereas the true *-u-mātrā* in *putra* draws a complete circle upwards.

6 Despite these paleaographical as well as lexical shortcomings, my reading *egaraṃña* was brushed aside and the hybrid "**yabgu-rāja* Kharahostes" maintained by Neelis (2007: 65, 73 n. 74 "the reading is clear"!)."

Falk (2010), p. 5. See also Salomon (1996), pp. 440-441.

This title, *yavuga*, could be originally derived from the Chinese *xihou* eventually finding its way into Turkic and other languages:

> "ιαβγο, title of Kushan kings (= Pkt. *yavuga-*, *yaüa-*, Gk. Ζαοου) < 翕侯 *xihou* 'allied prince' (EMC *xip-ɣəw*); Toch. B *yabko*, Turkish *yabγu*, etc." Sims-Williams (2002), p. 229, Table 3.

Xihou was used to denote a semi-independent ruler, 'prince,' belonging to a confederation of other tribes. It is also recorded in its Chinese form, *xihou*, as being employed by the Wusun. It came to be used for a territory, presumably one ruled by a *xihou*, much in the way we talk of a "duchy" or a "principality." See: Appendix O.

• Kujula's other Kharoṣṭhī titles

Kujula used a variety of Kharoṣṭhī titles on his coins, and not all of them have yet been adequately translated. Some of these titles are: '*dhramathida*' and 'sacadharmathida' and '*satya-dharma-sthitasya*'.

On some of his coins Kujula Kadphises featured a humped zebu bull which is often used as a symbol for the Hindu god, Śiva. However, Baldev Kumar (1973), p. 33, states that he had, "adopted Buddhism as his religion." He gives as evidence: "The title "Dharmathida" (Skt. Dharmasthita = stead-fast in faith), and "Sachadharmathida" (Skt. *Satyadharmasthita* = steadfast in true faith) are essentially Buddhist epithets."

As the word *dharma* was used by Hindus, Buddhists, and Jains (albeit with slightly different implications in each religion), these titles can hardly be used to bolster the case for one religion over the other.

The Sanskrit term: *dharmasthiti or dharmasthita* is translated by Monier-Williams, p. 512b, as: "f. the constant nature of Dharma." In ibid. p. 1136a, he gives for *satyadharma*: "m. the law of truth, eternal truth. . . ; mfn. one whose ordinances are true." Another translation of this term could be: "Steadfast in the Law."

Harry Falk (personal communication, 19 November 2006) explains the title on the coins of Vima Kadphises as Sanskrit '*satya-dharma-sthitasya*' which, "simply means 'steadfast in the law of the truth', something asked for from all kings in all the Dharmaśāstras."

Therefore, it is impossible to say if Kujula was trying to indicate support for Hinduism, Buddhism or Jainism, or whether he was trying to make his coins appeal to them all.

• Sadaṣkaṇa - another son of Kujula.

The only known reference to Sadaṣkaṇa, the son of Kujula, is in the lengthy gold-leaf dedicatory inscription of Senavarma, one of the kings of Oḍi (probably Uḍḍiyāna/modern Swat). See: note 13.16.

To date there have been four translations of this Kharoṣṭhī inscription into European languages. The first was by H. W. Bailey, "A Kharoṣṭhī Inscription of Senavarma, King of Oḍi." *JRAS*, 1980/1, pp. 21-29. This was followed by Fussman (1982), and by Salomon (1986), while the most recent translation can be found on page 29 of von Hinüber (2001), who transcribes the passage which refers to Sadaṣkaṇa as:

> **"8g maharajarayatirayakuyula*kataphsa*putro *sadaṣkaṇo*devaputro**
> **9a. sadha aṇakaena *suhasomeṇa* aṣmaṇakareṇa**
> **9b. sayuga-savalavahaṇa sadha guśurakehi sturakehi ca puyita.**
>
> mahārājarājātirājakujulakataphsaputraḥ sadaṣkaṇo devaputraḥ saha anaṅkayena sutasomena aṣmanakareṇa sayuga-sabalavāhena saha guśurakaiḥ stūrakaiś ca pūjitaḥ"

Although none of the translators has been able to satisfactorily render the latter part of this short passage, which apparently lists some of Sadaṣkaṇa's retinue, war animals and equipment, there is no disagreement about the first part of the passage that may be confidently rendered:

> "May the son of the Great King, the King of Kings, Kujula Kataphtsa, Sadaṣkaṇa, Devaputra (Son of the Gods) . . . be honoured."

From this it is logical to assume that Senavarma, King of Oḍi was subservient to Kujula and that Kujula's son, Sadaṣkaṇa, was active while his father, Kujula, was still alive.

Whether or not Sadaṣkaṇa and Wima Tak[tu] were brothers or half-brothers, or which of them (if either) issued the famous 'Soter Megas' coinage, still awaits further finds. According to the Rabatak inscription we can be certain that Wima Tak[tu] was the father of Vima Kadphises and the grandfather of Kanishka.

- **'Soter Megas,' the so-called 'Nameless King' = Vema Takhtu**

> "This article tries to assemble all the known spellings of the name of the second king of the Kuṣāṇas. For its title "vema takhtu" was selected, the version which I would propose to use, since it can be shown to be the source of a wide range of variant forms in several languages, including *takho, tako, taktu, takhtuasa, takṣumasya,* TAKTOO and TAKΔOOY." Falk (2009), p. 105.

> ". . . both Wema Kadphises and the Nameless King used the title Soter Megas (lit. 'the Great Saviour'), but while the former calls himself Basileus Basileon (King of Kings), the latter describes himself as Basileus Basileuon (Reigning King), the participle indicating a subordinate rank." Kumar (1973), p. 43.

The varying forms of the titles make MacDowall's theory that the "Soter Megas" coins were a late issue of Kujula unlikely. See: MacDowell (2002), pp. 164-169. Moreover, the youthful looking profiles on many "Soter Megas" coins support the theory that they did not represent Kujula, but one of his sons, presumably Wema Tak[tu] or, possibly, Sadaṣkaṇa .

> "Gold gave to Eucratides new support for revolting successfully against Demetrios II. But it was not an easy conquest. Demetrios II was a young man but, as suggested by Justin, as main king he certainly controlled the main armed forces of Bactria. Justin (XLI, 6, 4) tells how Eucratides was besieged for three months with only 300 soldiers by an army of 60,000 and could resist and escape. He finally conquered Demetrios II, and took the title of Megas. This expression 'Great King' had a special meaning in Greek: it was, since the Medic wars, the way to call the Achaemenid king ([3]).
>
> ([3]) It may be related to the adoption of the same epiclese *Megas* by the contemporary and rival Arsacid king Mithradates I, but the uncertainties in chronology does not allow to be sure it happened before or after Eucratides did it."
>
> Widemann (2007), pp. 14-15.

> "Vema Takhtu as an individual king of the Kuṣāṇa lineage became known as such only after the Bactrian inscription from Rabatak was edited by the jubilarian.[2] Seeing him mentioned as son of Kujula Kadphises and father of Vima Kadphises the question of his coinage arose. Kujula's various emissions have been well known for long, as were those of Vima Kadphises. Since it has likewise been known for a long time that the widely distributed coinage of an anonymous *sōtēr megas* comes in between Kujula and Vima Kadphises, it was natural to assume that Vema Takhtu is none other than *sōtēr megas* himself. CRIBB was the first to say so and thus paved the way out of many a calamity.[3] MAC DOWALL provided a reason for the irritating anonymity, by pointing[4] to the parallel behaviour of Octavian, who called himself "Caesar Augustus, *divi filius,*

Imperator" after his victory in 31 BC. The title *devaputra*, introduced in the last years of Kujula, also derives from this haloed antetype.[5] The regular succession from *sōtēr megas* to Vima Kadphises becomes obvious through a look at the metrology of the coinage, where Vima Kadphises adds his heavy copper issue weighing 17 grams to the retained volume of issues of *sōtēr megas*, weighing 2.1 and 8.5 grams in their standard forms.[6] The coinage of his father and predecessor is thus supplemented and not replaced by Vima Kadphises, a fact confirmed by numerous coin hoards where the coppers of both kings occurs side by side.

With the Rabatak genealogy at hand it was also possible to attribute successfully a series of coins where *vema* was read before, but where the letters forming *takho* had remained enigmatic.

2 Sims-Williams 1996, pp. 652–654; 1998, pp. 81–83; Sims-Williams/Cribb 1995–1996.
3 Cf. Göbl, who otherwise saw clearly that Kujula was the grandfather of Vima Kadphises, wrote in 1976, p. 51: "Since the coins of Soter Megas form the only available material to fill the numismatic gap between Kujula and Vima [Kadphises HF], only he can be, in my opinion, the famous Ch'iu-chiu-ch'üeh [= Kujula! HF] of the Chinese source."
4 Mac Dowall 2002, p. 167 b.
5 Mac Dowall, *ibid*."

Falk (2009), pp. 105-106.

• The Chinese title *gaozhen* 高珍 used for Vema Takhtu

The Yuezhi/Kushan king, and son of Qiujiuque (Kujula Kadphises), is called: 閻高珍 Yan Gaozhen in the *Hou Hanshu*. From the Rabatak Inscription and coins we know his name as Vima Takt[o] or Vima Takh[tu] – the final syllable is not clear.

The Chinese character Yan 閻, is commonly used to represent the Indo-Iranian god Yima/Yama as well as Sanskrit *ya(m) and ja(m)*. However, it is not clear if or how this character may be related to the personal name Wema/Vima.

> "閻 **yán MC yem** . . . .
> **2.** (Budd) ~淳提 *yánfútí* (MC yem-bjuw-dej), trsc. of Skt. *Jambudvīpa*, continent situated south of Mt. Sumeru; ~羅 *yánluó* (MC yem-la), trsc. of Skt. *Yama*, name of god of the dead, regent of hell." Kroll (2015), p. 527.

However, Professor Nicholas Sims-Williams has pointed out to me that neither '*w*' or '*v*' in Bactrian or any other Persian language, would be represented by a '*y*' in Chinese – so he considers this interpretation was very unlikely.

The second character of the Chinese name or title, 高珍 *gaozhen*, appears to be either an honorary title given by the Chinese, or a translation of a foreign title:

> Gao 高 can mean: "tall; high; superior; excellent; eminent; sublime; noble; to honour or to respect." *GR* Vol. III, No. 5891. Kroll (2015), p. 129 adds:
>
> "**1.** Tall; high, lofty; elevated. **2.** Lofty in character or reputation, eminent, exalted; high-minded."
>
> Zhen 珍, according to *GR* Vol. I, p. 301, means: 'treasure,' 'precious,' 'beautiful,' 'excellent'; 'perfect'; 'rare'. Kroll (2015), p. 598 gives:
>
> "**1.** Precious, esp. because of rarity (cf. 寶 *bǎo*, precious, treasured, because of value or importance.
> **a.** exquisite, fine, admirable.
> **2.** rare, rarity; choice, select, nonpareil, of unusual quality or provenance.
> **3.** prize, value, esteem, regard as special. . . ."

The title could, therefore, mean something like: *His Excellency*; *Honourable Precious (One)*; or *Noble Treasure*. Refer to note 13.16. Thus, the Chinese name Yangaozhen might tentatively be rendered as something like: "We(ma) the Excellent."

On the other hand, Harry Falk suggests that *Gaozhen* may have been an attempt to phonetically transcribe a form of Wema's title, *kuṣāṇa* or *guṣāṇa*:

> "It seems possible that the Chinese envoys heard about the history of the five tribes of the Yüe Chi, including the Kuṣāṇas, spelled Kuei-Shuang (貴霜), from one source and about the ruling king in India, i.e. Vema Kuṣāṇa, from another, without realizing that both terms contain a common element. Spelling variations are more or less the rule when it comes to Indian place names in early Chinese literature. A further spelling variation in Chinese regarding the Kuṣāṇas would not surprise given the many ways Kuṣāṇa names occur even in Indian sources. Although *kuṣāṇa* or *khuṣāṇa* (Taxila silver scroll) is the most common Kharoṣṭhī spelling for the family name, another informant may have used *guṣāṇa*, as the name is spelled in Panjtar, Manikiala or Kamra. Since the form Vema Kuṣā<ṇa> was actually used at Dasht-e Nāwur by the Kharoṣṭhī scribe, this occasional variant address, when pronounced *vema guṣāṇa*, may well have lead to *yen gao chen*, if we presuppose diffent [*sic*] informants with different spelling habits." Falk (2009), p. 114.

At first look, the modern pinyin form *gaozhen* suggests a plausible reconstructed pronunciation for *kuṣāṇa* or *guṣāṇa*, but an examination of the reconstructions make it look less likely as reconstructed Han pronunciations suggest something like: '*kawtingi*' or '*kawtrin*,' It is impossible at this stage to say that either theory is definitive.

• Vema Takhtu (and Takshama?)

There is no satisfactory explanation of the names or titles: "Takhtu" and "Takshama," so far, nor can we be certain they refer to the same king.

The names are reminiscent of (but not definitely connected to), the name of the important city and kingdom of Taxila (ancient forms: Greek Τάξιλα, Gāndhārī *Taksaïla*, Sanskrit *Takṣaśilā*, Pali *Takkasilā*), and also that of *Ta-kṣa-ka* (Skt. *Takṣaka*), the name of a *nāga*-king mentioned in the Khotanese Buddhist "history," the so-called 'Prophecy of the Li Country.' See: Emmerick (1967), pp. 39 and 96, or 'The Annals of the Li Country,' and: Thomas (1935), p. 113; Salomon (2005), p. 265.

• Vema Kadphises' titles

Vema Kadphises issued large quantities of copper, gold, and some silver coins. The images and Kharoṣṭhī legends on his coins are difficult to interpret.

All of Vema Kadphises' coins depict a god with an erect penis on the reverse. The lingam is usually associated with Śiva - or his bull, and/or representations of other attributes and symbols commonly associated with Śiva, such as a trident or trident-axe, water pot, thunderbolt, lion skin, and what is possibly a hoof-print symbol. Cribb (1997), pp. 46-47.

> "The bull was considered as the theriomorphic form ['animal form of'] as well as the mount of the god Śiva. If the suggestion that a statement of Hesychius alludes to the bull as the god of Gandhāra[18] is found acceptable, it may be interpreted as indicating Śiva was worshipped in that area, which included Pushkalāvatī [modern Chārsada].
>
> 18. See K. A. Nilakanta Sastri (editor), *A Comprehensive History of India*, vol. II, p. 400."
>
> Mukherjee (1969), p. 73.

Vema's coins have Greek legends (in the nominative case) on the obverse and Kharoṣṭhī (in the possessive case) on the reverse. The most common Kharoshṭḥī legend has usually been read as:

Maharajasa Rajadirajasa Sarvaloga Iśvarasa Maheśvarasa Vvima Kathpisasa Tratarasa

The title *Maheśvarasa* may be interpreted in several ways, so this legend can be translated as either:

— *(Of the) Great King, King of Kings, Universal Monarch, Śiva Devotee Vvima Kadphises, the Protector.*

— *(Of the) Great King, King of Kings, Universal Monarch, the Great Lord Vvima Kadphises, the Protector.*

In Sanskrit, *mahêśvara,* means: 'a great lord, sovereign, chief; a god, while the principal meanings of the similar and closely related title *māheśvara* (from *māhêśvara*) means: 'of or relating to Śiva.' (See: Monier-Williams, pp. 802b, 815b).

In the Kharoṣṭhī script used for the local Gandharan Prakrit of the time, there were no long vowel signs, such as the Sanskrit *ā*, so it is impossible to determine which of the two forms of the Sanskrit word was intended in Vima Kadphises' coin inscriptions.

However, Harold Falk said (personal communication 19 November 2006) that he has re-examined a number examples of these coins and they: "ALL read mahiśvarasa and this is not referring to maheśvara = Śiva, it exclusively means "lord of the earth", a title Vema assumes for himself (and, by the way, a VERY common title in India, used by kings, some much inferior to the Great Kushans). Medial -i and -e cannot be mistaken if written properly as on Vima's coins." He therefore transcribes and translates the legend as:

mahrajasa rajatirajasa sarvaloga-iśvarasa mahiśvarasa vvima-kaphthiśasa tradara

'of the Great King, King of Kings, Lord of all worlds, Lord of the earth, Vvima-Kaphthiśa' [i.e.] the saviour'

Falk adds:

"There is nothing irrefutably shivaite in the words of this text.

The interpretation of Īśvara as 'Lord' or 'King,' and Mahīśvara as: 'the Lord of the earth', makes them more compatible with other Kushan titles of the period – none of which, to my knowledge, specify that a king or emperor was a 'devotee' of a particular god.

The title *īśvara*, with the meaning of "Lord," is also found in the name of the famous Buddhist deity representing compassion, Avalokiteśvara. For a discussion of the translation of this name (i.e. 'Lord Avalokit') into Chinese, see Brough (1970b), pp. 83-84.

The images on Wima's coins have proved to be more difficult to interpret than the legends.

The same god is portrayed "on coins of each Kushan king from Wima Kadphises through to Vasudeva II, together with the representations of most of these kings making an identifiable act of worship of the god, or holding one of his attributes . . . ." Cribb (1997), p. 28.

On some coins of Kanishka I, Huvishka, and the later Kushans this god is named OHÞO ('Oesho' or 'Wesho' with variants OOHÞO or OHÞA), the name of a Bactrian god.

Of interest, on at least two examples of Kanishka's early issues, a Greek inscription on the dies, apparently naming the god as HPAKAHΣ (Heracles), were overcut with the Bactrian name OHÞO. It is worth noting that the animal skin featured (a lion's or tiger's?) is also reminiscent of Heracles. Cribb (1997), p. 36.

> Other aspects of the symbology (particularly the bull and trident), certainly seem to indicate a connection with Śiva, although he is not actually named as such."

To make sense of this confusing picture one might assume that the images are composites of the three gods and may represent a deliberate attempt to appeal to various ethnic groups and religions within the Kushan dominions, especially Greek, Bactrian and Indian.

- **Vāsudeva I**

Vasudeva is the only one of the "Great Kushan" kings to have had a distinctly Indian name – it is the name of the father of Krishna, the popular Hindu god.

According to the epigraphic evidence available, Vasudeva I ruled from years 64 to 98 of Kanishka's era, or from 191 to at least 225 CE. The last named inscription of his predecessor, Huvishka, is dated 60 (or 187 CE). Vāsudeva's coins bear the legend BAZOΔHO ("Bazodēo") in Graeco-Bactrian script. The *Sanguozhi* 三國志 *Weizhi* 3.6a under the 12th month of the 3rd Taihe year, says that:

> "On the Guimao day (26 January, 230 CE), the king of the Da Yuezhi, Bodiao (波調) sent an embassy with tribute. (Bo)diao was endowed with the title of 'King of the Da Yuezhi, Affectionate towards the Wei'." Also, consult Zürcher (1968), p. 371.

Vāsudeva is the final Kushan emperor mentioned in the Chinese sources, and the fragmentation of the Kushan Empire began soon after his rule ended. He was the last of the "Great Kushan kings." The end of his reign coincided almost exactly with the break-up of the Han Empire into three kingdoms, and the destruction of Parthian power by the Sasanians to the west.

Appendix R: *Qingbi* = Azurite/Lapis lazuli?

The *qingbi* 青碧 mentioned here in the *Hou Hanshu*, probably refers to azurite, a blue pigment used for paintings and in traditional Chinese medicine.

Azurite is thought to have been the only natural blue pigment used in ancient China. However, the identification is not certain, and *qingbi* may also possibly refer to ultramarine – a pigment made from lapis lazuli, which is often confused with azurite. See: note 12.10.

The common word, 青 *qing*, means 'blue' or 'green,' and is regularly used to describe the colour of the sky or sea.

The second character, 碧 *bi*, as a 'bound form,' means 'bluish/emerald green,' 'azure,' or a 'green stone'. In this context, though, it should probably be read as a noun with 青 *qing* as a qualifier or adjective describing the colour.

The *ABC* dictionary p. 39, gives for 碧 *bi*, as a noun in *wenyan* (文言), or 'classical language': 'green jade'; 'jasper'. The *OCD*, p. 39 gives: A. 'green jade.' *GR*, Vol. IV, p. 986 gives (translated from the French:

> "**1.** *Name* of a green-blue stone, resembling jade; **nephrite**; jasper. **2. Blue-green**, green jade, jade blue; azure [colour]. Azure [adjective]." See also: Kroll (2015), p. 18.

GR, Vol. IV, p. 986, interestingly, gives for the reverse form *biqing* 碧青: "(*Chinese painting*) Blue-green colour (derived from azurite)."

> "Azurite, like malachite, is formed by the weathering of other copper minerals. The copper gives its basic colour, but the presence of water in the crystal helps it turn bright blue rather than green. It was this brilliant blue that made it so popular with painters in the Renaissance as a pigment. It probably gets its name from *lazhward*, the ancient Persian word for 'blue' and in the past it was often confused with blue lapis lazuli and lazurite." Farndon (2006), p. 175.

Qingbi 青碧 is defined in the *OCD*, pt. II, p. 591 as: 1. 'dark green' and, 2. 'azure.' Azure is a deep blue pigment made from azurite (or its colour) and is often confused with ultramarine, the pigment derived from lapis lazuli. Qingbi may very well represent either, but it *could* instead refer to practically any other green or blue stone.

> "The ancient Chinese revered azurite as the *Stone of Heaven*, able to open spiritual doorways." Downloaded from: http://gemologyonline.com/azurite.html, 9 March 2012.

There is an interesting article in English discussing the varying forms of azurite found in China and their uses. It includes a large number of Chinese names. While it does not specifically mention q*ingbi* 青碧 – it does mention some obviously related names, such as: "*Bishiqing*, 碧石青 [gem stone blue] An indefinite substance from azurite." Downloaded from: http://www.chinamatters.nl/chinamatters.nl/Minerals/Entries/2010/5/11_Azurite,_qing,_qing.html on 30 March 2012.

Chavannes (1907), p. 182, n. 5, accepts Geert's identification of *qingbi* as a type of blue-green jasper. Nevertheless, in the context of Roman trade at this period, it more probably refers to azurite, which was already being used as a pigment in paintings by the Romans in the 1st century CE, if not earlier. Pliny (XXXV.12) refers to it as a 'florid pigment' called *armenium*. Siddall (2006), p. 21. However, other sources refer to *armenium* as ultramarine, which is derived from lapis lazuli:

> "It appears that ultramarine (lapis lazuli) was known to the ancients under the name of Armenium, 'Αρμένιον, from Armenia, whence it was procured." Wornam (1875), p. 321.

"*. . . a fine blue color, derived from an Armenian stone, ultramarine . . . .*" *LD* (1875), p. 163.

"Azurite's primary use since prehistoric times has been as a pigment. . . .

The ancient Chinese were also familiar with natural deposits of azurite and malachite. Detailed observations of malachite in nodular form with large holes and in stratified form with azurite have been found in Chinese texts dating to about 400 B.C.E. (Needham 1974). Azurite was used in wall paintings of the Song (960-1279) and Ming (1368-1644) dynasties and remains a commonly used pigment in Chinese art today.

Azurite was the most important blue pigment in Europe beginning in the Middle Ages, particularly from the fourteenth to the seventeenth century. In easel painting, azurite was often used as an underpainting for natural ultramarine. Germany was the principal supplier of azurite during the sixteenth century, with mines in Saxony, Tyrol, and Saarland; the last source was known from Roman times (Burmester and Krekel 1998)." Scott (2002), pp. 108-109.

"Following Wu-ti's conquest of Nan-yüeh in 111 B.C., southern overseas trade gradually extended to countries in Southeast Asia and the Indian Ocean which, in exchange for Chinese gold and silks, sent pearls, jade, lapis lazuli, and glass." Nishijima (2008), pp. 579-580.

"Blue pigments also played a special role in the history of China. Chinese Blue and Purple, also termed Han Blue and Purple (FitzHugh, 1992), which are chemically related to, but nevertheless different from Egyptian Blue appeared in China during the Warring States period about 500 B. C. Their presence in China must be taken as a strong indication of very high technical and scientific levels of skill in ancient Chinese civilization. Chinese Blue and Purple differ from Egyptian Blue in that they lack calcium, and are instead solid barium copper silicate compounds with defined chemical compositions (FitzHugh, 1983; FitzHugh, 1992; Wiedemann, 1997a: 145; Wiedemann, 1997b: 379):

Chinese Blue: $BaCuSi_4O_{10}$ brilliant blue
Chinese Purple: $BaCuSi_2O_6$ bluish purple

As can be seen from their composition, both compounds differ chemically in quartz content, a fact that is of great importance for their synthesis. It should be mentioned that BaCuSi4O10 is found as a mineral, effenbergerite, recently discovered in the Kalahari Manganese Field, South Africa (Giester, 1994). It is, however, so rare in nature that any cultural significance of the mineral can be ruled out." Berke and Wiedemann (2000), pp. 95-96. See also: Kakoulli (2007), p. 84.

"One of the world's oldest concentrations of lapis paintings is in the Kizil caves, 80 kilometers (50 mi) or so from the Silk Road trading town of Kucha in China's Xinjiang Province. Beginning as early as the third century, upward of 5000 Buddhist monks, occupying a thousand caves in the cliffs above the Muzat River, vibrantly depicted parables, called the Jataka tales, which trace the life of the Buddha. Teacher-disciples known as *bodhisattvas,* dancers and winged musicians are all portrayed in brilliant lapis hues." Covington (2013), p. 34.

"As mentioned before, natural stable blue pigments are rare. Among them, the most stable and valuable was lapis lazuli (Reinen, 1999), which was mined in the Antique World in areas of today's Afghanistan. To the best of our knowledge lapis lazuli was not found in China. Ancient China's demand for blue pigment was apparently mainly satisfied, apart from by Chinese Blue, by the minerals azurite (a basic copper carbonate), cobalt oxide (in glasses and glazes) and perhaps also to a certain extent by indigo blue, nowadays referred to as Maya Blue (José-Yacaman, 1996), since it was extensively produced and used by native American cultures. The quite abundant mineral azurite was mined in ancient China largely for the production of copper and copper based alloys (Golas, 1999, pp. 58 ff.). Azurite is relatively unstable and deteriorates in the open air, and even in a protected environment it tends to slowly transform into the more stable green mineral malachite. All these minerals for producing blue pigments were not easily available for widespread use due to various severe specific disadvantages. This lack of appropriate blue minerals from natural resources, which not only applied specifically to China but also to other places in the world, was presumably the motivation behind China's and mankind's search for self-made blue pigments displaying improved properties over those derived from mineral sources." Berke and Wiedemann (2000), p. 96.

"Commenting on some of Zhang's [Zhang Sengyou, active *circa* 490–540] paintings in a temple at Nanjing, a Tang author wrote: "All over the gate of the temple 'flowers-in-relief' are painted . . . Such flowers are done in a technique brought here from India. They are painted in Vermillion, malachite greens, and azure blues." Sullivan (2000), p. 178.

"The general's son, **Li Chao-tao** (*c.* 675-740 ?), though known as Little General Li, had no military rank, his position being that of Under-Secretary to the Heir-Apparent. As a painter, therefore, he was a non-professional like Li Ssu-hsün, and no less celebrated than his father for colourful 'blue-and-green' landscapes, often heightened with gold contours and abounding with fine detail. . . . But the hall-mark of this school is a combination that is always present—in the mountains and cliffs, rocks and terrain—of two mineral pigments : azurite blue and malachite green. The blue may be intense and dark ; the green is usually bright and fresh." Loehr (1980), p. 64.

• Could *qingbi* have been lapis lazuli?

Although the evidence points to azurite as the probable product indicated here by *qingbi* 青碧, we have seen in the quotes above that it was sometimes confused with ultramarine, the pigment produced from lapis lazuli. I have gathered information together on lapis lazuli and ultramarine. Also, see: Appendix T on the joining of the ancient jade and lapis lazuli routes.

The confusion between azurite (azure) and lapis lazuli and the pigment derived from it, ultramarine, is very common and has even entered scholarly literature:

"The real home of lapis lazuli was salubrious and well-pastured Badakhshan, its ancient and classical source. Here in the valley of the Kokcha, a branch of the Oxus River, the mineral azure, sometimes fine indigo-blue, sometimes pale blue, sometimes green or gray, was chopped out of its limestone matrix." Schafer (1963), p. 231.

"Ultramarine is a very fine blue powder, almost of the colour of the corn-flower or blue-bottle, which has this uncommon property, that, when exposed to the air or a moderate heat, it neither fades nor becomes tarnished. On this account it is used in painting; but it was employed formerly for that purpose much more than at present, as smalt, a far cheaper article, was not then known. It is made of the blue parts of the lapis lazuli, by separating them as much as possible from the other coloured particles with which they are mixed, and reducing them to a fine powder." Beckmann (1846), p. 467.

"Though the ancient names of precious stones have neither been examined with sufficient accuracy nor distinguished with the greatest possible certainty, I think I can discover among them lapis lazuli. I consider it as the sapphire of the ancients, and this opinion has been entertained by others; but I hope to render it more probable than it has hitherto appeared. In the first place, the sapphire of the Greeks and Romans was of a sky-blue colour with a violet of almost blackish-blue colour. Secondly this stone was not transparent. Thirdly, it had in it a great many gold points, or golden-yellow spots, but that which had fewest was most esteemed. Fourthly, it was polished and cut; but when it was not perfectly pure, and had mixed with it extraneous particles, it was not fit for the hands of the lapidary. Fifthly, it appears that it was procured in such large pieces that it could be employed for inlaid or mosaic-work. Sixthly, it was often confounded with, or compared to, copper-blue, copper-ore, and earth and stones impregnated with that metal. Seventhly, such medicinal effects were ascribed to it as could be possessed only by a copper salt; and lastly, it formed veins in rocks of other kinds of stone, as we are informed by Dionysius[1].

That a stone with these properties cannot be the sapphire of our jewellers is beyond all doubt. Our real sapphire does not form veins in other fossils, but is found among sand in small crystals, shaped like diamonds; although they sometimes have rather the figure of columns. Like other precious stones, they are always transparent; they have never got gold points in them; their blue colour resembles more or less that of blue velvet, and it is often very pale, and approaches seldom, or very little, to purple. Powder of sapphire appears like fine powdered glass, exhibits no trace of copper, and can in no manner produce a blue pigment, or be confounded with mountain-blue. . . .

On the other hand, we can affirm with the greatest certainty, that the sapphire of the ancients was our lapis lazuli. The latter is of a blue colour, which inclines sometimes to violet or purple, and which is often very dark. It is altogether opake, yet its colour will admit of being compared to a sky-colour; in mentioning of which Pliny had no idea of transparency, for he compares the colour of an opake jasper to a sky-blue. The lapis-lazuli is interspersed with small points, which were formerly considered as gold, but which are only particles of pyrites or marcasite. It can be easily cut and formed into articles of various kinds, and at present it is often used for seals. Pliny, however, informs us that it was not fit for this purpose when it was mixed with hard foreign particles, such as quartz; and that which was of one colour was therefore much more esteemed. Many cut stones of this kind, which are considered as antiques, may be found in collections. . . . The sapphire also mentioned in the oldest writings of the Hebrews, appears to be no other than the sapphire of the Greeks, or our lapis lazuli; for it was said likewise to be interspersed with gold points.

[1] See Plin. lib. xxxvii. cap. 9 and 10.—Isidori Orig. xvi. 9.—Throphrast. de Lapid. § 43.—Dioscorides, v. 157.—Dionys. Orb. Desc. v. 1195.—Epiphanius de xii gemmis, § 5.—Marbodeus de Lapidibus, 53, p. 46."

Beckmann (1846), pp. 469-472.

Lapis lazuli or lazurite has been mined since very ancient times in the rugged mountainous region south of Jurm at Sar-i Sang in Badakhshan, in Afghanistan. This mine has remained the world's main source of high quality lapis lazuli ever since.

The *Oxford Chinese Dictionary* (2010), p. 426, gives under **lapis lazuli**: 1. (gem) 杂青金石; 2. (pigment) 天青石颜料; (colour) 天青石色.

Lapis lazuli was never as popular in China as it was in Mesopotamia and Egypt – its place as a valued blue stone is overtaken by jade or turquoise. In fact, we do not know the early Chinese name for this gemstone and there are various interpretations of later names, making the identification in early sources next to impossible. However, it was not unknown in early China, being found at various archaeological sites, for example:

> "There is a lapis lazuli cicada of late Chou [770-256 BCE] in the British Museum (from the Eumorfopoulos Collection); if the raw material came all the way from Badakhshan, it is a remarkable instance of the extent of ancient trade relations, before the opening of the "silk routes" through Serindia." Schafer (1963), pp. 333-334, n. 92.

> "The role of lapis lazuli in Far Eastern civilization has been a mystery, largely because no Chinese word for the mineral could be identified in texts earlier than the Mongol period. It now appears that the word *se-se* (Ancient Chinese **ṣɒt- ṣɒt*) [瑟瑟], given to deep blue gemstones by the men of T'ang, usually meant "lapis lazuli" (lazurite), but sometimes the blue feldspathoid "sodalite," which is hardly to be distinguished from it, and occasionally even "sapphire." The argument for the identification will be suppressed here to a longish note, but in what follows, all reference to lapis lazuli based on *Chinese* sources assumes the correctness of the identification." Schafer (1963), pp. 230-231.

However, this proposed identification of *sese* with lapis lazuli is suspect. *Sese* 瑟瑟 is defined in the *GR*, Vol. V, p. 70, as: "2. (*Jade – anc.*) Name of a jade-green precious stone" (translated by author); *ABC*, p. 796 as "① trembling (of a person) ② turquoise."

> "**瑟 sè MC srit . . . .**
> **4.** Rdup. [reduplicated] onom. Soughing and sighing of wind, esp. in autumn; also (med.) [medieval] a blue-gem, mostly lapis lazuli with some sodalite and possibly sapphire > deep-blue color, deep azure, lapis-blue." Kroll (2015), p. 397.

> "The most conspicuous of the [Buddhist] Seven Treasures in the ruins of Yongning [Pagoda in Luoyang – built in 516 CE] was lapis lazuli. In the ancient world, this dark blue stone had already been a highly valued commodity for 2,000 years. Since one of the Mahayana Buddhist texts had described the hair of the Buddha as the color of lapis lazuli, Buddhist artists used a pigment made by grinding the lapis lazuli stone into a powder, from which they made blue pigments in order to paint the hair of the Buddha and, in some places, even that of the bodhisattvas and other heavenly beings. From the cave murals in Central Asia to the cave sculptures in China, the hair of the Buddha was consistently painted in this lapis lazuli blue. From the time of the Kushan Empire, this shade of blue became the most notable color in all Buddhist art." Liu and Shaffer (2007), p. 116.

> "金精 *kin tsiṅ* [pinyin: *jinjing*] ("essence of gold") appears to have been the term for lapis lazuli during the T'ang period. The stone came from the famous mines of Badaxšān.
>
> At the time of the Yüan or Mongol dynasty a new word for lapis lazuli springs up in the form *lan-č'i* 蘭赤. The Chinese traveller Č'aṅ Te, who was despatched in 1259 as envoy by the Mongol Emperor Mangu to his brother Hulagu, King of Persia, and whose diary, the *Si ši ki*, was edited by Liu Yu in 1263, reports that a stone of that name is found on the rocks of the mountains in the south-western countries of Persia. The word *lan-č'i* is written with two characters meaning "orchid" and "red," which yields no sense; and BRETSCHNEIDER is therefore right in concluding that the two elements represent the transcription of a foreign name. He is inclined to think that "it is the same as *landshiwer*, the Arabic name for lapis lazuli. In New Persian it is *lāšvard* or *lājvard* (Arabic *lāsvard*). Another Arabic form *lanjiver* is not known to me.

"There is also in the same country [Badakshan] another mountain, in which azure is found; 'tis the finest in the world, and is got in a vein like silver. There are also other mountains which contain a great amount of silver ore, so that the country is a very rich one." Thus runs Marco Polo's account. YULE comments as follows: "The mines of Lájwurd (whence l'Azur and Lazuli) have been, like the ruby mines, celebrated for ages. They lie in the upper valley of the Kokcha, called Korán, within the tract called Yamgán, of which the popular etymology is Hamah-Kán, or 'All Mines,' and were visited by Wood in 1838. The produce now is said to be of very inferior quality, and in quantity from thirty to sixty pud (thirty-six lbs. each) annually. The best quality sells in Bokhara at thirty to sixty tillas, or 12 *l.* to 24 *l.* the pud (Manphúl). In the Dictionary of Four Languages, lapis lazuli is styled *ts'iṅ kin ši* 青金石; in Tibetan *mu-men*, Mongol and Manchu *nomin*." Laufer (1919), pp. 520-521. [Note: Kroll (2015), p. 213 defines 金精 as: "*jīnjīng*, "germ of gold," realgar, orpiment . . . ."]

The common Chinese terms for ultramarine (the pigment made from lapis lazuli), include 群青, 海外的, and 佛青色.

"The first noted use of the stone [lapis lazuli] as a pigment can be seen in sixth and seventh century AD cave paintings in Afghanistan temples where the stone was most predominantly mined. Lapis Lazuli ultramarine pigment has also been found in some Chinese paintings dating from the tenth and eleventh centuries AD and in a few Indian murals dating from the eleventh, twelfth and seventeenth centuries AD. Italian painters of the fourteenth through the fifteenth centuries AD used the brilliant ultramarine color to complement their vermilion and gold illuminated manuscripts and panel paintings." "Lapis Lazuli Used as a Pigment." Downloaded 8 March 2011 from: http://academic.emporia.edu/abersusa/go340/students/haltom/pigment.htm .

The English name is derived from Arabic *lāzaward*, *lāzuward* 'lapis lazuli', 'blue'; *via* Persian *lāzhuward*, for 'blue.' Lapis lazuli is the source of the pigment, ultramarine.

"This was BADAKHSĀN, Afghanistan's northernmost province, and one of its wildest. Eskāzer lay at the junction of three valleys. One headed southwest along the route we had followed back to Panjshīr. Another led east via Kerān o Monjān to Pakistan (via Zeebak and its lung-splitting pass), Tajikistan (via Ishkashem on the river Panj), and China (via the Wakhān corridor). The other led north, following the Monjan river, via the ruby and lapis mines, to Faizābad. . . .

That inimitably coloured stone, lapis lazuli, has been mined in the Monjan valley for centuries, millennia perhaps; the mines are certainly pre-Islamic and the mountains are peppered with tunnels. During the war the stone was an important source of revenue. Mujaheddin carried it over the high passes to Pakistan to raise money for weapons. Today there is none of the equipment to cut and polish the stone, so it is carried out on horseback in raw lumps. The best stone is a pure and striking cyanic blue; inferior pieces are flecked with calcite, the crystalline matrix in which the stone is found, or iron pyrite that resembles gold.

Halfway up the mountain about a mile away was a black spot like the entrance to a cave. A procession of ant-like shapes was toiling up and down a thousand feet of zigzagging track that spilled from it; men and animals making their way from the mine to the village below, and back. It was a faintly sinister sight, as if we had uncovered some primitive and demonic industry hidden from the eyes of the ordinary population.

A creaking bridge of poplars crossed the river below the village, and a track led upwards towards a corral where a flock of miserable beasts of burden gathered in forlorn huddles. There we left Clockwork among his own to rest from the day's trials, entrusted my bag to the keeper of the local *serai*, and set off to cruise the main street, Ma'dān. The first thing I noticed about the place was the ground; all around us were lumps of white stone veined with blue streaks of the gem, each one a treasure but worthless in the garden of their original home." Elliot (1999), pp. 177-179.

"Lapis lazuli is one of the oldest, most treasured of all gemstones. Its name is a combination of the Latin *lapis* for 'stone' and the Arabic *azul* for 'sky' or the Persian *lazhuward* for 'blue'. It usually occurs as lenses and veins in white marble. Consisting largely of lazurite with spots of pyrite, it has a mottled look. Crystals are sometimes found, but more usually it is massive, and is carved to make jewellery, cups and other decorative objects. It was first mined over 6,000 years ago at Sar-e-Sang in the Kokcha valley in Afghanistan, still the source of the world's finest lapis lazuli. The ancient royal tombs of the Sumerian city of Ur contained over 6,000 beautifully carved lapis lazuli statues, and it was a favourite stone of the Ancient Egyptians, much used in the tomb decorations of Tutankhamun. The Roman writer Pliny the Elder described it as 'a fragment of the starry firmament'. Today, lapis lazuli is mined near Lake Baikal in Siberia and at Ovalle in Chile as well as in Afghanistan. Chilean lapis contains flecks of calcite." Farndon (2006), p. 209.

"The best known and probably the most important locality is in Badakshan. There it occurs in limestone, in the valley of the river Kokcha, a tributary to the Oxus, south of Firgamu. The mines were visited by Marco Polo in 1271, by J B Fraser in 1825 and by Captain John Wood in 1837-1838. The rock is split by aid of fire. Three varieties of the lapis lazuli are recognized by the miners: *nili* of indigo-blue colour, *asman* sky-blue, and *sabzi* of green tint." *EB* (1911), Vol. XVI, p. 200.

"Much of thc material that is sold as lapis is an artificially coloured jasper from Germany that shows colourless specks of clear, crystallized quartz and never the goldlike flecks of pyrite that are characteristic of lapis lazuli and have been compared with stars in the sky." *Encyclopædia Britannica*, Online Library Edition. Downloaded on 8 March, 2012, from: http://www.library.eb.com.au/eb/article-9047165.

"Lajvard" (Lapis lazuli) is got from Yumgan, a village in the mountain above Jirm in Badakhshan. "Lajvard" is sold at a rupee of a Rupee size. (Gold streaks are often found in it.)" Leitner (1893), Appendix VI, p. 7.

Lapis lazuli beads were found in a child's grave at Abydos in Egypt associated with the burial of the early 1st Dynasty ruler, King Aha, *circa* 2900 BCE. See: "Egypt's First Pharaohs" by John Calvin, *National Geographic*, Vol. 207, No. 4, p. 111.

"Lapis lazuli is insufficiently homogeneous, almost as hard as feldspar, and seems as if it were incapable of being finely worked. Yet the Egyptians have used it for images of certain goddesses – Isis, Nephthys, Neith, Sekhet, – which are marvels of delicate cutting. The modelling of the forms is carried out as boldly as if the material were more trustworthy, and the features lose none of their excellence if examined under a magnifying glass." Maspero (1895), p. 262.

"Lapis lazuli has consistently reflected significance in ritual contexts in Mesopotamia and in Egypt. It was considered to be a powerful apotropaic substance and a healing stone in Babylonian magical texts, particularly when worn around the neck or strung onto a thread as an amulet. This is attested from textual evidence (see, for discussion, Reiner 1995) as well as archaeological and art historical study (see Winter 1995). Lapis lazuli significantly shaped conceptual notions of truth within the Mesopotamian world, where it was used within sacred contexts. The physical nature of this stone, for early Dynastic Sumerians in particular (the most valued being luminous, dark and blue), represented the sacred, the sky and masculinity. It was often paired with red carnelian in burial contexts, reflecting both masculine and feminine . . . . This red-blue pairing is also found in burials of bronze and early iron age peoples in the Tarim Basin of Xinjiang, as red and blue cords were used to bind the hands of mummified bodies (see Good 2005; for further literature on the Tarim Basin mummies see Mallory and Mair 2000; Barber 1999; Mair 1998). This red/blue male/female connection may reflect a shared colour symbolism with a deep history." Good (2008), p. 34.

Until recently, most scholars presumed that *all* the lapis lazuli found in early Mesopotamian, Indian and Egyptian archaeological sites had its origin in the Badakhshan region. This led to the premise of the early development of extensive ancient trade routes. While now we know that not all ancient lapis lazuli came from the one source – it is still true that most of the lapis lazuli, and that of the best quality, did indeed come from Badakhshan.

Other stones which look like lapis lazuli, such as sodalite, have sometimes been assumed to be real lapis lazuli. Some reassessment of the actual nature of this ancient trade will need to be undertaken, especially now that tools have been developed for the non-destructive identification of the origins of specimens:

". . . the stone which we assume to be rare, from a specific source in northeastern Afghanistan, may well be another, equally rare but more widely distributed mineral, namely sodalite. This mineral occurs worldwide, and in fact is found in the lapis mines as well as regions in Southeast Asia, Siberia, the Russian Far East, the Urals region, Kazakhstan and Kyrgizstan. Sodalite is related to lapis as it, like lazurite, is in the feldspathoid group. The possibility of sodalite rather than lapis being a source of some of the blue stone that was so important to ancient Mesopotamia and Egypt must be addressed more closely. ...
There are several mines [of lapis lazuli], however, in the Pamirs further to the north; for example the Koh-e Lal mine in Tajikistan, which is orogenically related though is likely to have a distinctive elemental signature (see figure 4). Related geological structures in the Chagai Hills in Pakistan, the southern shore of Lake Baikal in Siberia, the Shugnan Range of the western Pamir in Tajikistan, and southwestern Badakshan in northern Afghanistan each carry veins of lapis lazuli; there is also a possible source in Iran. However for the present purpose, it is sufficient to simply call into question the assumptions made about lapis and its distribution in antiquity, and to point to new methods of analysing the components of lapis that make possible the sourcing of ancient stone." Good (2008), pp. 28-30.

"From the late 4th millennium B.C.E. and continuing (with gaps) across the millennia lapis lazuli was much sought after in all areas of the Near East (Brown). Cylinder seals, jewelry, inlays, fittings, and the like were manufactured from it. Lapis objects are first attested archeologically from Mesopotamia and documented in texts—with references to an eastern derivation—from the mid-3rd millennium B.C.E. Until recent times the only known source of the mineral was in northeastern Afghanistan. It has recently been noted, however, that, according to ancient Near Eastern, Roman, and Islamic records, there were also several sources in western Persia; there is also a modern geological report for this region (Brown, pp. 7ff.), but it remains to be confirmed. At any rate, whether Afghanistan was the only source for lapis lazuli or the material also came from Īrān, Iranian politics played a role in distributing it to the west. Lapis lazuli was traded across Iran and also by sea from the Indus valley, paralleling the tin route." Downloaded from *Encyclopædia Iranica* online from: http://www.iranicaonline.org/articles/commerce-i on 26 September, 2011.

"By applying atomic absorption to the lapis samples, trace element analysis revealed that barium and strontium levels differed distinctly in samples from different mines, thereby making a testable signature for sources of ancient lapis. This important discovery has indeed helped to clarify ancient lapis sources and the implications of its exchange. . . .

More recent study of trace elements in lazurite promises to help increase the accuracy of sourcing through another physical test, Prompt Gamma Activation Analysis (PGAA). This type of analysis has been applied to the study of lapis lazuli for its potential in discerning source areas . . . . One advantage of this technique is that it can examine independent trace elements, which may more effectively eliminate the problem of heterogeneity in the matrix of lapis lazuli stone . . . . Moreover it can be used completely non-destructively. This will encourage more museum objects to be tested, which will help to develop a more accurate and refined view of early lapis availability and concomitant contact and exchange. This type of study promises to produce important insights into early resources use and interaction in prehistory.

On the question of Iranian lapis, there are two points that need to be stressed. First there are most certainly at least two sources of lapis present in Iran, one from Khamesh (Zanjan), and the other from mount Rudbar Alamut (near Tafrish, also in Zanjan). These are well documented mines though their antiquity has not been investigated. However, the earliest known lapis found in the ancient Near East comes from Zagheh (grave 15, level VIII) on the Qazvin Plain in ca. 6000 BC (Shahmirzadi 1988; Abdi 2000) very close to the Khamesh mines." Good (2008), pp. 32-34.

Other mines may have been worked in ancient times. One such is near the town of Ghiamda (modern Gyimda), about 200 km directly northeast of Lhasa:

"The lapis lazuli, stag's horn, and rhubarb, are also materials of a great commercial intercourse with Lha-Ssa and the neighbouring provinces." Huc (*circa* 1915), p. 98.

For those with further interest in lapis lazuli, there is a detailed essay on the ancient sources and trade of lapis lazuli in Moorey (1999): No. 43, pp. 85-92. For information on the lapis lazuli trade by the Sakas (Scythians) and Sogdians, see: de la Vaissière (2002), pp. 22-26; 46-47; Myrdal and Kessle (1971), p. 48. Also, see: note 13.7; Ciolek (2005); Sarianidi (1971), pp. 12-14; Bancroft (1984); Good (2008), pp. 1-60; Shaikh (1987), p. 72, and (1988), pp. 127-139.

Appendix S: Jade

For thousands of years Khotan and Yarkand have been renowned for their production of large quantities of high-quality nephrite jades, or 玉 *yu*, much of which was traded to China.

> "Jade was as precious as water to the oasis, and as intimately joined to its survival. In the Chinese histories, Khotan is known as Yutian, the Kingdom of Jade. Trade may have begun as early as the third millennium BC and certainly flourished during the second, contributing significantly to the wealth of the oasis. When Fu Hao, the consort of the Yin-Shang emperor of China, was buried at the close of the thirteenth century BC in Anyang, then the capital of the Shang dynasty (1765-1123 BC), in northern Honan province, 750 Khotan jade carvings were entombed with here. Not only Khotan, but all the oases located on the commercial routes must have benefited from this activity. Every year when the water subsided after the summer melt, the king of Khotan would ritually wade into the river to find the first crude jade rock, swept the floods into the valleys. Now all the finds belong to the government.
>
> Khotan jade is graded according to its colour, Ahmet explained to me, with white being the best and the most expensive. There is also yellow, green, dark green, red, purple, and blue jade." Paula (1994), p. 98.

> "A piece of nephrite jade is one of the toughest stones in the world, rich with fibrous layers like a well-rooted soil: it can scarcely be destroyed with a hammer, even though it is only 6.5 on Moh's scale. Yet, if you attack diamonds in the same way, the crystals will shatter into shards." Finlay (2006), p. 368.

> "*Nephrite jade*: a green stone, less luminous than the Burmese jade or *jadeite*, which is mineralogically no relation. Named by Nicholas Mondares of Seville, a sixteenth-century doctor, who used it to treat kidney problems, and named it '*piedras de hijades*', or 'flank stone'. Believed in Ancient China to confer immortality, and still treasured there. A prestige stone in Maori and ancient American cultures. Found in western China, near Khotan, as well as all around the Pacific Rim, including Japan, New Zealand, California and Peru. One of the toughest, least breakable stones, because of its fibrous structure. Often faked and dyed." Finlay (2006), pp. 402-403.

Liu points out that numerous jade pieces dating to the Shang dynasty (traditionally: 1765-1122 BCE) can be traced to the region of Khotan and there is evidence of very early involvement of the Yuezhi in this trade:

> "The Yuezhi resided on the border of agricultural China even earlier than the Xiongnu. While the Xiongnu were famous in history because of their conflicts with Chinese empires, the Yuezhi were better known to the Chinese for their role in long-distance trade. Ancient economist Guan Zhong (645 B.C.E.) referred to the Yuezhi, or Niuzhi, as a people who supplied jade to the Chinese. It is well known that ancient Chinese rulers had a strong attachment to jade. All of the jade items excavated from the tomb of Fuhao of the Shang dynasty [a royal consort of the early 12th century BCE], more than 750 pieces, were from Khotan in modern Xinjiang. As early as the mid-first millennium B.C.E. the Yuezhi engaged in the jade trade, of which the major consumers were rulers of agricultural China." Liu (2001), p. 265.

> "Nephrite had already achieved a notable place in the Neolithic culture of China, but only as part of a general polished stone industry. By Chou times the mineral was already rich in royal and divine associations, and was reserved mainly for ceremonial

and magical objects. Among these were the old pointed royal sceptres, descended, it may be, from archaic axes; there were the "astronomical jades" with which the royal stargazers took their sightings; there were the tablets, full of mana, which announced the accession of the Son of Heaven; there were 'funerary jades" which closed the apertures of the dead man's body; there were cap and girdle ornaments for men, and buckles, sword fittings, scabbard mounts, and finger rings. Perhaps these last mentioned objects, secular and personal in purpose, had once been talismanic and apotropaic in function too. A great deal of their meaning was lost by Han times, but much of the archaic sense of these things was saved, though greatly altered. The king-shaman, who compelled the attendance of the rain-dragons with his wand of green nephrite, still remained, but encrusted with the newer paraphernalia of the monarchy. Moreover, a set of poetic and metaphorical images had grown up around the beautiful stone: its glossy luster typified the beneficent, mostly enriching character of the Confucian virtue of "humanity," and its toughness and fine texture symbolized the virtues of the upright man. In less elevating literature, jade, especially suet-white jade, stood for the physical beauty of women, representing the ideal appearance of their flesh, as if they were marble goddesses of the Mediterranean world." Schafer (1985), pp. 224-225.

"This [Khotan] was the ancient source of all the nephrite used in China,[19] and the white jade and deep green jade required by the lapidaries of T'ang continued to come from that city. Pebbles of the precious nephrite were picked from the beds of two rivers, which join near Khotan before they empty into the Tarim River. These are the Kara-kāsh ("Black Jade") and the Yurung-kāsh ("White Jade") rivers.

[19] Other localities may have existed in antiquity; if so, they have vanished. In later times, the jade quarries of Yarkand were to become more important than the Khotan deposits. Dr. Cheng Te-k'un has drawn my attention to the exploitation of jade (nephrite?) in southern Manchuria (reported in *Chung-kuo hsin-wen* for March 23, 1961). A huge piece, found in 1960, was partly yellow-green, partly turquoise green."

Schafer (1963), p. 224 and p. 331, n. 19.

"Recent excavations reveal how attempts of a very different nature were sometimes made to provide for the well-being of the dead. These were designed to preserve the body intact as long as possible, presumably so that the *p'o* [human soul] could live there happily, and not be tempted to return to the world of the living and wreak harm upon mankind for wrongs that had been suffered. The measures in question were of two types. In some cases the body was enclosed in a tailor-made suit, made up of rectangular pieces of jade. These were sewn together to fit the body, and it was hoped that by being encased in this life-giving substance the body would survive unimpaired. Regrettably, it must be recorded that in none of the cases of burial where this method was adopted was it successful; but this was not so with other methods, as has been dramatically demonstrated at the tomb of the countess of Tai, at Ma-wang-tui. Here effective results were achieved by encasing the body in no less than four massive timber coffins, at the foot of a deep pit; the surround had been dextrously sealed with layers of clay and charcoal. A further example of the discovery of a well-preserved corpse was found in a tomb of 167 BC. In addition there is a literary reference to the discovery of an undecayed body in about AD 225, which was identified as one of the Han kings who had died in 202 BC." Loewe (1982), pp. 121-122.

"In Khotan there are two rivers, called Kará Kásh and Urung Kásh,[4] in both of which jade is met with, and it is found nowhere else in the world. The waters of these two rivers are preferred [by some] to that of Yárkand, but personally, I could never find the superiority in them. Khotan is among the most famous towns in the world, but at the present time its jade is the only thing that remains worth writing about.

[4] The Yurung Kásh of ordinary maps, and according to modern pronunciation. On and near its upper waters, jade is still quarried. The late Mr. W. H. Johnson, who was at Karánghu-tágh on the Upper Yurung in 1865, wrote : "It is noted for the Yashm which is met with in the stream." (See J. R. G. S., 1867, p. 7)."

From the *Tarikh-i-Rashidi* [composed in 1541-42 CE]. See Elias (1895), p. 298.

Hanshu 96A mentions that "the soil" of Zihe 子合, which I have identified as being the region of modern Shahidulla, produced jade. In the 19th century, old abandoned Chinese jade quarries were found some 24 kilometres southeast of Shahidulla in the Upper Karakash valley. See: note 6.1; also, *CICA*, p. 101.

"One of the most valuable productions of Eastern Toorkistân used to be jade. The quarries are about six miles above the camping-ground of Balakchee on the right (or northern) bank of the River Karakash in the Kuen Luen Mountains (in latitude 36° 18' N., and longitude about 78° 15' E). The central mass of the range consists of granite. The chief quarry is situated some distance up the mountain side, but a quantity of débris has been washed down to the level of the river, forming a bank in which there are many marks of digging, the refuse being thrown up in heaps, while many fragments of raw jade, inferior in quality, are exposed. At the quarry itself the galleries run for some distance into the mountain, and pieces of wood, wedges &c., were seen by Dr. Cayley – lying about, abandoned by the workmen at the time of the Mussulman insurrection, by which the Chinese rule was ended in 1863-64. Further up the Karakash River are marks of the former traffic. At one place there is a piece of a path built up with a wall to support it on the precipice side, elsewhere there is a group of stone huts. These signs all lead up to the Elchee Dewan (or Pass) further up the Karakash, by which Mr. Johnson crossed over to Khoten in 1865. This must have been the route usually taken by the Chinese miners to reach the quarries.

All down the River Karakash pieces of jade are found among the pebbles in the stream. These are estimated at three times the value of the quarry stones; they are called 'Soo Tash' or 'Water Stones.' The probability is that constant knocking about in the rapid stream would have developed any cracks that there might be in the stone, and split off the extra pieces. Hence all "water stones," are pretty sure to be free from flaws. It is this which gives them their value; for with the quarry stones the workmen are always liable to have many days or months of labour wasted by the sudden appearance of a crack in the material, which would prevent all further carving. The chief value of jade seems to have been in the workmanship which it would bear owing to its hardness and toughness. I cannot learn that the raw uncarved jade bore any value at all in proportion to the finished article. The industry is now entirely extinct. The carving is said to have been done in Khoten and Yârkand by Chinese workmen. I believe none is carved in India, although some of the patterns bear a certain resemblance to Indian models. But the raw stone is not to my knowledge ever imported into India, although a considerable number of trifling articles made of jade are brought over every year. And I have seen in Yârkand itself jade carved in the form said to be Indian.

This quarry on the Karakash is not the only place in the locality where jade is found. On the summit of the Sanjoo Pass (The Grim Dewân) over the northern crest of the Kuen Luen Mountains I found coarse jade in situ, forming a saw-shaped cliff. Jade is found also in a river called Yooroong-Kash, draining into Khoten from the same mountains, as does the Karakash. The termination kash in each of these words signifies jade in Toorkee.

Marco Polo mentions that "jasper" is found in the bed of a river which may be identified with the Karakash. He probably means jade. Benedict Goez also visited the jade mines during his stay at Khoten [in 1603]. . . ." Shaw (1871), pp. 473-475. See also note 2.5.

"As the main source of jade, the Khotan envoys carried pounds (kīna) of the stone for presentation to the heads of states. They used the word īra- 'stone' for their stone par excellence, the 'jade', and the Bud. Skt. word śilā. Hence they could call their river the Śailodā and in Khotan-Saka ranījai ttāji 'the river of precious stone (ratna-)'. The īra- in the adjective form īrīnaa- was also used to render the mountain name Vajraka. The rivers in Khotan were in Turkish times called the yörüng qaš öküš and qara qaš öküš 'the white and black jade rivers'." Bailey (1985), p. 14; and also p. 58.

"The different occurrences in this zone [Central Asia and China] have been outlined by S.C. Nott (1936): (i) the dark green variety was obtained mainly from Barkul, Manas in Sungeria, the country surrounding lake Baikal and the mountain slopes of western Yunnan; (ii) an emerald green variety could be obtained from Lan t'ien on the borders of Shensi province; (iii) jadeite occurs *in situ* in the Pamir region, in the valley of the Tunga which is a tributary on the left bank of the Kaskem Darra; (iv) the nephrite variety of jade is known to occur in Khotan and Yarkand in eastern Turkestan, the jade mountains in Belurtag on the upper waters of the Tisnab river about eight miles [13 km] from Yarkand being possibly the most notable source of supply. Nott (1936:1) has also quoted the testimony of a Manchu author (Hsi Yu Wen Chien Liu, published in 1777 A.D.) in this regard: 'There is a river in Yarkand in which are found Jade pebbles. The largest are as big as round fruit dishes, or square peck measures, the smallest are the size of a fist or chestnut and some of the boulders weigh more than five hundred pound. There are many different colours, among which snow white, kingfisher green, beeswax yellow, Cinnabar red, and ink black, are all considered valuable.' It is also well known that jade was exploited in China from the Neolithic period onwards. The jade artefacts in what Alfred Salmony (1963:15) calls the Pre-Anyang period i.e. from the nebulous Hsia period (2205 BC) till 1200 BC include Neolithic axes, from Siberia, and flat ring ornaments, knives, chisels, adzes, rings, beads and segmented and whole slit discs from Kansu, Honan and Shansi." Lahiri (1992), pp. 78-79. Refer also to note 4.1.

"The acknowledged classic source of nephrite for both the Chinese and Western Asian worlds for millennia was Khotan, near the foot of the Kunlun mountains, on the southwest side of the Tarim Basin. The mineral appears in a wide range of greens (typically more or less dull and blending with other colors), as well as colors ranging from a pure, translucent white (the rarest and the most sought after both in western and eastern Asia) through various shades of off-white, to yellowish, tan, iron-red (normally occurring in the pebble's rind, where the iron content is strongly oxidized), to brown and black (the last almost invariably a very dark green when viewed through strong transmitted light). Even relatively small pieces of nephrite are very often variegated both in color and degree of translucency. Biruni states: "Jade (*yašm*) is extracted from two river valleys in Khotan where the reeds (or canes) form thickets. One of the river valleys is called Qāš, and there *the superior white material* is extracted, and it is not taken from its ultimate source [i.e., it is found as rollers in the streambed and not at its origin, from which it is washed down]. *The big pieces of it are*

reserved for the king personally, and the small ones are for the populace" (p. 198; italics added). The author of the *Ḥodud al-ʿālam* (372/982) had earlier reported that "the jade stone (*sang i yashm*) comes from the rivers of Khotan" (*Ḥodud al-ʿālam*, tr. p. 86)
It seems now established that in early times the Chinese had other sources of nephrite in China itself (Middleton and Freestone, pp. 414 and 417, apud Guang and Zhichun). Another major source, Kashghar, seems to have been feeding jade into the supply stream, probably starting as early as the 11th century, and in any case not later than the 13th. In a Persian panegyric from the late 11th or early 12th century by Lāmeʿi of Gorgān, a warrior wears "Kashghar jade" on his arms (Melikian-Chirvani, 1997/2000, p. 132). But as indicated above, Kashghari does not expand on Biruni's information. Jawhari of Nishapur, writing about a hundred years after Kashghari, also repeats Biruni, and adds that Khotan is the only known source of jade (*yašb*, p. 219). Aḥmad b. Yusof al-Tifāši (1184-1253), however, indicates only Kashghar as the source of jade, from where it was exported "to all countries" (p. 195). Although for a number of reasons Tifāši is not the best-informed of authorities, his account, in a manner similar to and combined with literary evidence like the aforementioned panegyric, indicates that Kashghar was a source of jade, whose deposits must have been exploited in a significant manner before his time in order for him to have heard of it. At the beginning of the 14th century, Kāšāni (p. 139) observes that jade (*yašb*) "comes in varieties, and its mines are in Ḵitāy and Ṭuḡmāj." Ḵitāy/ Khitay, Anglicized to Cathay, is an old name for northern China, and was derived from the name of the Ḵitāʾ confederation, while Ṭuḡmāj, also spelled Ṭuḡmāj, is a region in Turkistan. Kāšāni's usage of "Ḵatāy" may not, however, have referred to northern China but to the former territory of the Qārā Ḵatāy, a branch of the Ḵatāʾ who moved to the south and west in the 12th century and were the overlords of much of Turkistan in the period leading up to the conquests of Chingiz Khan. Nevertheless, the possibility that northern China may have been an important source of nephrite is suggested by the fact that on a recent visit to Mongolia the author became aware that jade is retrieved there and was able to acquire significant amounts of rough nephrite, including sizable pieces of fine white material. Its source does not seem to be officially documented, but according to word of mouth this material is sold on the Chinese market. It appears plausible that this source was already exploited long ago, but escaped scholarly attention." "JADE i. Introduction." Manuel Keene. In: *Encylopædia Iranica* online. Downloaded from: http://www.iranicaonline.org/articles/jade-i on 26 September, 2011

As well as being gathered from the stony beds of certain rivers, jade is still mined today in the regions of Yarkand, Khotan and Keriya. Large chunks are brought into town on the back of pickup trucks. People can still be seen every day searching for the highly prized river-tumbled pieces of jade in the bed of the Yurung-kāsh ("White Jade") river at Khotan, which are sold in the large thriving jade market on the right bank of the river.

Appendix T: The linking of the Jade and Lapis lazuli routes

The ancient lapis lazuli routes from Badakhshan to India, Mesopotamia and Egypt were linked with the eastern jade route from the western Tarim Basin to China in the second half of the 1st millennium BCE. This was one of the most important factors giving rise to the emergence of regular, organised trade between the Chinese, Parthian and Roman Empires.

> "By 2500 BCE a web of permanent trade routes connected the cities of the Mediterranean with those in western India. Around 1500 BCE a second network, centred on north-eastern China, was established. Around 1 CE, the two webs were bridged for the first time by commercial pathways formed across Central Asia, and across South East Asia." Ciolek (2005).

> "Early sources of jade are a critical area of research . . , but one likely candidate seems to be the major source at Khotan (Yutian/Hetian) on the southern margin of the Tarim Basin. By the end of the third millennium jade workshops are known (e.g., Xinhua, Shenmu county, Shanxi)[14] that may have been supplied from this source. If this is so, then the scale of the Yellow River catchment area for raw materials already encompassed much of the eastern segment of what was later (in a very different economic context) to become the Silk Route, through Xinjiang to Gansu and down to the heartland of cultural and political development below the Wei confluence. Indeed, there is a striking parallelism in this respect with what was already happening farther west, almost in mirror image, on the western segment of the future Silk Route between Bactria and Mesopotamia. Here, from the fourth millennium onward, supplies of lapis lazuli had traveled from their sources in the Chagai Hills and Badakhshan, across the Iranian Plateau (by the route known in medieval times as the Great Khorasan Road), to reach consumers in the Mesopotamian lowlands.[15] Both of these rare minerals had their origin in the extreme conditions created by the upthrust of the Himalayas, and their occurrences lay only 900 kilometers apart; but, separated by the formidable barrier of the Pamirs, one moved east and the other west – only in the closing centuries of the first millennium B.C.E. were the two paths united into a single route.
>
> This remarkable symmetry is doubly significant, for the Pamirs divided Eurasia into two cultural worlds, aptly symbolized by the contrasting colors of the two minerals: blue and green, lazurite and jade. As Fred Hiebert and Nicola di Cosmo have pointed out (1996, and emphasized in the title of their helpful collection of translations on Central Asian archaeology), appreciation of these two minerals was mutually exclusive. Blue stones were highly regarded and much sought after in the older metal-using communities of western Asia, where dark green stones had relatively little appeal after their vogue in the Neolithic; but, even today, jade is a fundamental part of Chinese culture, in a way unparalleled elsewhere – although it was equally prized among the civilizations of Central America before their extinction.
>
> [14] Information from Yang Jianhua (see *Shoucangjia* 2001, 6).
>
> [15] Small quantities of this precious material had even reached Egypt in the closing centuries of the fourth millennium."
>
> Sherratt (2006), pp. 38-39 and notes 14-15.

> "At present no one doubts the fact that separate sections of the route began to function as far back as the Bronze Age. Since the third millennium BCE, one of the sections of the route was used to export lapis-lazuli (Sarianidi 1968) to the Near East and India from Badakhshan. Turquoise was also exported from Sogdiana and Bactria, the exchange being realized through the steppe people. . . .

> In the third millennium BCE, the "Jade Road" appeared: jade, extracted in Khotan and Yarkand, was delivered to China where it was widely used in the Lungshan culture . . . and especially during the reign of the Zhou dynasty." Kuzmina (1998), p. 64.

China gained control of the main caravan routes around the Tarim Basin and into the rich lands along the Oxus River (Amu Darya) after Zhang Qian's journey to the Da Yuezhi in the late 2nd century BCE.

With larger, stronger horses from the 'Western Regions' to help the Chinese to keep the nomads at bay, and camels to carry bulk long-distance freight, the Chinese were able to link up with the old lapis lazuli routes controlled by the Da Yuezhi and Parthians. Together, these empires worked to keep the major caravan routes open all the way India and the Roman Empire, encouraging an ever-increasing flow of goods between China, india and the West in spite of sporadic periods of conflict between them.

> "This combination of military, political, and economic effort on the part of the Chinese Empire in its Central Asian expansion policies led to the opening of a remarkable network of land routes connecting China to many distant centers of civilization in the West. The ancient network of caravan routes
>
> ran around the rim of the Taklamakan [desert] like a loop of string, on which the oases hung like beads. Historically, the first line of communication is that known as the Silk Road. It ran from the western point of Kansu toward Lob Nor and then along the foot of K'unlun all the way to Khotan, Yarkand, and Kashgar. Later the Chinese began to open up communication with the oases north of the Taklamakan. . . .
>
> [The road] . . . north of the Taklamakan ran east and west the whole length of the southern foot of the Tien Shan, from Hami [Qomul] to Kashgar, and was accordingly known to the Chinese as the Tien Shan Nan Lu, the Road south of the Tien Shan. At Kashgar it converged with the Silk Road, thus closing the loop around the Taklamakan. From Kashgar a pass traversed the mountains westward to the oasis region of Ferghana, Khokand, and Samarkand, in the south of Russian Turkistan of today, and thence in turn roads led to Persia and the whole Near East. [Lattimore 1951, pp. 172-73. See map on p. 23]
>
> After the convergence of the Tien Shan Nan Lu and the Silk Road at Kashgar, there were at least two alternative routes in use across the Pamirs to the Amu Darya region and beyond. The first route was directly west from Kashgar across the Pamirs to the Karategin, Fergana, and Kokand oases in Russian Turkistan mentioned by Lattimore. The second route was due south and west from Kashgar and west southwest from Yarkand. The road from both of these two cities converged at Tashkurghan, the nearest town to the Afghan Pamirs and the Wakhan in Chinese Turkistan. Speaking of roads passing through Tashkurghan, over a century ago T. G. Montgomerie wrote, "Tashkurghan commands the roads from Badakhshan and Chitral to Kokhan [Kokand], Yarkand and Kashgar, and is still considered a place of importance" (1871, p. 163). Therefore, it is the southwestern branch of the Silk Road passing through Tashkurghan that is of significance for our purposes." Shahrani (2002), pp. 21-22.

With the routes joined, it was more practical and efficient to use pack camels for such long-distance trade. The east-west caravans generally used the two-humped 'Bactrian' camel, native to Central Asia, and better adapted to the cold than the one-humped dromedary, or 'Arabian' camel. Cable and French (1958), pp. 169-172.

> "Thus, archaeological data has established that in Central Asia, the Bactrian camel was domesticated in the fourth millennium B.C. and in the third to second millennium B.C., was widely employed as draft power for harnessing to vehicles with

solid wheels, a distinguishing feature of wheeled transport in Central Asia in the Bronze Age...." Kuzmina (2008), p. 70.

"Only half a pound (0.22 kg) a day of rape seed oil was enough to keep their stamina high during desert marches which required them to go for days without grazing, fodder and sometimes water. Full grown Bactrian Camels can carry as much as 220-270 kg about 30-40 km daily, though in difficult desert conditions this can be considerably slower. They do well in the cold climate of the Central Asian winters, but do not tolerate heat as well as their Arabic cousins. But even so, as Potts emphasises, they must have been the major beast of burden throughout the Tarim Basin and Central Asia in ancient times." Høisæter (2013), p. 43.

At some point, it was discovered that first generation hybrids between the two had significantly more strength and stamina than either of the original breeds, but it was centuries before a cold-resistant one-humped variety was bred. Bulliet (1975), pp. 141-175.

Camels can carry half as much as a horse and cart, and twice as much as a mule. They travel long distances with minimal water and fodder. Carts and formed roads were unnecessary, substantially reducing transport costs, and increasing the routes available to caravans.

A standard camel load in Roman times was about 195 kg (430 pounds) and over 227 kg (500 pounds) could be carried for shorter distances. A pack camel could travel 24 to 32 kilometres (15 to 20 miles) a day, and go for long periods without food or water. Bulliet (1975), pp. 20, 24, and 281, n. 35.

"Movement across land was limited chiefly by travelers' stamina and the reliability of access to food, fodder and drinking water. Land trade routes always lead from one re-victualling place to another. Where both fodder and water were plentiful so that only food needed to be carried, and where provisions represented no more than 70% of the total load, exactly one metric ton (2,200 lb.) of merchandise could be transported by 133 porters walking some 168 miles (270 km) in nine days. Under the same conditions, a team of four drivers and 23 pack camels could move the same cargo across some 660 miles (1060 km) and do so in 38 days. However, where neither fodder nor water were available *en route*, and the weather was hot, the maximum operating ranges would shrink dramatically. Porters would walk only one day and cover a mere 14 miles (23 km), while the camels and their handlers would walk only for five days and cover no more than 90 miles (150 km). In short . . . land routes were governed ruthlessly by the spacing of dependable sources of drinking water and the prevailing temperatures." Ciolek (2005).

"Pure-bred Bactrians stand 1.5-2.4 m high to the top of the humps and are normally 1.68-1.63 m long, with a mean weight of 460 kgs (Epstein 1969: 118). They have been known to carry loads of 220-270 kgs some 30-40 kms daily, or 80-100 kms if pulling a loaded cart (Walz 1954: 56). Bactrian camels, which can live to be 35-40 years old, are generally put to work at the age of four and can expect to have 20-25 years of productivework (Epstein 1969: 120). They are at their best in the dry cold of the winter and spring months in Inner Asia, when their thick coats provided them with ample warmth. Able to withstand extremes of heat and cold, Bactrians prefer temperatures below 21° C but are capable of tolerating a 70°-broad range between winter lows and summer highs (Manefield and Tinson 2000: 38). Consistent heat, however, is intolerable for Bactrians and the caravans which once set out from C hina westwards across the Gobi desert always traveled in winter (Walz 1954: 55-56). Bactrians have been known to function at altitudes of up to 4000 m. above sea level, e.g. in the Pamirs (Gauthier-Pilters and Dagg 1981: 6). After a long journey they were typically rested for 1-2 weeks and were pastured for the summer months on the steppe, where they built up their fat reserves again in anticipation of further caravan crossings the following winter (Walz 1954: 56)." Potts (2013), p. 2,

"Although larger and stronger, hybrids look like dromedaries in that they have one hump, though this is normally not very symmetrical and often has a small indentation between 4 and 12 cm deep which divides the rear portion of the hump — often 2-3 times as large as the front — from the front part. Alternatively, the hump may end up looking quite flat, and has been compared to a flattened pyramid. Hybridization produces a large animal, which can stand 2.32 m high at the hump or 2.15 m high at the shoulder (Kolpakow 1935: 618, n. 5). The legs are long, the height of the camel often greater than its length, and the weight sometimes in the 900-950 kg range, though more often approaching an average of c. 650 kg (Kolpakow 1935: 620).

All of the sources confirm the greater strength and load-bearing abilities of the hybrids and indeed references to hybrids able to carry 400-500 kgs, roughly double that of a dromedary and more than double that of an ordinary Bactrian, are not uncommon. It should not be a surprise then that the sources are also consistent in recording the substantially higher price of hybrids vs dromedaries (Tapper 1985: 57, 59). There is a considerable body of evidence concerning subsequent generations of hybrids crossed with pure-bred or other hybrid individuals, all of which points to their bad temper, inadequate size and generally poor quality. For this reason, hybrid males were usually castrated (Tapper 1985: 61). As Tapper (1985: 63) notes, "The hybrids were not allowed to breed, as their offspring would be vicious and dangerous." Statements to the effect that the dromedary-Bactrian crosses were infertile (Gray 1972: 161) are incorrect, and ample evidence demonstrates the contrary (Peters and von den Driesch 1997: 654). Already in the early nineteenth century Eduard Friedrich Eversmann reported seeing fertile offspring in Turkestan (Hartmann 1869: 70).

"To sum up, Tapper (1985: 67) notes, "in my experience, the main advantage of the hybrid over the purer species, to both nomadic and commercial users, is less its supposed versatility than its vastly greater size, strength and carrying capacity, its aesthetically pleasing appearance, and its correspondingly greater value, in both financial and ceremonial terms." In view of the evidence just reviewed, which extends from Anatolia and Syria in the west to Afghanistan in the east, we can safely say that small numbers of Bactrian camels have been kept, over the past 300-400 years, by groups which, in the main, raised dromedaries, for the purpose of producing hybrids of outstanding strength. Further, these hybrids were used specifically as caravan and draught animals. It can at least be suggested, therefore, that the reason why Assyrian kings seized Bactrian camels and demanded them as tribute from Iranian lands to the east of Assyria was to acquire studs and breeding females in order to practice the same sort of hybridization as just outlined, with a view to developing stronger pack animals for a variety of purposes (military, commercial, agricultural). While we have as yet no archaeological evidence of camel hybridization from the Assyrian period, we do have some from later periods in the Near East, which demonstrates that hybridization was practiced in antiquity.

In recent years, archaeo-zoologists have identified faunal evidence of camel hybrids at Mleiha in the United Arab Emirates, Troy in western Turkey, and Pella in Jordan. Chronologically, the earliest evidence dates to the Roman or Parthian period. In 1994, Dr. S.A. Jasim excavated an important cemetery near Mleiha, in the interior of Sharjah, United Arab Emirates, which contained the graves of at least 12 camels, most of which, judging from associated finds, date to the first two centuries CE (Jasim 1999). The faunal remains, studied by H.-P. Uerpmann, included three hybrids. Identification of these individuals as hybrids was based on the morphometric analysis of selected bones (axis, astragalus, first phalanx) as compared with dromedary and Bactrian material. In addition to this material, Uerpmann (1999: 111-113) has identified the phalanx of a probable hybrid from a Roman context at Troy." Potts (2005b), pp. 5-6. See also: Potts (2004), pp. 143-165.

"Kazakh herdsmen allow their camels to wander freely and unsupervised into the Annanba Reserve; where they wander, they invariably cross-breed with wild Bactrian stock. The result is a hybrid with an adulterated wild Bactrian camel genetic make-up. Both Kazakhs and Mongolians do not like to handle pure wild Bactrian camel calves because they are too dangerous. They frequently kill them. One two-year-old wild camel calf scalped a young Mongolian of my acquaintance; the problems are very real. A hybrid calf is different matter. The herdsmen welcome a diluted addition of wild blood into their domestic herds. The problem has grown to such large proportions, that it has become difficult to recognize which animals in the Annanba Nature Reserve are wild and which are domestic." Hare (2009), p. 57.

"Temperatures can plummet to -40°Celsius in January and February in this part of the Gobi and it is a tribute to the remarkable versatility of the wild Bactrian camel that it survives at all, especially in places where the only water that bubbles up from under the ground has a salt content that is greater than that of seawater. No other large mammal in the world, not even the domestic Bactrian camel, can tolerate such a high salt content. This is why we had to carry water for our domestic camels." Hare (2009), pp. 28-29.

See: Bulliet (1975), pp. 28-86, for more information on dromedaries, and pp. 141-175 for Bactrian (two-humped) camels and the superior hybrids.

For further discussions about the early development of the transcontinental land routes, see "Silk Roads or Steppe Roads? The Silk Roads in World History." *Journal of World History* 11.1 (2000), pp. 1-26; Sherratt and Sherratt (1998), pp. 329-342; Ciolek (2000); Ciolek (2005); Frank and Thompson (2005); Beaujard (2005).

Appendix U: The *xuandu* - the 'hanging passages'

It has long been agreed that the Chinese word 縣度 *xuandu* refers to the narrow pathways, locally known as *rafiqs* or *rafiks* (and as *ovring* in Wakhan – Middleton and Huw (2008), p. 602), which are built by jamming sticks into clefts in the rocks and then placing flat stones upon them - often at lofty heights across bare cliff faces. Also, see the description in the quote from Wylie (1889), in Appendix F.

The term *xuandu* 縣度 (sometimes incorrectly transcribed *xiandu*) comes from: 縣 *xuan* (which is an alternative form of 懸) 'to suspend,' 'hang,' 'dangerous' + 度 *du* = *GR* Vol. VI, No. 11640a: "7. – To cross (the water by ferry). To cross (over)." From this come the English renderings: 'hanging passages' or 'suspended crossings'.

Xuandu is obviously a descriptive geographical term. It is never listed as the name of a *guo* - 'kingdom' or 'country' - in any of the ancient Chinese texts. However, it has occasionally been confused with the names for India such as Shendu (身譯), Tianzhu (天竺), Juandu (身毒), and so on. This is partly due to the similarity of the names, and/or because the 'hanging passages' were often the first "Indian" territories reached by Chinese arriving from the north:

> "Hsüan-tu (懸度) originally means "hanging bridge," and it was mentioned in this sense by the Chinese travellers in the course of their passage from the Ts'ung-ling (Pamir) region to the upper Indus valley. Some authors either through confusion or on account of the similarity of the names used it to mean the country [India]. This is fully explained by Kuo Yi-kung as quoted by Li Tao-yüan in the *Shui-ching chu* (chüan 1): "To the west of Wu-ch'a (烏秅) there is the country of Hsüan-tu (懸度). The river in the hills cannot be crossed except with rope bridges. Hence the name of the country." ["郭義恭曰：烏秅之西，有懸度之國，山溪不通，引繩而度，故國得其名也。"] Li Tao-yüan says that the region in question is Chi-pin (Kashmir). This is confirmed by the account of Fa-hsien." Bagchi (1948), p. 370. **NOTE:** The Chinese text from the *Shuijing zhu* chapter 1, was downloaded on 12 December, 2011 from: http://zh.wikisource.org/wiki/%E6%B0%B4%E7%B6%93%E6%B3%A8/01

The exact location of the *xuandu*, has remained a subject of controversy. Some scholars thought they must be located in the deep chasms of the Hunza Valley. Others made a convincing case for their location in the gorges through which the Indus River makes a sharp bend around Nanga Parbat, and then flows south onto the plains of the Punjab. See, for example: the discussion in Jettmar and Kattner (2002), pp. 174-181 in Chapter 8. "The Suspended Crossing: Where and why?"

I believe the confusion is due to the fact that both scenarios were correct, that there were at least two places where long sections of *rafiqs* were built on major trade routes leading from Chinese territory into India, and a series of *rafiqs* were described as *xuandu* 縣度 by Chinese authors.

When the extant texts are carefully compared it becomes obvious that the early references in the *Hanshu* and *Hou Hanshu* refer to the region of Hunza, while the *xuandu* the Chinese monk Fa Xian crossed in 400 CE were the *rafiqs* found in the Indus Gorge itself.

The only *rafiqs* mentioned during the Han dynasty, were in the northern Hunza Valley, south of the junction of the Misgar and the Hunza rivers, and east of Baltit. See: Chavannes (1905), p. 529, n. 5.

The second set of *rafiqs*, those used by Fa Xian, were to the southwest, along the route through the gorges at the great bend in the Indus Valley, "a few miles west of the modern village of Sazin, the region where the Indus turns southwards to break through the last barrier of mountains before reaching the plains." Jettmar (1987), p. 96.

A route is described in the *Hou Hanshu* as running from the town of Pishan in the Tarim Basin to Wuyishanli (Arachosia, centred near modern Kandahar), and there is a similar passage in the *Hanshu* 96A — see: *CICA*, p. 99. By far the shortest and most direct route from Pishan to Wuyishanli would have been via Tashkurghan, Hunza and Gilgit, and then southeastwards via Mastuj, Chitral, and Jalalabad to Wuyishanli.

Although it was impossible to take pack animals over the Hunza section of this route - being arduous and risky even for people on foot - it was by far the shortest and quickest route from the Tarim Basin to Gandhara and Jibin. The *Hanshu* describes the *xuandu* as follows:

> "What is termed the Suspended Crossing is a rocky mountain; the valley is impenetrable, and people traverse the place by pulling each other across with ropes." From: *Hanshu* 96A in *CICA*, pp. 99-100.

> "The 22 miles [35.4 km] of track between Baltit [the present capital of Hunza] and the next inhabited settlement, Galmit ['valley of flowers' or 'a nest amidst flowers,' which Skrine spells 'Ghalmit' further on, and is usually now rendered 'Gulmit' in English], lie through the most terrific country imaginable. The turbid Hunza River rushes through a gorge of which the sides are mountains 24,000 and 25,000 feet high [7,315-7,620m]. The pathway, which is entirely native-built, varies from 18 inches to 4 feet [0.46 to 1.22 m] in width and is in many places carried for hundreds of yards at a stretch on stakes let into the cliff-face. Elsewhere it climbs narrow steeply-pitched clefts in the rock by means of a ladder-like arrangement of small branches and stones called *rafik*. The cliffs along the face of which so much of the track is thus laid are known as *paris*. Every time the path reaches the outside of a curve of the river, it has to climb high up the *pari* to avoid the water which laps against the perpendicular and sometimes overhanging rock ; on the inside of the next bend it drops down no less steeply to the stony river-bank for a stretch ; then comes another *pari*, and so on. One of these on our first march took an hour to cross, and we climbed 800 feet in the process. I was not sorry that the whole march was only 9 miles [14.5 km] in length, so that we did it comfortably enough ; leaving Baltit at noon we lunched in deep beds of clover under apricot trees on the way and were in by half-past five. We camped near the river under a waterfall at a place called Ata'abad ; we were told that there was a village of that name, but it was perched on a ledge of the cliffs 900 feet [274 m] almost vertically above our heads, so that we could not see it. . . .
>
> On the next day's march the grandeur of the Hunza gorges came to a climax. At each corner it was more difficult than at the last to believe that any way could be found through the apparently solid wall of cliff, thousands of feet high in front of us. Except for a mile of stony hill-track at Bulchidas in the middle of the day, the path was one continuous succession of rafiks or ladders. It was too bad even for led horses, and our three had to be taken to the village of Ata'abad and thence by a long *detour* high up in the mountains. As a matter of fact from Hafiz's account the track they went by cannot have been so very much better than ours, for in several places they had to take the horses over one by one, two men at the head and two at the tail. However, they all arrived safely late in the evening.
>
> Ghalmit is an attractive village boasting about 300 acres [121 ha] of fields and orchards well shaded with planes and poplars. It is walled round with lofty jagged peaks of a yellowish tint, fantastically fretted and carved into minarets and towers. The villagers, curiously enough, are mostly Wakhis who came originally from Guhyal near the headwaters of the Oxus, away up on the Roof of the World beyond the Hindu Kush ; hence the name of this part of Hunza, Little Guhyal." Skrine (1926), pp. 29-30.

NOTE: Galmit/Ghalmit is now usually spelt 'Ghulmet' or 'Gulmit' and pronounced 'goohl-MET.' See: King (1989), p. 114. (JEH)

"At a little beyond Baltit the valley of the Hunza river, which from Chalt has pursued an easterly course, turns due north, and the river cuts a deep gash or furrows an uproarious channel along its bottom in its descent from the watershed of the Pamirs. The scenery also changes. In place of the richly cultivated terraces of both the Hunza and Nagar slopes in the lower valley, we find only rare villages and rarer cultivation, and are in a region of rocks and stones. Big glaciers propel their petrified cascades to the very edge of the river. In many places this required to be forded. Sometimes the road is only conducted round the edge of the precipices that overhang the torrent by artificial ladders and ledges, built out from the cliff with stones loosely laid upon supports of brushwood and timber jammed into the interstices of the rock. This sounds very dreadful, but in practice is much less alarming, the galleries, though only lasting for a few days, being sufficiently strong at the beginning, and being slightly inclined inwards toward the cliff. In the course of a very few days I underwent the bodily labours of a Parliamentary session, and parted with the superfluous physical accretions of an entire London season. Over this vile stretch of country there are two tracks, the upper or summer track, which avoids the river-bed, then filled with a fierce and swirling torrent, and climbs to the summit of the cliffs, several thousand feet above the water; and the lower or winter track, which can only be pursued when the melting of the snow by the hot summer suns being over, the current dwindles to a number of fordable channels, across and amid the boulder-piled fringes of which the traveller picks his way. The second track is not commonly available till the beginning of October . . . ." Curzon (1896), pp. 8-10.

The section on this region from the lost text, the *Guangzhi* 廣志 by Guo Yigong (W-G: Kuo I-kung) 郭義恭 (who wrote during the Jin dynasty 265-420 CE), has fortunately been preserved as a quote in the *Shuijingzhu*:

"Kuo I-kung says that west of Wu-ch'a 烏秅 there is the country of the Hanging Passages. It is a mountain gorge which is impassable; only by drawing out ropes one may cross it; hence the country has received its name. The natives dwell in the mountains. They cultivate [their fields] between stone walls. Heaped rocks are employed for building houses. The people join their hands for drinking; it is what we call monkey drinking. They have white goats[2] and short-stepping horses. They have donkeys, but no oxen. . . .

Another quotation from Kuo I-kung is given by Ma Kuo-han: "In the Hanging Passages the tombs are in the dwelling huts. [The traveller] enters a stretch of about ten *li*, and [this] difficult crossing is the Hanging Passages. Once they are crossed, [the traveller] eventually reaches a plain of about 100 *li*. Its population is not different." The plain of 100 *li* [41.6 km] below the hanging passages must be the valley of Gilgit. It cannot be defined as a plain, but it is the greatest widening in the Indus valley between Baltistan and the Punjab.

[2] ST, SW and SY have 白草 "white grass" which seems out of place here so I have followed SS (白羊)."

Petech (1950), p. 18 and note 2. **NOTE:** Petech should have retained the literal 'white grass,' instead of proposing 'white goats' as a translation, which has nothing to recommend it. "White grass" 白草 is mentioned in a number of passages in the *Hanshu* and *Hou Hanshu*, and was used to prepare an arrow poison. I believe it was a species of aconite. See note 5.3. (JEH)

Ban Chao's biography (*HHS* chap. 77) states that: "(Ban) Chao then crossed the Congling [Mountains] and got as far as (the) *xuandu*." There are no other details. One assumes that the reference was to a brief foray by Ban Chao to the borders of Kushan territories – perhaps to deliver a message – or just to scout the area. See: Chavannes (1906), p. 237.

The *xuandu* of Hunza, and the Indus gorges, formed natural frontiers between the Indian subcontinent and the territories of Central Asia. Indeed, the *Weilüe* notes that after crossing the *xuandu* in Hunza, one entered the territory of the Da Yuezhi who controlled northern India at the time. See: Chavannes (1905), p. 529.

"But there remains something I absolutely could not understand. . . . Coming from the North the traveller was forced to ascend a high pass either the Kilik (4755 m) or the Mintaka (4629 m) or the Shimshal (4787 m) and to march through the difficult Hunza valley. A roundabout trek via the Mustagh pass in the East or the Karumbar valley in the West would have been by no means easier. Only the long detour leading to the Wakhan and then crossing the Baroghil and the Darkot passes would make some difference. So there was no choice. But why should Chinese envoys and pilgrims have chosen a route skirting the precipices of the Indus valley? Compared with this gorge all passes crossing the ridges in this 35° latitude are completely harmless. The Babusar pass is (almost) a low promenade (only 4148 m high) and the approach through the Thor valley is also without problems. It did not make any sense to me that an extremely tiring and dangerous passage was preferred to traverses which are perfectly fit for horses.

In the meantime I learned on the spot that there were very good reasons why the more comfortable passes could not be used. I will try to explain the reason as concisely as possible.

The best time for travelling through the mountain valleys via the passes north of the 36° latitude was — until recently — late autumn and early winter, before it becomes really cold and snowfall (never as heavy as farther south) closes the high passes. In this season the rivers are already reduced and can rather easily be forded. The raids of the Hunza men robbing caravans in the Tarim Basin and on the track to the Karakorum pass were deliberately adapted to this time-table (Müller-Stellrecht 1978: 86). As the best illustration of the difference between travelling in summer and in winter we may use the statistical material handed over to Prof. Haserodt by the WAPDA Lahore, the Agency for planning dams and irrigation systems. They indicate that the monthly quantity of water, passing the water gauge at "Dainyour", (i.e. the discharge of the Hunza river at its mouth) is extremely changing according to season. Here I want to compare the relevant figures only: In 1971 the relation between the defluxion during the travel period (November-January) and the summer maximum between June and September was 1:25. 1972 was a rather moderate year, the winter quantity was surpassed in summer 20 times, but in 1973 the difference was 1:40. This gives me an explanation why in the Northern Areas of Pakistan normally more people are killed by drowning than by falling from the mountain tracks. Only climber expeditions and jeep-traffic have somewhat distorted the statistic evidence.

In the mountains south of the great furrow (Gilgit valley-Rondu-Shyok) the situation is quite different. The area is affected by clouds brought by winds from the South. Satellite photographs are the best proof. The result is early and heavy snowfall, not as much as in the valleys but on the mountains, closing the passes.

The range immediately south of the Gilgit valley is impassable for a short period only. The higher ranges to the East and to the West of the southern flank of the Nanga Parbat however, are blocked by snow for most of the year. In fact, the jeep-road via the

Babusar pass, now in bad repair and practically out of use, was open only from May/June to August/September. Even men on foot were endangered by avalanches.

That means that travellers from the South had to start not later than August. Afterwards they had to stay in the Transhimalyas for three months, and only then they could venture to continue to the North crossing the rivers, now already at low level, while the passes were still open.

The way back needed an expanded interval as well. Starting from the northwestern corner of the Tarim Basin in November, wanderers reached the Indus valley west of the Nanga Parbat in January, and then they had to stay there until May/June.

Certainly many travellers accepted the rule of the game. Among them were the foreign artists who for a while lived near Chilas or Shatial in local monasteries. They had plenty of time to produce petroglyphs using the local technique (picking or engraving the rock), but following the stylistic tradition of their homelands (Jettmar 1980a, 1980b, 1980c, 1982, 1983a, 1983b).

The pre-historic and early historic migrants, for instance the Saka tribes who brought their cattle with them, certainly appreciated the slow and discontinued kind of migration. They had better arms than the locals and could require provisions if needed. Some of them settled down as "lords of the mountains." (The problem is dealt with in my forthcoming article *Prähistorische Wanderrouten in den Zentralasiatischen Hochgebirgen*, Smolla-Festschrift).

Diplomatic missions, merchants, and Buddhist pilgrims had a time-saving but dangerous way to shorten the procedure. They could use the only permanent open connection between the Transhimalayan zone and the South, namely the Suspended Crossing. In this way they could start in October/November and reach their destination area in January. Such journeys were feasible in both directions.

A few ethnographic observations may be added.

The footpath to the gorges of the Indus was used until the first unmetalled road replaced it at the end of the sixties. When the footpath was used by pedlars coming from the North, they had to leave the bank of the Indus between Shatial and Sazin and to climb up to a place near the village of Sazin, approximately 300 metres higher than the bottom of the Indus valley. Here a group of stone slabs marked the beginning of the most dangerous part of the track. It was practicable only because tree branches had been fixed in "fissures in the rock supporting galleries", steps had been carved out, on many places there were logs with notches to be used as ladders. The Sazinis were in charge of the repair, therefore, they had the right of toll to be paid at the place marked by the menhirs. The travellers tried to avoid the expenses so they made detours and were many times picked up by youths of the village. This was considered as a sport, the toll did not increase much after detection. Most of the time, the track climbed up and down through the precipices. Only at Jalkot, at the mouth of two large valleys, the dangerous part of the journey came to an end. Here and in some places farther south, it was possible to cross the Indus. During winter-time cliffs in the middle of the river were connected by tree-trunks forming temporary foot-bridges. From such places, the track to Swat was not too difficult.

Many of the passengers were pedlars from the South, from Pattan. They made their tours to the North late in the year, when agricultural work was finished and the villagers lived in compact settlements situated in the lower parts of the valleys. The pedlars always went on in groups carrying their loads in barrows which could be raised or let down by ropes at places where the men had to use the ladders.

Maybe this confirmation that the Suspended Crossing was indeed identic [*sic*] with the gorges of the Indus will help us to solve other problems. Since the Suspended Crossing is so far to the South. Wu-ch'a corresponding to an original *Uḍa

(Hulsewé 1979: 97-99, 101-104) was certainly not located somewhere between Badakhshan and Sarikol. The text says clearly that it is east of the Suspended Crossing. Only the Kaghan valley, or parts of Azad Kashmir fit into this description. According to the Han-shu it is east of Chi-pin (Hulsewé 1979: 99). Now in the *Records of the Western Lands* translated and interpreted for instance by Watters (1904/1905 – 1973: I, 239) there is an enigmatic notice that Ta-li-lo was formerly the seat of government of Uḍḍyāna/Wu-ch'ang. Ta-li-lo is identified with Darel, and the adjacent parts of the Indus valley.

Wu-ch'a and Wu-ch'ang were perhaps not only mixed up by modern authors (Lüders cf. Petech 1950: 18) but also by their ancient predecessors. If *Uḍa was the Kunhar-valley, also called Kaghan, it had perhaps a northern capital hidden behind the ranges, well protected against all enemies coming from the West or South. This would make more sense than a political connection with Swat, separated from Darel not by one but by several ridges. I don't dare to suppose an identification of *Uḍa with Oḍi, the country where the vassals of the Kushans ruled and deposited a most important document in the centre of a stupa (Bailey 1980)." Jettmar (1987), pp. 97-100.

Wucha (Wu-ch'a) and Wuchang (Wu-ch'ang or Uddiyana in modern Swat) have been often confused in later times – but I disagree with Jettmar that the ancient authors might have "mixed them up." The earliest Chinese texts make it perfectly clear that Wucha and Wuchang were separate states, located well apart. See: note 8.2.

In the early 5th century, when Fa Xian travelled southwest across the *xuandu* ('hanging passages') and through the Indus Valley he reached the country of Wuchang/Uddiyana immediately *after* crossing the river. Legge (1886), pp. 26-28. In the account of the *Hou Hanshu*, the traveller crossed Wucha *before* reaching the *xuandu*:

"Southwest of Pishan, you pass through Wucha, cross over the 'hanging passages' and Jibin and, at the end of more than 60 days march, you reach the kingdom of Wuyishanli."

Therefore, there can be no question of Wucha being mistaken for Wuchang/Uddiyana. For my identification of Wucha as Upper Hunza and the Tāghdumbāsh Pamir, see: note 8.2.

"If we follow the itinerary of Alexander to Swāt we meet a series of tribes, (and some of them having homologous names): Aspásioi < Aspioi? >, Assakenói, the Guréioi; Swāt is Soasténē for the Greeks, Suvāstu 'having a good dwelling" for the Vedas and Pāṇini IV, 2, 771 (Hu-asp for the Iranians?). But we find in Swāt another people: the Urdi, Aurddi, Uḍi (Tucci 1958, p. 326); then a name Wu ch'a, which could be taken as an older transcription, is found in the Commentary (*chu*) by Li Tao-yüan († 527) on the *Shui-ching-chu* "The classic of the Waters" (written in the 3rd century): « Kuo I-kung [lived under the Chin dynasty (265-420)] says that west of Wu ch'a (u̯o-d'ȧ, Uḍa) there is the country of "the hanging passages" » (cf. Hsüan-tsang).

In another passage Kuo I-kung also says that after crossing the "Hanging passages" there is a plain, which prof. Petech ([43]) identifies, rightly to my mind, with Gilgit (or better Yasin?). Wu ch'a here = Uḍa; but it has nothing to do with Uḍḍiyāna ([44]) which is much to the south of it.

([43]) PETECH 1950, p. 18.

([44]) As LÜDERS thought 1940, p. 496." Tucci (1977), p. 39 and notes 43-44.

The 'Karakoram Highway' from Pakistan to Xinjiang travels up the Indus Valley and around the base of Nanga Parbat, and through the Gilgit and Hunza Valleys. Travellers can still see the remnants of the terrifyingly narrow *rafiqs* crossing the bare cliff faces. The valley floors are often impassable in spring and summer, as they are filled with rushing torrents formed by the melting snowdrifts and glaciers.

Appendix V: Rhinoceroses and Rhinoceros Horn

Rhinoceroses (犀 *xi*) have long been in demand and hunted in China and Southeast Asia. At least two species survived in China into historical times: the two-horned 'Sumatran Rhinoceros' (*Dicerorhinus sumatrensis*), and the one-horned 'Javan' ('Sundan' or 'Lesser One-horned Rhinoceros'), *Rhinoceros sondaicus*.

> "*Re* the Rhinoceros : the difficulty arising from the mention in the *Hou-han-shu* of this animal as "coming from" T'iao-chih together with lions, zebus, peacocks and ostriches is not removed by placing T'iao-chih in any of the countries with which others have associated it, nor by giving it a position farther south on the coast of the Persian Gulf; the countries producing rhinoceros at the present day are altogether out of the question. Dr. Bretscheider (*Notes and Queries on China and Japan*, Vol. IV, p. 60 seq.), in trying to identify T'iao-chih with ancient Persia (Susa, Persepolis), assumes that, in this case, the term *hsi-niu* should be translated by *buffalo*; buffaloes being found in great numbers all over western Asia. But the difference between this animal and the rhinoceros is far too great ; and I would certainly not credit the Chinese writer, who must have known the former from his own experience and the latter from detailed descriptions of the Annamese species occurring in contemporaneous and older Chinese works, with such a confusion. If we possess no positive proof of the rhinoceros having existed in Chaldaea, I am also not aware of ancient authors stating that it did *not* exist there ; for, ancient literature, as it now exists, is mainly of an accidental nature and cannot fairly be expected to contain an exhaustive picture of the geographical range of each animal. Whether the rhinoceros did or did not occupy a prominent position in the Chaldaean fauna, there is no doubt that the low, swampy soil of the inundated fields near the lower course of the Euphrates must have been as good a habitat for this pachyderm as any other part of the world. Our knowledge in this respect is very incomplete, and the faith I place in the accuracy of ancient Chinese records has been so much strengthened in the course of my studies that I consider their mention of the rhinoceros in T'iao-chih quite as reliable as if the animal was stated by Ktesias, Pliny or Strabo to have been seen in Chaldaea. Is not our knowledge of the old fauna of countries much nearer our own civilisation equally doubtful? Who would have looked for rhinoceros' bones in the caves of Mount Libanon near Beirût where they have actually been seen together with the relics of the ure-ox, the bear, the Capricorn, the aboriginal goat (Urziege), the gazelle and the antelope? (Frass, *Drei Monate im Libanon*, Stuttgart, 1876, p. 66) Brehm (*Thierleben*, 2nd ed., Vol. III, p. 520) mentions a rhinoceros seen by Chardin at Ispahan, though I am not able to say how the animal had got to that place." Hirth (1875), pp. x-xii.

A rock relief near the village of Shamarq in Baghlan Province in central Afghanistan dating to circa 3rd to 4th centuries CE, depicts a Sassanian king hunting rhinoceroses. See: Cassar (2004), pp. 3-4.

As far as I know, they have not been recorded further to the west, although the wet swamplands of the lower Euphrates, as Hirth suggests, would seem to have been an ideal habitat for them, as would the wetlands near Kandahar and in Seistan. The Indian Rhinoceros was used in the circus "games" in Rome for the first, but not the last time, in 55 BCE under Augustus. See: Wiedemann, p. 3; Prothero & Schoch (2003), p. 277.

As Hirth said, Sir John Chardin reported that he saw a rhinoceros during his stay at Isfahan between 1664 and 1677 being used in Royal "games." It may not have been local but imported especially for this purpose. There is no indication as to its species. Chardin (1720), p. 84.

The Indian Rhinoceros (*Rhinoceros unicornis*) was still present in the 17th century as far west as the Indus River and the Afridi Hills near Peshawar:

> "Bábar Bádshah [1483-1541 CE] repeatedly mentions Pes'háwar by the name of Bagrám. In his day the rhinoceros was common in the *jangals* ['jungles'] of the district. On one occasion he found and killed one in a small wood near the township. Jahán-gír Bádsháh also says that he hunted the rhinoceros in the Begrám district, in company with his father, Akbar [1542-1605 CE]." Raverty (1880), p. 36.

Rhinoceroses said to have come from Tiaozhi could have been imported from Parthian territories in Sind and/or Gandhara, or from eastern Africa. In 2 CE one or more rhinoceroses were sent to the Chinese court from Huangzhi (Huang-chih) – usually thought to be in eastern India:

> "In the second year [of Pingdi = 2 CE], in the spring, the state of Huang-chih offered a rhinoceros [in tribute].[4.8]
>
> [4.8] Yen Shih-ku explains, "The rhinoceros has the shape of a water buffalo and a head like a pig, with four legs; it is like an elephant in its black color. It has one horn in front of its forehead, and on its nose has another small horn." For a translation of the passage in *HS* describing trading voyages into the Indian Ocean and the location of this place, cf. Glossary *sub* Huang-chih. Also cf. C. W. Bishop, "Rhinoceroses and Wild Ox in Ancient China," *China Journal XVII*, no. 6 (June 1933), p. 330. Wang Mang had sent a messenger with an order to the king of Huang-chih that he should present a live rhinoceros. Cf. *HS* 28 Bii: 68a, b; *Tzu-chih T'ung-chien* 35: 18b."
>
> Dubs (1955), p. 71 and note 4.8.

Compare the reference to this same event in a memorial of 5 CE, in which Huangzhi (which is said to be 30,000 *li* or 12,474 km from China), offered a live rhinoceros as tribute, in Dubs (1955), pp. 214-215. This would have been an Indian Rhinoceros.

Rhinoceroses were once widespread throughout Asia, ranging from Indonesia, through Southeast Asia, and into India and China, but the two-horned 'Sumatran Rhinoceros' (*Dicerorhinus sumatrensis*) and the one-horned 'Javan' ('Sundan' or 'Lesser One-horned') Rhinoceros – *Rhinocewros sondaicus*) are now restricted to two tiny populations, one in western Java, the other in a national park about 150 km north of Ho Chi Minh City (Saigon). There have been recent unconfirmed reports by locals of sightings of between twelve and fifteen Javan Rhinoceros in Vietnam. Chapman (1999), p. 43.

Daltry et al (2000), p. 3, report that there were still between three and eight individuals at Dong Nai in Vietnam and no other confirmed populations left in the country.

It is probable that the 'Indian' or the 'Great One-horned Rhinoceros' (*Rhinoceros unicornis*) was previously found in China. The Indian Rhinoceros once ranged from Pakistan to Burma but now only survives in small numbers in Nepal, Bhutan and Assam.

> "During the Bronze Age (around 3000 BC), when China was warmer than it is today, all three types of Asian rhino were found in China: the Indian (or one-horned) rhino, the Sumatran, and the Javan rhino. The horns, dried and powdered, were (and still are) believed by the Chinese to be a "cold drug," a preventative against hot ailments, such as poisons and fevers.
>
> The properties of "unicorn horn" were recognized in China long before they occurred to Europeans, probably because there were "unicorns" in China long before there were any in the West. In his fifty-volume pharmacological encyclopedia, the fourth-century Chinese author Li Chih-chen stated that the main ailments that could be treated with rhinoceros horn were snakebites, hallucinations, typhoid fever, headaches, boils, carbuncles, vomiting, food poisoning, and "devil possession," but in addition, "the unicorn horn is a safe guide to tell the presence of poison: when

poisonous medicines of liquid form are stirred with a horn, a white foam will bubble up, and no other test is necessary." (In their 2002 book *Rhinos,* Ann and Steve Toon suggested that, "improbable as it sounds, there may be some justification for the belief, as the alkaloids present in some poisons do react strongly with the keratin and gelatine in horn.")" Ellis (2005), pp. 77-78.

"The rhinoceros, like the elephant, was a familiar animal in north China in prehistoric and perhaps early historic times, but was already a rarity by the time of the ages illuminated by books. It is likely that two of the three Asian species of rhinoceroses were familiar to the archaic Chinese: we have small sculptures of both a one – and a two-horned kind surviving from Shang, Chou, and Han times; these must represent the Javanese (or Sunda) rhinoceros and the Sumatran rhinoceros respectively, both once widespread on the mainland and in the islands, but now restricted to remote parts of Indonesia, and on the verge of extinction." Schafer (1963), p. 83.

"Although nowadays the three species [of Asian rhinoceroses] are widely separated in habitat, both the one-horned and the two-horned species were once to be found living in the South-West of China, specifically in the province of Sichuan." Chapman (1999), p. 27.

"Another thick-skinned wanderer from the Pliocene (as it seems) was the Chinese rhinoceros, which can be no longer seen in China. Widely spread there in antiquity, in T'ang times it was found only in parts of Nam-Viet, especially the fastnesses of Jung Administration (Tang and Yü-lin), and in the remote woodlands of western and southern Hunan; it was apparently still common in Annam. The animal carried two horns, on its brow and nose, and Liu Hsün gives as its proper name "gaur rhinoceros" (*szu hsi*), presumably because its horns resembled those of that classical wild ox. He also tells of a single-horned rhinoceros, the Westerner's Cap Rhinoceros (*hu mao hsi*), doubtless so called because its horn looked like a Phyrgian cap, but not as a resident of the T'ang empire." Schafer (1967), p. 226.

"The fact is that the rhinoceros was hunted for its horn, then as now, and that the present-day tragedy of chase and slaughter reflects a situation that is at least two thousand years old. One of the earliest Chinese writings on the subject, dating from the second century BCE [*sic* – should read third century BCE] relates how the first Emperor of China, the notorious Qin Shihuang who reigned between 221 and 209 BCE, sent out five hundred thousand men to open up south-east trade routes in order to acquire rhinoceros horn and elephant tusks. The text in question goes on to say that there was a tremendous growth in the popularity of articles made from rhinoceros horn." Chapman (1999), p. 26.

"Rhinoceros horns are conical in shape, with a hollow in the base which originally fitted over the fleshy pad on the rhino's head. . . .

Because of this, they were used in ancient China as cups for fermented rice wine. In the poem "Juan'er" from the *Shijing* (Poetry Classic) it says "I will now take a cup (of wine) from that rhinoceros' horn, hoping I may not have long to sorrow" (Legge, 1960, Bk.1 Ode 3). This literary evidence confirms the fact that by the Eastern Zhou Dynasty at the latest, the Chinese were using wine cups made out of rhinoceros horn. Later they came to believe that when drinking from a rhino horn cup, its curative elements would be dissolved into the wine, thereby easing their pain and lengthening their lives. This belief may have arisen as a result of the growing interest in finding "The Elixir of Life" which became the focus of "The Search for Immortality" during the

third century B.C.E. Thus two of the most ancient uses of rhino horn, as a medicine, and as a wine cup, became linked together in people's minds. . . .
This evidence of the early use of rhino horn cups for wine and the use of dice made of rhino horn is intriguing, because it clearly links rhinoceros horn with games of chance in ancient China. Fate and good luck, which were also closely associated with the mythic unicorn *zhi* because of its uncanny ability to determine one's guilt or innocence in a court of law, also played an important role in such games." Parker (2007): Chapter 17. "The Ancient Uses of Rhinoceros Horn."

"Then again, we must not forget the fact that rhinoceros horn was already being used in China as a detector of poison. How and why the horn originated as a means of detecting poison and also as its antidote is lost in the mists of antiquity. The first written reference goes back to the fourth century and concerns a Daoist chemist named Ge Hong who wrote many books on the search for immortality. He said:
The horn is a safe guide to tell the presence of poison; when poisonous medicines of liquid form are stirred with a horn, a white foam will bubble up and no further test is necessary; when non-poisonous substances are stirred with it, no foam will arise. In this manner, the presence of poison can be detected.

Popular songs dating back long before 500 BCE demonstrate that rhinoceros horn cups were used when drinking toasts to wish for 'long life.' These songs suggest that in the minds of the people rhinoceros horn was already linked with the concept of immortality." Chapman (1999), p. 32.

"There are five species of rhinoceroses. Three of them live in Asia and two in Africa. *The Indian rhinoceros* is the largest of the three Asian species. It stands about 5 feet 8 inches (1.7 meters) high at the shoulder and weighs about 2 short tons (1.8 metric tons). It has one great blue-black horn, very thick at the base and about 1 foot (30 centimeters) long. In rare cases, the animal may stand up to 6 1/2 feet (2 meters) with a horn 2 feet (61 centimeters) long. The skin of the Indian rhinoceros is sprinkled with round knobs. It hangs in such definite folds that the animal looks as though it were wearing armor plate. But the hide can be pierced by a knife or bullet. The animal lives in marshy jungles among reeds and tall grass, on which it feeds morning and evening. Ancient peoples of Asia knew this rhinoceros well. It was even used in the circus games in Rome before the time of Christ. The similar one-horned *Javan rhinoceros* once ranged from eastern Bengal into Burma, and southward to Java, Borneo, and Sumatra. It is now nearly extinct. The *Sumatran* species is smaller than any other rhinoceros and has two horns. It stands about 4 ½ feet (1.4 meters) tall and weighs about 1 short ton (0.9 metric ton). It is hairy, especially on the tail and ears. The young have more body hair than the adults. This species lives in Sumatra, Borneo, and on the Malay Peninsula. It too is nearing extinction. Both the Javan and Sumatran rhinoceroses are found in forested hills. Less than 2,000 rhinoceroses live in the wild in Asia." Downloaded from: http://tourkenya.5u.com/RHINOCEROS.html on 17 November, 2004.

"During the late Warring States and the early Han Dynasty an extraordinary transmutation occurred whereby images of the mythic goat-unicorn zhi began to merge with images of the only other one-horned animal known to the ancient Chinese, and that, of course, was the rhinoceros. This melding of images was only made possible by the fact that by that time rhinos were rarely seen in central China anymore. And just as familiarity may breed contempt, extinction often gives birth to myth. So it was that by the Western Han Dynasty at the latest, the rhinoceros had acquired the status of a mythic beast in China. But how did this happen, when, as we have seen, the Rhinocerotidae had such a tremendously long ancestry in China stretching back into the Tertiary period?

Today the five surviving species of rhinoceros are found mainly in the tropical regions of Africa, India, Sumatra and Java. Yet rhinoceros bones found in Chinese Neolithic sites of six thousand years ago clearly indicate that rhinos flourished in both north and south China at that time (Sun, 1982, 80). During the Bronze Age, when the climate of northern China was warmer than it is at present, various species of Asian rhinoceros were known, including the two-horned Sumatran (*Dicerorhinus sumatrensis*) and the one-horned Javan (*Rhinoceros sondaicus*). In addition, a three-horned variety with one horn on the nose and two small horns on the forehead is mentioned in early Chinese texts. This three-horned tendency appears to be genetic, as it is now localized in different parts of Africa (Hillman-Smith and Groves, 1994, 5).

There is an ancient character *si* which appears in many oracle bone inscriptions and shows an animal with one large variegated horn on its head. . . ." Parker (2007); Kindle Edition Locations: 1444-1450.

"During Shang and Zhou times the rhinoceros was captured and killed mainly for its tough, thick skin. When dried, this became extremely hard and provided excellent protection against bronze weapons. Rhinoceros hide was considered to be the ideal material for making the helmets, body armour and shields commonly worn by soldiers throughout the Bronze Age period (Laufer, 1914, 174–200). At first, Shang armour was made from large single pieces of leather (fig. 42)....

From ancient times, in addition to their use in the manufacture of protective body armour and shields, rhinoceros hides and horns were melted down to make glue for the construction of Chinese compound bows. In the *Zhouli* (Rites of Zhou) it is recorded that this glue was made by boiling the skins and horns of various animals (Werner, 1932, 17), and in another ancient text, *Guo pu Mao shi shi yi* (Fragments of the Mao Commentary to the Shu jing) it says "the people of the west country use deer antlers and rhinoceros horn to make bows" (ibid., 20). Even as late as 1830, native Siberians were still using fossil rhino horns as raw material to increase the elasticity of their bows, since rhino horn was apparently excellent for this purpose (Fortelius, 1983, 126).

As a result of the increasing demand for rhinoceros hide armour during the turbulent Spring and Autumn period and the horrific conflicts of the Warring States period, the indigenous rhinoceros population in China was decimated. The gradual cooling of the climate throughout the Bronze Age probably also affected the rhino's habitat, and caused a southward migration towards Vietnam and Laos, similar to that undertaken by the Saola. But the unprecedented slaughter of the rhinoceros over the many centuries of the Eastern Zhou Dynasty dealt the death blow to the survival of this species in China. As a result, the rhinoceros entered the realm of legend, and came to be considered a mythic beast." Parker (2007). Kindle Edition: Locations 1489-1531.

"Though some old-fashioned rhinoceros-hide armor was still being made [in Tang times], the real demand was for the wonderful horn. Its uses were similar to those of ivory. It was carved into elegantly designed cups, boxes, bracelets, paperweights, knife hilts, chopsticks, note tablets, belt plaques, wish-fulfilling wands, and women's head ornaments. The various kinds of horn available were evaluated on the basis of their natural patterning. In particular, the image of a bird or animal in the venation of the horn greatly enhanced its value. . . . But even beyond this, rhinoceros horn was held in esteem as an antidote to poison. It would heal the wound caused by a poisoned arrow in an instant. . . ." Schafer (1967), pp. 226-227.

"Since ancient times in China, the most important use of rhinoceros horn ... has been as an antipyretic medicine to reduce fever." Parker (2007): Kindle Edition: Location 1541.

"Contrary to a universally held Western misconception, the rhino's horn is not widely considered to be an aphrodisiac. Only the Romans (and, nowadays, a few Indians) believed it to have this property, presumably either because it is long, hard and pointed upwards or because the rhino itself is so generously endowed by the size of its penis and takes over an hour to complete its copulation. . . .

In the Far East, however, it is another story and rhino horn has been on the books of traditional herbalists and exponents of folk-medicine since well before the time of Christ. . . .

Depending upon where one looks in the Far East, rhino horn has a variety of wonderful properties. In India, it is still – though very infrequently – offered as an aphrodisiac when mixed with herbs and swallowed in milk or honey: it was from the East that the Romans heard of this supposed property. Similarly taken, it is also said to cure arthritis, muscular pains and spasms and paralysis: fat and stomach lining are also said to cure polio and skin diseases. In the past, the horn was burnt under the anus of hæmorrhoid sufferers to alleviate their condition and to counteract constipation....

Rhino horn shavings are given as a treatment for the lowering of fever such as typhus and malaria. The idea, as is so often the case with such traditional brews, is that the liquid cleanses the body of poisons. Additionally, it is regarded as a cure for laryngitis, bronchitis, tuberculosis and poor eyesight. Dried and powdered rhino's blood is sold as a tonic for sufferers of anæmia which it probably does help to cure being, like snake's blood, rich in iron." Booth (1988), pp. 156–159.

"The horn of the rhinoceros played a role in the minor arts of T'ang very similar to that of ivory, and indeed the two substances were regularly linked in language, particularly in parallel verse. The demand for rhinoceros horn was very great, so that, although many rhinoceroses still lived in Hunan, as we have seen, and their horns were submitted to the court as tribute, it was also necessary to import them. From close at hand, they were obtained in Nan-chao and Annam; more remotely, they came to the port of Canton from the Indies, and in such quantities that the near extinction of the Indochinese rhinoceroses in modern times can in large part be attributed to the China trade of the T'ang. . . .

Rhinoceros horn was important in medieval Chinese medicine, especially as an antidote for all kinds of poison. Belief in its efficacy goes back to the fourth century, and may have originated in China, to spread to Western Asia and the Roman empire." Schafer (1963), p. 241; also p. 83.

"We have no means of scientifically establishing the identity of the kind of rhinoceros horn which was known to the Chinese as the *tongtianxi*. It may be that it was simply a term they used to designate a particularly rare type of rhino horn. Nevertheless, it was probably the horn of an Asian species, since all Asian rhinoceros horns have, in addition to their traverse banding, a distinctive groove on the exterior which runs longitudinally toward the tip, a feature which does not appear on African rhino horns (Chapman, 1999, 51). This unique groove may have provided the inspiration for the idea of the vein running through the *tongtianxi* with which it communicated with the sky." Parker, (2007). Kindle Edition: Locations 2348-2353.

In spite of Parker's comment above, it seems very probable that *Haiji* Rhinoceroses 駭雞犀, at least at times, referred to one or both of the two large African species - *Ceratotherium simum* (Burchell, 1817), the so-called 'White Rhinoceros, and/or the *Diceros bicornis* (Linnaeus, 1758) known as the 'Black Rhinoceros." Their exceptionally large horns were in high demand as trade items from the 1st century BCE, if not earlier.

Possibly, in spite of the comments linking them in the Chinese literature, the *Tongtian* and the *Haixi* were separate species – with the *Haixi* rhinos coming from Africa, while the *Tongtian* rhinoceros (通天犀) came from Asia, as Parker suggests above. If so, the *Tongtian* rhinoceros was clearly not one of the two commonly known species to the Chinese - the Sumatran and Javan Rhinoceroses and, if it wasn't one of the African species, it must have been the Indian Rhinoceros (*Rhinoceros unicornis*) – the only other extant species.

There are several reasons for identifying the *Haiji* rhinoceroses with the African species, including the telling fact that '*haiji*' is only used to describe rhinoceroses (or, more accurately, their horns) from Da Qin/the Roman Empire, and never those from Southeast Asia or India.

The *haiji* rhinoceroses are specifically mentioned as a product of Da Qin in the *Weilüe*, and therefore not from Asia. The two African species had by far the largest horns. The horns of the White Rhinoceros averaged 46 cm to 1.22 m (18 in to 4 ft), sometimes reaching 1.52 m (5 ft). According to Chapman 1999, p. 54, the record for the Black Rhinoceros seems to be 136 cm (4 ft 5.6 ins), although Ellis says that the record rhino horns for both species were nearly 5 feet (152.4 cm) in length. Ellis (2005), pp. 90, 99.

These horns dwarf the horn of the Indian Rhinoceros – the largest Asian species - of which the record size is only 20.6 in. (52.3 cm.). Ellis (2005), p. 112.

The Barbarā Coast of northeast Africa was well known to the Chinese for large rhinoceros horns in the 12th – 13th centuries, and probably far earlier:

> "The (other) products [of Pi-p'a-lo/Bipaluo = the Berbera Coast] are ambergris, big elephants' tusks and big rhinoceros horns. There are elephants' tusks which weigh over one hundred catties, and rhinoceros horns of over ten catties weight. [6 catties]" Hirth and Rockhill (1911), p. 128. **NOTE** See: ibid. p. 149, for more on the export of rhinoceros horns from islands far to the south along the African coast, perhaps Pemba and Madagascar.

The connection between the two names *haiji* and *tongtian* is first found in Ge Hong's *Baopuzi nei pian*, Chapter 17: "Climbing Mountains and Crossing Rivers," written in the early 5th century CE. He says:

> ". . . the Southern people also called the *Tongtian xi* (rhinoceros) the *Haiji xi* (chicken scaring rhinoceros) (故南人或名通天犀為駭雞犀)." Downloaded on 26 November 2005 from: http://venus.unive.it/dsao/pregadio/textbase/bpz_17.html.

The reference to the identification of *haiji* and *tongtian* rhinoceros horn by Ge Hong (W-G: Ko Hung), is quoted in *P'ei wên yün fu* – see the passage from Laufer (1914), p. 137, n. 1, and p. 138, and nn. 1-4, in Section V.

> "1 The allusion to the *hiai ki si* occurs in Ch. 108 of *Hou Han shu* (compare CHAVANNES, Les pays d'Occident d'après le Heou Han Chou, *T'oung Pao*, 1907, p. 182; and HIRTH, China and the Roman Orient, p. 79), where this kind of horn is ascribed to the country of Ta Ts'in (the Roman Orient). The legend given in explanation as above is derived from the famous Taoist writer Ko Hung, who died about 330 A.D.; and it is not accidental that the Taoist T'ao Hung-king here copies his older colleague, for the legend is plainly Taoistic in character. It is quoted in the commentary to *Hou Han shu*, but not in the text of the Annals. The view of Hirth, that it has arisen in consequence

of a false etymology based on the Chinese characters transcribing a foreign word, seems to me unfounded. First, as Chavannes remarks, the foreign word supposed to be hidden in *hiai-ki* has not yet been discovered, and in all probability does not exist. Second, as will be seen from *P'ei wên yün fu* (Ch. 8, p. 87 b), the term *hiai ki si* does not occur in *Hou Han shu* for the first time, but is noted as early as the *Chan kuo ts'e* at the time of Chang I, who died in B.C. 310, when the King of Ch'u despatched a hundred chariots to present to the King of Ts'in fowl-scaring rhinoceros-horns and jade disks resplendent at night (*ye kuang pi*). It is certainly somewhat striking to meet here these two names, which are identical with those in *Hou Han shu*, and occur there close together; and it cannot be denied that the passage of *Chan kuo ts'e* might be an interpolation. Huai-nan-tse, who died in B.C. 122, alludes to a rhinoceros-horn frightening foxes (*si kio hiai hu*, quoted in *P'ei wên yün fu*, *l. c.*, p. 89 a, "when placed in the lair of a fox, the fox does not dare return"), which is a case analogous in word and matter to the fowl-frightening horn. These notions must be taken in connection with the other legends regarding the rhinoceros, which all seem to spring from indigenous Taoist lore. The text of Ko Hung, as quoted in *P'ei wên yün fu* and translated by Hirth and Chavannes, is fuller than cited above in the *Pên ts'ao*, while the final clause in regard to placing the horn on the roof does not occur in Ko Hung. The latter links the *hiai ki si* with the t'ung t'ien, which Hirth and Chavannes translate "communicating with Heaven." This is certainly all right; but I prefer to avoid this term, because it may give rise to misunderstandings, as we are wont to think of Heaven as the great cosmic deity. A comparative study of all passages concerned renders it clear that the rhinoceros is not associated with spiritual, but with material heaven; that is, the sky. It is the stars of the sky which are supposed to be reflected in the veins of the horn. This means that the designs of the horn gave the impetus to the conception of connecting the rhinoceros with the phenomena of the sky,— again a thoroughly Taoistic idea, in which no trace of an outside influence can be discovered. Father ZOTTOLI (Cursus litteraturae sinicae, new ed., Vol. I, p. 301) renders the term *t'ung t'ien si tai by* "penetrantis coelum rhinocerotis cingulum."— Chao Ju-kua (Hirth's and Rockhill's translation, p. 103) attributes *hiai ki si* or *t'ung t'ien si* also to Baghdad (but I see no reason why these words should denote there a precious stone, instead of rhinoceros-horn). On p. 108 (note 10) the two authors represent the matter as though this reference might occur in *Ling-wai tai ta*, but in fact it is not there (Ch. 3, p. 1 b); it must therefore be due to Chao Ju-kua, who seems to indulge in a literary reminiscence taken from *Hou Han shu*. The passage, accordingly, affords no evidence for a trade in rhinoceros-horns from Baghdad to China, which *per se* is not very likely.—In the illustrations to the *Fêng shên yen i* (ed. of *Tsi ch'êng t'u shu*, p. 9, Shanghai, 1908), T'ung t'ien kiao chu (see W. GRUBE, Die Metamorphosen der Götter, p. 652) is seated astride a rhinoceros (outlined as a bull with a single striped horn), apparently because his name *T'ung t'ien* has been identified with *t'ung t'ien si*." Laufer (1914), p. 137, note 1.

The term 通天 *Tongtian* (*t'ung t'ien*) is defined in *GR* as: "1. To reach the sky : immense ; high . . 3. abbreviation of 通天犀 *tongtian xi* (*t'ung t'ien hsi*) – entirely white rhinoceros horn. . . ." *GR* Vol. VI, p. 386. Also, see: *GR* Vol. VI, p. 382.

The first definition suggests that the term as applied to rhinoceros (horn), indicates a very large horn – larger than those o the Indian rhinoceroses, which was the largest rhinoceros previously known to the Chinese.

The *tongtian* rhinoceros must, therefore, have been one of the two African species, both of which had horns larger that the Indian Rhinoceros. The so-called 'White' or 'Square-lipped' rhinoceros (*Ceratotherium simum*), was the most likely as it has the largest and very long horn that curves up pointing towards the sky even when it has its head lowered.

This can be clearly seen in a series of comparative profiles of each of the extant species of rhinoceroses in Gwin (2012), p. 114. In this article, a photo of one of these impressive horns, weighing 8 pounds (3.6 kg) is shown on page 112 with an estimated value on the black market of "up to US $360,000". The largest horns were more than three times as long as the one pictured here.

It is not at all clear what *le Grand Ricci* means by its reference to "entirely white rhinoceros horn." Perhaps it comes from a misreading of the claim that it had white "veins" (as in the quote from Chavannes – see below).

> "Regarding the expression 駭雞犀 *haijixi*, the commentary of the *Hou Hanshu* quotes a passage of the *Baopozi* of *Ge Hong* (4th cent. CE) where it is said that: "(The horn of the) rhinoceros communicating with Heaven 通天犀 [*tongtian xi*] has white veins resembling those used to string pearls. If one places it covered with rice in the middle of a flock of chickens, the chickens come to get the rice, but once they get there they recoil immediately in terror and this is why the Southern peoples call (the rhinoceros) *haiji* (that is to say, it frightens the chickens)." As Hirth commented, this legend must have developed later from a false etymology based on the Chinese characters which were used to transcribe a foreign word. Nevertheless, no one has yet found the foreign word which lies hidden behind the transcription of *haiji* of the term *haijixi*. It is known that the Arab voyagers of the ninth century gave the name *kerkedden* as another term for rhinoceros. On the other hand, the Sanskrit word for rhinoceros is *khadgin*. Cf. Reinard, *Relation des voyages faits par les Arabes et les Persanes*, Bk. I, pp. 28–30, and, in Bk. II, pp 65–70, the remarks of the naturalist Roulin." Translated and adapted from Chavannes (1907), p. 182, n. 1.

> "The native products [of Ta-ts'in = Da Qin] comprise . . . ; also (the precious stone called) hié-ki-si (駭雞犀) or túng-t'ién-si (通天犀)." Hirth and Rockhill (1911), p. 103. Also see p. 233.

The translators' interpretation of these two names as "precious stones" is mistaken. The Chinese names specifically refer to types of rhinoceros (horns).

The identification of *haiji xi* in the commentary of the *Hou Hanshu* as a "chicken-frightening rhinoceros" is clearly a case of a mistaken folk etymology based on a legend started by Taoist writers (probably Liu Xiang) during the Former Han dynasty.

The Chinese were importing rhinoceros horn and live rhinoceroses prior to the Later Han dynasty.

The "Westerner's Cap Rhinoceros" (*hu mao hsi*) was written: 胡帽犀. The so-called "gaur rhinoceros" (*szu hsi*) was written: 兕牛, and, according to William's Dictionary, p. 729, referred to: "The Malayan rhinoceros, the 兕牛 described as having a horn three cubits long ; its body is black, and weighs a thousand catties [597 kg] ; its skin is fit for making armor."

It is of interest that the rhinoceroses mentioned in the *Hou Hanshu* as products of Tiaozhi (Characene and Susiana – see: note 9.4), and Tianzhu (northern India) are referred to as *xi* 犀, and not described at all (presumably because they were already well known to the Chinese), while *haiji* rhinoceroses are mentioned *only* in connection with Da Qin (The Roman Empire). This again supports the theory that *haiji* rhinoceroses were different from the Indian and Southeast Asian species.

According to the *Hanshu*, the kingdom of Huangzhi (which was probably a kingdom at the mouth of the Ganges – Colless (1980), pp. 164-172), sent one or more live rhinoceroses to the court of Wang Mang in 2 CE, and perhaps again in 5 CE. Dubs (1955), pp. 71, 214-215. These are clearly listed as plain *xi* 犀, not *haiji xi*. See: note 9.4.

1. *Haiji* 駭雞 may have been another attempt to transcribe "Egypt," from where the Roman trading ships left on their way to India and ports further east. The phonetic reconstructions for *haiji* are:

2. 駭 *hai* – K. 937y *g'ɛg / γăi; EMC. ɣəɨj'/ɣɛːj'
   雞 *ji* – K. 876n *kieg / kiei; EMC. kɛj

The *Hou Hanshu* gives the name for Egypt as: Haixi 海西 – literally, 'West of the Sea.' See notes 10.13 and 12.25. As mentioned in note 10.13, the modern Chinese name of Egypt, *Aiji* 埃及, is also similar. All three forms may well have served as transcriptions of the same name.

We know Roman ships traded significant quantities of African rhinoceros horn to India by the 1st century CE. Their horns are mentioned as a trade item in the *Periplus of the Erythraean Sea*, which was written about the middle of the 1st century CE. This makes it likely that they would have found their way to China as well.

> "Rhinoceros horn was exported only from Africa—Adouli [the only port for the kingdom of Axum, which was in the Red Sea] and Rhapta [in south-eastern Africa; probably near the mouth of the Rufiji River]. It is possible that much of it went to India." Huntingford (1980), p. 124.

> "The mass of elephants and rhinoceroses that are slaughtered all inhabit the upland regions, although on rare occasions they are also seen along the shore around Adulis itself. . . . Exports from this region are: ivory, tortoise shell, rhinoceros horn." Casson (1989), pp. 53 and 55.

> "The area [serviced by Rhapta] exports: a great amount of ivory but inferior to that of Adulis; rhinoceros horn; best-quality tortoise shell after the Indian; a little nautilus shell." Casson (1989), p. 61.

> "Another commodity which was fed into the trade of the Indian Ocean from the *Barbarā* coast was rhinoceros horn, possibly the single most valuable item in the Chinese pharmacopoeia, a veritable apotropaion of apotropaia, which could also afford raw material for the jeweler. The Chinese could, of course, obtain horns from their own southern provinces and from South and Southeast Asia, but the market was so elastic that from time to time Arab merchants found it worth their while to bring to China the horn of the African rhinoceros." Wheatley (1975), p. 106.

On the other hand, Jeannie Thomas Parker speculates that *tongtianxi* probably referred to one of the Asiatic forms of rhinoceros horn:

> "The *tongtianxi* (communicating with the sky rhinoceros horn): This type of rhino horn was further defined in the commentaries on *Baopuzi* which were also written during the fourth century C.E. There, alchemists speculated that this particular horn was perforated from top to bottom and contained a marvellous substance which grew towards the tip of the horn, creating a star-shaped opening from which was emitted *qi*. By means of this *qi*, the magical horn of the rhinoceros was able to communicate with heaven and the world of the spirits.
>
> We have no means of scientifically establishing the identity of the kind of rhinoceros horn which was known to the Chinese as the *tongtianxi*. It may be that it was simply a term they used to designate a particularly rare type of rhino horn. Nevertheless, it was probably the horn of an Asian species, since all Asian rhinoceros horns have, in

addition to their traverse banding, a distinctive groove on the exterior which runs longitudinally toward the tip, a feature which does not appear on African rhino horns (Chapman, 1999, 51). This unique groove may have provided the inspiration for the idea of the vein running through the *tongtianxi* with which it communicated with the sky." Parker (2013): Kindle Version, Locations 2342-2353. "

"Li Shih-chên does not refer to Ko Hung, the famous Taoist adept of the fourth century,[1] who is the first author to impart a fantastic account in regard to rhinoceros-horn. He is likewise the first to set forth its [supposed] quality of detecting poison. His text is here translated, as given in *Tu shu tsi ch'êng.*[2]

"Mr. Chêng[3] once obtained a genuine rhinoceros-horn of the kind 'communicating with the sky,' three inches long, the upper portion being carved into the form of a fish. When a man carries such a piece in his mouth and descends into the water, the water will give way for him and leave a vacant space three feet square, so that he has a chance to breathe in the water.[4] The horn 'communicating with the sky' has a single red vein like a silk string running from base to the tip. When a horn filled with rice is placed among a flock of chickens, the chickens want to peck the grains. Scarcely have they approached the horn to within an inch when they are taken aback and withdraw. Hence the people of the south designate the horn 'communicating with the sky' by the name 'fowl-frightening horn.' When such a horn is placed on a heap of grain, the birds do not dare assemble there. Enveloped by a thick fog or exposed to the night dew, when placed in a courtyard, the horn does not contract humidity. The rhinoceros (*si*) is a wild animal living in the deep mountain-forests. During dark nights its horn emits a brilliant light like torch-fire. The horn is a safe guide to tell the presence of a poison: when poisonous medicines of liquid form are stirred with a horn, a white foam will bubble up, and no other test is necessary; when non-poisonous substances are stirred with it, no foam will rise. . . .

[1] He died in 330 A.D. at the age of eighty-one; see GILES (Biographical Dictionary, p. 372); MAYERS (Chinese Reader's Manual, p. 86); BRETSCHNEIDER (Bot. Sin., pt I, p. 42); and PELLIOT (*Journal asiatique*, 1912, Jullet-Août, p. 145).

[2] Chapter on Rhinoceros (*hui k'ao*, p. 3), introduced by the author's literary name Pao-p'u-tse, and the title of his work *Têng shê p'ien*, which is not included in the Taoist Canon.

[3] Presumably Chêng Se-yūan, a relative and spiritual predecessor of Ko Hung (L. WIEGER, Taoisme, Vol. I, Le canon, p. 16; PELLIOT, *l. c.*, p. 146.

[4] It is interesting to note that this belief is still upheld in the modern folk-lore of Annam: "Celui qui peut se procurer une corne de rhinocéros et la sculpt en forme de poisson, s'il la met entre ses dents, peut descender sans danger, comme le rhinoceros, ou le poisson, tout au fond de l'eau" (P. GIRAN, Magie et Religion Annamites, p. 104, Paris."

From the *T'u shu tsi ch'êng,* translated in Laufer (1914), p. 138, and notes 1-4.

"*Baopuzi* [the *Baopuzi nei pian* by Ge Hong (284-363 or 283-343 CE)] provides many other examples of sympathetic magic. The horn of a certain species of rhinoceros, called *tongtianxi* 通天犀, for example, was believed to be a powerful antidote of various sorts of poison because the animal was supposed to feed on poisonous plants. If a fish was carved on a piece of rhinoceros horn three inches or more in length, a person holding the horn in the mouth would be able to breath [*sic*] normally under water, as water would recede three feet from the horn forming a volume of air. Perhaps the charging power of the rhinoceros with the horn at the front and the ability of the fish to live in water were believed to produce this magical power." Ho (1985), p. 179.

"Su Sung, author of the *T'u king pên ts'ao*, published by imperial order in the age of the Sung dynasty, has the following: "Of rhinoceros-horn, that coming from the regions of the Southern Sea (*Nan hai*) takes the first place; that from K'ien and Shu[6] ranks next.

[6] Ancient designations for the present territory of the provinces of Kuei-chou and Sze-ch'uan."

Laufer (1914), p. 140, and n. 6. Consult the detailed notes on grades of rhinoceros horn in ibid. pp. 141, and n. 1; 142 and nn. 2-4; 143 and n. 4.

"The allusion to the *hiai ki si* [= *haiji xi* 駭雞犀] occurs in Ch. 108 of *Hou Han shu* (compare CHAVANNES, Les pays d'Occident d'après le Heou Han Chou, *T'oung Pao*, 1907, p. 182; and HIRTH, China and the Roman Orient, p. 79), where this kind of horn is ascribed to the country of Ta Ts'in (the Roman Orient). The legend is given in explanation as above is derived from the famous Taoist writer Ko Hung, who died about 330 A.D.; and it is not accidental that the Taoist T'ao Hung-king here copies his older colleague, for the legend is plainly Taoist in character. It is quoted in the commentary to *Hou Han shu*, but not in the text of the Annals. The view of Hirth, that it has arisen in consequence of a false etymology based on the Chinese characters transcribing a foreign word, seems to me unfounded. First, as Chavannes remarks, the foreign word supposed to be hidden in *hiai-ki* has not yet been discovered, and in all probability does not exist. Second, as will be seen from *P'ei wên yün fu* (Ch. 8, p. 87 b), the term *hiai ki si* does not occur in *Hou Han shu* for the first time, but is noted as early as the *Chan kuo ts'e* at the time of Chang I, who died in B.C. 310, when the King of Ch'u despatched a hundred chariots to present to the King of Ts'in fowl-scaring rhinoceros horns and jade disks resplendent at night (*ye kuang pi*). It is certainly somewhat striking to meet here these two names, which are identical with those in *Hou Han shu*, and occur there close together; and it cannot be denied that the passage of *Chan kuo ts'e* might be an interpolation. Huai-nan-tse, who died in B.C. 122, alludes to a rhinoceros-horn frightening foxes (*si kio hiai hu*, quoted in *P'ei wên yün fu*, *l. c.*, p. 89 a, "when placed in the lair of a fox, the fox does not dare return"), which is a case analogous in word and matter to the fowl-frightening horn. These notions must be taken in connection with the other legends regarding the rhinoceros, which all seem to spring from indigenous Taoist lore. The text of Ko Hung, as quoted in *P'ei wên yün fu* and translated by Hirth and Chavannes, is fuller than cited above in the *Pên ts'ao*, while the final clause in regard to placing the horn on the roof does not occur in Ko Hung. The latter links the *hiai ki si* with the *t'ung t'ien*, which Hirth and Chavannes translate "communicating with Heaven." This is certainly all right; but I prefer to avoid this term, because it may give rise to misunderstandings, as we are wont to think of Heaven as the great cosmic deity. A comparative study of all passages considered renders it clear that the rhinoceros is not connected with spiritual, but with material heaven; that is, the sky. It is the stars of the sky which are supposed to be reflected in the veins of the horn. This means that the designs of the horn gave impetus to the conception of connecting the rhinoceros with the phenomena of the sky, – again a thoroughly Taoistic idea, in which no trace of an outside influence can be discovered. Father ZOTTOLI (Cursus litteraturae sinicae, new ed., Vol. I, p. 301) renders the term *t'ung t'ien si tai* by "penetrantis coelum rhinocerotis cingulum." – Chao Ju-kua (HIRTH's and ROCKHILL's translation, p. 103) attributes *hiai ki si* or *t'ung t'ien si* also to Baghdad (but I see no reason why these words should denote there a precious stone, instead of rhinoceros-horn). On p. 108 (note 10) the two authors represent the matter as though this reference might occur in *Ling-wai tai ta*, but in fact it is not there (Ch. 3, p. I b); it must therefore be due to Chao Ju-kua, who seems to indulge in a literary reminiscence taken from *Hou Han shu*. The passage, accordingly, affords no evidence for a trade in rhinoceros-horns from Baghdad to China, which *per se* is not very likely. –In the illustrations to the *Fêng shen yen i* (ed. of *Tsi ch'eng t'u shu*, p. 9, Shanghai, 1908). T'ung t'ien kiao chu (see W. GRUBE, Die Metamorphosen der Götter, p. 652) is seated astride a rhinoceros (outlined as a bull with a single striped horn) apparently because his name *T'ung t'ien* has been identified with *t'ung t'ien si*." Laufer (1914), p. 137, n. 1.

The earliest apparent reference to *haiji* rhinoceroses is in the *Zhanguo ce* (*Chan kuo ts'e*), as mentioned by Laufer (see above). However, Victor Mair (personal communication, 16 Nov. 2005) states that, while the *Zhanguo ce* (or *Chan kuo ts'e*) certainly contains material from the Warring States Period, it was compiled and edited by Liu Xiang (*circa* 71-6 BCE). Therefore, we cannot be certain that the term *haiji* was used prior to the 1st century BCE.

Wang Yi (*circa* 89–*circa* 158), the commentator and compiler of the *Chuci*, defines *jihai* 雞駭 – described as a variant of *haiji* 駭雞 – as *wenxi* 文犀, or "veined rhinoceros horn" – see: *GR* Vol. VI, p. 588.

From this, it seems plausible that the name *haiji* might be a reference to a rare type of rhinoceros horn with visible 'vein' patterns showing in the horn.

"I am often asked whether there are any craftsmen working in this material today. As far as I am aware, the craft of rhinoceros horn carving died out in China somewhere around the year 1900 and the only country in the world where the craft has been practiced in volume in recent years has been in the Yemen Arab Republic. I visited North Yemen in 1984 . . . . During my visit I was fortunate to see some of the best carvers at work and learned a great deal about their handling of huge African horns, but I found that the Yemeni carvers knew nothing about dyeing the horn and even less about the type of skilled carving practiced by Chinese craftsmen between the twelfth and nineteenth centuries. In fact, when I showed them photographs of the beautiful flower bowl from the Chester Beatty collection (see 70) they could not believe it was made of rhinoceros horn." Chapman (1999), pp. 21-22.

"There is no reason to believe that the trade in African horn did not continue through the first millennium, since in the year 1226 the Commissioner for Foreign Trade in Fujian province reported that African as well as Asian horns were being imported through the Fujian ports. Discussing the products of the Berbera Coast (nowadays known as Somalia) he says that there are 'rhinoceros horns of over ten catties in weight' [6 kg].

By the Ming dynasty, large quantities of African horn were being imported into the south-east coastal ports of China and the value of these horns depended on two attributes: weight and patterning. Since African horns were so much larger than Asiatic horns the African horns would have been preferred. The most desirable type of horn, therefore, would be large and heavy with a light and dark patterning. The local gazetteer of Zhangzhou prefecture in Fujian province states that in the year 1615 the authorities distinguished between patterned white horn and black horn, taxing the former at almost three times the rate of the latter.

I had long been puzzled how the custom authorities of the Ming dynasty could grade the various horns for tax purposes without stripping off the protective outer sheath known as bark. The answer to the question came in 1988, when I was invited to examine a trunkful of twenty-five African Black rhinoceros horns recently arrived at the Museum of Natural History in Paris. The horns had been taken from animals shot by poachers and subsequently seized by the customs authorities. Of the twenty-five horns thirteen had black cores whilst twelve were of a uniformly dirty, pale-yellow colour, indicating that no black core was present. It is clear, therefore, that it was not necessary for the Chinese customs authorities to strip off the bark from imported horns in order to assess their value. The patterning effect of black against a pale background would have been visible at a glance and even these patterns varied from a small, round, central black mark to a large, wide-spreading mark sometimes with smaller spots of black at the periphery. Since I had never previously seen this black and white effect in the numerous museum specimens I had examined, I can only assume that the surface of the horn base loses its two-toned appearance as it dries out.

This black patterning which occurs on some rhinoceros horns has been of value since at least the Tang dynasty, for we learn that:

If the specks are deep in colour the horn is suitable for making into plaques for girdle ornaments. If the specks are scattered here and there, and light in colour, the horn can be made only into bowls and dishes.[27]

27: Laufer, B. (1914), p. 148 and note 7."

Chapman (1999), pp. 38-39 and note 27.

"The largest rhinoceros-horn is that of the *to-lo-si* [墮落犀], a single horn of which weighs from seven to eight catties. This is identified with the horn on the forehead of the male rhinoceros. It has numerous decorations conveying the impression of scattered beans. If the specks are deep in color, the horn is suitable to be made into plaques for girdle-ornaments; if the specks are scattered here and there, and light in color, the horn can be made only into bowls and dishes." Laufer (1914), p. 141, n. 1. See also p. 143, and note 4; Hirth and Rockhill (1911), p. 233, note.

"While both Europe and China bought the ivory, the biggest customer was India, as African ivory was superior to Indian ivory for carving into jewelry and ornaments." Kearney (2004), p. 93; Kindle Edition Location, No. 1374.

"The rhinoceros is already mentioned in Shan-hai-king, 10, 4, where it is called *si-ṇiu* (犀牛), Ling-piau-lü:i (written in the T'ang dynasty) gives (2, 10) an interesting description of the different varieties of rhinoceros of Indo-China and of the peculiarities of the horns of each. . . . The largest kind of rhinoceros is the *to-lo-si* (墮落犀), or *to-ho-lo* (墮和羅) rhinoceros, as the name is written in the T'ang-shu, 222[C], 10[a], whose horns attain a weight of seven or eight catties. Gerini, Researches, 830—831, says To-ho-lo was a district on the Gulf or Martaban." Hirth and Rockhill (1911), p. 233, note.

"When it comes to the quality of raw material, rhinoceros horns were graded by its chromatic mutations and configurations in ancient times. "Tongxi", for instance, is known for its superior quality. The cross-section of a "tongxi" horn shows a yellowish-beige interior that gradually turns black towards the core. In terms of type-form, the majority of the rhinoceros horns are carved into vessels, the most common kind being the libation cup. This is because the form of the libation cup coincides with the natural tapering form of the horn, making the best use of this very rare material. A second reason is based on the common belief that the cup may exude antidotal and mind-pacifying medicinal properties of the rhinoceros horn into the liquid it contains." From: "Rhinoceros horn carvings featured at Museum of Art." (2003). Accessed from: http://www.lcsd.gov.hk/en/ppr_release_det.php?pd=20030116&ps=02 on 10 November, 2008.

"On the question of *tongxi* and *tongtianxi*, according to the research of Mr Thomas Fok in his publication "Connoisseurship of Rhinoceros Horn Carving in China" (Thomas Fok: Hong Kong, 1999, p. 31), these terms are used for qualifying good horns in ancient China. *Tongxi*, as you noticed on our press release, has a cross-section showing a yellowish colour gradually turning black towards the core. *Tongtianxi* not only has the quality of *tongxi*, it also has a white streak running through the axis of the horn. *Tongtianxi* is extremely rare. These terms are commonly referred to grade the horns. We are not acquainted with material identifying them with a particular species. We do know that ancient Chinese had a strong preference for Asiatic horns versus African horns which they considered inferior both in aesthetic and medicinal quality." Information kindly supplied by Maria Mok, Assistant Curator (Chinese Antiquities), Hong Kong Museum of Art (personal communication, 25 November 2004).

"The horn surface, after the removal of the protective bark, is often graded in colour, usually black at the tip and a yellow-grey colour near the base. In the horns of the Black rhinoceros, for example, there is often a black core which runs the length of the horn. It measures in the region of 4 centimetres or more at the centre of the stem. Thus, whilst the tip end of the horn is completely black in colour, inside the 'well' of the cavity there is a black splash effect out from the centre. Although I know from personal experience that only a proportion of African Black horns possess this black core, I have not yet been able to discover whether it is present in all or only some of the four remaining rhinoceros horn types. A glance through the colour plates in this volume will, however, demonstrate that many Asian horns do have naturally black tip ends." Chapman (1999), p. 67.

Mr. Angelo Chung of Shen-Nong Limited, Kowloon (personal communication, 8 December 2004), advised:

"According to Dictionary of Chinese Materia Medica (Shanghai Scientific and Technical Publishers), the listed species for Rhinoceros horn includes:

1. *Rhinoceros unicornis*
2. *Rhinoceros sondaicus* Desmarest
3. *Rhinoceros sumatrensis* (Fischer)

Other species used include:

1. *Rhinoceros biconris* (Black Rhinoceros)
2. *Rhinoceros simus* Burchell (White Rhinoceros)

We are sorry we are really not familiar with the characteristics of different species of the rhinoceros. But we have attached the paragraph about Rhinoceros in Bencaogangmu *(Compendium of Materia Medica)* written by Dr. Li Shi Zhen in Ming Dynasty for your reference. Perhaps some ancient descriptions of rhinoceros horns may give you hints on the species. Although Bencaogangmu is written in Ming Dynasty, the quotations used in the book sometimes date back to Han Dynasty.

In Bencaogangmu, Dr. Li Shi Zheng has stated one paragraph written by Mr Kou Zong Shi (a herbalist in the 12th century) [on p. 1854] which mentioned the comparison of rhinoceros horns coming from different regions. He said rhinoceros coming from Sichuan (a province in China) and the south have small "lines" (on the horn). "Black" rhinoceros horns have prominent lines. "Yellow" rhinoceros horns lines are rare. But all of the above are not as good as rhinoceros horns coming from West "foreign region". Their lines are high. And the "rain-pattern" foot/base (of the horn) is prominent.

Perhaps by comparing different possible species of the rhinoceros and examining whether their horns matched the characteristics mentioned in the ancient texts may provide some more indirect hints. . . ."

"The populations of surviving rhinoceros species have dropped dramatically in the past 200 years, due to poaching for use in traditional medicines and dagger handles. Fortunately, through heroic efforts, some populations are increasing. The Southern White Rhinoceroses have recovered from less than 1,000 animals in 1900 to about 17,000 at the present, but the Northern White Rhinoceros is almost extinct. Javan Rhinos now number about 30-50, while the Sumatran Rhino is close to extinct. Black Rhinoceroses, numbering 300,000 to million in 1900, are now limited to a few, though there are some signs of recovery. Although the once-common Greater One-horned Indian Rhinoceros dropped to less than 100 in 1900, its stocks are now projected to reach 3,000 by 2020!" Dinerstein (2011).

"In the *Hsi shih chi* of 1263, a paragraph is devoted to <<ambergris», which reads as follows (WANG Kouo-wei's edition, 9-10; BRETSCHNEIDER's translation in *Br*, I, 152-153, is extremely inaccurate) : «. . . . The false product is made of rhinoceros excrements.» Pelliot (1959), p. 33.

The *Zhufan Zhi* (W-G: *Chu-fan-chi*) by Zhao Rugua (Chau Ju-Kua) *circa* 1225 CE has a short but interesting section on rhinoceros which may be found translated, with notes, in Hirth and Rockhill (1911), p. 233.

Appendix W: Notes on the Saka or Se/Sai peoples

There are very few references to the various 塞 Se/Sai (Old Chinese **sək*), or Saka, groups in the chapter on the Western Regions in the *Hou Hanshu*, although they played a critical role in the history of the period. It is, essential to understand what is known about them to enable us to follow the story of the different peoples involved in the development of the early Silk Routes.

To my knowledge, there has not been any serious question that 塞 Se/Sai (Old Chinese **sək*) refers to the Saka peoples of Western sources since Franke's succinct discussion of the connections between the Sai or Se of the Chinese, and the Saka of Western sources: "*There cannot be, therefore, the slightest doubt about the identity of the names Sök and Sakai, Sacae, or Saka* [and the Chinese name 塞]." Franke (1907), p. 677.

This appendix outlines what is known about the Saka to help make the events in the *Hou Hanshu* text more comprehensible in following the development of the Silk Routes.

Most writers have used *Sai* to romanise the Chinese word 塞. Thierry (2005), p. 437, however, correctly points out that the form *Se* (ancient **sək*) should be used for the nomadic peoples commonly identified as 'Saka,' and *sai* for when it is used to signify 'frontier.'

> "On the two passages from the Han annals quoted above, Yen Shi Ku (the commentator) remarks that the pronunciation of the character 塞 given by the fan-ts'ie 先, i.e. s(ien), and 得, i.e. the Cantonese (t)êk or (t)ök (Japanese toku), that is to say, the pronunciation is Sêk or Sök (*ê* or *ö* is to represent a sound, which lies between *a* and *o*). Should there, however, still remain any doubt as to the right pronunciation, this is completely removed by a most interesting mistake of Yen Shi Ku. In further explaining the name Sök, he goes on to say (loc. cit., ch. 61, fol. 4 v°):— "It (Sök) is the name of a country in the western regions, and is the same with what is called in Buddhist Sūtras 釋種, Shij- or Sik-chung. The sounds Sök and Sik are very close to each other. It is originally the name of a family or clan." Now Shik or Sik is the first part of the Chinese transliteration of Buddha's clan-name Śākya, whilst chung means 'tribe or race' : Shik or Sik-chung, therefore, is 'the tribe or race (or clan) of the Śākya.' In other words: *Yen Shi Ku has confused the Śaka (Sök) with the Śakya (Sik).* Here one of the etymological blunders of the learned commentator has proved to be of undesigned utility, for he could not possibly have stated more clearly the pronunciation of the character 塞. *There cannot be, therefore, the slightest doubt about the identity of the names Sök and Sakai, Sacae or Śaka.*" Francke (1907), p. 677.

> "The term 'Tūra' is the name by which the Central Asian nomadic tribes were known in one of the earliest parts of the *Avesta*. The Tūras are portrayed as the enemies of the sedentary Iranians and described, in *Yašt* XVII (prayer to the goddess Aši), 55-6, as possessing fleet-footed horses. As early as 641 or 640 B.C. the nomads were known in Assyrian sources as the Sakas.
>
> Many Greek writers referred to all the nomads of Eurasia, including those of Central Asia, as Scythians; and the Persians designated all the nomadic tribes of the Eurasian steppes, including the Scythians, as Sakas. These broad classifications were based on the similarity of the culture and the way of life of all the nomads who spoke Iranian languages. The question of the actual distribution of the different nomadic tribes or tribal groups is debatable, largely because of the dearth of written sources. Moreover, it is well to remember that nomadic life characteristically entailed frequent migrations, with the result that different tribes successively occupied one and the same territory. When it is considered that these tribes were culturally very close to one another it is easy to understand why classical writers sometimes

associated different tribes with the same historical events. For example, in their description of Cyrus' war against the Central Asian nomads, Cyrus fought against the Massagetae according to Herodotus; against the Sakas according to Strabo; against the Abiae according to Quintus Curtius; against the Derbices according to Ctesias; and against the Dahae according to Berossus.

It is now generally agreed that the ancient nomads of Central Asia were descendants of the Bronze Age cattle-breeding tribes who had inhabited the same territory, which does not exclude, however, the probability of considerable ethnic intermingling and movement within and beyond the borders of the region. These trends must have become particularly marked at the start of the first millennium B.C., when a number of tribes changed from cattle-breeding to a purely nomadic way of life.

This view is confirmed by anthropological studies. Between the seventh and fifth centuries B.C., the Sakas of the Aral Sea region seem to have a mixed population, consisting of a Europoid, mainly Andronovo stratum with a significant admixture of Mongoloid forms of Central Asian origin. Anthropological materials of the Saka period from eastern Kazakhstan are heterogeneous, showing genetic similarities with the population of the T'ien Shan and the Altai mountains with a Mongoloid admixture already apparent. The Sakas of the eastern Pamirs occupied a place apart, among the other Saka tribes or those akin to them." Abetekov and Yusupov (1994), pp. 23-24. See also Yablonsky (1995b), pp. 213-214.

"The term 'Andronovo culture' is a blanket name for a collection of similar Bronze Age tribes that flourished ca. 2300–1000 BCE in western Siberia from the southern Urals, to the Yensie River and the west Asiatic steppe. The term applies to communities that were largely nomadic pastoralists as well as those settled in small villages, especially in Central Asia. The Andronovo culture is strongly associated with the Indo-Iranians and is often credited with the invention of the spoke-wheeled chariot around 2000 BCE. Archaeological data from Bactria and Margiana shows that Andronovo tribes penetrated into Bactria and the Margianian oases. The Andronovo cultures are generally considered to be the ancestors of the Scythian Haomavarga, discussed in the next Chapter, and it is through this group, as we shall show, that the Haoma cult became surprisingly widespread...." Bennett (2010), Kindle Locations 2865-2871.

"Both modern and fossil evidence suggests that hunter-gatherers led longer, healthier and more leisured lives than did farmers until less than a century ago. But farmers have numbers on their side. And numbers beget numbers, which in turn beget cities." Carr (2005), p. 10.

"On the basis of dendrologically calibrated radiocarbon dating, **Arzhan 1** has been dated to the late ninth/early eighth centuries BC and is the earliest known kurgan of the Scythians. This **Arzhan 1 phase** of Tuva (850-700 BC) can be synchronised with the Tagar-Bainov phase in the Minusinsk Basin. From this dating and the discoveries made, despite the extensive plundering, highly significant conclusions can be drawn regarding the early Iron Age of Central Asia:

1. The kurgan of Arzhan 1 reveals a mature form of nomadic Scythian culture more than a century before the earliest Scythian kurgans of the Eastern European Black Sea region, such as the Kurgans of Kelermes in the Kuban region, [at the base of the northern slopes of the Caucasus Mountains], from the mid-seventh century BC. Herodotus was right: the Scythians and their culture originated in Central Asia.

2. Both the Scythians and the Saka belonged mainly to Europid peoples, descendants of representatives of the cultures of Andronovo and Karasuk. Neither the Scythians nor the Saka were homogeneous peoples, however, but rather a cultural community of mostly Europid nomadic horsemen who spoke Iranian dialects. From the perspective of the Pontic Scythians, one may concur with Parzinger that 'farther to the east of the European steppe belt there lived similarly structured bands of nomadic horsemen, who were progressively less ethnically related to the Scythians of the Black Sea region but remained culturally connected to them'.
3. The early Iron Age horse-based nomadism of the steppe belt of Central Asia arose in Tuva in the tenth/ninth centuries BC. In the following centuries the early Scythian material culture as well as their customs and rituals, spread through migrations from the Tuvan epicentre westward as far as Crimea. In the Pontic region Scythian material culture was influenced by the Near East and Greece.
4. Between the Altai and the Pontic region there was intense trade contact, something like a transcontinental steppe road used for gold.
5. The common thread that drew together all the Scythian groups of the Central Asian steppe belt, the so-called 'Scythian triad', had its start in Tuva, as can already be seen in Arzhan 1. This encompassed a particular composition of grave goods, consisting of three elements: first, Scythian weapons such as double-edged, straight daggers, arrowheads and a gorytos (a combined case for a bow and arrows); second, parts of the horse-gear such as bronze bits with stirrup-shaped psalias and pierced bid rods, and third, animal-style artwork.
6. The unique motif of a coiled predatory animal, first a panther and later, during the Sarmatian period, a wolf, arose in north-eastern Central Asia, with the earliest influences perhaps originating in northern and north-eastern China. There, depictions of coiled animals were common not only during the contemporaneous epoch of the Western Zhou (*ca.* eleventh century-771 BC) on cheek pieces for draught horses but also in the C-shaped jade dragons of the Neolithic Hongshan Culture (fourth millennium BC).
7. The third element of the Scythian triad, the Scytho-Siberian animal style, also began in north-eastern Central Asia. These animal images, portrayed according to a strict code, emphasise certain features of the animal that had particular symbolic content in the Scythians' hierarchy of values. In the animal style there is the representation in animal form of elements of a worldview that is difficult for us to decipher today. The animal-style discoveries at Arzhan 1 refute hypotheses that the animal style developed first out of decisive influences from Assyria and Urartu, Anatolia or the Maeotian Kuban region. The inspirations for the animal style should be sought in the east; in southern Siberia, in the petroglyphs and deer-stones of Mongolia and, as the Russian historian Rostovtzeff (1870-1952) surmised as long ago as 1929, in northern China, especially in the hunting and stockbreeding cultures in north-eastern Inner Mongolia. Even before Rostovtzeff, in 1913, the archaeologist Ellis Minns (1874-1953) had emphasised the tight relations between the Scytho-Pontic animal style and the Siberian animal style and spoken of 'Scytho-Siberian art.' Beginning in the seventh century BC the Scythian animal style began to adopt iconographic elements from Urartu, Assyria and later Iran.
8. A few of the most striking burial rituals described by Herodotus are confirmed by Arzhan 1. After the deceased ruler assumed his final resting place in the grave, 'various members of the king's household are buried beside him: one of his concubines, his butler, his cook, his groom, his steward and his chamberlain

> [messenger] – all of them strangled. Horses are buried too and gold cups [...] This ceremony over, everybody with great enthusiasm sets about raising a mound of earth.' The younger woman buried at Arzhan 1, the eight attendants in the central chamber and the eight attendants in the central chamber and the approximately 160 sacrificed, uneaten horses correspond with Herodotus's account. By comparison, the 38 largest kurgans of the fourth century BC in the northern Pontic region contained between three and ten additional corpses. In the Kuban region the contemporaneous Elisavetinskaja Kurgan held 200 sacrificed horses and kurgan 1 at Ul'skji contained 360 horses." Baumer (2012), pp. 178-180.

"Herodotus (VI, I, 64, 2) wrote that "the Persians refer to all the Scythians as Saka." Pliny (VI, 17) also knew this but made the distinction that the Saka were "Scythian tribes" who "lived on the other side of the Jaxartes." The authors of antiquity, each in his turn, used the name "Scythian" to mean all of the nomads in both the western and eastern Eurasian steppes.

In modern scientific literature, the term Saka designates the Iranian-speaking cattle breeding tribes who inhabited the steppe regions of Central Asia and Eastern Turkestan in the 1st millennium B.C. The Massagetae, frequently mentioned by ancient authors, are treated as a Saka tribe who populated the western areas of Central Asia.

The Saka have left us no script and historians are obliged to use fragmentary passages. Moreover, information about the Saka in the works of the ancient authors is not too reliable. This fragmentary and poorly constructed information sheds no light on the formative stages of the Saka-type communities. Also, some data are mythological in nature. Therefore, we must rely on archaeology and paleoanthropology to supply objective scientific data to solve the general problems of the early nomadic history of Central Asia.

Archaeological studies of Early Iron Age sites in the western Black Sea region began in the 19th century A.D. Because of the incredible finds from the royal Scythian kurgans the public's interest was peaked and the Scythians have assumed a prominent position in the cultural legacies of the world. The eastern steppe lands, however, have remained blank on the archaeological map. Scholars made the erroneous assumption, which only recently has been corrected, that the steppes north of the Black Sea were always the cultural and political center of the Scythian world and that the Asian lands were, at best, its hinterland.

It was only in the late 1920s that M.V. Voevodsky and M.P. Gryaznov began organized archaeological studies in the eastern steppe belt. As new scientific data, including that of the Neolithic, and material from excavated cemeteries and settlements accumulated, scholars began to realize that the historical and cultural developmental processes throughout the great Eurasian steppes showed many parallels with those from the more western steppe lands. Animal breeding economies were established in the European and Asian steppes at essentially the same time. Between the 14th-11th centuries B.C. horse riding equipment appeared. Toward the end of this period, and probably as a result of climatic changes, an alpine-type cattle breeding economy developed across the steppes. By the beginning of the 1st millennium B.C, as indicated by similar traits in material and spiritual culture, a new type of community, composed of cattle breeding tribes, had developed across the entire steppe zone. In our literature this community type is known as the "Scythian world of Siberia." This terminology is only partially appropriate because, although it adequately reflects the cultural similarities between peoples of the western and eastern steppes, it inappropriately combines the ethnic term "Scythian" with the geographic area "Siberia." From an archaeological point of view, the "Scythian world of Siberia" indicates, above all, the presence in the burial rite of the "Scythian triad," a combination of burial items which must include weaponry, horse harness items, and at least one artifact exhibiting the Scythian "animal style" tradition.

At the same time, analyses of archaeological remains indicates that Saka communities were not always culturally homogenous. Equally interesting is the fact that the populations, as evidenced by paleoanthropological materials, were not physically heterogeneous. We are, therefore, obliged to observe a system of local variations. Each variation was bound to a specific geographical area within the entire steppe zone. The results of ethnological studies lead us to conclude that the particular ecological conditions of the habitat leave a strong imprint on the material culture. Therefore, before attempting an archaeological description of the Saka communities we should briefly describe the natural geographical conditions of their habitat." Yablonsky (1995), pp. 194-195.

"Scythian Culture came into the ancient world came through three major phases of migration. First, the 'proto-Scythian'or'Timber Grave Culture' originating from the Urul Mountains of Western Russia (which divides Europe and Asia), began a westward expansion around 1800 B.C. This was followed around 1100 B.C. when another Scythian migration through the Pontic Steppes took place, and these nomads incorporated indigenous agricultural communities into their fold, leading to their classification as "Agricultural Scythians." "Then, ca. 600-550 B.C.E., a third wave migrated westward out of southern Siberia. These latecomers, who eventually pushed west along the north coast of the Black sea as far as Bulgaria and who invaded Iran as well, bore several ethnic labels... among them were the Massagetae (southeast of the Aral sea), the Saka (northeastern Iran, Western Afghanistan), the Thyssagetae (the central Urals), and... the 'Sauromatae..'." (Littleton & Malcor, 1994-2000)." Bennett (2010), Kindle Locations 2912-2919.

"Referring to the Scythians under their alternate name of the 'Sakas,' Guive Mirfendereski notes "etymologically, many have concluded that the name Massagetae meant 'Great Saka'... Massagetae, the reasoning goes, referred to Saga/Saka and 'ma' meant 'big' or 'great' so the whole name meant 'Great Saka'...." (Mirfendereski, 2005). This was a conclusion that Mirfendereski rejected, noting that Scythians of eastern Central Asia are called 'haumavarka' (Haoma-gatherers)[7]; "I believe the key to the meaning of 'Massagetae' then ought to be in the possibility of it being a Greek rendition of Homavarka - in which 'homa' appears in the form of the first syllable 'ma'[8] and Saka is represented in 'sagetae' or 'saketae.' Herodotus's Massagetae therefore was a direct translation of 'Homa Saka'" (Mirfendereski, 2005)." Bennett (2010), Kindle Locations 3017-3023.

"Prior to their arrival in northwestern India, Sakas (as they are known in Iranian sources) appear in Old Persian inscriptions and monumental art of the Achaemenid empire as tributary neighbors. The Naqš-i-Rustam inscription of Darius I (reigning from 522–486 B.C.) distinguishes three groups of Sakas:

1) *Saka Paradraya* or Sakas "who are across the sea" inhabited the Pontic steppe areas north of the Black Sea. The attempt by Darius I to conquer this group of Sakas around 513 B.C. is described at length by Herodotus (4.1–162), who also provides many fascinating (although not necessarily reliable) details about the lifestyle, economy, and religious beliefs of these Scythians (as they are known in Greek sources).

2) *Saka Tigraxauda*, Sakas "wearing the pointed cap," probably inhabited areas in western Central Asia between the Caspian Sea and the Aral Sea. A Saka chief (Skunkha) with a distinctive high pointed cap is depicted last in a line of rebellious supporters of Gaumāta subjugated by Darius I in 522–521 B.C. in a rock relief at Behistun and other *Saka Tigraxauda* are shown bearing tribute in the *apadana* (grand hall) at Persepolis. Herodotus (7.64) describes Sakas or Scythians who were "clad in trousers" and had "on their heads tall stiff caps rising to a point" among the Persian forces led by Xerxes during his invasion of Greece in 479/80 B.C., although he classifies them as Amyrgian Scythians.
3) *Saka Haumavarga* are the "hauma-drinking" or "hauma-preparing" Sakas referred to as Amyrgian Scythians by Herodotus (7.64). These Sakas originally seem to have been located in the regions around the Syr Darya (Jaxartes River), particularly in the Ferghana and Alai valleys in proximity to Sogdia.[16] However, Haumavarga Sakas were also likely to have settled in the southeastern Iranian province of Drangiāna (around the Helmand valley) which later became known as Sakastān/ Śakasthāna/Sejistān/Seistan following conflicts with the Parthians after the death of Mithradates I in 138 B.C. Sakas from this region (on the borders between modern eastern Iran and southern Afghanistan) come to play important roles in the history of the Indian subcontinent in the first century B.C. and early centuries A.D.

[16] According to Frye, the Saka *haumavarga* ". . . inhabited the eastern part of Central Asia, probably from Ferghana into Chinese Turkestan" (1963, 66). L.V. P'iankov ("The Ethnic History of the Sakas," *Bulletin of the Asia Institute* 8 (1994 [but appearing in 1996]): 37–38 summarizes arguments for localizing the Amyrgians in Ferghana and the Alai valleys, but supports the view that this group migrated across the western Pamir mountains to Badakhshan and eventually to the eastern Iranian plateau and northwestern India in the second and first centuries B.C."

Neelis (2007), pp. 57-58.

"In Darius' time both the *Tigraxauda* ["Sakas who wear pointed caps"] and the *Haumavarga* ["the 'Preparers of Haoma', generally transcribed as 'Amyrgian' Sakas"] were described (somewhat vaguely) as living *para Sugdam* ('beyond Sogd' or southern Sogdia) i.e. anywhere from the Syr Darya south towards Sodgia/northern Bactria, and as far east as the Ferghana Valley. Ptolemy located the seat of the *Sacaraucae* (presumably the *Tigraxauda*) as being 'south of the Syr Darya'.[56] These *Sacaraucae* were well known to the Greeks, having furnished horsemen wearing mailed armor to the army of Darius III at the Battle of Gaugamela,[57] and later supplying Alexander with cavalry to assist in his invasion of India.[58] As will be shown in Chapter Five, by the time the Yuezhi passed through Sogdia in *c.* 131, the *Tigraxauda* Saka were probably in occupation of northern Bactria, and may have undermined the last substantial vestiges of Greek power in Bactria proper and established hegemony over it. The Yuezhi defeated the northern Bactrian Sakas in *c.* 130, and in so doing gained *de facto* suzerainty over Bactria.

[56] Ptol., vi, 14, 14.
[57] Arrian, *Anabasis*, iii, 8, 3; 11, 4; 13, 4.
[58] *Ibid*, v, 12.2.
[59] Pulleyblank (1962), *op. cit.*, pp. 58-144, 206 - 265; Pulleyblank (1983) *op. cit.*, p. 451. See also N. Egami, *Yurashya kodai hoppo bunka* (Tokyo 1948)."

Benjamin (2007), p. 99.

"The lower Syr Darya Saka were extremely heterogeneous. The craniological series from Uigarak is marked with a distinctly expressed Mongolian admixture, which, as in central Kazakhstan, is more prominent among the female skulls (Ginzburg and Trofimova, 1972, pp. 118-119). The initial cultural and genetic heterogeneity of the early Saka population of the lower Syr Darya River area is stressed once again by the presence of burial rites contrasting sharply with those described above. The so-called "slag kurgans" (Levina, 1979) contained cremated bodies which were lying on special earthen platforms. Circular ditches were dug around the burial mound and filled with blocks of slag. Judging by the bronze arrowheads, these kurgans date to the 6th-5th centuries B.C.

The distinct Mongoloid admixture found in the early Saka population in the lower Syr Darya River area seems to be strong evidence of eastern genetic ties. Moreover, archaeological evidence also confirms cultural contacts with the eastern regions. The lower Syr Darya Saka populations shared common cultural and genetic components with the steppe populations of Central Asia, Kazakhstan, and the Southern Siberian steppes dating from the Bronze Age which accounts for the strong contacts during the Early Iron Age. Moreover, the strong connections between the Saka of the lower Syr Darya River area and FIG. 69 area and those from the southern Ural steppe region have been discussed frequently (Vishnevskaya and Itina, 1971; Vishnevskaya, 1973)." Yablonsky (1995b), pp. 222-223 and also see: pp. 238; 252.

"One group of Indo-European speakers that makes an early appearance on the Xinjiang stage is the Saka (Ch. Sai). Saka is more a generic term than a name for a specific state or ethnic group; Saka tribes were part of a cultural continuum of early nomads across Siberia and the Central Eurasian steppe lands from Xinjiang to the Black Sea. Like the Scythians whom Herodotus describes in book four of his *History* (*Saka* is an Iranian word equivalent to the Greek *Scythos*, and many scholars refer to them together as Saka-Scythian), Sakas were Iranian-speaking horse nomads who deployed chariots in battle, sacrificed horses, and buried their dead in barrows or mound tombs called *kurgans*. Royal burials included rich inventories of metal objects, often decorated in 'animal style' motifs—one famous example is the trove that yielded the gold fittings known as 'Golden Man', of which a reproduction now stands on a pillar in downtown Almaty. There are Saka sites across Central Eurasia. In Xinjiang sites with Saka artefacts and Europoid remains have been dated from *c.* 650 BCE through the latter half of the first millennium BCE in Tashkurgan (west of Kashgar, in the Pamirs), in Yili, and even near Toqsun, south of the Tianshan. This latter site, dated to between the fifth and second centuries BCE, yielded a statuette of a kneeling warrior wearing a tall conical hat coming to a curved point—headwear associated in Persian sources with Sakas, and well known in classical Greek and Roman writings as a 'Phrygian cap', after another group of steppe invaders who sported it. An identical hat, fashioned from felt, was found in a tomb near Cherchen in the southern Tarim, dating to *c.* 1000 BCE, and on the heads of three women buried in Subashi [literally: 'Water-head'] in the Turfan Basin in the fourth or third century BCE. Very similar hats would centuries later adorn the heads of Soghdians in Tang depictions of these Central Asian, Iranian-speaking merchants." Millward (2007), pp. 13-14.

"The Sakas who invaded Bactria appear in the sources under different names, namely, Indian *Śaka-muruṇḍa-*, Chinese *Sai-wang*, Greek **Sakaraukai*, Latin **Sa<ca>raucae*. Of these both Indian *Śaka-muruṇḍa-* and Chinese *Sai-wang* mean 'Saka king' and 'Saka [king or] kings', respectively, in so far as *muruṇḍa-* can be regarded as the Saka title for 'lord, king' and Chinese *wang* as the translation of it. As both the Chinese and the Graeco-Latin sources mention the same peoples as conquerors of Bactria, we have to regard the *Sakaraukai* as identical with the *Śaka-muruṇḍa-* and the

Sai-wang respectively. Accordingly, the element *-rauk-* in the name *Sakaraukai* must have the same meaning as Saka *muruṇḍa-* and Chinese *wang.* In fact the word can be compared to Khotanese Saka *rūkya-* 'commander, lord', going back to **raukya-*. Saka *muruṇḍa-*, too, has an equivalent in Khotanese Saka: *rrund-* 'possessing power, lord, king'. As it is proved by Saka *muruṇḍa-*, both Khotanese terms *rrund-* and *rūkya-* derive from the root **mrav-/*mru-* 'to declare, to order" as **mrav-ant-* and **mrav-aka-/*mrau-ka-* respectively. Old Iranian **mr-* was reduced to *r-* in Khotanese Saka, while in the language of the Sakas of Gandhāra the initial **mr-* was preserved. It is a remarkable fact that the outcome of Old Iranian **mrav-ant-* and **mrav-aka-* was different in the Western and Eastern Saka groups. This phenomenon clearly supports the theory according to which the **Śakā mravakā-* (> **Śakā raukā*) and the **Śakā mravantah* (> **Śakā murunda*) both meaning 'Saka lords' or 'Saka kings' – invaded Bactria and Gandhāra separately. The name 'Saka lords/Saka kings' originally denoted the Saka tribal aristocracy who were alone able to wander away from their territory while the common people remained at home." Harmatta (1994a), p. 409.

"It [the Yüeh-chih migration into Bactria] also set in motion the Saka tribes again. After several successful wars against the Parthians, the western branch of the Sakas settled in Sistan where a Saka kingdom was established. About the same time, the Sakas using the Karakorum route established a Saka kingdom in Gandhāra. They eventually conquered Mathura and, advancing south, later became masters of Surashtra and Malwa.

The Sakas quickly abandoned their nomadic way of life and adapted themselves to local social and economic customs. They adopted many elements of Parthian, Greek and Indian cultures and became Hellenized or Indianized. They issued coins modelled on the Graeco-Bactrian coinage, took part in the worship of their Indian subjects and patronized both Brahmanic sanctuaries and Buddhist monasteries. But they retained their armaments and art of warfare – the deployment of armoured cavalry which began to spread from them throughout the ancient world." Harmatta (1994c), pp. 488-489.

"In 129 BCE a crisis arose in the affairs of the Arsacid kingdom. The ruler of the time, Phraates II, was engaged in a war against the Seleucid Antiochus VII Sidetes, who had moved from Babylonia with a powerful army to regain Media for his kingdom.[6] At the same time. Phraates was threatened by the arrival on his eastern border of a large horde of the Sacae, displaced from what is today Kazakhstan by the formidable Yuezhi or Tocharian confederacy, in turn expelled from China's Gansu Province after a crushing defeat by the Huns. By a clever manoeuvre, Phraates enlisted the nearest group of Sacae as mercenaries for his war against the Greeks, but before the contingents arrived, Antiochus was trapped and killed by the Parthian forces, and the war in the west was at an end. When the mercenaries arrived, they were too late to take part, and Phraates committed the fatal blunder of refusing these levies their pay. When he rejected their proposal either for compensation, or employment against another enemy, the mercenaries turned against him, and ranged across Iran ravaging the countryside. Phraates marched against them, bolstering his forces by the incorporation of Greek prisoners from the army of Antiochus, but these too had been cruelly treated, and at the height of the battle they deserted to the Sacae. The Parthians were routed, and Phraates himself was killed in the debacle.

With the Tocharians pressing on behind, the Sacae moved southwards into Drangiana, thenceforth to be known by their name as Sakastan, today Sistan. Next it was the Tocharians who collided with the Parthian eastern frontier, and in a battle to oppose them in 124/3 BCE the next Arsacid ruler, Artabanus II, was in turn killed, surprisingly as a result of a wound to his arm.[7] The next Parthian king Mithradates II, titled "the Great", was a powerful ruler. His personal campaigning seems to have been confined to the west, where he secured Babylonia, and overthrew the ruler of Characene, Hyspaosines, before pressing on to the Euphrates, where he defeated the late Seleucid ruler Antiochus X.

Events on the eastern border are not well attested, but the fighting continued between the Iranians and the nomads – probably, at this stage, again the Tocharians. A clue may be derived from the *Shāh-nāma* stories of the battles between the Iranians and Afrasiāb in the time of Kay Ka'ūs. The Iranians, commanded by Tūs, Godarz and Faziburz, sustain a series of reverses, and are eventually besieged on the mountain of Hamāvān. In their extremity, they are eventually relieved by the invincible Rustam, already apparently installed in Sistan, and commanding the forces of the Parthian southeast border. The episode may reflect some bias from the Sitan epic, but it seems clear that in the aftermath of the nomad invasion, the stabilisation of the eastern frontier was entrusted to the family of the Suren, who were successful in restoring the situation, and repelling the invaders.

From the outcome it is evident that the Suren chiefs, whose names are not clearly transmitted, succeeded in expelling the Saca horde from Drangiana, and drove them eastwards into Arachosia and the Punjab. There the invaders established a powerful kingdom, known as Sakastan, and attested for us by inscriptions and a copious coinage. We can construct a list of the Saca kings: Vonones, Spalirises, Spalagadames, Azes I, Azilises, and Axes II.

Chronological pegs for this series are provided by two fixed dates. The date of the Vikrama Era, BCE 57, marks, as we shall see, the formal installation of the first Azes [note that Falk and Bennett (2009) seem to have finally disproven this assumption, by assigning the Azes era to *circa* 47 CE]. The demise of Azes II appears to fall very close to 9 CE,* though this date[8] cannot be fully substantiated. It is the event laconically reported in Prologue 42 of Trogus: *Interitus Sa(ca)raucarum*, "The destruction of the Sacaraucae".[9] We lack the full text to tell us by whom, and how, the Sacaraucae were destroyed, whether by the Kushans or by the Suren — that is to say, by the Indo-Parthians — though their copious coinage disintegrates at around this moment.

[6] Justin Epitome: 42, 1-2.

[7] Justin Epitome: 42, 2. Artabanus Tochariis bello inlato bracchio vulneratus statim decedit. See Curtis, V. S. in this volume: where this ruler is referred to as Artabanus I. This is due to different chronologies for the early Arsacid period.

[8] Quoted by the medieval chronicler Roger of Wendover (d. 1237): Anno divinae incarnationis nono . . . Trogus Pompeius chronica sua terminavit. Cf. Otto Seel (ed) Pompei Trogi Fragmenta, Teubner, Leipzig 1956, p. viii, who, however, rejects the dating. This, whatever its source, remains plausible in the South Asian context."

Bivar (2007), pp. 27-28 and nn. 6-8. ***NOTE:** Date *circa* 19 CE according to Falk and Bennett. Azes II likely did not exist, so this probably refers to Azes I – see Senior (2008a). (JEH)

During the early centuries CE, people of Saka descent still controlled the upper Alai Valley at Xiuxun 休循 (written Xiuxiu 休脩 in the *Weilüe*) and Juandu 捐毒 (written Sundu 損毒 in the Weilüe) located at modern Irkeshtam, about 200 km west of Kashgar, close to Ptolemy's 'Stone Tower'. This information is upheld in both in Western and Eastern sources. See: Appendix E and notes 2.16.

Appendix X: The Significance and Use of Skull Cups

According to the *Hanshu*, the drinking cup made from the skull of the king of the Yuezhi was used when the Xiongnu concluded a treaty with two Han ambassadors during the reign of Emperor Yuan (49-33 BCE).

> "More than a century after this event [the defeat of the Yuezhi by Jizhu or 'Laoshang' Chanyu of the Xiongnu in 165 BCE], when Chinese ambassadors came to sign a treaty of alliance with the Chanyu Houhanxie, they drank blood from the cranium of the ancient king of the Yuezhi to solemnly ratify the convention." From: *Qian Hanshu*, chap. XCIV, 2nd part, p. 4b. Translated and adapted from: Chavannes (1895-1905), Introduction, LXX, pp. 44, and 156, n. 112.

> "At a somewhat later date, when two Chinese envoys were sent to the Hiung-nu [Xiongnu] to conclude a treaty, they drank blood with the Turkish chiefs out of the same skull-bowl, in order to solemnize their vows. The sacrificial animal in this case was a white horse. Blood, as is well known, was of great significance with many peoples in affirming sacred agreements and keeping faith. According to the philosopher Huai-nan-tse, the ancient Chinese in such cases rubbed their lips with blood, while the inhabitants of Yüe (in southern China) made an incision in their arms." Laufer (1923), p. 12.

The preparation and use of skull cups is extremely ancient and widespread:

> "***Background:*** The use of human braincases as drinking cups and containers has extensive historic and ethnographic documentation, but archaeological examples are extremely rare. In the Upper Palaeolithic of western Europe, cut-marked and broken human bones are widespread in the Magdalenian (15 to 12,000 years BP) and skull-cup preparation is an element of this tradition. . . .
> ***Conclusions:*** Three skull-cups have been identified amongst the human bones from Gough's Cave [Somerset, England]. New ultrafiltered radiocarbon determinations provide direct dates of about 14,700 cal BP, making these the oldest directly dated skull-cups and the only examples known from the British Isles. . . .
>
> The act of collecting and modifying human body parts after the death of an individual for trophy or ritual use is well documented. Although examples of post-cranial modification are known, the majority of modified human remains are cranial elements. In these examples, skinning of the skull and removal of brain and facial tissues has been attributed to cannibalism, trophy display or secondary burial. The use of skull vaults as drinking cups is known from recent ethnographic studies as well as historical accounts. Herodotus in *The Histories* (5th Century BC) portrayed the Scythians as people who drank from the skulls of their enemies. Similar traditions were described for China in *The Record of Great Historian* by Sima Qian (1st–2nd Centuries BC) and for Viking tribes by Mágnus Ólafsson in the *Krakumal* written in 1636. Human skull-bowls, known as *kapala* in Sanskrit, were fashioned from the oval upper section of a human cranium and used as a libation vessel for a number of Vajrayana deities in tantric Buddhist rituals. Laufer documented Historic evidence of the use of human calvariae as drinking bowls in India, where the ritual seems to be still practiced by the Aghori sub-sect. Skull-cups have been reported as being used by Australian aborigines, and in the nineteenth century human skulls were used as drinking cups in Fiji and other islands in Oceania." Bello et al. (2011), p. 1.

> "It is not surprising that a people as militaristic as the Scythians had special war rituals. In order to strengthen cohesion, pairs of warriors would swear blood brotherhood. They mixed their blood with wine in a cup, dipped their weapons in it

and drank it in the presence of witnesses. On the battlefield young warriors also drank the blood of the first enemy killed, in order to incorporate his strength. Such a warrior's share of the spoils was determined by the number of heads of decapitated enemies, they collected these and brought them to their king or chieftain. The collecting of heads on the battlefield brought not only spoils but also honour, since the district rulers gathered all the warriors annually and each warrior who had killed at least one enemy was honoured with a cup of wine. The unsuccessful, however, 'have to sit by themselves in disgrace.' The Scythians further 'made use' of fallen enemies by making drinking vessels out of their skulls and clothing out of their tanned scalps or tying the scalps on the reins of their horses." Baumer (2012), p. 237. On the early practice of scalping, see: Murphy et al (2002), pp. 1-10.

".... there is a visible survival of the ancient custom still preserved in our language. German *kopf* ("head") corresponds to English *cup* (Anglo-Saxon *cuppe),* both being derived from Latin *cuppa* ("cup"). In Italian, *coppa* means a "cup;" but in Provençal, the same word in the form *cobs* means a "skull." Latin *testa* refers to a pottery vessel or sherd, as well as to the brain-pan and head. In Provençal, *testa* signifies a "nut-shell;" in Spanish, *testa* denotes "head" and "bottom of a barrel." In Sanskrit, *kapāla* means both a "skull" and a "bowl." This correlation is still extant in many other Indo-European languages." Laufer (1923), p. 24.

"The historic texts record the sacrifice of a horse to solemnize alliance between the Han and Xiongnu; participants mixed some of the horse's blood with their own in wine which was drunk from a vessel made of a Yuezhi skull." Psarras (2003), pp. 129-130.

"In the *Shijia* of *Wei* (Mém. hist., chap. XLIV), under the date of 266, one finds an interesting indication on the manner in which Wei and Han, who had been allies of *Zhibo* besieging *Zhao* in *Jinyang*, suddenly realised that the ambition of *Zhibo* threatened them, and, making an about-face, abruptly united themselves with Zhao. – In the book of Huainan Ze (d. 122 BCE), one reads the following account (chap. XII, p. 340.420) . . . .

Ten months later, *Zhibo* besieged (*Zhao*) *Ziangze* in *Jinyang*; (*Zhao*) Ziangze deployed some battalions and fought against him; he inflicted a great defeat on Zhibo; he smashed his head and made a drinking cup of it.

The same anecdote is reported in the *Shuoyuan* (chap. III, at the end) of *Liu Xiang* (80-9 BCE); in this second drafting, the final sentence becomes:

"He coated his head with varnish and made a drinking cup of it."

To take the skull of an enemy to make a drinking cup is a rare trait amongst the Chinese but, on the other hand, is found among the Turkic peoples, and this seems to prove that the country of Zhao had strongly come under the influence of the barbarian tribes which it had annexed while conquering the country of Tai."
Translated and adapted from: Chavannes (1899-1905), Vol. V, p. 185, n. 43.232.

"The *jinglu* (or, later, *qinglü* 輕呂) divinity is attributed to the Xiongnu by Yan Shigu 顏師古 in his commentary on the origin of a temple consecrated [sic] to *jinglu* located in the Han district of Yunyang 雲陽 (in modern Shaanxi). The *Hanshu* passage in which this reference occurs describes religious rites in China during the reign of the Emperor Xuan (73-49 B.C.) and specifies that the Ceremonies performed at the *jinglu* temple were held in honor of the King Xiuchu.[258] The term *jinglu* appears only once in the *Hanshu* chapter on the Xiongnu, and refers to the knife used by Huhanye I during the Ceremony sealing his alliance with China: Huhanye cut himself with the *jinglu* so that his blood would run into the cup fashioned from the skull of a Yuezhi defeated by the Chanyu Laoshang.[259] This knife with its ritual status, may be assumed to have held some sacred value, which led to its description as a divinity in the *Hanshu* passage on Chinese religious rites under Xuandi. The god *jinglu* and his temple in the district of Yunyang reappear later in the Hanshu in an enumeration of religious sites closed by Chengdi.[260]

[257] E.G. Pulleyblank, personal communication.
[258] *HS*, p. 1250, note 7.
[259] *HS*, p. 3801.
[260] *HS*, p. 1250."

Psarras (2003), p. 131 and nn.

"The custom of consecrating an oath by the exchange of some drops of blood which one produced by making a cut on the forearms of the two contracting people came from the country of Yue if one believes the testimony of *Huainan ze* (chap. XI, p. 7 b):

> "Thus, the *Hou* held up a bone (according to the commentary there was an allusion here to the custom of the Barbarians of the North to consecrate an oath by drinking wine in the cranium of a dead enemy; cf. Tome V, n. 43.232, at the end), the people of Yue cut their forearms, the Middle Kingdoms (the people of Chinese race) rub the lips with blood; the tradition by which each is inspired is different, but the idea is the same."

"The Scythian soldier drank the blood of the first man he overcame in battle. The heads of all slain enemies were cut off and triumphantly carried to the king; in this case only was he entitled to a share of the booty, whereas he forfeited all claim, did he not produce a head. The scalps were likewise captured and suspended from the horse's bridle; the more scalps a man was able to show, the more highly he was esteemed. Cloaks were made by many from a number of scalps sewed together. The skulls of their most hated enemies [of the Scythians] were turned into drinking-cups, the outside being covered with leather, the inside being lined with gold by the rich. They did the same with the skulls of their own kith and kin if they had been at feud with them and vanquished them in the king's presence. When strangers of any account came to visit them, they handed these skulls around, the host telling how these were his relations who made war upon him, and how he defeated them; all this was regarded as proof of bravery. The practice of the Scythians in capturing and preserving the skulls of slain enemies was doubtless inspired by the widely prevalent belief in the transference of the powers of the deceased to the victor, who, in accordance with this conception, was enabled to add the skill, prowess and courage of his dead enemy to his own." According to Herodotus (IV, 64-65), in Laufer (1923), pp. 10-11.

> "66. Once a year the governor of each district, at a set place in his own province, mingles a bowl of wine, of which all Scythians have a right to drink by whom foes have been slain; while they who have slain no enemy are not allowed to taste of the bowl, but sit aloof in disgrace. No greater shame than this can happen to them. Such as have slain a very large number of foes, have two cups instead of one, and drink from both. . . .
>
> 70. Oaths among the Scyths are accompanied with the following ceremonies: a large earthen bowl is filled with wine, and the parties to the oath, wounding themselves slightly with a knife or an awl, drop some of their blood into the wine; then they plunge into the mixture a scimitar, some arrows, a battle-axe, and a javelin, all the while repeating prayers; lastly the two contracting parties drink

each a draught from the bowl, as do also the chief men among their followers." Herodotus, Chap. IV. Quoted in Godolphin (1973-1974), p. 136-138.

"Herodotus considered the Scythians militarily invincible. According to him, they drank the blood of their slain foes, whose heads they brought to their king. The warriors fashioned napkins and clothing from the scalps of those they had killed and made drinking goblets from their skulls. Scythians swore oaths by consuming a mixture of blood (contributed by the oath-takers) and wine into which they first dipped their arrows or other weapons. In annual tribal or clan gatherings, those who had killed their enemies were permitted to join the chief in drinking a specially brewed wine. Those that had not were barred from participation in this ceremony, a signal dishonor.

Herodotus reports that the kindred Issedones consumed the flesh of their deceased fathers, mixing it with chopped sheep and goat meat. The deceased's head was then cleaned and gilded, serving afterwards "as a sacred Herodotus reports that the kindred Issedones consumed the flesh of their deceased fathers, mixing it with chopped sheep and goat meat. The deceased's head was then cleaned and gilded, serving afterwards "as a sacred image" to which they made sacrifices annually." Golden (2011), p. 24; Kindle Edition, locations 427-433.

"Having related the legend [about Hercules], Herodotus adds: "And from the circumstance of the goblet which hung from the belt, the Scythians to this day wear goblets on their girdles." A warrior had to kill some enemies and show personal heroism to be awarded with such a cup, and only the most respected men were allowed to wear one with gold appliqué. (These goblets were in some periods also made from a human skull recovered from the body of a dead enemy, reminiscent of the skull cups used by Shiva and his devotee saddhus to drink *bhang* [cannabis] from.)" Bennett (2010), Kindle Locations 3226-3231.

The oldest record in the Chinese accounts of the skull cup tradition is dated in the final years of the Spring and Autumn period, when the victors of the Battle of Jinyang in 453 BCE made the skull of Zhi Bo Yao (智伯瑤) into a wine cup. *Shiji* 86: 趙襄子最怨智伯，漆其頭以為飲器。

Skull cups were widely used across Eurasia. Chavannes gives a translation of a passage from Livy' *History of Rome*, 23.24, dated 216 BCE, regarding their use among the Boii, a Galatian Celtic tribe living in Europe at the time:

"The skin and the head of the consul (Postumius) was carried in triumph by the Boii into the most honoured temple of their nation, then the head was cleaned out and, according to the custom of their people, the skull, decorated with a circle of gold served as a sacred vessel to offer libations at festivals, it was also the cup of the pontiff and the priests of the temple." (From the French translation by Bertrand). Translated and adapted from: Chavannes (1899-1905), Vol. V, pp. 185-186. See also: Livy (1905), Bk. 23.24. English translation by Rev. Canon Roberts.

"Boii (Boi; Boyards)

The Boii are classified as a Celtic people. They lived in various parts of Europe and are discussed as CELTS or GAULS. The ancestral homeland of the Boii was the region that came to be known as Bohemia, named after them, in what is now the western Czech Republic.

Probably in the fifth century B.C.E. some among the Boii migrated south of the Po River to present-day northeastern Italy around the modern city of Bologna, also named after them. In Italy the Boii were associated with the ANARES, CENOMANI, INSUBRES, LINGONES, SENONES, and other Celtic peoples who settled the region. They were influenced culturally by the ETRUSCANS. The ROMANS defeated them along with the Insubres at Telemon west of Lake Bolsena in 225 B.C.E., ending Celtic power." Waldman and Mason (2006), p. 70.

"The Huns [who invaded Europe] had the practice, similar to that of the Scythians, of making the skulls of their enemies into drinking cups; this may have had a ritual basis." Waldman and Mason (2006), p. 397.
"To the north the Bulgars, who had moved into the power vacuum created by the collapse of the Avar state and had assumed control of the Slavic population, defended their territory against the Byzantines, defeating and killing Emperor Nicephorus in 811 and making his skull into a drinking cup." Waldman and Mason (2006), p. 119.

Similar skull cups are still used in Tantric Hindu and Tibetan Buddhist ceremonies today. They are known in Sanskrit as *kapala* (Sanskrit: 'skull'), and as *thod pa* in Tibetan.

"[A kapala is a] cup made of a human skull, frequently offered by worshipers to the fierce Tantric deities of Hindu India and Buddhist Tibet. In Tibet the skull cup is displayed on the Buddhist altar and is used in ritual to offer to the ferocious *dharmapala* ("defender of the faith") divinities either wine, which symbolizes blood, or dough cakes, which are shaped to resemble human eyes, ears, and tongues. The skull cup is often a handsomely worked object and rests on a triangular pedestal representing a sacrificial fire with skulls. The cup is mounted in metal, usually heavily embossed silver or gilt bronze, and topped with a lid shaped like half a skull, with a *vajra-* ("thunderbolt-") shaped handle." *Encyclopædia Britannica Online Library Edition*. Downloaded on the 26 February 2012 from: http://www.library.eb.com.au/eb/article-9044643.

In the Tibetan tradition, these cups are made from the skulls of particularly holy and revered donors who, of course, have died naturally. For excellent photos and descriptions of two fine Tibetan skull cups decorated in gold, see *MCTBAF*, plates 24, 25 and p. 79.

"It would be erroneous to believe that this "barbarous" practice was limited to prehistoric times and the "savage" tribes of ancient Europe, Asia, America, and Australia. Like so many other pagan customs, it has persisted until recently among Christian, civilized nations. Even within the pale of Christianity, the skulls of saints have been preserved and worshipped. The village of Ebersberg east of Munich, Bavaria, for instance, boasts of possessing for a thousand years the skull of St. Sebastian. It is kept in a special chapel erected in 1670; there, a silver bust of the saint which hides the relic is placed on an altar. On his name-day, the 20th of January, pilgrimages were made to this chapel, and the pilgrims received consecrated wine from the saint's skull, believing they would be cured from any disease. This is but one example out of many; it was an ancient usage of the church to have the faithful drink out of bowls which formerly were in the possession of saints, and particularly out of their skulls." Laufer (1923), p. 15.

Appendix Y: The Adventures of Zhang Qian

Zhang Qian 張騫 (?–113 BCE), one of the greatest explorers in the annals of history, was a native of Hanzhong in southwest Shaanxi, Central China. His daring journeys of exploration and detailed observations greatly increased Chinese knowledge of distant countries and cultures, and laid the foundations for opening the transcontinental trade routes now referred to as the 'Silk Routes'. Thus began an era of rapid expansion of Chinese power and influence.

Zhang Qian was a *lang* or 'Court Attendant' during the Jianyuan era (140-135 BCE) when he responded to the Emperor's quest to find someone willing to attempt the perilous journey to the Yuezhi to arrange an alliance with them against the Xiongnu.

There is a brief biographical notice on Zhang Qian in *Shiji* 111, which reads:

> "General Zhang Qian. Sent [in the spring of 139 BCE] as envoy to Bactria [literally, Daxia]; on return [summer, 126 BCE] was appointed subordinate commander in campaign under Wei Qing [123 BCE?]. Won merit and was enfeoffed as Bowang marquis [123 BCE]. Three years later was made general and went on campaign out of Youbeiping [summer of 121 BCE]. Failed to arrive at rendezvous point on time; condemned to death but allowed to pay fine and become a commoner. Later sent as an envoy to Wusun barbarians [ca. 119 BCE]. Became grand messenger [*circa* 115 BCE] and died in office [113 BCE]. Grave situated in Hanzhong [his birthplace]." Watson (1993), p. 181.

> "At this time [after the Xiongnu defeat of the Yuezhi in 166 BCE] the emperor [Wu Di – reigned 141-87 BCE] questioned various Xiongnu who had surrendered to the Han and they all reported that the Xiongnu had defeated the king of the Yuezhi people . . . and made his skull into a drinking vessel. As a result the Yuezhi had fled and bore a constant grudge against the Xiongnu, though as yet they had been unable to find anyone to join them in an attack on their enemy.
>
> The Han at this time was engaged in a concerted effort to destroy the Xiongnu and therefore, when the emperor heard this, he decided to try to send an envoy to establish relations with the Yuezhi. To reach them, however, an envoy would have to pass through Xiongnu territory. The emperor accordingly sent out a summons for men capable of undertaking such a mission. Zhang Qian, who was a palace attendant at the time, answered the summons and was appointed as envoy to the Yuezhi." *Shiji* 123 in Watson (1993), p. 231. For the parallel passage in *Hanshu* 61, see: *CICA*, p. 207.

• The Dating of Zhang Qian's first mission to the West

Soon after setting out in 139 BCE, Zhang Qian and his company of 100 men, including a disaffected Xiongnu archer, Ganfu, were captured by the Xiongnu and taken before the Chanyu:

> "The *Shanyu* "detained [留 *liu*] them and refused to let them proceed. "The Yuezhi people live to the north of me," he said. "What does the Han mean by trying to send an envoy to them! Do you suppose that if I tried to send an envoy to the kingdom of Yue in the southeast the Han would let my men pass through China?" Watson (1993), p. 231. Also, *Hanshu* 61, *CICA*, p. 208.

The statement by the Chanyu that the Yuezhi people were living to the north of him indicates that the Yuezhi were still in control of the Ili Valley and the region of Issyk Kul.

Zhang Qian and his company were detained there for "over ten years." The Chanyu gave Zhang Qian a wife by whom he had a son. *Shiji* 123 in Watson (1993), p. 232. The translation from *Hanshu* 61 in *CICA*, p. 208, says "by whom he had children." This is an unnecessarily loose translation, as both the Chinese texts clearly state that she bore him a son or sons [it is impossible to be certain if there was one or more sons, as the Chinese text does not indicate number – though one would expect that if he had more than one son that this would been specified] – but there is certainly no mention of any daughter.

Some years later, in 129 BCE, Zhang Qian found an opportunity to flee on foot with some of his men and his Xiongnu wife and continued on his interrupted mission to contact the Yuezhi. "After hastening west for twenty or thirty days, they reached the kingdom of Dayuan." Watson (1993), p. 232.

All this time Zhang Qian had managed to keep his imperial credentials with him. The king of Dayuan gave him an escort of guides and interpreters to lead him to the Kangju who, in turn, led him to the Da Yuezhi, who, by this time, had just conquered Daxia.

Many scholars have dated Zhang Qian's visit to the Da Yuezhi to about 129 and/or 128 BCE. However, Chris Dorn'eich has, I believe, for the first time, managed to outline the chronology of his great journey more accurately and in greater detail:

> "Various texts in the *Shiji* unmistakably state that Zhang Qian — the first Chinese envoy who traveled so far west — was sent out in a secret mission by Emperor Wu, and eventually returned to the Chinese capital Chang 'an 長安 in the spring of 126 BCE.
>
> It is narrated in the *Shiji* that this mission lasted 13 years. And Zhang Qian spent:
>
> — "more than 10 years" 十餘歲 in captivity with the Xiongnu;
>
> — "more than 1 year" 留歲餘 with the Ruzhi (Yuezhi) 月氏 in *Daxia* (i.e. in the eastern half of Bactria);
>
> — "more than 1 year" 歲餘 a second time as captive of the Xiongnu.
>
> To this we have to add short periods of time for four journeys:
>
> — starting from *Longxi* 隴西, the border town, until being arrested by the Xiongnu;
>
> — escaping from the Xiongnu (near *Shule*, i.e. Kashgar) until reaching the 月氏;
>
> — returning from *Daxia* until being arrested by the Xiongnu again;
>
> — escaping from the *ordos* of the Xiongnu *chanyu* 單于 until reaching Chang'an.
>
> All four journeys together must have lasted less than 1 year. Of the first we can surmise that it lasted only days or weeks. The second one across the Pamirs and Sogdiana may have lasted some 3–4 months. The third one is not so easy to estimate, but cannot have been shorter than 3 months. The fourth should have been a matter of weeks as the distance was short and Zhang Qian this time escaped in the company of *Yudan* 於單, the deposed Xiongnu crown prince and the two men were able to help each other effectively: Yudan in the Xiongnu empire and Zhang Qian in Han China.
>
> With this information, it is clear that the historic mission started in the spring of 139 BCE — and not in 138, as even some Chinese and Japanese scholars believed or still believe. It is clear, therefore, that our Chinese Ulysses arrived at the *ordos* or court of the 月氏 in the company of just his Xiongnu servant *Gan Fu* 甘父 "after more than 10 years" as a captive of the Xiongnu and some three or four months traveling, i.e. in the summer of 129 — and not 128 as most modern texts erroneously tell us. This is a particularly important correction.
>
> Zhang Qian left *Daxia* in the fall of 128 and spent all of 127 with the Xiongnu again, and then escaped a second time in late winter or early spring of 126 BCE.
>
> In exile, the Xiongnu crown prince *Yudan* was made a "marquis" by Han Emperor *Wu* on May 2, 126 BCE, but soon afterwards [the next month] he [Yudan] died." Dorn'eich (2008), p. 2.

Both *Hanshu* 61 and *Shiji* 123 clearly say that Zhang Qian was away for 13 years on his mission, so approximate dates for his journey can be calculated.

> "At the time [Chang] Ch'ien had started his journey, over a hundred men set out, but thirteen years later only two succeeded in returning. The states reached by [Chang] Ch'ien in person comprised Ta Yüan, Ta Yüeh-chih, Ta Hsia and K'ang-chü, and those of whom he heard tell included five or six large states at their side." *Hanshu* 61 2A from *CICA*, p. 210.

> "When Zhang Qian first set out on his mission, he was accompanied by over 100 men, but after thirteen years abroad, only he and Gaofu managed to make their way back to China." *Shiji* 123 – see Watson (1993), p. 233.

The 13 years can be roughly confirmed by adding together each portion of his journey as described in the *Shiji* and the *Hanshu*:

1. "Over ten years" in captivity among the Xiongnu.
2. "Over a year" among the Yuezhi and in Daxia.
3. "Over a year" while detained for a second time by the Xiongnu.
4. Plus travelling time.

See Watson (1993), p. 232, and Hulsewé (1979), pp. 208-209.

The only evidence against accepting these dates for Zhang Qian's 13-year adventure is to be found in *Shiji* 116, and the similar passage in the much later *Zizhi tongjian* – completed in 1084 CE - see: Yap (2009), p. 176, which was possibly copied from the *Shiji*. They state that Zhang Qian returned to China in the 1st Yuanshou year, i.e. sometime between 15th November, 123 to 6 October, 122 BCE:

> "In the first year of *yuanshou* (122 BC) Zhang Qian, the Bowang marquis, returned from his mission to the land of Daxia (Bactria) [及元狩元年，博望侯張騫使大夏來], and reported that while he was there he had seen cloth produced in Shu and bamboo canes from Qiong [in Sichuan]. . . ." Watson (1993), pp. 256-257.

The date given here must be an error. I believe the meaning implied in this passage is: "In the first year of *yuanshou* (122 BC) Zhang Qian, the Bowang marquis, [sometime *after* he had] returned from his mission to the land of Daxia, reported that . . . ."

All other surviving early accounts indicate he returned to China *circa* 126 CE, soon after the death of Chanyu Junchen in late 127 or early 126 BCE.

I suspect that a scribe confused the date that Zhang Qian returned from the West with the date that he was made a Marquis, by mistaking the Yuanshuo 元朔 era (128-123 BCE) with the following Yuanshou 元狩 era (122-117 BCE).

After Zhang Qian's return, both *Hanshu* 61 and *Shiji* 123 claim he advised the Emperor that it should be possible to reach countries such as Dayuan, Daxia and Anxi by travelling southwest. Accordingly, four expeditions from Shu (Sichuan) and Chien-wei commanderies were sent out on different routes to find a way. All were unsuccessful.

He also participated in a major campaign against the Xiongnu *before* he was enfeoffed as Marquis of Bowang in the sixth Yuanshuo year (123 BCE). *HSPC* 17, 10a specifies that his enfeoffment as Bowang Marquis took place in March/April of 123. From: *Hanshu* 61 in *CICA*, p. 213, n. 790.

> "As a colonel [Chang] Ch'ien had accompanied the Supreme General [Wei Ch'ing] in campaigns against the Hsiung-nu, and thanks to his acquaintance with [the resources of] water and the pasture grounds, the army had been able to get by without a shortage. [Chang] Ch'ien was thereupon invested with the title of noble of Po-wang.[790] This year was the sixth year of the *Yüan-shuo* reign-period [123 B.C.]. Two years later [after he had been made Bowang Marquis - i.e. in the 2nd Yuanshou year =

121 BCE], as superintendent of the Guards, [Chang] Ch'ien set out from Yu-pei-p'ing [commandery] to attack the Hsiung-nu, in company with Li Kuang. The Hsiung-nu surrounded General Li, and the army suffered severe losses. Being late for the rendezvous, [Chang] Ch'ien was deemed worthy of beheading, but he redeemed himself from punishment by degradation to commoners' status [i.e. he had to give up his recently appointed title of Bowang (Po-wang) Marquis].

[790] Po-wang was a prefecture in Nan-yang commandery, see *HSPC*, 28A ii, 16b. According to *HSPC* 17, 10a, Chang Ch'ien was enobled in March-April 123 B.C., but the cyclical date indicated seems impossible."

Hanshu 61 4A, from *CICA*, p. 213. See also *Zizhi tongjian* in: Yap (2009), p. 180.

The key is that more time would have been needed to conduct these two major expeditions – one to the south and one to the north - between the sixth Yuanshou year (123 BCE) and when he was demoted in the first Yuanshou year (121 BCE).

"Seleucid rule in Persia ended in 129 BC when the Parthians defeated the Seleucids and killed Antiochus VII in battle. Just at that point in time the Parthians were suffering from an invasion of Sakas who may have been fleeing from the Tokharians (Τόχαροι, Yüeh-chih). The latter [i.e. the Tocharoi – who are not, I believe, to be identified with the Yuezhi] killed Ardawân (Artabanus II or I, ca. 128-124/123 BC) in battle and conquered Bactria. The Parthians recovered, however, and their empire was firmly established under Mithridates II (the Great, r. ca. 124/123-87 BC)." Beckwith (2009), pp. 83-84.

"The time of Zhang Qian's travel to Central Asia coincided with a crucial period in the Parthian history. In about 129/128 BCE, the Parthians were fighting on two fronts: the Seleucids in the west, and the Scythians in the east. The Parthian army killed the Seleucids in the west, and the Scythians in the east. The Parthian army killed the Seleucid ruler Antiochus VII, but the Parthian king, Phraates II (r. 138-128 BCE), was killed by the Scythians. But in Zhang Qan's [sic – Qian's] account there is no mention at all of this dramatic event. Many scholars assume that it is because that the [sic] his main interest was to report to his emperor the location, customs and products of the countries and peoples from this region, but not historical events. Others suggest that he may have left the [region] before conflict occurred. A third explanation is that Zhang Qian may have had some knowledge of the event, but for some reason it was left out of the present chapter." Wang (2007a), p. 92.

"Chang Ch'ien announced that although he had failed to enlist the Yueh-chih as allies, he returned with much more to offer the Emperor: he had found the progeny of the heavenly horses of Muh Wang in the valley of Ferghana, a valley he had named Ta-yuan. He had known at once that they were heavenly horses, he said, because they did not sweat like ordinary horses, they sweated blood.

The blood-sweating of the Bactrian horses was caused by parasites under their skins; a fact he did not mention. Chang Ch'ien, acknowledged as an expert judge of horses, was an even better judge of emperors.

Han Wu-ti decreed the failed mission a success and bestowed on Chang Ch'ien the tile of Po-wang, Marquis.

The Horses of Heaven were not gifts for the asking. Twenty-three years marked war, east in Korea, and unabatingly, west in the lands of khanates. Grand Historian Ssu-ma Chien wrote of his own times: 'From day to day I can report only of wars and rumours of wars and again of wars.'

The wars raged on across the deserts. One by one, oasis khanates fell before the onslaughts of the Han. Garrisons of Han soldier-settlers were exiled to the deserts to man the fortresses and watchtowers of the captured oases. China spread westward.

By 102 BC, the Pamirs to the west and the Pamir Knot from the Karakoram to the Hindu Kush in the south-west had been claimed by the Han, and the way towards the Western world had been opened.

Of more significance to Han Wu-ti, he had achieved his main objective. Ferghana had fallen: the Horses of Heaven had become his.

If Han Wu-ti subsequently set off in a chariot drawn by heavenly horses to visit the Mountains of the Immortals, his journey was never recorded." Martyn (1987), pp. 68-69.

"From the magnificent Nisaean horses pastured by the old Persian kings in the rolling lands south of the Caspian, the Parthians had bred a strain of 'great horses'; chargers of unprecedented size and strength. Fed on dried alfalfa to keep up their condition year round, these enormous animals could not only carry a lance-wielding rider encased in armour plate, but could also wear chain-mail themselves. To field this heavily armoured cavalry in significant numbers it was necessary to impose a military form on large sectors of the Parthian economy: to squeeze the towns for metals and smiths, to foster in the countryside great estates where the labour of the peasantry was devoted to breeding and maintaining the great mounts for their lordly riders. It was necessary, as well, to reorganize the Parthian army. The infantry was relegated to garrison duties, and in their place two classes of horsemen rode into battle: the barons, with the sun glinting on their armour, on their gold accoutrements, on the mail slapping the sleek sides of their gigantic horses, moving forward to halt and turn the oncoming archer hordes; and their retainers, gathered around them and equipped like their enemies as mounted bowmen, to counter-attack and pursue. This formidable answer to steppe warfare suffered from only one serious drawback: the Parthian lancer, like his Sarmatian prototype, had no stirrups, and the weight he could put behind the thrust of his lance was thus limited.

But the Parthian great horse not only stopped the momentum from the Heartland launched by the Hiung-nu. It served as a model for the later Byzantine cataphracts; and by onward transmission, for the knights of western Europe. And as in Iran it demanded a landed baronage for its maintenance, so in Europe the availability of the mounted knight and his retainers could only be ensured by the king's grant of estates required for their upkeep. Between the weapon acquired by the Parthians from the steppes and the feudal system of medieval Europe there was a direct link." Legg (1970), pp. 98-99.

Shiji 123 reports that Zhang Qian reached the court of the Da Yuezhi on the Oxus after their king had been killed by the *hu* (presumably the Xiongnu, although it possibly refers here to the Wusun or some other group), and the Crown Prince had been made king: 大月氏王已為胡所殺，立其太子為王。

In an otherwise identical parallel passage from *Hanshu* 61, after the king of the Da Yuezhi was killed by the "*Hu*," his *wife* (夫人 *furen*) *was* made 'King': 大月氏王已為胡所殺，立其夫人為王。 The term 夫人 *furen* or 'Madame' in the *Hanshu*, which replaces 太子 *taizi* or 'crown prince' in the *Shiji*, is a term of address for a lady of high rank. *GR*, Vol. II, p. 685 specifies: "**b.** *Title of* the principal wife of a feudatory prince or of the wives of the second rank of the Emperor." (Translated by the author from the French).

The later *Zizhi tongjian* 18 (completed in 1084 CE), agrees with the *Shiji*, saying that the Crown Prince was made King of the Da Yuezhi: 大月氏太子為王。

This must have been a deliberate change to the record, not just a scribal error, as the characters 太子 for 'Crown Prince,' and 夫人 for 'Principal Wife,' are not easily mistaken. Perhaps it was considered inappropriate to have a female ruler, or possibly, there was a period of joint rule or as a regent until the prince was old enough to rule alone?

> "Narain finds in this range of variant readings evidence of Chinese 'misinformation'. He offers a possible reconciliation of the textual ambiguity by suggesting that the slain king of the Da Yuezhi was 'survived by his principal consort who was probably pregnant at the time'. Thus, as the texts can be variously interpreted to refer to one or two persons, the pregnant widow would have acted in effect as a queen-regent, and ruled 'vicariously' until the 'crown-prince' was old enough to rule on his own. Even if the prince had been born before his father was executed by the Xiongnu, he would still probably have been only a baby, and thus the 'regency of the Yuezhi queen-mother need not be doubted'." Benjamin (2007), pp. 92-93.

It is uncertain which report came first, as some scholars, notably A.F.P. Hulsewé, believe that chapter 123 from the *Shiji* was actually reconstructed from the *Hanshu* account (see: *CICA*, pp. 11-25), while others, for example, Edwin Pulleyblank, believe the opposite is true:

> "In an appendix to the article 'Chinese and Indo-Europeans' it was shown that, contrary to the view put forward but never demonstrated by the eighteenth-century scholar Ts'ui Shih, and adopted by the eminent sinologists Paul Pelliot and G. Haloun, chapter 123 of the *Shih-chi* on 'Ta-yüan' could not have been reconstituted from parallel passages in the *Han shu* but must have been the source for the latter—as one would naturally assume if doubts had never been raised." Pulleyblank (1970), p. 154.

None of the texts actually specifies that it was the Xiongnu who murdered the king. The term used in the both the *Shiji* and the *Hanshu* is simply "胡" *hu* - although both Hulsewé and Watson translate this as "Xiongnu," apparently considering that the reference is to the Yuezhi king murdered by the Xiongnu Chanyu Jizhu (= 'Laoshang,') in late 161 BCE.

About 33 years had passed from the time the Da Yuezhi king was murdered in 162 until Zhang Qian arrived at the Da Yuezhi court in 129. It seems unlikely, though possible, that the Queen Mother would still be ruling so long after his death; and by then even her son could have also died. There could, therefore, have been another, unrecorded, ruler of the Da Yuezhi during their long migration to the west.

Perhaps the widow ruled for some time immediately after her husband's death and was followed by (or possibly married) a brother or close relative of the former king, who then became king of the Da Yuezhi. This king could then have been the one killed by the "*Hu*," as stated in both texts.

His son, the "Crown Prince", could have followed this assumed second king. The lack of detail in the records, however, makes other scenarios equally possible.

The term "*Hu*" was certainly used sometimes to refer to the Xiongnu, but only occasionally, being more frequently used for peoples with Caucasoid features (typically described as hairy people with big noses and deep-set eyes). It would, therefore, be more likely to be used to refer to the Wusun than the Xiongnu. Further notes on the successor(s) to the slain Da Yuezhi king can be accessed in Benjamin (2007), pp. 92-93.

Zhang Qian's expedition is illustrated among the famous frescoes of the Mogao cave-temples at Dunhuang, painted many centuries later (*circa* 618-712 CE):

> "Zhang Qian led on his horse, carrying the insignia of his imperial mission: a bamboo pole over two metres long, with three tufts of yak-tail hair attached to it. This yak hair can reach two metres in length, and has always been an emblem of power across a large part of continental Asia." Boulnois (2004), p. 62.

Although unable to draw the king of the Da Yuezhi into coordinating an attack with China against the Xiongnu, he did manage to cross into Daxia and gathered a wealth of information on the area and neighbouring countries, including their products and trade.

Zhang Qian stayed in the region of the Da Yuezhi, and their subjects the Daxia "for over a year." *Hanshu* 61 in *CICA*, p. 209, and *ZZTJ*. Watson (1993), p. 232, translates the phrase in parallel text in the *Shiji* to read "for a year or so," but the original Chinese text actually reads: "for more than a year."

After this, Zhang Qian attempted to return to China through the territory of the Qiang to the south of the Tarim Basin, but he was arrested by the Xiongnu again and held for "over a year" - from *circa* 128. *Shiji* 123 informs us that:

> "Just at this time the *Shanyu* died and the Luli King of the Left attacked the *Shanyu*'s heir and set himself up as the new *Shanyu* (126 BC). As a result of this the whole Xiongnu nation was in turmoil and Zhang Qian, along with his Xiongnu wife and the former slave Ganfu, was able to escape and returned to China." Watson (1993), p. 232.

> "The following winter [after the 2nd Yuanshuo year; i.e. between 31 October, 127 and 26 January, 126 BCE] the *Shanyu* Junchen died and his younger brother, the Luli King of the Left, Yizhixie, set himself up as *Shanyu*. He attacked and defeated Junchen's heir, Yudan, who fled and surrendered to the Han. The Han enfeoffed Yudan as marquis of Shean, but he died several months later.
>
> The summer after Yizhixie became *Shanyu* [i.e. 14 May to 12 July, 125 BCE] the Xiongnu invaded the province of Dai with 20,000 or 30,000 cavalry, murdering the governor, Gong You, and carrying off over 1,000 persons." Watson (1993), pp. 150-151; Also, see: p. 166.

This detailed account, with mutually supporting dates for the death of Junchen and the following invasion headed by the new Chanyu, his younger brother Yizhixie, makes it most probable that Zhang Qian returned to China in 126 BCE; most likely early in the year.

> "[In 126 BCE] *Liu Che* [sic - Liu Zhi or Emperor Huan] promoted *Zhang Qian* to the position of Senior Counsellor of the Palace, and *Gan Fu* was bestowed the title of Sir *Fengxi* [sic – should read *Fengshi jun* 奉使君]. When *Zhang Qian* departed from *Han* the envoy group was made up of more than one hundred members, thirteen years later upon his return to the *Han* capital, only two members survived." *Zizhi tongjian, juan* 18. Yap (2009), p. 168. **NOTE:** de Crespigny (2007a), p. 1223, translates the title 太中大夫 *Taizhong Dafu* as 'Grand Palace Grandee.' See also the report of Zhang Qian's journey in *Zizhi tongjian, juan* 18. Yap (2009), pp. 167-168. (JEH)

> "Zhang Qian in person visited the lands of Dayuan, the Great Yuezhi, Daxia, and Kangju, and in addition gathered reports on five or six other large states in the neighbourhood. All of his information he related to the emperor on his return. . . ." *Shiji* 123. Watson (1993), p. 233.

• Zhang Qian's later adventures

There are later accounts, in both the *Shiji* and *Hanshu*, of what Zhang Qian allegedly heard while living among the Xiongnu and reported to the Emperor some years after his return:

> "After his triumphant return from the west Chang Ch'ien's [Zhang Qian's] career had ups and downs. In 123 he received the rank of marquis (*hou*) for his success as a general in a military expedition against the Hsiung-nu [Xiongnu]. The following year, however, he was late for a rendezvous with another general in a new expedition against the Xiongnu. For this he should have received the death penalty but, in

accordance with Han law, he was able to redeem his life with his rank [plus a fine] and was merely reduced to a commoner. A few years later (119 B.C. or thereafter) he found an opportunity to recover his lost fortunes by persuading the emperor to send him on a second embassy to the west. This time it was not the Yüeh-chih but the Wusun whom he hoped to persuade to move east to Gansu and become China's ally against the Hsiung-nu [Xiongnu]. The Kansu [Gansu] corridor had recently come under Chinese control because of the surrender of the Hun-ya [Hunye] King, a Hsiung-nu prince who had held it as his appanage from the *shan-yü*. The Hun-ya King and his people had been moved eastwards into the Ordos, leaving the territory empty. The *Shih-chi* records Chang Ch'ien's proposal to the emperor as follows.[3]

> 'When I was living among the Hsiung-nu [Xiongnu], I heard that the king of the Wusun was called K'un-mo [Kunmo]. K'un-mo's father (ruled over) a small country on the western borders of the Hsiung-nu. The Hsiung-nu attacked and killed his father. K'un-mo was abandoned alive in the wilderness. A crow brought meat in its bill and flew over him. A wolf came and suckled him. The *chanyu* marvelled, thinking him divine, and received him and brought him up. When he was full grown (the *shan-yü* [*chanyu*]) put him in charge of troops. He frequently won distinction. The *shan-yü* gave K'un-mo back his father's people and ordered him to defend forever the Western Regions (?).[4] K'un-mo gathered together and fostered his people and attacked small countries round about. He had several 10,000 bowmen practised in warfare.
>
> When the *shan-yü* died, K'un-mo led his people and moved far away. He made himself independent and was no longer willing to go to the Hsiung-nu court. The Hsiung-nu sent crack troops to attack him but they were not victorious. They regarded him as divine and avoided him. So they treated him as a dependency but did not make major attacks on him.
>
> Now the *shan-yü* has recently been hard pressed by Han and the former territory of the Hun-ya (King) is empty and depopulated. The barbarians by nature covet the goods of Han. If now we take this occasion and bribe the Wu-sun richly, inviting them to fill up the east and live in the old territory of the Hun-ya (King) and join in brotherhood with Han, they will likely agree. If they agree, it will cut off the right arm of the Hsiung-nu. When we have made an alliance with the Wu-sun, the peoples to the west around Ta-hsia [Daxia] can all be invited to come and be our outer subjects.'
>
> [3] *Shih-chi*, 123.19-20.
>
> [4] Taking 西城 in the text to be a corruption of 西域. I can discover no other reference to a Western Fort or Wall in the Hsiung-nu territory and the use of such fortifications by the nomads seems highly unlikely. On the other hand, the term Western Regions does not begin with Chinese penetration of the Tarim Basin but is found with reference to the period of Hsiung-nu domination. See *Han shu pu-chu* [*Hanshu buzhu*], 96A, p. 5437 (*Kuo-hsüeh chi-pen ts'ung-shu* [*Guoxue jiben congshu*])."
>
> Pulleyblank (1970), pp. 154-155 and notes. For an alternative translation, see: *CICA*, pp. 237-238.

Soon after his return, Zhang Qian reported to the Emperor discoveries he had made on his journeys to the powerful and rich kingdoms to the west. Later:

> "He [the Emperor] ordered Zhang Qian to start out from Jianwei in Shu on a secret mission to search for Daxia. The party broke up into four groups proceeding out of the regions of Mang, Ran, Xi, and Qiong and Po. All the groups managed to advance

1,000 or 2,000 li [416 or 832 km] but they were blocked on the north by the Di and Zuo tribes and on the south by the Sui and Kunming tribes. The Kunming tribes have no rulers but devote themselves to plunder and robbery, and as soon as they seized any of the Han envoys they immediately murdered them. Thus none of the parties were ever able to get through to their destination. They did learn, however, that some 1,000 or more *li* to the west there was a state called Dianyue whose people rode elephants and that the merchants from Shu sometimes went there with their goods on unofficial trading missions. In this way the Han, while searching for a way to Daxia, first came into contact with the kingdom of Dian....

Zhang Qian was made a subordinate commander and sent to accompany the commander in chief Wei Qing [died 106 BCE] on expeditions against the Xiongnu. Because he knew where water and pasture were to be found in Xiongnu territory, he was able to save the army from hardship. He was enfeoffed as Bowang Marquis or "Broad Vision" Marquis. This occurred in the sixth *yuanshuo* era (123 BC)." *Shiji* 123. From Watson (1993), pp. 236-237.

Shiji 123 reports that Zhang Qian was sent on a final mission to the Wusun, *circa* 119 BCE:

"Zhang Qian dispatched his assistant envoys to Dayuan, Kangju, the Great Yuezhi, Daxia, Anxi, Shendu, Yutian, Yumo, and the other neighbouring states, the Wusun providing them with guides and interpreters. Then he returned to China [*circa* 115 BCE], accompanied by twenty or thirty envoys from the Wusun and a similar number of horses which the Wusun had sent in exchange for the Han gifts. The Wusun envoys thus had an opportunity to see with their own eyes the breadth and greatness of the Han empire.

On his return Zhang Qian was honoured with the post of grand messenger [115 BCE], ranking him among the nine highest ministers of the government. A year or so later he died [in 113 BCE]." *Shiji* 123 from Watson (1993), pp. 239-240. For the dates, see: *CICA*, p. 218, n. 819. See also: Perkins (1999), p. 615.

The same events are recorded with some differences of detail in *Hanshu* 96B and 61:

"The Son of Heaven frequently asked [Chang] Ch'ien about the states such as Ta Hsia. Since he had already lost his noble rank, [Chang] Ch'ien took the opportunity to report as follows: ...." From: *Hanshu* 61 in CICA, pp. 213-214.

There is an account given to the Emperor of stories Zhang Qian (Chang Ch'ien) had heard about the Wusun during his captivity among the Xiongnu. At the end of the report, Zhang Qian said:

"At present the Shan-yü has recently suffered at the hands of the Han and the *K'un-mo*'s lands[809] are empty. Barbarians love their old homelands and are also greedy for Han goods. If we could only make use of the present opportunity to send generous presents to Wu-sun and induce [its people] to move east and live in their old lands; and if the Han would send a princess to be the consort of [the king] and establish brotherly relations, the situation would be such that they would agree, and this would result in cutting off the right arm of the Hsiung-nu. Once a link had been forged with Wu-sun, the states such as Ta-Hsia to its west could all be induced to come to court and become outer subjects of Han.

[809] *Shih-chi* 123.10a has "the old lands of (the king of) K'un-yeh", the latter being of course, not a Wu-sun but a Hsiung-nu leader, who surrendered to the Han together with his followers in 121 B.C.; see *HFHD* II, p. 62 and *Urkunden* I, p. 126ff., and cf. p. 75 above."

CICA, p. 217-218 and n. 809.

"The Son of Heaven agreed with this [advice] and appointed [Chang] Ch'ien to be leader of the gentlemen of the palace, with a force of three hundred men; each man had two horses, and the cattle and sheep were counted by the ten thousand. He took gold, valuables and silk which was worth an enormous amount; and there were a large number of deputy envoys bearing their insignia to be sent to the neighbouring states if the roads were feasible. As soon as he reached Wu-sun,[813] [Chang] Ch'ien presented his gifts and a message [from the emperor], but he was not able to obtain a decision from Wu-sun. An account of this is given in the Chapter on the Western Regions.

[Chang] Ch'ien forthwith sent his deputy envoys on separate missions to Ta Yuan, K'ang-chü, the Yüeh-chih and Ta Hsia. Wu-sun provided interpreters and guides to accompany [Chang] Ch'ien, together with a mission from Wu-sun; this comprised men and horses, each numbered by the ten, and was to render thanks [to the emperor]. The mission was ordered to use the opportunity to make a thorough observation of Han and find out its extent. On his return [Chang] Ch'ien was appointed superintendent of state visits, and after about a year he died. About a year later the deputy envoys whom he had sent to make contact with states such as Ta Hsia all came to court, in many cases with people from those places.

For the first time the states of the north then came into communication with Han. It was [Chang] Ch'ien who had pioneered the way, and all those who subsequently went there as envoys mentioned the name of the noble of Po-wang as a pledge of good faith among the outer states, who then trusted them. Subsequently, Wu-sun finally contracted a matrimonial alliance with Han....

[815] Here *SC* inserts the passage which occurs in *HS* 96B. 2a-b. *HSPC* 96B. 2b-3a (transl. p. 145) [see below]."

From: *Hanshu* 61 in *CICA*, pp. 218-219, and note 315.

- **Zhang Qian's Xiongnu family**

"He [the Xiongnu Chanyu after the first capture of Zhang Qian] ordered to have *Zhang Qian* and his men detained. However, the *Chanyu* had great admiration for the courage of the men; they were each given a *Xiongnu* wife. Ten years later when *Zhang Qian* realised he had a chance to escape and continue with his mission he deserted his wife. On the occasion of his second capture by the *Xiongnu* he was reunited with his *Xiongnu* wife. Whereupon a second chance arose to get away, he escaped. His wife realising he had escaped hurriedly rode with their two children to join up with her husband. The *Xiongnu* army went in hot pursuit of the escaping prisoners. *Zhang Qian* managed to escape with his elder son, his *Xiongnu* wife and the younger son were captured by the pursuing army. The husband and wife never saw each other again. However different accounts vary, another account claims that he returned to *Han* with his wife. N.B. The above accounts about *Zhang Qian* and his Xiongnu wife are from informal chronicles." Yap (2009), pp. 168-169. **NOTE:** Underlining replaced with italics.

- **Zhang Qian's death in 113 BCE**

"The indications regarding the year of his death differ, but Shih Chih-mien (1961), p. 268 shows beyond doubt that he died in 113 B.C. His tomb is situated in Chang-chia ts'un 張家村 near Ch'eng-ku . . . ; during repairs carried out in 1945 a clay mold with the inscription 博望家造 [Home of the Bowang (Marquis) - he was enfeoffed as Bowang Marquis or "Broad Vision" Marquis in 123 BCE] was found, as reported by Ch'en Chih (1959), p. 162." Hulsewé and Loewe (1979), p. 218, note 819.

• Conflicting accounts in the *Shiji* and the *Hanshu* of Zhang Qian and his Discoveries.

The *Hanshu* contains more information than the *Shiji*, and includes accounts of the Da Yuezhi displacing some Se/Sai/Saka people when moving into the Ili region; and, later, being defeated by the Wusun before moving on to Daxia.

This additional material is sometimes difficult to follow, and often, contradictory. As I have mentioned earlier, some scholars suspect that the *Shiji's* account is an unreliable later reconstruction, while others think the account in the *Hanshu* was, perhaps, deliberately distorted. Deciding which text was the primary one is extremely complex.

Two distinguished professors, have held opposing views of this problem for years. Hulsewé claims that the account in the *Hanshu* should be considered primary to that in the *Shiji*, while Pulleyblank has maintained the contrary point of view in a series of long and detailed articles.

More recently, a Chinese scholar, Professor Zongli Lu, has reconsidered this unhappy standoff and, in another detailed article reviewing all the evidence, has come to a conclusion similar to that propounded by Pulleyblank.

After careful study of all these articles I find myself agreeing with Zongli Lu's conclusions:

> "This paper has made no attempt to prove that the present *Shih chi* 123 could not be a later reconstruction, or to reject the challenge to rectify errors in the *Shih chi* text. The most we can claim is that there is no conclusive evidence, either external or internal, to support Hulsewé's hypothesis on the spuriousness of *Shih chi* 123. There are further arguments in Hulsewé's article which have not been discussed here, but his crucial points have all been dealt with at length in this paper.
>
> If the loss of the *Shih chi* from 100 (or 200) to 400 A. D. could be proven, it would be crucial supporting evidence for Hulsewé's hypothesis. In fact, his theory that the present *Shih chi* 123 is a Six Dynasties' reconstruction is largely based on this unproven assumption. Since the transmission of the *Shih chi* during the period mentioned in this paper is so evident, much more substantial textual evidence would be required to show that any of the *Shih chi* has undergone the reconstruction Hulsewé suggests.
>
> The emphasis of Hulsewé's article is on textual criticism. Hulsewé has discovered many questionable points in the present *Shih chi* text, which will be helpful to the future study of *Shih chi* 123. However, as Hulsewé himself realized, proving the authenticity or lack thereof of *Shih chi* 123 is a hazardous undertaking. Besides the difficulty of determining which of two almost identical passages is the original and the other a copy, justifying the claim that certain expressions in a work are anachronistic requires a painstaking investigation and examination of texts contemporary with it. This paper, therefore, limits its discussion to refuting Hulsewé's theory. We conclude that there are no firm linguistic grounds to support the suggestion that *Shih chi* 123's language is later, or less grammatical, than that of the *Han shu.* Nor do the stylistic differences warrant any observation other than the fairly obvious point that they come from the hands of different authors." Lu (1993), pp. 67-68.

For more detail consult the discussion and numerous references in Professor Zongli Lu's "Problems concerning the Authenticity of Shih chi 123 Reconsidered" in *Chinese Literature: Essays, Articles, Reviews (CLEAR)*, Vol. 17 (Dec., 1995), pp. 51-68, from which I have quoted above.

Appendix Z: Lijian (Ptolemaic and Roman Egypt)

The name *Lijian* 犂鞬 originally referred to the Ptolemaic Empire based in Egypt, and later to Roman Egypt.

As is often the case, there has been extensive debate in academic circles regarding the identification of the territory referred to as Lijian/Lixian, with many suggestions made (see: note 11.2), but no consensus has been reached.

I believe it may be possible to clear up this confusion on the basis of my recent identifications of Tiaozhi as Characene/Mesene and Susiana (see: note 9.1), and Haixi as Egypt (see: note 10.13). As I have dealt with these matters previously in the notes mentioned, I will consider them as established for the sake of this discussion of Lijian.

Even if I am wrong about the identification of Tiaozhi, and it originally referred to the Seleucid Empire, these arguments should still hold true.

As outlined in note 9.1, there were many ways of transcribing the name of this region in the Chinese histories. They are all closely related both in terms of the characters used and their reconstructed pronunciations - so it is probable that these were attempts to transcribe an ancient foreign name. See: note 11.2, and the discussion in Yu (2013), pp. 237-249.

I tend to agree with Pelliot (1915), pp. 690-691, and Dubs (1957) - especially see pp. 2-3 and nn. 6 and 8, pp. 25-26, that all the variants in the Chinese histories and possibly even the 'Alasandra' of the Pali *Milindrapañha* (given as 阿荔散 A-li-san in the Chinese versions: see: Pelliot 1914, pp. 359-419, esp. p. 413), were early attempts to represent the name of Alexandria, the capital of the Ptolemaic Empire. This empire was based in Egypt and included neighbouring territories in the centuries following Alexander's conquests.

> "On the other hand, in spite of the variant characters, the several phonetic glosses which from early times have been added to these names show that they all ought to be read, in modern pronunciation, Lijian. Thus the Mediterranean Orient had been known in China since the return of Zhang Qian [W-G: Chang Chien] in 126 BCE, under the name of Lijian, and that this name had been replaced during the first century of our era by that of Da Qin." Translated and adapted from Pelliot (1915), p. 690.

> "The name Li-jien was almost surely a Chinese transcription and abbreviation of the Greek word "Alexandria" and originally denoted Alexandria in Egypt. We may even perhaps be able to tell how this word came into use in China.
>
> Between 110 and 100 B.C., there arrived at the Chinese capital an embassy of the King of Parthia. Among the presents to the Chinese emperor are stated to have been fine jugglers from Li-jien. The jugglers and dancers, male and female, from Alexandria in Egypt were famous and exported to foreign countries. Since the King of Parthia obviously esteemed highly the emperor of China, he naturally sent the best jugglers he could secure. When these persons were asked whence they came, they of course replied "from Alexandria," which word the Chinese, who disliked polysyllables and initial vowels and could not pronounce certain Greek sounds, shortened into "Li-jien." When they also learned that this place was different from Parthia, the Chinese naturally used its name for the country of these jugglers. No Chinese had been to the Roman empire, so they had no reason to distinguish a prominent place in it from the country itself. The Romans moreover had no name for their empire other than, *orbis terrarium, i.e..*, "the world," so that these jugglers would have found it difficult to explain the name of the Roman empire! In such a fashion there probably arose the Chinese name Li-jien which, for them, denoted the Roman empire in general." Dubs (1957), pp. 2-3.

While I agree with Dubs' argument here, it must be noted that he has made one serious error: Egypt was not annexed by the Romans until 30 BCE, so the jugglers here would have been referring to Alexandria, the capital of the Ptolemaic Empire. It was only sometime after 30 BCE,when Rome took control of Egypt, that the merging of the name Lijian with Da Qin (the Roman Empire) could have taken place.

Lijian and variations of the name appear in all the main Chinese histories from the *Shiji* to the *Weilüe*, as well as in other documents. One of the difficulties in identifying Lijian has been that the *Shiji* appears at first glance to say that Lijian is *north* of Anxi (Parthia) – see, for example, Watson (1961), p. 235 - while the *Hanshu, Hou Hanshu* and *Weilüe* all indicate it is to the *west* of Wuyishanli (Arachosia), or Tiaozhi and Anxi.

This apparent contradiction is explained by a probable misreading of the Chinese text of the *Shiji*, as Hulsewé clarifies:

> "It is to be noted that the vast difference between the location of Li-kan in the North, viz. in Hyrcania, and its location somewhere in the West, is due to the ambiguity of the *Shih-chi* text. *SC* 123.2b (*Chien-yu* ed.), when describing An-hsi, i.e. Arsacid Persia, writes 其西則條枝北有奄蔡黎軒條枝安息西數千里, "to the West there is T'iao-chih. In the North there is Yen-ts'ai [and?] Li-kan [and?] T'iao-chih is? are? several thousand *li* West of An-hsi". *HS* 96A.13a (Ching-yu ed.), however, when speaking about Wu-i-shan-li, leaves no room for doubt when writing 西與犁靬條支接 "it adjoins Li-kan and T'iao-chih in the West". Herrmann (1941), pp. 222-223, believed that Pan Ku made a mistake when copying the *Shih-chi*; concerning the unreliability of the *Shih-chi* see our Introduction, p. 12f.; to Herrmann Li-kan is Vehrkāna, i.e. Hyrcania." See n. 275.7 in CICA, pp. 117-118.
>
> **NOTE:** the quote from the *Shiji* ends: 臨西海 or "close to the Western Sea," [the Arabian Sea, including the Persian Gulf and the Red Sea]. See: *CICA*, pp. 113, 235, n. 916. (JEH)

I believe the accounts in the *Hou Hanshu* and *Weilüe* are clear that Lijian originally referred to Alexandria in Ptolemaic Egypt. The *Hou Hanshu* reports:

> 大秦國一名犂鞬以在海西亦云海西國地方數千里有四百餘城小國役屬者數十。

I have translated this as:

> "[Part of] the kingdom of Da Qin [the Roman Empire] was also named Lijian. As it is found to the west of the sea, it is also called the kingdom of Haixi [lit. 'West of the Sea' = Egypt]. Its territory extends for several thousands of *li*. It has more than four hundred walled towns. There are several tens of smaller dependent kingdoms."

The parallel passage from the *Weilüe* states:

大秦國一號犂靬在安息條支西大海之西。

> "[Haixi which is now part of] the kingdom of Da Qin (Roman Empire), also called Lijian, (and was) west of Anxi (Parthia) and Tiaozhi (Characene and Susiana), and west of the Great Sea [here referring to the Red Sea]."

I feel these two passages identify Lijian beyond doubt - originally as the region of the Ptolemaic Empire, and later retained to refer to Roman Egypt along with the other, newer, name of Haixi during the period of the Later Han..

ABBREVIATIONS

AAC: *Afghanistan: Ancien carrefour entre l'est et l'ouest.* (2005) Eds. Osmund Bopearachchi and Marie Françoise Boussac. Brepols Publishers, n.v., Turnhout, Belgium.

AACABI: *After Alexander: Central Asia before Islam.* Eds. Georgina Hermann and Joe Cribb. (2007). *Proceedings of the British Academy* **133**. Oxford University Press.

ABC: *ABC Chinese-English Comprehensive Dictionary.* Editor: John de Francis. (2003) University of Hawai'i Press.

ACE: *Atlas of the Chinese Empire.* (1908). Prepared by Edward Stanton for the China Inland Mission. Morgan & Scott, Ltd., London.

AGRSR: *Ancient Glass Research along the Silk Road.* Editor-in-Chief, Gan Fuxi. (2009). World Scientific Publishing Co. Pte. Ltd., Singapore.

AHTNMK: *Afghanistan: Hidden Treasures from the National Museum, Kabul.* (2008). Eds., Friedrik Hiebert, Pierre Cambon. National Geographic, Washington, D.C.

AOS: *Archaeology of Seafaring: The Indian Ocean in the Ancient Period.* (1999). Edited by Himanshu Prabha Ray. Pragati Publications, Delhi.

ARAI: *Ancient Rome and India: Commercial and cultural contacts between the Roman world and India.* (1994) Edited by Rosa Maria Cimino. New Delhi, Munshiram Manoharlal Publishers Pvt. Ltd.

ATR: *Asian Trade Routes.* Edited by Karl Reinhold Haellquist. Studies on Asian Topics No. 13. 1991. London: Scandinavian Institute of Asian Studies. Curzon Press.

BAI: *Bulletin of the Asia Institute: The Archaeology and Art of Central Asia. Studies From the Former Soviet Union.* New Series. Edited by B. A. Litvinskii and Carol Altman Bromberg. Translation directed by Mary Fleming Zirin.

BEFEO: *Bulletin de l'École Française d'Extrême-Orient.*

BSOAS: *Bulletin of the School of Oriental and African Studies, University of London.*

CAC: *The Contemporary Atlas of China.* (1989). Sydney, Collins. 1st edition, 1988, London, Marshall Editions.

CAOC: *The Contemporary Atlas of China.* (1988). London: Marshall Editions Ltd. Reprint: 1989. Sydney: Collins Publishers Australia.

CEAW: *Contact and Exchange in the Ancient World.* (2006). Edited by Victor Mair. University of Hawai'i Press.

CED: *A Chinese-English Dictionary* (Revised Edition). (1997). Foreign Language Teaching and Research Press

CHC: *The Cambridge History of China. Volume I. The Ch'in and Han Empires, 221 B.C. - A.D. 220.* (1986). Edited by Denis Twitchett and Michael Loewe. Cambridge University Press.

CHEIA: *The Cambridge History of Early Inner Asia*, (1990). Edited by Denis Sinor, Cambridge University Press.

CHI: *The Cambridge History of Iran. Volume 3 (1) and (2).* The Seleucid, Parthian and Sasanian Periods. (1983). Edited by Ehsan Yarshater. Cambridge University Press.

CICA: *China in Central Asia: The Early Stage 125 BC - AD 23: an annotated translation of chapters 61 and 96 of the History of the Former Han Dynasty.* Hulsewé, A. F. P. and Loewe, M. A. N., (1979). Leiden: E. J. Brill.

CID: *Cassell's Italian-English, English-Italian Dictionary.* Compiled by Piero Rebora with Francis M. Guercio and Arthur L. Hayward. 2nd Edition (1960). Cassell & Company, London.

DEABT: *Dictionary of East Asian Buddhist Terms.* Chief Editor, Charles Muller. Downloaded 4 Jan 2000 from: http://www.human.toyogakuen-u.ac.jp/-acmuller/dicts/deabt/data/

DOBCT: *A Dictionary of Chinese Buddhist Terms: With Sanskrit and English Equivalents and a Sanskrit-Pali Index.* Compiled by William Edward Soothill and Lewis Hodous. 1st edition 1937. Paperback edition, RoutledgeCurzon, London. 2004.

EB (1911): *Classic Encyclopaedia* based on the 11th Edition of the *Encyclopaedia Britannica* (1911). Accessed on various dates from: *LoveToKnow 1911 Online Encyclopedia.* © 2003, 2004 LoveToKnow, at: http://1911encyclopedia.org/index.htm. Website now defunct.

EB (2011): *Encyclopædia Britannica.* Online Home Edition.

EDB: The *Earthquake Data Bank.* International Institute of Earthquake Engineering and Seismology. [Iranian] Seismology Research Centre. Downloaded 31 December 2002, from: http://www.iiees.ac.ir/English/bank/eng_bank_historic_inIslam.html. Website now defunct, but the information is in: Ambraseys and Melville (1982).

EDOC: *ABC Etymological Dictionary of Old Chinese.* Axel Schuessler (2007). University of Hawai'i Press, Honolulu.

EIT: *Explorations in Turkestan: With an Account of The Basin of Eastern Persia and Sistan.* Expedition of 1903, under the Direction of Raphael Pumpelly. Carnegie Institute of Washington, April, 1905. Downloaded from: http://dsr.nii.ac.jp/toyobunko/ on 18 December 2004.

GEL: *A Greek-English Lexicon.* Compiled by Henry George Liddell and Robert Scott. 1843. Ninth Edition Revised and Augmented by Henry Stuart Jones, 1940. Reprint: 1953, Oxford at the Clarendon Press.

GR: *Grand dictionnaire Ricci de la langue chinoise.* 7 volumes. Instituts Ricci (Paris – Taipei). Desclée de Brouwer. 2001.

HCCA, Vol. II: *History of civilizations of Central Asia*, Volume II. The development of sedentary and nomadic civilizations: 700 B.C. to A.D. 250. Harmatta, János, ed., 1994. Paris: UNESCO Publishing.

HCCA, Vol. III: *History of civilizations of Central Asia*, Volume III. The crossroads of civilizations: A.D. 250 to 750. Litvinsky, B. A., ed., 1996. Paris: UNESCO Publishing.

HCCA, Vol. IV: *History of civilizations of Central Asia*, Volume IV. The Age of Achievement: A.D. 750 to the End of the Fifteenth Century. Part Two: The Achievements. Eds. C.E. Bosworth and M.S. Asimov. 2000. Paris: UNESCO Publishing.

HDC: *Hanyu Da Cidian* 漢語大詞典 [Unabridged Dictionary of Sinitic]. 1995. Luo Zhufeng. Originally 13 volumes. 3 Volume Compact Edition (whole text in condensed font).

Hucker: *A Dictionary of Official Titles in Imperial China.* Charles O. Hucker. 1985. Stanford University Press. Stanford, California.

ISCH: *Indo-Greek and Indo-Scythian Coins and History*. Robert C. Senior. 3 vols. 2001. Classical Numismatic Group, Lancaster, PA.

ITLOTG: *In the Land of the Gryphons: Papers on Central Asian archaeology in antiquity*. Edited by Antonio Invernizzi. Le Lettere. Firenze, Italy. 1995.

IRLP: *Indo-Iranian Languages and Peoples.* Edited by Nicholas Sims-Williams. Proceedings of the British Academy – 116. Oxford University Press. 2002.

JA: *Journal asiatique.*

JAOS: *The Journal of the American Oriental Society*. University of Michigan.

JOSA: *Journal of the Oriental Society of Australia.* University of Sydney.

JRSOP: *Journal of the Research Society of Pakistani.* Research Society of Pakistan. University of the Punjab.

JWH: *Journal of World History*. University of Hawai'i.

K: Karlgren, Bernhard, 1940. *Grammata Serica.* Stockholm: Bulletin of the Museum of Far Eastern Antiquities. Reprint: Taipei: Ch'eng-wen Publishing Company. 1966.

KSU: *Kushan Studies in U.S.S.R. Papers presented by Soviet Scholars at the UNESCO Conference on History, Archaeology and Culture of Central Asia in the Kushan Period.* Dushanbe, 1968. Calcutta: *Soviet Indology Series No. 3.* Indian Studies Past & Present. 1970.

LD: *A Latin Dictionary*. Founded on Andrews' Edition of Freund's Latin Dictionary. Revised, enlarged and rewritten by Charlton T. Lewis and Charles Short. 1879. Reprint 1958. Oxford at the Clarendon Press.

LYT: *Lin Yutang's Chinese-English Dictionary of Modern Usage*. Lin Yutang. 1972. Reprint 1980. The Chinese University Press. Hong Kong.

MCTBAF: *Masterpieces of Chinese Tibetan Buddhist Altar Fittings in the National Palace Museum*. (1971) National Palace Museum, Taipei, Taiwan, Republic of China.

MTB: *Memoirs of the Research Department of the Toyo Bunko*.

NEB (1977): *New Encyclopædia Britannica*. 1977. 15th edition. 32 vols. Chicago: Encyclopædia Britannica, Inc.

NGAOC: *Atlas of China* (2007). The National Geographic Society. Washington, D.C.

NGAME: *Atlas of the Middle East*. (2003). The National Geographic Society. Washington, D.C.

NSAE: *Nomads et sédentaires en asie centrale: apports de l'archéologie et de l'ethnologie*. Actes du colloquy franco-soviétique. Alma Alta (Kazakhstan) 17-26 Octobre 1987. CNRS, Paris. 1990.

OED: *The Compact Edition of the Oxford English Dictionary*. Complete Text Reproduced Micrographically. 2 volumes. 1977. Oxford University Press.

OCD: *Oxford Chinese Dictionary*. 2010. Chief Editors: Julie Kleeman, Harry Yu. OUP, Oxford.

OTCOFE: *On the Cusp of an Era: Art in the Pre-Kuṣāṇa World*, edited by Doris M. Srinivasan. Leiden: Brill, 2007.

PDK: *Papers on the Date of Kaniṣka*. Basham, A. L., ed., 1968. Leiden: E. J. Brill.

RAI: *Rome and India: The Ancient Sea Trade*. 1991. V. Begley and R. D. De Puma, eds. University of Wisconsin Press.

RPGD: *Greek Dictionary: Greek-English and English-Greek Pocket Dictionary*. (1985). Compiled by Paul Nathanail. Routledge & Kegan Paul, London, Boston and Henley.

SOAS: School of Oriental and African Studies, London.

SAW: *Saudi Aramco World*. Saudi Aramco.

TAA: *Tradition and Archaeology: Early Maritime Contacts in the Indian Ocean*. Proceedings of the International Seminar *Techno-Archaeological Perspectives of Seafaring in the Indian Ocean 4th cent. B.C. - 15th cent. A.D.* New Delhi, February 28 – March 4 1994. Edited by Himanshu Prabha RAY, New Delhi, and Jean-François SALLES, Lyon. First published: 1996. Reprinted: 1998. Manohar Publishers & Distributors, New Delhi.

TAB: *The Times Atlas of the Bible*, 1987. Edited by James B. Pritchard, Sydney, Bay Books.

TAWH: *The Times Atlas of World History*, 1978. Edited by Geoffrey Barraclough, Sydney, William Collins Publishers.

TCAW: *The Times Comprehensive Atlas of the World*. Twelfth Edition. 2007. Times Books Group Ltd. London.

TGJ: *The Geographical Journal*. Royal Geographical Society. U.K.

TP: *T'oung pao*.

TSOB: *The Spread of Buddhism*. (2007). Edited by Ann Heirman and Stephan Peter Bumbacher. Handbook of Oriental Studies. Section Eight, Central Asia. Edited by Denis Sinor and Nicola Di Cosmo. Brill, Lieden; Boston.

WTNID: *Webster' Third New International Dictionary: Unabridged*. G. & C. Merriam & Co., 1967.

ZZTJ: *Zizhi tongjian* 資治通鑒卷 (*juan*) 18. Downloaded on 13 November 2011, from: http://zh.wikisource.org/wiki/%E8%B3%87%E6%B2%BB%E9%80%9A%E9%91%91/%E5%8D%B7018

BIBLIOGRAPHY

Abdullaev (1995): "Nomadism in Central Asia. The archaeological evidence (2nd–1st centuries B.C.)." K. Abdullaev. In: *ITLOTG*, pp. 151-161.

Abdullaev (2007): "Nomad Migration in Central Asia." Kazim Abdullaev. *Proceedings of the British Academy* **133**, 73-98.

Abel-Rémusat (1836): *The Pilgrimage of Fa Hian; from the French Edition of the Foe Koue Ki of MM. Remusat, Klaproth and Landresse with Additional Notes and Illustrations.* Translated by J. Thomas. Baptist Mission Press, Calcutta. The original French edition by Jean-Pierre Abel-Rémusat was published posthumously in Paris in 1836.

Abetekov and Yusupov (1994): "Ancient Iranian Nomads in western Central Asia." A. Abetekov and H. Yusupov. In: *HCCA*, (1994), pp. 23-33.

Abramson (2008). *Ethnic Identity in Tang China.* Marc S. Abramson. University of Pennsylvania Press, Philadelphia.

Achaya (1994): *Indian Food: A Historical Companion.* K. T. Achaya. 1994. Oxford University Press. Oxford University Paperbacks. New Delhi. Second Impression, 1998.

Adams (1988): *Tocharian Historical Phonology and Morphology*. Douglas Q. Adams. New Haven: American Oriental Society.

Adams (2002): "Silk in Ancient Nubia: One Road, Many Sources," by Nettie K. Adams. *Silk Roads, Other Roads.* 2002. CD: "Proceedings of the 8th Biennial Symposium of the Textile Society of America, Inc. 2003.

Adams (2007): *Land Transport in Roman Egypt: A Study of Economics and Administration in a Roman Province.* Colin Adams. Oxford University Press, USA (May 17, 2007).

Agarwal (1986): "A Cultural Study of the Western Kshatrapa Inscriptions." Aashi Agarwal. *Journal of Indian History*, Vol. LXIV. April, August, December 1986, Parts 1 – 3, pp. 53-67.

Alderton (1988): *Turtles & Tortoises of the World.* David Alderton. Blanford Press. First published 1988. Paperback reprint, 1993.

Allchin and Hammond (1979): *The Archaeology of Afghanistan from Earliest Times to the Timurid Period.* F. Allchin and N. Hammond. New York. Academic Press.

Alemany (2002): "Maes Titianos I la Torre de Pedra (I): una font grega sobre els orígens de la ruta de la seda." Augustí Alemany i Vilamajó. *Faventia* 24/2, 2002, pp. 105-120. (In Catalan).

Allen (1982): *A Mountain in Tibet: The Search for Mount Kailas and the Sources of the Great Rivers of India.* Charles Allen. André Deutsch Limited, Great Britain. Reprint: Futura Publications, London. 1991.

Allen (1999): *The Search for Shangri-la : A Journey into Tibetan History.* Charles Allen. Abacus Books. London.

Allen (2000): "Imra, Pentads and Catastrophes." Nick J. Allen. *Ollodagos* (Brussels) 2000, 14: 278-308.

Almgren (1962): "Geographical Aspects of the Silk Road especially in Persia and East Turkestan." Bertil Almgren. 1962. *Museum of Far Eastern Antiquities Bulletin* No. 34, pp. 93-108.

Alonso-Núñez (1988-1989): "The Roman Universal Historian Pompeius Trogus on India, Parthia, Bactria and Armenia." J. M. Alonso-Núñez. *Persica* XIII (1988-1989), pp. 125-145.

Aly (1956): *De Strabonis Codice Rescripto: Cuius Reliquiae in Codicibus Vaticanis Vat. Gr. 2306 et 2061A servatae sunt.* Wolfgangus Aly. Studi e Testi 188. Città del Vaticano. Biblioteca Apostolica Vaticana (in Latin).

Aly (1957): *Strabonis Geographica.* Strabons Geographika in 17 Büchern. Text, Übersetzung und erläuternde Anmerkungen von Wolfgang Aly. Band 4: Strabon von Amaseia. Untersuchungen über Text, Aufbau und Quellen der Geographika. Rudolf Habelt Verlag, Bonn, (in German).

A.M. (1900): "On the Afghan Frontier: A Reconnaissance in Shugnan." Author: "A.M." *The Geographical Journal*, Vol. 16, No. 6 (Dec., 1900), pp. 666-679.

Ambolt (1939): *Karavan: travels in Eastern Turkestan*. Nils Ambolt. Translated from the Swedish by John Bulman. Blackie & Son Limited, London and Glasgow.

Ambraseys et al. (1981): "The Pattan (Pakistan) earthquake of 28 December 1974: field observations." N. Ambraseys, G. Lensen, A. Moinfar and W. Pennington. *Quarterly Journal of Engineering Geology and Hydrogeology*. 1981 volume 14, pp. 1-16.

Ambraseys and Melville (1982): *A History of Persian Earthquakes*. N. N. Ambraseys and C. P. Melville, Cambridge Earth Science Series, Cambridge University Press.

Ames and Hall (2001): ***Focusing the Familiar***. A Translation and Philosophical Interpretation of the *Zhongyong*. Roger T. Ames and David L. Hall. University of Hawaii Press. Electronic version from Google Play Books.

Anthony (2007): *The Horse the Wheel and Language: How Bronze-Age Riders from the Eurasian Steppes Shaped the Modern World*. David W. Anthony. Princeton University Press.

Anonymous (1842), "The Bolan Pass." *Journal of the Royal Geographical Society of London*, Vol. 12 (1842), pp. 109-112.

Appleby (1997): "The Royal Society and the Tartar Lamb." John H. Appleby. *Notes and Records of the Royal Society of London*, 51 (1), pp. 23-34.

Apte (1963): *The Practical Sanskrit-English Dictionary* [Fourth Revised & Enlarged Edition]. Vaman Shivram Apte. Delhi, 1963. Reprint: Motilal Banarsidass, Delhi. 1978.

Arbach (2002): "La chronologie du royaume de Qatabân du 1er siècle avant J.-C. au 1er siècle après J.-C." Mounir Arbach. *Chroniques yéménites* (2002). Downloaded, from: http://cy.revues.org/document135.html?format=print on 1 Sept. 2005.

Arnaud-Lindet (2003): *Epitoma Historiarum Philippicarum*. Ed. and Trans. Marie-Pierre Arnaud-Lindet (2003). Downloaded 3 June 2007 from: http://www.forumromanum.org/literature/justin/index. html.

Aujac and Lasserre (1969): *Strabon. Géographie*. Vol. 1. Germaine Aujac and François Lassere. Paris. Les Belles Lettres (Association Guillaume Budé).

Aujac (2000) : "Strabon et son temps." Germaine Aujac. First published in: Wolfgang Hübner (Eds.), *Geographie und verwandte Wissenschaften*, Franz Steiner Verlag Stuttgart, 2000, pp. 103-139. Downloaded from: http://www.strabon.org/edito/article105.html on 16 May 2007.

Bachhofer (1941): "On Greeks and Śakas in India." Ludwig Bachhofer. *Journal of the American Oriental Society*, Vol. 61, No. 4 (Dec. 1941), pp. 223-250.

Bachhofer (1949): Review of "La vieille route de l'Inde de Bactres à Taxila" by A. Foucher. Ludwig Bachhofer in *Journal of the American Oriental Society*, Vol. 69, No. 2 (Apr. - Jun., 1949), pp. 100-103.

Bagchi (1948): "Ancient Chinese Names of India." P. C. Bagchi. *Monumenta Serica*, Vol. 13 (1948), pp. 366-375.

Bagrow (1945): "The Origins of Ptolemy's Geographica." Leo Bagrow. *Geografiska Annaler*, Vol. 27. (1945), pp. 318-387.

Bailey (1937): "Ttaugara." H. W. Bailey. *Bulletin of the School of Oriental Studies*. Vol. VIII, Part 4, pp. 883-921.

Bailey (1946): *Mission to Tashkent*. F. M. Bailey. Published by Jonathan Cape. Folio Society reprint with amended version of Introduction and epilogue by Peter Hopkirk, 1999.

Bailey (1952): "Kusanica." H. W. Bailey. *BSOAS* XIV (1952), pp. 420-434.

Bailey (1958): "Languages of the Saka." H. W. Bailey. *Handbuch der Orientalistik*, I. Abt., 4. Bd., I. Absch., Leiden-Köln.

Bailey (1979): *Dictionary of Khotan Saka*. H. W. Bailey. Cambridge University Press. PB reprint, 2010.

Bailey (1979b): "North Iranian Problems." H. W. Bailey. *BSOAS* (1979), 42 : pp. 207-210.

Bailey (1985): *Indo-Scythian Studies being Khotanese Texts Volume VII*. H. W. Bailey. Cambridge University Press.

Baines and Málek (1984): *Atlas of Ancient Egypt*. John Baines and Jaromir Málek. Equinox, Oxford.

Baldick (2000): *Animal and Shaman: Ancient Religions of Central Asia*. Julian Baldick. New York University Press.

Ball (2000): *Rome in the East: The transformation of an empire*. Warwick Ball. Routledge. London & New York.

Banchich (2000): *De Imperatoribus Romanis* (published *c.* 361). Sextus Aurelius Victor. Translated by Thomas M. Banchich as: *A Booklet about the style of life and the manners of the Imperatores*. Downloaded from: http://www.roman-emperors.org/epitome.htm on 21 April 2007.

Bancroft (1984): "Lapis Lazuli from Afghanistan." Peter Bancroft. A chapter taken from his book: *Gem and Crystal Treasures*. Western Enterprises/Mineralogical Record, Fallbrook, California. Downloaded from: http://www.palagems.com/lapis_lazuli_bancroft.htm, 30 October 2008

Bao, et al. (2004): "Evidence for a late Holocene warm and humid climate period and environmental characteristics in the arid zones of northwest China during 2.2 ~ 1.8 kyr B.P." Bao, Y., Braeuning, A., Yafeng, S. and Fahu, C., *Journal of Geophysical Research* **109**: 10.1029/2003 JD003787." Downloaded on 23 March 2004 from: http://www.co2science.org/journal/v7/v7n11c2.htm.

Barber (1999): *The Mummies of Ürümchi*. Elizabeth Wayland Barber. 1999. London. Pan Books.

Barfield (1981): "*The Hsiung-nu Imperial Confederacy: Organization and Foreign Policy*." Thomas J. Barfield. *The Journal of Asian Studies*, Vol. 41, No. 1 (Nov., 1981), pp. 45-61.

Barger (1939): "Exploration of Ancient Sites in Northern Afghanistan." Evert Barger. *The Geographical Journal*, Vol. 93, No. 5 (May 1939), pp. 377-391.

Barnwell (2013): "The Evolution of the Concept of De 德." Scott A. Barnwell. *Sino-Platonic Papers*. Number 235, March 2013.

Basham (1953): "A New Study of the Śaka-Kusāṇa Period." A. L. Basham. *BSOS* 15, 1953, pp. 80-97.

Basirov (2001): "The Origin of the Pre-Imperial Iranian Peoples." Oric Basirov. CAIS series of lectures, *SOAS*, 26/4/2001. Downloaded on 9 August 2007, from: http://www.cais-soas.com /CAIS/Religions/iranian/Zarathushtrian/Oric.Basirov/origin_of_the_iranians.htm

Baumer (2000): *Southern Silk Road: In the Footsteps of Sir Aurel Stein and Sven Hedin*. Christoph Baumer. 2000. White Orchid Books. Bangkok.

Baumer (2012): *The History of Central Asia. Volume One: The Age of the Steppe Warriors*. Christoph Baumer. I. B. Tauris. London. New York.

Beal (1884): *<u>Si-Yu-Ki</u>: Buddhist Records of the Western World*, by Hiuen Tsiang. 2 vols. Trans. by Samuel Beal. London. 1884. Reprint: Delhi. Oriental Books Reprint Corporation. 1969.

Beal (1911): *The Life of Hiuen-Tsiang*. Translated from the Chinese of Shaman Hwui Li by Samuel Beal. London. 1911. Reprint Munshiram Manoharlal, New Delhi. 1973.

Beaujard (2005): "The Indian Ocean in Eurasian and African World-Systems before the Sixteenth Century." Philippe Beaujard. *JWH* Vol. 16, Issue 4, pp. 411-465.

Beckwith (1991); "The Impact of the Horse and Silk Trade on the Economies of T'ang China and the Uighur Empire." Christopher I. Beckwith. *Journal of the Economic and Social History of the Orient*, Vol. XXXIV, pp. 183-198.

Beckwith (1993): *The Tibetan Empire in Central Asia: A History of the Struggle for Great Power among Tibetans, Turks, Arabs, and Chinese during the Early Middle Ages*. Christopher I. Beckwith. (Princeton: Princeton University Press, 1987). First paperback edition, with new afterword, 1993.

Beckwith (2005). "On the Chinese Names for Tibet, Tabghatch, and the Turks." Christopher I. Beckwith. *Archivum Eurasiae Medii Aevi* 14: 7-22.

Beckwith (2006). "Old Tibetan and the Dialects and Periodization of Old Chinese." Christopher I. Beckwith. *In: Medieval Tibeto-Burman Languages II.* C.I. Beckwith, ed., pp. 179-200. Leiden: Brill.

Beckwith (2009): *Empires of the Silk Road: A History of Central Eurasia from the Bronze Age to the Present.* Christopher I. Beckwith. Princeton University Press.

Been (1992): "Aconitum: Genus of Powerful and Sensational Plants." Anita Been. *Pharmacy in History*, Vol. 34, No. 1 (1992), pp. 35-39.

Beeston (1981): A review of *The Periplus of the Erythraean Sea, by an unknown author* by G.W.B. Huntingford (ed. and trans.). A. L. F. Beeston. London. 1980. *JSOAS*, No. 44.

Bell (1890): "The Great Central Asian Trade Route from Peking to Kashgaria." Mark S. Bell. *Proceedings of the Royal Geographical Society and Monthly Record of Geography*, New Monthly Series, Vol. 12, No. 2 (Feb., 1890), pp. 57-93.

Bello et al. (2011): "Earliest Directly-Dated Human Skull-Cups." Silvia M. Bello, Simon A. Parfitt, Chris B. Stringer, *PLoS One.* 2011; 6(2): e17026. Published online 2011 February 16. Downloaded 31 January, 2012 from: 10.1371/journal.pone.0017026.

Benjamin (2003): "The Yuezhi Migration and Sogdia." Craig Benjamin. *Transoxiana: Ērān ud Anērān - Webfestschrift Marshak 2003.* Downloaded on 12 October 2003 from: www.transoxiana.com.ar/Eran/Articles/benjamin.html

Benjamin (2007): *The Yuezhi: Origin, Migration and the Conquest of Northern Bactria.* Craig G. R. Benjamin. Silk Road Studies XIV. Brepols, Belgium.

Benn (2002): *China's Golden Age: Everyday Life in the Tang Dynasty.* Charles Benn. Oxford University Press.

Bennett (2010*): Cannabis and the Soma Solution.* Chris Bennett. Trine Day. Kindle Edition.

Berggren and Jones (2000): *Ptolemy's **Geography**: An Annotated Translation of the Theoretical Chapters.* J. Lennart Berggren and Alexander Jones. Princeton University Press, Princeton, N.J.

Bergman (1939): *Archaeological Researches in Sinkiang, especially in the Lop-Nor Region.* Folke Bergman. Reports from the Scientific Expedition to the North Western Provinces of China under the leadership of Dr Sven Hedin – The Sino-Swedish Expedition, Publication 7. Stockholm.

Berke and Wiedemann (2000): "The Chemistry and Fabrication of the Anthropogenic Pigments Chinese Blue and Purple in Ancient China." Heinz Berke and Hans G. Wiedemann. *EASTM* 17 (2000): 94-120.

Bernard (1980): "Une nouvelle contribution soviétique à l'histoire des kushans : la fouille de Dal'verzin-tépé (Uzbékistan)." Paul Bernard. *BEFEO*, LXVIII, 1980, pp. 313-348.

Bernard (1994a): "Alexander and his successors in Central Asia." P. Bernard. In: *HCCA* II, pp. 88-97.

Bernard (1994b): "The Greek Kingdoms of Central Asia." P. Bernard. In: *HCCA* II, pp. 99-129.

Bernard (2005): "De la Euphrate à la Chine avec la caravane de Maès Titianos (c. 100 ap. n. è.)." Paul Bernard. *Comptes rendus des séances de l'Académie des inscriptions et Belles-Lettres*, 149e année, N 3, 2005. pp. 929-969.

Bernard (2008a): "The Greek Colony at Ai Khanum and Hellenism in Central Asia." Paul Bernard. In: *AHTNMK*, pp. 81-105.

Bernard (2008b): "Ai Khanum Catalog." Paul Bernard. In: *AHTNMK*, pp. 106-129.

Biddulph (1875): "Visit to Maralbashi." J. Biddulph. In: *Report of a Mission to Yarkund in 1873, with Historical and Geographical Information Regarding the Possessions of the Ameer of Yarkand.* T. D. Forsyth. The Foreign Department Press. Calcutta. Pages 217-221.

Bielenstein (1980): *The bureaucracy of Han times.* Hans Bielenstein. Cambridge University Press. Digital Version. 2008.

Bielenstein (1986): "The institutions of Later Han." Hans Bielenstein. *CHC*, pp. 491-519.

Bielenstein (2005): *Diplomacy and Trade in the Chinese World, 589-1276.* Hans Bielenstein. Brill. Leiden and Boston.

Bivar (1963); "The Kaniṣka dating from Surkh Kotal." A. D. H. Bivar. *BSOAS*, Vol. 26, No. 3, (1963), pp. 498-502.

Bivar (1976): "The Kusana Trilingual." A. D. H. Bivar. *BSOAS*, Vol. 39, No. 2. (1976), pp. 333-340.

Bivar (1981): "Gondophares and the Shāhnāma." A. D. H. Bivar. *Iranica antiqua*, 16 (1981), pp. 141-151.

Bivar (1983a): "The political history of Iran under the Arsacids." A. D. H. Bivar. *CHI* 3 (1), pp. 21-99.

Bivar (1983b): "The history of eastern Iran." A. D. H. Bivar. *CHI* 3 (1), pp. 181-231.

Bivar (2000): "A Current Position on Some Central and South Asian Chronologies." A. D. H. Bivar. *BAI, NS*, Vol. 14, (2000) pp. 69-75.

Bivar (2007): "Gondophares and the Indo-Parthians." A. D. H. Bivar. In: *The Age of the Parthians* (*The Idea of Iran*, Vol. 2). Ed. by Vesta Sarkhosh Curtis and Sarah Stewart. I. B. Tauris. London, pp. 26-36.

Bonavia (1988): *An Illustrated Guide to the Silk Road.* Judy Bonavia. 1988. William Collins. Great Britain.

Bonavia (2004): *The Silk Road From Xi'an to Kashgar.* Judy Bonavia – revised by Christoph Baumer. 2004. Odyssey Publications.

Booth (1988): *Rhino Road: The Black and White Rhinos of Africa.* Martin Booth. 1988. London. Constable.

Bopearachchi (1993): *Indo-Greek, Indo-Scythian and Indo-Parthian Coins in the Smithsonian Institution.* Osmund Bopearachchi. The National Numismatic Collection, Smithsonian Institution, Washington, D.C.

Bopearachchi & Raman (1995): *Pre-Kushana Coins in Pakistan.* Osmund Bopearachchi & Aman ur Rahman. IRM Associates Ltd., Islamabad.

Bopeararchichi (2002): "Archaeological Evidence on Shipping Communities of Sri Lanka." Osmund Bopeararchichi. In: *Ships and the Development of Maritime Technology on the Indian Ocean.* Eds. David Parkin, Ruth Barnes. Routledge (U.K.), pp. 92-127.

Bopearachchi (2006) : « Chronologie et Généalogie des premiers rois Kouchans : Nouvelles Données », Osmond Bopearachchi. *Comptes-rendus des séances de l'Académie des Inscriptions et Belles-Lettres.* 2006. Volume 150 Issue 3, pp. 1433-1447.

Bostock & Riley (1855): *The Natural History* by Pliny the Elder. Translated by John Bostock and H. T. Riley. Taylor and Francis, Fleet St., London. Downloaded on the 10 March 2013 from: http://www.perseus.tufts.edu/hopper/text?doc=Perseus:text:1999.02.0137 and ff.

Bosworth (1983): "Iran and the Arabs before Islam." C. E. Bosworth. In: *CHI*, pp. 593-612.

Bouchet (1998): "Gandhari and the early Chinese Buddhist translations reconsidered: the case of the Saddharmapundarikasutra." Daniel Boucher. *JAOS*, Vol. 118, No. 4, Oct. 1988, pp. 471-506.

Boulnois (1992): *La Route de la Soie.* Luce Boulnois. 1963. Arthaud. 3rd Edition. 1992. Genève. Editions OLIZANE.

Boulnois (2004): *Silk Road: Monks, Warriors & Merchants on the Silk Road.* Luce Boulnois. Translated by Helen Loveday. Odyssey Books, Hong Kong.

Bowersock (1996): *Roman Arabia.* G. W. Bowersock, Harvard University Press, 1983. First paperback edition. Harvard University Press.

Bowles (1977): *The People of Asia.* Gordon T. Bowles. 1977. London. Weidenfield and Nicolson.

Braund (1991): "New "Latin" Inscriptions in Central Asia: Legio XV Apollinaris and Mithras?" David Braund. Zeitschrift für Papyrologie und Epigraphik, Bd. 89 (1991), pp. 188-190.

Braund (1994): *Georgia in Antiquity: A History of Colchis and Transcaucasian Iberia 550 BC - AD 562.* David Braund. Clarendon Press, Oxford. 1994.

Bretschneider (1870): "Ta-ts'in-kuo." E. Bretschneider. *The Chinese Recorder and Missionary Journal*, Vol. 3. No. 2. Foochow, China. July, 1870, pp. 29-31.

Briant (2012): "From the Indus to the Mediterranean: The Administrative Organization and Logistics of the Great Roads of the Achaemenid Empire." Pierre Briant. In: *Highways, Byways, and Road Systems in the Pre-Modern World.* First Edition, pp. 185-201. Edited by Alcock, Bodel and Talbert. John Wiley & Sons, Inc.

Brosser (1828): *Relation du pays de Ta ouan; traduite du chinois par* M. BROSSET jeune (2). *JA*, Tome II, 1828, pp. 418-450.

Brough (1965): "Comments on 3rd Century Shan-shan and the History of Buddhism." J. Brough. *BSOAS*, XXVIII, pp. 582-612.

Brough (1970a): "Supplementary Notes on Third-Century Shan-Shan." J. Brough. *BSOAS*, XXXIII, pp. 39-45.

Brough (1970b): "Nugae Indo-Sericae." John Brough. In: *W. B. Henning Memorial Volume.* Editors: Mary Boyce and Ilya Gershevitch. London, 1970, pp. 81-88.

Brown (2001): *Israel and Hellas: The Legacy of Iranian Imperialism and the Individual.* Vol. III. John Pairman Brown. Walter De Gruyter Inc.

Browne (1832): *The Naturalist*, Vol. II. Edited by D. J. Browne. Boston: Allen & Ticknor; New York: P. Hill.

Browning (1989): *Petra.* Iain Browning. 1st edition, 1973. 3rd edition, 1989. Chatto & Windus, London.

Bruemmer (1997): "Promised land of the ostrich: can this biblical bird return to its ancestral home in Israel?" Fred Bruemmer. *International Wildlife*, Vol. 27, No. 6, November-December 1997

Bulliet (1975): *The Camel and the Wheel.* Richard W. Bulliet. Cambridge, Massachusetts, Harvard University Press.

Bumbacher (2007): "Early Buddhism in China: Daoist Reactions." Stephan Peter Bumbacher. In: *TSOB*, pp. 203-246.

Bunker (1993): "Gold in the Ancient Chinese World: A Cultural Puzzle." Emma C. Bunker, *Artibus Asiae*, Vol. 53, No. 1/2 (1993), pp. 27-50.

Bunker (1998): "Cultural Diversity in the Tarim Basin Vicinity and Its Impact on Ancient Chinese Culture." Emma C. Bunker. In: *The Bronze Age and Early Iron Age Peoples of Eastern Central Asia*, Vol. Two, pp. 604-618. Edited by Victor H. Mair. Institute for the Study of Man, with The University of Pennsylvania Museum Publications.

Burnett (1836): *Magazine of botany and gardening British and foreign, comprehending figures carefully coloured from nature of flowers, fruits, & cryptogamia with descriptions thereof, together with original & select papers & reviews on the principles and practice of cultivation.* James Burnett. Thordarson Collection.

Burrow (1940): *A Translation of the Kharosthi Documents from Chinese Turkestan.* T. Burrow. Royal Asiatic Society. Downloaded on 17 August 2006 from: http://depts.washington.edu/silkroad/texts/niyadocts.html.

Burton (1996): "Itinéraires commerciaux et militaires entre Boukhara et l'Inde." Audrey Burton. *Cahiers d'Asie central.* Numéro 1/2 (1996), pp. 13-32. Downloaded on 11 September 2011, from: http://asiecentrale.revues.org/index415.html

Bussagli (1996): *L'Art du Gandhara.* Mario Bussagli. Originally published in Italian, 1984. Torino, Unione Tipografico - Editrice Torinese. Translated into French by Béatrice Arnal. Librairie Générale Française. 1996.

Cable (1934): "The Bazars of Tangut and the Trade-Routes of Dzungaria." Mildred Cable. *TGJ*, Vol. 84, No. 1 (Jul., 1934), pp. 17-31.

Cable and French (1958): *The Gobi Desert*. Mildred Cable and Francesca French. First edition, Hodder & Stoughton 1943; "reprint" (with changed pagination) by Four Square Books, Landsborough Publications, 1958. London.

Califano (2011): "Museums in Afghanistan – A Roadmap into the Future (with an appendix on Samangan/Takht-e Rostam)." Alessandro Califano. *The Silk Road*, Volume 9, 2011, pp. 88-103.

Cambon (2008): "Begram: Alexandria of the Caucasus, Capital of the Kushan Empire." Pierre Cambon. In: *AHTNMK*, pp. 145-161.

Campany (1995): *Strange Writing: Anomaly Accounts in Early Medieval China*. Robert Ford Campany. State University of New York Press.

Cang (1991): *Shiji cidian* 史记词典 ["Dictionary to the Records of the Historian"]. Cang Xiuliang. Jinan. Shandong jiaoyu, CBS.

Capon and MacQuitty (1973): *Princes of Jade*. Edmund Capon and William MacQuitty. Sphere Books. London.

Carr (2005): "The proper study of mankind: A survey of human evolution." Geoffrey Carr. *The Economist*. December 24, 2005, Christmas survey, pp. 3-12.

Carter (2005): *The History and Prehistory of Pearling in the Persian Gulf*. Robert Carter. *Journal of the Economic and Social History of the Orient*. 662, 5/23/2005, pp. 139-209.

Cary (1956): "Maes, Qui et Titianus." M. Cary. *The Classical Quarterly*, New Series, Vol. 6, No. 3/4. (Jul. – Oct., 1956), pp. 130-134.

Cassar (2004): "The rock relief discovered in the village of Shamarq, Baghlan province." Brendan J. Cassar. SPACH. 2004, pp. 2-7.

Casson (1974): *Travel in the Ancient World*. Lionel Casson. 1974. Paperback reprint: 1994. Baltimore, Johns Hopkins University Press.

Casson (1983): "Sakas versus Andhras in the *Periplus maris erythraei*. Lionel Casson. *Journal of the Economic and Social History of the Orient*, 26 (1983), pp. 164-177.

Casson (1989): *The Periplus Maris Erythraei*. Lionel Casson. (Translation by H. Frisk, 1927, with updates and improvements and detailed notes). Princeton, Princeton University Press.

Cerasetti (2004). "Reasoning with GIS : Tracing the Silk Road and the Defensive Systems of the Murghab Delta (Turkmenistan)." Barbara Cerasetti. *The Silk Road*, Volume 2, Number 2, December 2004, pp. 39-42.

Chahin (1991): *The Kingdom of Armenia*. M. Chahin. New York, Dorset Press.

Chakravarti (1930): "Naval Warfare in Ancient India." Prithwis Chandra Chakravarti. *The Indian Historical Quarterly*, Vol. 4, No. 4. 1930.12, pp. 645-664. Downloaded on 19 December 2004 from: http//ccbs.ntu.edu.tw/FULLTEXT/JR-ENG/cha.htm.

Chan (2004): "Early Middle Chinese: Towards a New Paradigm." Abraham Chan. *T'oung Pao* XC, Nos. 1-3, pp. 122-162.

Chang (2007): *The Rise of the Chinese Empire: Nation, State, and Imperialism in Early China, ca. 1600 B.C.-A.D. 8*. Chun-shu Chang. University of Michigan Press.

Chandra (1977): *Trade and Trade Routes in Ancient India*. Moti Chandra. New Delhi. Abhinav Publications.

Chapman (1999): *The Art of Rhinoceros Horn Carving in China*. Jan Chapman. Christie's Books, London.

Chardin (1724): *Travels in Persia 1673-1677*. Two Volumes. Sir John Chardin. Reprint in One Volume: The Argonaut Press. London, 1927.

Chattopadhyay (1975): *Kushāna State and Indian Society: A Study in Post-Mauryan Polity & Society*. Bhaskar Chattopadhyay. Punthi Pustak, Calcutta.

Chattopadhyay (1979): *The Age of the Kushānas - A Numismatic Study*. Second (*Enlarged*) Edition. Bhaskar Chattopadhyay. Punthi Pustak, Calcutta.

Chavannes (1895-1905): *Les mémoires historiques de Se-ma Ts'ien*, 5 Vols. Édouard Chavannes. On line version by Pierre Palpant of l'Université du Québec à Chicoutimi. Accessed 15 November 2008: http://classiques.uqac.ca/classiques/chine_ancienne/auteurs_chinois.html

Chavannes (1900): *Documents sur les Tou-kiue (Turcs) occidentaux*. Édouard Chavannes. 1900. Paris, Librairie d'Amérique et d'Orient. Reprint: Taipei. Reprint: Cheng Wen Publishing Co. 1969.

Chavannes (1903): "Voyage de Song Yun dans l'Udyāna et le Gandhāra 518-522 p. C." Édouard Chavannes. *BEFEO* (1903), pp. 379-441.

Chavannes (1905): "Les pays d'Occident d'après le Wei lio." Édouard Chavannes. *T'oung pao* (1905) 6, pp. 519-571.

Chavannes (1905b): "Les livres chinois avant l'invention du papier." Édouard Chavannes. *JA* (Jan-Feb 1905), pp. 5-75.

Chavannes (1906): "Trois Généraux Chinois de la dynastie des Han Orientaux. Pan Tch'ao (32-102 p.C.); - son fils Pan Yong; - Leang K'in (112 p.C.). Chapitre LXXVII du *Heou Han chou*." Édouard Chavannes. *T'oung pao* 7, (1906), pp. 210-269.

Chavannes (1907): "Les pays d'Occident d'après le *Heou Han chou*." Édouard Chavannes. *T'oung pao* 8, (1907) pp. 149-244.

Chavannes (1911): "Divination par l'écaille de tortue dans la haute antiquité chinoise (d'après un livre de M. *Lo Tchen-yu*). *JA* 1911, series X, bk. xvii, pp. 127-137.

Ch'en (1964): *Buddhism in China: A Historical Survey*. Kenneth Ch'en. Princeton University Press. First Paperback Edition 1972..

Chen (2002): "Son of Heaven and Son of God: Interactions among Ancient Asiatic Cultures regarding Sacral Kingship and Theophoric Names." Sanping Chen. *JRAS*, Series 3, 12, 3 (2002), pp. 289-325.

Childs-Johnson, ed. (2002): *Enduring Art of Jade Age China: Chinese Jades of Late Neolithic Through Han Periods*. Ed: Elizabeth Childs-Johnson. University of Hawaii Press.

Choksy (2003). "The enigmatic origins of the Tokharians." Jamsheed K. Choksy. In: *Jamshid Soroush Soroushian Commemorative Volume*. Volume II. Eds. Carlo G. Cereti and Farrokh Vajifdar. pp. 107-119.

Christian (2000): "Silk Roads or Steppe Roads? The Silk Roads in World History." David Christian. *JWH* 11.1 (2000) 1-26.

Christie (1979): "Lin-I, Fu-nan, Java." A. H. Christie. In: *Early South East Asia: Essays in Archaeology, History and Historical Geography*. Edited by R. B. Smith and W. Watson. Oxford University Press, New York, Kuala Lumpur, pp. 281-287.

Churchill (1898): *The Story of the Malakand Field Force An Episode of Frontier War*. Winston S. Churchill. Downloaded on 29 March 2012 from: http://infomotions.com/etexts/gutenberg/dirs/etext05 /mkdff10.htm.

Ciancaglini (2001): "Sciti, iranici, nomadi: problemi di etnonimia in Strabone." Claudia A. Ciancaglini. In: *STUDI SULL'XI LIBRO DEI GEORAPHIKA DI STRABONE*. Ed. Giusto Traina, et al. Congedo Editore. Studi di filologia letteratura 6, Università di Lecce, Italia, pp. 1-83.

Ciolek (2000): *Old World Trade Routes (OWTRAD): 'Intelligence' Notebook*. T. Matthew Ciolek, downloaded from: http://www.ciolek.com/OWTRAD/notebook.html on 1 November, 2000.

Ciolek (2005): "Trade Routes." T. Matthew Ciolek. Last revised: 17 May 2005. Downloaded 7 Nov. 2005. http://www.ciolek.com/PAPERS/trade-routes-enc2005.html.

Clarysse and Thompson (2007): "Two Greek Texts on Skin from Hellenistic Bactria." Willy Clarysse and Dorothy J. Thompson. *Zeitschrift für Papyrologie und Epigraphik*, Bd. 159 (2007), pp. 273-279.

Codrington (1944): "A Geographical Introduction to the History of Central Asia." K. de B. Codrington. *TGJ*, Vol. 104, No. 1/2. (Jul.- Aug. 1944), pp. 27-40.

Codrington (1944b): "A Geographical Introduction to the History of Central Asia (Continuation)." K. de B. Codrington. *TGJ*, Vol. CIV Nos 3-4. Sept.-Oct. 1944, pp. 73-91.

Colledge (1967): *The Parthians.* Malcolm A. R. Colledge. *Ancient Peoples and Places*, Vol. 59. General Editor: Dr. Glyn Daniel. Frederick A. Praeger, New York; Washington.

Colless (1980): "Han and Shen-tu – China's Ancient Relations with South Asia." Brian Colless. *East and West*, n. s. Vol. 30, Nos. 1-4, (Dec. 1980), pp. 157-177.

Compareti (2009): *Samarcanda Centro del Mondo: Proposte di lettura del ciclo di Afrāsyāb.* Matteo Compareti. Mimesis Edizioni (Milano – Udine).

Cotterell (2008): *The Imperial Capitals of China: An Inside View of the Celestial Empire.* Arthur Cotterell. Pimlico, London.

Couvreur (1890): *Dictionnaire Classique de la Langue Chinoise.* F. S. Couvreur. Reprint: Taiwan, Kuangchi Press (1966).

Covington (2013): "The Celestial Stone." Richard Covington. *SAW*, March/April, 2013, pp. 24-36.

Creasy (1854): *History of the Ottoman Turks: From the Beginning of their Empire to the Present Time.* Vol. I. E. S. Creasy. London: Richard Bentley. 1854.

Creel (1965): "The role of the Horse in Chinese History." H. G. Creel. *The American Historical Review*, Vol. 70, No. 3. (Apr. 1965), pp. 647-672.

Cribb (1984): "The Sino-Kharosthi Coins of Khotan, their Attribution and Relevance to Kushan Chronology. Part 1." Joe Cribb. *Numismatic Chronicle* Vol. 144 (1984), pp. 128-152.

Cribb (1985): "The Sino-Kharosthi Coins of Khotan, their Attribution and Relevance to Kushan Chronology. Part 2." Joe Cribb. *Numismatic Chronicle* Vol. 145 (1985), pp. 136-149, plus plates.

Cribb (1992): "Numismatic evidence for the date of the Periplus." Joe Cribb. *Indian Numismatics, History, Art and Culture, Essays in the honour of Dr. P. L. Gupta,* (edited by D. W. MacDowall, S. Sharma and S. Garg), Delhi, pp. 131-145.

Cribb (1993): "The Heraus Coins: their attribution to the Kushan king Kujula Kadphises, c. C.E. 30-80." Joe Cribb. In: M. Price et al., eds., *Essays in honour of Robert Carson and Kenneth Jenkins*, London, 1993, pp. 107-34.

Cribb (1995): "Western Satraps and Satavahanas: old and new ideas of chronology." Joe Cribb. In: *Ex Moneta: Essays on Numismatics, History, and Archaeology in Honour of Dr. David W MacDowall,* (edited by A. K. Jha and S. Garg), Nashik, pp. 151-164.

Cribb (1997): "Shiva images on Kushan and Kushano-Sassanian coins." Joe Cribb. In: *Studies in Silk Road Coins and Culture: Papers in honour of Professor Ikuo Hirayama on his 65th birthday.* Edited by Katsumi Tanabe, Joe Cribb, and Helen Wang. The Institute of Silk Road Studies, Kamakura, Japan.

Cribb (1999): "The Early Kushan Kings: New Evidence for Chronology: Evidence from the Rabatak Inscription of Kanishka I." Joe Cribb. In: *Coins, Art, and Chronology: Essays on the pre-Islamic History of the Indo-Iranian Borderlands.* Edited by Michael Alram and Deborah E. Klimburg-Salter. Verlag Der Osterreichischen Akademie Der Wissenschaften, Wein 1999. Downloaded from: http://www.griftrerrec.com/y/cribb/ekk_cribb_01.html on July 7 2003.

Cribb (2005): "The Greek Kingdom of Bactria, its coinage and its collapse." Joe Cribb. In: *AAC*, pp. 207-225.

Cribb (2007): "Money as a Marker of Cultural Continuity and Change in Central Asia." Joe Cribb. In: *AACABI*, pp. 333-375.

Cunningham (1871): *The Ancient Geography of India. I. The Buddhist Period, Including the Campaigns of Alexander, and the Travels of Hwen-Thsang.* Alexander Cunningham. Trübner and Co., London. Complete and unabridged reprint (2006): Low Price Publications, Delhi.

Curiel and Fussman (1965): *Le trésor monétaire de Qunduz. (Mémoires de la Délégation archéologique française en Afghanistan* t. XX): Raoul Curiel and Gérard Fussman. Librairie C. Klincksieck, Paris (1965).

Curtis (2007): "The Iranian Revival in the Parthian Period." Vesta Sarkosh Curtis. In: *The Age of the Parthians (The Idea of Iran, Vol. 2)*. Edited by Vesta Sarkhosh Curtis and Sarah Stewart. I. B. Tauris. London, pages 7-25.

Curzon (1896): *The Pamirs and the Source of the Oxus*. George Nathaniel Curzon. Royal Geographical Society, London. Reprint: Elibron Classics Series, Adamant Media Corporation. 2005. Assembled from the original in *The Geographical Journal*, Vol. 8, No. 1 (Jul., 1896), pp. 15-54, Vol. 8, No. 2 (Aug., 1896), pp. 97-119, and Vol. 8, No. 3 (Sept. 1896), pp. 239-260.

Dabrowa (1984): "Vologèse Ier et l'Hyrcanie." E. Dabrowa. *Iranica antiqua*, 19 (1984), pp. 141-147.

Daffinà (1972): "The Return of the Dead." Paolo Daffinà. *East and West* Nos. 1-2 (March-June 1972), pp. 87-92.

Daffinà (1982): "The Han Shu Hsi Yü Chuan Re-translated. A Review Article." Paolo Daffinà. *T'oung pao* 68 (1982), pp. 309-339.

Daltry et al (2000): "Cardamom Mountains biodiversity survey." Daltry, J.C. et al., Cambridge, Fauna and Flora International. Downloaded on 10 November 2014 from: http://www.rhinoresourcecenter.com/index.php?s=1&act=pdfviewer&id=1349057957&folder=134.

D'Ancona (1949): "Is the Kaniṣka Reliquary a work from Mathurā?" Mirella Levi d'Ancona. *Art Bulletin*, Vol. 31, No. 4 (Dec. 1949), pp. 321-323.

Dandamayev (1994): "Media and Achaemenid Iran." M. A. Dandamayev. *HCCA*. Vol. II (1994), pp. 35-65.

Dani (1973): *Alberuni's Indica*. Abbreviated and annotated by Ahmad Hasan Dani. University of Islamabad Press.

Dani and Litvinsky (1996): "The Kushano-Sassanian kingdom." A. H. Dani and B. A. Litvinsky. In: *HCCA* Vol. III, pp. 103-118.

Dani, Litvinsky and Safi (1996): "Eastern Kushans, Kidarites in Gandhara and Kashmir and Later Hephthalites." A. H. Dani, B. A. Litvinsky and M. H. Zamir Safi.

Dar (undated): "The Question of Roman Influence in Gandhara Art : Numismatic Evidence" (typed draft article), pp. 1-37. Saifar Rahman Dar.

Dar (1979): "Epigraphical Evidence from Taxila. Part I." Saifar Rahman Dar. *JRSOP*, Vol. XVI, October 1979, No. 4, pp. 1-31.

Dar (1980a): "Epigraphical Evidence from Taxila. II. Aramaic Inscription by Asoka Priyadari." Saifar Rahman Dar, *JRSOP*, Vol. XVII, No. 1, pp. 1-18.

Dar (1980b): "Epigraphical Evidence from Taxila. Part III: Kharosthi, Brahmi, Greek Tokharian and Pahlavi Inscriptions." Saifar Rahman Dar, *JRSOP*, Vol. XVII, July 1980, No. 3, pp. 1-41.

Dar (2007): "Pathways Between Gandhara and North India during Second Century B.C.- Second Century A.D." Saifur Rahman Dar. In: *OTCOFE*, pp. 29-54.

Darian (1978): *The Ganges in Myth and History*. Steven G. Darian. The University Press of Hawaii, Honolulu.

Daryaee (2003): "The Persian Gulf Trade in Late Antiquity." Touraj Daryaee. *JWH*, Vol. 14, No. 1 (2003), pp. 1-16.

Davis-Kimball (2000): "Enarees and Women of High Status: Evidence of Ritual at Tillya Tepe (Northern Afghanistan)." Jeannine Davis-Kimball. In: *Kurgans, Ritual Sites, and Settlements: Eurasian Bronze and Iron Age*, pp. 223-239. BAR International Series 2000. Eds. Jeannine Davis-Kimball et al. Downloaded on 9 March 2008 from: http://www.csen.org/BAR%20Book/BAR.%20Part%2001.TofC.html.

Davis-Kimball (2002): *Warrior Women: An Archaeologist's Search for History's Hidden Heroines.* Jeannine Davis-Kimball with Mona Behan. Warner Books, New York. First Trade Printing, 2003.

Deasy (1900): "Journeys in Central Asia (Continued)." H. H. P. Deasy. *TGJ*, Vol. 16, No. 5 (November 1900), pp. 501-523.

Deasy (1901): *In Tibet and Chinese Turkestan: Being a Record of Three Years' Exploration.* H. H. P. Deasy. T. Fisher Unwin, London.

de Clavijo (2005): *Embassy to Tamerlane: 1403-1406.* Ruy González de Clavijo. Translated from the Spanish by Guy Le Strange. RoutledgeCurzon London and New York. 2005. First published 1928.

de Crespigny (1965): "The Second Year of Yen-hsi: notes to the Han chronicle of A.D. 159." Rafe de Crespigny. *JOSA*, vol. 10, Nos. 1 and 2, June 1965, pp. 7-25.

de Crespigny (1973): "Universal Histories." Rafe de Crespigny. In: *Essays on the Sources for Chinese History.* Editors: Donald Leslie, Colin Mackerras, Wang Gungwu. Australian National University Press, Canberra. 1973, pp. 64-70.

de Crespigny (1977): *The Ch'iang Barbarians and the Empire of Han: A Study in Frontier Policy.* Rafe de Crespigny. 1977. *Papers on Far Eastern History 16*, Australian National University. Canberra.

de Crespigny (1984): *Northern Frontier. The Policies and Strategies of the Later Han Empire.* Rafe de Crespigny. 1984. Faculty of Asian Studies, Australian National University. Canberra.

de Crespigny (1989): "South China under the Later Han Dynasty" [Chapter One from *Generals of the South: the Foundation and early history of the Three Kingdoms state of Wu.* Rafe de Crespigny, in Asian Studies Monographs, New Series No. 16 Faculty of Asian Studies, The Australian National University, Canberra 1989]. Downloaded on 28 September 2003, from: http://www.anu.edu.au/asianstudies/south_china.html

de Crespigny (1989b): "Later Han Civil Administration: An Outline of the Civil Administration of the Later Han Empire." Rafe de Crespigny. Originally published in the *Asian Studies Monographs*, New Series No. 12, Faculty of Asian Studies, The Australian National University, Canberra 1989. Downloaded on 4 February 2004 from: www.anu.edu.au/asianstudies/decrespigny/lhca.html.

de Crespigny (1991): "The Three Kingdoms and Western Jin: A History of China in the Third Century AD." Rafe de Crespigny. *East Asian History*, no. 1 [June 1991], pp. 1-36 & no. 2 [December 1991], pp. 143-164. Australian National University, Canberra. Downloaded from: http://www.anu.edu.au/asianstudies/decrespigny/3KWJin.html on 4 February 2004. Last updated January 2004. [This version does not include footnotes or characters].

de Crespigny (1996): "Later Han Military Administration: An Outline of the Military Administration of the Later Han Empire." Rafe de Crespigny. *Asian Studies Monographs*, New Series No. 21, The Australian National University, Canberra. Downloaded on 4 February 2004 from: http://www.anu.edu.au/asianstudies/decrespigny/mil_org.html.

de Crespigny (2004): "The Government & Geography of Later Han." Rafe de Crespigny. Accessed from: https://digitalcollections.anu.edu.au/html/1885/42048/northern_front.html. Rechecked on 10 January 2014.

de Crespigny (2006): "Some Notes on the Western Regions 西域 in Later Han." Rafe de Crespigny. *JAH*, 40 (2006) 1, pp. 1-30.

de Crespigny (2007a) *A Biographical Dictionary of Later Han to the Three Kingdoms* (23-220 AD) (Handbook of Oriental Studies, Section 4). Rafe de Crespigny. Brill, Leiden.

de Crespigny (2007b): *Political Protest in Imperial China: The Great Proscription of Later Han 167-184.* Rafe de Crespigny. First edition 1981. Second edition [Internet]. Downloaded 16 Oct. 2008 from: http://asianstudies.anu.edu.au/Early_Imperial_China.

de Crespigny (2007c): *Inspection and Surveillance Officials Under The Two Han Dynasties.* Second edition [Internet]. 1st edition (1981). Rafe de Crespigny. Downloaded 16 October 2008, from: http://asianstudies.anu.edu.au/Early_Imperial_China.

Defen (636): *Zhou shu* Dynastic History of the Northern Zhou (557-581), Chapter 50. Compiled by Linghu Defen. Downloaded on 5 August 2011 from: http://zh.wikisource.org/wiki/%E5%91%A8%E6%9B%B8/%E5%8D%B750.

Deferrari (1964): *The Seven Books of History against the Pagans* by Paulus Orosius. Translated by Roy J. Deferrari, The Catholic University of America Press, Washington, D.C.

de la Vaissière (2002): *Histoire des marchands sogdiens.* Étienne de la Vaissière. Collège de France. Institut des hautes études chinoises. Paris. 2002.

de la Vaissière (2003): "Sogdians in China: A Short History and Some New Discoveries." Étienne de la Vaissière. *Silk Road Newsletter* Vol. 1, No. 2. December 2003. Downloaded from: http://www.silkroadfoundation.or/yoc/newsletter_dec.html on 13 February 2004.

de la Vaissière (2005): *Sogdian Traders: A History.* Étienne de la Vaissière. Translated By James Ward. Brill, Leiden, Boston.

de la Vaissière (2013): "Iranian in Wusun? A tentative reinterpretation of the Kultobe inscriptions" In: S. Tokhtasev, P. Lur'e (ed.), *Commentationes Iranicae. Vladimiro f. Aaron Livschits nonagenario donum natalicium*, pp. 320-325.

de Rodrigo (2001): *Relaciones de Intercambio entre Egipto y el Mediterraneo Oriental* (Spanish Edition). Alicia Daneri De Rodrigo (Apr. 2001). Biblos.

de Vingo (2000): "Historical and Archaeological Sources Relating to the Migration of Nomadic Peoples Toward Central and Southern Europe During the Imperial Age." By Paolo de Vingo. In: *Kurgans, Ritual Sites, and Settlements: Eurasian Bronze and Iron Age*, pp. 153-159. BAR International Series 2000. Eds. Jeannine Davis-Kimball et al. Downloaded on 9 March 2008 from: http://www.csen.org/BAR%20Book/BAR.%20Part%2001.TofC.html

Dharmananda (undated): "Tortoise Shell: with Brief Reports on Treating Aplastic Anemia and Parkinson's Disease." Subhuti Dharmananda. Downloaded on 13 January 2005 from: http://www.itmonline.org/arts/tortois2.htm

Diamond (1996): "Empire of Uniformity." Jared Diamond. *Discover*, March 1996, pp. 79-85.

Di Cosmo (1994): "Ancient Inner Asian Nomads: Their Economic Basis and Its Significance in Chinese History." Nicola Di Cosmo. *The Journal of Asian Studies* 53, no. 4 (November 1994): pp. 1092-1126.

Di Cosmo (2002): *Ancient China and its Enemies: The Rise of Nomadic Power in East Asian History.* Nicola Di Cosmo. Cambridge University Press. First Paperback Edition, 2004. Quotes reprinted with the permission of Cambridge University Press.

Diller (1958): Review by Aubrey Diller of: *De Strabonis codice rescripto cuius reliquiae in codicibus* by Wolfgang Aly; Franciscus Sbordone; *Strabon von Amaseia. Untersuchungen über Text, Aufbau und Quellen der Geographika* by Wolfgang Aly. *Gnomon*, 30. Bd., H. 7 (1958), pp. 527-532.

DiMarco (2008): *War Horse: A History of the Military Horse and Rider.* Louis A. DiMarco. Chicago Distribution. Also available in Kindle Edition.

Dinerstein (2011): *Handbook of the Mammals of the World*, Volume 2. Eric Dinerstein, "Rhinocerotidae (Rhinoceroses)." Lynx Editions. Downloaded February 2011, from: http://www.lynxeds.com/hmw/family-text/hmw-2-family-text-rhinocerotidae-rhinoceroses.

Diodorus (ca. 36 BCE): *Diodorus of Sicily in Twelve Volumes.* Vol. II. Loeb Classical Edition. Translated by Oldfather. London and Cambridge, Massachusetts, 1967.

Dobbins (1968): "Two Gandhāran Reliquaries." K. Walton Dobbins. *East and West*, 18, 1968, pp. 151-165.

Dobbins (1971): *The Stūpa and Vihāra of Kanishka I.* K. Walton Dobbins. The Asiatic Society of Bengal Monograph Series, Vol. XVIII. Calcutta.

Dobbins (1971b): "The Commerce of Kapisene and Gandhāra after the fall of Indo-Greek Rule." K. Walton Dobbins. *Journal of the Economic and social History of the Orient*, 14 (1971), pp. 286-302.

Dobson (1964): *Late Han Chinese: A Study of the Archaic-Han Shift*. W.A.C.H. Dobson. University of Toronto Press.

Doerfer (1998): "Tatar and Bashkir." Gerhard Doerfer. In: *The Turkic Languages* pp. 283-300. Ed. Lars Johanson. Routledge, New York.

Donato and Seefried (1989): *The Fragrant Past: Perfumes of Cleopatra and Julius Caesar. Giuseppe Donato and Monique Seefried*. Emory University Museum of Art and Archaeology, Atlanta. Instituto Poligrafico e Zecca Dello Stato.

Dorn'eich (1999): "Minar-i chakari: Afghanistan lost an unsolved architectural enigma of great antiquity." Chris M. Dorn'eich. *Spach* NewsLetter, 5 May 1999, pp. 1-16.

Dorn'eich (2003): *HS 96: BAN GU ANNALEN DER ÄLTEREN HAN DIE WESTLÄNDER: IM CHINESISCHEN ORIGINAL UND WESTLICHEN ÜBERSETZUNGEN*. Chris M. Dorn'eich. Berlin.

Dorn'eich (2008): 張騫 *Zhang Qian: The Secret Mission of Han Emperor Wu in search of the Ruzhi (Yuezhi) and the fall of the Græco-Bactrian Kingdom (annotated compilation of Eastern and Western sources)*. Unpublished. Chris Dorn'eich. Berlin.

Dorn'eich (2009): *Chinese Sources on the History of the Wuzhi/Asi-Asioi/Asiani-Rishika-Arsi/Arshi, or Pinyin Ruzhi/Yuezhi People and their Guishuang/Kushan Dynasty. Volume I : Shiji 110 / Hanshu 94A. The Xiongnu. Synopsis of the Original Chinese Text and Various Western Translations with Full Annotations.* Chris M. Dorn'eich. Berlin. Downloaded from: www.chrisdorneich.tumblr.com.

Dorn'eich (2010): "The Great Yuezhi / A(r)si Exodus of 月氏西遷 166 BCE." Chris M. Dorn'eich. Berlin.

Dorn'eich (2011): ***CHINESISCHE QUELLEN*** *zur Geschichte der Yuèzhð/Arsi und ihrer Kuschan-Dynastie. (Chinesische Originaltexte mit westlichen Übersetzungen)*. Christof Michael Dorn'eich, Berlin.

Dorn'eich (2013): 蕭關 *The Xiao Guan Gateway and Early Yuezhi/Rouzhi History Before the Great Exodus of 166 BCE.* (First draft — Unfinished). Including Ancient Notes to *Shiji* 110 by the SAN JIA commentators (5th -8th century). Translated by Wan Xiang and Wen Jing in 2009; revised and annotated by Chris M. Dorn'eich. Berlin.

Drekmeier (1962): *Kingship and Community in Early India*. Charles Drekmeier. Stanford University Press, Stanford, California.

Drew (1877): *The Northern Barrier of India: a popular account of the Jammoo and Kashmir Territories with Illustrations*. Frederic Drew. 1st edition: Edward Stanford, London. Reprint: Light & Life Publishers, Jammu. 1971.

Dreyer (2008): "Zhao Chongguo: "A Professional Soldier of China's Former Han Dynasty." Edward L. Dreyer. *The Journal of Military History*, Vol. 72, No. 3, July 2008, pp. 665-725.

Du and Wang (2005): *Dunhuang & Silk Road*. Compiled by: Du Doucheng and Wang Shuqing. Sea Sky Publishing House, Shenzen, China.

Dubs (1938): *The History of the Former Han Dynasty by Pan Ku*. Vol. One. Translator and editor: Homer H. Dubs. Baltimore. Waverly Press, Inc.

Dubs (1942): "An Ancient Chinese Mystery Cult." Homer H. Dubs. *Harvard Theological Review*. Vol. XXXV, Oct., 1942, No. 4, pp. 221-240.

Dubs (1944): *The History of the Former Han Dynasty by Pan Ku*. Vol. Two. Translator and editor: Homer H. Dubs. Baltimore. Waverly Press, Inc.

Dubs (1955): *The History of the Former Han Dynasty by Pan Ku*. Vol. Three. Translator and editor: Homer H. Dubs. Ithaca, New York. Spoken Languages Services, Inc.

Dubs (1957): *A Roman City in Ancient China*. Homer H. Dubs. London. The China Society.

Dubs and de Crespigny (1967): *Official Titles of the Former Han Dynasty*, translated and compiled by H. H. Dubs and Rafe de Crespigny. Australia National University Press.

Dupree (1977): *An Historical Guide to Afghanistan*. Nancy Hatch Dupree. 1st Edition: 1970. 2nd Edition. Revised and Enlarged. Afghan Tourist Organization, 1977. Downloaded from: http://www.zharov.com/dupree/index.html on 2 April 2007.

Duyvendak (1949): *China's Discovery of Africa: Lectures given at the University of London on January 22 and 23, 1947*. J. J. L. Duyvendak, Arthur Probsthain, London.

Ebrey (1980): "Later Han Stone Inscriptions." Patricia Ebrey. *Harvard Journal of Asiatic Studies* 40, 1980, pp. 325-353.

Ecsedy (1975): "Böz – An Exotic Cloth in the Chinese Imperial Court." Hilda Ecsedy. *Altorientalische Forschungen 3*: pp. 145-153.

Edwards (1891): *Egypt and its Monuments: Pharaohs, fellahs and explorers*. Amelia B. Edwards. 1891. New York. Harper & Brothers.

Egan (1979): "The Prose Style of Fan Yeh." Ronald C. Egan. *Harvard Journal of Asiatic Studies*, Vol. 39, No. 2. (Dec. 1979), pp. 339-401.

Eggermont (1966): "The Murundas and the ancient trade-route from Taxila to Ujjain." P. H. L. Eggermont. *Journal of the Economic and Social History of the Orient*, 9 (1966), pp. 257-296.

Eisen (1916)" "The Origin of Glass Blowing." Gustavus Eisen. *American Journal of Archaeology*, Vol. 20, No. 2 (Apr. - Jun. 1916), pp. 134-143.

Eisenberg (1991): "Retired Emperorship in Medieval China: The Northern Wei." Andrew Eisenberg. *T'oung Pao*, Second Series, Vol. 77, Livr. 1/3 (1991), pp. 49-87.

Eitel (1888): *Handbook of Chinese Buddhism: Being a Sanskrit – Chinese Dictionary*. Ernest J. Eitel. Reprint: New Delhi. Cosmo Publications, 1981.

Elias (1895): *The Tarikh-i-Rashidi of Mirza Muhammad Haidar, Dughlát: A History of the Moghuls of Central Asia. An English Version*. [Originally composed in Persian in 1541-42]. Edited, with Commentary, Notes, and Map by N. Elias. Translation by E. Denison Ross. London. Sampson, Low, Marston and Company Ltd.

Elisseeff (1998): "Approaches Old and New to the Silk Roads" Vadime Elisseeff in: *The Silk Roads: Highways of Culture and Commerce*. Paris (1998) UNESCO. Reprint: Berghahn Books (2000), pp. 1-2.

Elisseeff and Elisseeff (1983): *New Discoveries in China: Encountering History Through Archaeology*. Danielle and Vadime Elisseeff. Translated by Larry Lockwood. Chartwell Books Inc., Secaucus, New Jersey.

Elliot (1999): *An Unexpected Light: Travels in Afghanistan*. Jason Elliot. Picador, London. Reprint: 2000.

Ellis (2005): *Tiger Bone & Rhino Horn : The Destruction of Wildlife for Traditional Chinese Medicine*. Richard Ellis. Shearwater Books, Washington, D.C.

Emmerick (1967): *Tibetan Texts Concerning Khotan*. R. E. Emmerick. London. Oxford University Press.

Enoki (1955): "Sogdiana and the Hsiung-nu." Kazuo Enoki. *Central Asiatic Journal* (1955). Vol. I, pp. 43-62.

Enoki (1959): "On the Nationality of the Ephthalites." Kazuo Enoki. *MTB* 18 (1959), pp. 1-58.

Enoki (1963): "The location of the capital of Lou-lan and the date of the Kharoṣṭhi Inscriptions." Kazuo Enoki. *MTB* 22 (1963), pp. 125-171.

Enoki (1968): "Hsieh 謝, Fu-Wang 副王, or Wang 王 of the Yüeh-shih 月氏 : A Contribution to the Chronology of the Kushans." Kazuo Enoki. *MTB* 26 (1968), pp. 1-13.

Enoki (1983): "On the Relationship between the *Shih-chi* 史記, Bk. 123 and the *Han-shu* 漢書, Bks. 61 and 96." Kazuo Enoki. *MTB*, 41 (183), pp. 1-31.

Enoki, *et al.*, (1994): "The Yüeh-chih and their migrations." K. Enoki, G. A. Koshelenko and Z. Haidary. *HCCA* Vol. II, pp. 171-189.

Eremeev and Semashko (1992): "Pastoral and Nomadic Peoples in Ethnic History." Dmitriy E. Eremeev and Irina M. Semashko. In: *Foundations of Empire: Archaeology and Art of the Eurasian Steppes*. Ed. Gary Seeman. Vol. 3 Proceedings of the Soviet-American Academic Symposia in Conjunction with the Museum Exhibitions. 1989. Ethnographics Press, Centre for Visual Anthropology, University of Southern California, Los Angeles.

Fairley (1975): *The Lion River: The Indus*. Jean Fairley. 1975. 1st Pakistan Edition: 1979. S. I. Gillani, Lahore.

Falconer (1857): Geography, *Strabo*. Chapter XI. Literally translated, with notes. The first six books by H.C. Hamilton, esq., the remainder by W. Falconer. From: *The Geography of Strabo*. Literally translated, with notes, in three volumes. London. George Bell & Sons. 1903. Downloaded on 27 December 2011 from: http://www.perseus.tufts.edu/hopper/text?doc=Perseus:text: 1999.01.0239:book=11:chapter =11

Falk (2001): "The *yuga* of Sphujiddhvaja and the era of the Kuṣâṇas." Harry Falk. *Silk Road Art and Archaeology* VII, pp. 121-136.

Falk (2003): "Five new Kharoṣṭhī donation records from Gandhāra." Harry Falk. *Silk Road Art and Archaeology* IX, pp. 71-86.

Falk (2004): "The Kaniṣka era in Gupta records." Harry Falk. *Silk Road Art and Archaeology* X (2004), pp. 167-176.

Falk (2005): "The introduction of stūpa-worship in Bajaur." Harry Falk. In: *AAC*, pp. 347-358.

Falk (2008): "Money can buy me heaven: Religious donations in late and post-Kushan India." Harry Falk. In: *Archäologische Mitteilungen aus Iran und Turan* 40, 2008, pp. 137-148.

Falk (2009): "The Name of Vema Takhtu." Harry Falk. In: *Exegisti monumenta: festschrift in honour of Nicholas Sims-Williams*. Werner Sundermann, Almut Hintze, François de Blois (2009), *Iranica*, 17, pp. 105-116.

Falk (2010): "Names and Titles from Kuṣāṇa Times to the Hūṇas: The Indian Material." Harry Falk. In: *Coins, Art and Chronology II: The First Millennium C.E. in the Indo-Iranian Borderlands*. Austrian Academy of Sciences (December 31 2010). Michael Alram (Author), Deborah E. Klimburg-Salter (Author). Pages 73-89. Downloaded from: http://scholar.googleusercontent.com/scholar?q=cache:z1uHpl-jk2oJ:scholar.google.com/ &hl=en&as_sdt=0,5 on 15 November 2011.

Falk (2012): *Ancient Indian Eras: An Overview*. Harry Falk. *BAI*, N. S./Volume 21, 2007, pp. 131-145.

Falk and Bennett (2009). "Macedonian Intercalary Months and the Era of Azes." Harry Falk and Chris Bennett. *Acta Orientalia* 70, pp. 197-215.

Fang (1965): *The Chronicle of the Three Kingdoms (220-265): Chapters 69-78 from the Tzŭ chih t'ung chien of Ssŭ-ma Kuang (1019-1086)*. Vols. I and II. Translated and annotated by Achilles Fang. Harvard-Yenching Institute Studies VI. Harvard University Press. Cambridge, Massachusetts.

Farndon (2006): *The Complete Guide to Rocks & Minerals*. John Farndon. Hermes House, London.

Farrock (2005): *Sassanian Elite Cavalry AD 224-642*. Kaveh Farrock. Osprey Publishing. Also: Kindle Edition.

Federov (2004): "On the origin of the Kushans with reference to numismatic and anthropological data." Michael Federov. *Oriental Numismatic Society Newsletter* No. 181, pp. 30-32.

Ferber (1907): "An Exploration of the Mustagh Pass in the Karakoram Himalayas." Aug. C. F. Ferber. *The Geographical Journal*, Vol. 30, No. 6. (Dec. 1907), pp. 630-643.

Ferguson (2005): *Rome and Parthia: Power politics and diplomacy across cultural frontiers*. R. James Ferguson. Centre for East-West Cultural and Economic Studies, Bond University. Downloaded 1 January 2014 from:

http://epublications.bond.edu.au/cgi/viewcontent.cgi?article=1009&context=cewces_papers

Ferrier (1856): *Caravan Journeys and Wanderings in Persia, Afghanistan, Turkistan and Beloochistan with Historical Notices of the Countries lying between Russia and India.* J. P. Ferrier. John Murray. London. Translated by Captain William Jesse.

Ferrier (1858). *History of the Afghans.* J. P. Ferrier. John Murray. London. Translated by Captain William Jesse.

Filippi (1924): *Storia della Spedizione scientifica italiana nel Himàlaia, Caracorùm e Turchestàn Cinese (1913-1914).* Filippo de Filippi. Featuring additional essays by Ciotto Dainelli and J.A. Spranger. Nicola Zanichelli, Bologna. Accessed: http://dsr.nii.ac.jp/toyobunko/VIII-1-A-100/V-1/on 26 February 2006.

Filliozat (1956): *Les relations extérieures de l'Inde (I).* Jean Filliozat. Institut français d'indologie, Pondichéry.

Findley (2005): *The Turks in World History.* Carter Vaughn Findley. Oxford University Press.

Finlay (2006): *Buried Treasure: Travels Through the Jewel Box.* Victoria Finlay. Sceptre Books, London.

Fitzsimmons (1996): "Chronological Problems at the Temple of the Dioscuri, Dil'berdžin Tepe (North Afghanistan)." Tom Fitzsimmons. *East and West* Vol. 46. Nos. 3-4 (Dec. 1996), pp. 271-298.

Fleet (1914): "The Name Kushan." J. F. Fleet. *Journal of the Royal Asiatic Society of Great Britain and Ireland,* (Apr. 1914), pp.369-381.

Fok (1999): *Connoisseurship of Rhinoceros Horn Carving in China.* Thomas Fok. Tai Yip Co., Hong Kong.

Foltz (1999): *Religions of the Silk Road : Overland Trade and Cultural Exchange from Antiquity to the Fifteenth Century.* Richard C. Foltz. St. Martin's Press. New York.

Foraboschi (2002): "VICINO ED ESTREMO ORIENTE: FORME DELLO SCAMBIO MONETALE." Daniele Foraboschi. In: *Atti della Fondazione Canusio,* pp. 137-146. Available for download at: http://www.fondazionecanussio.org/atti2002/foraboschi.pdf

Forsyth (1875): *Report of a Mission to Yarkund in 1873, with Historical and Geographical Information Regarding the Possessions of the Ameer of Yarkand.* T. D. Forsyth. The Foreign Department Press. Calcutta.

Fracasso (1988): "Holy Mothers of Ancient China: A New Approach to the Hsi-wang-mu Problem." Ricardo Fracasso. *T'oung pao* LXXXIV, (1988), pp. 1-45.

Francfort (1990): Une proto-route de la Soie a-t-elle existé aux 2e-1er millénaires? H.-P. Francfort. *NSAE,* pp. 121-129.

Francis (2002): *Asia's Maritime Bead Trade : 300 B.C. to the Present.* Peter Francis, Jr. University of Hawai'i Press.

Francke (1907): "The Identity of the Sok with the Sakas." O. Francke. *Journal of the Royal Asiatic Society of Great Britain and Ireland,* (Jul. 1907), pp. 675-677.

Frank and Thompson (2005): "Afro-Eurasian Bronze Age Economic Expansion and Contraction Revisited." Andre Gunder Frank and William R. Thompson. *JWH* 16.2 (2005). Downloaded on 2 December 2005, from: http://www.historycooperative.org/journals/jwh/16.2/frank.html.

Franke (1907): "The identity of the Sok with the Saka." Q. Franke. *Journal of the Royal Asiatic Society of Great Britain and Ireland.* (Jul. 1977), pp. 675-677.

Franke (1916/1918): "Einige Bemerkungen zu F.W.K. Müllers 'Toχrï und Kuišan (Küšän)'." Otto Franke. In: *Osteasiatische Zeitschrift,* Fünter und Sechster Jahrgang, Berlin, pp. 83-86.

Franke (1920): "Das alte Ta-hia der Chinesen. Ein Beitrag zur Tocharer-Frage." Von O. Franke. IN: Festschrift für Friedrich Hirth. Berlin, 1920, pp. 117-136.

French (1998): "Pre- and Early-Roman Roads of Asia Minor. The Persian Royal Road." David French. *Iran,* Vol. 36 (1998), pp. 15-43.

Frye (1962): "Some Early Iranian Titles." Richard N. Frye. *Oriens*, Vol. 15. Dec. 31 1962), pp. 352-359.

Frye (1963): *The Heritage of Persia*. Richard N. Frye. Reprint: Toronto. Mentor Books. 1966.

Frye (1975): *The Golden Age of Persia: The Arabs in the East*. Richard N. Frye. Weidenfeld and Nicholson, London. Paperback reprint: 1988.

Frye (1984): *The History of Ancient Iran*. Richard N. Frye. München : Beck.

Frye (1996): *The Heritage of Central Asia: From Antiquity to the Turkish Expansion*. Richard N. Frye. Marcus Weiner Publishers, Princeton.

Frye (1999): "Persia/Fars from Alexander to the Sasanians." Richard N. Frye. *The Iranian World: Art and Archaeology*. Presented to Ezat O. Negahbar. Edited by Abbas Alizadeh, Yousef Majidzadeh, Sadegh Malek, Shahmn Zadi. Tehran, 1999, pp. 194-199.

Fussman (1980) : "Nouvelles inscriptions Saka : ère d'Eucratide, ère d'Azès, ère Vikrama, ère de Kaniṣka." Gérard Fussman. *Bulletin de l'Ecole française d'Extrême-Orient*. Tome 67, 1980. pp. 1-44.

Fussman (1982): "Documents épigraphiques kouchans (III): l'inscription kharoṣṭhī de Senavarma, roi d'Oḍi : Une nouvelle lecture." Gérard Fussman. *BEFEO*, Vol. 71, pp. 1-46.

Fussman (1991): "Le *Périple* et l'histoire politique de l'Inde." Gérard Fussman. *JA* CCLXXIX (1991), pp. 31-38.

Fussman (1993): "L'indo-grec Ménandre ou Paul Demiéville revisité." *JA* 281, pp. 61-138.

Fussman (1996): "Notes sur la topographie de l'ancienne Kandahar." Gérard Fussman. In: *Arts asiatiques*. Tome 13, 1966. pp. 33-57.

Fussman (1998): "L'inscription de Rabatak et l'origine de l'ère saka." Gérard Fussman. *JA* 286.2 (1998), pp. 571-651.

Fussman (2013): "Une publication bienvenue : le premier inventaire complet et commenté des reliquaries du Gandhāra. Gérard Fussman. *Arts Asiatiques*, Tome 68 – 2013, pp. 129-134.

Gan (2009): "Origin and Evolution of Ancient Chinese Glass." Gan Fuxi. In: *AGRSR*, pp. 1-40.

Gardiner (1920): "The Ancient Military Road between Egypt and Palestine." Alan H. Gardiner. *The Journal of Egyptian Archaeology*, Vol. 6, No. 2 (April 1920), pp. 99-116.

Gardiner (1973): "Standard Histories, Han to Sui." K. H. J. Gardiner. In: *Essays on the Sources for Chinese History*. Editors: Donald Leslie, Colin Mackerras, Wang Gungwu. Australian National University Press, Canberra, pp. 42-52.

Garzetti (1976): *From Tiberius to the Antonines: A History of the Roman Empire AD 14-192*. Albino Garzetti (1st edition, 1960, *L'Impero da Tiberio agli Antonini* by Istituto di Studi Romani, Rome). English translation, including author's revisions and additions, first published in 1974. London, Methuen & Co Ltd.

Gettens, Feller and Chase (1972): "Vermilion and Cinnabar." Rutherford J. Gettens, Robert L. Feller and W. T. Chase. *Studies in Conservation*, Vol. 17, No. 2. (May, 1972), pp. 45-69.

Ghirshman (1954): *Iran: From the Earliest Times to the Islamic Conquest*. R. Grishman. French version, Paris, 1951. 1st English version, 1954. 1978 Reprint: Hammondsworth, Middlesex, Penguin Books.

Ghosh (1947-1948): "Taxila (Sirkap), 1944-45." A. Ghosh. *Ancient India: Bulletin of the Archaeological Survey of India*, Number 4, July 1947 – January 1948, pp. 41-84 + map. Published by the Director General, Archaeological Survey of India, New Delhi, 1984.

Gibbon (1867): *The History of the Decline and Fall of the Roman Empire*, Vol. IV. Edward Gibbon. Bell & Daldy, Covent Garden, London.

Gibbon (undated): *The History of the Decline and Fall of the Roman Empire*, Vol. VII. Edward Gibbon. With Notes by the Rev. H. H. Milman. Thomas Y. Cromwell & Co. New York.

Giles (1930-1932): "A Chinese Geographical Text of the Ninth Century." Lionel Giles. *Bulletin of the School of Oriental Studies London Institution*, VI, (1930-1932), pp. 825-846.

Giuliani, et al (2000): "Oxygen Isotopes and Emerald Trade Routes Since Antiquity." Gaston Giuliani, Marc Chaudisson, Henri-Jean Schubnel, Daniel-H. Piat, Claire Rollion-Bard,

Christian France-Lanord, Didier Giard, Daniel de Narvaez, Benjamin Rondeau. *Science*, January 28 2000, pp. 631-633.

Glass (2000): "A Preliminary Study of Kharoṣṭhī Paleography." Andrew Glass. A thesis. University of Washington, Seattle.

Glueck (1959): *Rivers in the Desert: A History of the Negev*. Nelson Glueck, 1959. New York. Farrar, Straus and Cudahy.

Gnoli (2002): "The "Aryan" language." Gherardo Gnoli, *JSAI* 26 (2002), pp. 84-90.

Golden (2006): "The Origins and Shaping of the Turkic Peoples." Peter B. Golden. In: *CEAW*, pp. 136-157.

Golden (2011): *Central Asia in World History*. (*The New Oxford World History*). Peter B. Golden. Oxford University Press. Also available In Kindle format.

Goldin (2002): "On the Meaning of the Name Xi wangmu, Spirit-Mother of the West." Paul R. Goldin. *JAOS*, Vol. 122, No. 1/January-March 2002, pp. 83-85.

Godolphin (1973-1974): "Herodotus: On the Scythians." Francis R. B. Godolphin. The *Metropolitan Museum of Art Bulletin*, New Series, Vol. 32, No. 5, From the *Lands of the Scythians: Ancient Treasures from the Museums of the U.S.S.R. 3000 B.C.-100 B.C.* (1973 - 1974), pp. 129-149.

Good (1995): "On the question of silk in pre-Han Eurasia." Irene Good. *Antiquity*, Vol. 69, Number 266, December 1995, pp. 959-968.

Good (2008): "When East Met West: Interpretive Problems in Assessing East-West Contact and Exchange in Antiquity." In: Vth ICAANE Congress, Madrid. Edited by Allison Betts and Fiona Kidd. *Ancient Near Eastern Monograph series*. Peeters, Louvain.

Good, et al. (2009): "New Evidence for Early Silk in the Indus Civilization." I. L. Good, J. M. Kenoyer and R. H. Meadow. Published online 21 January 2009. Later published in *Archaeometry*, Vol. 51, Issue 3, June 2009, pages: 457–466, I. L. GOOD, J. M. KENOYER and R. H. MEADOW

Good (2011): "Exploring Inner Asia's High Alpine Frontier: : High Alpine Transhumant Pastoralism, Vertical Cultivation and Environmental Archaeology." Irene Good. In: Frenez, D. and Tosi, M. (eds.), *The Lower Vakhsh-Panj Confluence and Gorno-Badakhshan Regions, Southern Tajikistan 19th European Association of South Asian Archaeologists Conference Proceedings*, Ravenna 2007, pp. 1-10."

Gopal (1961): "Textiles in Ancient India." Lallanji Gopal. *Journal of the Economic and Social History of the Orient*, 4 (1961), pp. 53-69.

Gopal (1964): "Sugar—making in Ancient India." Lallanji Gopal. *Journal of the Economic and Social History of the Orient*, 7 (1964), pp. 57-72.

Gordon (1876): *The Roof of the World: Being the Narrative of a Journey over the high plateau of Tibet to the Russian Frontier and the Oxus sources on Pamir*. T. E. Gordon. Edinburgh. Edmonston and Douglas. Reprint by Ch'eng Wen Publishing Company. Taipei. 1971.

Gourret (1997): "Taxila: the cradle of Gandharan art." Laurence Gourret. *UNESCO Courier* Oct. 1997. Downloaded on 13 September 2011 from:
http://findarticles.com/p/articles/mi_m1310/is_1997_Oct/ai_20150234/?tag=content;col1

Graf (1996): "The Roman East from the Chinese Perspective." David T. Graf. 1996. In: *Les Annales Archéologiques Arabes Syriennes. Revue d'Archéologie*, Vol. XLII, pp. 199-216. Damascus.

Graham (2001): *Chuang-Tzŭ: The Inner Chapters*. Translated by A. C. Graham. Hackett Publishing Company, Inc. Indianapolis/Cambridge. 2001 edition.

Grant (1986): *A Guide to the Ancient World*. Michael Grant. Michael Grant Publications. 1986. Reprint: New York, Barnes & Noble, 1997.

Grant (1973): *The Jews in the Roman World*. Michael Grant. Scribner. Reprint: New York, Barnes & Noble, 1995.

Gray (1878): *China: A History of the Laws and Customs of the People.* Vols. I-II. John Henry Gray. Originally published by Macmillan, London. Reprint: Dover Publications, Mineola, New York, 2002.

Gregoratti (2012): "The Parthians between Rome and China. Gan Ying's mission into the West (1st century AD)." Leonardi Gregoratti. *Akademisk Kvarter*, Volume 04, Spring 2012, pp. 109-119.

Grenard (1904): *Tibet: The Country and its Inhabitants.* Fernand Grenard. Translated by A. Teixeira de Mattos. Originally published by Hutchison and Co., London. 1904. Reprint. Cosmo Publications. Delhi. 1974.

Grenet (1995): "DRÁPSKA". Frantz Grenet. Entry in *Encyclopedia Iranica.* Downloaded on 25 April, 2008 from: *http://frantz.grenet.free.fr/index.php?coix=publications.*

Grenet (2005): "KIDARITES: a dynasty which ruled Tukharistan and later Gandhāra, probably also part of Sogdiana; the initial date is disputed (ca 390 CE for some modern authors, ca. 420-430 for others)." Franz Grenet. Downloaded from *Encyclopedia Iranica* on 15th October, 2011 from: *http://www.iranicaonline.org/articles/kidarites*

Grenet (2006): "Nouvelles données sur la localisation des cinq *yabgus* des Yuezhi: l'arrière plan politique de l'itinéraire des marchands de Maès Titianos." Frantz Grenet. *JA* 294.2 (2006): 325-341.

Grenet et al. (2007): "The Sasanian relief at Rag-i Bibi (northern Afghanistan)." In: *AACABI*, pp. 241-267.

Griffiths (2010): *The Lotus Quest: In Search of the Sacred Flower.* Mark Griffiths. St. Martin's Press.

Grousset (1970): *The Empire of the Steppes: A History of Central Asia.* René Grousset. Translated from the French by Naomi Walford. Rutgers University Press, New Brunswick, N. J., U.S.A.

Gupta and Kulashreshthạ (1994): *Kuṣāṇa Coins and History.* Parmeshwari Lal Gupta and Sarojini Kulashreshthạ. D. K. Printworld. New Delhi.

Gwin (2012): "Rhino Wars." Peter Gwin. *National Geographic Magazine.* Volume 221, No. 3, March 2012, pp. 106-127.

Haloun (1949-50): "The Liang-chou Rebellion 184-221 A.D." G. Haloun. *Asia Major* I, pp. 119-132.

Hamilton and Falconer (1903): *Strabo* 11.10.2. Translated by H. C. Hamilton and W. Falconer. Downloaded on 26 April 2013 from: http://www.perseus.tufts.edu/hopper/text?/hopper/text?doc=Strab.+11.10.2&fromdoc=Perseus%3Atext%3A1999.01.0198

Hansen (undated): "An Analysis of *Dao*." Chad Hansen. Dept. of Philosophy, University of Hong Kong. Downloaded on 31 August 2011 from: www.hku.hk/philodep/ch/Dao.html.

Hansen (2001): "What We Can Learn from One Hundred Years of Studying Niya (Summary)." Valerie Hansen. In: *Between Han and Tang: Cultural and Artistic Interaction in a Transformative Period* pp. 295-298. Edited by Wu Hung. Cultural Relics Publishing House. Beijing.

Hansen (2004): "Religious Life in a Silk Road Community: Niya During the Third and Fourth Centuries," pp. 279-315. Valerie Hansen. In: *Religion and Chinese Society: Volume I: Ancient and Medieval China.* Edited by John Lagerwey. The Chinese University Press and École française d'Extrême-Orient.

Hansman (1967): "Charax and the Karkheh." John Hansman. *Iranica antiqua*, 7 (1967), pp. 21-58.

Hansman (1968): "The Problems of Qūmis." J. Hansman. *Journal of the Royal Asiatic Society* (1968), pp. 111-139.

Hansman (undated): "**CHARACENE** and **CHARAX** (Spasinou) in pre-Islamic times." John Hansman. In: *Encyclopædia Iranica*, pp. 363-365. Downloaded on 13 February 2006 from: http://www.iranicaonline.org/articles/characene-and-charax-spasinou-in-pre-islamic-times

Hansman (1980): "The land of Meshan." John Hansman. *Iran*, Vol. 22 (1984), pp. 161-166.

Hansman (1981): "The Measure of Hecatompylos." John Hansman. *Journal of the Royal Asiatic Society* (1981), pp. 3-9.
Hansman and Stronach (1974): "Excavations at Shahr-i Qūmis, 1971." John Hansman and David Stronach. *JRAS* (1974), pp. 8-22.
Harada (1971): "East and West (II)." Yoshito Harada. *MTB*, No. 29 (1971), pp. 57-79.
Hare (1998): *The Lost Camels of Tartary: A Quest Into Forbidden China.* John Hare. Abacus, London.
Hare (2009): *Mysteries of the Gobi: Searching for Wild Camels and Lost Cities in the Heart of Asia.* John Hare. I. B. Tauris. London & New York.
Hargreaves (1910-11): "Excavations at Shāh-jī-kī Dhērī." F. Hargreaves. *Archaeological Survey of India, 1910-11*, pp. 25-32.
Harmatta (1970): *Studies in the History and Language of the Sarmatians.* J. Harmatta. Acta Universitatis de Attila József Nominatae. Acta antique et archaeologica Tomus XIII. Szeged 1970. Downloaded from: http://www.kroraina.com on 28 July 2008.
Harmatta (1994a): "Languages and scripts in Graeco-Bactria and the Saka kingdoms." J. Harmatta. *HCCA*, (1994), pp. 397-416.
Harmatta (1994b): "Languages and literature in the Kushan Empire." J. Harmatta. *HCCA*, (1994), pp. 417-440.
Harmatta (1994c): "Conclusion." J. Harmatta. *HCCA*, (1994), pp. 485-492.
Harmatta, et al (1994): "Religions in the Kushan Empire." J. Harmatta, with contributions of B. N. Puri, L. Lelekov, S. Humayun and D. C. Sircar. *HCCA*, (1994), pp. 313-329.
Harrell (2004): "Archaeological Geology of the World's First Emerald Mine." *Geoscience Canada*, Volume 31, Number 2.
Hauser (2001): Review by Stefan R. Hauser of Monika Schuol, *Die Charakene: Ein mesopotamisches Königreich in hellenistisch-parthischer Zeit (Oriens et Occidens, Band 1).* Stuttgart: Franz Steiner Verlag, 2000. Pp. 554. In: *Bryn Mawr Classical Review* 2001.12.20. Downloaded on 12 May, 2007 from: http://ccat.sas.upenn.edu/bmcr/2001/2001-12-20.html.
Haye & Crone (1933): "Demarcation of the Indo-Afghan Boundary in the Vicinity of Arandu." W. R. Hay and D. R. Crone. *TGJ*, Vol. 82, No. 4 (Oct. 1933), pp. 351-354.
Heather (2005): *The Fall of the Roman Empire: A New History of Rome and the Barbarians.* Peter Heather. Oxford University Press. Kindle Edition.
Hedin (1903): "Three years' exploration in Central Asia, 1899-1902." Sven Hedin. *TGJ*, Vol. XXI, No. 3, pp. 221-257, plus map on p. 318.
Hedin (1925): *My Life as an Explorer.* Sven Hedin. First published Boni & Liveright, New York. Republished: National Geographic Adventure Classics. Washington, D.C. 2003.
Hedin (1936): *The Trail of War: On the Track of 'Big Horse' in Central Asia.* Sven Hedin. Macmillan and Co., 1936; The Sven Hedin Foundation, Stockholm, 2009.
Hedin (1938): *The Silk Road: Ten Thousand Miles Through Central Asia.* Sven Hedin. Macmillan and Co., 1938; Reprint: 2009, with Foreword by John Hare. Tauris Parke Paperbacks.
Hedin (1938b): *The Wandering Lake: Into the Heart of Asia.* Sven Hedin. First published in English in 1940, George Routledge & Sons. Reprint: 2009, with Foreword by John Hare. Tauris Parke Paperbacks.
Helms (1983): "Kandahar of the Arab Conquest." S. W. Helms. *World Archaeology*, Vol. 14, No. 3, Islamic Archaeology. (Feb. 1983), pp. 342-354.
Helms, et al (2001): "Five seasons of excavations in the Tash-K'irman oasis of ancient Chorasmia, 1996-2000. An interim report." S. W. Helms, V. N. Yagodin, A.V. G. Betts, G. Khozhaniyazov and F. Kidd. *Iran: Journal of the British Institute of Persian Studies*, Volume XXXIX, 2001, pp. 119-144.
Henning (1956): "Notes and Communications. 'Surkh Kotal'." W. B. Henning. *Bulletin of the School of Oriental and African Studies, University of London*, Vol. 18, No. 2 (1956), pp. 366-367.

Henning (1960): "The Bactrian Inscription." W. B. Henning. *Bulletin of the School of Oriental and African Studies, University of London,* Vol. 23, No. 1. (1960), pp. 47-55.

Herrmann (1941): "Ta-ch'in 大秦 Oder das China des Fernen Westens." Albert Herrmann. *Monumenta Serica*, Vol. 6, No. 1/2 (1941), pp. 212-272.

Hiebert (2008): "The Lost Worlds of Afghanistan." Fredrik Hiebert. In: *AHTNMK*, pp. 55-64.

Hildinger (1997): *Warriors of the Steppe: A Military History of Central Asia 500 B.C. to 1700 A.D.* Erik Hildinger. First Da Capo Press edition, Cambridge, MA, 2001.

Hill (1988): "Notes on the Dating of Khotanese History." John E. Hill. *Indo-Iranian Journal* 31 (1988), pp. 179-190.

Hill (2004): *The Peoples of the West* from the *Weilüe* 魏略 by Yu Huan 魚豢: A Third Century Chinese Account Composed between 239 and 265 CE. Quoted in *zhuan* 30 of the *Sanguozhi*. Published in 429 CE. Draft English translation by John E. Hill available online at: http://depts.washington.edu/silkroad/texts/weilue/weilue.html

Hill (2009): *Through the Jade Gate to Rome : A Study of the Silk Routes During the Han Dynasty 1st to 2nd Centuries CE.* John E. Hill. BookSurge. Charleston, South Carolina.

Hirth (1875): *China and the Roman Orient.* Friedrich Hirth. Shanghai and Hong Kong. Unchanged reprint: Chicago, Ares Publishers, 1975.

Hirth (1889): "Contributions to the History of Ancient Oriental Trade." A Lecture delivered before the Geographical Society at Berlin on 8th December 1888. Friedrich Hirth. *The China Review.* Vol. 18 No. 1 (1889) July, pp. 41-54.

Hirth (1909): "Mr. Kingsmill and the Hiung-nu." Friedrich Hirth, *JAOS*, Vol. 30, No. 1. (Dec. 1909), pp. 32-45.

Hirth and Rockhill (1911): ***Chau ju-kua**: His work on the Chinese and Arab Trade in the twelfth and thirteenth Centuries, entitled **Chu-fan-chï**.* Translated from the Chinese and annotated by Friedrich Hirth and W. W. Rockhill, St. Petersburg. Reprint: Literature House, Ltd., Taiwan. 1965.

Hitch (1988): "Kushan Tarim Domination." Doug Hitch. *Central Asiatic Journal* 32, No. 3-4, pp. 170-193. Downloaded from: http://www.ynlc.ca/ynlc/staff/hitch/hitchindex.html on 4 September 2011.

Hitch (2009): "The Special Status of Turfan." Doug Hitch. 7 January 2009. Unpublished but may appear in the proceedings of the May 2008 Central and Inner Asian Studies Conference at the University of Toronto. Personal communication, 22 January 2009.

Ho (1985): *Li, Qi and Shu: An Introduction to Science and Civilization in China.* Ho Peng Yoke. Hong Kong: Hong Kong University Press. Reprint: Dover Publications, New York. 2000.

Hoernle (1916): *Manuscript Remains of Buddhist Literature Found in Eastern Turkestan: Facsimiles with Transcripts Translations and Notes Edited in Conjunctions with other Scholars* by A. F. Rudolf Hoernle. First Edition, Oxford 1916. Second Edition, Sri Satguru Publications, New Delhi.

Høisæter (2013): *Beyond the White Dragon Mounds: the polities of the Tarim Basin in the first three centuries CE, their rise and importance for trade on the Silk Road.* Tomas Larsen Høisæter. A master thesis in History. University of Bergen, Norway.

Holcombe. (1994): *In the Shadow of the Han: Literati Thought and Society at the Beginning of the Southern Dynasties.* Charles Holcombe. University of Hawaii Press, Honolulu.

Holdich (1901): "The Geography of the North-West Frontier of India." Thomas Holdich. *TGJ*, No. 5, May 1901, Vol. XVII.

Holdich (1910): *The Gates of India.* Thomas Holdich. Macmillan and Company, Limited, London.

Holmgren (1982): *Annals of Tai. Early T'o-pa history according to the first chapter of the Wei-shu.* Jennifer Holmgren. 1982. Canberra, Australian National University Press.

Holt (1988): *Alexander the Great and Bactria: The Formation of a Greek Frontier in Central Asia*. Brill. Leiden.

Holt (1999): *Thundering Zeus: The Making of Hellenistic Bactria*. Frank Lee Holt. University of California Press, Berkeley, Los Angeles and London.

Holt (2005): *Into the Land of Bones: Alexander the Great in Afghanistan*. Frank L. Holt. University of California Press. Berkeley, Los Angeles, London.

Holt (2012): *Lost World of the Golden King: In Search of Ancient Afghanistan*. Frank L. Holt. University of California Press.

Honey (1937): "Early Chinese Glass." W. B. Honey. *The Burlington Magazine for Connoisseurs*, Vol. 71, No. 416 (Nov. 1937), pp. 211-213+216-219+221-223.

Honey (1999): "The Han-shu, Manuscript Evidence, and the Textual Criticism of the Shih-chi: The case of the "Hsiung-nu lieh-chuan"." David B. Honey. *Chinese Literature: Essays, Articles, Reviews (CLEAR)*, Vol. 21. (December 1999), pp. 67-97.

Honeychurch and Amartuvshin (2007): "Hinterlands, urban centers, and mobile settings: the "new" Old World archaeology from the Eurasian steppe." William Honeychurch and Chunag Amartuvshin. *Asian Perspectives: the Journal of Archaeology for Asia and the Pacific* 46.1 (Spring 2007), pp. 36.

Hooker (1854): *Himalayan Journals or Notes of a Naturalist*. Joseph Dalton Hooker. John Murray, London. Project Gutenberg Ebook edition. 2004.

Hoppál (2011): "The Roman Empire according to the Ancient Chinese Sources." Krisztina Hoppál. *Acta antiqua Academiae Scientiarum Hungaricae* (2011), 51, pp. 263-305.

Howland (1940): "Crossing the Hindu Kush." Felix Howland. *Geographical Review*, Vol. 30, No. 2 (Apr. 1940), pp. 272-278.

Huc (*circa* 1915): *The Land of the Lamas* by Abbé Huc. The Romance of Travel Series. Taken from: *Travels in Tartary, Thibet and China, 1844-1846*. MM. Huc and Gabed, translated by William Hazlitt.

Hulsewé (1961): "Han measures." A. F. P. Hulsewé. *T'oung pao Archives*, Vol. XLIX, Livre 3, 1961, pp. 206-207.

Hulsewé (1975): "The problem of the authenticity of "Shih-chi" ch. 123, the Memoir on Ta Yüan", A. F. P. Hulsewé. *T'oung pao, 61* (1975), pp. 83-147.

Humbach (1966): *Baktrishe Sprachdenkmäler*. Helmut Humbach. Wiesenbaden.

Hummel (2000): *On Zhang-zhung*. Siegbert Hummel. Edited and translated by Guido Vogliotti. Library of Tibetan Works and Archives.

Huntingford (1980): *The Periplus of the Erythraean Sea*. G. W. B. Huntingford. The Hakluyt Society, 2nd series 151. London.

Huntington (1905): "The Basin of Eastern Persia and Sistan." Ellsworth Huntington. In: *EIT*, pp. 219-305.

Huntington (1907a): "Lop-Nor. A Chinese Lake. Part I. The Unexplored Salt Desert of Lop." Ellsworth Huntington. *Bulletin of the American Geographical Society*, Vol. 39, No. 2 (1907), pp. 65-77.

Huntington (1907b): "A Chinese Lake. Part II. The Historic Lake (Lop-Nor)." Ellsworth Huntington. *Bulletin of the American Geographical Society*, Vol. 39, No. 3 (1907), pp. 137-146.

Hutton (1924): "The occurrence of the Blow-Gun in Assam." J. H. Hutton. *Man*, Vol. 24 (Jul. 1924), pp. 104-106.

Hyde (1984): "The Queen of Textiles." Nina Hyde. *National Geographic*. Vol. 165, No. 1, January 1984, pp. 2-49.

Invernizzi (2007): "The Culture of Parthian Nisa between Steppe and Empire." Antonio Invernizzi. In: *AACABI*, pp. 163-177.

Jackobsson (2009): "Who Founded The Indo-Greek Era of 186/5 B.C.E.?" Jens Jakobsson. *Classical Quarterly* 59.2 (2009).

Jacquesson (2004): "Les langues indo-iraniennes des Pamirs et de l'Hindou Kouch." François Jacquesson. Cahiers d'Asie central. Numéro 11/12 (2004), pp. 15-60. Downloaded from: http://asiecentrale.revues.org/index687.html on 11 September 2011

Jacquet (1832): "Origine d'un des noms sous lequels l'Empire romain a été connu à la Chine." E. Jacquet. *JA* (1832) t. IX, pp. 456-464.

Jain (1964): *The Jaina Sources of the History of Ancient India (100 B.C. - A.D. 900)*. Jyoti Prasad Jain. Munshi Ram Manohar Lal, Delhi.

Jairazbhoy (1963): *Foreign Influence in Ancient India*. R. A. Jairazbhoy. Asia Publishing House, Bombay. 1963.

James (1995): "An Iconographic Study of Xiwangmu during the Han dynasty." Jean M. James. *Artibus Asiae*, Vol. 55, No. 1/2. (1995), pp. 17-41.

Jettmar (1987): "The "Suspended Crossing" — Where and Why?" Karl Jettmar. In: *India and the Ancient World: History Trade and Culture before A.D. 650*. Festschrift Eggermont. Ed. Gilbert Pollet. (Orientalia Lovaniensia Analecta, 25; Leuvin: Department Oriëntalistik), pp. 95-102.

Jettmar, et al. (1985): *Zwischen Gandhara und den Seidenstrassen: Felsbilder am Karakorum Highway: Entdeckungen deutsch-pakistanischer Expeditionen 1979-1984*. Karl Jettmar, A. H. Dani and Volker Thewalt. 1985. Mainz am Rhein, Philipp von Zabern.

Jettmar and Kattner (2002): *Beyond the Gorges of the Indus: Archaeology before Excavations*. Karl Jettmar and Ellen Kattner. Oxford University Press. ISBN 0-19-577979-7.

Jila (2006): "Myths and Traditional Beliefs about the Wolf and the Crow in Central Asia: Examples from the Turkic Wu-Sun and the Mongols." Namu Jila. *Asian Folklore Studies*, Volume 65, 2006: 161-177.

Jones (2001): "Apollonius of Tyana's Passage to India." Christopher P. Jones. *Greek, Roman, and Byzantine Studies* 42 (2001), pp. 185-189.

Jones (1924): *The Geography of Strabo*. Ed. H. L. Jones. Cambridge, Mass.: Harvard University Press; London: William Heinemann. 1924. Downloaded on 18 February 2012 from: http://www.perseus.tufts.edu/.

Josephus (75-79 CE): *History of the Jewish War*. Flavius Josephus. Translated by William Whiston, revised by D. S. Margoliouth in: *The Great Roman-Jewish War: A.D. 66-70*. First Harper Torchbook Edition. 1960.

Josephus (93 CE): *The Antiquities of the Jews*. Flavius Josephus. Trans. by William Whiston. Downloaded from: http://www.ccel.org/j/josephus/works/ant-20.htm on 29 July 2002.

Juliano and Lerner (2002): *Monks and Merchants: Silk Road Treasures from Northwest China*. Annette L. Juliano and Judith A. Lerner with essays by: Michael Alram, Chen Bingying, Albert E. Dien, Luo Feng, Boris I. Marshak. The Asia Society, N.Y.

Julien (1846): "Sur les pays et les peoples etrangers, tirées des géographes et des historiens chinois." Stanislas Julien. *JA* (1846), t. VIII, pp. 228-252; 385-445.

Julien (1847): "Sur les pays et les peoples étrangers, tirées des géographes et des historiens chinois: Les Oïgours." Stanislas Julien. *JA* (1846), t. IX, pp. 50-66.

Kakoulli (2007): "Intercultural links and trade of painting materials in the Greco-Roman Period." Ioanna Kakoulli. In: *Mural Paintings of the Silk Road: Cultural Exchanges Between East and West*, pp. 81-88. Eds. Kazuya Yamauchi, Yoko Taniguchi and Tomoko Uno. Archetype Publications. Tokyo.

Karlgren (1923): *Sound and Symbol in Chinese*. Bernhard Karlgren. 1923. Revised edition: 1940. Reprint: Oxford University Press. Hong Kong. 1971.

Keall (1975): "Parthian Nippur and Vologases' Southern Strategy: A Hypothesis." E. J. Keall. *JOAS*, Vol. 95, No. 4. (Oct. - Dec. 1975), pp. 620-632.

Kearney (2004). *The Indian Ocean in World History (Themes in World History)*. Milo Kearney. Taylor and Francis, and Kindle Edition.

Keay (1977): *When Men and Mountains Meet.* John Keay. 1977. Reprint: Karachi. Oxford University Press. 1993.

Keay (2005): *The Spice Route: A History.* John Keay. John Murray (Publishers), London.

Keay (2008): *China: A History.* John Keay. Harper Press, Great Britain.

Kessler (1993): *Empires Beyond the Great Wall: The Heritage of Genghis Khan.* Adam T. Kessler. Natural History Museum of Los Angeles County.

Keyser-Tracqui, et al. (2003): "Nuclear and mitochondrial DNA analysis of a 2,000-year-old necropolis in the Egyin Gol valley of Mongolia." *Christine Keyser-Tracqui; Eric Crubezy; Bertrand Ludes. American Journal of Human Genetics*, August 2003 v73 i2 pp. 247-260.

Keown (2003): *A Dictionary of Buddhism.* Damien Keown. Oxford University Press, Oxford.

Khan (undated): *Buddhist Art and Architecture in Pakistan.* Ahmad Nabi Khan. Ministry of Information and Broadcasting, Directorate of Research, Reference and Publications, Government of Pakistan, Islamabad.

Kim et al (2010): "A Western Eurasian Male Is Found in 2000-year-Old Elite Xiongnu Cemetery in Northeastern Mongolia." Kijeong Kim, et al. *American Journal of Physical Anthropology* 142:429-440 (2010).

King (1989): *Karakoram Highway : the high road to China.* John King. Hawthorn, Victoria, Lonely Planet Publications.

King, et al. (1996): *Central Asia.* John King, John Noble and Andrew Humphries. Hawthorn, Victoria. Lonely Planet Publications.

Kingsmill (1882): "The Intercourse of China with Eastern Turkestan and the Adjacent Countries in the Second Century B.C." Thomas W. Kingsmill. *Journal of the Royal Asiatic Society of Great Britain and Ireland.* New Series. Volume 14, pp. 74-104.

Klaproth (1823): "Sur les Boukhares." Julius von Klaproth. *JA* (1823) t. II, pp. 154-163.

Klaproth (1823b): *Critique littéraire*: HISTOIRE DE LA VILLE DE KHOTAN, *tirée des annals de la Chine et traduite du chinois, suivie de recherches sur la substance minéral, appelée par les Chinois* pierre de Iu, *et sur le* jaspe *des anciens* ; par M. ABEL-RÉMUSAT. — Paris, in-8°, xvi et 240 pages (1). J. von Klaproth, *JA* (1823), bk. III, pp. 293-309.

Klaproth (1826): *Tableaux historiques de l'Asie, depuis la monarchie de Cyrus jusqu'a nos jours.*" Julius von Klaproth. Lachevardiere fils, Paris.

Klimkeit (1993): *Gnosis on the Silk Road: Gnostic Texts from Central Asia.* Translated & Presented by Hans-Joachim Klimheit. Harper, San Francisco.

Knauer (2006): "The Queen Mother of the West: A Study of the Influence of Western Protoypes on the Iconogaphy of the Taoist Deity." Elfried Regina Knauer. In: *CEAW*, pp. 62-115.

Knight (1893): *Where Three Empires Meet.* E. F. Knight. 1893. London, Longmans, Green, and Co. 3rd Edition. Reprint: Taipei, Ch'eng Wen Publishing Company, 1971.

Konow (1929): *Kharoshsthī Inscriptions: with the exception of those of Aśoka.* Corpvs Inscriptionvm Indicarvum Vol. II, Part I. Edited by Sten Konow. First published in Calcutta, 1929. Reprint: Indological Book House, Varanasi. 1969.

Konow (1934): "Notes on Indo-Scythian Chronology." Sten Konow. *Journal of Indian History.* Vol. XII 1933, Parts I to III, pp. 1-146. Published: Madras, 1934.

Koshelenko and Pilipko (1994): "Parthia." G. A. Koshelenko and V. N. Pilipko. In: *HCCA*, Vol. II, pp. 131-150.

Kramers (1986): "The development of the Confucian schools." Robert P. Kramers. 1986. *CHC*, pp. 747-765.

Kremmer (2002): *The Carpet Wars.* Christopher Kremmer. Flamingo – an imprint of HarperCollins *Publishers.* Australia. 2002.

Krist (1939): *Alone through the Forbidden Land: Journeys in Disguise through Soviet Central Asia.* Gustav Krist. Translated by E. O. Lorimer. Readers' Union Limited, Great Britain.

Kroll (2015): *A Student's Dictionary of Classical and Medieval Chinese.* (2015). Paul W. Kroll. Brill. Leiden/ Boston.

Kuhn (1995): "Silk Weaving in Ancient China: From Geometric Figures to Patterns of Pictorial Likeness." Dieter Kuhn. *Science* 12 (1995), pp. 77-114.

Kunz (2003): *Curious Lore of Precious Stones.* (1912). George Frederick Kunz. Reprint: Kessinger Publishing LLC.

Kurbanov (2010): "The Hephthalites: Archaeological and Historical Analysis." Aydogdy Kurbanov. PhD thesis submitted to the Department of History and Cultural Studies of the Free University, Berlin, 2010.

Kuzmina (1998): "Cultural Connections of the Tarim Basin People and Pastoralists of the Asian Steppes in the Bronze Age." Elena E. Kuzmina. In: In: *The Bronze Age and Early Iron Age Peoples of Eastern Central Asia,* Vol. One, pp. 63-93. Edited by Victor H. Mair. Institute for the Study of Man, with The University of Pennsylvania Museum Publications.

Kuzmina (2008): *The Prehistory of the Silk Road.* E. E. Kuzmina. Edited by Victor H. Mair. University of Pennsylvania Press, Philadelphia.

Kyzlasov (1996): "Northern Nomads." L. R. Kyzlasov. In: *HCCA,* Vol. III, pp. 315-325.

Lacouperie (1891): "On the ancient history of Glass and Coal and the Legend of Nü-kwa's coloured stones in China." T. De Lacouperie, *T'oung pao* 2 (1891), pp. 234-243.

Lahiri (1992): *The Archaeology of Indian Trade Routes up to c. 200 BC: Resource Use, Resource Access and Lines of Communication.* Nayanjot Lahiri. Oxford University Press, 1992. First Indian Reprint, Oxford Indian Paperbacks, 1999.

Laing (1995): "Recent finds of western-related glassware, textiles and metalwork in Central Asia and China." Ellen Johnston Laing. *BAI,* Vol. 9. 1995, pages 1-9.

Lal (1949): "**Śiśupālgarh 1948:** An Early Historical Fort in Eastern India." B. B. Lal. *Ancient India: Bulletin of the Archaeological Survey of India,* Number 5 (1949). Republished by: The Director General, Archaeological Survey of India, New Delhi, 1984, pp. 62-105.

Landström (1966): *The Quest for India: A History of Discovery and Exploration from the Expedition to the Land of Punt in 1493 B.C. to the Discovery of the Cape of Good Hope in 1488 A.D. in Words and Pictures.* Björn Landström. Stockholm, Doubleday.

Lang (1980): *Armenia. Cradle of Civilisation.* David Marshall Lang. 1st Edition, London, George Allen & Unwin, 1970. 3rd Edition (Corrected). London, George Allen & Unwin.

Lariche and Pidaev (2007): "Termez in Antiquity." Pierre Leriche & Shakir Pidaev. In: *AACABI,* pp. 179-211.

Latham (1982): *The Travels of Marco Polo.* Translated and introduced by Ronald Latham. First published 1958 by Penguin. Reprint: Abaris Books. New York. 1982. Based on Folio Society Edition.

Lattimore (1929): *The Desert Road to Turkestan.* Owen Lattimore. Boston, Little, Brown, and Company. Reprinted with new introduction, 1972, New York, N.Y., AMS Press.

Lattimore (1930): *High Tartary.* Owen Lattimore. Boston, Little, Brown, and Company. 1930. Reprint: Kodansha International, New York. 1994.

Lau and Ames (1998): *Yuan Dao:* Tracing *Dao* to its Source. Translated by D. C. Lau and Roger T. Ames. Introduction by Roger T. Ames. Ballantine Books, New York.

Laufer (1912): *Jade: A Study in Chinese Archaeology & Religion.* Berthold Laufer. 1912. Field Museum of Natural History. Chicago, Publication 154 (Anthropological Series, Vol. X), Paperback edition: New York. Dover Publications. 1974.

Laufer (1914): *Chinese Clay Figures, Part 1, Prolegomena on the History of Defensive Armor.* Berthold Laufer. Chicago, Field Museum of Natural History.

Laufer (1915): "Asbestos and Salamander, an Essay in Chinese and Hellenistic Folk-lore." Berthold Laufer. *T'oung pao,* Vol. 16 (1915), pp. 299-373.

Laufer (1917): *The Language of the Yüe-chi or Indo-Scythians.* Berthold Laufer. Chicago. R.R. Donnelley & Sons Company, pp. 3-14. Reprinted in: *Kleinere Schriften von Bethold Laufer.*

Teil 2: Publikationen aus der Zeit von 1911 bis 1925. Hartmut Walravens (ed.). Franz Steiner Verlag, Wiesbaden. 1979, pp. 1107-1118.

Laufer (1919): *Sino-Iranica: Chinese Contributions to the History of Civilization in Ancient Iran With Special Reference to the History of Cultivated Plants and Products.* Berthold Laufer. Chicago. *Field Museum of Natural History Publication 201.* Anthropological Series. Vol. XV, No. 3.

Laufer (1923): "Use of Human Skulls and Bones in Tibet." Berthold Laufer. Chicago. *Field Museum of Natural History Leaflet No. 10,* 24 pp.

Laufer (1925): "Ivory in China." Berthold Laufer. Chicago. *Field Museum of Natural History Leaflet No. 21,* pp. 1-78.

Law (1932): *Geography of Early Buddhism,* 2nd edition. Bimala Churn Law. 1932. New Delhi. Oriental Books Reprint Corporation. 1979.

Leake (1839): "On the Stade, as a Linear Measure." W. Martin Leake. *Journal of the Royal Geographical Society of London,* Vol. 9 (1939), pp. 1-25.

Lebedynsky (2006): *Les Saces: Les « Scythes » d'Asie. VIIIe siècle av. J.-C.-IVe siècle apr. J.-C.* Iaroslav Lebedynsky. Editions Errance, Paris.

Legg (1970): *The Barbarians of Asia.* Stuart Legg. Originally published as *The* Heartland. 1990 edition by Dorset Press, New York.

Legge (1886): *A Record of Buddhistic Kingdoms: Being an account by the Chinese Monk Fa-Hien of his travels in India and Ceylon (A.D. 399-414) in search of the Buddhist Books of Discipline.* James Legge. 1886. Oxford, Clarendon Press. Reprint: New York, Paragon Book Reprint Corp., 1965.

Leitner (1893): *Dardistan in 1866, 1886 and 1893: Being An Account of the History, Religions, Customs, Legends, Fables and Songs of Gilgit, Chilas, Kandia (Gabrial) Yasin, Chitral, Hunza, Nagyr and other parts of the Hindukush, as also a supplement to the second edition of The Hunza and Nagyr Handbook. And An Epitome of Part III of the author's "The Languages and Races of Dardistan."* G. W. Leitner. First Reprint: 1978. Manjusri Publishing House, New Delhi.

Le May (1943): "The Bimaran Casket." Reginald Le May. *The Burlington Magazine for Connoisseurs,* Vol. 82, No. 482. (May 1943), pp. 116-120+123.

Lendering (undated): "Ancient Persia." Chapter on Drangiana. Jona Lendering. Downloaded from: http://www.livius.org/do-dz/drangiana/drangiana.html on 11 June 2007.

Lendering (undated b): "Babylonian Chronicles: Dictionary." Jona Lendering. Downloaded from: http://www.livius.org/cg-cm/chronicles/reading2.html on 12 June 2007.

Lendering (2014): "Royal Road." Jona Lendering. Iran Chamber Society. Downloaded on 4 April 2014 from: http://www.iranchamber.com/history/achaemenids/royal_road.php

Leriche (undated): "**Bactria**: i. Pre-islamic period." F. Leriche. In: *Encyclopaedia Iranica,* pp. 339-343. Downloaded from: http://www.iranica.com/articlenavigation/index.html on 13 February 2006.

Leriche (1993): "L'Extrême-Orient hellénistique : Le monde de la brique crue." Pierre Leriche. *Les dossiers d'archeologie,* No. 179, Feb. 1993, pp. 75-83.

Leriche (2007): "Bactria: Land of a Thousand Cities." Pierre Leriche. In: *AACABI,* pp. 121-153.

Leriche and Pidaev (2007): "Termez in Antiquity." Pierre Leriche and Shakir Pidaev. In: *AACABI,* pp. 179-211.

Lerner (1998): "Ptolemy and the Silk Road: from Baktra Basileion to Sera Metropolis." Jeffrey D. Lerner. *East and West* 48, Nos. 1-2 (June 1998), pp. 9-25.

Lerner (1999): "The Impact of Seleucid Decline on the Eastern Iranian Plateau: The Foundations of Arsacid Parthia and Graeco-Bactria." Jeffrey D. Lerner. *Historia* 123, pp. 1-139.

Lerner (2010): "Revising the Chronologies of the Hellenistic Colonies of Samarkand-Marakanda (Afrasiab II-III) and Aï Khanoum (Northeastern Afghanistan). Jeffrey D. Lerner. *Anabasis* 1 (2010), pp. 58-79.

Lerner (2011): "A Reappraisal of the Economic Inscriptions and Coin finds from Aï Khanoum." Jeffrey D. Lerner. *Anabasis* 2 (2011), pp. 103-147.

Leslie and Gardiner (1996): *The Roman Empire in Chinese Sources.* D. D. Leslie and K. H. J. Gardiner. 1996. Università di Roma, Pubblicati dal Dipartimento di Studi Orientali, Volume XV.

Le Strange (1905): *The Lands of the Eastern Caliphate: Mesopotamia, Persia, and Central Asia from the Moslem Conquest to the Time of Timur.* Guy Le Strange. Oxford 1905. Reprint: Adamant Media Corporation, 2005.

Levey (1966): "Medieval Arabic Toxicology: The Book on Poisons of ibn Wahshīya and Its Relation to Early Indian and Greek Texts." Martin Levey. Transactions of the American Philosophical Society, New Series, Vol. 56, No. 7 (1966), pp. 1-130.

Levi (1972): *The Light Garden of the Angel King: Journeys in Afghanistan.* Peter Levi. The Bobbs-Merrill Company, Indianapolis/New York.

Lévi and Chavannes (1895): "L'itinéraire d'Ou-K'ong (751-790)." M. Sylvain Lévi and Édouard Chavannes. *JA*, (1895) Sept.-Oct., pp. 341-384.

Lévi (1896): "Note rectificative sur le *Ki-pin.*" M. Sylvain Lévi. *JA* (1896) Janv.-juin (Sér. 9), pp. 161-162.

Lévi (1913): "Le 'tokharien B,' langue de Koutcha." Sylvain Lévi. *JA*, (1913) 11th Ser., Sept.-Oct., 1913, pp. 311-380.

Lévi (1933): "Le "tokharien"," Sylvain Lévi. *JA*, (1933). Vol. 222 (Janv.-mar. 1933), pp. 1-30.

Lévi (1934): "Devaputra." Sylvain Lévi. *JA*, (1934). Vol. 224 (Janv.-mar. 1934), pp. 1-21.

Lévi (1936): "Kaniṣka et Śātavāhana, deux figures symboliques de l'inde au premier siècle." Sylvain Lévi. *JA*, (1936). Vol. 228 (Janv.-déc. 1936), pp. 62-121.

Lewis (1983): *Life in Egypt under Roman Rule.* Naphtali Lewis. First published 1983. Paperback reprint 1985. Clarendon Press. Oxford.

Lewis (2000): "The Han Abolition of Universal Military Service." Mark E. Lewis. In: *Warfare in Chinese History*, edited by Hans van de Ven, Brill Academic Publishers, Leiden, pp. 33-75.

Lewis (2007): *The Early Chinese Empires: Qin and Han.* Mark Edward Lewis. The Belknap Press of Harvard University Press. Kindle Edition.

Li (1995): *A Biography of the Tripiṭaka Master of the Great Ci'en Monastery of the Great Tang Dynasty.* Translated by Li Rongxi. Numata Center for Buddhist Translation and Research. Berkeley, California.

Li (1996): *The Great Tang Dynasty Record of the Western Regions.* Translated by Li Rongxi. Numata Center for Buddhist Translation and Research. Berkeley, California.

Li (2004): *China's Cultural Relics.* Li Li, translated by Li Zhurun. China Intercontinental Press.

Li (2005): "Jibin, Jibin Route and China." Li Chongfeng. Xi'an, World Publishing Corporation, 2005. Pp. 985-990. In: Proceedings of the ICOMOS 15th General Assembly and Scientific Symposium. Vol. 2. Downloaded 11 November 2008 from: http://www.international.icomos.org/xian2005/papers/4-26.pdf

Li et al (2008): "Evidence that a West-East admixed population lived in the Tarim Basin as early as the early Bronze Age." Chunxiang Li, et al. *BMC Biology* 2010, 8:15. Downloaded 6 March 2011 from: http://www.biomedcentral.com/1741-7007/8/15

Lieberman (1957): "Who Were Pliny's Blue-Eyed Chinese?" Samuel Lieberman. *Classical Philology*, Vol. 52, No. 3 (July 1957), pp. 174-177.

Lieu (2011): "Places and Peoples in Central Asia and in the Graeco-Roman Near East: A Multilingual Gazetteer Compiled for the Serica Project." Samuel N.C. Lieu. Ancient Cultures Research Centre, Macquarie University, Sydney, N.S.W., Australia. Downloaded on 5 November 2011 from: www.acrc.mq.edu.au/serica/Gazetteer.pdf

Lin (1972): "Lin Yutang's Chinese-English Dictionary of Modern Usage." Lin Yutang. The Chinese University Press, Hong Kong. Second printing 1980.

Littledale (1892): "A Journey across the Pamir from North to South." *Proceedings of the Royal Geographical Society and Monthly Record of Geography*, New Monthly Series, Vol. 14, No. 1 (Jan. 1892), pp. 1-35.

Litvinsky (1996): "The Hephthalite Empire." B. A. Litvinsky. In: *HCCA*, Vol. III, pp. 135-162.

Litvinskij (2002): "Copper Cauldrons from Gilgit and Central Asia. More about Saka and Dards and Related Problems." Boris A. Litvinskij. *East and West*, Vol. 52 (2002), pp. 127-149.

Liu (1988): *Ancient India and Ancient China: Trade and Religious Exchanges AD 1-600*. Xinru Liu. 1988. Reprint: New Delhi, Oxford India Paperbacks. 1994.

Liu (1996): *Silk and Religion: An Exploration of Material Life and the Thought of People, AD 600-1200*. Xinru Liu. Oxford University Press. 1996.

Liu (2000): "Eastern Central Asia." Liu Yingsheng. In: *HCCA*, Vol. IV, pp. 574-584.

Liu (2001): "Migration and Settlement of the Yuezhi-Kushan: Interaction and Interdependence of Nomadic and Sedentary Societies." Xinru Liu. *Journal of World History*, Volume 12, No. 2, Fall 2001. University of Hawaii Press, pp. 261-292. Available at: http://muse.jhu.edu/journals/journal_of_world_history/toc/jwh12.2.html.

Liu and Shaffer (2007): *Connections Across Eurasia: Transportation, Communication, and Cultural Exchange on the Silk Roads*. Xinru Liu and Lynda Norene Shaffer. McGraw Hill, New York.

Livy (1905): *History of Rome*. Titus Livius. Chap. 23.24. Translated by Rev. Canon Roberts. J. M. Dent & Sons, Ltd., London, 1905. Downloaded on 15 November 2008 from: http://mcadams.posc.mu.edu/txt/ah/Livy/Livy23.html

Loehr (1980): *The Great Painters of China*. Max Loehr. Phaidon Press Limited, Oxford.

Loeschner (2008). "Notes on the Yuezhi – Kushan Relationship and Kushan Chronology." Hans Loeschner. 28 pp. Downloaded on 24 April 2008, from: http://www.osnumis.org.

Loeschner (2013): "Kanishka in Context with the Historical Buddha and Kushan Chronology." Hans Loeschner. Draft 2009-06-28_update-2010-06-28 (final inputs) edited w.r.t. typing errors 2013-12-26. 66 pages.

Loewe (1960): "The Orders of Aristocratic Rank of Han China." Michael Loewe. *TP* 48, pt. 1, 1960, pp. 97-174.

Loewe (1967): *Records of Han Administration*, Vol. 1. Michael Loewe. Cambridge University Press.

Loewe (1982): *Faith, Myth and Reason in Han China*. Michael Loewe. Hackett Publishing Company, Indianapolis. Reprint: 2005.

Loewe (1986): "The Former Han dynasty." Michael Loewe. In: *CHC* Vol. I, pp. 103-222.

Loewe (1994): "China's sense of unity as seen in the early empires." Michael Loewe. *T'oung pao* LXXX (1994), pp. 6-26.

Loewe (2006): *The Government of the Qin and Han Empires: 221 BCE - 220 CE*. Michael Loewe. Hackett Publishing Company, Inc. Indianapolis/Cambridge.

Lohuizen-De Leeuw (1949): *The "Scythian" period: an approach to the history, art, epigraphy and palaeography of north India from the 1st century B.C. to the 3rd century. A.D.* J. E. van Lohuizen-De Leeuw. E. J. Brill. Leiden.

Long (1833): "On the site of Susa." G. Long. *Journal of the Royal Geographical Society of London*, Vol. 3 (1833), pp. 257-267.

Longden (1931): "Notes on the Parthian Campaigns of Trajan." R. P. Longden. *The Journal of Roman Studies*, Vol. 21, (1931), pp. 1-35.

Lovell (2006): *The Great Wall: China Against the World, 1000 BC—AD 2000*. Jane Lovell. Atlantic Books, London.

Lozinski (1984): "The Parthian Dynasty." B. Philip Lozinski. *Iranica antiqua*, 19 (1984), pp. 119-139.

Lu (1995): "Problems Concerning the Authenticity of *Shih chi* 123 Reconsidered." Zongli Lu. *Chinese Literature: Essays, Articles, Reviews (CLEAR)*, Vol. 17 (Dec. 1995), pp. 51-68.

Lucan (39-65 CE): *Lucan: Civil War*. Translated by Susan H. Braund. Clarendon Press, 1992. Paperback, Oxford World Classics, 1999.

Luce (1925): "Fu-kan-tu-lu." G. H. Luce. *Journal of Burma Research Society*, No. 14 (1925), pp. 91-99.

Luckner (1994): "Ancient Glass." Kurt T. Luckner. *Art Institute of Chicago Museum Studies*, Vol. 20, No. 1, 1994, pp. 78-91.

Ma and Sun (1994): "The Western Regions under the Hsiung-nu and the Han." Ma Yong and Sun Yutan. In: *HCCA*, Vol. II, pp. 227-246.

Ma (1371): *Wenxian Tongkao*, chapter 50. Ma Duanlin. Downloaded 5 August 2011 from: http://www.uus8.com/China/%E5%9B%9B%E5%BA%93%E5%85%A8%E4%B9%A6%E7%B1%BB/%E5%8F%B2%E9%83%A8/%E5%85%B6%E4%BB%96/%E6%96%87%E7%8C%AE%E9%80%9A%E8%80%83/338.html

McCrindle (1885). *Ancient India as Described by Ptolemy*. Reprinted from the *"Indian Antiquary, 1884"*. J. W. McCrindle. Calcutta: Thacker, Spink & Co., Bombay: B.E.S. Press, London: Trübner & Co.

MacDowall (1977): "The Context of Rajuvula the Satrap." David W. MacDowell. *Acta Antiqua, Academiae Scientiarum Hungaricae*, XXV. Budapest, 1977, pp. 187-195.

MacDowall (1996): "The Evidence of the Gazetteer of Roman Artefacts in India." David W. MacDowall. In: *TAA*, pp. 79-95.

MacDowall (2002): "The Rabatak Inscription and the nameless Kushan king." David W. MacDowell. In: *Cairo to Kabul: Afghan and Islamic Studies presented to Ralph Pinder-Wilson*. Edited by Warwick Ball and Leonard Harrow. Melisende, London, 2002, pp. 163-169.

McDowell (1939): "The Indo-Parthian Frontier." Robert H. McDowell. *The American Historical Review*, Vol. 44, No. 4. (Jul. 1939), pp. 781-801.

Mac Dowell and Taddei (1978a): "The Early Historic Period: Achaemenids and Greeks." D. W. Mac Dowall and M. Taddei. In: Allchin and Hammond (1978), pp. 187-232.

Mac Dowell and Taddei (1978b): "The Pre-Muslim Period: Achaemenids and Greeks." D. W. Mac Dowall and M. Taddei. In: Allchin and Hammond (1978), pp. 233-299.

McKinley (1988): *Pinna and Her Silken Beard: A Foray Into Historical Misappropriations*. Daniel L. McKinley. *Ars Textrina: A Journal of Textiles and Costumes*, Vol. 29, June, 1998, Winnipeg, Canada, pp. 9-223.

Maeder (2002): "The project Sea-silk – Rediscovering an Ancient Textile Material." Felicitas Maeder. *Archaeological Textiles Newsletter*, Number 35, Autumn 2002, pp. 8-11.

Maeder, Hänggi and Wunderlin (2004): ***Bisso marino*** *: Fili d'oro dal fondo del mare –* ***Muschelseide****: Goldene Fäden vom Meeresgrund*. Eds. by Felicitas Maeder, Ambros Hänggi, and Dominik Wunderlin. Naturhistoriches Museum and Museum der Kulturen, Basel.

Maenchen-Helfen (1945): "The Yüeh-chih Problem Re-examined." Otto Maenchen-Helfen. *JAOS*, Vol. 65, No. 2 (Apr. – Jun. 1945), pp. 71-81.

Magee et al (2005): "The Achaemenid Empire in South Asia and Recent Excavations in Akra in Northwest Pakistan." Peter Magee, Cameron Petrie, Robert Knox, Farid Khan, and Ken Thomas. *American Journal of Archaeology*, 109 (2005), pp. 711-741.

Mahajan (1978): *Ancient India*. Vidya Dhar Mahajan. Eighth Edition (Revised & enlarged). S. Chand & Co., New Delhi.

Maillart (1937): *Forbidden Journey – From Peking to Kashmir*. Ella K. Maillart. 1937. Translated from the French by Thomas McGreevy. London, William Heinemann Ltd.

Mair (1990): "Old Sinitic **M^y^ag*, Old Persian *Maguš*, and English "Magician." Victor H. Mair. *Early China* 15 (1990), pp. 27-47.

Mair (2005): "Genes, Geography, and Glottochronolgy: The Tarim Basin during Late Prehistory and History." Victor H. Mair. With Appendix: "Proto-Tocharian, Common Tocharian, and Tocharian – on the value of linguistic connections in a reconstructed language," by Gerd Carling. *Journal of Indo-European Monograph Series*, No. 50. Washington, DC.

Mair (2006): "The Rediscovery and Complete Excavation of Ördek's Necropolis." Victor H. Mair. *The Journal of Indo-European Studies*. Vol. 34, Nos. 3 & 4, Fall/Winter 2006, pp. 273-318.

Mair (2007): "Horse Sacrifices and Sacred Groves among the North(west)ern Peoples of East Asia." Victor Mair. *Eurasian Studies* Vol. 6, pp. 22-53.

Mair and Cheng (2013): *Kungang* (昆岗): *The Making of an Imaginary Archaeological Culture.* Victor H. Mair and Cheng Fangyi. *Sino-Platonic Papers*. Number 237, April 2013.

Mairs (2008): "Greek identity and the settler community in Hellenistic Bactria and Arachosia." Rachel Mairs. *Migrations & Identities* 1.1 (2008), pp. 19–43.

Mairs (2011): "*The Archaeology of the Hellenistic Far East: A Survey. Bactria, Central Asia and the Indo-Iranian Borderlands, c. 300 BC - AD 100.*" Rachel Mairs. Downloaded 2 March 2012 from: http://bactria.org/Publications.html.

Majumdar (1981): *The Classical Accounts of India*. R. C. Majumdar. Firma KLM Private Ltd., Calcutta.

Mallory and Mair (2000): *The Tarim Mummies: Ancient China and the Mystery of the Earliest Peoples from the West*. J. P. Mallory and Victor H. Mair. Thames & Hudson. London.

Man (1997): *Gobi : Tracking the Desert*. John Man. Weidenfield & Nicolson. Paperback by Phoenix, Orion Books. London. 1998.

Man (2005): *Attila: A Barbarian King and the Fall of Rome*. John Man. Bantam Press. London.

Mansfield (1991): *A History of the Middle East*. Peter Mansfield. 1991. Reprint, Penguin Books.

Maricq (1968): "The date of Kanika." André Maricq. Translated by J. G. de Casparis. *PDK*, pp. 179-203.

Markham (1879): "The Mountain Passes on the Afghan Frontier of British India." C. R. Markham. *Proceedings of the Royal Geographical Society and Monthly Record of Geography*, New Monthly Series, Vol. 1, No. 1. (Jan. 1879), pp. 1-19.

Markham (1894): "Himalayan Trade Routes." Clements R. Markam. *The Journal of the Manchester Geographical Society*. 1894. Vol. 10. Nos. 1-8. January to March, pp. 12-18.

Marshak (2003): "The Archaeology of Sogdiana." Boris I. Marshak. *Silk Road Newsletter* Vol. 1, No. 2, December 2003.

Marshak and Raspopova (1994): "Worshipers from the Northern Shrine of Temple II, Panjikent." B. I. Marshak and V. I. Raspopova. *BAI*. Vol. 8, pp. 187-207.

Marshak and Negematov (1996): "Sogdiana." B. I. Marshak and N. N. Negmatov. In: *HCCA*, III, pp. 233-280.

Marshall (1909): "Archælogical Exploration in India, 1908-9." (Section on: "The stūpa of Kanishka and relics of the Buddha"). John H. Marshall. *Journal of the Royal Asiatic Society*, 1909, pp. 1056-1061.

Marshall (1947): "Greeks and Sakas in India." John Marshall. *Journal of the Royal Asiatic Society of Great Britain and Ireland*, No. 1 (Apr. 1947), pp. 3-32.

Marshall and Cooke (1997): *Tibet Outside the TAR*. Steven D. Marshall and Susette Ternent Cooke. On CD ROM: The Alliance for Research in Tibet.

Martindale (1958): *The Extra Pharmacopœia*, Volume I. William Martindale. 1881. Updated 24th edition, London, The Pharmaceutical Press.

Martyn (1987): *The Silk Road*. Norma Martyn. Methuen. North Ryde, Sydney, Australia.

Maspero (1895): *Manual of Egyptian Archaeology and Guide to the Study of Antiquities in Egypt*. Gaston Camille Charles Maspero. Originally published in French in 1887. Fourth and Revised Edition. Translated by Amelia B. Edwards. Reprint: BiblioBazaar (August 14, 2007).

Maspero (1901): "Le songe et l'ambassade de le'empereur Ming." M. H, Maspero. *BEFEO*, X (1901), pp. 95-130 + Correspondence from M. le Commandant Harfeld and reply from Maspero, pp. 282-283.

Maspero (Undated): "The Mythology of Modern China." Henri Maspero. *Asiatic Mythology: A Detailed Description and Explanation of the Mythologies of All the Great Nations of Asia*. New York, Crescent Books, pp. 252-384.

Masson (1970): "Toward the problem of the northern borders of the state of the "Great Kushans". M. E. Masson. (Abstract). *KSU*, pp. 167-168.

Mather (2002): *Shih-shuo Hsin-yü*: A new Account of Tales of the World." 2nd Edition. Liu I-ch'ing (403-444) ; with commentary by Liu Chü; translated with introduction and notes by Richard B. Mather. The University of Michigan, Ann Arbor.

Mathers and Shaw (1993): *Treasure of the Concepción*. William M. Mathers and Nancy Shaw. Hong Kong. APA Publications (HK) Ltd.

Mathew (1975): "The Dating and the Significance of the *Periplus of the Erythrean Sea*." Gervase Mathew. In: *East Africa and the Orient. Cultural Syntheses in Pre-Colonial Times*. Neville H. Chittick and Robert I. Rotberg, eds., New York, Africana Publishing Company, pp. 147-163.

Matthews (2003): *The archaeology of Mesopotamia: theories and approaches*. Roger Matthews. Routledge.

Matsuda (1981): "The T'ien-shan Range in Asian History." Hisao Matsuda. *Acta Asiatica. Bulletin of the Institute of Eastern Culture*, No. 43, (1981), pp. 1-28.

Maunder (1878): *The Treasury of Natural History*. Samuel Maunder. New Edition. London, Longmans, Green, and Co.

Mayor (2009): *Greek Fire, Poison, Arrows and Scorpion Bombs: Biological & Chemical Warfare in the Ancient World*. Adrienne Mayor. Overlook Duckworth. New York & London.

Mayor (2014): *The Amazons: Lives and Legends of Warrior Women across the Ancient World. Adrienne Mayor. Princeton University Press.*

Mazumi (2006): "The Zhufoyaojijing at the Lüshun Museum." Mitani Mazumi. *International Dunhuang Project News*. Issue No. 28, Winter 2006.

Meakin (2011a): "Qiang 羌 references in the Book of the Later Han 后汉书 Rachel Meakin. Downloaded from: http://www.qianghistory.co.uk/ on 8 December 2011.

Meakin (2011b): "Hou Han Shu Chapter 117, Biography of the Western Qiang." Rachel Meakin. Downloaded from: http://www.qianghistory.co.uk/ on 8 December 2011.

Maenchen-Helfen (1945): "The Yüeh-Chih Problem Re-Examined." Otto Maenchen-Helfen. *Journal of the American Oriental Society*, Vol. 65, No. 2 (Apr. - Jun. 1945), pp. 71-81.

Mehendale (1996): "Begram: along ancient Central Asian and Indian trade routes." Sanjyot Mehendale. *Cahiers d'Asie central*. Numéro 1/2 (1996), pp. 47-64. Downloaded on 11 September 2011 from: http://asiecentrale.revues.org/index419.html

Mehendale (2001): "The Begram Ivory and Bone Carvings: Some Observations on Provenance and Chronology." Sanjyot Mehendale. *Topoi* 11 (2001) [2003], pp. 485-514.

Mehendale (2008a): "Begram: At the heart of the Silk Roads." Sanjyot Mehendale. In: *AHTNMK*, pp. 131-143.

Mehendale (2008b): "Begram Catalog." Sanjyot Mehendale. In: *AHTNMK*, pp. 162-209.

Melyukova (1990): "The Scythians and Sarmatians." A. I. Melyukova. Translated by Julia Crookenden, *CHEIA*, (1990), pp. 97-117.

Merzliakova (2003): Searchable database of Mountain Passes by Irina Merzliakova of the Russian Academy of Sciences, Institute of Geography, Moscow. Downloaded April 2003 from: http://195.19.12.125/pass1.htm.

Mesny (1894): *Tungking*. William Mesny. Hong Kong, Noronha & Co.

Mesny (1895): *Mesny's Chinese Miscellany. A Text Book of Notes on China and the Chinese*. Vol. I, William Mesny. Shanghai.

Mesny (1896): *Mesny's Chinese Miscellany. A Text Book of Notes on China and the Chinese*. Vol. II, William Mesny. Shanghai.

Mesny (1899): *Mesny's Chinese Miscellany. A Text Book of Notes on China and the Chinese.* Vol. III, William Mesny. Shanghai.

Mesny (1905): *Mesny's Chinese Miscellany. A Text Book of Notes on China and the Chinese.* Vol. IV, William Mesny. Shanghai.

Middleton and Huw (2008): *Tajikistan and the High Pamirs: A Companion and Guide.* Robert Middleton and Thomas Huw. Odyssey Books & Guides. Hong Kong.

Mielczarek (1997): "Remarks on the numismatic evidence for the northern Silk Route." Mariusz Mielczarek. In: *Studies in Silk Road Coins and Culture: Papers in honour of Professor Ikuo Hiryama on his 65th birthday.* Edited by Katsumi Tanabe, Joe Cribb and Helen Wang. The Institute of Silk Road Studies, Kamakura, pp. 131-147.

Miksic (1985): "Traditional Sumatran Trade." John N. Miksic. *BEFEO*, 74, (1985), pp. 423-467.

Millar (1993): *The Roman Near East 31 BC - AD 337.* Fergus Millar. Third Printing, 1996. Harvard University Press. Cambridge, Mass.

Miller (1959): *Accounts of Western Nations in the History of the Northern Chou Dynasty.* Roy Andrew Miller. University of California Press.

Mills (1970): *Ying-yai Sheng-lan: 'The overall survey of the ocean's shores.'* Ma Huan [1433], translated and annotated. J. V. G. Mills. Cambridge, at the University Press.

Millward (2007): *Eurasian Crossroads: A History of Xinjiang.* James A. Millward. Columbia University Press, New York.

Milton (1999): *Nathaniel's Nutmeg: How One Man's Courage Changed the Course of History.* Giles Milton. Hodder and Stoughton, London.

Minorsky (1937): *Ḥudūd al-'Ālam - 'The Regions of the World'*, A Persian Geography 372 A.H. – 982 A.D. Translated and Explained by V. Minorsky, Oxford, Oxford University Press.

Minyaev (1985): "The Origin of the Hiung-nu." S. Minyaev. *International Association for the Study of the Cultures of Central Asia Information Bulletin*, Issue 9 (1985). Moscow, Nauka Publishers. pp. 69-78.

Minyaev (Undated). "Archaeology of the Hsiung-nu in Russia – new discoveries and some problems." S. Minyaev. From: http://www.silk-road.com/artl/minayaev1.shtml. Copyright 1997, Silkroad Foundation. Accessed 27 May 1999.

Mirsky (1977): *Sir Aurel Stein: Archaeological Explorer.* Jeannette Mirsky, 1977. Chicago, University of Chicago Press. Paperback edition: 1998.

Mock (undated): *Dards, Dardistan, and Dardic: an Ethnographic, Geographic, and Linguistic Conundrum.* John Mock. Downloaded on 28 October 2002 from: http://www.monitor.net/~jmko/karakoram/dard.htm

Mock and O'Neil (1996): *Trekking in the Karakoram & Hindukush.* John Mock and Kimberley O'Neil. Hawthorn, Victoria, Lonely Planet Publications.

Mock & O'Neil (2004): "Expedition Report. The Source of the Oxus River: A Journey to the Wakhan Pamir & Across Dilisang Pass to Misgar (July-August 2004)." John Mock & Kimberley O'Neil. Downloaded from: http://www.mockandoneil.com/stg04tc.htm on 31 October, 2011.

Molè (1970): *The T'u-yü-hun from the Northern Wei to the time of the Five Dynasties.* Gabriella Molè. 1970. Rome, Instituto Italiano per il Medio ed Estremo Oriente.

Monier-Williams (1899): *A Sanskrit-English Dictionary.* Oxford at the Clarendon Press. Monier Monier-Williams. Reprint: London, Oxford University Press, 1974.

Montgomerie (1871): "Report of "The Mizra's" Exploration from Cabaul to Kashgar." T. G. Montgomerie. *Journal of the Royal Geographical Society of London.* Vol. 41 (1871), pp. 132-193.

Moorcroft and Trebeck (1841): *Travels in the Himalayan Provinces of Hindustan and the Panjab; in Ladakh and Kashmir, in Peshawar, Kabul, Kunduz, and Bokhara... from 1819 to 1825*, Vol. II. William Moorcroft and George Trebeck. 1841. Reprint: New Delhi, Sagar Publications, 1971.

Moorey (1999): *Ancient Mesopotamian Materials and Industries: The Archaeological Evidence.* Peter Roger Stuart Moorey. Eisenbrauns (November 1999), Warsaw, Indiana, U.S.A.

Moorhouse (1984): *To the Frontier.* Geoffrey Moorhouse. Hodder and Stroughton, Great Britain. Sceptre edition: 1988.

Morgan (1891): "Expedition of the Brothers Grijimailo to the Tian Shan Oases and Lob-nor." E. Delmar. *Proceedings of the Royal Geographical Society and Monthly Record of Geography*, New Monthly Series, Vol. 13, No. 4 (Apr. 1891), pp. 208-226.

Morriss (2012): *Islands in the Nile Sea: the Maritime Cultural Landscape of Thumis, an Ancient Delta City.* A Master of Arts Thesis by Veronica Marie Morriss at the Texas A&M University. May 2012.

Moshref (2000): "History of Old Balkh." R. J. Moshref. Downloaded on 6 October 2000 at: http://www.afghan-network.net/oldbalkh.html

Motomura (1991): "An Approach towards a Comparative Study of the Roman Empire and the Ch'in and Han Empires." MOTOMURA Ryoji. *Kodai* 2, 1991, pp. 61-69.

Mukhamedjanov (1994): *Economy and social system in Central Asia.* A. R. Mukhamedjanov. In: *HCCA*, Vol. II, pp. 265-290.

Mukherjee (1967): *The Kushāṇa Geneology: Studies in Kushāṇa Geneology and Chronology*, Vol. I. B. N. Mukherjee. Sanskrit College, Calcutta.

Mukherjee (1968): *Kanishka I and the Deccan (A Study in the Problem of Relationship).* B. N. Mukherjee. Pilgrim Publishers, Calcutta.

Mukherjee (1969): *Nanā on Lion: A Study in Kushāṇa Numismatic Art.* B. N. Mukherjee. The Asiatic Society, Calcutta.

Mukherjee (1969b): "Ta-hsia and the Problem Concerning the Advent of Nomadic Peoples in Greek Bactria." B. N. Mukherjee. *East and West* 1969, Nos. 3-4, Sept – Dec., pp. 395-400.

Mukherjee (1970): *The Economic Factors in Kushāṇa History.* B. N. Mukherjee. Pilgrim Publishers, Calcutta.

Mukherjee (1973): *Central and South Asian Documents on the Old Śaka Era.* B. N. Mukherjee. Bharat Bharati, Varanasi.

Mukherjee (1977): "The Kushāṇa epithet *Kara.*" B. N. Mukherjee. *Acta Antiqua Academiae Scientiaum Hungaricae* 25, 1977, pp. 8-9.

Mukherjee (1978): *Kushāṇa Coins of the Land of the Five Rivers.* B. N. Mukherjee. Indian Museum, Calcutta.

Mukherjee (1981): *Mathurā and its Society: The Śaka-Pahlava Phase.* B. N. Mukherjee. Firma K. L. M. Private Limited, Calcutta.

Mukherjee (1988): "Chinese Ideas about the Geographical Connotation of the Name Shen-tu." B. N. Mukherjee, *East and West* 38 (1988), pp. 297-303.

Muller (1998): "East Asian Apocryphal Scriptures: Their Origin and Role in the Development of Sinitic Buddhism." Charles Muller. *Bulletin of Toyo Gakuen University*, vol. 6 (1988), pp. 63-7. Downloaded from: http://www.human.toyogaken-u.ac.jp/-acmuller/articles/apocrypha.htm on 27 November 1999.

Müller and Sieg (1916): "Maitrisimit und >Tocharisch<", pp. 395-417. Friedrich Wilheim Karl Müller and Emil Sieg. In: *Sitzungsberichte der Königlich Preussischen Akademie der Wissenschaften.* Berlin.

Mullie (1969): "Les Sien-pi." Jos. L. M. Mullie. *Central Asiatic Journal*, Vol. 13, (1969), pp. 24-51.

Murphy et al (2002): Prehistoric Old World Scalping: New Cases from the Cemetery of Aymyrlyg, South Siberia." Eileen Murphy et al. *American Journal of Archaeology*, Vol. 106, No. 1 (Jan. 2002), pp. 1-10.

Murowchick (2002): "The Political and Ritual Significance of Bronze Production and Use in Ancient Yunnan. Robert E. Murowchick. *JEAA* 3, 1-2 (2002), pp. 133-192.

Murty (1969): "A Re-appraisal of the Mon-legend in Himalayan Tradition." T. S. Murty. *Central Asiatic Journal* 13, (1969), pp. 291-301.

Musil (1926): *THE NORTHERN ḤEĞĂZ: A Topographical Itinerary.* Alois Musil. American Geographical Society. New York.

Musselman (2012): *A Dictionary of Bible Plants.* Lytton John Musselman. Cambridge University Press.

Myrdal and Kessle (1971): *Gates to Asia : A Diary from a Long Journey.* Jan Myrdal & Gun Kessle. Translated from the Swedish by Paul Britten Austin. Pantheon Books. New York.

Nagaswamy (1995): *Roman Karur: A peep into Tamils' past.* R. Nagaswamy. Brahad Prakashan, Madras.

Nanjio (1883): *A Catalogue of the Chinese Translation of the Buddhist Tripitaka: The Sacred Canon of the Buddhists in China and Japan.* Bunyiu Nanjio. Oxford at the Clarendon Press.

Narain (1957): *The Indo-Greeks.* A. K. Narain. Oxford University Press. Reprint: Delhi. 1980.

Narain (1958): "The Greeks of Bactria and India." A. K. Narain. In: *The Cambridge Ancient History*, Volume XIII, Second Edition. Rome and the Mediterranean to 133 B.C., pp. 388-421.

Narain (1968): "A Postscript on the Date of Kaniṣka." In: *PDK*, pp. 240-246.

Nath (1995): "Antiquities of Graeco-Roman Affinity from Adam: An Inland Mart of Central India." Amarendra Nath. *East and West* Vol. 45, Nos. 1-4 (December 1995), pp. 149-171.

Nebenzahl (2011): *Mapping the Silk Road and Beyond: 2,000 Years of Exploring the East.* Kenneth Nebenzahl. Phaidon Press.

Needham (1978): *The Shorter Science & Civilisation in China: An abridgement by Colin A. Ronan of Joseph Needham's original text*, Vol. 1. Cambridge University Press. Paperback Edition 1980.

Neelis (2007): "Passages to India: Śaka and Kuṣāṇa Migrations in Historical Contexts" by Jason Neelis. In: *OTCOFE*, pp. 55-94.

Negmatov and Saltovskaya (1970): "Material culture of Kushan times in Ustrushana and West Ferghana." N. N. Negmatov and E. D. Saltovskaya (Abstract), *KSU*, pp. 174-175.

Negmatov (1994): "States in north-western Central Asia." N. N. Negmatov. *HCCA*, pp. 441-456.

Neusner (1983): "Jews in Iran." J. Neusner. *CHI*, 3(2), pp. 909-923.

Neva (2003): "Ancient jewelry from Central Asia." Elena Neva. *Transoxiana* 6, Julio 2003. Downloaded on 7 July 2003 from: http://www.transoxiana.org.

Neve (1945): *The Tourist's Guide to Kashmir, Ladakh, Skardo, &c.* Arthur Neve. 18th edition. Lahore, The Civil & Military Gazette, Ltd.

Nicholson and Shaw (2000): *Ancient Egyptian materials and technology.* Paul T. Nicholson and Ian Shaw. Cambridge University Press, 2000.

Nishijima (2008): "The economic and social history of Former Han." In: *The Cambridge History of China. Volume I. The Ch'in and Han and Han Empires, 221 B.C.—A.D. 220.* General editors: Denis Twitchett and John K. Fairbank, pp. 551-607.

Noble (1930-32): "A Kharoṣṭhī Inscription from Endere." Peter S. Noble. *Bulletin of the Society of Oriental Studies*, VI, (1930-32), pp. 445-455.

Nodelman (1960): "A preliminary history of Characene." S. A. Nodelman. *Berytus* 13 (1960), pp. 83-123.

Noelle (1997): *State and tribe in nineteenth-century Afghanistan: The Reign of Amir Dost Muhammad Khan (1826-1863).* Christine Noelle. RoutledgeCurzon.

Norman and Coblin (1995): "A New Approach to Chinese Historical Linguistics." Jerry L. Norman and W. South Coblin. *JAOS*, Vol. 115, No. 4. (Oct.-Dec. 1995), pp. 576-584.

Olmstead (1948): *History of the Persian Empire.* A. T. Olmstead. 1948. University of Chicago. Reprint: University of Chicago Press. 1978.

Olufsen (1904): *Through the Unknown Pamirs: The Second Danish Pamir Expedition, 1898-99.* Ole Olufsen. W. Heinemann, London.

Osbaldeston and Wood (2000): *Dioscorides de Materia Medica. Being an Herbal with many other Medicinal Materials written in Greek in the First Century of the Common Era. A New Indexed Version in Modern English* by Tess Anne Osbaldeston and R.P.A. Wood. Ibidis Press, Johannesburg. Downloaded from: http://www.ibidispress.scriptmania.com/box_widget.html on 29 July 2011.

Osborne (1975): *River Road to China: The Mekong River Expedition 1866-1873*. Milton Osborne. 1975. Reprint: Newton Abbot, Devon, ReadersUnion Limited. 1976.

Osborne (2000): *The Mekong: Turbulent Past, Uncertain Future*. Milton Osborne. Atlantic Monthly Press, New York.

Outram et al (2009): "The Earliest Horse Harnessing and Milking." Alan K. Outram, Natalie A. Stear, Robin Bendrey, Sandra Olsen, Alexei Kasparov, Victor Zaibert, Nick Thorpe, Richard P. Evershed. *Science* 6 March 2009: Vol. 323. no. 5919, pp. 1332-1335.

Padwa (2004): "Archaeological GIS and Oasis Geography in the Tarim Basin." Mariner Padwa. *The Silk Road*, Volume 2, Number 2, December 2004, pp. 26-29.

Pahlen (1964): *Mission to Turkestan: Being the Memoirs of Count K.K. Pahlen, 1908-1909*. Konstantin Konstanovich Pahlen. Translated by N. Couriss. Oxford University Press. Accessed from: http://www.iras.ucalgary.ca/~volk/sylvia/Pahlen.htm on 11 December 2005.

Pan (1992): "Early Chinese Settlement Policies towards the Nomads." Pan Yihong. *Asia Major*, 3rd series, Vol. V, Part 2, (1992), pp. 41-78.

Panchenko (2000): *The City of the Branchidae and the question of Greek contribution to the intellectual history of India and China*. Dmitri Panchenko. *Hypoboreus* Vol. 8 (2000) Fasc. 2, pp. 244-255. Downloaded from: wsw@yahoogroups.com on 18 March 2003.

Parker (1885): "Contributions towards the Topography and Ethnology of Central Asia. 1. Extracts from the P'êi-wên Yün-fu." E. H. Parker. *The China Review*. Vol. 13 No. 5, pp. 337-346; Vol. 13 No. 6, pp. 375-386; Vol. 14 No. 1, pp. 39-49.

Parker (1892, 1894): "The Turko-Scythian Tribes." E. H. Parker. *The China Review*. Vol. 20 No. 1 (1892), pp. 1-24; Vol. 20 No. 2, pp. 109-125; Vol. 21 No. 2 (1894), pp. 100-119; Vol. 21 No. 3, pp. 129-137.

Parker (1895): "Turko-Scythian Tribes – After Han Dynasty." E. H. Parker. *The China Review*. Vol. 21 No. 4, pp. 253-267; Vol. 21 No. 5, pp. 291-301.

Parker (1905): "China and the Ancient Cabul Valley." E. H. Parker. *The English Historical Review*, Vol. 20, No. 80. (Oct. 1905), pp. 625-636.

Parker (2002):□"Ex Oriente Luxuria: Indian Commodities and Roman Experience." Grant Parker. *Journal of the Economic and Social History of the Orient*, Vol. 45, No. 1 (2002), pp. 40-95.

Parker (2007): *Chinese Unicorn: all about the Zhi* (廌). Jeannie Thomas Parker. Toronto. Downloaded from http://www.chinese-unicorn.com/qilin/about/ on May 28 2009. Also, see: Kindle version (2013).

Parry-Jones and Vincent (1998): "Can we tame wild medicine?" Rob Parry-Jones and Amanda Vincent. *New Scientist*, Vol. 157, No 2115, 3 January 1998, pp. 26-29.

Parsons (2007): *City of the Sharp-Nosed Fish: Greek Lives in Roman Egypt*. Peter Parsons. Weidenfeld and Nicolson, London.

Partridge (1958): *ORIGINS: A Short Etymological Dictionary of Modern English*. Eric Partridge. 1958. Reprint: Greenwich House, New York, 1983.

Parzinger (2008): "The 'Silk Roads' Concept Reconsidered: About Transfers, Transportation and Transcontinental Interactions in Prehistory." Hermann Parzinger. In: *The Silk Road*. Vol. 5, No. 2, Winter 2008, pp. 7-15.

Paul (1952): *The Cross Over India*. Rajaiah D. Paul. SCM Press Ltd., London.

Paula (1995): *The Road to Miran: Travels in the Forbidden Zone of Xinjiang*. Christa Paula. HarperCollins, Great Britain. 1994. Flamingo edition 1995.

Pearce (2003): *Justin, Epitome of Pompeius Trogus*. Translation by Roger Pearse based Seel's text and consulting Yardley's translation. Downloaded on 18 October 2008, from: http://www.tertullian.org/fathers/justinus_08_prologi.htm

Peissel (1984): *The Ants' Gold. The Discovery of the Greek El Dorado in the Himalayas*. Michel Peissel. London, Harvill Press.

Peers (2006): *Soldiers of the Dragon: Chinese Armies 1500 BC - AD 1840*. C. J. Peers. Osprey Press, Oxford, U.K.

Pelliot (1904a): Review article on: *Document sur les Tou-kiue (turcs) occidentaux* (Sbornik trudov orkhonskoï ekspeditsii, t. VI). St Pétersbourg, 1903, gr, in-8°, IV-378 pp. avec carte. – *Notes additionelles sur les Tou-kiue (Turcs) occidentaux* (*TP*, 1904, série II, t. V, pp.1-110). Paul Pelliot. *BEFEO* 1-2 Jan-Jun (1904), pp. 479-483.

Pelliot (1904b): "Deux itinéraires de Chine en Inde à la fin du viiie siècle." Paul Pelliot. *BEFEO* 4 (1904), pp. 131-413.

Pelliot (1906): Review article on: *Les pays d'Occident d'auprès le Wei lio* by Édouard Chavannes (*T'oung pao*, II, vi, décembre 1905, pp. 519-571). Paul Pelliot. *BEFEO*, 6, (1906), pp. 361-400.

Pelliot (1912): "Kao-tch'ang, Qočo, Houo-tcheou et Qarâ-khodja." Paul Pelliot, with an additional note by Robert Gauthiot. *JA* Series 10, Bk 19, May-June 1912, pp. 579-603.

Pelliot (1914): "Les noms propres dans les traductions chinoises du Milindapañha." Paul Pelliot. *JA*, 1914, II, pp. 359-419.

Pelliot (1915): "Li-kien, autre nom du Ta-Ts'in (Orient méditerranéen)." Paul Pelliot. *T'oung pao, 16* (1915), pp. 690-691.

Pelliot (1920): "À propos des comans." Paul Pelliot. *JA* April-June 1920, pp. 125-183.

Pelliot (1920b): "Meou-tseu ou les doutes levés." Traduit et annoté par Paul Pelliot. *TP*, 19 (1920), pp. 255-433.

Pelliot (1921): "Note sur les anciens itinéraries chinoise dans l'orient romain." Paul Pelliot. *JA* XVIII, XIe, Jan-Mar 1921, pp. 139-145

Pelliot (1923): "Note sur les anciens noms de Kučā, d'Aqsu et d'Uč-Turfan." Paul Pelliot. *TP*, 22 (1923), pp. 126-132.

Pelliot (1929): "Neuf notes sur des questions d'asie centrale." Paul Pelliot. *TP*, 26 (1929), pp. 201-266.

Pelliot (1934): "Tokharien et Koutchéen." Paul Pelliot. *JA*. CCXXIV, Janv.-juin, pp. 23-106.

Pelliot (1936): "A propos du «Tokharien»." Paul Pelliot. *TP*, vol. XXXII, 1936, pp. 259-284.

Pelliot (1959): *Notes on Marco Polo*, vol. I. Paul Pelliot. Paris. Imprimerie Nationale.

Pelliot (1963): *Notes on Marco Polo*, vol. II. Paul Pelliot. Paris. Imprimerie Nationale.

Pelliot (1973): *Notes on Marco Polo*, vol. III. Paul Pelliot. Paris. Imprimerie Nationale.

Pelliot (2002): "Notes sur Kumārajīva." Paul Pelliot (posthumous) In: *A Life Journey to the East: Sinological Studies in Memory of Giuliano Bertuccioli* (1923-2001). Edited by Antonio Forte and Federico Masini. Italian School of East Asian Studies. Essays: Volume 2. Kyoto. Pages 1-19.

Peng and Zhu (1995): *New Research on the Origins of Cowries Used in Ancient China*. Ke Peng and Yanshui Zhu. *Sino-Platonic Papers*, No. 68, May 1995. Dept. of Asian and Middle Eastern Studies, University of Pennsylvania.

Perkins (1999): *Encyclopedia of China: The Essential Reference to China, Its History and Culture*. Dorothy Perkins. Roundtable Press, New York.

Petech (1950): *Northern India According to the Shui-ching-chu*. L. Petech. Rome. Istituto Italiano per il Medio ed Estremo Oriente.

Petech (1951): "Rome and Eastern Asia." Luciano Petech. *East and West*, Vol. 2, No. 2 (July 1951), pp. 72-76.

Peters (2002): "Ethnicity along China's southwestern frontier." Heather A. Peters. *Journal of East Asian Archaeology*, Vol. 3, 1–2, pp. 75-102.

Phillips (1955): *Qataban and Sheba: Exploring Ancient Kingdoms on the Biblical Spice Routes of Arabia*. Wendell Phillips. London, Victor Gollancz Ltd. 1955. Also published as: *Sheba's Buried City*. London, 1958, Pan Books (paperback).

P'iankov (1994): "The Ethnic History of the Sakas." I. V. P'iankov. *BAI*, Vol. 8, (1994) [but appearing in 1996], pp. 37-46.

Piankov (2010): *The Tochari - Who Are They?* Igor V. Piankov, *Anabasis* I, 2010, pp. 97-106.

Piankov (2014): "The "Stone Tower" on the Great Silk Road." I.V. Piankov. In: *Scripta Antiqua - Ancient History, Philology, Arts and Material Culture. The Almanac. Volume Three.*

Edward Rtveladze Felicitation Volume. Sobranie. Moscow 2014, pp. 204-219. In Russian with English Summary.

Pickworth (2002): "The role of seals in trade across the Red Sea." Diana Pickworth. In: *Red Sea Trade and Travel.* The British Museum. Sunday 6 October 2002. Organised by The Society for Arabian Studies. Downloaded 20 July 2003 from: www.thebritishmuseum.ac.uk/ane/fullpapers.doc

Pickworth (2003): "Sheba@Saba-Trading. com: A Yemeni Trading Link Three Thousand Years Old." Diana Pickworth. *The Silk Road Newsletter* Vol. 1, No. 1. January 15, 2003. Downloaded from: http://www.silkroadfoundation.org/toc/newsletter_jan.html on 13 February 2004.

Pilipko (1994): "Excavations of Staraia Nisa." V. N. Pilikpo. *BAI*, Vol. 8, (1994), pp. 101-116.

Pinault (2002b): "Tocharian and Indo-Iranian: Relations between two linguistic areas." Georges-Jean Pinault. In: *IRRLP*, pp. 243-284.

Pliny *NH* (77 CE) (a): *Natural History - A Selection.* Pliny the Elder. Translated by John F. Healy. London. Penguin Books. (1991).

Pliny *NH* (77 CE) (b): *Natural History*. Pliny the Elder (77 CE). Translation by W. H. S. Jones, Loeb Classical Library, London/Cambridge, Mass. (1961).

Poidebard (1929): "Coupes de la chausée romaine Antioche-Chalcis." A. Poidebard. *Syria* X, 1929, pp. 22-29.

Poidebard (1934): *La trace de Rome dans le désert de Syrie : le limes de Trajan a la conquête arabes : recherches aériennes (1925-1932).* A. Poidebard. Paris, Librairie Orientaliste Paul Geuthner.

Pokora (1973): "Pre-Han Literature." Timoteus Pokora. In: *Essays on the Sources for Chinese History*, eds. Donald Leslie, Colin Mackerras, Wang Gungwu. Australian National University Press, pp. 23-35.

Pothecary (1995): "Strabo, Polybios, and the Stade." Sarah Pothecary. *Phoenix*, Vol. 49, No. 1 (Spring 1995), pp. 49-67.

Potts (1988): "Arabia and the Kingdom of Characene." D. T. Potts. In: *Araby the Blest: Studies in Arabian Archaeology.* Edited by D. T. Potts. The Carsten Niebuhr Istitute of Ancient Near Eastern Studies, University of Copenhagen. Museum Tusculanum Press, pp. 137-167.

Potts (1988b): "Trans-Arabian Routes of the Pre-Islamic Period." Daniel T. Potts. In: *L'Arabie et ses mers bordières I. Itinéraires et voisinages.* Séminaire de recherche 1985-1986 / J.-F. SALLES (dir.) TMO 16, 1988, pp. 127-162.

Potts (1990): *The Arabian Gulf in Antiquity Volume II: From Alexander the Great to the Coming of Islam.* D. T. Potts. Oxford, Clarendon Press.

Potts (1991-1992). "A note on rice cultivation in Mesopotamia and Susiana." D.T. Potts. *NABU*, 1991-2. Carsten Niebuhr Institute, Copenhagen. Downloaded on 14 September 2002 from: www.achemenet.com/pdf/nabu/nabu1991-002.pdf

Potts (1999): *The Archaeology of Elam : Formation and Transformation of an ancient Iranian State.* D.T. Potts. Cambridge, Cambridge University Press.

Potts (2001): "Ostrich Distribution and Exploitation in the Arabian Peninsula." D. T. Potts. *Antiquity* 75 (2001), pp. 182-190.

Potts (2004): "Camel Hybridization and the role of *Camelus Bactrianus* in the Ancient Near East." D. T. Potts. *Journal of the Economic and Social History of the Orient*, 47 (2004): 143-165.

Potts (2005): "Persian Gulf in Antiquity." Daniel T. Potts. Downloaded on 12 May 2007 from: http://www.iranica.com/newsite/articles/ot_grp7/ot_pers_gulf_ant_200503223.html

Potts (2005b): "Bactrian Camels and Bactrian-Dromedary Hybrids." Daniel Potts. *Silkroad Journal*, Vol. 3, no. 1 (2013), pp. 1-13. Accessed on 24 December 2013 from: www.silkroadfoundation.org/newsletter/vol3num1/7_bactrian.php.

Prasad (1977): *Foreign Trade and Commerce in Ancient India.* Prakash Charan Prasad. New Delhi, Abhinav Publications.

Prasad (1980): "India's Contacts with Africa from the Earliest Times." Amba Prasad. In: *Imprints of Indian Thought and Culture Abroad. Vivekananda Kendra Patrika* Vol. 9, No. 1. February 1980, pp. 190-203. Madras.

Prasad (1984): *Cities, Crafts and Commerce under the Kuśāṇas.* Kameshwar Prasad. Delhi, Agam Kala Prakashan.

Prasad (1988): *History of the Andhras up to 1565 A.D.* Durga Prasad. P. G. Publishers, Guntur-10, A.P., India.

Pregadio (undated): *Glossaire de l'alchimie chinoise.* Fabrizio Pregadio. Accessed 12 December 2006 from: http://venus.unive.it/dsao//pregadio/articles/glossary.html.

Prothero & Schoch (2003): *Horns, Tusks, and Flippers: the Evolution of Hoofed Mammals.* Donald R. Prothero, Robert M. Schoch. John Hopkins University Press.

Průšek (1971): "Chinese statelets and the Northern Barbarians in the period 1400-300 B.C." Jaroslav Průšek. Dordrecht, Holland, Reidel.

Psarras (1994): "Exploring the North: Non-Chinese Cultures of the Late Warring States and Han." Sophia-Karin Psarras. *Monumenta Serica,* 42 (1994), pp. 1-125.

Psarras (2003): "Han and Xiongnu: a Reexamination of Cultural and Political Relations I." Sophia-Karin Psarras. *Monumenta Serica* 51 (2003), pp. 55-236.

Psarras (2004): "Han and Xiongnu: a Reexamination of Cultural and Political Relations II." Sophia-Karin Psarras. *Monumenta Serica* 51 (2004), pp. 37-93.

Ptolemy (1932): *The Geography.* Claudius Ptolemy. Translated and edited by Edward Luther Stevenson. New York, The New York Public Library, 1932, (Published as the *Geography of Claudius Ptolemy).* Reprint New York, Dover Publications, Inc., 1991.

Ptolemy (1971): *Ptolemaios. Geographie 6,9-21. Ostiran und Zentralasien.* Teil I. Containing Greek and Latin texts. Translated and annotated in German with English translation by Italo Ronca. Instituto Italiano per il medio ed estremo Oriente. Rome 1971.

Pugachenkova, *et al.,* (1994): "Kushan Art." G. A. Pugachenkova, S. R. Dar, R. C. Sharma and M. A. Joyenda, in collaboration with H. Siddiqi. *HCCA* (1994), pp. 331-395.

Pulleyblank (1952): "A Sogdian Colony in Inner Mongolia." Edwin G. Pulleyblank. *TP* 41, 1952, pp. 317-356.

Pulleyblank (1963): "The consonantal system of Old Chinese." Edwin G. Pulleyblank. *Asia Major* 9 (1963), pp. 58-144, and 206-265.

Pulleyblank (1966): "Chinese and Indo-Europeans." Edwin G. Pulleyblank. *JRAS,* 1965, pp. 9-39.

Pulleyblank (1968): "Chinese Evidence for the Date of Kanishka." Edwin G. Pulleyblank. *PDK,* pp. 247-258.

Pulleyblank (1970): "The Wu-sun and Sakas and the Yüeh-chih Migration." Edwin G. Pulleyblank. *BSOAS,* 33 (1970), pp. 154-160.

Pulleyblank (1981): "China in Central Asia." A Review Article. Edwin G. Pulleyblank. *The International History Review,* Vol. 3, No. 2 (Apr., 1981), pp. 278-286

Pulleyblank (1990): "The "High Carts": A Turkish-Speaking People Before the Turks." Edwin G. Pulleyblank. *Asia Major* 3rd Series, Vol. III, Part I, pp. 21-26.

Pulleyblank (1991): *Lexicon of Reconstructed Pronunciation in Early Middle Chinese, Late Middle Chinese and Early Mandarin.* Edwin G. Pulleyblank. UBC Press. Vancouver.

Pulleyblank (1999): "The Roman Empire as known to Han China." A review article on *The Roman Empire in Chinese Sources.* D. D. Leslie and K. H. J. Gardiner. Rome (1996). Review by Edwin G. Pulleyblank. *JAOS* 119.1 (1999), pp. 71-9.

Pulleyblank (2000) "The Nomads in China and Central Asia in the Post-Han Period," in: Hans Robert ROEMER (Hg.), *History of the Turkic Peoples in the Pre-Islamic Period. Histoire des Peuples Turcs à l'Époque Pré-Islamique.* Philologiae et Historiae Turcicae Fundamenta Tomus Primus. Berlin: Klaus Schwarz Verlag, S. pp. 76–94. (Philologiae Turcicae Fundamenta; III).

Pumpelly (1905): "Physiographic Observations Between the Syr Darya and Lake Kara Kul, on the Pamir, in 1903." Raphael W. Pumpelly. In: *EIT*, pp. 123- 155.

Puri (1987): *Buddhism in Central Asia*. B. N. Puri. Motilal Banarsidass, Delhi.

Puri (1994): "The Sakas and Indo-Parthians." B. N. Puri. In: *HCCA* II, pp. 191-207.

Pusch (1996): "Qantir, Pi-Ramsès." Edgard Pusch. *Les Dossiers d'Archeologie*, No. 213, (1996), pp. 54-59.

Raguin (1979): "Taoism and Taoist Religion." Unpublished notes for a course given by Fr. Yves Raguin, S.J. at the Faculty of Theology of Fujen University, Taiwan.

Raman (1991): "Further Evidence of Roman Trade from Coastal Sites in Tamil Nadu." K. V. Raman. *RAI*, (1991), pp. 125-133.

Ranov (1984): "L'exploration archéologique du pamir." V. A. Ranov. *BEFEO*, LXXIII, (1984), pp. 67-97.

Rante (2008): "The Iranian city of Rayy: Urban Model and Military Architecture." R. Rante. *Iran*, Vol. 46 (2008), pp. 189-211.

Rapin (1996): "Relations entre l'Asie centrale et l'Inde à l'époque hellénistique." Claude Rapin. *Cahiers d'Asie central*. Numéro 1/2 (1996), pp. 13-32. Downloaded as pdf file on 11 September 2011 from: http://asiecentrale.revues.org/index417.html

Rapin (1998): "L'incompréhensible Asie centrale de la carte de Ptolémée. Propositions pour un décodage." Claude Rapin. *BAI, NS* 12 (1998), pp. 201-225.

Rapin (2001): "La tombe d'une princesse nomade à Koktepe prés de Samarkand." Claude Rapin, in collaboration with Mukhammadjon Isamiddinov and Mutallib Khasanov. *Comptes Rendue de l'Academie des Inscriptions et Belles Lettres* (*CRAI*) Jan.-Mar. 2001, pp. 33-92.

Rapin (2004): "After Alexander : Central Asia Before Islam : Nomads and the shaping of Central Asia." Claude Rapin. Abstract. Downloaded on 24 April 2008 from: http://www.britac.ac.uk/events/programmes/2004/abstracts/asia-rapin.html.

Rapin (2005): "L'Afghanistan et l'Asie centrale dans la géographie mythique des historiens d'Alexandre et dans la toponymie des géographes gréco-romains." Claude Rapin in: *AAC*.

Rapin et al (2006): Rapin, C., A. Baud, F. Grenet, Sh.A. Rakhmanov, «Les recherches sur la région des Portes de Fer de Sogdiane: bref état des questions en 2005», *IMKU*, No. 35, Tashkent, 2006, p. 91-101 (texte en russe) et 102-112 (texte en français). Downloaded from: http://www.google.com.au/search?hl=en&q=Les+recherches+sur+la+r%C3%A9gion+des+Portes+de+Fer+de+Sogdiane%3A+bref+%C3%A9tat+des+questions+en+2005&btnG=Google+Search&meta= on 25 April 2008.

Rapin (2007): "Nomads and the Shaping of Central Asia from the Early Iron Age to the Kushan Period. Claude Rapin. In: *AACABI*, pp. 29-72.

Rapoport (1994): "The Palaces of Topraq-Qal'a." IU. A. Rapoport. *BAI*. Vol. 8. (1994), pp. 161-185.

Rapson (1897): "Two notes on Indian Numismatics." E. J. Rapson. *Journal of the Royal Asiatic Society* (1897), pp. 319-324.

Rapson, ed., (1922): *The Cambridge History of India. Vol I: Ancient India*. Edited by E. J. Rapson. 1922. Cambridge University Press. Reprint: Delhi. S. Chand & Co. 1968.

Raschke (1976): "New Studies in Roman Commerce with the East." Manfred G. Raschke. Aufsteig und Niedergang der Römischen Welt II (Principat), ed. H. Temporini, bd. 92, Berlin/N.Y., pp. 604-1233.

Raunig (1984): "Forever amber." Walter Raunig. *The UNESCO Courier*. Paris. June 1984, pp. 13-15. b.

Raunig (1991a): "Some aspects of trade in Badakhshan (Afghanistan) between 1880 and 1980." Walter Raunig. *ATR* (1991), pp. 61-68.

Raunig (1991b): "Problems of settlement of the eastern Wakhan Valley and the discoveries made there in 1975." Walter Raunig. *ATR* (1991), pp. 69-77.

Raverty (1880): *Notes on Afghánistan and part of Balúchistán: Geographical, Ethnological, and Historical, extracted from the writings of little known Afghán and Tájzik Historians, Geographers, and Genealogists, the Histories of the Ghúris, the Turk Sovereigns of the Di.* Henry George Raverty. First Printed in 1880 by order of the Secretary of State for India in Council. Reprint by Nabu Public Domain Reprints, 2010.

Rawlinson (1842): "Comparative Geography of Afghanistan: Extract of a Letter from Major Rawlinson, dated Kandahar, May 1st, 1841." George Rawlinson. *Journal of the Royal Geographical Society of London.* Vol. 12 (1842), pp. 112-114.

Rawlinson (1866-1867): "On the Recent Journey of Mr. W. H. Johnson from Leh, in Ladakh, to Ilchi in Chinese Turkistan." H. C. Rawlinson. *Proceedings of the Royal Geographic Society of London,* Vol. 11, No. 1. (1866-1867), pp. 6-15.

Rawlinson (1862): *The Seven Great Monarchies of the Ancient Eastern World,* Vols. I-III. George Rawlinson. 1st Edition, 1862. 2nd Edition. New York, Hurst and Company.

Rawlinson (date unknown): *The Seven Great Monarchies of The Ancient Eastern World.* Vol. 6 (of 7), Parthia. Parthia the History, Geography and Antiquities of Chaldaea, Assyria, Babylon, Media, Persia, Parthia and Sassanian or New Persian Empire. Republished by the Library of Alexandria through Kindle Books.

Rawlinson (1899): *The Seven Great Monarchies of The Ancient Eastern World.* Vol. 2 (of 3). Persia, George Rawlinson. Revised Edition. New York Colonial.

Rawlinson (1910): *Herodotus: Histories.* Herodotus. (Born perhaps 484 BCE, died *circa* 430 - 420 BCE). Translated with notes by George Rawlinson. 1st Edition, 1858. Revised edition, 1910, reprinted by Ware, Hertfordshire, Wordsworth Editions Limited, 1996.

Rawlinson (1912): *Bactria: The History of a Forgotten Empire.* H. G. Rawlinson. Probsthain & Co., London.

Ray (2003): *The Archaeology of Seafaring in Ancient South Asia.* Himanshu Prabha Ray. Cambridge University Press.

Reddy (2001): "Maritime Trade of Early South India: New Archaeological Evidences from Motupalli, Andhra Pradesh." P. Krishna Mohan Reddy. *East and West* Vol. 51 – Nos. 1-2 (June 2001), pp. 143-156.

Redford (1996): "Le Wadi Tumilat." Donald Redford. *Les Dossiers d'Archeologie.* No. 213, (1996), pp. 50-53.

Reinhart-Waller (Undated): *The Alekseev Manuscript.* Geraldine Reinhart-Waller. Downloaded from www.esittmann.de/ alexseev.mainframe.html on 21 May 2000.

Rice (1965): *Ancient Arts of Central Asia.* Tamara Talbot Rice. New York, Frederick A. Praeger, Publishers.

Richter (1929): "Silk in Greece." Gisela M. A. Richter. *American Journal of Archaeology,* Vol. 33, No. 1. (Jan.-Mar. 1929), pp. 27-33.

Ricotti (1994): "Indian Products in Roman Cuisine." E. Slaza Prina Ricotti. *ARAI,* pp. 101-108.

Rivard, Foster and Sidebotham (2002): "Emerald City." Jean-Louis Rivard, Brandon C. Foster, *and* Steven E. Sidebotham. *Archaeology.* May/June 2002, pp. 36-41.

Rizvi (1983): *Ladakh: Crossroads of High Asia.* Janet Rizvi. Oxford University Press. Reprint: Oxford University Press, New Delhi (1996).

Rizvi (1999): *Trans-Himalayan Caravans : Merchant Princes and Peasant Traders in Ladakh.* Janet Rizvi. Oxford University Press. New Delhi.

Robin (1991): "L'Arabie du sud et la date du *Périple de la mer Érythrée* (nouvelles données)." Christian Robin. *JA* CCLXXIX (1991), pp. 1-30.

Roerich (1931): *Trails to Inmost Asia: Five Years of Exploration with the Roerich Central Asian Expedition.* George N. Roerich. 1931. First Indian Reprint. Book Faith India, Delhi. 1996.

Rogers (1968): *Chronicle of Fu Chien: A Case of Exemplar History.* Michael C. Rogers. 1968. Berkeley and Los Angeles. University of California Press.

Rolfe (1935-1939): *Ammianus Marcellinus – History.* Translated by J. C. Rolfe. Loeb Classical Library, 3 vols. London/Cambridge, Mass.

Rolls (1992): *Sojourners.* Eric Rolls. St. Lucia, Queensland. University of Queensland Press.

Rong (2004): "Land Route or Sea Route? Commentary on the Study of the Paths of Transmission and Areas in which Buddhism Was Disseminated during the Han Period." Rong Xinjiang. Translated by Xiuqin Zhou. *Sino-Platonic Papers*, Number 144, July 2004. Edited by Victor H. Mair.

Rong (2004)b: "Khotanese Felt and Sogdian Silver: Foreign Gifts to Buddhist Monasteries in Ninth- and Tenth-Century Dunhuang." pp. 15-34. Rong Xinjiang. *Asia Major*, Series III. Volume 17, Part I. 2004.

Root, *et al.* (1982): *Wondrous Glass: Reflections on the World of Rome c. 50 B.C. - A.D. 650*. M. C. Root, *et al.* Downloaded 21 August 1999 from: http://www.umich.edu/~kelseydb/Exhibits/WondrousGlass/MainGlass.html.

Rosen (2007): *Justinian's Flea: Plague, Empire, and the Birth of Europe.* William Rosen. Viking books, London.

Rosewater (1961): "The Family Pinnidae in the Indo-Pacific." Joseph Rosewater. *Indo-Pacific Mollusca*, vol. 1, no. 4. September 28, 1961, pp. 175-176.

Rosewater (1965): "The Family Tridacnidae in the Indo-Pacific." Joseph Rosewater. *Indo-Pacific Mollusca*, vol. 1, no. 6. April 30, 1965, pp. 347-396.

Ross (1883): *The Land of the Five Rivers and Sindh.* David Ross. London. Reproduced by Sani Hussain Panhwar. Copyright © www.panhwar.com

Rowell (1983): *Mountains of the Middle Kingdom: Exploring the High Peaks of China and Tibet.* Galen Rowell. San Francisco. Sierra Club Books.

Rtveladze (1994): "Kampir-Tepe: Structures, Written Documents, and Coins." E. V. Rtveladze. *BAI*, Vol. 8 (1994), pp. 141-154.

Rtveladze (1995): "Parthia and Bactria." E. V. Rtveladze. In: *ITLOTG*, pp. 181-190.

Rtveladze (2007): "Monetary Circulation in Ancient Tokharistan." Edward Rtveladze. In: *AACABI*, pp. 389-397.

Ruegg (2005): "The Kalawān Copper-Plate Inscription: Early Evidence for Mahāyāna-type Thinking?" D. Seyfort Ruegg. *Journal of the International Journal of Buddhist Studies*, Volume 28, Number 1, pp. 3-9.

Rusanov (1994): "The Fortification of Kampir-Tepe: A Reconstruction." D. V. Rusanov. *BAI*, Vol. 8 (1994), pp. 155-160.

Russo et al. (2008): "Phytochemical and genetic analyses of ancient cannabis from Central Asia." Ethan B. Russo et al. *Journal of Experimental Botany, Vol. 59, No. 15*, pp. 4171-4182.

Sadakata (1996): "Inscriptions kharoṣṭhī provenant du marché aux antiquités de Peshawar." Akira Sadakata. *JA*, 284.2 (1996), pp. 301-324.

Saha (1970): *Buddhism and Buddhist literature in Central Asia.* Kshanika Saha. Calcutta, Firma K. L. Mukhopadhyay.

Saint-Denys (1876): *Ethnographie des peuples étrangers à la chine. Ouvrage composé au XIII siècle de notre ère par Ma-Touan-lin.* Marquis d'Hervey de Saint-Denys. Paris.

St. George (1974): *Soviet Deserts and Mountains.* George St. George. Amsterdam, Time-Life International.

Salomon (1982): "The "Avaca" Inscription and the Origin of the Vikrama Era." Richard Salomon. *Journal of the American Oriental Society*, Vol. 102, No. 1. (Jan. – Mar. 1982), pp. 59-68.

Salomon (1986): "The Inscription of Senavarma, King of Oḍi." *Indo-Iranian Journal*, Vol. 29, No. 4 (Oct., 1986), pp. 261-293.

Salomon (1991): Epigraphic remains of Roman traders in Egypt." Richard Salomon. *Journal of the American Oriental Society 111.4* (1991), pp. 731-736.

Salomon (2003): "Three Kharoṣṭhī Reliquary Inscriptions in the Institute of Silk Road Studies." Richard Salomon. *Silk Road Art and Archaeology* IX, pp. 39-69.

Salomon (2005): "The Indo-Greek Era of 186/5 B.C. in a Buddhist Reliquary Inscription." Richard Salomon. In: *AAC*, pp. 359-401.

Saran (2005): *Chasing the Monk's Shadow: A Journey in the Footsteps of Xuanzang*. Mishi Saran. Penguin/Viking, New Delhi.

Sarianidi (1971): "The Lapis Lazuli Route in the Ancient East." V. I. Sarianidi. *Archaeology Magazine*, January 1971, pp. 12-15.

Sarianidi (1980): "The Treasure of Golden Hill." *American Journal of Archaeology*, Vol. 84, No. 2 (Apr. 1980), pp. 125-131.

Sarianidi (1985): *The Golden Hoard of Bactria: From the Tillya-tepe Excavations in Northern Afghanistan*. Victor Sarianidi. 1985. Harry N. Abrams, New York.

Sarianidi (1989): "Early Kushan Jeweller's Art." Victor Sarianidi. *International Association for the Study of the Cultures of Central Asia Information Bulletin*, Issue 15. Moscow, Nauka Publishers, pp. 124-134.

Sarianidi (1990-1992): "Tilya Tepe: The Burial of a Noble Warrior." V. Sarianidi. *PERSICA XIV*, 1990-1992, pp. 103-130.

Sarianidi (2008): "Ancient Bactria's Golden Horde." Viktor Ivanovitch Sarianidi. In: *AHTNMK*, pp. 211-217.

Sarianidi and Kowalski (1971): "The Lapis Lazuli Route in the Ancient East." V. I. Sarianidi and Luba H. Kowalski. *Archaeology*, Vol. 24, No. 1 (Jan. 1971), pp. 12-15.

Sawyer (2004): *Fire and Water: The Art of Incendiary and Aquatic Warfare in China*. Ralph D. Sawyer with the collaboration of Mei-chün Lee Sawyer. Westview Press, Cambridge, MA.

Schafer (1950): "The Camel in China down to the Mongol Dynasty." Edward H. Schafer. *Sinologica* II, (1950), 3, pp. 165-194, 263-290.

Schafer (1952): "The Pearl Fisheries of Ho-p'u." Edward H. Schafer. *JAOS*, Vol. 72 (1952), pp. 155-168.

Schafer (1955): "Orpiment and Realgar in Chinese Technology and Tradition." Edward H. Schafer. *JAOS*, Vol. 75 (1955), pp. 73-89.

Schafer (1957): "Rosewood, Dragon's Blood, and Lac." Edward H. Schafer. *JAOS*, Vol. 77 (1957), pp. 129-136.

Schafer (1963): *The Golden Peaches of Samarkand: A study of T'ang Exotics*. Edward H. Schafer. University of California Press. Berkeley and Los Angeles. First paperback edition: 1985.

Schafer (1965): "The Origin of an Era." Edward H. Schafer. *JAOS*, Vol. 85, No. 4 (Oct.-Dec. 1965), pp. 543-550.

Schafer (1967): *The Vermilion Bird: T'ang Images of the South*. Edward H. Schafer. University of California Press. Berkeley and Los Angeles.

Scheidel (2009): *Rome and China: Comparative Perspectives on Ancient World Empires*. Edited by Walter Scheidel. Oxford University Press.

Schettler (1981): *Kashmir, Ladakh & Zanskar*. Rolf Schettler. Lonely Planet Publications. South Yarra, Victoria, Australia.

Schiltz (2008a): "Tillya Tepe: The Hill of Gold: A Nomad Necropolis." Véronique Schiltz. In: *AHTNMK*, pp. 219-231.

Schiltz (2008b): "Tillya Tepe Catalog." Véronique Schiltz. In: *AHTNMK*, pp. 232-298.

Schindel (2011): "The Era of the Bactrian Documents: A Reassessment." Nickolaus Schindel. 2011. Gandhāran Studies, No. 5, pp. 1-10.

Schmidt (1991): *Himalayan Passage: Seven Months in the High country of Tibet, Nepal, China, India & Pakistan*. Jeremy Schmidt. The Mountaineers Books, Seattle.

Schmitthenner (1979): "Rome and India: Aspects of Universal History during the Principate." Walter Schmitthenner. *The Journal of Roman Studies*, Vol. 69 (1979), pp. 90-106.

Schoff (1912): *The Periplus of the Erythræan Sea*. Wilfred H. Schoff. 1912. New York, Longmans, Green, and Co. 2nd Edition. Reprint: New Delhi. Oriental Books Reprint Corporation. 1974.

Schoff (1913): "The Name of the Erythraean Sea." Wilfred H. Schoff. *Journal of the American Oriental Society*, Vol. 33. (1913), pp. 349-362.

Schoff (1914): *Parthian Stations by Isidore of Charax: An account of the overland trade route between the Levant and India in the first century B.C.* The Greek text, with a translation and commentary by Wilfred H. Schoff. 1914. Reprint by Ares Publishers, Chicago. 1989.

Schuessler (2007): *ABC Etymological Dictionary of Old Chinese.* Axel Schuessler. University of Hawai'i Press. 2007.

Schuessler (2009): *Minimal Old Chinese and Later Han Chinese: A Companion to Grammata Serica Recensa.* Axel Schuessler. University of Hawai'i Press. 2009.

Schwarz and Giuliani (2001): "Emerald Deposits – A Review." D. Schwarz and G. Giuliani. *Australian Gemmologist* (2001) **21**, pp. 17-23.

Scott (1998): "The Perennial Message of 'the Goddess': Enduring Themes down the Ages in Bactria." David Scott. *East and West*, Vol. 48, (1998), No. 1, pp. 27-39.

Scott (2002): *Copper and bronze in art: corrosion, colorants, conservation.* David A. Scott, Getty Conservation Institute.

Scott-Moncrieff (1924): "The Roads of the North-West Frontier." George K. Scott-Moncrieff. *Blackwood's Magazine*, No. MCCCIV, Vol. CCXV, June 1924, pp. 743-757.

Sear (1988): *Roman Coins and Their Values.* David R. Sear. 4th Revised Edition, Seaby.

Sedlar (1980): *India and the Greek World. A Study in the Transmission of Culture.* Jean W. Sedlar. Totowa, New Jersey, Rowman and Littlefield.

Seel (1972a): *Pompeius Trogus: Weltgeschichte von den Anfängen bis Augustus. Im Auszug des Justin.* Otto Seel. Artemis Verlag, Zürich/München. (In German – with Introduction, Translation, and Notes).

Seel (1972b): *M. Iuniani Iustini epitoma Historiarum Philippicarum Pompei Trogi, Accedunt prologi in Pompeium Trogum.* Otto Seel. (Stuttgart 1972). (Latin text based on edition of Franz Ruel).

Sehrai (1979): *Hund: The Forgotten City of Gandhara.* Fidaullah Sehrai. Peshawar, Pakistan.

Sehrai (1980): *A Brief Guide to Peshawar Museum.* Fidaullah Sehrai. Peshawar, Pakistan.

Seland (2010a): "Ports and Political Power in the *Periplus*: complex societies and maritime trade on the Indian Ocean in the first century A.D." Eivind Heldaas Seland. *BAR International Series 2102.* 2012.

Seland (2010b): "The *Liber Pontificalis* and the Red Sea trade of the early-mid fourth century AD: a working paper from the project Palmyrena: City, Hinterland and Caravan Trade between Orient and Occident." Eivind Heldaas Seland. Accessed on 10 October 2011 from: http://www.org.uib.no/palmyrena/

Seland (2013): "Ancient Afghanistan and the Indian Ocean: Maritime Links of the Kushan Empire ca 50-200 CE." Eivind Heldaas Seland. *Journal of Indian Ocean Archaeology* No. 9, 2013, pp. 66-74.

Sellwood (1983a): "Parthian coins." David Sellwood. *CHI*, 3 (1), (1983), pp. 279-298.

Sellwood (1983b): "Minor states in southern Iran." David Sellwood. *CHI*, 3 (1), (1983), pp. 299-321.

Semenov (1998). *Travels in the Tian'-shan' 1856-1857.* Peter Petrovich Semenov. Edited and annotated by Colin Thomas. Translated by Liudmila Gilmour, et al. The Hakluyt Society, London, 1998.

Sen (2003): *Buddhism, Diplomacy, and Trade: the Realignment of Sino-Indian Relations, 600-1400.* Tansen Sen. University of Hawaii Press and the Association for Asian Studies.

Senior (2004): "The Indo-Greek and Indo-Scythian King Sequences in the Second and First Centuries BC." Robert C. Senior. *Oriental Numismatic Society Newsletter* No. 179, Spring 2004, Supplement, pp. 1-24.

Senior (2008a): "The Final Nail in the Coffin of Azes II." R. C. Senior. *Journal of the Oriental Numismatic Society* 197 (2008), pp. 25-27.

Senior (2008b): "Gondophares-Sases and Nahapana." R. C. Senior. *Journal of the Oriental Numismatic Society* 197 (2008), pp. 27-28.

Shafer (1947): "Linguistics in History." Robert Shafer. *JAOS*, Vol. 67, No, 4. (Oct. – Dec. 1947), pp. 296-305.

Shaffer (1996): *Maritime Southeast Asia to 1500*. Lynda Norene Shaffer. Armonk, New York, M.E. Sharpe, Inc.

Shahrani (2002): *The Kirghiz and Wakhi of Afghanistan: Adaptation to Closed Frontiers and War*. M. Nazif Shahrani. University of Washington Press, Seattle and London. 1st edition 1979. With new preface and epilogue. 2002.

Shaikh (1987): "Early Trade in Indus Valley." Nilofer Shaikh. *Journal of Central Asia*, Vol. X, No. 2, December, 1987, pp. 61-96. Note: Nilofer Shaikh's name is misspelled "Sheikh" in a couple of places in this issue of the journal.

Shaikh (1988): "Lapis Lazuli in Indus Valley (From 6th Millennium to Early 2nd Millennium BC)." Nilofar Shaikh. *Journal of Central Asia*, Vol. XI, No. 1, July 1988, pp. 127-139.

Sharma (1953): "Exploration of Historical Sites." Y. D. Sharma. *Ancient India: Bulletin of the Archaeological Survey of India*, Number 9, 1953. Special Jubilee Number. Published by the Director General, Archaeological Survey of India, New Delhi, 1984, pp. 116-169.

Sharma (1969): *Excavations at Kausāmbī 1949-50*. G. R. Sharma. *Memoirs of the Archaeological Survey of India No. 74*. Delhi, 1969.

Sharifi (2011): "New Evidence on Cultural Relations in Northeastern Iran in the Parthian Period: Results of Archaeological Excavations at Dibaj Damghan." Mahnaz Sharifi. *The Silk Road*, Volume 9, 2011, pp. 42-52.

Shamir (1999): "Textiles, Basketry and Cordage from 'En Raḥel." Orit Shamir. *'Atiqot* XXXVIII, 142-999, pp. 91-123.

Shamir (2001): "Byzantine and Early Islamic Textiles Excavated in Israel." Orit Shamir. *Textile History*, **32** (1), pp. 93-105.

Shamir (2002)a: "Textiles found along the Spice Route joining Petra and Gaza from the Find Spots." Orit Shamir. Unpublished (emailed by author).

Shamir (2002)b: "Coloured Textiles found along the Spice Route joining Petra and Gaza." Orit Shamir. Unpublished (emailed by author).

Sharma (1976): *Mathura Museum and Art (A Comprehensive Pictorial Guide Book)*, Second Revised and Enlarged Edition. R. C. Sharma. 1976. Government Museum, Mathura.

Shastri (1998): *The Sātavāhanas and the Western Kshatrapas: A Historical Framework*. Ajay Mitra Shastri. Dattsons, Nagpur.

Shastri (1999): "The Kṣaharātas of Western India : Fresh Light." Ajay Mitra Shastri. *The Indian Historical Review*. Volume XXVI (July 1999), pp. 23-59.

Shaw (1871): *Visits to High Tartary, Yarkand and Kashgar*. Robert Shaw. 1871. Reprint: Oxford University Press, 1984.

Shaw (1876): "A Prince of Kâshghar on the Geography of Eastern Turkistan." R. B. Shaw. *Journal of the Royal Geographical Society of London*, Vol. 46 (1876), pp. 277-298.

Shaw and Nicholson (1995): *British Museum Dictionary of Ancient History*. Ian Shaw and Paul Nicholson. BCA by arrangement with the British Museum Press, London.

Shchutskii (1980): *Researches on the I Ching*. Iulian K. Schchutskii. Translated and edited by William L. MacDonald, Tsuyoshi Hasegawa and Hellmut Wilheim. Originally published in Moscow, 1960. 1st English version: Princeton University Press, 1979. Paperback edition: Routledge & Kegan Paul, London, 1985.

Sheldon (2006): "The Ethnic and Linguistic Identity of the Parthians: A Review of the Evidence from Central Asia." John Sheldon. *Asian Ethnicity*, Vol. 7, No. 1, February 2006, pp. 1-17.

Sheppard (2008): *Alexander the Great at War: His Army ♦ His Battles ♦ His Enemies*. Edited by Ruth Sheppard. Osprey Publishing, Oxford.

Sherkova (1990): "Hoards of Roman coins in India as a manifestation of the Empire's eastern trade: on the methodology of research." T. Sherkova. *International Association for the Study of the Cultures of Central Asia Information Bulletin*, Issue 17 (1990). Moscow, Nauka Publishers, pp. 100-113.

Sherratt and Sherratt (1998): "Small worlds: interaction and identity in the ancient Mediterranean." Andrew and Susan Sherratt. In: Cline, E. and Harris-Cline, D. (eds.), *The Aegean and the Orient in the second millennium BC* (Liège), pp. 329-343. Downloaded from: http://web.arch.ox.ac.uk/archatlas/Trade/SmallWorlds.pdf on 7 November 2005.

Sherratt (2006): "The Trans-Eurasian Exchange: The Prehistory of Chinese Relations with the West." Andrew Sherratt. In: *CEAW*, pp. 30-61.

Sherwin-White and Kuhrt (1993): *From Samarkhand to Sardis : A new approach to the Seleucid empire.* Susan Sherwin-White and Amélie Kuhrt. University of California Press, Berkeley and Los Angeles.

Shi, Yao and Yang. (1998): "Decadal climatic variations recorded in Guliya ice core and comparison with the historical documentary data from East China during the last 2000 years." SHI Yafeng, YAO Tandong and YANG Bao. *Science in China (Series D)*, Vol. 42 Supp., August 1999, pp. 91-100.

Shiba (1970): *Commerce and Society in Sung China*. Originally published in Japanese as *Sōdai shōgyō-shi kenkyū*. Tokyo, Kazama shobō, 1968. Yoshinobu Shiba. Translation by Mark Elvin, Center for Chinese Studies, University of Michigan.

Shimazaki (1969): "Ku-shih 姑師 and the Anterior and Posterior Kingdoms of Kü-shih 車師." Akira Shimazaki. *MTB*, No. 27 (1969), pp. 27-81.

Shiratori (1923): "Sur l'origine des Hiong-nou." Kurakichi Shiratori. *JA*, CCII, Jan-Mar, 1923, pp. 71-81.

Shiratori (1956a): "A Study on T'iao-chih 條支." Kurakichi Shiratori. *MTB*, 15 (1956), pp. 1-23.

Shiratori (1956b): "Chinese Ideas Reflected in the Ta-ch'in 大秦 Accounts." Kurakichi Shiratori. *MTB*, 15 (1956), pp. 25-72.

Shiratori (1956c): "The Geography of the Western Region Studied on the Basis of the Ta-ch'in Accounts." Kurakichi Shiratori. *MTB*, 15, (1956), pp. 73-163.

Shiratori (1956d): "A New Attempt at the Solution of the Fu-lin 拂林 Problem." Kurakichi Shiratori. *MTB*, 15 (1956), pp. 165-329.

Shiratori (1957): "On the Ts'ung-ling 蔥嶺 Traffic Route Described by C. Ptolemaeus." Kurakichi Shiratori. *MTB*, No. 16 (1957), pp. 1-34.

Siddall (2006): "Not a day without a line drawn: Pigment and painting techniques of Roman Artists." Ruth Siddall. *Infocus* Issue 2, 2006, pp. 18-31.

Sidebotham & Zitterkopf (1995): "Routes Through the Eastern Desert of Egypt." Steven E. Sidebotham and Ronald E. Zitterkop. *E X P E D I T I O N* Volume 37, No. 2 (1995), pp. 39-52.

Sieg (1918): "Ein einheimischer Name für Toχrï." Emil Sieg. In: *Sitzungsberichte der Königlich Preussischen Akademie der Wissenschaften*. Berlin.

Sieg and Siegling (1908): *Tocharisch, die Sprache der Indoskythen. Vorläufige Bemerkungen über eine bisher unbekannte indogermanische Literatursprache.* Emil Sieg and Wilhelm Siegling. Sitzungsberichte der Königlich Preussischen Akademie der Wissenschaften. 1908, 39. Akademie der Wissenschaften, Berlin 1908, 1916.

Simonetta (1958): "A New Essay on the Indo-Greeks The Śakas and the Pahlavas." Alberto M. Simonetta. *East and West*, Vol. 9, No. 3 (September 1958), pp. 154-183.

Simonetta (1978): "The Chronology of the Gondopharean Dynasty." Alberto M. Simonetta with comments by François Widemann. *East and West*, Vol. 28, Nos. 1-4 (Dec. 1978), pp. 155-191.

Simonin (2011): *Hellénisme et phénomènes d'acculturation en Asie Centrale à travers la numismatique* (250 av. n.è. – 150 de n.è.). Two Volumes. Antoinine Simonin. Mémoire de Master, Présenté par A. Simonin sous la direction de M. C. Brélaz. Université de Strasbourg.

Sims-Williams and Cribb (1995/6): "A New Bactrian Inscription of Kanishka the Great." Nicholas Sims-Williams & Joe Cribb. *Silk Road Art and Archaeology* 4 (1996), pp. 75-142.

Sims-Williams (1997): "New Findings in Ancient Afghanistan – the Bactrian documents discovered from the Northern Hindu-Kush." A lecture given by Nicholas Sims-Williams in Tokyo in 1997. Downloaded 16 April 2002 from: http://www.gengo.l.u-tokyo.ac.jp/~hkum/bactrian.html

Sims-Williams (1998): "Further notes on the Bactrian inscription of Rabatak, with an Appendix on the names of Kujula Kadphises and Vima Taktu in Chinese." Nicholas Sims-Williams. Proceedings of the Third European Conference of Iranian Studies Part 1: Old and Middle Iranian Studies. Edited by Nicholas Sims-Williams. Wiesbaden. 1998, pp. 79-93.

Sims-Williams (2000): "The Iranian Inscriptions of Shatial." Nicholas Sims-Williams. *Indologica Taurinensia*, Volume XXIII-XXIV. Edizioni A.I.T., Torina. 1997-98 [2000], pp. 524-541.

Sims-Williams (2002): "Ancient Afghanistan and its invaders: Linguistic evidence from the Bactrian documents and inscriptions." Nicholas Sims-Williams. In: *IILP, Proceedings of the British Academy*, **116,** 225-242.

Sims-Williams (2008): "The Bactrian Inscription of Rabatak: A New Reading." Nicholas Sims-Williams. *Bulletin of the Asia Institute* 18, 2008, pp. 53-68.

Sims-Williams (2012): "Bactrian Historical Inscriptions of the Kushan Period." Nicholas Sims-Williams. *The Silk Road* 10 (2012): 76-80.

Sims-Williams (undated): "Bactrian Language." N. Sims-Williams. In: *Encyclopaedia Iranica*, pp. 344-349. Downloaded from: http://www.iranica.com/articlenavigation/index.html on 20 April 2007.

Sims-Williams and de la Vaissière (2007). "**JABḠUYA**, Arabo-Persian form of the Central Asian title *yabḡu*." Nicholas Sims-Williams and Etienne de la Vaissière. In: *Encyclopædia Iranica*. Accessed from: http://www.iranicaonline.org/articles/jabguya on 5 September 2011.

Sinor (1990): "The establishment and dissolution of the Türk empire." Denis Sinor. In: *CHEIA* (1990), pp. 285-316.

Sinor (1996): "The Türk Empire. Part One: The First Türk Empire (553-682)." D. Sinor. In: *HCCA*, Vol. III, pp. 327-335.

Sircar (1971): *Studies in the Geography of Ancient and Medieval India* (1960), Dineshchandra Sircar. Second Edition Revised and Enlarged. 1971. Motilal Banarsidass, Delhi.

Sircar (1975): *Inscriptions of Aśoka*. D.C. Sircar. Third Edition (Revised). Ministry of Information and Broadcasting, Government of India, New Delhi, Bombay, Calcutta, Madras.

Sircar (1980): "Indian Influence on the Geographical Names of South-East Asia." D. C. Sircar. In: *Imprints of Indian Thought and Culture Abroad. Vivekananda Kendra Patrika* Vol. 9, No. 1. February 1980, pp. 51-56. Madras.

Sitwell (1984): *The World the Romans Knew*. N. H. H. Sitwell. 1984. London, Hamish Hamilton.

Skaff (2005): "Survival in the Frontier Zone: Comparative Perspectives on Identity and Political Allegiance in China's Inner Asian Borderlands during the Sui-Tang Dynastic Transition (617-630)." Jonathan Karam Skaff. *JWH* 15.2 (2004).

Skrine (1926): *Chinese Central Asia*. C. P. Skrine. Methuen, London. Reprint: Barnes & Noble, New York. 1971.

Slane (1991): "Observations on Mediterranean Amphoras and Tablewares Found in India." Kathleen Warner Slane. *RAI*, pp. 204-215.

Smith (1856): *Dictionary of Greek and Roman Geography*. 2 Volumes. Edited by William Smith. Walton and Maberly, London.

Smith and Anthon (1860): *A New Classical Dictionary of Greek and Roman: Biography, Mythology and Geography*. William Smith and Charles Anthon. Harper & Brothers, New York.

Smith (1903): *The Kushān, or Indo-Scythian, Period of Indian History, B.C. 165 to A.D. 320*. Vincent Smith. *Journal of the Royal Asiatic Society of Great Britain and Ireland*, (Jan. 1903), pp. 1-64.

Smith (1908): *The Early History of India*. From 600 B.C. to the Muhammadan Conquest including the Invasion of Alexander the Great. Vincent A. Smith. 1908. Oxford. The Clarendon Press.

Smith (1914): *The Early History of India*: From 600 B.C. to the Muhammadan Conquest including the Invasion of Alexander the Great. Third Edition, Revised and Enlarged. Vincent A. Smith. Oxford. The Clarendon Press.

Smith (1931): *The Historical Geography of the Holy Land*. George Adam Smith. 1st Edition 1894, Hodder & Stroughton Ltd. 25th edition, paperback reprint of the 1931 edition, Fontana Library Edition, London, Collins, 1973.

Smith (1958): *Akbar the Great Mogul 1542-1605*. Vincent A. Smith. 2nd edition. Oxford University Press.

So (2006): "Travels, Contact, and Conversion: Chinese Rediscovery of the West." Francis K. H. So. *Monumenta Serica*, Vol. 54 (2006), pp. 165-184.

Soma (1978): "Studies on the Country of T'iao-Chih." Takashi Soma. 1978. *MTB* No. 36, pp. 1-26.

Sonderegger (2002): "Words in the Desert: the Story of Tocharian and the Tocharians." Morgan Sonderegger. Downloaded from: http://web.mit.edu/smore/www/tocharian-paper.ps on 7 June 2006.

Specht (1883): "Études sur l'asie centrale, d'après les historiens chinois." Édouard Specht. *JA*, Oct.-Dec., 1883, pp. 326-350.

Spooner (1908-9): "Excavations at Shāh-jī-kī-Dhērī." Dr. D. B. Spooner. *Archaeological Survey of India, 1908-9*, pp. 38-59.

Srinivasan (2007): "Pre-Kuṣāṇa Art: A New Concept." Doris Meth Srinivasan. In: *OTCOFE*, pp. 1-28.

Stark (1966): *Rome on the Euphrates: The Story of a Frontier*. Freya Stark. 1966. Reprint: New York, Harcourt, Brace & World, Inc.

Stark (2012): "Nomads and Networks: Elites and Their connections to the Outside World." Sören Stark. In: Stark et al (2012), pp. 106-138.

Stark et al (2012): *Nomads and Networks: the Ancient Art and Culture of Kazakhstan*. Edited by Sören Stark, Karen S. Rubinson with Zainolla S. Samashev and Jenniofer Y. Chu. Princeton University Press, Princeton and London.

Staviskij (1995): "Central Asian Mesopotamia and the Roman world: evidence of contacts." B. J. Staviskij. In: *ITLOTG*, pp. 191-202.

Stein (1900): *Kalhaṇa's Rājataraṅgiṇī - A Chronicle of the Kings of Kaśmīr*, 2 vols. M. Aurel Stein. London, A. Constable & Co. Ltd. 1900. Reprint, Delhi, Motilal Banarsidass, 1979.

Stein (1902): "A Journey of Geographical and Archæological Exploration in Chinese Turkestan." M. A. Stein. *The Geographical Journal*, Vol. 20, No. 6 (Dec. 1902), pp. 575-610.

Stein (1903): *Sand-Buried Ruins of Khotan: Personal narrative of a journey of archaeological and geographical exploration in Chinese Turkestan*. M. A. Stein. T. Fisher Unwin, London.

Stein (1907): *Ancient Khotan: Detailed report of archaeological explorations in Chinese Turkestan*, 2 vols. M. Aurel Stein. 1907. Clarendon Press. Oxford.

Stein (1912): *Ruins of Desert Cathay: Personal narrative of explorations in Central Asia and westernmost China*, 2 vols. M. Aurel Stein. 1912. Reprint: Delhi. Low Price Publications. 1990.

Stein (1921): *Serindia: Detailed report of explorations in Central Asia and westernmost China*, 5 vols. M. Aurel Stein. 1921. London. Oxford. Clarendon Press. Reprint: Delhi. Motilal Banarsidass. 1980.

Stein (1922): "A Chinese expedition across the Pamirs and Hindukush, A.D. 747." M. Aurel Stein. *Indian Antiquary* 1923. 05-07, pp. 98-103, 139-145, 173-177. Downloaded 13 Jan. 1999 from: http://www.pears2.lib.ohio-state.edu/FULLTEXT/TR-ENG/%20aurel.htm.

Stein (1928): *Innermost Asia: Detailed report of explorations in Central Asia, Kan-su and Eastern Iran*, 5 vols. M. Aurel Stein. 1928. Oxford. Clarendon Press. Reprint: Cosmo Publications. New Delhi. 1981.

Stein (1929) *On Alexander's Track to the Indus: Personal Narrative of Explorations on the North-west Frontier of India.* M. Aurel Stein. London. 1929. Reprint, Benjamin Blom. New York. 1972.

Stein (1932): *On Ancient Central Asian Tracks: Brief Narrative of Three Expeditions in Innermost Asia and Northwestern China.* M. Aurel Stein. Reprinted with Introduction by Jeannette Mirsky. Book Faith India, Delhi. 1999.

Stein (1937): *Archaeological Reconnaissances in North-western India and South-eastern Īrān.* Sir Aurel Stein. Macmillan and Co., London.

Stein (1944): *Archaeological Notes from the Hindukush Region.* Sir Aurel Stein. *Journal of the Royal Asiatic Society* (1944) Parts 1 and 2, pp. 5-24.

Stein (1961): *Les tribus anciennes des marches sino-tibétaines.* R. A. Stein. Paris. Presses Universitaires de France.

Stein (1972): *Tibetan Civilization.* R. A. Stein. First published as *La Civilisation tibétaine.* Dunod Editeur, Paris, 1972. This edition by Faber and Faber Ltd., London, 1972. Paperback reprint: Stanford University Press, 1972

Stephens (1837): *Incidents of Travel in Egypt, Arabia Petræa and the Holy Land.* John Lloyd Stephens. New York, Harper and Brothers. Reprint: Mineola, N.Y., Dover Books. 1996.

Stern (1991): "Early Roman Export Glass in India." E. Marianne Stern. In: *Rome and India: The Ancient Sea Trade.* Edited by Vimala Begley and Richard Daniel de Puma. University of Wisconsin Press. pp. 113-124.

Stride (2004): "An Archaeological GIS of the Surkhan Darya Province (Southern Uzbekistan)." Sebastian Stride. *The Silk Road*, Volume 2, Number 2, December 2004, pp. 30-35.

Stride (2007): "Regions and Territories in Southern Central Asia; What the Surkhan Darya Province Tells Us about Bactria." Sebastian Stride. In: *AACABI*, pp. 99-117.

Strong (1930): *The Road to the Grey Pamir.* Anna Louise Strong. Robert M. McBride & Company, New York. 1931.

Sullivan (2000): *The Arts of China*, 4th Edition. Michael Sullivan. University of California Press.

Sun (2000): "The Development of China's Navigation Technology and of the Maritime Silk Route." Sun Guangqi. In: *The Silk Roads: Highways of Culture and Commerce.* 2000. Edited by Vadime Elisseeff. UNESCO Publishing, Berghahn Books, Oxford. New York, pp. 288-303.

Sung (1637): *T'ien kung k'ai wu.* Sung Ying-hsing. 1637. Published as *Chinese Technology in the seventeenth century.* Translated and annotated by E-tu Zen Sun and Shiou-chuan Sun. 1996. Mineola. New York. Dover Publications.

Sutton (1990): *A Thousand Years of East Africa.* John Sutton. Nairobi, British Institute in Eastern Africa. Reprint: 1992.

Swinson (1967): *North-west Frontier: People and Events 1839-1947.* Arthur Swinson. Frederick A. Praeger. New York.

Sykes (1902): "A Fourth Journey in Persia, 1897-1901." P. Molesworthy Sykes. *The Geographical Journal*, Vol. XIX, No. 2, February 1902.

Szemerényi (1980): "Four Old Iranian Ethnic Names: Scythian – Skudra – Sogdian – Saka." Oswald Szemerényi. *Österreichischen Akademie der Wissenschaften, Philosophisch-Historische Klasse*, Wein. Vol. 371, pp. 1-47.

Szynkiewicz (1989): *Interactions between the nomadic cultures of central Asia and China in the Middle Ages.* Slawoj Szynkiewicz. Excerpt from "CENTRE AND PERIPHERY –

Comparative Studies in archaeology." From: http://www.silk-road.com/artl/szynkiewicz 27 May 1999.

Tacitus (109 CE): *The Annals*. Cornelius Tacitus. Trans. by Alfred John Church and William Jackson Brodribb. Downloaded from: http://classics.mit.edu/Tacitus/annals.mb.txt on 28 July 2002.

Takakusu (1896): *A Record of The Buddhist Religion as practised in India and the Malay Archipelago (A.D. 671-695)*. J. Takakusu. An annotated translation of the work by I-tsing, late 7th - early 8th century. London, Clarendon Press. Reprint Delhi, Munshiram Manoharlal, 1966.

Tamot and Alsop (1996): "A Kushan-period Sculpture from the reign of Jaya Varma-, A.D. 184/185, Kathmandu, Nepal." Kashinath Tamot and Ian Alsop. Accessed 6th Jan 1999, from: www.asianet.com/articles/jaka/king.html .

Tanabe (1993): *Silk Road Coins: The Hirayama Collection* by Katsumi Tanabe. A loan exhibition at the British Museum Gallery 69A 1st April to 31st May, 1993. The Institute of Silk Road Studies, Kamakura. English Translation by K. Tanabe, revised by J. Cribb and H. Wang.

Tarn (1901): "Patrocles and the Oxo-Caspian Trade Route." W. W. Tarn. *The Journal of Hellenic Studies*, Vol. 21, (1901), pp. 10-29.

Tarn (1902): "Notes on Hellenism in Bactria and India." W. W. Tarn. *The Journal of Hellenic Studies*, Vol. 22. (1902), pp. 268-293.

Tarn (1940): "Two notes on Seleucid History: 1. Seleucus' 500 elephants, 2. Tarmita." W. W. Tarn. *The Journal of Hellenic Studies*, Vol. 60 (1940), pp. 84-94.

Tarn (1984): *The Greeks in Bactria and India*. William Woodthorpe Tarn. 1st Edition, 1938; 2nd Updated Edition, 1951. 3rd Edition, updated with a Preface and a new bibliography by Frank Lee Holt. Ares Publishers, Inc., Chicago. 1984.

Tatár (1991): "Through the Sayan mountains: trade routes between Mongolia and Siberia." Magdelena Tatár. *ATR*, pp. 51-60.

Taylor (1893). *Central Asia: Travels in Cashmere, Little Thibet and Central Asia*. Compiled and arranged by Bayard Taylor. Revised by Thomas Stevens. New York. Charles Scribner's Sons.

Teggart (1939): *Rome and China*. Frederick J. Teggart. University of California Press.

Temple (1999): *The Crystal Sun: Rediscovering a Lost Technology of the Ancient World*. Robert Temple, 1st edition, 1999. Reprint: Century. Arrow Books edition, 2000.

Thapar (1961): *Aśoka and the Decline of Mauryas*. Romila Thapar. Oxford University Press. 1961. Third Impression. New Delhi. 1980.

Thapar (2002): *The Penguin History of Early India: From the Origins to AD 1300*. Romila Thapar. First published as: *Early India* by Allen Lane, Penguin Press (2002). Published under present title by Penguin Books, 2003.

Thapliyal (1979): *Foreign Elements in Ancient Indian Society: 2nd century BC to 7th century AD*. Uma Prasad Thapliyal. Munshiram Manoharlal Publishers Pvt. Ltd. Delhi,

Theroux (1977): "The Imperiled Nile Delta." Peter Theroux. *National Geographic Magazine*, January, 1997, pp. 2-35.

Thierry (2005): "Yuezhi et Kouchans. Pièges et dangers des sources chinoises." François Thierry. In: *AAC*, pp. 421-539.

Thomas (1906): "Sakastana." F. W. Thomas. *Journal of the Royal Asiatic Society* (1906), pp. 181-216.

Thomas (1913): "The Date of Kanishka." F. W. Thomas. *Journal of the Royal Asiatic Society* (1913), pp. 627-650.

Thomas (1935): *Tibetan Literary Texts and Documents Concerning Chinese Turkestan*. Part I. Selected and translated by F. W. Thomas. Royal Asiatic Society. London.

Thomas (1944): "Sandanes, Nahapāna, Caṣṭana and Kaniṣka : Tung-li P'an-ch'i and Chinese Turkestan." F. W. Thomas. *New Indian Antiquary* VII. 1944, pp. 81-100.

Thomas (1943-46): "Some Notes On Central-Asian Kharoṣṭhī Documents." F. W. Thomas. *Bulletin of the Society of Oriental Studies*, 11, pp. 513-549.

Thorley (1969): "The Development of Trade between the Roman Empire and the East under Augustus." J. Thorley. *Greece & Rome*, 2nd Ser., Vol. 16, No. 2. (Oct. 1969), pp. 209-223.

Thorley (1971): "The Silk Trade between China and the Roman Empire at its height, *circa* A.D. 90-130." J. Thorley. *Greece & Rome*, 2nd Ser., Vol. 18, No. 1. (Apr. 1971), pp. 71-80.

Thorley (1979): "The Roman Empire and the Kushans." John Thorley. *Greece & Rome*, 2nd Series, Vol. 26, No. 2 (Oct. 1979), pp. 181-190.

Thornton (1844): *A* gazetteer *of the* countries adjacent *to* India *on the* north-west. Volume 1. Edward Thornton. Wm. H. Allen and Co. London.

Thornton & Schurr (2004a). C. P. Thornton & T. G. Schurr. "Genes, language, and culture: An example from the Tarim Basin." *Oxford Journal of Archaeology* 23(1): 83-106.

Thornton & Schurr (2004b). "Prehistoric 'Europeans' in Xinjiang? A Case for Multiple Interpretations." C. P. Thornton & T. G. Schurr. *In*: (H. Bolin, ed.) "The Interplay of Past and Present." Stockholm: Södertörn. *Archaeological Studies* 1, pp. 85-98.

Tod (1829-1832): *Annals and Antiquities of Rajasthan.* (1829-1832) James Tod, edited with introduction and notes by William Crooke, Reprint: Low Price Publications, Delhi (1990), Three Volumes.

Tolstov (1961): "Les Scythes de l'Aral et le Khorezm." S. P. Tolstov. *Iranica antiqua*, 1 (1961), pp. 42-92.

Tortchinov (1998): "Science and magic in Ge Hong's "Baopu-zi nei pian." Evgueni A. Tortchinov. A paper presented at The 8th International Conference on the History of Sciences in China, Berlin, August 23–27, 1998. Downloaded on 26 Nov. 2005 from: http://www.levity.com/alchemy/ge_hong.html.

Toynbee (1958): *East to West : A Journey Round the World.* Arnold J. Toynbee. Oxford University Press, London.

Toynbee (1961): *Between Oxus and Jumna.* Arnold J. Toynbee. 1961. London. Oxford University Press.

Townsend (2005): "China and Afghan Opiates: Assessing the Risk." Central Asia-Caucasus Institute & Silk Road Studies Program. Washington, D.C. Jacob Townsend. June 2005. Downloaded from: www.silkroadstudies.org/new/inside/publications/Townsend_Total.pdf on 28 October 2014.

Travis (2008): "Trail of Mare's Milk Leads To First Tamed Horses." John Travis. *Science*, Vol. 322, 17 October 2008, p. 368.

Tremblay (2001) *Pour une histore de la Sérinde. Le manichéisme parmi les peoples et religions d'Asie Centrale d'apré les sources primare*, Xavier Tremblay, Vienna, 2001, Appendice D : Notes sur l'origine des Hephthalites, pp. 183-88.

Tremblay (2005): "Irano-Tocharia et Tocharo-Iranica." Xavier Tremblay. *BSOAS*, 68, 3 (2005), pp. 421-449.

Tremblay (2007): "The Spread of Buddhism in Serindia— Buddhism among Iranians, Tocharians and Turks before the 13th century." Xavier Tremblay. In: *TSOB*, pp. 75-129.

Tschanz (1988): "Unsung Crossroads." David W. Tschanz. *Aramco World* March/April 1988, pp. 24-31.

Ts'en (1981): *Han Shu Hsi Yü Chuan ti li chiao shih.* Ts'en Chung-mien. 1981. Beijing. China Library.

Tucci (1977): "On Swāt. The Dards and Connected Problems." Giuseppe Tucci. *East and West*, Vol. 27, No. 1/4 (December 1977), pp. 9-103.

Tung (1960): *Chronological Tables of Chinese History.* Tung Tso-pin. Hong Kong University Press.

Turner and Rosewater (1958): "The Family Pinnidae in the Western Atlantic." Ruth D. Turner and Joseph Rosewater. *Johnsonia*, Vol. 3 No. 38, June 28 1958, pp. 285-326.

Tupikova, Schemmel and Geus (2014): "Travelling along the Silk Road: A new interpretation of Ptolemy's coordinates." Irina Tupikova, Matthias Schemmel, Klaus Geus. Max Planck Institute for the History of Science, Berlin.

Tyndale (1849): *The Island of Sardinia, including Pictures of the Manners and Customs of the Sardinians,…*" Three Volumes. John Warre Tyndale. London: Richard Bentley.

Uberti (1988): "Glass." Maria Luisa Uberti. In: *The Phoenicians*. Edited: Sabatino Moscati. First published, Venice, 1988. Reprint: I. B. Tauris &Co. Ltd., London & New York, (2001), pp. 536-561.

Uphill (1988): "An Ancient Egyptian Maritime Link with Arabia." E. P. Uphill. *Proceedings of the Seminar For Arabian Studies* Vol. 18 (1988), pp. 163-170.

Uphill (1988b): *Egyptian Towns and Cities*. Eric P. Uphill. Shire Publications Ltd., Bucks, U.K.

Uphill (2000): "The Butic Canal : Its Date and Functions." E. P. Uphill. *Eighth International Congress of Egyptologists - Cairo* (2000), pp. 186-187.

Ustinova (2000): "New Latin and Greek Rock-Inscriptions from Uzbekistan." Yulia Ustinova. *Hephaistos: New Approaches in Classical Archaeology and related Fields.* 18/2000, pp. 169-179.

Vaillant (1725): *Arsacidarum imperium sive Parthorum historia. Ad sidem Numismatum accomodata.* Tomus Primus. J. Foy Vaillant. Canoli Moette, Parisiis. (In Latin).

Vajira (1961): *Mahā-Parinibbāna Sutta*, the 16th text of the Digha-Nikāya of the Pāli Canon translated by Sister Vajira, *Last Days of the Buddha*, 1961, *Selected Buddhist Texts.* Vol. II, part 2, 2nd Impression, 1974, Kandy, Sri Lanka, Buddhist Publication Society.

Valbelle and el-Maksoud (1996): "La marche du Nord-Est." Dominique Valbelle and Mohamed Abd el-Maksoud. *Les Dossiers d'Archeologie*, No. 213 (1996), pp. 60-65.

van der Spek (2001): "The Theatre of Babylon in Cuneiform." R. J. Van der Spek. *Veenhof Anniversary Volume: Studies Presented to Klaas R. Veenhof on the occasion of his sixty-fifth birthday.* Ed. W. H. Soldt. Leiden, pp. 445-456.

van der Sprenkel (1964): *Pan Piao, Pan Ku, and the Han History.* O. B. van der Sprenkel. Canberra, Occasional Paper 3, Australian National University, Centre of Oriental Studies.

van Ess (1999): "The apocryphal texts of the Han dynasty and the old text / new text controversy." Hans van Ess. *T'oung pao* LXXXV (1999), pp. 29-64.

van Wijk (1927): "On dates in the Kaniṣka era." W. E. van Wijk. *Acta Orientalia*, V, pp. 168-170.

Vaux (2001): "Disharmony and derived transparency in Uyghur Vowel Harmony." Bert Vaux. From: *Proceedings of the North East Linguistic Society*. 2000. Pages 1-28.

Venetis & Mozdoor (2003): "The Establishment and Development of Christianity in the Parthian Empire (1st cent.-224/6 A.D.)." Evangelos Venetis and M. Alinia Mozdoor. *Transoxiana* 6, Julio 2003. Downloaded from: http://www.transoxiana.org on 7 July 2003.

Veniukof and Michell (1866): "The Pamir and the Sources of the Amu-Daria." M. Veniukof and J. Michell. *Journal of the Royal Geographic Society of London*, Vol. 36 (1866), pp. 248-263.

Verma (1978): *Medieval Routes to India: Baghdad to Delhi.* H. C. Verma. 1978. Naya Prokash. Calcutta.

Vigne (1842): *Travels in Kashmir, Ladak, Iskardo, the Countries Adjoining the Mountain-course of the Indus, and the Himalaya, North of the Panjab.* 2 Vols. Godfrey Thomas Vigne. H. Colburn, London.

Vissière (1914): "Les designations ethniques: Houei-houei et Lolo." A. Vissière. *JA*, 1914. 11th series, III, pp. 175-182.

Vogelsang (1985): "Early historical Arachosia in South-east Afghanistan; Meeting-place between East and West." W. Vogelsang. *Iranica antiqua, 20 (1985)*, pp. 55-99.

Vogelsang (1988): Book review by Willem Vogelsang of "*La Bactriane sous les Kushans*". *Problèmes d'histoire et de culture.* Translated from the Russian by P. Bernard, et al, 1986. Paris, Libraire d'Amerique et d'Orient. Original title: *Kushanskaja Baktrija, problemy istorii i kul'tury*. Moscow, 1977. *Persica* XIII (1988-1989), pp. 161-166.

Vogelsang (2002): *The Afghans.* Willem Vogelsang. Blackwell Publishers. Oxford.

Volbach (1969): *Early Decorative Textiles.* W. Fritz Volbach. Translated by Yuri Gabriel from the Italian original, *Il Tessuro nell'Arte Antica* 1966 Fratelli Fabbri Editore, Milan. This edition: Paul Hamlyn. Middlesex.

Vollmer *et al.*, eds. (1983): *Silk Roads ♦China Ships. An Exhibition of East-West Trade.* John Vollmer, *et al., eds.* Toronto, Royal Ontario Museum.

von Hagen (1967): *The Roads that led to Rome.* Victor W. von Hagen. Cleveland and New York. The World Publishing Company.

von Hinüber (2001): "Beiträge zur Erklärung der Senavarma-Inschrift." Oskar von Hinüber. Akademie der Wissenschaften und der Literatur 2001, pp. 1-56. Stuttgart: Franz Steiner Verlag.

von Le Coq (1928): *Buried Treasures of Chinese Turkestan: An Account of the Activities and Adventures of the Second and Third German Turfan Expeditions.* Albert von Le Coq. Translated by Anna Barwell. London George Allen & Unwin Ltd. 1928. Reprint: Oxford University Press, 1985.

von Saldern (1966): "Ancient Glass." Axel von Saldern. *Boston Museum Bulletin*, Vol. 64, No. 335 (1966), pp. 4-17.

Wada (1978): "On the Date of the Spread of Buddhism to the East." Sei Wada. *MTB* 36 (1978), pp. 27-38.

Wagner (1998): *A Classical Chinese reader: The Han shu biography of Huo Guang with notes and glosses for students.* Donald B. Wagner. Curzon Press, Richmond, Surrey.

Wainwright (1943): Review of *Egypt in the Classical Geographers* by J. Ball. G. A. Wainwright. *The Journal of Hellenic Studies*, Vol. 63 (1943), pp. 125-126.

Waldman and Mason (2006): *Encyclopedia of European Peoples.* Carl Waldman and Catherine Mason. Facts on File. New York, N.Y.

Walter (1998): *Tocharian Buddhism in Kucha: Buddhism of Indo-European Centum Speakers in Chinese Turkestan before the 10th Century C.E.* Mariko Namba Walter. *Sino-Platonic Papers* Number 85. October 1998, pp. 1-30.

Walter (2006): *Sogdians and Buddhism.* Mariko Namba Walter. *Sino-Platonic Papers* No. 174. Nov 2006. Dept. of East Asian Languages and Civilizations, University of Pennsylvania.

Waltham (1971): *Chuang Tzu; Genius of the Absurd.* Clae Waltham. Arranged from the translation of James Legge. New York, Ace Books.

Wang (1900): *Hanshu Buzhu* 漢書補注 (Commentaries on the *Hanshu*). 2 Volumes. Wang Xianqian 王先謙. Changsha: Xushou tang 虛受堂.

Wang (1949): "An Outline of the Central Government of the Former Han Dynasty." Wang Yü-ch'üan. *Harvard Journal of Asiatic Studies* 12, 1949, pp. 134-187.

Wang (1973): "Some Comments on the Later Standard Histories" Wang Gungwu. In: *Essays on the Sources for Chinese History.* Editors: Donald Leslie, Colin Mackerras, Wang Gungwu. Australian National University Press, Canberra. 1973, pp. 53-63.

Wang (1984): *A Record of Buddhist Monasteries in Lo-yang.* Wang Yi-t'ung. Princeton, N.J., Princeton University Press. (Translation with notes of the *Lo-yang ch'ieh-lan chi* by Yang Hsüan-chih, first published in 547 A.D.)

Wang (1991): "T'ang Maritime Trade Administration." Wang Zhenping. *Asia Major, Third Series*, Vol. IV, 1991, pp. 7-38.

Wang (1996): "The Most Important Findings of Niya in Taklamakan." Wang Binghua. Originally published in *China Culture Pictorial* Vol. 1.2 April 1996. Downloaded on 27 May 1999, from: http://www.silk-road.com/artl/niya.shtml

Wang (1999): "History, Space, and Ethnicity: The Chinese Worldview." Q. Edward Wang. *Journal of World History* 10.2 (1999) 285-305. Downloaded on 17 October 2001, from: http://muse.jhu.edu/demo/jwh/ 10.2wang.html

Wang (1999b): "From the Qiang Barbarians to the Qiang Nationality: The Making of a New Chinese Boundary." Wang Ming-ke. In: *Imaging China: Regional Division and National Unity*, edited by Shu-Min Huang and Cheng-Kuang Hsu Institute of Ethnology, Academia Sinica. Taipei. pp. 43-80.

Wang (2004a): "Cheap fluorite can never be the night-shining jewel." Chunyun Wang. *Jewellery Science and Technology*, Vol. 16 (Serial No. 54), pp. 42-48 (in Chinese with English abstract).

Wang, (2004b). "Night-shining jewel in the mouth of Empress Dowager Cixi: material, nomenclature and source." Chunyun Wang. *Jewellery Science and Technology*, Vol. 16, No. 5 (Serial No. 57), pp.1-8 (in English with Chinese abstract).

Wang (2004c): "A conspectus about historical tracing study of diamond in China." Chuyun Wang. *Superhard Material Engineering*, Vol. 16, No. 4 (Serial No. 56) (in press) (in Chinese with English abstract).

Wang (2007a): "Parthia in China: a Re-examination of the Historical Records." Wang Tao. In: *The Age of the Parthians (The Idea of Iran, Vol. 2)*. Edited by Vesta Sarkhosh Curtis and Sarah Stewart. I. B. Tauris. London, pp. 87-104.

Wang (2007b): "Money in Eastern Central Asia before AD 800." Helen Wang. In: *AACABI*, pp. 399-409.

Wang (2008): "Official Salaries and Local Wages at Juyan, North-West China, First Century BCE to First Century CE." Helen Wang. In: *Wages and Currency: Global Comparisons from Antiquity to the Twentieth Century*. Jan Lucassen. Peter Lang AG, pp. 59-76.

Ward (1989): "The Kun Lun Shan: Desert Peaks of Central Asia." Michael Ward. *The Alpine Journal* (1989-90), pp. 84-96.

Warder (1970): *Indian Buddhism*. A. K. Warder. Reprint: Delhi, Motilal Barnasidass, 1980.

Watson (1961): *Records of the Grand Historian of China*. Burton Watson. New York, Columbia University Press.

Watson (1968): *The Complete Works of Chuang Tzu*. Translated by Burton Watson. Columbia University Press. New York.

Watson (1972): *Transport in Transition : The evolution of traditional shipping in China*. Andrew Watson. Center for Chinese studies, The University of Michigan.

Watson (1974): *Courtier and Commoner in Ancient China: Selections from the* ***History of the Former Han*** *by Pan Ku*. Translated by Burton Watson. Columbia University Press. New York and London.

Watson (1983): "Iran and China." William Watson. *CHI* 3 (1), (1983), pp. 537-558.

Watson (1993): *Records of the Grand Historian of China. Han Dynasty II*. (Revised Edition). Burton Watson. Columbia University Press. New York.

Watters (1904-1905): *On Yuan Chwang's Travels in India*. Thomas Watters. 1904-1905. London. Royal Asiatic Society. Reprint: Delhi. Munshiram Manoharlal. 1973.

Waugh (1999): "The 'Mysterious and Terrible Karatash Gorges': Notes and Documents on the Explorations by Stein and Skrine." Daniel C. Waugh. *The Geographical Journal*, Vol. 165, No. 3. (November, 1999), pp. 306-320.

Waugh (2007): "Richthofen's "Silk Roads": Toward the Archaeology of a Concept." *The Silk Road*. Volume 5, Number 1, Summer 2007, pp. 1-10.

Waugh (2013): "A Road Less Taken?" Daniel C. Waugh. *The Silk Road*. Volume 11, 2013, pp. 188-191.

Weed (2002): "First to Ride." William Speed Weed. *Discover Magazine* (March, 2002), pp. 54-61.

Weinstein (2000): "Biblical evidence of spice trade between India and the land of Israel : a historical analysis." Brian Weinstein. *The Indian Historical Review*. Volume XXVII (January 2000), pp. 12-28.

Wendrich, et al. (2003): "Berenike Crossroads: The Integration of Information." W. Z. Wendrich, et al. *Journal of the Economic and Social History of the Orient*. Volume 46, Number 1, 2003, pp. 46-87.

Weatherford (2004): *Genghis Khan and the Making of the Modern World*. Jack Weatherford. Three Rivers Press, New York.

Wheatley (1975): "Analecta Sino-Africana Recensa." Paul Wheatley. 1975. In: *East Africa and the Orient. Cultural Syntheses in Pre-Colonial Times*. Neville H. Chittick and Robert I. Rotberg, eds., 1975. New York. Africana Publishing Company, pp. 76-114.

Wheeler and Piggott (1945): "Iran and India in Pre-Islamic Tines: A Lecture." R. E. M. Wheeler, with an Appendix by Stuart Piggott. Lecture first delivered in Tehran in 1945. Published in *Ancient India: Bulletin of the Archaeological Survey of India*, New Delhi, Number 4, July 1947 – January 1948, pp. 85-103.

Wheeler, Ghosh and Deva (1946): "Arikamedu: an Indo-Roman Trading-station on the East Coast of India." R. E. M. Wheeler, A. Ghosh and Krishna Deva. *Ancient India: Bulletin of the Archaeological Survey of India* Number 2, 1946. Reprint: Archaeological Survey of India, New Delhi, 1983, pp. 17-124.

Wheeler (1947-48): "Iran and India in pre-Islamic Times: a Lecture." R. E. M. Wheeler with an Appendix by Stuart Piggott. *Ancient India: Bulletin of the Archaeological Survey of India* Number 4, July 1947-January 1948, pp. 85-103.

Whitehouse (1991): "Epilogue: Roman Trade in Perspective." David Whitehouse. *RAI*, pp. 216-218.

Whitehouse (1997): "Looking Through Roman Glass." David Whitehouse. *Archaeology*, September/October 1997, pp. 79-82.

Whitehouse (2000): "Did the Vikings make a telescope?" David Whitehouse. *BBC News*. Downloaded from: http://news.bbc.co.uk/hi/english/sci/tech/newsidx702000/702478.stm on 3 December 2001.

Widemann (2000): "Scarcity of Precious Metals and Relative Chronology of Indo-Greek and Related Coinages (1st Century B.C-1st Century A.D.)." François Widemann. *East and West*, Vol. 50 – Nos. 1-4 (December 2000), pp. 227-258.

Widemann (2003): "Maues King of Taxila: An Indo-Greek Kingdom with a Saka King." François Widemann. *East and West*, Vol. 53, No. 1/4 (December 2003), pp. 95-125

Widemann (2007): "Civil Wars and Alliances in Bactria and North-Western India after the Usurpation of King Eucratides." François Widemann. *East and West*, Vol. 57, No. 1/4 (December 2007), pp. 9-28.

Wieger (1927): *Chinese Characters: Their origin, etymology, history, classification and signification*. L. Wieger, S.J. English translation by L. Davrout, S.J. 2nd Edition, enlarged and revised according to the 4th French edition. 1927. Reprint Paragon Book Reprint Corp. and Dover Publications New York. 1965.

Weins (1963): "The Historical and Geographical Role of Urumchi, Capital of Chinese Central Asia." Herold J. Wiens. *Annals of the Association of American Geographers*, Vol. 53, No. 4 (Dec., 1963), pp. 441-464.

Wiedemann (1995): *Emperors and Gladiators*. Thomas E. J. Wiedemann. Routledge.

Williams (1909): *A Syllabic Dictionary of the Chinese Language*. Revised Edition. S. Wells Williams. North China Union College, Tung Chou, near Peking, China.

Williamson (1966): *Procopius: The Secret History*. G. A. Williamson. Penguin Books. London. The Folio Society, 1990.

Wilkinson (2012): *Chinese History: A New Manual*. Endymion Wilkinson. Harvard Yenching Institute Monograph Series 84. Harvard University Asia Center.

Wilson (undated): *The Wall of Alexander against Gog and Magog and the Expedition sent out to find it by the Khalif Wāthiq in 842 A.D.* C. E. Wilson. Asia Major, Introductory Volume. Reprint, London, Probasthain & Co.

Wilson (1840): *The Vishnu Purana: A System of Hindu Mythology and Tradition*. Translated by Horace Hayman Wilson. Accessed from: http://www.sacred-texts.com/hin/vp/index.htm.

Wilson (2004): "Demetrios II of Bactria and hoards from Ai Khanoum." L. M. Wilson. ONS Newsletter 180, pp. 12-13.

Winchester (2008): *The man who loved China: The Fantastic Story of the Eccentric Scientist Who Unlocked the Mysteries of the Middle Kingdom.* Simon Winchester. HarperCollins*Publishers.* New York.

Wimmel (1996): *The Alluring Target : In Search of the Secrets of Central Asia.* Kenneth Wimmel. Trackless Sands Press. Washington, Palo Alto.

Witzel (2000): "The Home of the Aryans." Michael Witzel. Muenchener Studien zur Spachwissenschaft Beihaft NF 19, 2000, pp. 283-388. Downloaded on 2 August 2003 from: http://www.people.fas.harvard.edu/~witzel/AryanHome.pdf

Witzel (2001): "Autochthonous Aryans? The Evidence from Old Indian and Iranian Texts." Michael Witzel. *Electronic Journal of Vedic Studies* 7-3 (EJVS) 2001, pp. 1-115.

Witzel (2003): *Linguistic Evidence for Cultural Exchange in Prehistoric Western Central Asia.* Michael Witzel. *Sino-Platonic Papers*, 129 (December, 2003).

Witzel (2006): "Early Loan Words in Western Central Asia: Indicators of Substrate Populations, Migrations, and Trade Relations." Michael Witzel. In: *CEAW*, pp. 158-190.

Wolski (1982): "Le problème de la foundation de l'État gréco-bactrien." Józef Wolski. *Iranica antiqua*, 17 (1982), pp. 131-146.

Wolters (1967): *Early Indonesian Commerce: A study of the origins of Śrīvijaya.* O. W. Wolters. Cornell University Press, Ithaca, New York.

Wong (1984): "Peoples of China's Far Provinces." Wong How-man. *National Geographic*, Vol. 165, No. 3, pp. 283-333.

Wood (1872): *A Journey to the Source of the River Oxus.* Captain John Wood. With an essay on the Geography of the Valley of the Oxus by Colonel Henry Yule. London: John Murray.

Wood (1959): *The Gold Types of the Great Kushāṇas.* Allen H. Wood III, *Numismatic Notes and Monographs* General Editor: A. K. Narain, No. 9. The Numismatic Society of India, Varanasi, 1959.

Wood (1997): *In the footsteps of Alexander the Great: A Journey from Greece to Asia.* Michael Wood. BBC, London. First published 1997. Paperback Edition. 2001.

Wood (2002): *The Silk Road.* Frances Wood. The Folio Society. London.

Woodcock (1966): *The Greeks in India.* George Woodcock. Faber and Faber, London.

Wornam (1875): "Colores." Ralph Nicholson Wornum. In: *A Dictionary of Greek and Roman Antiquities.* William Smith. John Murray publishers, London, 1875, pp. 320-322.

Wriggins (1996): *XUANZANG. A Buddhist Pilgrim on the Silk Road.* Revised and updated. Sally Hovey Wriggins. Boulder, Colorado, WestviewPress.

Wriggins (2004): *The Silk Road Journey with XUANZANG.* Sally Hovey Wriggins. Boulder, Colorado. WestviewPress.

Wright (1978): *The Sui Dynasty.* Arthur F. Wright. New York, Alfred A. Knopf.

Wrigley (1997): "The *Periplus* and Related Matters." Christopher Wrigley. *Azania, Vol.* XXXII (1997), pp. 112-117.

Wu (1982): *The Chinese Heritage.* K. C. Wu. New York. Crown Publishers, Inc.

Wylie (1881) "Description of the Western Regions from the *Ts'een Han Shoo* [*Han Shu*], Bk. 96." Alexander Wylie. *Journal of the Anthropological Institute of Great Britain and Ireland*, Vol. X (1881), pp. 20-73.

Wylie (1990): "How did Trajan Succeed in Subduing Parthia where Mark Anthony failed?" Graham Wylie. *The Ancient History Bulletin* 4.2 (1990), pp. 37-43. Downloaded from: http://collection.nlc-bnc.ca/100/201/ancient_history/2001-04-27/ahb-4-42d.html, on 28 Feb. 2003.

Xiang (2006): *The Story of Gold.* Xiang Zhonghua. Foreign Languages Press, Beijing.

Xiong (2008): *Historical Dictionary of Medieval China.* Victor Cunrui Xiong. Scarecrow Press.

Xu (1995): "The Discovery of the Xinjiang Mummies and Studies of the Origin of the Tocharians." Xu Wenkan. *The Journal of Indo-European Studies* Volume 23, Number 3 & 4, Fall/Winter 1995, pp.357-369.

Xu (1996): "The Tokharians and Buddhism." Xu Wenkan, In: *Studies in Central and East Asian Religions* 9, pp. 1-17 (1996). Downloaded on June 14 2003, from: http://61.54.131.141:8010 /Resource/Book/Edu/JXCKS/TS010057/0001_ts010057.htm

Xu (2002): "The Archaeology of the Great Wall of the Qin and Han dynasties." Xu Pingfang. *Journal of East Asian Archaeology*, Vol. 3, 1–2, pp. 259-281.

Yablonsky (1995): "Written Sources and the History of Archaeological Studies of the Saka in Central Asia. Leonid T. Yablonsky. In: *Nomads of the Eurasian Steppes in the Early Iron Age*. Edited by Jeannine Davis-Kimball, Vladimir A. Bashilov and Leonid T. Yablonsky. Zinat Press, Berkeley, California, pp. 193-200.

Yablonsky (1995b): "The Material Culture of the Saka and Historical Reconstruction." Leonid T. Yablonsky. In: *Nomads of the Eurasian Steppes in the Early Iron Age*. Edited by Jeannine Davis-Kimball, Vladimir A. Bashilov and Leonid T. Yablonsky. Zinat Press, Berkeley, California, pp. 201-240.

Yang (1961): "Hostages in Chinese History." Lien-sheng Yang. In: *Studies in Chinese Institutional History*, Harvard-Yenching Institute Studies XX, Harvard University Press, Cambridge, Mass., pp. 507-521.

Yap (2009): *Wars with the Xiongnu: A Translation from the Zizhi tongtian*. Joseph P. Yap. AuthorHouse, Bloomington, Indiana.

Yardley (1994): *Justin: Epitome of the Philippic History of Pompeius Trogus*. Translated and with introduction by J. C. Yardley. The American Philological Association.

Yonge (1862): *The Roman History of Ammianus Marcellinus during the reigns of the Emperors Constantius, Julian, Jovianus, Valentinian, and Valens*. Translated by Charles Duke Yonge. London: Bohn. Reprint 1902: George Bell & Sons, London.

Yoshida (2003): "On the origin of the Sogdian surname Zhaowu 昭武 and related problems." Yutaka Yoshida. *JA*, 291.1-2 (2003), pp. 35-67.

Young (2001): *Rome's Eastern Trade : International Commerce and Imperial Policy, 31 BC – AD 305*. Gary K. Young. Routledge. London and New York. August 2001.

Younghusband (1890): "Journeys in the Pamirs and Adjacent Countries" F. E. Younghusband. *Proceedings of the Royal Geographical Society and Monthly Record of Geography*, New Monthly Series, Vol. 14, No. 4 (Apr., 1892), pp. 205-234.

Younghusband (1896): *The Heart of a Continent*. Francis E. Younghusband. John Murray, London. Facsimile reprint: (2005) Elbiron Classics.

Younghusband (1909): *KASHMIR*. Francis Younghusband. Illustrations painted by E. Molyneux. 1909. 2nd reprint. London. A. & C. Black, Ltd. 1917.

Younghusband (1924): *Wonders of the Himalayas*. Francis Younghusband. 1924. 1st Indian Reprint: Chandigarh. Abhishek Publications. 1977.

Yu (1998): *A Study of Saka History*. Taishan Yu. *Sino-Platonic Papers* No. 80. July 1998. Dept. of Asian and Middle Eastern Studies, University of Pennsylvania.

Yu (2000): *A Hypothesis about the Source of the Sai Tribes*. Taishan Yu. *Sino-Platonic Papers* No. 106. September 2000. Dept. of Asian and Middle Eastern Studies, University of Pennsylvania.

Yu (2004): *A History of the Relationships between the Western and Eastern Han, Wei, Jin, Northern and Southern Dynasties and the Western Regions*. Taishan Yu. *Sino-Platonic Papers* No. 131. March 2004. Dept. of East Asian Languages and Civilizations, University of Pennsylvania.

Yu (2006): *A Study of the History of the Relationship Between the Western and Eastern Han, Wei, Jin, Northern and Southern Dynasties and the Western Regions*. Taishan Yu. *Sino-Platonic Papers*, No. 173.

Yu (2006b): "月氏" 读音考. "The Textual Research into the Pronunciation of "Rou Zhi". Lu Yu. *Journal of Anhui Agricultural University* (Social Science Edition) 2006, 03. Abstract.

Downloaded on 28 May 2007 from: http://scholar.ilib.cn/Abstract.aspx?A=ahnydxxb-shkxb 200603030.

Yu (2011): *The Origin of the Kushans.* Taishan Yu. *Sino-Platonic Papers* No. 212 July, 2011. Dept. of East Asian Languages and Civilizations, University of Pennsylvania. Downloaded on 24 Sept 2011 from: http://sino-platonic.org/complete/spp212_kushan_guishuang.pdf

Yu (2011): *China and the Ancient Mediterranean World: A Survey of Ancient Chinese Sources.* Taishan Yu. *Sino-Platonic Papers* Number 242. November 2013. Dept. of East Asian Languages and Civilizations, University of Pennsylvania.

Yü (1986): "Han foreign relations." Yü Ying-shih. In: *CHC* (1986), pp. 377-462.

Yule (1866): *Cathay and the way thither: being a collection of Medieval Notices of China.* Translated and edited by Colonel Henry Yule with a preliminary essay. 2 vols. Hakluyt Society, London. Downloaded from: http://dsr.nii.ac.jp/toyobunko/III-2-F-b-2/V-1/ and http://dsr.nii.ac.jp/toyobunko/III-2-F-b-2/V-2/ on 22 December 2004.

Yule (1873): "Art. V.—Notes on Hwen Thsang's Account of the Principalities of Tokháristán, in which some Previous Geographical Identifications are Reconsidered." *Journal of the Royal Asiatic Society of Great Britain & Ireland (New Series)* (1873), Vol. 6: pp. 92-120.

Yule (1903): *The Travels of Marco Polo: The Complete Yule-Cordier Edition*, Vol. I. Henry Yule. Reprint: with Henri Cordier's later volume of notes and addenda (1920); Dover Publications, Mineola, N.Y., 1993.

Yule and Burnell (1886): *Hobson-Jobson The Anglo-Indian Dictionary*. Henry Yule and A. C. Burnell. 1886. Reprint: Ware, Hertfordshire. Wordsworth Editions Limited. 1996.

Zadneprovskiy (1994): "The Nomads of northern Central Asia after the invasion of Alexander." Y. A. Zadneprovskiy. 1994. *HCCA*, pp. 457-472.

Zarins (1997): "Atlantis of the Sands." Juris Zarins. *Archaeology*, Vol. 50, No. 3, May/June 1997, pp. 51-53.

Zeimal (1983): "The Political History of Transoxiana." E. V. Zeimal. *CHI* 3 (1), (1983), pp. 232-262.

Zeimal (1996): "The Kidarite kingdom in Central Asia." E. V. Zeimal. In: *HCCA*, Vol. III, pp. 119-133.

Zhang (1996): "The city-states of the Tarim basin." Zhang Guang-de. In: *HCCA*, Vol. III, pp. 281-301.

Zuev (1960): *K etnicheskoĭ istorii usuneĭ.* Üry Aleksey Zuev. Works of Kazakh SSR Academy of Sciences. Institute of History, Archaeology and Ethnography, Vol.8. Kazakh SSR Academy of Sciences Publishing House, Alma-Ata. English title: *Ethnic History of the Wusun.* (Draft translation by Norm Kisamov).

Zuev (2002): *Rannie tyurki. Ocerki istorii i ideologii.* Üry Aleksey Zuev. Daik-Press, Almaty, Kazakhstan. In Russian. English title: *Early Türks: Essays of History and Ideology.* (Draft translation by Norm Kisamov).

Zufferey (2008): "Traces of the Silk Road in Han-Dynasty Iconography: Questions and Hypotheses." Nicolas Zufferey. In: *The Journey of Maps and Images on the Silk Road.* Edited by Philippe Forêt and Andreas Kaplony. Brill. Leiden • Boston.

Zürcher (1968): "The Yüeh-chih and Kaniṣka in the Chinese sources." E. Zürcher. 1968. *PDK*. pp. 346-393.

Zürcher (1972): *The Buddhist Conquest of China.* E. Zürcher. Leiden. E. J. Brill.

34758765R20197

Made in the USA
San Bernardino, CA
06 June 2016